The Enjoyment of
MUSIC

Ninth Edition/Shorter

The Enjoyment of
MUSIC

An Introduction to Perceptive Listening

Joseph Machlis

Late Professor of Music Emeritus,
Queens College of The City University of New York

Kristine Forney

Professor of Music, California State University, Long Beach

W. W. NORTON & COMPANY
NEW YORK · LONDON

W. W. Norton & Company has been independent since its founding in 1923, when William Warder Norton and Mary D. Herter Norton first published lectures delivered at the People's Institute, the adult education division of New York City's Cooper Union. The Nortons soon expanded their program beyond the Institute, publishing books by celebrated academics from America and abroad. By mid-century, the two major pillars of Norton's publishing program—trade books and college texts—were firmly established. In the 1950s, the Norton family transferred control of the company to its employees, and today—with a staff of four hundred and a comparable number of trade, college, and professional titles published each year—W. W. Norton & Company stands as the largest and oldest publishing house owned wholly by its employees.

For Earle Fenton Palmer

The text of this book is composed in Photina

Composition by UG / GGS Information Services, Inc.

Manufacturing by Courier, Kendallville

Cover illustration: Helmut Preiss. *Jazz*, 1997. Courtesy of the artist.

Cover design: Andrew M. Newman Graphic Design, Inc.

Editor: Maribeth Payne

Managing Editor—College: Marian Johnson

Director of Manufacturing—College: Roy Tedoff

Associate Art Director—College: Rubina Yeh

Page Layout by Alice Bennett Dates and Brad Walrod

Copy Editor: Kathryn Talalay

Project Editor: Kathryn Talalay

Photograph editors: Neil Ryder Hoos and Penni Zivian

Assistant Editor: Claire McCabe

Editorial Assistant: Allison Benter

Indexer: Marilyn Bliss

Library of Congress Cataloging-in-Publication Data

Machlis, Joseph, 1906-
    The enjoyment of music : an introduction to perceptive listening / Joseph Machlis, Kristine Forney.—9th ed., shorter.
        p. cm.
    Includes bibliographical references and index.
    ISBN 0-393-97879-6 (pbk.)
    1. Music appreciation.   I, Forney, Kristine.   II. Title.

MT90.M23 2003a
780—dc21   2002045466

ISBN 0-393-97879-6 (pbk.)

W. W. Norton & Company, Inc. 500 Fifth Avenue, New York, NY 10110

www.wwnorton.com

W. W. Norton & Company Ltd., Castle House, 75/76 Wells Street, London W1T 3QT

2 3 4 5 6 7 8 9 0

CONTENTS

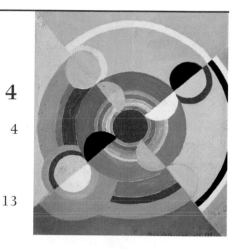

PART 2 Medieval and Renaissance Music

Timeline: Medieval/Renaissance Era

PART 4 The Baroque Era

Timeline: Baroque Era

PART 5 More Materials of Form

UNIT IX Focus on Form   180

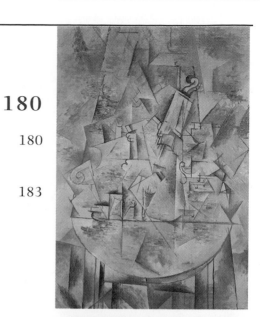

PART 6 Eighteenth-Century Classicism

Timeline: Classical Era

UNIT X The Classical Spirit   190

UNIT XI Classical Chamber Music   199

UNIT XII The Classical Symphony   209

PART 7 The Nineteenth Century

Timeline: Romantic Era

Part 8 The Twentieth Century

Timeline: Post-Romanticism, Impressionism, and Early Twentieth Century

UNIT XXI The Impressionist and Post-Impressionist Eras   356

Listening Guides

Cultural Perspectives

Preface: *The Enjoyment of Music* Package

You have just purchased what is perhaps the most comprehensive package of materials available for the study of music appreciation and literature. This book is a classic—it's been around for nearly half a century—but its contents and pedagogical approach are very much up-to-date, featuring appealing musical repertory, the latest scholarship, an eye-catching design, and an unparalleled package of electronic ancillaries. This preface introduces you to some of the important pedagogical features in your text, on the CDs, and on the Web. Knowing how to use and integrate these resources will enhance your music listening and study skills and ultimately your performance in class.

Using the book

The Enjoyment of Music is designed for maximum readability. The narrative is accompanied by many useful and instructive features that will facilitate your study of music. These features are described below.

- The **eLearning** lists at the beginning of each Unit provide an overview of Web and CD-ROM resources that integrate with your text.
- **Marginal icons**, placed throughout the book, direct you to relevant Web and CD-ROM resources.
- **Key Points,** at the beginning of each chapter, provide a brief summary of the terms and main points in each chapter.
- **Marginal sideheads** identify key terms defined in the text and focus attention on important concepts.

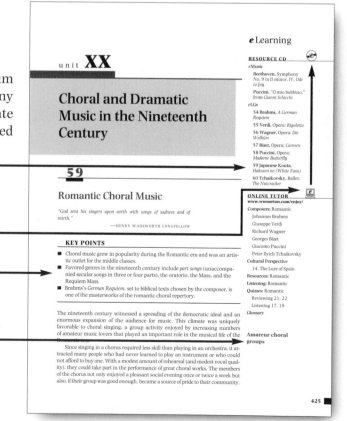

- **Cultural Perspectives** expand on issues discussed in the text and allow you to view music within a larger cultural framework.
- **Full-color photographs** and illustrations bring to life the figures and events discussed in the text.
- **Listening Guides** for each piece on the CD set enhance your understanding of the musical selection with a moment-by-moment description of the work. (See **About the Listening Guides** and also read about the **eLGs** on the **Student Resource CD**.)
- **What to Listen For boxes**, featured in each Listening Guide, offer helpful suggestions for what to focus on while hearing the music.
- **In His/Her Own Words**, placed throughout all chapters, offer interesting and relevant quotes from composers and important historical figures.
- **Timelines**, placed at the beginning of each Part or era, provide a chronological orientation for world events, principal literary and artistic figures, as well as composers.

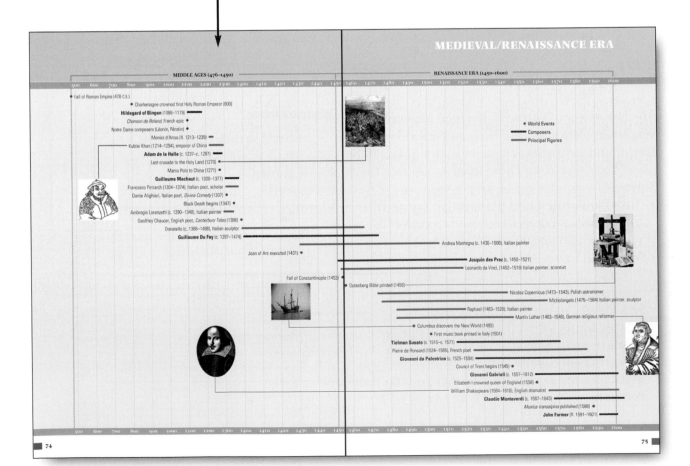

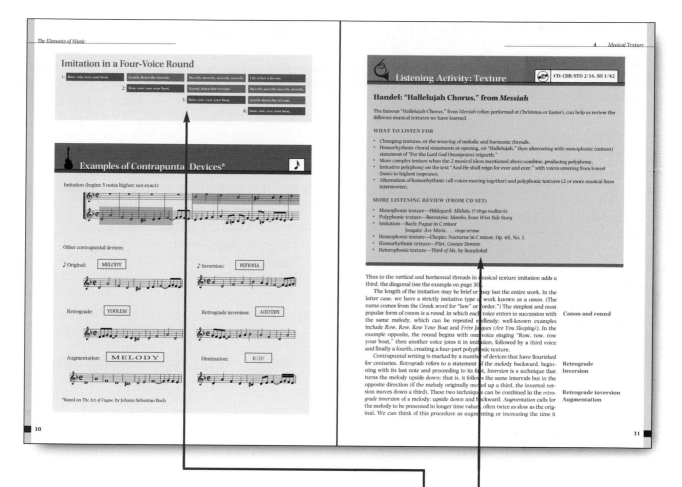

- **Colorful charts** visually reinforce concepts presented in the text.
- **Musical Activities**, bulleted points at the end of each "Elements of Music" chapter, provide suggested listening exercises to check your understanding of concepts relating to the building blocks of music.
- **Era introductions**, opening each Part or era, provide overviews of major artistic and intellectual trends in each historical period.

Some other useful reference tools are provided in the text to help in your studying.
- A **Glossary** (Appendix II) offers clear, concise definitions of all musical terms.
- The **Musical Notation** section (Appendix I) gives explanation of musical symbols used for pitch and rhythm to assist in understanding musical examples.
- A **Table of Listening Guides and Recordings** (inside the front and back covers) provides quick reference for locating Listening Guides in the book, as well as pieces on the recording packages.
- A **World map** (at the back of the book) offers a quick view of the location of continents, countries, and major cities. Inserts provide detail on Europe, the United States, and Canada.
- The **Index** (at the back of the book) gives the page number in boldface for definitions, and in italics for illustrations.

About the Listening Guides

The **Listening Guides** are an important feature of your textbook; they should be used while listening to a work from the CD set. They are easy to follow and will enhance your knowledge and appreciation of each piece. Refer to the sample **Listening Guide** and numbers on the facing page as you read through the following points:

❶ The CD locator, boxed in the upper right-hand corner of each Listening Guide, provides CD and track numbers for both the 8-CD set (to accompany Chronological/Standard version) and the 4-CD set (to accompany Shorter version).

> **CHR** = Chronological version
> **STD** = Standard version
> **SH** = Shorter version

❷ The composer and title of each piece is followed by some basic information about the work in outline format at the top of each Listening Guide.

❸ The total duration of each piece is given in parentheses to the right of the title.

❹ The **What to Listen For** box offers helpful study tips while listening.

❺ Music examples of main theme(s) are provided. (For help with reading music, see Appendix I, "Musical Notation.")

❻ CD track numbers, boxed and running down the left side of each Listening Guide, provide the specific track in the CD set that coordinates with your text. Inclusive tracks are listed at the top of each Listening Guide (see 1, above).

❼ Cumulative timings, starting from zero in each movement, are provided throughout the Listening Guide.

❽ Text and translations are given for all vocal works; a moment-by-moment description is generally provided as well to assist you in following the music.

❶

Choral and Dramatic Music in the Nineteenth Century

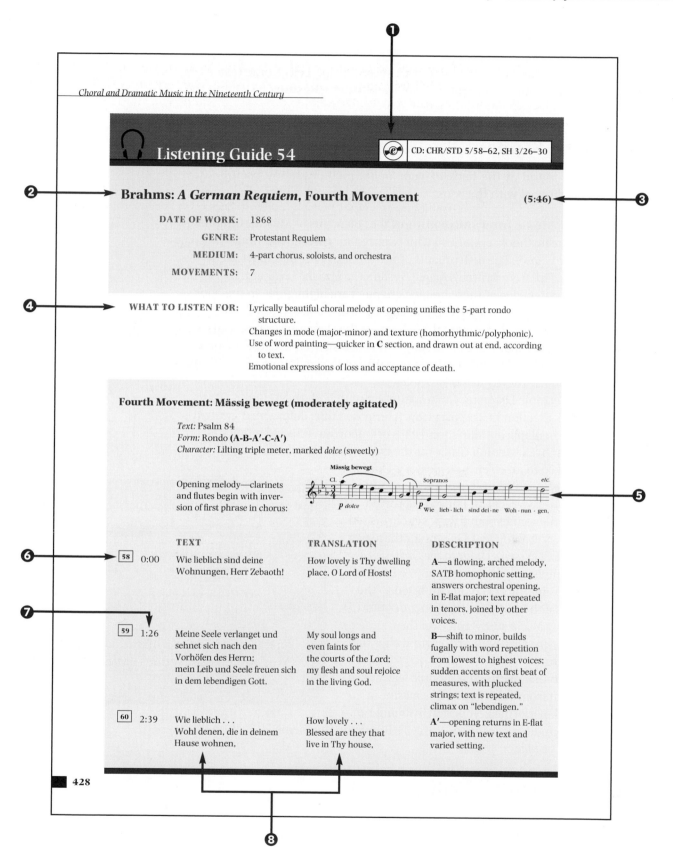

Listening Guide 54

CD: CHR/STD 5/58–62, SH 3/26–30

❷ **Brahms:** *A German Requiem,* **Fourth Movement**   **(5:46)** ◄ **❸**

DATE OF WORK:	1868
GENRE:	Protestant Requiem
MEDIUM:	4-part chorus, soloists, and orchestra
MOVEMENTS:	7

❹ WHAT TO LISTEN FOR: Lyrically beautiful choral melody at opening unifies the 5-part rondo structure.
Changes in mode (major-minor) and texture (homorhythmic/polyphonic).
Use of word painting—quicker in **C** section, and drawn out at end, according to text.
Emotional expressions of loss and acceptance of death.

Fourth Movement: Mässig bewegt (moderately agitated)

Text: Psalm 84
Form: Rondo **(A-B-A'-C-A')**
Character: Lilting triple meter, marked *dolce* (sweetly)

Opening melody—clarinets
and flutes begin with inver-
sion of first phrase in chorus: **❺**

	TEXT	TRANSLATION	DESCRIPTION
❻ **58** 0:00	Wie lieblich sind deine Wohnungen, Herr Zebaoth!	How lovely is Thy dwelling place, O Lord of Hosts!	**A**—a flowing, arched melody, SATB homophonic setting, answers orchestral opening, in E-flat major; text repeated in tenors, joined by other voices.
❼ **59** 1:26	Meine Seele verlanget und sehnet sich nach den Vorhöfen des Herrn; mein Leib und Seele freuen sich in dem lebendigen Gott.	My soul longs and even faints for the courts of the Lord; my flesh and soul rejoice in the living God.	**B**—shift to minor, builds fugally with word repetition from lowest to highest voices; sudden accents on first beat of measures, with plucked strings; text is repeated, climax on "lebendigen."
60 2:39	Wie lieblich . . . Wohl denen, die in deinem Hause wohnen,	How lovely . . . Blessed are they that live in Thy house,	**A'**—opening returns in E-flat major, with new text and varied setting.

❽

428

xxiii

Using the eLearning

The Enjoyment of Music is coordinated with several helpful electronic resources that will enhance your learning; these are the **Student Resource CD** and the **Online Tutor**.

About the Student Resource CD

This CD-ROM, found at the back of your book, includes many useful study resources coordinated with the book.

- **Materials of Music Interactive** features the "Elements of Music" (Chapters 1-10) from the textbook, enhanced with twenty-four **eMusic** listening examples (see below). The instruments of the orchestra are also illustrated here by video clips from Britten's *Young Person's Guide to the Orchestra.* In addition, the outer edge of these first ten chapters are highlighted in the book by a $^1/_4$ -inch light-blue strip, which is visible when the book is closed.
- **eMusic**, short musical examples that illustrate the elements, or materials, of music, features familiar traditional songs and accessible classical selections. Each selection is listed by title in the **eLearning** at the beginning of each Unit and marked in the text by a musical note (♪).
- **eLGs**, the electronic Listening Guides, interact with both the 4- and 8-CD set. Each musical selection has an overview (composer, title, date, genre, context), translation when appropriate, sound clips of important musical moments, and an interactive Listening Guide for the entire work. In addition, all the terms are linked to an electronic glossary. Once the software is installed, the menu will prompt you to insert the correct CD. The **eLGs** provide moment-by-moment explanations, synchronized with the music, making learning easier than ever.
- **Britten**'s *Young Person's Guide to the Orchestra* features a complete audio recording (see **LG 1** in text, p. 62). Using the **eLG**, you can listen to the musical work either on your computer or your CD player. There is also a study guide on the *Instruments of the Orchestra*, with sound clips and various images.
- The **Baroque-era orchestra** module features a video segment from Telemann's *Tafelmusik*—a Baroque work performed on period instruments— as well as an audio recording of Purcell's Rondeau, the theme for Britten's *Young Person's Guide.*

About the Online Tutor

Available at www.wwnorton.com/enjoy, this Web site offers helpful study guides and quizzes as well as Web resources for further exploration of music, including:
- **Overview** of each period, with historical themes, musical context, and discussion of style.

- **Quizzes** that are computer graded, for reviewing terms, concepts, and listening.
- **Composer biographies**, with illustrations, audio examples, and links to online resources.
- **Cultural Perspectives** from the text, with useful links for further research.
- **Transitions** between historical periods, with comparative charts, audio examples, and drag-and-drop exercises.
- **Resources**, or links, to useful Web sites for each historical period.
- **Listening** examples to illustrate the musical style of each period.
- **Musical excursions**, including interviews with musicians and information on current musical events.
- A **Glossary**, from the text, with definitions that can be accessed from the main menu or from linked terms.
- **Timelines**, from the text, that help with chronological orientation of key figures and events.
- **Chapter-by-chapter assignments** to help you learn the material and prepare for exams.

To the Instructor

The Enjoyment of Music, Ninth Edition, presents a comprehensive teaching and learning package that integrates innovative technological resources with the traditional book and audio CDs. If you have not already done so, please review the previous section (pp. xix–xxv) and be sure to have your students read this as well. We encourage you and your students to take full advantage of the features we have developed. As with previous editions, *The Enjoyment of Music* text is available in three formats: the **Chronological** and **Shorter**, both of which take a sequential historical approach, and the **Standard**, which begins with the accessible music of the Romantic era.

We have addressed many pedagogical issues in this new Ninth Edition, with a goal of providing innovative teaching and learning resources; these include the following:

- Increased computer and Web resources for classroom and individual use
- More "Elements of Music" resources for students
- Improved balance of genres
- Updated content, including film music, popular and traditional music, jazz, and contemporary examples
- Accessible and highly "teachable" repertory
- Inclusion of five complete multimovement works
- Excellent quality recordings, including more period-instrument performances
- "Front-loading" of information in each chapter (**Key Points**)
- Clear guidelines for listening (**What to Listen For**)
- Integration of women musicians (as composers, musicians, and patrons) in each era.
- Focus on comparative cultures (Western vs. non-Western/traditional musics)
- Increased emphasis on traditional and art music of the Americas
- New, colorful design that reinforces learning

About the Repertory and Listening Guides

This new edition is accompanied by two CD sets: a longer 8-CD version, which has ninety-five pieces, and a shorter 4-CD set, with fifty-five pieces. Every work on the CD is supported by both an in-text Listening Guide and an electronic Listening Guide (*e*LGs on the **Student Resource CD**).

The electronic Listening Guides have been redesigned to meet the needs of today's students and faculty. These interactive guides are ideal for use in lectures and for individual study; they help students follow the music closely, while focusing on key structural and stylistic features.

Highlights of the repertory are provided below (boldface text designates a new selection or recording).

Repertory

95 works with Listening Guides in the Chronological and Standard versions of the book
- 28 of these are new to the Ninth Edition.
- All are recorded on the 8-CD set.

55 works with Listening Guides in the Shorter version of the book
- 16 of these are new to the Ninth Edition.
- All are recorded on the 4-CD set.

World/traditional music examples set against Western pieces influenced by the style:
- **Japanese kouta (geisha song)**, following **Puccini, *Madame Butterfly***
- **Javanese gamelan work**, following **Cage, *Sonatas and Interludes***
- Chinese traditional music, following **Tan Dun film score (*Crouching Tiger, Hidden Dragon*)**
- Eastern African drumming, following Ligeti piano étude

Traditional and art music of the Americas:
- **Cajun dance tune (*Think of Me*), performed by BeauSoleil**
- **Symphonic work by Mexican composer Silvestre Revueltas (*Homenaje a Federico García Lorca*)**

Film music, in a new chapter dedicated to the genre:
- Prokofiev: *Alexander Nevsky*
- **Tan Dun: *Crouching Tiger, Hidden Dragon***

More complete coverage of music by women composers (spanning the full chronological range):
- **Hildegard of Bingen chant: *Alleluia, O virga mediatrix***
- **Barbara Strozzi cantata: *Begli occhi***
- Fanny Mendelssohn Hensel Lied: *Bergeslust*
- Clara Schumann piano work: Scherzo, Op. 10
- Amy Beach chamber work: Violin Sonata
- **Billie Holiday piece: *Billie's Blues***
- **Joan Tower orchestral work: *For the Uncommon Woman***

Improved, more comprehensive coverage of jazz (including its influence on art music):
- Ragtime—Joplin: *Maple Leaf Rag*
- **Blues—Holiday: *Billie's Blues***
- **Big band—Strayhorn/Ellington: *Take the A Train***
- **Bebop—Gillespie/Parker: *A Night in Tunisia***
- Merger of classical and jazz styles:
    - **Gershwin: Piano Prelude No. 1**
    - **Baker: *Through This Vale of Tears***

Five complete multimovement pieces representing major genres:
- Baroque concerto—Vivaldi, *La primavera*
- Chamber music (string quartet)—Mozart: *Eine kleine Nachtmusik*
- Classical symphony—Beethoven: Symphony No. 5 in C minor
- Classical concerto—Mozart: Piano Concerto in G major, K. 453
- Classical sonata—Beethoven: Piano Sonata, Op. 13 *(Pathétique)*

Improved early music examples (with excellent recordings):
- New examples of Gregorian chant representing Mass Ordinary and Proper, medieval polyphony (organum and motet) and Renaissance secular music
- New works by Hildegard of Bingen, Notre Dame School, Adam de la Halle, Josquin, and Susato
- Continuing works by Machaut, Du Fay, Josquin, Palestrina, Monteverdi, Farmer, representing all major genres (Mass, motet, chansons, madrigals, instrumental music)

Excellent coverage of period-instrument performances—many new to this edition—representing wide-ranging eras:
- Medieval and Renaissance dance; Baroque opera, oratorio, trio sonata, concerto, and suite; Classical chamber, keyboard, and orchestral music, as well as oratorio; and early Romantic symphony
- Exceptional performances by the New London Consort, Philharmonia Baroque, London Baroque, Tafelmusik, English Baroque, Boston Baroque, Los Angeles Baroque, Quatuor mosaiques, Orchestra of the 18th Century, Academy of Ancient Music, Orchestre romantique, as well as solo performances by Davitt Moroney and Anthony Newman

Expanded coverage of contemporary music, including four new works from the last decade:
- **Tower: For the *Uncommon Woman* (1992)**
- **Adams: *Chamber Symphony* (1992)**
- **Pärt: *Cantate Domino canticum novum* (1977; rev. 1996)**
- **Tan Dun: *Crouching Tiger, Hidden Dragon* (2000)**

We also offer the new ***Norton Digital Music Collection, 2003 Edition***, which features six additional hours of music in Windows Media Format, including Stravinsky's ever-popular *Rite of Spring*, Part I; Ravel's *Bolero*; and Gershwin's *Rhapsody in Blue.* The pieces were selected to support and enhance the core repertory of the Ninth Edition. For the complete contents see www.wwnorton.com/college/music/ndmc.

Outstanding Ancillaries for Both Students and Instructors

In addition to the Student Resource CD, Online Tutor, two CD sets with *e*LGs, and the Norton Digital Music Collection—all described above—Norton offers a pedagogically rich array of ancillary materials unique to this text.

The Norton Scores

This two-volume anthology includes scores for nearly all the works on both CD sets. A unique highlighting system—long a hallmark of this collection—assists students in following full orchestral scores. A stylistic commentary for each piece is new to this edition. These scores are essential for instructor use in the classroom and for the preparation of lectures.

The Study Guide

This is a workbook that assists students with reviewing and listening exercises as well as cultural explorations. It also includes some projects for groups and individuals as well as concert report outlines.

Norton Media Library CD ROM

This resource features over 130 digital music sound excerpts illustrating key concepts in the text; a video segment from Georg Phillip Telemann's *Tafelmusik* performed by the Los Angeles Baroque Orchestra; PowerPoint slides for every chapter of the text; and Peter Schickele's *New Horizons in Music Appreciation* (a humorous narrated version of Beethoven's Fifth Symphony).

The Norton Resource Library

An online collection of lecture and quiz materials, this valuable resource also includes the complete Instructor's Manual in pdf format, ready to download.

Music Example Bank

This unique and highly useful ancillary consists of four fully indexed audio CDs that illustrate—with examples from classical, folk, and popular music—all the musical concepts discussed in the text.

Instructor's Manual

Available in paper and downloadable from the Norton Resource Library Web site, this resource includes an overview of ancillaries to accompany *The Enjoyment of Music;* suggested approaches to teaching, a sample course syllabus, and exam schedule; lecture notes to accompany PowerPoint slides (see above, *Norton Media Library CD ROM*); resources (books, videos, recordings) for enhancing key units; and answers to the student Study Guide questions.

Test-Item File

Featuring over 2,400 multiple-choice, true/false, and essay questions, the Test-Item File is available in print (TIF) and in computerized dual-platform (CTIF) formats that enable the instructor to edit questions and add new ones.

Britten, Young Person's Guide to the Orchestra video (49 minutes)

This popular video is now available in VHS and DVD formats.

Transparencies

All in-text Listening Guides are available as transparencies for in-class projection in "nonsmart" classrooms.

Videos

This collection of music, opera, and dance videos, offers instructors an exceptional library of video resources. Consult the Instructor's Manual for a list of specific works and performances distributed by W. W. Norton.

So what's new in the Ninth Edition? The answer is a lot—more technology, more pedagogical resources, more diversity, and more visual and aural stimulation—within the same dependable package of teaching materials. You will find a greater breadth of musical styles than ever before, and music repertory that speaks to today's student in this diverse, multicultural society. Although this edition continues to focus on Western art music, it addresses issues and events in the contemporary world around us. The Ninth Edition of *The Enjoyment of Music* combines an authoritative text, a stimulating new design that integrates text, pedagogy, and emedia, and unparalleled print and online ancillaries. The result is an exceptional teaching—and learning—package.

Any project of this size is dependent on the expertise and assistance of many individuals to make it a success. First, we wish to acknowledge the many loyal users of *The Enjoyment of Music* who have taken the time to comment on the text and ancillary package. As always, their suggestions help us shape each new edition. We also wish to thank those instructors who participated in focus groups held at several American Musicological Society meetings and at the University of California, Santa Barbara, and at California State University, Long Beach. These forums encouraged a free exchange of ideas on teaching methods, repertory, and the instructional use of technology.

The list of specialists who offered their expertise to this text continues to grow. In addition to those acknowledged in the last several editions, whose insights have helped shape the book, we wish to thank Roger Hickman (California State University, Long Beach), for contributing the new chapter on film music in this edition; Revell Carr (University of California, Santa Barbara), for updating the rock chapter and for his analysis of the Javanese gamelan piece; Gregory Maldonado (California State University, Long Beach), for providing audio and video segments performed by the Los Angeles Baroque Orchestra, which he directs; Carol Hess (Ball State University), for sharing research materials on Silvestre Revueltas and Mexican art music; and Carla Reisch (Orange County High School for the Arts), for lending her expertise to the music technology chapter.

The team assembled to prepare the ancillary materials accompanying this edition is unparalleled: it includes our Webmaster Russell Murray (University of Delaware); Irene Girton (Occidental College), author of the electronic Listening Guides; John Husser (Virginia Technological Institute and State University), who designed and programmed the emedia; John Muller (Juilliard School of Music), James Forney (St. Lawrence University), and Tom Laskey (Sony Special Products), who assembled, licensed, and mastered the recording package; Richard Birkemeier (California State University, Long Beach), who updated and edited the Test-Item File; Alicia Doyle (University of Texas, El Paso), who prepared the new Instructor's Manual and PowerPoint slides for classroom presentation; Roger Hickman (California State University, Long Beach), who prepared the new commentary in the Norton Scores; Gregory Maldonado (California State University, Long Beach), who highlighted the new scores for this edition; and our team of research assistants, including Carla Reisch, Jeanne Scheppach, Denise Odello, and Patricia Dobiesz.

This new edition would not have been realized without the capable assistance of the W. W. Norton team. We owe profound thanks to Maribeth Payne, new music editor at W. W. Norton, for her dedication and counsel to the whole project; to Kathy Talalay, for her expert copyediting, as well as her patience, encouragement, and advice; to technology editor Steve Hoge, for creating and coordinating our outstanding emedia package; to Claire McCabe, for her able editing of *The Norton Scores* and her coordination of many of the ancillaries; to Allison Benter, for overseeing innumerable details of the package; to Rubina Yeh, for her stunning and pedagogically sound design; to Penni Zivian and Neil Ryder Hoos, for their excellent illustration research; to Alice Bennett Dates and Brad Walrod, for their artistic and eye-catching layout; to Roy Tedoff, for his expert oversight of the production for the entire *Enjoyment* package; and to Peter Lesser, for his insightful marketing strategies.

We wish finally to express our deep appreciation to three former music editors at Norton, Michael Ochs, Claire Brook, and David Hamilton, who over the years have guided and inspired *The Enjoyment of Music* to its continued success.

Joseph Machlis
Kristine Forney

The Enjoyment of
MUSIC

Sonia Delaunay
(1885–1979), *Rhyth*
Circulaire no. 4 (1939
(Fijnaut & Paol Fine A

The Materials of Music

e Learning

unit **I**

The Elements of Music

Prelude

Listening to Music Today

"Ah, Music . . . a magic beyond all we do here!"

—ALBUS DUMBLEDORE, HEADMASTER, HOGWARTS SCHOOL OF
WITCHCRAFT AND WIZARDRY

Our lives are constantly changing, with new avenues of the supertechnology highway opening to us every day. This technological revolution significantly influences our work and our leisure activities; it further conditions how, when, and where we listen to music. From the moment we are awakened by our clock radios, our days unfold against a musical background. We hear music while on the move—in our cars, on planes, or at the gym—and at home for relaxation. We can hardly avoid it in grocery and department stores, in restaurants and elevators, at the dentist's office or at work. We experience music at live concerts—outdoor festivals, rock concerts, jazz clubs, the symphony hall, the opera stage—and we hear it on television, at the movies, and on the Internet. MTV (Music Television) has forever changed the way we "listen" to popular music; it is now a visual experience as well as an aural one. This increased dependency on our eyes makes our ears work less actively, a factor we will attempt to counteract in this book. Music media too are rapidly changing. We now have more choices than ever before—streaming audio, Internet radio, and Webcasting, to name only a few (see CP 1).

Composers have welcomed the technological revolution; the basic tools of music composition—formerly, a pen, music paper, and perhaps a piano—now include a computer and laser printer. In short, modern technology has placed at our disposal a wider diversity of music from every period in history, from every kind of instrument, and from every corner of the globe than has ever been available before.

Given this diversity, we must choose our path of study. In this book, we will focus on the classics of Western music while paying special attention to the important influences that traditional, popular, and non-Western musics have had on the European and American heritage. Our purpose is to expand the listening experience through a heightened awareness of many styles of music, including those representing various subcultures of the American population. We will hear the uniquely American forms of ragtime, blues, jazz, and musical theater, as well as rock and contemporary world music. The book seeks to place music, whether art, traditional, or popular, within its cultural context, and to highlight the relationships between different styles. To this end, the Cultural Perspectives, informative boxed texts placed throughout the book, open windows onto other cultures and their musics. You can also explore these topics further on the *Enjoyment* Web site (www.wwnorton.com/enjoy), which provides links to related sites of interest.

The language of music cannot be translated into the language of words. You cannot deduce the actual sound of a piece from anything written about it; as the great violinist Yehudi Menuhin notes in the quote above, the ultimate meaning lies in the sounds themselves and in the ears of the listener. While certain styles are immediately accessible without any explanation, the world of music often brings us into contact with sounds and concepts that we grasp more slowly. What, you might wonder, can prepare the nonmusician to understand and appreciate an eighteenth-century symphony, a contemporary opera, or an example of African drumming? A great deal. We can discuss the social and historical context in which a work was born. We can explore the characteristic features of the various styles throughout the history of music, so that we can relate a particular piece or style to parallel developments in literature and the fine arts. We can read about the lives of the composers who left us so rich a heritage, and take note of what they said about their art. (Engaging comments by composers appear throughout the book, labeled "In His/Her Own Words.") We can acquaint ourselves with the elements out of which music is made, and discover how the composer combines these into any one work. And we can come to understand music as an art form, as a means of expression that is created by the composer, interpreted by the

There is no such thing as music divorced from the listener. Music as such is unfulfilled until it has penetrated our ears.
—YEHUDI MENUHIN

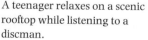 **Web site**

A teenager relaxes on a scenic rooftop while listening to a discman.

Music and Today's Listener: The State of the Art

In the last half of the twentieth century, technology has allowed us to hear music in many different ways. Some of us still listen to music through radio, television broadcasts, live concerts, and from recorded media such as the compact disc. But our options have expanded considerably with the advent of the Internet and digital technology. Today's listener is just as likely to listen to an Internet radio station, located hundreds of miles away, as download MP3 files from a new artist on the other side of the world. Global technology of the twenty-first century has forever changed our relationship with music.

Recorded music has historically been bought and sold in the traditional brick-and-mortar music store. Now we can buy a CD directly from an online retailer whose selection is far greater than any one music store. Music by obscure artists and composers, as well as by their well-known counterparts, is readily available, which in turn increases sales and visibility for those who would not have had that chance in store sales alone. In addition, most online retailers of music allow customers to preview part or all of the CD via streaming audio before buying.

A student listens to music on his MP3 player.

(Streaming audio plays directly from the Web site in real time and does not require downloading.)

Internet radio is in its infancy but is growing steadily. There are some advantages to listening to music online: first, geographical location is irrelevant; second, the listener can readily identify the artist and song title from the computer display and, in some cases, purchase the music instantly; and finally, the Internet provides some degree of interactivity between the listener and the program manager. The program manager can monitor Internet traffic and determine what music or artists is drawing in listeners—and keeping them there. In other words, statistics on audience preferences are instantaneous. Listeners now have many more choices than the handful of radio stations broadcasting in their immediate area. As bandwidth (the amount of data that can travel through a transmission line) improves, Internet radio may replace our traditional radio, or at the very least, compete with the new satellite radio services that transmit signals to a wide region via low-earth-orbit satellites.

Internet radio (a type of Webcasting) has also brought us another innovation: listening to concerts online. It may not be possible or practical to fly to Europe to attend the Haydn festival at the Esterháza Palace, but thanks to Webcasting, classical music enthusiasts can listen to the concert online. Many Internet radio stations carry broadcasts from the New York Metropolitan Opera on a weekly basis, making it possible for anyone with a computer and Internet connection to listen in. (In some areas, listeners have been able to hear the Metropolitan broadcasts on traditional radio every Saturday for years.) Other venues, such as the House of Blues, which features popular music, blues, and jazz concerts, also program audio (and sometimes video) Webcasts of concerts online. Often these broadcasts are made available for a specified period of time (from several days to a week), encouraging listeners to check in regularly for new Webcast listings.

A new technology that has gained immense popularity is the MP3 file, which has widened the possibilities for artist and listener alike. MP3 (short for

Moving Pictures Expert Group 1 Layer 3) is simply a file-compression format applied to digital audio files. A compressed MP3 file is about one-tenth the size of an original audio file (which may be thirty or forty megabytes in size), enabling users to download many more files at a faster rate than would otherwise be possible (not to mention taking up less space on a user's hard drive). This technology has become so widespread that manufacturers are now making CD and DVD players that can read the MP3 file format. In fact, a CD can hold up to twelve hours worth of music, once it has been compressed by the MP3 file format—a far cry from the seventy-four minutes of audio available on a traditional CD. This is possible thanks to inexpensive CD burners, which are standard components of most new computer systems.

Performers, composers, and songwriters have taken advantage of the possibilities open to them with these new technologies. The Internet has provided artists with a new promotional tool that is commercially effective and extremely economical. Many artists now market and sell their music directly to the consumer via their own Web sites, or make MP3 files of their music available on sites devoted to file sharing. Although MP3 file sharing is welcomed by many, some industry groups and artists feel they have been cheated out of royalty payments, and thus have fought bitterly against it. Napster, an Internet file-sharing service that catered specifically to users swapping their favorite tunes, was involved in one of the most talked about and controversial lawsuits of our century. The Recording Industry Association of America (RIAA) accused Napster of copyright infringement and demanded that the courts shut down the service. The question is who infringed on the copyright: Napster or the people using the service? Many issues were raised regarding copyright and intellectual property rights in that lawsuit, none of which have

Twenty-year-old Napster founder Shawn Fanning (center) at a press conference in San Francisco, February 12, 2001, shortly after the court ruling preventing file swapping of copyrighted music.

been completely resolved. Although copyright issues are more clear-cut with printed music and recorded media, the application of the laws to web-based media and intellectual property are still fuzzy. For the time being it may be possible (and even legal) to download copyrighted music, but is it ethical?

While the courts are hearing cases and Congress is busy trying to draft new laws concerning Internet technology issues, millions of computer users are shaping the future of music online. Peer-to-peer (P2P) networks, in the tradition of Napster, are springing up everywhere, and users are still sharing files on a grand scale, using technology that makes it easy to hide their activities from those wanting to ban the practice. Some would suggest that we are headed for a new business model: free, downloadable music paid for by online advertising. Others have catered to the concerns of the RIAA by charging a monthly fee for downloading MP3 files from their sites. While today's music listener watches this controversy unfold, tomorrow's listener will see the results of technology's growing pains and will reap the benefits of a whole new world of music listening.

TERMS TO NOTE

Internet radio
Webcasting
Streaming audio

MP3
peer-to-peer (P2P)
Napster

Members of the musical theater show BLAST!, a celebration of instrumental music (drum and bugle corps) featuring dramatic staging, intricate choreography, and spectacular pagentry.

performer(s), and processed by the listener. All this knowledge—social, historical, biographical, technical, artistic, and analytical—can be interrelated. What emerges is a total picture of a work, one that will clarify, in far greater degree than you may have thought possible, the form and meaning of a composition.

There are people who claim they prefer not to know anything technical about the music they hear, that to intellectualize the listening experience destroys their enjoyment of the music. Yet most sports fans would hardly suggest that the best way to enjoy football is to avoid learning the rules of the game. A heightened awareness of musical processes and styles brings listeners closer to the sounds and allows them to hear and comprehend more.

Some Practical Suggestions

It takes practice to become good listeners. Most of us "listen" to music as a background to another activity—perhaps reading or studying—or for relaxation. In either case, we are probably not concentrating on the music. The approach set out in this book is intended to develop your listening skills and expand your musical memory. In order to accomplish this, you should listen to the examples repeatedly, focusing solely on what you are hearing. As you play the music, you will also find it helpful to follow the Listening Guides distributed throughout the book or use the electronic guides on your Resource CD. (Be sure to read pages xix–xxx, "*The Enjoyment of Music* Package," in order to understand all the electronic study tools available to you with this book.) Since the Listening Guides are outlines, they should not divert your attention from the sounds you hear. The music examples printed in the Listening Guides may be useful if you can follow the **Appendix I**   general line of the music (see Appendix I, "Musical Notation"). Don't worry if you can't read music; the verbal descriptions of each piece and its sections will tell you what to listen for. An explanation of the format for the Listening Guides is found on pages xxii-xxiii.

It is also important to hear music in live performance. Why not try something new and unfamiliar? There are many possibilities. You will want to read the upcoming section, "Attending Concerts," to learn some of the conventions followed in the concert hall and to learn about concerts in general. The goal is to open up a new world of musical experiences that you can enjoy for the rest of your life.

You will notice that each historical era begins with a general discussion of the culture, its arts, and its ideas. This chapter should help you integrate the knowledge you have gained from other disciplines into the world of music and help you understand that developments in music are closely related to the art, literature, philosophy, religion, and scientific knowledge of the time as well as the social background of the era.

You may be surprised at how technical the study of music can be, and how many new terms you will learn. Studying music is not easier than studying other **Glossary**   subjects, but it can be more fun. Make use of the Glossary in Appendix II, and note that the most important terms, when introduced in the book, are printed in italics. Some of these terms may be familiar to you from another context ("texture," for example, is a term commonly used to describe a surface or cloth); we will learn to associate these words with different, often more specific, meanings. Many others, such as the directions for musical expression, tempo, and dynamics, come from foreign languages. We will begin building this vocabulary in the first chapters by breaking music into its constituent parts—its building blocks, or elements. Listening Activities based on the CDs accompanying the book appear at the end of each elements chapter, and a collection of traditional songs (**eMusic** on your Resource CD) will help reinforce the terminology and concepts presented there. We will then analyze how a composer proceeds to shape a melody, how that melody is fitted with accompanying harmony, how music is organized in time, and how it is structured so as to assume logical, recognizable forms. In doing so, we will become aware of the basic principles that apply to all styles of music (classical and popular, Western and non-Western), to music from all eras and countries, and beyond that, to the other arts as well.

 **Resource CD**

"To understand," said the painter Raphael, "is to equal." When we come to understand a musical work, we grasp the "moment of truth" that gave it birth and thus become worthy of keeping company with its creator. We receive the message of the music, we recognize the intention of the composer. In effect, we listen perceptively—and that is the one sure road to the enjoyment of music.

Attending Concerts

Even with the many ways now available to hear fine-quality performances, nothing can equal the excitement of a live concert. The crowded hall, the visual as well as aural stimulation of a performance, even the element of unpredictability—of what might happen on a particular night—all contribute to the unique communicative powers of people making music. There are, however, certain traditions surrounding concerts and concertgoing: the location of the most desirable seats, the way performers dress, the appropriate moments to applaud, are but a few. These conditions differ somewhat between concerts of art music and of popular styles. Understanding the various traditions can contribute to your increased enjoyment of the musical event.

> *Music must never offend the ear, but must please the listener, or, in other words, must never cease to be music.*
> —W. A. MOZART

Choosing Concerts, Tickets, and Seats

Many types of musical events can be found in most parts of the country, with choices ranging from zydeco bands and Chinese opera to professional and college orchestras and choirs. To explore musical events in your area, check with the Music Department for on-campus concerts, read local and college newspapers for a calendar of upcoming events in the area, consult Web sites for nearby concert venues and calendars, or scan bulletin boards at your local university or college and in public buildings for concert announcements.

Ticket prices vary, depending on the event. For university events, including both popular and classical music, tickets are usually reasonable (under $20). For a performance in a major concert hall, you will probably pay more, generally $25 to $75, depending on the location of your seat. Orchestra section seats—those closest to the stage—are usually the most expensive; balcony seats are more

Summary: Attending Concerts

- Consult your local and college newspapers, the Music Department, Web sites, and bulletin boards on campus to learn about upcoming concerts in your area.
- Determine if it is necessary to purchase your tickets in advance or if you can acquire them at the door.
- Read about the works in advance in your textbook, at your library, or on the Internet.
- Consider what to wear; the degree of formality in your attire should suit the occasion.
- Arrive at least twenty minutes early to purchase or pick up your ticket.
- Review the program before the concert starts to learn what you can about the music and the performers.
- Be respectful to the performers and those sitting near you by not making noise during the concert (turn off cell phones and pagers).
- Follow the program carefully so that you know when to applaud (after complete works or sets of pieces).
- Be aware of and respect the traditions of the concert hall.
- Enjoy the event!

economical and the sound is as good or sometimes better than seats on the main floor, depending on the hall. It is also sometimes easier to see the performers from the balcony. Today, most new concert halls are constructed so that virtually all the seats are satisfactory. Where you choose your seats depends on the type of the event. For small, chamber groups, front orchestra seats, close to the performers, are best. For large ensembles—orchestras and operas, or even popular concerts—the best places are probably near the middle of the hall or the front of the balcony, where you also have a good view. For some concerts, you may need to purchase tickets in advance, either by phone or online, paying with a credit card. Be sure to ask for student discounts when appropriate.

Preparing for the Concert

Researching the concert

Before you attend a concert, especially if the musical style is unfamiliar to you, you may want to do some advance reading. First, find out what works will be performed at the upcoming concert. Then, check your textbook for information about the composers, works, genres, or styles. You may also look for information about the music in your campus library and on the Internet, or you can ask your instructor. There are several excellent reference books available that contain useful program notes on standard concert music and opera plots. It is especially important to read about an opera before the performance because it may be sung in the original language (Italian, German, or French).

What you choose to wear to a concert should depend on the degree of formality and the location of the event. For opening night at a large concert hall, some people may wear formal attire; most will generally wear a nice dress or a coat and tie. But more often, dress will be less formal, especially for university concerts. Whatever the occasion, it is best to dress nicely out of respect for the performers. If you are attending a jazz or pops concert, however, or an outdoor event, very casual dress is appropriate.

Arriving at the Concert

When attending a concert, you should plan to arrive at least twenty minutes before the event starts, especially if it is open seating or if you have ordered your tickets by phone or online and must pick them up at the box office. The time before a performance is often when people meet with friends or enjoy a beverage at the lobby bar. On the way to your seat, be sure to pick up a concert program—they are usually free—from the usher in order to read about the music and the performers before the event begins. You will enjoy the music more if you know a little about each work. Translations into English of vocal texts are generally provided as well. If you arrive after the concert has begun, you may not be able to enter the hall until after the first piece is finished or an appropriate break in the music occurs. It is important to be respectful of the performers and those around you by not talking and not leaving your seat except at intermission (the break that usually occurs about halfway through the performance).

Understanding the Concert Program

One key aspect of attending a concert is understanding the program. Here is a sample program for an orchestra concert, such as you might find at your college or in your community.

The concert program

PROGRAM

Overture to *A Midsummer Night's Dream*   Felix Mendelssohn (1809–1847)

Symphony No. 41 in C major, K. 551 (*Jupiter*)   W. A. Mozart (1756–1791)
    Allegro vivace
    Andante cantabile
    Menuetto (Allegretto) & Trio
    Finale: Molto allegro

INTERMISSION

Concerto No. 1 for Piano and Orchestra   P. I. Tchaikovsky
    in B-flat minor, Op. 23   (1840–1893)
    Allegro non troppo e molto maestoso;
      Allegro con spirito
    Andantino simplice; Prestissimo; Tempo I
    Allegro con fuoco

Barbara Allen, piano

The University Symphony Orchestra
Eugene Castillo, conductor

A glance at the program confirms that three works will be performed. The concert will open, as is often the case, with an overture. The title of this work implies that it has a literary basis: Shakespeare's well-known play *A Midsummer Night's Dream*. In other words, this is a programmatic piece. Since no subdivisons or internal tempo markings are noted, you can expect it to be a one-movement work.

The Los Angeles Philharmonic Orchestra performing at the Dorothy Chandler Pavilion.

The program also provides dates for the composer, Felix Mendelssohn, which establish him as an early Romantic master. (Since we study Mendelssohn, you could read about him in advance in this book.)

The concert will continue with a symphony by the eighteenth-century composer Mozart. The work's title suggests that Mozart wrote many symphonies; what we would not know without reading about him is that this is his last. You can further note that the symphony is in the key of C major and has a catalog number of 551 (assigned by a bibliographer named Köchel).

The program reveals that the symphony is in four sections, or movements, with contrasting tempo indications for each movement. The tempo pattern of fast (Allegro vivace)-slow (Andante cantabile)-moderate dance (Menuetto & Trio)-fast (Molto allegro) is typical in its overall structure. (You can read more about the multimovement instrumental cycle and the forms of individual movements in Chapter 28.)

The second half of the concert will be devoted to a single multimovement work—a piano concerto by the late-nineteenth-century composer Tchaikovsky. (You may notice different spellings for Tchaikovsky and other Russian composers on some programs, owing to varied ways of transcribing their names.) This concerto appears to be a three-movement work, falling again into a standard format (fast-slow-fast). The tempo markings for each movement are, however, much more descriptive than those for the Mozart symphony, using words like *maestoso* (majestic), *con spirito* (with spirit), and *con fuoco* (with fire). This is typical of the Romantic era, as is the work's somber minor key. In the concerto, your interest will be drawn sometimes to the soloist, performing virtuoso passages and cadenzas, and at other times to the orchestra.

In addition to the works to be performed, the printed program may include short notes about each composition and biographical sketches of the soloist and the conductor. Traditionally, the names of all the ensemble members are also listed, along with upcoming concert dates.

During the Performance

Concert etiquette There are certain concert conventions and rules of etiquette during a performance of which you should be aware. The house lights are usually dimmed just before the concert begins. Out of consideration for the performers and those around you, be sure your cell phone or pager is turned off before the concert begins, and that you do not make noise with candy wrappers or shuffling papers while taking notes. It is customary to applaud at the entrances of performers, soloists, and conductors. In an orchestra concert, the concertmaster (the first violinist) may also make an entrance and then tune the orchestra by asking the oboe player to play a pitch, to which all the instruments tune in turn. When the orchestra falls silent, the conductor enters, and, after another round of applause, the performance begins.

Knowing when to applaud during a concert is important. Generally, one applauds after complete works such as a symphony, a concerto, a sonata, or a song cycle; it is inappropriate to clap between movements of a multimovement work. Sometimes, short works are grouped together on the program, suggesting that they are a set. In this case, applause is suitable at the close of the group. If you are unsure, follow the lead of others in the audience. One notable exception to the rule of avoiding applause during a work is at the opera, where it is traditional to interrupt with applause after a particularly fine delivery of an aria or an ensemble number.

The Performers

Onstage decorum

Newcomers to the concert hall are often surprised at the way the performers are dressed. For many years, it has been traditional for ensemble players to wear black—long dresses or pantsuits for the women, tuxedos or tails for the men. While this may seem overly formal, it is still customary, since dark, uniform clothing minimizes visual distraction. Soloists may dress more colorfully.

The behavior of the performers on stage is often as formal as their dress. The entire orchestra may stand at the entrance of the conductor, who shakes the hand of the first violinist before beginning. A small group, such as a string quartet, will often bow to the audience in unison. Normally a performer will directly address the audience only if, at the close of the program, an additional piece or two is demanded by the extended applause. In this case, the *encore* (French for "again") is generally announced.

It may surprise you to see that some musicians, particularly pianists, singers, and other soloists, perform from memory. To perform without music requires intense concentration and necessitates many arduous hours of study and practice.

This brief explanation is intended to remove some of the mystery surrounding concertgoing. The best advice that can be given is to take full advantage of the opportunities available—try something completely unfamiliar, perhaps the opera or the symphony, and continue enjoying concerts of whatever music you already like!

For more information about concertgoing and for sample concert reports visit our Web site at www.wwnorton.com/enjoy.

1

Melody: Musical Line

"It is the melody which is the charm of music, and it is that which is most difficult to produce. The invention of a fine melody is a work of genius."

—JOSEPH HAYDN

KEY POINTS

■ A musical *sound* (or *tone*) has *pitch* and *duration*, shown symbolically in a *note*.
■ A *melody* is the line in music, a concept shared by all cultures.
■ A melody is defined by *pitches* and *intervals*.
■ It can have a narrow to wide span of pitches *(range)*.

- Melody can move in different directions (up or down).
- It can move by connected steps *(conjunct)* or by leap *(disjunct)*.
- The units of a melody are *phrases*, and the phrases end in *cadences*.
- A melody may be accompanied by a secondary melody *(countermelody)*.

Melody is often the element in music that makes the most direct appeal to the listener. It is usually what we remember and whistle and hum. We know a good melody, or tune, when we hear it, and we recognize its power to move us, although we may not be able to explain why it does. Millions of melodies have been written around the world, but no matter how different they may sound, all music cultures share the concept of melody as a musical line.

Musical Sound

Frequency

Duration

Before we can define the term melody, we must have a common understanding of several terms. *Sound* is produced by vibrations perceived by the human ear. A musical sound, or a *tone,* can be defined in terms of its pitch and its duration, and is represented by a musical symbol called a *note. Pitch* refers to the highness or lowness of a sound, measured in *frequency* (the number of vibrations per second), which depends on the vibrating body. A short string, or column of air, vibrates faster than a longer one and thus produces a higher pitch. *Duration* depends on the length of time that the vibration continues. We will see that pitch relates to the musical element of melody while duration influences the music's movement through time (rhythm).

Defining Melody

The familiar architectural line of the *Pyramid of Cheops* at Giza, in Egypt (2680–2258 B.C.E.), relates to the upward and downward turns that shape a melody.

A *melody* is a coherent succession of single pitches. We perceive the pitches of a melody in relation to each other, in the same way we hear the words of a sentence—not singly but as an entire thought. As mentioned above, pitch refers to the highness or lowness of a tone, depending on the rate of vibration (or frequency)—the faster the vibration, the higher the pitch. The distance between two different pitches is called an *interval.* Intervals may be large or small. The intervals of Western music are familiar to us, while certain world musics use intervals so small as to be virtually indistinguishable to our ears.

Characteristics of Melody

Melodies may rise and fall with bold movement, or change slowly, subtly, almost imperceptibly. The melodies of each music culture have their own distinctive character. In some cultures, melody is closely bound to rhythm, and in others, including Western culture, a melody (more popularly called a *tune*) is nearly inseparable from the sounds that are combined with it. (We will come to know this concept as harmony.)

We can describe some characteristics of any melody: its range, its shape, and the way it moves. A melody goes up and down, one tone being higher or lower than another; by *range,* we mean the distance between the melody's lowest and highest tones. This span can be very narrow, as in a children's song that is easy to sing, or it can be very wide, which is often true of melodies played on an instrument. The range of a piece is usually described in approximate terms— narrow, medium, or wide.

Range

Shape is determined by the direction a melody takes as it turns upward or downward or remains static. This movement can be charted on a kind of line graph, resulting in an ascending or descending line, an arch, or a wave.

Shape

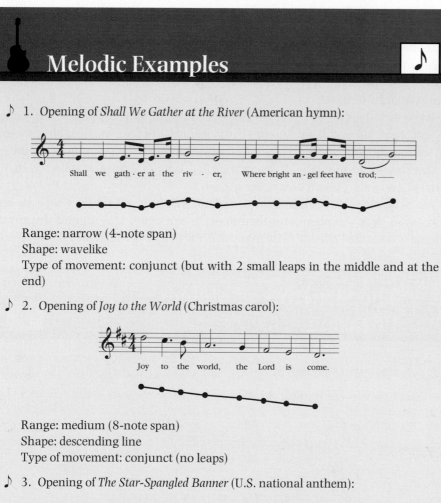

Melodic Examples

♪ 1. Opening of *Shall We Gather at the River* (American hymn):

Range: narrow (4-note span)
Shape: wavelike
Type of movement: conjunct (but with 2 small leaps in the middle and at the end)

♪ 2. Opening of *Joy to the World* (Christmas carol):

Range: medium (8-note span)
Shape: descending line
Type of movement: conjunct (no leaps)

♪ 3. Opening of *The Star-Spangled Banner* (U.S. national anthem):

Range: wide (10-note span)
Shape: wavelike
Type of movement: disjunct (many leaps)

A melody can move from pitch to pitch in small intervals, or it can move by leaps to more distant pitches. Melodies that move principally by small intervals in a joined, connected manner are called *conjunct,* while those that move in disjointed or disconnected intervals are described as *disjunct.* Melodies do not necessarily remain the same throughout. A melody may, for example, begin with a small range and conjunct motion and, as it develops, expand its range and become more disjunct.

Conjunct and disjunct movement

The Structure of Melody

**Phrase
Cadence**

Just as a sentence can be divided into its component units or phrases, so can a melody. A *phrase* in music, as in language, denotes a unit of meaning within a larger structure. The phrase ends in a resting place, or *cadence,* which punctuates the music in the same way that a comma or period punctuates a sentence. The cadence may be inconclusive, leaving the listener with the impression that more is to come, or it may sound final, giving the listener the sense that the melody has reached the end. The cadence is where a singer or instrumentalist pauses to draw a breath.

If the melody is set to words, the text line and the musical phrase will generally coincide. Many folk and popular tunes consist of four musical phrases that are set to a four-line poem. The first and third lines of the poem may rhyme, as do the second and fourth—this symmetrical type of stanza is reflected in the phrase-and-cadence structure of the melody.

An example is the well-known American folk hymn *Amazing Grace.* Its four phrases, in both the poem and the music, are of equal length, and the rhyme scheme is described *a-b-a-b.* (The *rhyme scheme* of a poem describes the similarity

Rhyme scheme

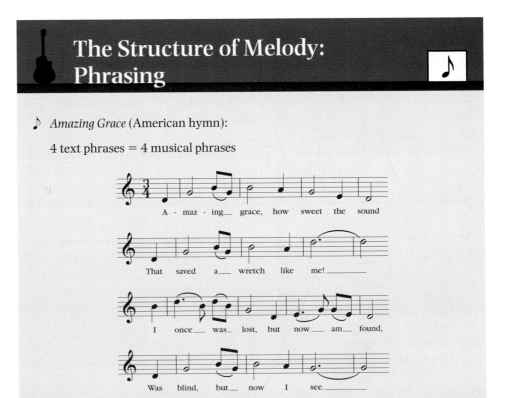

The Structure of Melody: Phrasing

♪ *Amazing Grace* (American hymn):

4 text phrases = 4 musical phrases

A - maz - ing — grace, how sweet the sound

That saved a — wretch like me! —

I once — was — lost, but now — am — found,

Was blind, but — now I see. —

Listening Activity: Melody

CD: CHR/STD 8/25, SH 4/54

Bernstein: *Tonight*, from *West Side Story*

Let's try out your understanding of terms relating to melody with a familiar musical-theater song from Leonard Bernstein's ever-popular *West Side Story*.

WHAT TO LISTEN FOR

- 4 symmetrical phrases, all the same length.
- How each phrase ends on a long note at the cadence.
  (Rhyming text words = "star," "are," "light," "night.")
- Wide range (spanning 12 notes) and disjunct movement.
  (Big jump up, then down, at opening; "Tonight, tonight.")
- How third phrase is more conjunct ("Today the minutes seem like hours").
- Countermelody in the violins (imitating the voice in the third phrase).

MORE LISTENING REVIEW (FROM CD SET)

- Conjunct movement, small range—Hildegard: *Alleluia, O virga mediatrix*
- Mostly conjunct movement, medium range—Mozart: "Non so più," from *The Marriage of Figaro*
- Disjunct movement, wide range—Schoenberg: *Pierrot lunaire*, No. 18
- Symmetrical phrasing—Mozart: *Eine kleine Nachtmusik*, third movement
- Countermelody—Haydn: Symphony No. 94 in G major *(Surprise)*, second movement (countermelody in violins begins about 1 minute into the work)

in sound of the last syllables in each line—here they are "sound," "me," "found," and "see.") The first three cadences (at the end of each of the first three lines) are inconclusive (incomplete), with an upward inflection like a question at the end of the second phrase. The fourth phrase, with its final downward motion, provides the answer; that is, it gives the listener a sense of finality. One pitch serves as home base, around which the melody revolves and to which it ultimately returns.

This same feeling of symmetry and balance can be achieved in melodies that do not rely on words but are played on instruments. Composers can also adapt asymmetrical melodies of irregular phrase length to both vocal and instrumental works. We will hear examples of all these structures in our study of various musical styles.

A world of variety is possible when it comes to forming melodies. In order to maintain the listener's interest, a melody must be shaped carefully, either by the composer who plans it out in advance or by the performer who invents it on the spot. What makes a striking effect is a climax, the high point in a melodic line, which usually represents a peak in intensity as well as in range. (Think of the stirring last phrase of *The Star-Spangled Banner*, when the line rises to the words "O'er the land of the free.")

We will also hear music that features several simultaneous melodies. Sometimes the relative importance of one over the other is clear, and the added tune is called a *countermelody* (literally, "against a melody"). In other styles, each melodic line is of seemingly equal importance.

Countermelody

For much of the music we will study, melody is the most basic element of communication between the composer or performer and the listener. As the twentieth-century composer Aaron Copland aptly put it, "The melody is generally what the piece is about."

2

Rhythm: Musical Time

"I got rhythm, I got music . . . "

—IRA GERSHWIN

KEY POINTS

- *Rhythm* is what moves music forward in time.
- *Meter,* marked off in *measures,* organizes the *beats* in music.
- Each measure begins with a strong *downbeat.*
- *Simple meters* are the most common: duple, triple, and quadruple.
- *Compound meters* subdivide each beat into three, rather than two, subbeats.
- Rhythmic complexities occur with *upbeats, offbeats, syncopation,* and *polyrhythm.*
- *Additive meters* are used in some world musics.
- Some music is *nonmetric* or has an obscured pulse.

Beat

Music is propelled forward by *rhythm,* the element that organizes movement in time. The term refers to the length, or duration, of individual notes. The basic unit we use to measure time is called the *beat*—the regular pulsation heard in most Western styles of music. Some beats are stronger than others; these are known as *accented,* or strong, beats. In much of the music we hear, these strong beats occur at regular intervals—every other beat, every third beat, every fourth, and so on—and thus we perceive all the beats in groups of two, three, four, or more. These patterns into which rhythmic pulses are organized are called *meters* and, in notation, are marked off in *measures,* each measure containing a fixed number of beats. The first beat of each measure generally receives the strongest accent.

Meter and measure

Meter is a broader term. While the term "rhythm" encompasses the overall movement of music in time, meter is the actual measurement of time. It refers to the number of beats in a measure, the placement of accents within the measure, and the way each beat in a measure is divided into smaller parts. A parallel may be drawn in the realm of poetry. For example, the following stanza by the American poet Robert Frost is in a meter that alternates a strong and weak beat. A metrical reading of this poem will bring out the regular pattern of accented (´) and unaccented (¯) syllables:

> Thē wóods āre lóve-lȳ, dárk ānd déep.
> Būt Í hāve próm-īs-és tō kéep,
> Ānd míles tō gó bē-fóre Ī sléep,
> Ānd míles tō gó bē-fóre Ī sléep.

When we read rhythmically, on the other hand, we bring out the natural flow of the language within the basic meter and the meaning of the words.

Metrical Patterns

Much of Western music is based on simple recurring patterns of two, three, or four beats grouped together in a measure. As in poetry, these patterns, or meters, depend on the regular recurrence of an accent. In music, the first accented beat of each pattern is known as a *downbeat*, referring to the downward stroke of a conductor's hand. Simplest of all patterns is a succession of beats in which a strong downbeat alternates with a weak beat: ONE-two, ONE-two, or, in marching, LEFT-right, LEFT-right. This common pattern of two beats to a measure is known as *duple meter*.

   Triple meter, another basic pattern, consists of three beats to a measure—one strong beat and two weak—and is traditionally associated with such dances as the waltz and the minuet.

   Quadruple meter, also known as *common time*, contains four beats to the measure, with a primary accent on the first beat and a secondary accent on the third. Although it is sometimes not easy to tell duple and quadruple meter apart, quadruple meter usually has a broader feeling.

   When duple, triple, and quadruple meters subdivide the beat into two or four, they are called *simple meters*. However, meters in which each beat is divided into three are known as *compound meters*. *Sextuple meter*, for example, with six beats to the measure, is usually heard as a duple-compound meter, in which the principal accents fall on one and four (ONE-two-three, FOUR-five-six). Marked by a gently flowing effect, this pattern is often found in lullabies.

   The following examples illustrate the four basic patterns.

The principles of symmetry and repetition of elements in architecture are comparable to the regular organization of rhythm into meters. *The Temple of the Warriors*, an eleventh-century structure in Chichén Itza, Yucatán.

Examples of Meters

' = primary accent
˘ = secondary accent
‾ = unaccented beat

SIMPLE METERS

Duple meter: *Twinkle, Twinkle, Little Star* (children's song)

Accents:	Twín-	klē,	twín-	klē,	lít-	tlē	stár,___	
Meter:	1	2	1	2	1	2	1	2
	Hów	Ī	wón-	dēr	whát	yōu	áre,___	
	1	2	1	2	1	2	1	2

Other examples of duple meter:

♪ *Yankee Doodle* (American Revolutionary War song)
  Oh, Susanna (19th-century American song by Stephen Foster)
  Dixie (American Civil War song)

♪ **Triple meter:** *America* (patriotic song)

Mý´	cōun-	trȳ	'tís_____		ōf	thēe,
1	2	3 |	1		2	3 |

Swéet	lānd	ōf	lí-		-	bēr-tȳ
1	2	3 |	1		2	3 |

Óf	thēe	Ī	síng._____		
1	2	3 |	1	2	3 |

Other examples of triple meter:

♪ *The Star-Spangled Banner* (U.S. national anthem)
  Happy Birthday (traditional American song)
♪ *Amazing Grace* (American hymn)
  Cielito lindo (traditional Spanish song)
♪ *Goodbye, Old Paint* (American cowboy song)

Quadruple meter: *America, the Beautiful* (patriotic song)

Ōh,	beaú-	-	tī -	fŭl	fōr	spá-	- ciōus	skĭes,
4 |	1	2		3	4 |	1	2	3

Fōr	ám-	bēr		wǎves	ōf	gráin,_____		
4 |	1	2		3	4 |	1	2	3

Fōr	púr-	-	plē	moŭn-	tāin	má-	-	jēs-tiĕs
4 |	1	2		3	4 |	1	2	3

Ā-	bóve	thē		frŭit-	ēd	pláin,_____		
4 |	1	2		3	4 |	1	2	3

Other examples of quadruple meter:

♪ *Shall We Gather at the River* (19th-century American hymn)
♪ *The Battle Hymn of the Republic* (American Civil War song)
  Auld Lang Syne (traditional Scottish song)
  O Canada (Canadian national anthem)

COMPOUND METER

Sextuple meter: *Rock-a-bye Baby* (children's lullaby)

Róck-	ā	bȳe	bǎ-	-	bȳ,	ón	thē	trēe-	tŏp,	
1	2	3	4	5	6 |	1	2	3	4	5	6|

Whén	thē	wīnd	blōws,		thē	crá-	dlē	wīll	rŏck,	
1	2	3	4	5	6 |	1	2	3	4	5	6|

Other examples of sextuple meter:

♪ *Greensleeves* (English folk song)
  Silent Night (Christmas carol)
  When Johnny Comes Marching Home (American Civil War song)

In certain cases, a piece might not begin with a downbeat. For example, *America, the Beautiful,* in quadruple meter, begins with an *upbeat,* or on the last beat of the measure—in this case, on beat 4. (Notice that the Frost poem cited earlier also begins with an upbeat.)

Composers have devised a number of ways to keep the recurrent accent from becoming monotonous. The most common is the use of *syncopation,* a deliberate upsetting of the normal pattern of accentuation. Instead of falling on the strong beat of the measure, the accent is shifted to a weak beat or to an *offbeat* (in between the beats). Syncopation has figured in the music of the masters for centuries, and is characteristic of the African-American dance rhythms out of which jazz developed. The examples on this page illustrate the technique.

Syncopation is only one technique that throws off the regular patterns. A composition may change meters during its course. Indeed, certain twentieth-century pieces shift meters nearly every measure. Another technique is the simultaneous use of rhythmic patterns that conflict with the underlying beat, such as "two against three" or "three against four"—in a piano piece, for example, the left hand might play two notes to a beat, while the right hand plays three notes to the same beat. This is called *polyrhythm* (many rhythms), and occurs frequently in the musics of many African cultures as well as in music influenced by those cultures, such as jazz and rock. In some non-Western

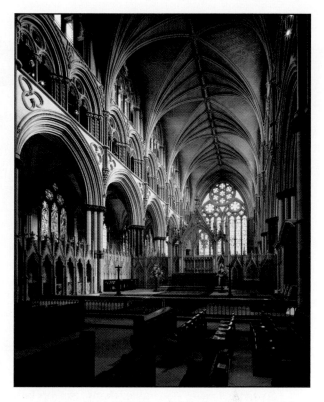

The duple subdivisions of the vaulted arches in the Angel Choir of Lincoln Cathedral (c. 1282), in England, can be compared to simple meters in music.

Examples of Syncopation

Try singing or speaking these songs in time with a regular beat (the numbers below).

♪ 1. Gently syncopated: *Sometimes I Feel Like a Motherless Child* (quadruple meter) (African-American spiritual)

Sometimes_____ I		feel_____like a	
1	2		3 4	

mo-ther-less child,_____	
1	2		3 4	

2. Accented and syncopated: *Hello! Ma Baby* (quadruple meter) (ragtime song)

Hel-lo!	ma' ba-	by,	Hel-lo!	ma' ho-	ney,
1	2	3	4	1	2	3	4	

Hel-lo!	ma' rag-	time	gal._____
1	2	3	4	1	2	3	4	

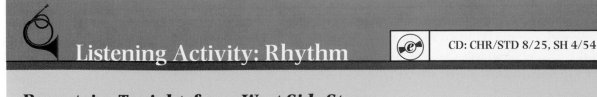

Listening Activity: Rhythm

CD: CHR/STD 8/25, SH 4/54

Bernstein: *Tonight,* from *West Side Story*

Let's return to *Tonight,* the same musical-theater song we listened to in Chapter 1, and see what rhythmic and metric characteristics you can hear,

WHAT TO LISTEN FOR

- Duple meter (strong beat, weak beat).
- Upbeat on opening text (To-**night** = weak-**strong**: upbeat-**downbeat**).
- Complex rhythms with offbeats and syncopation.
- Polyrhythm created in accompaniment.

MORE LISTENING REVIEW (FROM CD SET)

- Nonmetric—Hildegard: *Alleluia, O virga mediatrix*
- Duple meter—Haydn: Symphony No. 94 in G major *(Surprise),* second movement
- Triple meter—Mozart: *Eine kleine Nachtmusik,* third movement
- Quadruple meter—Mozart: *Eine kleine Nachtmusik,* first movement
- Compound meter—Smetana: *The Moldau* (opening)
- Changing meter—Bernstein: *Mambo,* from *West Side Story*
- Veiled pulse—Debussy: *Prelude to "The Afternoon of a Faun"*
- Syncopation—Joplin: *Maple Leaf Rag*
- Polyrhythm—Ligeti: *Disorder,* from *Etudes for Piano*
         Traditional: Ugandan drumming

Additive meter

musics, the rhythmic organization is even more complex, being based on an *additive meter,* or grouping of irregular numbers of beats that add up to a larger overall pattern. For example, a rhythmic pattern of ten beats common in the music of India divides into groupings of 2 + 3 + 2 + 3. We will see that certain folk styles employ similar additive patterns of accents.

Nonmetric

Some music moves without any strong sense of beat or meter. We might say that such a work is *nonmetric,* as some early Western music is, or that the pulse is veiled or weak, with the music moving in a floating rhythm that typifies certain non-Western styles.

Time is a crucial dimension in music, and its first law is rhythm. This is the element that binds together the parts within the whole: the notes within the measure and the measure within the phrase.

3

Harmony: Musical Space

*"We have learned to express the more delicate nuances of feeling by
penetrating more deeply into the mysteries of harmony."*
—ROBERT SCHUMANN

KEY POINTS

- *Harmony* describes the simultaneous happenings in music.
- A *chord* is the simultaneous sounding of three or more pitches.
- Chords are built from a particular *scale*, or sequence of pitches.
- The most common chord in Western music is a *triad*, which is built on alternate notes of a scale.
- Most Western music is based on *major* or *minor scales*, from which melody and harmony are derived.
- The *tonic* is the central tone around which a melody and its harmonies are built; this principle of organization is called *tonality*.
- *Diatonic* pitches belong to a major or minor scale; chromatic pitches draw from the full gamut of notes available in the octave.
- *Dissonance* is created by an unstable, or discordant, harmony.
- *Consonance* occurs with the resolution of dissonance, producing a concordant sound.
- In some cultures, a single sustained tone, or *drone*, constitutes the harmony.

To the linear movement of the melody, harmony adds another dimension: depth, or the simultaneous happenings in music. Harmony is to music what perspective is to painting—it introduces the impression of musical space. Not all musics of the world rely on harmony for interest, but it is central to most Western styles.

Harmony describes the movement and relationship of intervals and chords. We already know that an interval is the distance between any two tones. Intervals can occur melodically—that is, when one note follows another—or simultaneously. When three or more tones are sounded together, a *chord* is produced. **Chord**
The intervals from which melodies and chords are built are chosen from a particular *scale*, or collection of pitches arranged in ascending or descending order. **Scale**
For convenience, the tones of the most frequently used Western scales are assigned syllables, *do-re-mi-fa-sol-la-ti-do*, or numbers, 1-2-3-4-5-6-7-8 (both **Syllables**
ascending scales). Thus the interval *do-re* (1-2) is a second, *do-mi* (1-3) is a third, *do-fa* (1-4) is a fourth, *do-sol* (1-5) is a fifth, *do-la* (1-6) is a sixth, *do-ti* (1-7) is a seventh, and *do-do* (1-8) is an *octave*. As you can see from the example on page **Octave**
25, melody constitutes the horizontal aspect of music, while harmony, comprising blocks of tones (the chords), constitutes the vertical. We will consider the importance of the octave and scales in Chapter 17.

The Function of Harmony

Chords have meaning only in relation to other chords—that is, only as each chord leads into the next. Harmony therefore implies movement and progression. And the progression of harmonies in a musical work gives us a feeling of order and unity.

Triad   The most common chord in Western music is a certain combination of three tones known as a *triad.* Such a chord may be built on any step, or *degree,* of the scale by combining every other note. A triad built on the first degree consists of the first, third, and fifth pitches of the scale *(do-mi-sol);* on the second degree, steps 2-4-6 *(re-fa-la);* on the third degree, steps 3-5-7 *(mi-sol-ti);* and so on. The triad is a basic formation in our music. In the example below, the melody of *Old MacDonald* is harmonized with triads. The supporting role of harmony is apparent when a singer or solo instrument is accompanied by piano. As in *Old MacDonald,* a vocalist sings the melody while an instrument provides the harmonic background. Melody and harmony do not function independently of one another. On the contrary, the melody suggests the harmony that goes with it, and each constantly influences the other.

The Organization of Harmony

Tonic   In all musics of the world, certain tones assume greater importance than others. In Western music, the first tone of the scale, *do,* also called the *tonic* or keynote, serves as a home base around which the others revolve and to which they ultimately gravitate. We observed this principle at work earlier with the tune *Amazing Grace* (p. 16). It is this sense of a home base that helps us recognize when a piece of music ends.

Harmony lends a sense of depth to music, as perspective does in this photograph, by **Fernand Ivaldi,** of a view down a tree-lined canal in France. (Fernand Ivaldi/Getty Images)

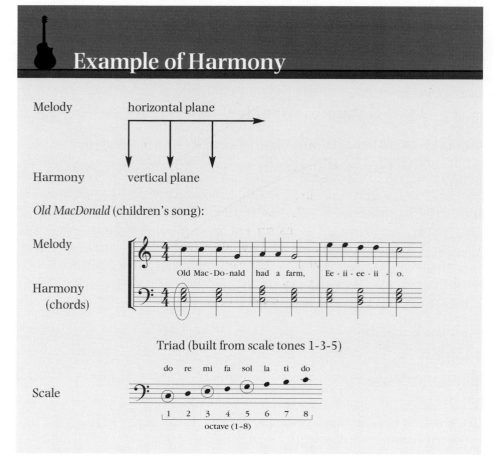

Example of Harmony

Melody — horizontal plane

Harmony — vertical plane

Old MacDonald (children's song):

Melody

Old Mac-Do-nald had a farm, Ee - ii - ee - ii - o.

Harmony (chords)

Triad (built from scale tones 1-3-5)

do re mi fa sol la ti do

Scale

1 2 3 4 5 6 7 8

octave (1–8)

The principle of organization around a central tone, the tonic, is called *tonality*. The particular scale chosen as the basis of a piece determines the identity of the tonic and the tonality. Two different types of scales are commonly found in Western music written between about 1650 and 1900: major and minor. What characterizes these two types are the intervals on which they are built. We will learn more about the formulation of scales later (in Chapter 17). For the moment, it is necessary to know only that there are certain perceived differences between scales: music in major is usually thought of as bright, while minor often sounds more subdued. Some people find that minor sounds sadder to them than major. Indeed, a nineteenth-century composer would hardly choose a minor tonality for a triumphal march or for the grand finale of a piece. We will regard major and minor as scale types and as tonalities, each with its own unique quality of sound.

Tonality

Major and minor scales

We distinguish between notes that belong to a particular scale and tonality and those that do not. The term *diatonic* describes melodies or harmonies that are built from the tones of a major or minor scale; *chromatic* (from the Greek word *chroma*, meaning "color") describes the full gamut of notes available in the octave.

Diatonic and chromatic

Consonance and Dissonance

Harmonic movement, as we will see, is generated by motion toward a goal or a feeling of resolution. This striving for resolution is the dynamic force in our

Listening Activity: Harmony

CD: CHR/STD 2/55, SH 2/1

Haydn: Symphony No. 94 in G major (*Surprise*)

Listening to this appealing orchestral work will help us recognize some aspects *of harmony* (the simultaneous happenings in music).

WHAT TO LISTEN FOR

- Simple, folklike melody with accompaniment.
- Melody and harmony centered on a major scale, sounding bright and cheery.
- Melody is diatonic, lacking in chromaticism.
- Melody hovers around a central tone, or tonic, serving as home base.
- "Surprise" is a loud crashing chord, or block of harmony.
- Changing mood when harmony moves to a minor scale at an increased volume level, now sounding more dramatic and emotional.
- Return to original melody on a major scale.
- Overall harmony is consonant; tension builds through changes from major to minor and through dynamics.

MORE LISTENING REVIEW (FROM CD SET)

- Major tonality—Mozart: *Eine kleine Nachtmusik,* third movement
- Minor tonality—Beethoven: Symphony No. 5 in C minor, first movement
- Consonance—Handel: "Hallelujah Chorus," from *Messiah*
- Dissonance—Ligeti: *Disorder,* from *Etudes for Piano*

Dissonance

music. It shapes the forward movement, providing focus and direction. Movement in music receives its maximum impetus from *dissonance,* a combination of tones that sounds discordant, unstable, in need of resolution.

Dissonance introduces the necessary tension into music in the same way suspense and conflict create tension in drama. Dissonance finds its resolution in **Consonance** *consonance,* a concordant (or agreeable) combination of musical tones that provides a sense of relaxation and fulfillment. At their extremes, dissonance can sound harsh, while consonance is more pleasing to the ear. Each complements the other, and each is a necessary part of the artistic whole.

In general, music has grown more dissonant through the ages. It is easy to understand why. A combination of tones that sounded extremely harsh when first introduced begins to seem less so as the sound became increasingly familiar. As a result, each later generation of composers uses ever more dissonant harmonies in order to create the same degree of excitement and tension as its predecessor.

Historically, harmony appeared much later than melody—about a thousand years ago—and its development took place largely in the West. In many Far Eastern cultures, harmony takes the subsidiary role of a single sustained **Drone** tone, called a *drone,* against which melodic and rhythmic complexities unfold. This harmonic principle also occurs in certain European folk musics, where, for example, a bagpipe might play one or more accompanying drones to a lively dance tune.

Our harmonic system has advanced steadily over the past millennium, continually responding to new needs. Composers have tested the rules as they have experimented with innovative sounds and procedures. Yet their goal remains the same: to impose order on the raw material of sound, organizing the pitches so that they reveal a unifying idea.

4

Musical Texture

"The composer . . . joins Heaven and Earth with threads of sound."
　　　　　　　　　　　—ALAN HOVHANESS

KEY POINTS

- *Texture* refers to the interweaving of the melodic and harmonic elements of music.
- The simplest texture is single-voiced music, or *monophony*.
- *Heterophony* refers to multiple voices elaborating the same melody at the same time.
- *Polyphony* describes a many-voiced texture based on *counterpoint*—one line set against another.
- *Homorhythm* is a texture in which all the voices, or lines, move in the same rhythm.
- A principal melodic voice with accompaniment is *homophony*.
- *Imitation*—when a melodic idea is presented in one voice, then restated in another—is a common unifying technique in polyphony; *canons* and *rounds* are two types of strictly imitative works.
- Some of the devices used in writing counterpoint manipulate the melody by stating it backwards *(retrograde)*, upside down *(inversion)*, upside down and backwards *(retrograde inversion)*, in elongated rhythmic values *(augmentation)*, and in shortened rhythmic values *(diminution)*.

Types of Texture

Another element of music is what we call its texture, or fabric. Melodic lines may be thought of as the various threads that make up the musical fabric. This texture may be one of several distinct types.

Monophony

The simplest texture is *monophony*, or single-voiced. ("Voice" refers to an individual part or line, even when we are talking about instrumental music.) Here, the melody is heard without any harmonic accompaniment or other melodic lines. It may be accompanied by rhythm and percussion instruments that embellish it, but interest is focused on the single line rather than on any accompaniment. Up to about a thousand years ago, the Western music we know about was monophonic, as much music of the Far and Middle East is to this day.

Line and texture are the subject of **Paul Klee's** (1879–1940) painting *Neighborhood of the Florentine Villas* (1926). (Musée National d'Art Moderne, Centre Georges Pompidou, Paris)

One type of texture that is found widely outside the tradition of Western art music is based on two or more voices (parts) simultaneously elaborating the same melody, usually in an improvised performance. Called *heterophony*, this technique usually results in a melody combined with an ornamented version of itself. It can be heard too in some folk musics as well as in jazz and spirituals, where *improvisation* (in which some of the music is created on the spot) is central to performance.

Distinct from heterophony is *polyphony* (or many-voiced texture), in which two or more different melodic lines are combined, thus distributing melodic interest among all the parts. Polyphonic texture is based on *counterpoint*. This term comes from the Latin *punctus contra punctum*, "point against point" or "note against note"—that is, one musical line set against another. Counterpoint is the art of combining two or more simultaneous melodic lines, usually with rules defined in a particular era.

In the fourth type of texture, *homophony*, a single voice takes over the melodic interest, while the accompanying parts take a subordinate role. Normally, they become blocks of harmony, the chords that support, color, and enhance the principal line. Here, the listener's interest is directed to a single melodic line, but this is conceived in relation to a harmonic background. Homophonic texture is heard when a pianist plays a melody in the right hand while the left sounds the chords, or when a singer or violinist carries the tune against a harmonic accompaniment on the piano. Homophonic texture, then, is based on harmony, just as polyphonic texture is based on counterpoint.

Finally, there is *homorhythm*, a texture where all the voices, or lines, move in the same rhythm, in a note-against-note style. Like homophonic structure, it is based on harmony moving in synchronization with a melody.

A composition need not use one texture or another exclusively. For example, a large-scale work may begin by presenting a melody against a homophonic texture, after which the interaction of the parts becomes increasingly polyphonic as more independent melodies enter. So too in a largely homophonic piece, the composer may enhance the effect of the principal melody through an interesting play of countermelodies and counterrhythms in the accompanying parts.

We have seen that melody is the horizontal aspect of music, while harmony is the vertical. Comparing musical texture to the weave of a fabric consequently has validity. The horizontal threads, the melodies, are held together by the vertical threads, the harmonies. Out of their interaction comes a texture that may be light or heavy, coarse or fine.

Contrapuntal Devices

Imitation

When several independent lines are combined (in polyphony), one method composers use to give unity and shape to the texture is *imitation*, in which a melodic idea is presented in one voice and then restated in another. While the imitating voice restates the melody, the first voice continues with new material.

Examples of Musical Texture

Monophonic—1 melodic line, no accompaniment
♪ Gregorian chant: *Alleluia, Emitte spiritum:*

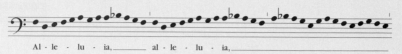

Polyphonic—2 independent melodic lines combined
♪ Bach: Organ chorale prelude, *Jesu, Joy of Man's Desiring:*

Homophonic—1 melody with accompaniment (melody on top)
♪ Mozart: Piano Concerto in C major, second movement (piano solo):

Homorhythmic—4 voices moving together
Handel: "Hallelujah Chorus," from *Messiah* (CD: CHR/STD 2/16, SH 1/42):

Imitation in a Four-Voice Round

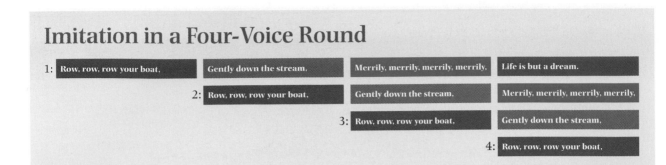

Examples of Contrapuntal Devices*

Imitation (begins 5 notes higher; not exact):

Other contrapuntal devices:

♪ Original: MELODY

♪ Inversion: YDOLEM

Retrograde: YDOLEM

Retrograde inversion: MELODY

Augmentation: MELODY

Diminution: MELODY

*Based on *The Art of Fugue*, by Johann Sebastian Bach

Listening Activity: Texture

CD: CHR/STD 2/16, SH 1/42

Handel: "Hallelujah Chorus," from *Messiah*

The famous "Hallelujah Chorus," from *Messiah* (often performed at Christmas or Easter), can help us review the different musical textures we have learned.

WHAT TO LISTEN FOR

- Changing textures, or the weaving of melodic and harmonic threads.
- Homorhythmic choral statements at opening, on "Hallelujah," then alternating with monophonic (unison) statement of "For the Lord God Omnipotent reigneth."
- More complex texture when the 2 musical ideas mentioned above combine, producing polyphony.
- Imitative polyphony on the text "And He shall reign for ever and ever," with voices entering from lowest (bass) to highest (soprano).
- Alternation of homorhythmic (all voices moving together) and polyphonic textures (2 or more musical lines interwoven).

MORE LISTENING REVIEW (FROM CD SET)

- Monophonic texture—Hildegard: *Alleluia, O virga mediatrix*
- Polyphonic texture—Bernstein: *Mambo*, from *West Side Story*
- Imitation—Bach: Fugue in C minor
             Josquin: *Ave Maria . . . virgo serena*
- Homophonic texture—Chopin: Nocturne in C minor, Op. 48, No. 1
- Homorhythmic texture—Pärt, *Cantate Domino*
- Heterophonic texture—*Think of Me*, by BeauSoleil

Thus to the vertical and horizontal threads in musical texture imitation adds a third, the diagonal (see the example on page 30).

The length of the imitation may be brief or may last the entire work. In the latter case, we have a strictly imitative type of work known as a *canon*. (The name comes from the Greek word for "law" or "order.") The simplest and most popular form of canon is a *round*, in which each voice enters in succession with the same melody, which can be repeated endlessly; well-known examples include *Row, Row, Row Your Boat* and *Frère Jacques (Are You Sleeping?)*. In the example opposite, the round begins with one voice singing "Row, row, row your boat," then another voice joins it in imitation, followed by a third voice and finally a fourth, creating a four-part polyphonic texture.

Canon and round

Contrapuntal writing is marked by a number of devices that have flourished for centuries. *Retrograde* refers to a statement of the melody backward, beginning with its last note and proceeding to its first. *Inversion* is a technique that turns the melody upside down; that is, it follows the same intervals but in the opposite direction (if the melody originally moved up a third, the inverted version moves down a third). These two techniques can be combined in the *retrograde inversion* of a melody: upside down and backward. *Augmentation* calls for the melody to be presented in longer time values, often twice as slow as the original. We can think of this procedure as augmenting or increasing the time it

Retrograde
Inversion

Retrograde inversion
Augmentation

Diminution   takes to play the melody. The opposite technique is called *diminution*, in which the melody is presented in short time values, thus diminishing the time it takes to be played. These structural devices are often difficult for the ear to pick out.

Musical Texture and the Listener

Different textures require different kinds of listening. Monophonic music with its single melodic line is, in principle, the simplest type of music, and we perceive it on a linear time line. Homophonic music is a familiar texture to most of us today, and we are therefore accustomed to focusing on the main melody and its subordinate harmonies, and following the interrelation of the two. Indeed, much of the music we have heard since childhood—including many traditional and popular styles—consists of melody and accompanying chords. Homorhythmic texture is familiar in its simple, vertical conception and hymn-like movement.

Polyphony and heterophony present the most challenging textures. Still, in heterophony, we are often aware of the principal melody, in spite of the linear fabric that surrounds it. In polyphony, we must be attentive to the independent lines as they flow against one another, each in its own rhythm. With practice and repeated hearings, we will learn to follow the individual voices within the contrapuntal web.

5

Musical Form

"The principal function of form is to advance our understanding. It is the organization of a piece that helps the listener to keep the idea in mind, to follow its development, its growth, its elaboration, its fate."

—ARNOLD SCHOENBERG

KEY POINTS

- *Form* is the organizing principle in music; its basic elements are repetition, contrast, and variation.
- Some music is created spontaneously in performance, through *improvisation*.
- *Binary form* (**A-B**) and *ternary form* (**A-B-A**) are basic structures in music.
- A *theme* is a melodic idea used as a building block in a musical composition. A theme can grow and be expanded through *thematic development* and through *sequences* (repetitions at different pitch levels).
- A theme's component parts are small melodic-rhythmic fragments, or *motives*.
- Many non-Western cultures use *call-and-response* (also called *responsorial music*) in performance; this formal structure features a soloist and group response.
- The repetition of a short musical pattern (melodic, rhythmic, harmonic), or *ostinato*, is a common structural procedure.
- Large-scale compositions, such as symphonies and sonatas, are divided into sections, or *movements*.

In all the arts, a balance is required between unity and variety, between symmetry and asymmetry, activity and repose. Nature too has embodied this balance in the forms of plant and animal life and in what is perhaps the supreme achievement—the human form. In music, *form* gives us an impression of conscious choice and rational arrangement. In other words, it is a work's structure or shape, the way the elements of a composition have been combined, or balanced, to make it understandable to the listener.

Structure and Design in Music

Our lives are composed of sameness and difference: certain details occur again and again, others are new. Music, regardless of its cultural origin, mirrors this dualism. Its basic structural elements are *repetition and contrast*—unity and variety. Repetition fixes the material in our minds and satisfies our need for the familiar. Contrast stimulates our interest and feeds our love for change. From the interaction between the familiar and the new—the repeated elements and the contrasting ones—results the contours of musical form. Every kind of musical work, from the nursery rhyme to the symphony, has a conscious structure.

Repetition and contrast

One principle of form that falls between repetition and contrast is *variation*, where some aspects of the music are altered but the original is still recognizable. We hear this formal technique when we listen to a new arrangement of a well-known popular song; the tune is recognizable, but many features of the version we know may be changed.

Variation

The variety of musical structures reflects procedures worked out by generations of composers. No matter how diverse the structures, they are based in one way or another on repetition and contrast. The forms, however, are not fixed molds into which composers pour their material. What makes a piece of music unique is the way it adapts a general plan to its own requirements. All faces have two eyes, a nose, and a mouth; in each face, though, these features make a wholly individual combination. Similarly, no two symphonies of Haydn or

(Left): the Trylon and Perisphere, symbols of the New York World's Fair of 1939, are a visual realization of binary (**A-B**) form. (Right): the Taj Mahal in Agra, India, one of the world's seven wonders, illustrates that three-part (**A-B-A**) form is as appealing to the eye as it is to the ear.

Mozart, no two sonatas of Beethoven, are exactly alike. Each is a fresh and unique solution to the problem of fashioning musical material into a logical and coherent form.

Improvisation   Performers sometimes participate in shaping a composition. In works based primarily on *improvisation* (pieces created in performance as opposed to being precomposed), such as most jazz tunes and rock songs, and in certain non-Western styles, all the elements described above—repetition, contrast, and

Binary and Ternary Form

Binary form: *Yankee Doodle*

Statement—**A**

Yan-kee Doo-dle went to town, a-rid-ing on a po-ny,

Stuck a fea-ther in his cap and called it ma-ca-ro-ni.

Departure—**B**

Yan-kee Doo-dle keep it up, Yan-kee Doo-dle dan-dy,

Mind the mu-sic and the step and with the girls be han-dy.

Ternary form: *Goodbye, Old Paint*

Statement—**A**
(Chorus)

Good-bye, Old Paint, I'm a-leav-in' Chey-enne, Good-

bye, Old Paint, I'm a-leav-in' Chey-enne. My

Contrast
(departure)—**B**
(Verse)

foot's in the stir-rup, my po-ny won't_ stand,_ I'm a-

leav-in' Chey-enne and I'm off to Mon-ta-na. Good-

Repetition—**A**
(Chorus)

bye, Old Paint, I'm a-leav-in' Chey-enne, Good-

bye, Old Paint, I'm a-leav-in' Chey-enne.

Motives and Sequences

♪ *America* (also *God Save the Queen*)

My coun-try 'tis of thee, Sweet land of li-ber-ty, Of thee I sing.
God save our gra-cious Queen, Long live our no-ble Queen; God save the Queen!

Land where our fa-thers died, Land of the pil-grim's pride,
Send her vic-to-ri-ous, Hap-py and glo-ri-ous,

From ev-'ry moun-tain-side, Let free-dom ring.
Long to reign o-ver us, God save the Queen!

variation—play a role. Thus, even when a piece is created on the spot, a balance of these structural principles is present.

Two-Part and Three-Part Form

Two of the most basic patterns in Western music are two-part, or *binary*, form, based on a statement and a departure, without a return to the opening section; and three-part, or *ternary*, form, which extends the idea of statement and departure by bringing back the first section. (In our example, opposite, the pattern of chorus-verse-chorus gives us a ternary form.) Formal patterns are generally outlined with letters: binary form as **A-B** and ternary form as **A-B-A** (illustrated in the chart opposite).

Binary form

Ternary form

Both two-part and three-part forms are common in short pieces such as songs and dances. Ternary form, with its logical symmetry and its balancing of the outer sections against the contrasting middle one, constitutes a simple, clear-cut formation that is favored by architects and painters as well as musicians (see illustration on p. 33).

The Building Blocks of Form

When a melodic idea is used as a building block in the construction of a musical work, we call it a *theme*. The theme is the first in a series of musical events, all of which must grow out of its basic idea as naturally as the plant does from the seed. Spinning out a theme, weaving and reweaving its lines, is the essence of musical thinking. This process of expansion has its parallel in prose writing, where an idea stated at the beginning of a paragraph is embroidered and enlarged upon until it has been explored as thoroughly as the author desires. Each sentence leads smoothly into the one that follows. In similar fashion, every

Theme

Thematic development

measure in a musical work takes up where the one before left off and brings us logically to the next.

The most tightly knit kind of expansion in music is known as *thematic development*—elaborating or varying a musical idea, revealing its capacity for growth. One of the most important techniques in musical composition, thematic development requires imagination, craftsmanship, and intellectual power. The principle of extended melodic elaboration is important also to the melody-oriented styles of many Far Eastern and Middle Eastern musics.

In the process of development, certain procedures have proved to be particularly effective. The simplest is repetition, which may be either exact or varied. Or the idea may be restated at a higher or lower pitch level; this restatement is known as a *sequence*.

Sequence

Motive

Another important technique of thematic development entails breaking up a theme into its component parts, or motives. A *motive* is the smallest fragment of a theme that forms a melodic-rhythmic unit. Motives are the cells of musical growth. By breaking themes into fragments, repeating and varying motives, and combining them in new patterns, composers impart to their works the qualities of evolution and growth.

These musical building blocks can be seen in action even in simple songs, such as the popular national tune *America* (see above). In this piece, the opening three-note motive ("My country") is repeated in sequence (at a different pitch level) on the words "Sweet land of." Another example of a sequence occurs later in the piece: the musical motive set to the words "Land where our fathers died"

Listening Activity: Musical Form

CD: CHR/STD 6/44–46, SH 3/43–45

Tchaikovsky: March from *The Nutcracker*

The march from the popular ballet *The Nutcracker* offers us a chance to test our musical memory in listening for the *form*, or structure, of a composition.

WHAT TO LISTEN FOR

- Catchy march in ternary form (3 sections **A-B-A**).
- Opening theme (melody) played by brass, answered by strings; repeated a number of times.
- Short middle section with rushing, descending lines, first heard in woodwinds, then strings.
- Return of opening music, but with variation in accompaniment.
- Use of basic formal components: repetition, contrast, and variation.

MORE LISTENING REVIEW (FROM CD SET)

- Variation and improvisation—Gillespie/Parker: *A Night in Tunisia*
- Binary form—Mozart: *Eine kleine Nachtmusik*, second movement (first section, about 1 minute long)
- Ternary form—Handel: "Rejoice greatly," from *Messiah*
- Motive, sequence, and thematic development—Beethoven: Symphony No. 5 in C minor, first movement
- Responsorial music—Hildegard: *Alleluia, O virga mediatrix*
- Ostinato (melodic)—Tan Dun: *Farewell*, from *Crouching Tiger, Hidden Dragon*

is repeated beginning on a lower note for the words "Land of the pilgrim's pride."

Whatever the length or style of a composition, it will show the principles of repetition and contrast, of unity and variety, that we have traced here. One formal practice linked to repetition that can be found throughout much of the world is *call and response,* or responsorial music. Heard in many African, Native American, and African-American musics, this style of performance is based on a social structure that recognizes a singing leader who is imitated by a chorus of followers. We will study the practice first as it occurs in early styles of Western church music (see p. 80). Yet another widely used structural procedure linked to the principle of repetition is *ostinato,* a short musical pattern—melodic, rhythmic, or harmonic—that is repeated continually throughout a work or a major section of a composition. This unifying technique is especially prevalent in many African musics as well as popular styles such as blues, jazz, rock, and rap.

Composed and improvised music displays the striving for organic form that binds together the individual tones within a phrase, the phrases within a section, the sections within a *movement* (a complete, comparatively independent division of a large-scale work), and the movements within the work as a whole—just as a novel binds together the individual words, phrases, sentences, paragraphs, chapters, and parts.

Call and response

Ostinato

Movement

6

Musical Expression: Tempo and Dynamics

"Any composition must necessarily possess its unique tempo. . . . A piece of mine can survive almost anything but a wrong or uncertain tempo."

—IGOR STRAVINSKY

KEY TERMS

- *Tempo* refers to the rate of speed, or pace, of the music.
- We use Italian terms to describe musical tempo: *allegro* (fast), *moderato* (moderate), *adagio* (quite slow), *accelerando* (speeding up the pace), and *ritardando* (slowing the pace) are a few examples.
- A *metronome* is a device that indicates the tempo, or beats per minute, by sounding a pulse.
- *Dynamics* describe the volume, or how loud or soft the music is played; Italian dynamic terms include *forte* (loud) and *piano* (soft).
- Composers indicate tempo and dynamics in the music as a means of expression.

The Pace of Music

In our musical system, meter tells us how many beats there are in a measure, but it does not tell us whether these beats occur slowly or rapidly. The *tempo,* or   **Tempo**

Dynamic contrasts in music may be compared to light and shade in painting. *The Concert* (1626), by **Hendrik Terbrugghen** (1588–1629). (National Gallery, London)

rate of speed, of the music provides the answer to this vital question. Consequently, the flow of music in time involves both meter and tempo.

Tempo carries emotional implications. We hurry our speech in moments of agitation or eagerness. Vigor and gaiety are associated with a brisk speed, just as despair usually demands a slow one. In an art that moves in time, as music does, the pace is of prime importance, drawing from listeners responses that are both physical and psychological.

Tempo markings   Because of the close connection between tempo and mood, tempo markings indicate the character of the music as well as the pace. The markings, along with other indications of expression, are given by tradition in Italian. This practice reflects the domination of Italian music in Europe during the period from around 1600 to 1750, when such performance directions were established. A list of some of the most common tempo markings follows:

grave	solemn (very, very slow)
largo	broad (very slow)
adagio	quite slow
andante	a walking pace
moderato	moderate
allegro	fast (cheerful)
vivace	lively
presto	very fast

Frequently, we also encounter modifying adverbs such as *molto* (very), *meno* (less), *poco* (a little), and *non troppo* (not too much). Of great importance are terms indicating a change of tempo, among them *accelerando* (getting faster), *ritardando* (holding back, getting slower), and *a tempo* (in time, or returning to the original pace).

Loudness and Softness

Dynamics denote the volume (degree of loudness or softness) at which music is played. Like tempo, dynamics can affect our emotional response. The main dynamic indications, listed below, are based on the Italian words for soft *(piano)* and loud *(forte)*.

pianissimo (**pp**)	very soft
piano (**p**)	soft
mezzo piano (**mp**)	moderately soft
mezzo forte (**mf**)	moderately loud
forte (**f**)	loud
fortissimo (**ff**)	very loud

Directions to change the dynamics, either suddenly or gradually, are indicated by words or signs. Among the most common are the following:

crescendo (<): growing louder
decrescendo or *diminuendo* (>): growing softer
sforzando (**sf**), "forcing": accent on a single note or chord

Tempo and Dynamics in a Musical Score

CD: CHR/STD 6/20, SH 3/1

From Clara Schumann's Scherzo, Op.10

Tempo: Very fast (Presto)
Dynamics: Soft *(p)*, then medium loud *(mf)*, then gradually growing softer in a long *decrescendo* (>)

Listening Activity: Tempo and Dynamics

CD: CHR/STD 2/55, SH 2/1

Haydn: Symphony No. 94 in G major (*Surprise*)

Let's return to the second movement of Haydn's *Surprise* Symphony to consider elements of *expression* in music.

WHAT TO LISTEN FOR

- How tempo (pace) and dynamics (volume) affect the listener's response.
- Moderate tempo *(Andante)*, a walking pace.
- Soft opening (marked *piano*), which is repeated very softly *(pianissimo)*.
- Jarring, loud chord, played *fortissimo*, which changes the mood.
- Alternation between quiet *(piano)* and loud *(forte)* sections.
- New characer of the middle section, set in minor key and played *fortissimo*.
- How sense of pace changes when the notes in the melody quicken.

MORE LISTENING REVIEW (FROM CD SET)

- *Grave*—Purcell: Dido's Lament, from *Dido and Aeneas*
- *Adagio*—Beethoven: Piano Sonata in C minor, Op. 13 *(Pathétique)*, second movement
- *Moderato*—Brahms: *A German Requiem*, fourth movement
- *Allegro*—Bartók: *Concerto for Orchestra*, fourth movement
- *Vivace*—Adams: *Roadrunner*, from Chamber Symphony
- *Piano*—Copland: *Street in a Frontier Town*, from *Billy the Kid*, opening
- *Fortissimo*—Beethoven: Symphony No. 5 in C minor, fourth movement
- *Crescendo/decrescendo*—Brahms: *A German Requiem*, fourth movement, opening

Tempo and Dynamics as Elements of Musical Expression

The composer adds markings for tempo and dynamics to help shape the expressive content of a work. These expression marks steadily increased in number during the late eighteenth and nineteenth centuries, as composers tried to make their intentions known ever more precisely, until in the early twentieth century few decisions were left to the performer.

If tempo and dynamics are the domain of the composer, what is the role of performers and conductors in interpreting a musical work? Performance directions can be somewhat imprecise—what is loud or fast to one performer may be moderate in volume and tempo to another. Even when composers give precise **Metronome** tempo markings in their scores (using a device known as a *metronome*, which measures the exact number of beats per minute), performers have the final say in choosing a tempo that best delivers the message of the music. And for the many styles of music—non-Western, folk, and popular, among others—that do not rely on composer directions or even printed music, the performer takes full responsibility for interpreting the music.

unit **II**

Musical Instruments and Ensembles

7

Voices and Musical Instruments I

"It was my idea to make my voice work in the same way as a trombone or violin—not sounding like them but 'playing' the voice like those instruments."

—FRANK SINATRA

KEY POINTS

- The properties of sound include pitch, duration, volume, and *timbre*, or tone color.
- An *instrument* generates musical vibrations and transmits them into the air.
- The human voice occurs in various ranges, including *soprano* and *alto* for female voices; *tenor* and *bass* for male voices.
- The world instrument classification system divides into *aerophones* (such as flutes or horns), *chordophones* (such as violins or guitars), *idiophones* (such as bells or cymbals) and *membranophones* (various drums).

Musical Timbre

Timbre

We have considered that a musical tone has pitch, duration, and volume. A fourth property of sound—known as tone color, or *timbre*—best accounts for the striking differences in the sound of instruments. It is what makes a trumpet sound altogether different from a guitar or a drum. Timbre is influenced by a number of factors, such as the size, shape, and proportions of the instrument,

***e* Learning**

RESOURCE CD

***e*Music**

Purcell, Rondeau, from *Abdelazar*

***e*LG**

Britten, *Young Person's Guide*

Instruments of the Orchestra

Study the Composition

ONLINE TUTOR

www.wwnorton.com/enjoy

Quizzes: Materials of Music

Cultural Perspective

2. The Roles of Music around the World

Glossary

the material it is made of, and the manner in which vibration is produced. A string, for example, may be bowed, plucked, or struck.

Instrument

People produce music vocally (by singing or chanting) or by playing a musical instrument. An *instrument* is a mechanism that generates musical vibrations and launches them into the air. Each voice type and instrument has a limited melodic range (the distance from the lowest to the highest tone) and dynamic range (the degree of softness or loudness beyond which the voice or instrument cannot go). We describe a specific area in the range of an instrument or voice, such as low, middle, or high, as its *register*. These and a host of similar considerations help determine the composer's and performer's choices.

Register

The Voice as a Model for Instrumental Sound

The human voice is the most natural of all musical instruments; it is also one of the most widely used—all cultures have some form of vocal music. Each person's voice has a particular quality, or character, and range. Our standard designations for vocal ranges, from highest to lowest, are *soprano*, *mezzo-soprano*, and *alto* (short for *contralto*) for female voices, *tenor*, *baritone*, and *bass* for male voices.

Vocal ranges

In earlier eras, Western social and religious customs severely restricted women's participation in public musical events. Thus young boys, and occasionally adult males with soprano- or alto-range voices, sang female roles in church music and on the stage. In the sixteenth century, women singers came into prominence in secular (nonreligious) music. Tenors were most often featured as soloists in early opera; the lower male voices, baritone and bass, became popular soloists in the eighteenth century. In other cultures, the sound of women's voices has always been preferred for certain styles of music; for example, in certain Muslim cultures of northern Africa, wedding songs are traditionally performed by professional women singers.

(Left): the blind Italian tenor Andrea Bocelli has received worldwide acclaim.

(Right): aerophone—a European bagpipe, often used in folk music, sounds a sustained drone under the melodic line.

Throughout the ages, the human voice has served as a model for instrument builders and players who have sought to duplicate its lyric beauty, expressiveness, and ability to produce *vibrato* (a throbbing effect) on their instruments.

(Above): a Native American dancer with rattles, a type of idiophone.

(Left): a Japanese woman plays the koto, a plucked chordophone.

The World of Musical Instruments

The diversity of musical instruments played around the world defies description. Since every conceivable method of sound production is used, and every possible raw material employed, it would be impossible to list them all here. However, specialists have devised a method of classifying instruments that is based solely on the way their sound is generated. Called the Sachs-Hornbostel System (after its inventors Curt Sachs and Erich von Hornbostel), there are four basic categories. *Aerophones* produce sound by using air as the primary vibrating means.

Aerophones

A drum ensemble from Burundi in Central Africa illustrates membranophones.

Listening Activity: Voices

CD: CHR/STD 6/17, SH 3/34

Verdi: Quartet, from *Rigoletto*

Let us investigate the musical character and range of the standard voice designations in a quartet from an opera by Verdi. This work allows us to hear four of the vocal ranges, first in quick succession and then singing together.

WHAT TO LISTEN FOR

- Voices that differ in timbre (tone color or character) and in range (soprano, alto, tenor, baritone).
- Opera ensemble beginning with the main soloist—a tenor, with a robust and powerful voice.
- Dramatic, emotional quality achieved in high range of tenor voice.
- Dialogue between 2 women's voices: the alto, with a dark and heavy voice, and the soprano, in a higher range and with a brighter timbre.
- Deep baritone voice entering as lowest and supporting voice of ensemble.
- How the ear is sometimes drawn to the tenor, then to the crystal-clear soprano, soaring above the other voices in the ensemble.

MORE LISTENING REVIEW (FROM CD SET)

- Soprano—Handel: "Rejoice greatly," from *Messiah*
- Mezzo-soprano—Purcell: Dido's Lament, from *Dido and Aeneas*
- Tenor—Bernstein: *Tonight* (solo in *Tonight* Ensemble), from *West Side Story*
- Baritone—Schubert: *Erlking*
- Bass—Wagner: Finale, from *Die Walküre*
- Ensemble (baritone, tenor, soprano)—Mozart: Act I, Scene 7, from *The Marriage of Figaro*
- Chordophone—*The Moon Reflected on the Second Springs* (bowed and struck)
- Aerophone—*Think of Me*, by BeauSoleil (accordion)
- Idiophone (cowbell) and membranophones (bongos)—Bernstein: *Mambo*, from *West Side Story*

Chordophones	Common instruments in this grouping are flutes, whistles, accordions, bagpipes, and horns—in short, nearly any wind instrument. *Chordophones* are instruments that produce sound from a vibrating string stretched between two points. The string may be set in motion by bowing, plucking, or striking, so the instruments are as disparate as the violin, harp, guitar, Japanese koto, Chinese hammered dulcimer *(yangqin)*, and Indian sitar.
Idiophones	*Idiophones* produce sound from the substance of the instrument itself. They may be struck, blown, shaken, scraped, or rubbed. Examples of idiophones are bells, rattles, xylophones, and cymbals—in other words, a wide variety of percussion instruments, among others. *Membranophones* are drum-type instruments that are sounded from tightly stretched membranes. These instruments can be struck, plucked, rubbed, or even sung into, thus setting the skin in vibration (see illustrations on p. 43).
Membranophones	

In the next chapter, the instruments used most frequently in Western music will be described and categorized. Throughout the book, however, you will see allusions to other instruments associated with popular and art music cultures around the world that have influenced the Western tradition.

8

Musical Instruments II

"In music, instruments perform the function of the colors employed in painting."

—HONORÉ DE BALZAC

KEY POINTS

- The four families of Western instruments are *strings, woodwinds, brass,* and *percussion.*
- String instruments (chordophones) are sounded by *bowing* and *plucking.*
- Bowed strings include *violin, viola, cello,* and *double bass;* plucked strings include *harp* and *guitar.*
- Woodwind instruments (aerophones) have differing sound production means; they include *flute, oboe, clarinet, bassoon,* and *saxophone.*
- Brass instruments (aerophones) include *trumpet, French horn, trombone,* and *tuba.*
- Percussion instruments include idiophones *(xylophone, cymbals, triangle)* and membranophones *(timpani, bass drum);* some instruments are pitched *(chimes)* while others are unpitched *(tambourine).*
- Keyboard instruments, such as *piano* and *organ,* do not fit neatly into the Western classification system.

The instruments of the Western world—and especially those of the orchestra—may be further categorized into four familiar groups: strings, woodwinds, brass, and percussion. We will see, however, that these categories, or families, of instruments are not entirely homogeneous; that is, all woodwinds are not made of wood, nor do they share a common means of sound production. Also, we will see that certain instruments do not fit neatly into any of these convenient categories (the piano, for example, is both a string and a percussion instrument).

String Instruments

The string family, like the grouping of chordophones, includes two types of instruments: those that are bowed and those that are plucked. The bowed string family has four principal members: violin, viola, violoncello, and double bass, each with four strings (double basses sometimes have five) that are set vibrating by drawing a bow across them. The hair of the bow is rubbed with *rosin* (a substance made from hardened tree sap) so that it will "grip" the strings. The bow is held in the right hand, while the left hand is used to "stop" the string by pressing a finger down at a particular point, thereby leaving a certain portion of the string free to vibrate. By stopping the string at another point, the performer changes the length of the vibrating portion, and with it the rate of vibration and the pitch.

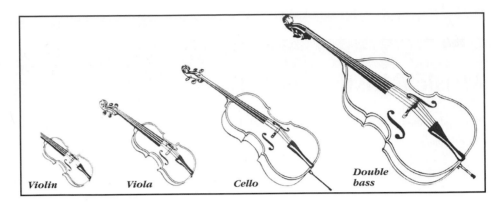

Violin   Viola   Cello   Double bass

Violin

The *violin* evolved to its present form at the hands of the brilliant instrument makers who flourished in Italy from around 1600 to 1750. Most famous among them were the Amati and Guarneri families—in these dynasties, the secrets of the craft were transmitted from father to son—and the master builder of them all, Antonio Stradivari (c. 1645–1737). A recent film, *The Red Violin* (1998), traces a fictional account of one such fine instrument. Preeminent as a melody instrument, the violin is capable of brilliance and dramatic effect, subtle nuances from soft to loud, and great agility in rapid passages throughout its extremely wide range.

Violinist Anne-Sophie Mutter.

The *viola* is somewhat larger than the violin and thus has a lower range. Its strings are longer, thicker, and heavier. The tone is husky in the low register, somber and penetrating in the high. The viola is an effective melody instrument that often balances the more brilliant violin by playing a countermelody. It usually fills in the harmony, or it may double another part. One instrument is said to *double* (reinforce) another when it plays the same notes an octave higher or lower.

Violoncello

The *violoncello*, popularly known as *cello*, is lower in range than the viola and is notable for its singing quality, which takes on a dark resonance in the low register. Cellos often carry the melody, they enrich the sound with their full timbre, and together with the double basses, they supply the foundation for the harmony of the string family.

Double bass

The *double bass*, known also as a *contrabass* or *bass viol*, is the lowest of the string instruments of the orchestra. Accordingly, it plays the bass part—that is, the foundation of the harmony. Its deep tones support the cello part an octave lower.

These four instruments constitute the string section, or what is often called "the heart of the orchestra," a designation that indicates the section's versatility and importance.

Special effects

Orchestral string instruments can be played in many styles and can produce many special effects. They excel at playing *legato* (smoothly, connecting the notes) as well as the opposite, *staccato* (with notes short and detached). A special effect, *pizzicato* (plucked), is created when a performer plucks the string with a finger instead of using the bow. *Vibrato*, a throbbing effect, is achieved by a rapid wrist-and-finger movement on the string that slightly alters the pitch. For a *glissando*, a finger of the left hand slides along the string while the right hand draws the bow, thereby sounding all the pitches under the left-hand finger, in

(Left): Yo-Yo Ma, cellist.

(Right): Milt Hinton playing the double bass.

one swooping sound. *Tremolo*, the rapid repetition of a tone through a quick up-and-down movement of the bow, is associated with suspense and excitement. No less important is the *trill*, a rapid alternation between a tone and one adjacent to it.

Double-stopping means playing two strings simultaneously; playing three or four strings together is called *triple-* or *quadruple-stopping*. Using this technique, the members of the violin family, essentially melodic instruments, become capable of producing harmony all by themselves. Another effect is created by the *mute*, a small attachment that fits over the bridge, muffling (and changing) the sound. *Harmonics* are crystalline tones in a very high register that are produced by lightly touching the string at certain points while the bow is drawn across the string.

Singer Bono and guitarist The Edge perform during a U2 concert, part of the Elevation Tour, July 17, 2001, Paris.

Banjo player Béla Fleck and
the Flecktones.

Two plucked string instruments, the harp and the guitar, are also widely used. The *harp* is one of the oldest of musical instruments, with a home in many cultures outside Europe. Its plucked strings, whose pitches are changed by means of pedals, produce an ethereal tone. Chords on the harp are frequently played in broken form—that is, the tones are sounded one after another instead of simultaneously. From this technique comes the term *arpeggio,* which means a broken chord (*arpa* is Italian for "harp"). Arpeggios can be created in a variety of ways on many instruments.

Guitar

The *guitar,* another old instrument, dating back at least to the Middle Ages, probably originated in the Middle East. It has always been a favorite solo instrument, and is associated today with folk and popular music as well as classical styles. The standard acoustical (as opposed to electric) guitar is made of wood and has a fretted fingerboard and six nylon strings, which are plucked with the fingers of the right hand or with a pick. The *electric guitar,* an electronically amplified instrument capable of many specialized techniques, comes in two main types: the hollow-bodied (or electro-acoustic), favored by jazz and popular musicians, and the solid-bodied, used more often by rock musicians. Related to the guitar are such traditional instruments as the *banjo* (see illustration above) and *mandolin.*

Woodwind Instruments

The tone of woodwind instruments (aerophones) is produced by a column of air vibrating within a pipe that has little holes along its length. When one or another of these holes is opened or closed, the length of the vibrating air column within the pipe is changed. Woodwind players are capable of remarkable agility on their instruments by means of an intricate mechanism of keys arranged to suit the natural position of the fingers.

Flutist James Galway.

This group is less homogeneous than the strings. Nowadays woodwinds are not necessarily made of wood, and they require several different methods of setting up vibration: blowing across a mouth hole (flute family), blowing into a mouthpiece that has a single reed (clarinet and saxophone families), or blowing into a mouthpiece fitted with a double reed (oboe and bassoon families). They do, however, have one important feature in common: the holes in their pipes. In addition, their timbres are such that composers think of them and write for them as a group.

The *flute* is the soprano voice of the woodwind family. Its tone is cool and velvety in the expressive low register, mellow in the middle, and often brilliant in the upper part of its range. The present-day flute, made of a silver alloy rather than wood, is a cylindrical tube, closed at one end, that is held horizontally. The player blows across a mouth hole cut in the side of the pipe near the closed end. The flute is used frequently as a melody instrument—its timbre stands out against the orchestra—and offers the performer great versatility in playing rapid repeated notes, scales, and trills. The *piccolo* (from the Italian *flauto piccolo,* "little flute") is actually the highest pitched instrument in the orchestra. In its upper register, it takes on a shrillness that is easily heard even when the orchestra is playing *fortissimo.*

Piccolo

The *oboe* continues to be made of wood. The oboist blows directly into a double reed, which consists of two thin strips of cane bound together so as to leave between them a very narrow passage for air. The oboe's timbre, generally described as nasal and reedy, is often associated with pastoral effects and nostalgic moods. As the oboe's pitch is reasonably stable, it traditionally sounds the tuning note for the other instruments of the orchestra. The *English horn* is an alto oboe. Its wooden tube is wider and longer than that of the oboe and ends in a pear-shaped opening called a *bell,* which largely accounts for its soft, expressive timbre. The instrument is not well named, for it is neither English nor is it a horn.

Oboe

English horn

The *clarinet* has a single reed, a small thin piece of cane fastened against its chisel-shaped mouthpiece. The instrument possesses a smooth, liquid tone, as well as a remarkably wide range from low to high and from soft to loud. Almost as agile as the flute, it has an easy command of rapid scales, trills, and repeated notes. The *bass clarinet,* one octave lower in range than the clarinet, has a rich tone, a wide dynamic range, and great flexibility.

Clarinet

Bass clarinet

The *bassoon,* another double-reed instrument, possesses a tone that is weighty and thick in the low register, crisp and sonorous in the middle, and reedy and intense in the upper. Capable of a hollow-sounding staccato and wide leaps that can sound humorous, it is at the same time a highly expressive instrument. The *contrabassoon* produces the lowest tone of the woodwinds. Its function in the woodwind section of supplying a foundation for the harmony may be compared with that of the double bass among the strings.

Bassoon

Contrabassoon

(Left): Pamela Pecha, oboist.

(Right): Richard Stolzman playing the clarinet in Carnegie Hall.

(Left): Anja Caffelle, bassoonist.

(Right): Joshua Redman playing tenor saxophone.

Saxophone   The *saxophone* is of more recent origin than the other woodwind instruments, having been invented by the Belgian Adolphe Sax in 1840. It was created by combining the features of several other instruments—the single reed of the clarinet along with a conical bore and the metal body of the brass instruments. The saxophone blends well with either woodwinds or brass. By the 1920s, it had become the characteristic instrument of the jazz band, and has remained a favorite sound in many styles of music today.

Brass Instruments

The main instruments of the brass family (also aerophones) are the trumpet, French horn (generally referred to simply as horn), trombone, and tuba. All these instruments have cup-shaped mouthpieces (except for the horn, whose mouthpiece is shaped like a funnel) attached to a length of metal tubing that flares at the end into a bell. The column of air within the tube is set vibrating by the tightly stretched lips of the player, which are buzzed like a kind of double reed. Going from one pitch to another involves not only mechanical means, such as a slide or valves, but also enough muscular control to vary the pressure of the lips and breath. Brass and woodwind instrument players often speak about their *embouchure,* referring to the entire oral mechanism of lips, lower facial muscles, and jaw.

Wynton Marsalis, trumpeter.

Trumpets and horns were widely used in the ancient world. At that time, they were fashioned from animal horns and tusks, which at a later stage of civilization were reproduced in metal, and were used chiefly for religious ceremonies and military signals. Their tone could be terrifying—remember that in the biblical account, the walls of

Jericho came tumbling down to the sound of trumpets.

The *trumpet,* highest in pitch of the brass family, possesses a brilliant timbre that lends radiance to the orchestral mass. It is often associated with ceremonial display. The trumpet can also be muted, using a pear-shaped, metal or cardboard device that is inserted in the bell to achieve a bright, buzzy sound. Trumpet players have experimented with various kinds of mutes that produce many different timbres.

The *French horn* is descended from the ancient hunting horn. Its mellow resonance lends itself to a variety of uses: it can be mysteriously remote in soft passages and nobly sonorous in loud ones. The timbre of the horn blends equally well with woodwinds, brasses, and strings. Although capable of considerable agility, the horn is often used in sustained, supportive parts. The muted horn has a distant sound. The horn is played with the right hand inserted in the bell and is sometimes "stopped" by plugging the bell with the hand, producing a somewhat eerie and rasping quality.

Christian Lindberg, trombonist.

The *trombone*—the Italian word means "large trumpet"—has a full and rich sound that combines the brilliance of the trumpet with the majesty of the horn, but in a lower range. In place of valves, it features a movable U-shaped slide that alters the length of the vibrating air column in the tube.

Trombone

The *tuba* is the bass instrument of the brass family. Like the string bass and contrabassoon, it furnishes the foundation for the harmony. The tuba adds body to the orchestral tone, and a dark resonance ranging from velvety softness to a rumbling growl.

Tuba

(Left): French hornist Barry Tuckwell.

(Right): Sue Bradley playing the tuba.

Evelyn Glennie, percussionist.

Other brass instruments are used in concert and brass bands as well as marching bands. Among these is the *cornet*, which makes a rounder, less brilliant sound than the trumpet. In the early twentieth century, the cornet was very popular in concert bands; today, however, the trumpet has replaced it in virtually all ensembles. The *bugle*, which evolved from the military (or field) trumpet of early times, has a powerful tone that carries well in the open air. Since it is not equipped with valves, it is able to sound only certain tones of the scale, which accounts for the familiar pattern of duty calls in the army. The *fluegelhorn*, much used in jazz and brass bands, is really a valved bugle with a wide bell. The *euphonium* is a tenor-range instrument whose shape resembles the tuba. And the *sousaphone*, an adaptation of the tuba designed by the American bandmaster John Philip Sousa, features a forward bell and is coiled to rest over the shoulder of the marching player.

Percussion Instruments

The percussion section of the orchestra is sometimes referred to as "the battery." Its members accentuate the rhythm, generate excitement at the climaxes, and inject splashes of color into the orchestral sound.

The percussion family (encompassing the vast array of idiophones and membranophones) is divided into two categories: instruments capable of being tuned to definite pitches, and those that produce a single sound in the realm between music and noise (instruments of indefinite pitch). In the former group are the *timpani*, or *kettledrums*, which are generally used in sets of two or four.

Pitched percussion instruments

The timpani is a hemispheric copper shell across which is stretched a "head" of plastic or calfskin held in place by a metal ring. A pedal mechanism enables the player to change the tension of the head, and with it the pitch. The instrument is played with two padded sticks, which may be either soft or hard. Its dynamic range extends from a mysterious rumble to a thunderous roll. The timpani first arrived in western Europe from the Middle East, where Turks on horseback used them in combination with trumpets.

Also among the pitched percussion instruments are several members of the *xylophone* family; instruments of this general type are used in Africa, Southeast Asia, and throughout the Americas. The xylophone consists of tuned blocks of wood laid out in the shape of a keyboard. Struck with mallets with hard heads, the instrument produces a dry, crisp sound. The *marimba* is a more mellow xylophone of African origin. The *vibraphone* combines the principle of the xylophone with resonators, each containing revolving disks operated by electric motors. Its highly unusual tone is marked by an exaggerated vibrato, which can be controlled by changing the speed of the motor. The vibraphone is often featured in jazz groups, and has been used by a number of contemporary composers.

The *glockenspiel* (German for "set of bells") consists of a series of horizontal tuned steel bars of various sizes, which when struck produce a bright, metallic, bell-like sound. The *celesta*, a kind of glockenspiel that is operated by means of a keyboard, resembles a miniature upright piano. The steel plates are struck by small hammers to produce a sound like a music box. *Chimes,* or *tubular bells,* a set of tuned metal tubes of various lengths suspended from a frame and struck with a hammer, are frequently called on to simulate church bells.

Unpitched percussion instruments

The percussion instruments that do not produce a definite pitch include the *snare drum* (or *side drum*), a small cylindrical drum with two heads (top and bottom) stretched over a shell of metal and played with two drumsticks. This instrument owes its brilliant tone to the vibrations of the lower head against taut snares (strings). The *tenor drum,* larger in size, has a wooden shell and no snares. The *bass drum* is played with a large soft-headed stick and produces a low, heavy sound. The *tom-tom* is a colloquial name given to Native American or African drums of indefinite pitch. The *tambourine* is a round, hand-held drum with "jingles"—little metal plates—inserted in its rim. The player can strike the drum with the fingers or elbow, shake it, or pass a hand over the jingles. Of Middle Eastern origin, it is particularly associated with music of Spain, as are *castanets,* little wooden clappers moved by the player's thumb and forefinger.

The *triangle* is a slender rod of steel bent into a three-cornered shape; when struck with a steel beater, it gives off a bright, tinkling sound. *Cymbals* came to the West from central Asia during the Middle Ages. They consist of two large circular brass plates of equal size, which when struck against each other produce a shattering sound. The *gong,* or *tam-tam,* is a broad circular disk of metal, suspended in a frame so as to hang freely. When struck with a heavy drumstick, it produces a deep roar. The gong has found its widest use in the Far East and Southeast Asia, where it is central to the ensemble known as the *gamelan.*

Other Instruments

Piano

Aside from the instruments just discussed, several others, especially those of the keyboard family, are frequently heard in solo and ensemble performances. The *piano* was originally known as the *pianoforte,* Italian for "soft-loud," which suggests its wide dynamic range and capacity for nuance. Its strings are struck with hammers controlled by a keyboard mechanism. The piano cannot sustain tone as well as the string and wind instruments, but in the hands of a fine performer, it is capable of producing a singing melody. Each string (except in the highest register) is covered by a damper that stops the sound when the finger releases the key. There are generally three pedals. If the one on the right, the damper pedal, is pressed down, all the dampers are raised, so that the strings continue to vibrate, producing a luminous haze of sound. The pedal on the left, known as the soft (or *una corda*) pedal, shifts the hammers to reduce the area of impact on the strings, thereby inhibiting the volume of sound. In between is the sustaining pedal (missing on upright pianos), which sustains only the tones held down at the moment the pedal is depressed.

Pianist André Watts.

The piano has a notable capacity for brilliant scales, arpeggios, trills, rapid passages, and octaves, as well as chords. Its range from lowest to highest pitch spans more than seven octaves, or eighty-eight semitones. Closely related is the *electric piano,*

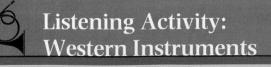

Listening Activity: Western Instruments

RESOURCE CD

Britten: *The Young Person's Guide to the Orchestra*

Britten's *The Young Person's Guide to the Orchestra* introduces the listener first to the sound of the entire orchestra, then to each of its instrument families. The work then passes the principal melody through each instrument individually, proceeding from the highest-ranged instrument to the lowest.

WHAT TO LISTEN FOR

- Entire orchestra playing together, then the 4 groups of instruments: *woodwinds, brass, strings, percussion.*
- Individual instruments in each family, playing in order from highest to lowest (see Listening Guide 1 on pp. 62–63).

If this is difficult to follow, locate a narrated recording or video in your college library.

MORE LISTENING REVIEW (FROM CD SET)

- Saxophone—Gillespie/Parker: *A Night in Tunisia*
- Piano—Beethoven: Piano Sonata in C minor, Op. 13 *(Pathétique)*, second movement
- Harpischord—Bach: Prelude and Fugue in C minor
- Guitar, drums—*Think of Me*, by BeauSoleil
        Gillespie/Parker: *A Night in Tunisia*

an electronically amplified instrument capable of producing piano-like sounds. The more generic electronic keyboard, commonly used in rock groups, can create numerous different sonorities.

Organ   The *organ*, once regarded as "the king of instruments," is a wind instrument. The air flow to each of its many pipes is controlled by the organist from a console containing two or more keyboards and a set of pedals. Gradations in the volume of tone are made possible by enclosing some of the pipes in shuttered cabinets called swell boxes. The organ's multicolored sonority can easily fill a huge space. Electronic keyboards, or synthesizers, capable of imitating pipe organs and other timbres, have become commonplace. (On early organ types and their music, see pp. 162 and 172.)

The instruments described in this and the previous chapter form a vivid and diversified group. To composers, performers, and listeners alike, they offer an endless variety of colors and shades of expression.

9

Musical Ensembles

KEY POINTS

- Choral groups often feature *a cappella singing,* with no accompaniment.
- *Chamber music* is ensemble music for small groups, with one player per part.
- Standard chamber ensembles include *string quartets* as well as *woodwind quintets* and *brass quintets.*
- The modern *orchestra* features eighty to one hundred players.
- Large ensembles generally use a *conductor* who beats patterns with a *baton* to help the performers keep the same tempo.

The great variety in musical instruments is matched by a wide assortment of ensembles, or performance groups. Some are homogeneous—for example, choral groups using only voices or perhaps only men's voices. Others are more heterogeneous—for example, the orchestra, which features instruments from the different families. Across the world, any combination is possible.

Choral Groups

Choral music—music performed by many voices in a chorus or choir—is sung around the world, both for religious purposes (sacred music) and for secular (nonspiritual) occasions. Loosely defined, a *chorus* is a fairly large body of singers who perform together; their music is usually sung in several voice parts.

Chorus

The Boy's Choir of Harlem performing in New York City.

The Colorado String Quartet (Julie Rosenfeld, violin; Diane Chaplin, cello; Deborah Redding, violin; Francesca Martin Silos, viola) enjoys an international reputation.

Most often the group consists of both men and women, but choruses can also be restricted to women's or men's voices only. A *choir* is traditionally a smaller group, often connected with a church or with the performance of sacred music. The standard voice parts in both chorus and choir correspond to the voice ranges described earlier: sopranos, altos, tenors, and basses (abbreviated as SATB).

In early times, choral music was often performed without accompaniment, a style of singing known as *a cappella* (meaning "in the chapel"). The organ eventually became coupled with the choir in church music, and by the eighteenth century, the orchestra also had established itself as a partner of the chorus.

Smaller, specialized vocal ensembles include the *madrigal choir* and *chamber choir*. The madrigal choir might perform *a cappella* secular works, known as *part songs.* The designation "chamber choir" refers to a small group of up to twenty-four singers, performing either *a cappella* or with piano accompaniment.

Instrumental Chamber Ensembles

Chamber music is ensemble music for a group of two to about a dozen players, with one player to a part—as distinct from orchestral music, in which a single instrumental part may be performed by as many as eighteen players or more. The essential trait of chamber music is its intimacy.

Many of the standard chamber music ensembles consist of string players. A standard combination is the *string quartet,* made up of two violins, viola, and cello. Other popular combinations are the *duo sonata* (soloist with piano); the *piano trio, quartet,* and *quintet,* each made up of a piano and string instruments; the *string quintet*; as well as larger groups—the *sextet, septet,* and *octet.* Winds

Sitarist Ravi Shankar and his daughter Anoushka perform in a charity concert in Kuala Lampur. The traditional Indian ensemble includes *tabla,* a hand drum (not shown).

Standard Chamber Ensembles

DUOS

Solo instrument
Piano

TRIOS

String trio
Violin 1
Viola or Violin 2
Cello

Piano trio
Piano
Violin
Cello

QUARTETS

String quartet
Violin 1
Violin 2
Viola
Cello

Piano quartet
Piano
Violin
Viola
Cello

QUINTETS

String quintet
Violin 1
Violin 2
Viola 1
Viola 2
Cello

Piano quintet
Piano
String quartet (Violin 1,
    Violin 2, Viola, Cello)

Woodwind quintet
Flute
Oboe
Clarinet
Bassoon
French horn (a brass instrument)

Brass quintet
Trumpet 1
Trumpet 2
French horn
Trombone
Tuba

too form standard combinations, especially *woodwind* and *brass quintets.* Some of these ensembles are listed below.

These chamber music combinations remain popular today. We will see that contemporary composers have experimented with new groupings that combine the voice with small groups of instruments and electronic elements with live performers. In some cultures, chamber groups mix what might seem to be unlikely timbres to the Western listener—in India, plucked strings and percussion are standard, and in some styles of Chinese music, plucked and bowed strings are normally combined with flutes.

The Orchestra

In its most general sense, the term "orchestra" may be applied to any performing body of diverse instruments—the Japanese ensemble used for court entertainments (called *gagaku*) or the *gamelan* orchestras of Bali and Java, made up largely of gongs, xylophone-like instruments, and drums (see illustration on p. 43). In the West, the term is now synonymous with *symphony orchestra,* an

(Above): the Orchestre Symphonique de Montréal, Charles Dutoit, conductor.
(Below): the seating plan of the orchestra.

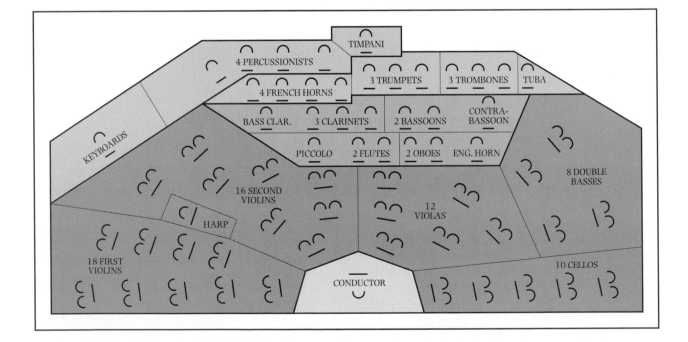

Typical Distribution of Orchestral Instruments

STRINGS	18 first violins 15 second violins 12 violas 12 cellos 9 double basses 1–2 harps, when needed
WOODWINDS	3 flutes, 1 piccolo 3 oboes, 1 English horn 3 clarinets, 1 bass clarinet 3 bassoons, 1 double bassoon
BRASS	4–6 French horns 4 trumpets 3 trombones 1 tuba
PERCUSSION	3–5 players 1 timpani player (2–4 timpani) 2–4 on other instruments

ensemble of strings coupled with an assortment of woodwinds, brass, and percussion instruments.

The symphony orchestra has varied in size and makeup throughout its history, but has always featured string instruments as its core. From its origins as a small group of twenty or so members, the orchestra has grown into an ensemble of more than a hundred musicians, approximately two-thirds of whom are string players. The list above shows the distribution of instruments typical of a large orchestra today.

The instruments of the orchestra are arranged to achieve the best balance of tone. Thus, most of the strings are near the front, as are the gentle woodwinds. The louder brass and percussion are at the back. A characteristic seating plan for the Orchestre Symphonique de Montréal is shown opposite; this arrangement varies somewhat from one orchestra to another.

Concert, Jazz, and Rock Bands

"Band" is a generic name applied to a variety of ensembles, most of which feature winds and percussion at their core. The band is a much-loved American institution, whether it is a concert, marching, or military band or a jazz or rock ensemble. The earliest wind and percussion groups (including Turkish "Janissary" bands—see p. 234) were used for military purposes: musicians accompanied soldiers to war, playing their brass and percussion instruments from horseback and their fifes and drums from among the ranks of the foot soldiers to spur the troops on into battle. Concert wind groups originated in the Middle Ages. In northern Europe, a wind band of three to five musicians played each evening, often from

The Indiana University marching band in formation for a football game.

the high tower of a local church or city hall. From these traditions grew the military bands of the French Revolution and American Civil War. One American bandmaster, John Philip Sousa (1854–1932), achieved worldwide fame with his concert band and the repertory of marches he wrote for it.

Concert band

In the United States today, the *concert band* (sometimes called a *wind ensemble*) ranges in size from forty to eighty or so players; it is an established institution in most secondary schools, colleges, and universities, and in many communities as well. Modern composers like to write for this ensemble, since it is usually willing to play new compositions. The *marching band*, well-known today in the United States and Canada, commonly entertains at sports events and parades. Besides its core of winds and percussion, this group often features remnants from its military origins, including a display of drum majors (majorettes), flags, and rifles.

Marching band

The precise instrumentation of *jazz bands* depends on the particular music being played, but generally includes a reed section made up of saxophones of various sizes and an occasional clarinet, a brass section of trumpets and trombones, and a rhythm section of percussion, piano, double bass, and electric guitar. *Rock bands* typically feature amplified guitars, percussion, and synthesizers. We will discuss jazz and rock bands in later chapters.

American conductor Leonard Bernstein in a performance of Beethoven's Ninth Symphony at the East Berlin Schauspielhaus, December 23, 1989, one month after the Berlin Wall fell.

The Role of the Conductor

Large ensembles, such as an orchestra, concert band, or chorus, generally need a conductor, who serves as the group's leader. Conductors beat time in standard metric patterns to help the performers keep the same tempo; many conductors use a thin stick known as a *baton*, which is easy to see. These conducting patterns, shown in the diagrams on page 61, further emphasize the strong and weak beats of the measure. Beat 1, the strongest in any meter, is always given a downbeat, or a downward motion of the hand; a secondary accent is shown by a change of direction; and the last beat of each mea-

Basic Conducting Patterns

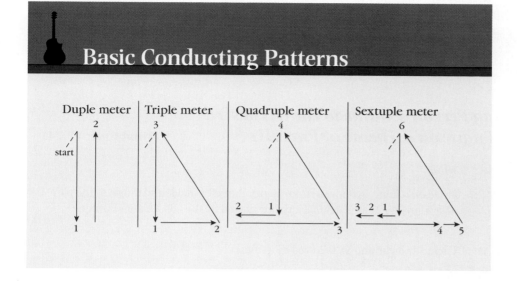

sure, a weak beat, is always an upbeat or upward motion, thereby leaving the hand ready for the downbeat of the next measure.

Equally as important is the conductor's role in interpreting the music for the group. This includes deciding the precise tempo—how fast or slow—and the dynamics—how soft or loud—for each section of the piece. In most cases, the composer's markings are relative (how loud is *forte?*) and thus open to interpretive differences. Conductors also rehearse ensembles in practice sessions, helping the musicians to learn and interpret their individual parts. String players depend on the conductor, or sometimes the *concertmaster* (the first-chair violinist), to standardize their bowing strokes so that the musical emphasis, and therefore the interpretation, is uniform.

Below is the process that a musical work undergoes before you hear it.

COMPOSITION	REHEARSAL	PERFORMANCE
Composer	Musician/conductor	Listener
↓	↓	↓
Creates the work	Practices/interprets the work	Hears/enjoys the work

The Orchestra in Action

A helpful introduction to the modern orchestra is Benjamin Britten's *The Young Person's Guide to the Orchestra,* which was written expressly to illustrate the timbre of each instrument. The work, composed in 1946 and subtitled *Variations and Fugue on a Theme of Purcell,* is based on a dance tune by Henry Purcell (1659–1695), a great seventeenth-century English composer. You can listen to Purcell's original dance tune—a rondeau in a broad triple meter, set in a minor key—on your Student Resource CD; the work is played here by the Los Angeles Baroque Orchestra, using Baroque-period string instruments (with gut rather than metal strings) and harpsichord. You will note that Britten uses only the first section of the dance as the basis for his composition. Compare the soft,

Listening Guide 1

🎧

📀 RESOURCE CD

Britten: *The Young Person's Guide to the Orchestra (Variations and Fugue on a Theme of Purcell)*

(Total time: 17:24)

DATE OF WORK: 1946

♪ **THEME:** Based on a dance (rondeau) from Henry Purcell's incidental music to the play *Abdelazar (The Moor's Revenge)*; theme played by the Los Angeles Baroque Orchestra

MUSICAL FORM: Theme and variations, followed by a fugue

WHAT TO LISTEN FOR:

Purcell
Original dance tune played on Baroque-period string instruments.
Difference in timbre between Baroque instruments and modern strings.

Britten
Stately dance theme, played first by the full orchestra.
Different timbres of each of the 4 instrument families.
Sounds of individual instruments, played in turn by each instrument family (highest to lowest).
Imaginative variations of the original theme.
Special orchestral effects *(pizzicato, glissando, trill)*.
Change from major to minor tonality; changing meters (duple, triple, compound).
Complex fugue at end, with overlapping statements of the theme.

1	0:00	**I. Theme:** 8 measures in D minor, stated 6 times to illustrate the orchestral families:

1. Entire orchestra
2. Woodwinds
3. Brass
4. Strings
5. Percussion
6. Entire orchestra

II. Variations: 13 short variations, each illustrating a different instrument.

		VARIATION	FAMILY	SOLO INSTRUMENT	ACCOMPANYING INSTRUMENTS
2	3:01	1	Woodwinds:	flutes, piccolo	violins, harp, and triangle
		2		oboes	strings and timpani
		3		clarinets	strings and tuba

		4		bassoons	strings and snare drum
3	6:13	5	Strings:	violins	brass and bass drum
		6		violas	woodwinds and brass
		7		cellos	clarinets, violas, and harp
		8		double basses	woodwinds and tambourine
		9		harp	strings, gong, and cymbal
4	10:33	10	Brass:	French horns	strings, harp, and timpani
		11		trumpets	strings and snare drum
		12		trombones, tuba	woodwinds and high brass
5	12:50	13	Percussion:	various	strings

(Order of introduction: timpani, bass drum, and cymbals; timpani, tambourine, and triangle; timpani, snare drum, and wood block; timpani, castanets, and gong; timpani, and whip; whole percussion section)

6   14:46   **III. Fugue:** Subject based on a fragment of the Purcell theme, played in imitation by each instrument of the orchestra in same order as variations:

Woodwinds: piccolo
flutes
oboes
clarinets
bassoons

Strings: first violins
second violins
violas
cellos
double basses
harp

Brass: French horns
trumpets
trombones, tuba

Percussion: various

7   16:32   Full orchestra at the end with Purcell's theme heard over the fugue.

sweet sound of the Baroque string instruments with the louder and richer sonorities of the modern orchestral strings.

In Britten's *Young Person's Guide*, the composer introduces the sound of the entire orchestra playing together, then the sonorities of each instrumental family as a group—woodwinds, brasses, strings, percussion—and finally repeats the statement by the full orchestra. Once the listener has the theme, or principal melody, well in mind, every instrument is featured in order from highest to lowest within each family. Next we encounter variations of the theme, each played by a new instrument with different accompanying instruments. (See Listening Guide 1 for the order of instruments.) The work closes with a grand fugue, a

Suggested Listening Examples

Choral groups
- Chorus—Pärt: *Cantate Domino canticum novum*
- Choir—Josquin: *Ave Maria . . . virgo serena*
- Madrigal choir—Farmer: *Fair Phyllis*
- Men's choir—Bernstein: *Tonight* Ensemble, from *West Side Story* (opening)

Chamber music
- String chamber ensemble—Mozart: *Eine kleine Nachtmusik,* first movement
- Voice and chamber ensemble (20th century)—Baker: *Sometimes I Feel Like a Motherless Child,* from *Through This Vale of Tears*
- Instrumental chamber ensemble (20th century)—Gershwin: Prelude No. 1 (violin and piano)

Orchestra
- Baroque orchestra—Handel: Alla hornpipe, form *Water Music*
- Classical orchestra—Haydn: Symphony No. 94 in G major *(Surprise),* second movement
- Romantic orchestra—Smetana: *The Moldau*
- Twentieth-century orchestra—Stravinsky: *The Rite of Spring*
                        Copland: *Street in a Frontier Town,* from *Billy the Kid*
- Choir with orchestra—Bach: Cantata No. 80, first movement
- Jazz band—Gillespie/Parker: *A Night in Tunisia*
- Chinese chamber ensemble—Abing: *The Moon Reflected on the Second Springs* (erhu and yangqin)
- African drum ensemble—*Ensiriba ya munange Katego*
- Traditional Cajun band—*Think of Me,* by BeauSoleil

For the location of each piece in your sound package, see the table on the front and back inside covers of this book.

polyphonic form popular in the Baroque era (1600–1750), which is also based on Purcell's theme. The fugue, like the variations, presents its subject, or theme, in rapid order in each instrument. (For a discussion of the fugue, see pp. 170–71.)

The modern orchestra, with its amplitude of tonal resources, its range of dynamics, and its infinite variety of color, offers a memorable experience to both the musician and the music lover. It is clearly one of the wonders of Western musical culture.

10

Style and Function of Music in Society

"A real musical culture should not be a museum culture based on music of past ages. . . . It should be the active embodiment in sound of the life of a community—of the everyday demands of people's work and play and of their deepest spiritual needs."

—WILFRID MELLERS

KEY POINTS

- Music provides different functions in societies around the world, including to accompany religious activities, work, and for entertainment.
- Most cultures have *sacred music,* for religious functions, and *secular music,* for entertainment or other nonreligious activities.
- There are many *genres,* or categories, of music; some works *cross over* categories, borrowing elements of one style for use in another (for example, combining jazz with the string quartet).
- The *medium* is the specific group (e.g., orchestra, chorus) that performs a piece.
- Some music is not written down, but is known through *oral transmission.*
- The distinctive features of any artwork make up its *style.*
- In a musical composition, style is created through individual treatment of the elements (melody, rhythm, harmony, texture, form, dynamics, tempo).
- We organize styles of artworks into *historical periods,* each with its own characteristics.
- Works created in any one historical period share some stylistic similarities.

In every culture, music is intricately interwoven with the lives and beliefs of its people. This is especially true of many non-Western societies where, just as in the West, the "classical" exists alongside the "popular" and both are nourished from the rich store of traditional music that is closely allied with daily living. (Later, we will study *The Moon Reflected on the Second Springs,* a piece written by a Chinese folk musician, that is today viewed as "classical" conservatory repertory.) Music serves different functions in different societies, though some basic roles are universal. It accompanies religious and civic ceremonies, it helps workers establish a uniform rhythm to get the job done more efficiently, and it provides entertainment through song and dance. The social organization of any particular culture has much to do with its musical types and styles. In some cultures, such as in the Western classical tradition, only a few people are involved with the actual performance of music; in others, such as that of the African Pygmies, cooperative work is so much a part of society that the people sing as a group, with each person contributing a separate part to build a complex whole.

There is music for every conceivable occasion, but the specific occasions celebrated vary from one culture to another. Thus musical *genres,* or categories of repertory, do not necessarily transfer from one society to the next, though

Genres

The Roles of Music around the World

Music enhances many of our activities, including work, worship, and even warfare. As we noted earlier, music can help synchronize group tasks; such songs tend to be rhythmic, and both the melody and words fit the activity. Work songs are most often responsorial, or sung call and response—a leader improvises lyrics and the group responds rhythmically ("Michael rowed the boat ashore, **Hallelujah**"). Blues and spirituals, for example, grew out of the field hollers of slaves brought to the United States from West Africa. Frederick Douglass, a former slave, wrote in his autobiography *My Bondage and My Freedom* (1855) that "Slaves are generally expected to sing as well as to work." With emancipation, the tradition of singing at work continued on projects such as the building of the transcontinental railroad ("John Henry was a steel-driving man"). You may remember that the opening scene of the 2001 award-winning film *O Brother, Where Art Thou?* featured a work song, *Po' Lazarus*, sung by James Carter and the Prisoners as they break up stones for a road surface.

Most lullabies are sung in the vernacular—that is, the language of the people—and many such songs use vocables, or nonsense syllables, and speak to the child in diminutive or endearing terms. For example, a native American Zuni lullaby from New Mexico refers to "little boy, little cottontail, little jack rabbit, little rat." Lullabies from around the world share some other common musical traits: they are often repetitive, slowly paced, with a gentle rhythmic motion. In Western tradition, many cradle songs are set in triple or sextuple meter to simulate a rocking motion ("Rock-a-bye baby, on the tree top"). One famous example, *Brahms's Lullaby* ("Lullaby and good night"), was written by the Romantic composer Johannes Brahms as an art song for voice and piano (entitled *Wiegenlied*); however, it has entered the realm of traditional music because it is so widely known, having been passed down through oral transmission.

"Lightin'" Washington, an African-American prisoner, singing with his group in the woodyard at Darrington State Farm, Texas, 1934.

Sacred and secular music

they may be similar. For example, Japanese *Noh* drama and Peking opera serve essentially the same social role as opera does in the Western world. And we can distinguish in most cultures between *sacred music,* for religious or spiritual functions, and *secular music,* for and about everyday people outside a religious context.

It is important to differentiate between genre and form: a *genre* is a more general term that suggests something of the overall character of the work as

Music for worship can take many forms, but whether it is sung, played, or danced, it helps shape rituals, or ceremonial acts. We will see later that the Roman Catholic Mass was celebrated for many hundreds of years with sung chant, and that other cultures around the world use their own forms of religious chant (see CP 4). Today, music for worship in America can be as diverse as a traditional Protestant hymn, such as *A Mighty Fortress Is Our God*, a Black gospel rendition of *Amazing Grace*, or a new contemporary Christian song by Michael W. Smith.

Since ancient times, horns (later trumpets) and drums have been associated with warfare. Music serves military campaigns as a means to signal and give orders, to mark the military day (*Reveille* is the wake-up call), and to excite troops in battle. The idea of a military band accompanying soldiers seems to have originated in India or the Middle East. The bagpipe, a popular folk instrument in various world cultures, spurred Scottish and Irish troops to battle from at least the sixteenth century; and in America, fife-and-drum corps accompanied Revolutionary and Civil War soldiers on the march. (A fife is a small wooden transverse flute with fewer holes than a piccolo.)

Much of the music we will hear is intended as entertainment, but not for a specific audience. In addition to the symphonies and art songs heard in our concert halls, we will explore great jazz and blues performances more typically enjoyed in night-clubs; the ceremonial drum ensemble of Uganda, who performed within the royal compound of the king; and a Japanese song traditionally sung in tea-

Actors performing in a Noh play (a Japanese theatrical genre of music and dance).

houses by geisha—a class of professional women entertainers.

TERMS TO NOTE:

work song	oral transmission
field holler	bagpipe
vocable	fife
vernacular	geisha

SUGGESTED LISTENING:

Work song or field holler (*Po' Lazarus,* from
   O Brother, Where Art Thou? soundtrack)
John Henry (traditional ballad)
Brahms's Lullaby (Wiegenlied)
A Mighty Fortress Is Our God (Protestant hymn)
Amazing Grace (hymn or Gospel version) ♪

well as its function. For example, the term *symphony* is a genre designation for a standard format—usually a four-movement orchestral work. As we will see later, each movement has a specific internal *form*, or structure. "Symphony" also implies the *medium*, or the specific group that performs the piece—in this case, an orchestra.

Medium

Titles for musical compositions occasionally indicate the genre and key, such as Symphony No. 94 in G major, by Joseph Haydn. Another way works

Reviewing Terms

TITLE: Symphony No. 5 in C minor, Op. 67 (Op.=opus=work number)
COMPOSER: Ludwig van Beethoven
GENRE: Symphony
FORM: 4-movement work for orchestra
MEDIUM: Symphony orchestra

TITLE: *Messiah*
COMPOSER: George Friedrich Handel
GENRE: Oratorio
FORM: Multimovement work for chorus and soloists, accompanied by orchestra
MEDIUM: Vocal soloists (SATB), chorus, orchestra

TITLE: *Wiegenlied*, Op. 49, No. 4 *(Brahms's Lullaby)*
COMPOSER: Johannes Brahms
GENRE: Romantic song (in German, *Lied*)
FORM: Strophic (2 stanzas sung to same music)
MEDIUM: Solo voice and piano

are identified is through a cataloguing system, often described by *opus number* (*opus* is Latin for "work"; an example is Nocturne, Opus 48, a piano work by Chopin). Other titles are more descriptive, such as *The Nutcracker* (a ballet by the Russian composer Tchaikovsky), *The Trout* (a song by Schubert, an Austrian composer), and *The Moon Reflected on the Second Springs* (by the Chinese musician Abing).

Just as the context for music—when, why, and by whom a piece is performed—varies from culture to culture, so do aesthetic judgments of what is beautiful and what is appropriate. For example, the Chinese consider a thin, tense vocal tone desirable in their operas, while the Italians prefer a full-throated, robust sound in theirs. Likewise, certain performers and styles gain or lose in popularity as cultural preferences change.

Not all music is written down and learned from books or formal lessons. Music of most cultures of the world, including some styles of Western popular and traditional music, is transmitted by example (through a master-apprentice relationship) or by imitation and is performed from memory. The preservation

Oral transmission

of music without the aid of written notation is referred to as *oral transmission.*

We will focus much of our study on Western art music—that is, the notated music of a cultivated and largely urban society. We often label art music as "classical," or serious, for lack of better terms. However, the lines that distinguish art music from other kinds are often blurred. Popular and traditional musics are art forms in their own right: performers of these styles may be as talented as those that present classical music; and both jazz and rock are considered by many to be new art forms, having already stood the test of time. To confuse these categories further, some composers and performing artists *cross over* from one type of music to another—from jazz to rock, from rock to Western classical—or simply borrow elements of one style to use in another, drawing these styles ever closer. Later we will hear elements of Latin-American dance music in the musical theater work *West Side Story* (Chapter 69) and some elements of contemporary chamber music accompanying a well-known Negro spiritual (in David Baker's work *Through This Vale of Tears*, in Chapter 68).

The Concept of Style

Style may be defined as the characteristic way an artwork is presented. We distinguish between the style of a novel and that of an essay, between the style of a cathedral and that of a palace. The word may also indicate the creator's personal manner of expression—the distinctive flavor that sets one artist apart from all others. Thus we speak of the literary style of Dickens or Shakespeare, the painting style of Picasso or Rembrandt, the musical style of Bach or Mozart. We often identify style with nationality, as when we refer to French, Italian, or German style; or with an entire culture, as when we contrast a Western musical style with one of China, India, or some other region.

What makes one musical work sound similar to or different from another? It is the individualized treatment of the elements of music. We have seen that Western music is largely a melody-oriented art based on a particular musical system, from which the underlying harmonies are also built. Musics of other cultures may sound foreign to Western ears, sometimes "out of tune," because they are based on entirely different musical systems, and many do not involve harmony to any great extent. One important factor in these differing languages of music is the way in which the octave is divided and scales are produced, an area we will explore in more detail in Chapter 17. Complex rhythmic procedures and textures set some world musics apart from Western styles, while basic formal considerations—such as repetition, contrast, and variation—bring musics of disparate cultures closer. In short, a style is made up of pitch, time, timbre, and expression, creating a sound that each culture recognizes as its own.

> *Music is never stationary; successive forms and styles are only like so many resting places—like tents pitched and taken down again on the road to the ideal.* —FRANZ LISZT

Suggested Listening Examples

- Sacred music—Palestrina: Gloria, from *Pope Marcellus* Mass
  Brahms: *A German Requiem*, fourth movement

- Secular music—Farmer: *Fair Phyllis*
  Schubert: *Erlking*

- Popular music—Joplin: *Maple Leaf Rag*

- Crossover—Bernstein: Excerpts from *West Side Story*

- Traditional music—*Think of Me*, by BeauSoleil

For examples of Western art music styles, see individual chapters.

Listening Activity: Musical Styles

A typical work from each historical style period is listed below. Listen to each, noting some of its unique characteristics.

- Early Middle Ages—Hildegard: *Alleluia, O virga mediatrix*
- Late Middle Ages—Machaut: *Puis qu'en oubli*
- Renaissance—Josquin: *Ave Maria . . . virgo serena*
- Baroque—Purcell: Dido's Lament, from *Dido and Aeneas*
- Classical—Mozart: *Eine kleine Nachtmusik,* first movement
- Romantic—Berlioz: *Symphonie fantastique,* fourth movement
- Impressionism—Debussy: *Prelude to "The Afternoon of a Faun"*
- Early twentieth century—Stravinsky: *The Rite of Spring*
- Later twentieth century—Adams: *Roadrunner,* from Chamber Symphony

Musical Styles in History

The arts change from one age to the next, and each historical period has its own stylistic characteristics. No matter how greatly the artists, writers, and composers of a particular era may vary in personality and outlook, when seen in the perspective of time, they turn out to have certain qualities in common. Because of this, we can tell at once that a work of art—whether music, poetry, painting, sculpture, or architecture—dates from the Middle Ages or the Renaissance, from the eighteenth century or the nineteenth. The style of a period, then, is the total art language of all its artists as they react to the artistic, political, economic, religious, and philosophical forces that shape their environment. We will find that a knowledge of historical styles will help us place a musical work within the context (time and place) in which it was created.

Historical periods
Scholars will always disagree as to precisely when one style period ends and the next begins. Each period leads by imperceptible degrees into the following one, dates and labels being merely convenient signposts. The timeline below shows the generally accepted style periods in the history of Western music. Each represents a conception of form and technique, an ideal of beauty, a manner of expression and performance attuned to the cultural climate of the period—in a word, a style!

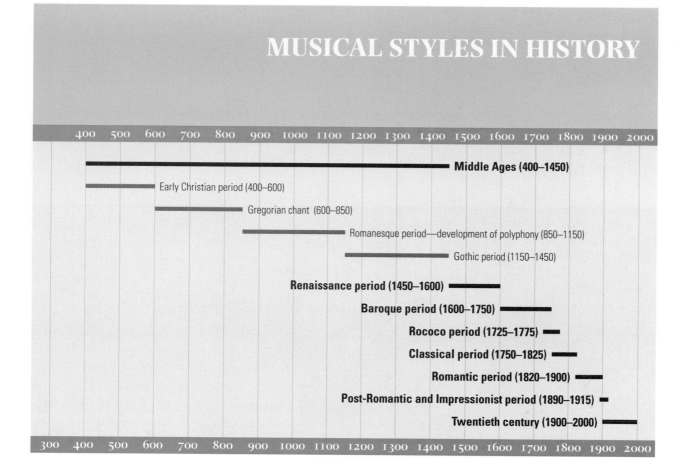

MUSICAL STYLES IN HISTORY

Middle Ages (400–1450)

Early Christian period (400–600)

Gregorian chant (600–850)

Romanesque period—development of polyphony (850–1150)

Gothic period (1150–1450)

Renaissance period (1450–1600)

Baroque period (1600–1750)

Rococo period (1725–1775)

Classical period (1750–1825)

Romantic period (1820–1900)

Post-Romantic and Impressionist period (1890–1915)

Twentieth century (1900–2000)

Andrea Mantegna (1431–1506), *Mars and Venus,* or *Parnassus* (1497). (Paris, The Louvre)

Medieval and Renaissance Music

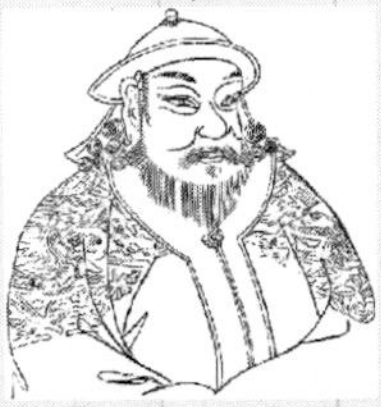

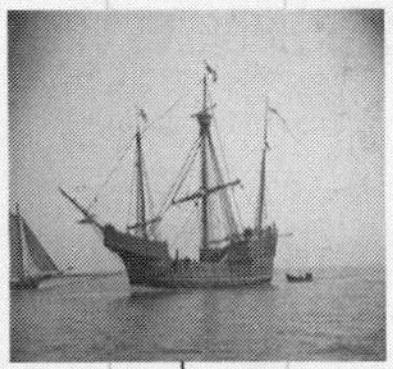

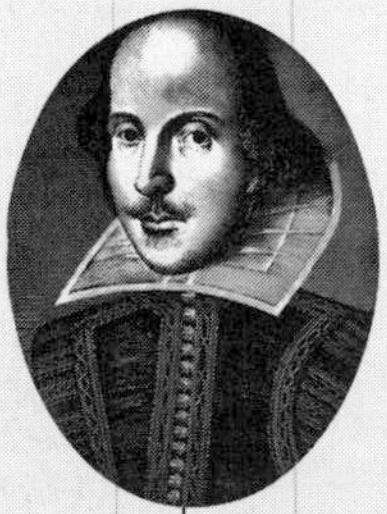

MIDDLE AGES (476–1450)

500 | 600 | 700 | 800 | 900 | 1000 | 1100 | 1200 | 1300 | 1400 | 1410 | 1420 | 1430 | 1440 | 145

- Fall of Roman Empire (476 C.E.)
- Charlemagne crowned first Holy Roman Emperor (800)
- **Hildegard of Bingen** (1098–1179)
- *Chanson de Roland,* French epic
- Notre Dame composers (Léonin, Pérotin)
- Moniot d'Arras (fl. 1213–1239)
- Kublai Khan (1214–1294), emperor of China
- **Adam de la Halle** (c. 1237–c. 1287)
- Last crusade to the Holy Land (1270)
- Marco Polo to China (1271)
- **Guillaume Machaut** (c. 1300–1377)
- Francesco Petrarch (1304–1374), Italian poet, scholar
- Dante Alighieri, Italian poet, *Divine Comedy* (1307)
- Black Death begins (1347)
- Ambrogio Lorenzetti (c. 1290–1348), Italian painter
- Geoffrey Chaucer, English poet, *Canterbury Tales* (1386)
- Donatello (c. 1386–1466), Italian sculptor
- **Guillaume Du Fay** (c. 1397–1474)
- Joan of Arc executed (1431)
- Fall of Constantinople (1453

500 | 600 | 700 | 800 | 900 | 1000 | 1100 | 1200 | 1300 | 1400 | 1410 | 1420 | 1430 | 1440 | 14

RENAISSANCE ERA (1450–1600)

| 1460 | 1470 | 1480 | 1490 | 1500 | 1510 | 1520 | 1530 | 1540 | 1550 | 1560 | 1570 | 1580 | 1590 | 1600 |

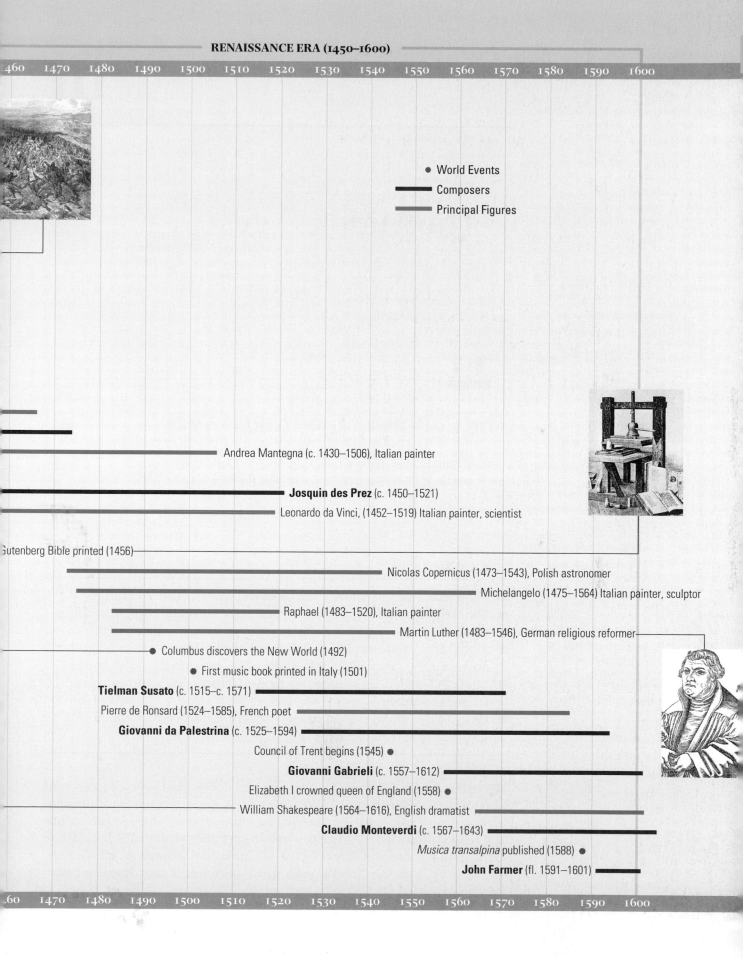

● World Events
━━ Composers
━━ Principal Figures

Andrea Mantegna (c. 1430–1506), Italian painter

Josquin des Prez (c. 1450–1521)

Leonardo da Vinci, (1452–1519) Italian painter, scientist

Gutenberg Bible printed (1456)

Nicolas Copernicus (1473–1543), Polish astronomer

Michelangelo (1475–1564) Italian painter, sculptor

Raphael (1483–1520), Italian painter

Martin Luther (1483–1546), German religious reformer

● Columbus discovers the New World (1492)

● First music book printed in Italy (1501)

Tielman Susato (c. 1515–c. 1571)

Pierre de Ronsard (1524–1585), French poet

Giovanni da Palestrina (c. 1525–1594)

Council of Trent begins (1545) ●

Giovanni Gabrieli (c. 1557–1612)

Elizabeth I crowned queen of England (1558) ●

William Shakespeare (1564–1616), English dramatist

Claudio Monteverdi (c. 1567–1643)

Musica transalpina published (1588) ●

John Farmer (fl. 1591–1601)

| 1460 | 1470 | 1480 | 1490 | 1500 | 1510 | 1520 | 1530 | 1540 | 1550 | 1560 | 1570 | 1580 | 1590 | 1600 |

e Learning

unit **III**

The Middle Ages

11

The Culture of the Middle Ages

"Nothing exists without music, for the universe itself is said to have been framed by a kind of harmony of sounds, and the heaven itself revolves under the tone of that harmony."

—ISIDORE OF SEVILLE

KEY POINTS

- The Middle Ages span nearly one thousand years (c. 476–1450).
- The early Christian church and the state were the centers of powers during this time.
- Much of the surviving music left from the Middle Ages is religious, or *sacred*, because of the sponsorship (*patronage*) of the church.
- The later Middle Ages saw the rise of cities, cathedrals, and great works of art and literature.
- Music held a central place in the cultures of ancient Greece, Rome, and in the Judaic world (CP 3).

The relics of the ancient civilizations—Sumer, Babylonia, Egypt, Greece—bear witness to a flourishing musical art. Only a few fragments of the music of antiquity have survived, however. The centuries have forever silenced the sounds that echoed through the Athenian amphitheater and the Roman circus. Those sounds and the attitudes they reflected, in Greece and throughout the Mediterranean world, were the foundation on which the music of later ages was based. They became part of the Western heritage (see CP 3).

The Middle Ages extended over the thousand-year period between the fall of Rome, commonly set in the year 476, and the cultural flowering of the Renaissance. The first half of this millennium, lasting from around 500 to 1000 and once referred to as the Dark Ages, should be viewed as a period not of decline but rather of ascent and development. In this society, all power flowed from the king, with the approval of the Roman Catholic Church and its bishops. The two centers of power, church and state, were bound to clash, and the struggle between them shaped the next chapter of European history. The modern concept of a strong, centralized government as the guardian of law and order is generally credited to Charlemagne (742–814), the legendary emperor of the Franks. This progressive monarch, who regretted until his dying day that he did not know how to write (he regarded writing as an inborn talent he simply did not possess), encouraged education and left behind him an ideal of social justice that illuminated the perceived "darkness" of the early medieval world.

Early Middle Ages

The culture of this period was largely shaped by the rise of monasteries. It was the members of these religious communities who preserved the learning of the ancient world and transmitted it, through their manuscripts, to European scholars. In their desire to enhance the church service, they supported music extensively, and because of their efforts as patrons, the art music of the Middle Ages was largely religious. Women as well as men played a role in preserving knowledge and cultivating music for the church, as nuns figured prominently in church society. One woman who stands out in particular is Hildegard of Bingen, head of a monastery in a small town in western Germany. She is remembered today for her writings on natural history and medicine and for her poetry and music for special church services. We will study a religious chant by Hildegard in Chapter 12.

The church as patron

The late Middle Ages, from around 1000 to 1450, witnessed the construction of the great cathedrals and the founding of universities throughout Europe. Cities emerged as centers of art and culture, and within them the townspeople—the bourgeoisie—played an ever expanding role in civic life. Developing national literatures helped shape the languages of Europe. Literary landmarks, such as the *Chanson de Roland* (c. 1100) in France, Dante's *Divine Comedy* (1307) in Italy, and Chaucer's *Canterbury Tales* (1386) in England, find their counterparts in painting: Lorenzetti's frescoes in Siena's Town Hall (1338–40, see below) and Orcagna's *Last Judgment* for Florence (c. 1355).

Music is a part of civic life as shown in a detail of **Ambrogio Lorenzetti's** (d. 1348?) fresco *Good Government in the City.* (Palazzo Pubblico, Siena)

Music of the Muses

How old is the art of music, and what role did it play in ancient societies? Archeologists have unearthed flutes and drums that date back 30,000 years and Neolithic cave paintings that provide pictorial evidence of a musical tradition among early humans. Looking back five or six millennia to Mesopotamia, the so-called cradle of civilization (modern-day Syria and Iraq; see map, end of book), we find the first threads of a musical culture that can be traced directly to modern times. By around 2500 B.C.E. (before the common era), the Sumerians had developed several types of plucked string instruments: the harp and its relative the lyre. A small-sized lyre favored by the Babylonians in the second millennium was exported to Egypt and later to Greece and Rome. Hand drums and clappers developed to accompany dancing, as did the earliest wind instrument: a double-reed pipe that was adopted by the Egyptians and later became a standard in Greek culture, known there as the aulos.

Music pervaded the lives of the Jews, as the Hebrew Scriptures (Old Testament) vividly describe. The Israelites' escape from slavery in Egypt was celebrated in Miriam's dance with timbrels (percussion instruments related to the tambourine; Exodus 15:20); David's harp soothed Saul's distemper (1 Samuel 16:14–23); and the sounds of military music felled the walls of Jericho (Joshua 11:4).

Our word "music" derives from the Greek *mousike,* which refers to the art of the Muses of Greek mythology. Each of the Muses, who were the nine daughters of Zeus, father of the gods, presided over an art: for example, Calliope was the Muse of epic poetry, Terpsichore guided dancing and choral singing, and Euterpe inspired lyric poetry and music. Text and music were linked, because most poetry was sung or recited to an instrumental accompaniment. The Greek philosopher Plato, in his dialogue the *Republic,* advised young people to develop skills in both gymnastics and music so they could be strong in war and express themselves through song. Thus, music was woven into all aspects of Greek life. It played a role in ceremonial rites—marriages, funerals, the harvest—and it served as the focus of singing competitions.

The study of music was a serious endeavor, taken up by philosophers such as Pythagoras, who discovered the mathematical ratios of musical intervals, and Aristotle, who recognized the influence of music's harmonies on the soul. In later antiquity, music was grouped with three mathematical arts—

King David, surrounded by his musicians, playing a psaltery. (Biblioteca communale "Maria Teresa," Mantua)

The Roman sun god Apollo sings of his triumph over the python, accompanying himself on the lyre. Fresco (c. 65–70) from the House of the Vettii at Pompeii.

arithmetic, geometry, and astronomy—into what was called the quadrivium; these subjects held an elevated status among the seven liberal arts well into the Middle Ages.

A link between theater and music that was established by the Greeks carried over to the culture of ancient Rome, where musical preludes and interludes were interspersed throughout theatrical comedies, and pantomime (in which an actor silently played all the parts in a show) was accompanied by singing. The Roman world produced both professional and amateur musicians. Among the gifted amateurs was the notorious Emperor Nero (r. 54–68), who, according to legend, "fiddled while Rome burned" in a fire he claimed to have set himself.

The ancient sounds of music have their direct descendants in today's world. The value we place on music and the emotional response we have to its appealing melodies, rhythms, and harmonies have also come down to us from early times, as part of our heritage. And the inclusion of music in school and college curricula, as both an applied art and an academic study, rests on a cultural tradition that is literally thousands of years old.

TERMS TO NOTE:

harp	Muses
lyre	quadrivium
aulos	pantomime
timbrel	psaltery

The age of knighthood

In an era of violence brought on by deep-set religious beliefs, knights embarked on holy—and bloody—Crusades to conquer the Holy Land from the Muslims. Although feudal society was male-dominated, idealizing as it did the figure of the fearless warrior, women's status was raised by the universal cult of Mary, mother of Christ, and by the concepts of chivalry that arose among the knights. In the songs of the court minstrels, women were adored with a fervor that laid the foundation for our concept of romantic love. This poetic attitude found its perfect symbol in the image of the faithful knight who worshipped his lady from afar and was inspired by her to deeds of great daring and self-sacrifice.

The Middle Ages, in brief, encompassed a period of enormous ferment and change. Out of its stirrings, faint at first but with increasing clarity and strength, emerged a profile of what we know today as Western civilization.

12

Sacred Music in the Middle Ages

"When God saw that many men were lazy, and gave themselves only with difficulty to spiritual reading, He wished to make it easy for them, and added the melody to the Prophet's words, that all being rejoiced by the charm of the music, should sing hymns to Him with gladness."

—ST. JOHN CHRYSOSTOM

KEY POINTS

- Many cultures around the world use a kind of chant, a monophonic (single-line) melody, in their worship (CP 4).
- The music of the early Christian church, called *Gregorian chant*, features monophonic, nonmetric melodies set in one of the church *modes*, or scale patterns.
- The melodies fall into three categories *(syllabic, neumatic, melismatic)* based on how many notes are set to each text syllable.
- The most solemn ritual of the Catholic Church is the *Mass*, a daily service with two categories of prayers: the *Proper* (texts that vary according to the day) and the *Ordinary* (texts that remain the same for every Mass).
- Some chants are sung alternating a soloist and chorus in a *responsorial* performance.
- The Cathedral of Notre Dame in Paris was a center for *organum*, the earliest type of polyphony, which consisted of two-, three-, or four-voice parts sung in fixed rhythmic patterns *(rhythmic modes)* that are repeated or varied.
- Preexistent chants formed the basis for early polyphony, including organum and the *motet*, the latter a form that featured multiple texts *(polytextual)*.

The early music of the Christian church was shaped in part by Greek, Hebrew, and Syrian influences. In time, it became necessary to assemble the ever growing body of music into an organized liturgy. The *liturgy* refers to the set order of services and the structure of each service. The task extended over several generations, though tradition credits Pope Gregory the Great (r. 590–604).

Like the music of the Greeks and Hebrews, *Gregorian chant* (also known as *plainchant* or *plainsong*) consists of a single-line melody; in other words, it is monophonic in texture, lacking harmony and counterpoint. Its freely flowing vocal line is subtly attuned to the inflections of the Latin text and is generally free from regular accent.

Gregorian chant

The Gregorian melodies, numbering more than three thousand, form an immense body of music, nearly all of it anonymous. Gregorian chant avoids wide leaps and dynamic contrasts, allowing its gentle contours to create a kind of musical speech. Free from regular phrase structure, the continuous, undulating vocal line is the counterpart in sound of the lacy ornamentation typical of medieval art and architecture. The melodies fall into three main classes, according to the way they are set to the text: *syllabic*, with one note sung to each syllable of text; *neumatic*, generally with small groups of up to five or six notes sung to a syllable; and *melismatic*, with long groups of notes set to a single syllable of text. The melismatic style, descended from the elaborate improvisations heard in Middle

Text settings

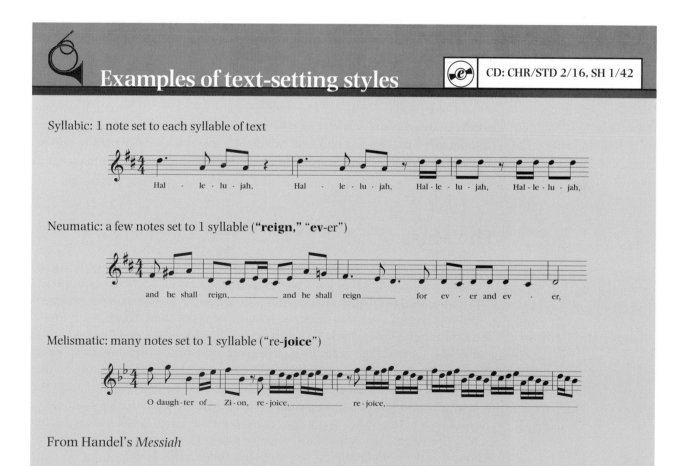

Examples of text-setting styles   CD: CHR/STD 2/16, SH 1/42

Syllabic: 1 note set to each syllable of text

Hal - le - lu - jah, Hal - le - lu - jah, Hal - le - lu - jah, Hal - le - lu - jah,

Neumatic: a few notes set to 1 syllable (**"reign,"** "**ev**-er")

and he shall reign,_____ and he shall reign_____ for ev - er and ev - er,

Melismatic: many notes set to 1 syllable ("re-**joice**")

O daugh-ter of ___ Zi - on, re - joice,_____ re - joice,

From Handel's *Messiah*

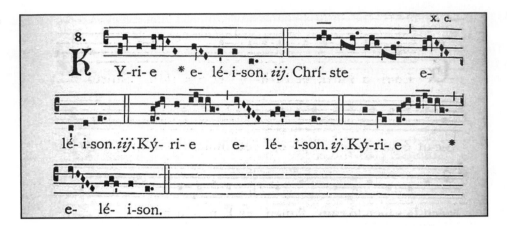

The opening of the Kyrie chant in Gregorian notation, from the *Liber Usualis*, p. 16.

Eastern music, became an expressive feature of Gregorian chant and exerted a strong influence on subsequent Western music.

At first the chants were handed down orally from one generation to the next. As the number of chants increased, singers needed help in remembering **Neumes** the general outlines of the different melodies. Thus *neumes*, little ascending and descending signs, were written above the words to suggest the contours of the melody. Neumes eventually developed into a musical notation consisting of square notes on a four-line staff (see above).

From Gregorian chant through Renaissance polyphony, Western music **Modes** used a variety of scale patterns, or *modes*. In addition to major and minor modes, which possess a strong sense of gravitation to a tonic note, there were others that lacked this sense. The modes served as the basis for European art music for a thousand years. With the development of polyphony—music for several independent lines—a harmonic system based on these scale patterns evolved. The adjective *modal* thus refers to various melodic and harmonic types that prevailed in the early and later Middle Ages. It is frequently used in opposition to *tonal*, which refers to the harmony based on major-minor tonality that came later.

The Mass

The services of the Roman Catholic Church can be divided into two categories: the daily Offices and the Mass. The *Offices* are a series of services celebrated at various hours of the day in monasteries and convents. The *Mass*, a reenactment of the sacrifice of Christ, is the most solemn ritual of the Church. Its name is **Proper and Ordinary** derived from the Latin words *ite, missa est* (go, the Mass is ended), recited at the end of the service. The collection of prayers that makes up the Mass (or its liturgy) falls into two categories: the *Proper*, texts that vary from day to day throughout the church year, depending on the feast being celebrated; and the *Ordinary*, texts that remain the same in every Mass. The Kyrie, for example, is the first item of the Ordinary, or fixed portion, of the Mass. While its text is from Greek, the rest of the Mass texts were in *Latin*, the language of the ancient Romans and the language of learning throughout the Middle Ages and the Renaissance. The Catholic Church continued the use of Latin for the Mass until the middle of the twentieth century. (A chart showing the organization of the

Mass with the individual movements of the Proper and Ordinary appears in Chapter 15, p. 104.) There are Gregorian melodies for each section of the ceremony. In this way, Gregorian chant has been central to the celebration of the Mass, which was and remains the primary service in the Catholic Church.

Life in the Medieval Cloister

One lifestyle available to men and women in the Middle Ages centered around the Catholic Church. Life in a cloister (a place for religious seclusion) allowed people to withdraw from secular society to the shelter of monasteries and convents, where they devoted themselves to prayer, scholarship, preaching, charity, or healing the sick, depending on the religious order they joined.

A life devoted to the church was not an easy one, because the discipline was arduous. A typical day began at 2:00 or 3:00 A.M. with the celebration of the first of the daily services (the Offices), the reading of lessons, and the singing of psalms. Each day in the church calendar had its own ritual and its own order of prayers. The members of the community interspersed their religious duties with work in the fields, in the library, in the workshop. Some produced items that could be sold—wine, beer, or cheese, for example—thus bringing in revenue to the order.

Despite the grueling schedule, many men and women in religious life dedicated themselves to writing and preserving knowledge from earlier times. Such a person was Hildegard of Bingen, one of the most remarkable women of the Middle Ages, who was renowned in her day as a poet and prophet and is immensely popular today for her serenely beautiful music.

The priest Volmar records Hildegard of Bingen's visions. The image, a miniature, is from her poetry collection *Scivias* (1141–51).

The Music of Hildegard of Bingen

"The words of the musical performance stand for the body, and the musical performance itself stands for the spirit. The celestial harmony announces the divinity, and the words truly uncover the humanity of the Word of God."

Hildegard of Bingen (1098–1179) was the daughter of a noble couple who promised her to the service of the church. Raised by a religious recluse, she lived in a stone cell with a single window and took her vows at the age of fourteen. From childhood, Hildegard experienced visions, which intensified in later life. She was reportedly able to foretell the future.

With the death of her teacher, Hildegard became head of the community, and about 1150 founded her own convent in Rupertsberg, Germany, on the Rhine River near Bingen. Her miracles and prophecies made her famous throughout Europe; popes, kings, and priests sought her advice on political and religious issues. She was also known for her scientific and medical writings. Although never officially canonized, Hildegard is regarded as a saint by the church.

Chant as Music for Worship

Many cultures employ music when worshipping or performing certain rituals. These sacred songs take many forms, including chant, a simple, monophonic melody sung or recited to a text. The chants and practices of the early Christian church owe much to Judaism, the religion from which Christianity sprang. In particular, the two religions are linked by the singing of the 150 texts from the Old Testament Book of Psalms. Many of these psalms celebrate singing; "O come, let us sing to the Lord," "Sing unto the Lord a new song," and "I will sing of loyalty and justice" are a few opening lines. In the Judaic tradition, the psalm texts are sung responsorially, by the cantor (soloist and singing leader) and the congregation. In the Roman Catholic Church, the recitation of the psalms, more like speaking than singing, became the core of many religious services; here, too, performances are often responsorial. We will see later that the practice of singing psalms was adopted in the services of the Protestant churches during the Reformation and after (see CP 6 on music and religion in the Americas). Another important musical influence on the early Christian church was from the Church of Byzantium (or Constantinople, now Istanbul in Turkey). This Eastern branch of the Christian church absorbed traditions from Greek and other Mediterranean cultures to form its own music and traditions. (As noted earlier, the text of the Kyrie, from the Mass, is Greek.)

Moving further east to the Islamic world, the texts of the Koran (the sacred text of Islam) are also recited rhythmically in a kind of chant. Two different styles prevail here: a simple, undecorated form for private devotion, and a more embellished form for public performance. The practice of chanting the Koran is governed by established oral traditions that specify the vocal timbre, rhythmic treatment of texts, pronunciation, and the use of a special vibrato (a wavering fluctuation of the pitch). One of the most familiar sounds in Islamic cultures is the call to prayer, which is sounded publically five times per day and helps regulate Muslim daily life. The Prophet Muhammad is credited with instituting the practice of the call to prayer, which is heard once from a minaret (a tower on a mosque, the Muslim house of worship), then from inside the mosque.

One type of religious music that has been popularized in recent years is Tibetan Buddhist chant. In 1988, the Gyütö Tantric choir traveled to the United States on a concert tour set up by Mickey Hart, drummer of the Grateful Dead. The monks agreed to perform

Illuminated initial from Psalm 114 (in Hebrew) depicting the exodus from Egypt, in which Moses led the Israelites from bondage. (From the Kaufmann Haggadah)

A muezzin, or crier, sounds the Muslim call to prayer from the minaret of a mosque.

in order to generate awareness of the oppression of Tibet and its people; their album *Freedom Chants from the Roof of the World* (1989) was recorded during this U.S. visit. Their singing features an unusual multiphonic vocal style, sometimes called throat singing, in which each monk produces a chord of two or three tones, including a deep fundamental pitch (the tone generating the overtone, or harmonic, series) and overtones (thus one voice can sound polyphonic). Sung to prayers, their otherwordly music is said to emanate from a trancelike state that helps the monks transcend their human state to be one with the deity.

On the other side of the world, the Afro-Cuban religion of Santeria is practiced in many Caribbean cultures. A combination of West African beliefs and Catholicism, Santeria is a "magical" religion in which humans communicate with an orisha, or saint, through song and trance. Unlike Gregorian chant, the music of Santeria is highly rhythmic and dance-like, accompanied by bata drums (hourglass shaped drums from Cuba), played in sets of three different-sized instruments, and various idiophones. Santeria groups have arisen in the United States in recent years, performing this engaging music outside the liturgical tradition from which it sprang.

The etheral sounds of chant—Western and Eastern alike—have drawn many listeners to this soothing, meditative music. Some performers have even popularized religious chant by creating "New Age" arrangements, launching, for example, the music of Hildegard of Bingen to the top of the classical charts.

TERMS TO NOTE:

Book of Psalms	overtone
Cantor	multiphonic
responsorial	throat singing
Gregorian chant	vibrato
Islam	fundamental
Koran	Santeria
mosque	orisha
minaret	idiophone

SUGGESTED LISTENING:

Gregorian chant
Jewish cantorial chant
Islamic call to prayer
Buddhist throat singing
Santeria chant

Moved to record her visions and prophecies, Hildegard completed three collections in manuscript entitled *Scivias*. After a particular vision she had in 1141, when "the heavens were opened and a blinding light of exceptional brilliance flowed through my flame," she claimed to understand fully the meaning of the Scriptures.

Hildegard also wrote religious poetry with music, which she collected in a volume entitled *Symphony of the Harmony of Celestial Revelations (Symphonia armonie celestium revelationum)*. These works form a liturgical cycle appropriate for singing at different religious feasts throughout the year. Hildegard's musical style is highly original; it resembles Gregorian chant, but unlike most other new music of the time, it does not draw on the existing repertory.

A Chant to the Virgin by Hildegard

Hildegard wrote many of the texts she set to music; her poetry is characterized by brilliant imagery and visionary language. Some of her songs celebrate the lives of local saints such as Saint Rupert, the patron of her monastery, while many praise the Virgin Mary, comparing her to a blossoming flower or branch and celebrating her purity. Our example is an Alleluia (Listening Guide 2), a movement from the Mass Proper, to be sung on a feast day for the Virgin. The performance here is *responsorial,* alternating between a soloist and a chorus. Despite the contrast between two such dissimilar bodies, the texture remains monophonic, with no harmonic accompaniment. The chant can be viewed as three-part, with the choral *Alleluia* framing the solo verse in an **A-B-A** structure. It is sung to a conjunct, or connected, melody with few leaps and with a free nonmetric rhythm. One of Hildegard's signatures can be heard here: an occasional upward leap of a fifth that gives the line a soaring feeling. It is the text that shapes the line, reaching its highest peaks on evocative words such as "holy womb," "flower," and "chastity." The setting is basically neumatic, with small groups of notes per syllable, but with occasional melismatic settings—especially on the last syllable of *Alleluia* and in the last text line, describing the Virgin's purity or chastity—where syllables are stretched over many notes.

Responsorial singing

Melismatic setting

The Rise of Polyphony: The Notre Dame School

Polyphony, the single most important development in the history of Western music, began to emerge toward the end of the Romanesque era (c. 850–1150). (*Polyphony*, you will remember, combines two or more simultaneous melodic lines.)

Polyphony helped bring about the use of regular meters, which was needed if the different voices were to keep together. Because this music had to be written down in a way that would indicate the precise rhythm and pitch, a more exact notational system was worked out, not unlike the one in use today. (For an explanation of our modern notational system, see Appendix I, "Musical Notation," p. A-1.)

Development of notation

With the development of a more precise notation, music progressed from being an art of improvisation and oral tradition to one that was carefully planned and preserved. During the Gothic era (c. 1150–1450), which saw the

Hildegard of Bingen: *Alleluia, O virga mediatrix* (Alleluia, O mediating branch)

(3:30)

GENRE:	Gregorian chant
CHANT TYPE:	Alleluia, from the Mass Proper
TEXT:	In praise of the Virgin Mary (poet, Hildegard of Bingen)
OCCASION:	For feasts of the Virgin Mary
PERFORMANCE:	Responsorial (solo and chorus; sung chorus-verse-chorus)
STYLE:	Opening melismatic, then neumatic

WHAT TO LISTEN FOR: Alternation between solo and chorus (responsorial).
Monophonic texture (unaccompanied) and free rhythm (nonmetric).
Text setting shifts between melismatic (many notes to a syllable) and neumatic (small groups of notes to a syllable).
Conjunct movement with a few leaps.
Range of 9 notes (just over an octave).
Climaxes (highest range) on words "holy flesh," "beautiful flower," "chastity."
Repeat of opening *Alleluia* at close.

		TEXT	TRANSLATION	PERFORMANCE
1	0:00	Alleluia.	Alleluia.	Solo intonation, then choral resonse with long extension on last syllable (*–ia*); very melismatic.
2	0:45	O virga mediatrix	O mediating branch	Solo verse, with several melismas.
		sancta viscera tua mortem superaverunt,	Your holy flesh has overcome death,	Higher range, neumatic text setting.
		et venter tuus omnes creaturas illuminavit	And your womb has illuminated all creatures	
		in pulchro flore de suavissima integritate	Through the beautiful flower of your tender purity	
		clausi pudoris tui orto.	That sprang from your chastity.	Melismatic at end.
3	2:56	Alleluia.	Alleluia.	Chorus; return to opening.

Opening of solo chant, with melismatic setting on *Alleluia*:

Higher range on "sancta viscera" (holy flesh), in neumatic setting:

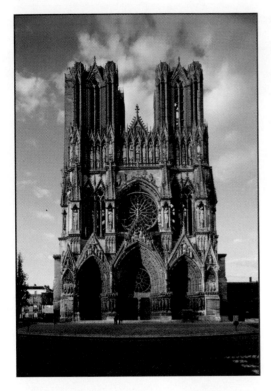

In both architecture and music, the Gothic period saw great advances in the techniques of construction. The Cathedral of Notre Dame, Paris (1163–1235).

rise of cathedrals with their choirs and organs, the period of anonymous creation drew to a close, and the individual composer came to be recognized. The learned musicians, mostly clerics in religious communities, mastered the art of writing extended musical works.

The earliest polyphonic music, called *organum*, developed from the custom of adding a second voice that ran above or below the Gregorian melody at the interval of a fifth or fourth. Soon a polyphonic art blossomed in which the individual voices moved with ever greater independence, not only in parallel but also in contrary motion. In the forefront of this evolution were the composers centered at the Cathedral of Notre Dame in Paris during the twelfth and thirteenth centuries. Their leader, Léonin (fl. third quarter of twelfth century), is the first composer of polyphonic music whose name is known to us. He wrote the *Great Book of Organum (Magnus liber organi)*, music for the entire church year, in this new musical style. His successor, Pérotin (fl. early thirteenth century), expanded the dimensions of organum by increasing the number of voice parts, first to three and then to four.

To the medieval mind, the new had to be founded on the old. Therefore composers of organum based their pieces on preexisting Gregorian chants. While the lower voice sang the fixed melody in extremely long notes, the upper voice sang a freely composed part that moved rapidly above it. In such a setting, the chant was no longer recognizable as a melody. Its presence was symbolic, anchoring the new in the old.

In the organum *Gaude Maria virgo* (Listening Guide 3), the opening polyphonic section features two voices singing in a *rhythmic mode*—a fixed pattern of long and short notes that is repeated or varied—over a sustained bottom voice, the *Tenor* (from Latin *tenere*, "to hold"), that is drawn from the chant of the same name. The setting, in the style of Pérotin (and possibly by him), is highly melismatic, with many notes sung to each syllable of text. The form of this organum is typical in that it alternates polyphony with chant. The text, a *responsory* (from the Offices rather than the Mass), is in praise of the Virgin Mary and thus appropriate for feasts of the Blessed Virgin.

The Early Medieval Motet

Motet

Polytextual

Toward the end of the thirteenth century, musicians began writing new texts for the previously textless upper voices of organum. The addition of these texts resulted in the *motet*, the most important form of early polyphonic music. The term "motet" derives from *mot* (French for "word"), referring to the words that were added to the vocal lines. Sometimes two different texts—in Latin or French—went on at the same time. The medieval motet, then, is a *polytextual* (more than one text) vocal composition, either sacred or secular; it may or may not have had instrumental accompaniment.

The early motet illustrates how medieval composers based their own works on what had been handed down from the past. As in organum, a composer selected a fragment of Gregorian chant for a particular voice part and, keeping the pitches intact, gave them precise rhythmic values, usually of very long notes.

Listening Guide 3

CD: CHR/STD 1/7–8, SH 1/4–5

Notre Dame School Organum: *Gaude Maria virgo* (*Rejoice Mary, virgin*)

(1:26)

GENRE:	Organum, in 3 voices
CHANT TYPE:	Responsory for one of the Offices
COMPOSER:	From the Notre Dame School, in the style of Pérotin (13th century)
TEXT:	In praise of the Virgin Mary
OCCASION:	For feasts of the Blessed Virgin Mary (especially Purification)

WHAT TO LISTEN FOR: 2 upper voices singing rhythmically over sustained bottom voice.
2 upper parts exchanging melodic ideas.
Long-short rhythm repeated, then faster, even notes.
Highly melismatic (only 2 words for whole example).
Open, hollow chords at cadences.
Shifts from organum to chant (sung monophonically).
Chant is melismatic (many notes) on "virgo," then neumatic
   (a few notes per syllable).

		TEXT	TRANSLATION	PERFORMANCE
4	0:00	Gaude Maria	Rejoice Mary,	Organum style; upper 2 voices moving rhythmically over sustained third voice.
5	1:07	virgo cunctas hereses sola interemisti.	O virgin, you alone have destroyed all heresies.	Monophonic chant, melismatic, then continuing in neumatic setting.

Opening of organum, with 2 rhythmic upper voices over long chant note:

Countermelody

This stretched-out chant served as the structural skeleton of the piece, to which the composer added one, two, or three freely composed, rhythmically active countermelodies. (A *countermelody*, as noted earlier, is a melody heard against another.) In the motet, a sacred text might be combined with one that is quite secular, even racy. The basic Gregorian tune, hidden among the voices, fused these disparate elements into a unity—if not in the listener's ear, at least in the composer's mind.

One such work is the late-thirteenth-century motet *Aucun se sont loé/A Dieu/Super te,* by the poet and musician Adam de la Halle (c. 1237–c. 1287). Here, the bottom voice sounds the notes of the chant *Super te* in a repeated rhythmic pattern known as an *ostinato,* over which two faster moving voices present differing French texts: one tells of the bitterness of love and the other laments the political scene in Northern France. The motet's triple meter symbolizes the Trinity (the Father, the Son, the Holy Ghost).

13

Secular Music in the Middle Ages

"A verse without music is a mill without water."
—ANONYMOUS TROUBADOUR

KEY POINTS

- Secular music arose in courts—performed by aristocratic *troubadours* and *trouvères* in France and by *Minnesingers* in Germany—and in cities, performed by wandering minstrels (*jongleurs*); women (*trobairitz* and *jongleuresses*) took part in music-making as well.
- Secular songs were sung monophonically, with improvised instrumental accompaniment.
- Guillaume de Machaut was an important poet-composer of the French *Ars nova* (new art of the fourteenth century), who wrote sacred music and polyphonic *chansons* (French secular songs) set to fixed text forms (*rondeau, ballade, virelai).*
- Instrumental music was generally improvised, performed by ensembles of soft *(bas)* or loud *(haut)* instruments, categorized by their use (indoor or outdoor).
- Dance music was one of the primary instrumental genres, and featured improvised musical decorations (*embellishments*) of simple tunes.
- The religious wars (Crusades) and medieval explorations enabled the exchange of musical instruments as well as theoretical ideas about music with Middle Eastern and Far Eastern cultures (CP 5).

Medieval minstrels

Alongside the learned (or art) music of the cathedrals and choir schools, a popular literature sprang up of songs and dances that reflected every aspect of medieval life. Minstrels emerged as a class of musicians who wandered among the courts and towns. Some were versatile entertainers who played instruments, sang and danced, juggled and showed tricks, presented animal acts, and performed plays. In an age that had no newspapers, they regaled their audience with gossip and news. These itinerant actor-singers—called *jongleurs* (male) and *jongleuresses* (female)—lived on the fringe of society.

On a different social level were the poet-musicians who flourished at the various courts of Europe. Those from the southern region of France known as Provence were called *troubadours*, a term applied to both men and women (women were also called *trobairitz*). In northern France, these musicians were called *trouvères*. Both terms mean the same thing—finders or inventors (in musical terms, composers). Troubadours and trouvères numbered among their ranks members of the aristocracy and even some royalty. They either sang their music and poetry themselves or entrusted its performance to other musicians. In Germany, they were known as *Minnesingers*, or singers of courtly love.

Secular music became an integral part of medieval court life, supplying the necessary accompaniment for dancing, dinner, and after-dinner entertainment. It was central to court ceremonies, to tournaments, and to civic processions. Military music supported campaigns, inspired warriors departing on the Crusades, and greeted them on their return.

The poems of the troubadour and trouvère repertory ranged from simple ballads to love songs, political and moral ditties, war songs, chronicles of the Crusades, laments, and dance songs. They praised the virtues recognized in the age of chivalry: valor, honor, nobility of character, devotion to an ideal, and the quest for perfect love. Like so many of our popular songs today, many of the medieval lyrics dealt with the subject of unrequited—or unconsummated—passion. The object of the poet's desire was generally unattainable, either because of rank or because the beloved was already wed to another. This poetry, in short, dealt with love in its most idealized form. The subjects of poems by women were similar to those by men, ranging from the sorrow of being rejected by a lover to the joy of true love, but they were approached from a feminine point of view. The songs in praise of the Virgin Mary were cast in the same style and language, sometimes even set to the same melodies, as those that expressed a more worldly kind of love.

One prominent poet-musician was Moniot d'Arras, a monk who wrote both secular and sacred music. His work marked the end of the trouvère tradition. Characteristic is his love song *Ce fut en mai* (It happened in May), a monophonic tune that tells of an unhappy lover who finds comfort in the joys of another couple; it was probably sung against an improvised accompaniment.

The Minnesinger Heinrich von Meissen, called "Frauenlob" (champion of ladies), is exalted by musicians playing drum, flute, shawm, fiddles, psaltery, and bagpipe. (Heidelberg University Library)

Moniot d'Arras

Guillaume de Machaut and the French *Ars Nova*

"Music is a science that would have us laugh, sing, and dance."

The breakup of the feudal social structure brought with it new concepts of life, art, and beauty. These changes were reflected in the musical style known as

in his own words

He who writes and composes without feeling spoils both his words and his music.

Opening Doors to the East

The Middle Ages was an era of religious wars and exploration, both of which opened doors to the East. Between 1096 and 1221, there were five organized Crusades, military expeditions undertaken by European Christians in an attempt to conquer the Holy Land of Palestine from the Muslims. Along the way, crusaders massacred local people, plundered their riches, and destroyed their artworks. Yet out of these violent episodes came a significant meeting of cultures. The crusading knights learned from the expert military skills and weapons of the Turkish and Moorish warriors. The advanced medical and scientific knowledge of the Arab world was imported to Europe, and the Arab number system was adopted in Western commerce and banking. (Until then, Europeans had used Roman numerals—I, II, III, IV, V; today, we primarily use Arabic numerals—1, 2, 3, 4, 5.)

What of the musical interaction of these cultures? Instruments of all kinds as well as music and theoretical ideas were brought back to western Europe. For example, the medieval rebec, a small, violin-like instrument, was derived from the Arab rabab, and the loud, double-reed shawm used for outdoor events was closely related to the Turkish

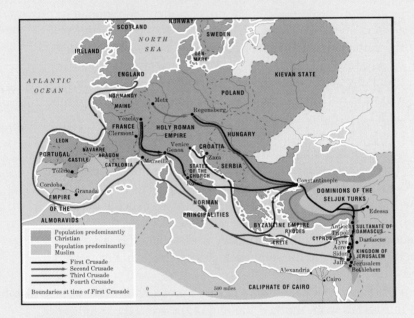

Boundaries at the time of the First Crusade.

Ars nova (new art), which made its appearance at the start of the fourteenth century in France and somewhat later in Italy. The music of the French *Ars nova* shows greater refinement than music of the *Ars antiqua* (old art), which it displaced. Writers such as Petrarch, Boccaccio, and Chaucer were turning to human subjects; painters would soon begin to discover the beauties of nature and the attractiveness of the human form. Similarly, composers turned increasingly from religious to secular themes. The *Ars nova* ushered in developments in rhythm, meter, harmony, and counterpoint that transformed the art of music.

zurna. We will see later that more Turkish instruments—especially percussion—found their way into Western ensembles in the eighteenth century. Crusaders heard the sounds of the Saracen military trumpets and drums and soon adopted these as their call to battle. The foundations of our Western system of modes (or scale forms) also felt the influence of Eastern theoretical systems.

In 1271, the Venetian merchant and explorer Marco Polo (1254–1324) made a historic journey to China. Polo was welcomed by the great Kublai Khan, a Mongol ruler who had conquered northern China and further modernized the already highly sophisticated civilization there. The Khan encouraged literature, the arts, and medical research, and established Buddhism as the official state religion. Polo and his entourage were much impressed by this society's technical advances; many, such as the making of gunpowder and the art of printing from movable type, were still unknown in western Europe. Polo's diary describes the importance of music to the Chinese military campaigns: "The Tartars never attack until they hear their commander's drums, but while waiting for the battle to begin, they always play and sing."

The information Marco Polo recorded throughout his travels helped open routes for the exchange of commerce (especially silks and spices), arts, and ideas from East to West. Although these early encounters were isolated, they helped immeasur-

In this miniature from the *Prayer Book* of Alfonso the Wise, King David is playing a rebec on his lap, in the manner of the Middle Eastern rabab.

ably in the centuries that followed to encourage communication between different nations and cultures. We see the results of this process today in the unprecedented freedom of exchange between different societies, making it possible for students from all regions of the globe to attend schools in foreign countries, and enabling audiences everywhere to enjoy performing artists from distant lands, in person or via the Internet.

TERMS TO NOTE:

rebec rabab
shawm zurna
mode

SUGGESTED LISTENING:

Turkish music (Janissary ensemble; see p. 234)
Medieval dance with shawm

Its outstanding figure was the French composer-poet Guillaume de Machaut (c. 1300–1377). His name—William from Machaut, a small town in northern France—was typical for the era. He took holy orders at an early age, became secretary to John of Luxembourg, king of Bohemia, and was active at the court of Charles, duke of Normandy, who subsequently became king of France. Machaut spent his old age as a canon at the Cathedral of Rheims, admired as the greatest musician of the time.

Machaut's double career as cleric and courtier inspired him to write both religious and secular music. His output includes more than twenty motets,

Guillaume de Machaut

many secular *chansons* (French for "songs"), and an important polyphonic setting of the complete Ordinary of the Mass. His own poetry reveals him as a proponent of the ideals of medieval chivalry. One of his writings, a long autobiographical poem of more than nine thousand lines in rhymed couplets, tells the love story of the aging Machaut and a young girl named Peronne. The two exchanged poems and letters, some of which the composer set to music.

The Chanson Puis qu'en oubli

Fixed forms

Machaut's music introduced a new freedom of rhythm, characterized by gentle syncopations and the interplay of duple and triple meters. Among secular genres, Machaut favored the chanson, which was generally set to courtly love poems written in one of several fixed text forms. These poetic forms—the *rondeau, ballade,* and *virelai*—established the musical repetition scheme of the chansons. We will study his love song *Puis qu'en oubli,* a rondeau for three voices with a refrain echoing the pain of unrequited love ("Since I am forgotten by you, sweet friend, I bid farewell to a life of love and joy"; see Listening Guide 4 for complete text and translation). In Machaut's elegant chanson, whose low melodic range makes it appropriate for three men's voices or a solo male voice accompanied by instruments, the two musical sections alternate in a pattern

A polyphonic chanson is performed with voice and lute in this miniature representing the Garden of Love, from a Flemish manuscript of *Le Roman de la Rose* (c. 1500).

Machaut: *Puis qu'en oubli (Since I am forgotten)*

(1:46)

DATE OF WORK: Mid-14th century

GENRE: Polyphonic chanson, 3 voices

POEM: Rondeau by the composer (with 2-line refrain)

MUSICAL FORM: 2 short musical sections, **A** and **B**, repeated as follows: **A-B-a-A-a-b-A-B**
(capital letters indicate refrain text)

WHAT TO LISTEN FOR: Low range—all 3 parts for men's voices.
2 short sections of music (**A-B**), repeated in set scheme *(rondeau)*.
Opening refrain text (2 lines of poetry) repeated in middle and at end.
Slow triple meter, with subtle rhythmic movement and syncopations.
Open, hollow cadences at ends of phrases.
3-part polyphonic texture.

Top-line melody of **A** section, with refrain text:

Top-line melody of **B** section, with refrain text:

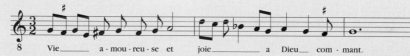

			TEXT	MUSICAL FORM	TRANSLATION
6	0:00	Refrain	Puis qu'en oubli sui de vous, dous amis,	**A**	Since I am forgotten by you,
			Vie amoureuse et joie a Dieu commant.	**B**	sweet friend, I bid farewell to a life of love and joy.
7	0:25	Verse	Mar vi le jour que m'amour en vous mis;	**a**	Unlucky was the day I placed my love in you;
8	0:38	Partial refrain	Puis qu'en oubli sui de vous, dous amis.	**A**	Since I am forgotten by you, sweet friend.
9	0:52	Verse	Mais ce tenray que je vous ay promis:	**a**	But what was promised you I
			C'est que jamais n'aray nul autre amant.	**b**	will sustain: That I shall never have any other love.
10	1:17	Refrain	Puis qu'en oubli sui de vous, dous amis,	**A**	Since I am forgotten by you,
			Vie amoureuse et joie a Dieu commant.	**B**	sweet friend, I bid farewell to a life of love and joy.

dictated by the poetry. The influence of this last great poet-composer was far-reaching, his music and poetry admired long after his death.

Early Instrumental Music

The fourteenth century witnessed a steady growth in the scope and importance of instrumental music. Though the central role in art music was still reserved for vocal works, instruments were put to more and more uses. As we have seen, they could play a supporting role in vocal music, doubling or accompanying the singers. Instrumental arrangements of vocal works grew increasingly popular. And instruments found their earliest prominence in dance music, where rhythm was the prime consideration.

Improvised music

Unlike the sophisticated vocal music of church and court, instrumental music was rarely written down; rather, it was improvised, much as jazz would be six centuries later. We can therefore only estimate the extent and variety of the instrumental repertory during the late Middle Ages. But our speculation can be guided by an ever growing body of knowledge acquired from paintings, historical documents, and surviving instruments. Early instruments fell into the same general families as modern ones—strings, woodwinds, brass, percussion, and keyboard—and were also divided into *soft* (*bas*), or indoor, and *loud* (*haut*), or outdoor, categories according to their use. Among the most commonly used soft instruments were the *recorder,* an end-blown flute with a breathy tone; the *lute,* a plucked string instrument with a rounded back (of Middle Eastern origin); the *harp* and *psaltery,* plucked string instruments of biblical fame; and the

Three shawms and a trombone accompany dancers in this detail from the Adimari wedding chest, c. 1450. (Galleria dell'Accademia, Florence)

rebec (also of Middle Eastern origin) and *vielle,* the two principal bowed string instruments of the Middle Ages.

The loud category of instruments, used mainly for outdoor occasions such as tournaments and processions, included the *shawm,* an ancestor of the oboe, with a loud, nasal tone; and the *slide trumpet,* which developed into the early trombone known as the *sackbut.* Percussion instruments of the time included a large cylindrical drum called the *tabor* and small drums known as *nakers,* usually played in pairs. Several of these instruments had their origins in the Middle East, and nakers are mentioned in Marco Polo's account of his travels in Asia.

Several types and sizes of organ were already in use in the Middle Ages. There **Organs** were large ones, requiring a team of men to pump their giant bellows and often several more men to manipulate the cumbersome slider mechanisms that opened and closed the pipes. At the other extreme were *portative* and *positive* organs— smaller instruments with keyboards and a few ranks of pipes.

Of the purely instrumental pieces left to us from this era, most are simple monophonic dance melodies. Common types include the *saltarello,* a lively, Italian **Saltarello and** "jumping" dance, and the *estampie,* a more stately French dance. The dance **estampie** melodies reflect, however, only the skeletal framework from which medieval musicians performed; they usually added *embellishments,* or melodic decorations, **Embellishments** to the written music to an improved percussion accompaniment and possibly a *drone* (a sustained single tone). Evidence suggests that professional musicians **Drone** were highly skilled, since their earnings were often quite high.

The revival of early music has grown in recent decades, as scholars and performers have worked to reconstruct some of the conditions under which the music was originally performed. Most of the ensembles that now specialize in this repertory boast players who have mastered the old instruments. Their concerts and recordings have made the public aware of the sound of these instruments to a degree that was undreamed of fifty years ago.

unit **IV**

The Renaissance

14

The Renaissance Spirit

"I am not pleased with the Courtier if he be not also a musician, and besides his understanding and cunning [in singing] upon the book, have skill in like manner on sundry instruments."

—BALDASSARE CASTIGLIONE

KEY POINTS

- The Renaissance was an era of exploration, scientific inquiry, and artistic awakening and marked the passing from a highly religious society to a more secular one.
- Artists and writers found inspiration in the cultures of ancient Greece and Rome.
- Renaissance musicians found employment in churches, cities, and courts or in the trades of instrument building, printing, and music publishing.
- The Renaissance is often regarded as the golden age of *a cappella* singing (unaccompanied vocal music).
- Renaissance music features a fuller and more consonant sound (using thirds and sixths) than music from the Middle Ages.
- Some Renaissance pieces are built on a fixed, preexistent melody *(cantus firmus)*, while others reflect the text through the music *(word painting)*.
- Musical influence between the Native Americans in the New World and Europeans (CP 6) was insignificant.

The Renaissance (c. 1450–1600) is one of the most beautiful if misleading names in the history of culture: beautiful because it implies an awakening of intellectual awareness, misleading because it suggests a sudden rebirth of learning and art after the presumed stagnation of the Middle Ages. History moves continuously rather than by leaps and bounds. The Renaissance was the next phase in a cultural process that, under the leadership of the church, universities, and princely courts, had long been under way.

The Arts in the Renaissance

The Renaissance marks the passing of European society from a predominately religious orientation to a more secular one, and from an age of unquestioning faith and mysticism to one of belief in reason and scientific inquiry. The focus of human destiny was seen to be life on earth rather than the hereafter. People began to rely more on the evidence of the senses rather than on tradition and authority, and they gained new confidence in their ability to solve their own problems and order their world rationally. This awakening found its symbol in the culture of Greek and Roman antiquity. Renaissance society, led by the humanists, discovered the summit of human wisdom not only in the Church Fathers and saints, as their ancestors had done, but also in the ancient philosophers and writers, including Plato and Virgil.

Philosophical developments

A series of momentous circumstances helped to set off the new era from the old. The introduction of gunpowder signaled the eventual end of the age of knighthood. The development of the compass made possible the voyages of discovery that opened up a new world and demolished old superstitions. While the great European explorers of this age—Christopher Columbus, Amerigo Vespucci, and Ponce de León, among others—were in search of a new trade route to the riches of China and the Indies, they stumbled on the unknown (to them) continents of North and South America. During the course of the sixteenth and seventeenth centuries, these new lands became increasingly important to European treasuries and society.

The Renaissance painter preferred realism to allegory and psychological characterizations to stylized stereotypes, as exemplified in the famous portrait of *Mona Lisa*, by **Leonardo da Vinci** (1452–1519). (The Louvre, Paris)

The revival of ancient writings mentioned earlier, spurred by the introduction of printing, had its counterpart in architecture, painting, and sculpture. The Renaissance lavished its constructive energy on palaces rather than on Gothic cathedrals. The gloomy fortified castles of the medieval princes gave way to spacious villas that displayed the harmonious proportions of the classical style. (The term "classical" in this context refers to the culture of the ancient Greeks and Romans, whose art was thought to embody the ideals of order, stability, and balanced proportions.)

So too the elongated saints and martyrs of medieval painting and sculpture were replaced by the realism of the David of Michelangelo and the gentle Madonnas of Leonardo. Even where artists retained a religious theme, the Mother of Sorrows and the symbols of grief gave way to smiling Madonnas—often posed for by very secular ladies—and dimpled cherubs. The nude human form, denied or covered for centuries, was revealed as a thing of beauty and used as an object of anatomical study. Nature entered painting as well, and with it an intense preoccupation with the laws of perspective and composition.

Medieval painting had presented life through symbolism; the Renaissance preferred realism. The medieval painters posed their figures frontally, impersonally; the Renaissance developed the art of portraiture and humanized its subjects. Medieval painting dealt in stereotypes; the Renaissance concerned itself with individuals. Space in medieval painting was organized in a succession of planes that the eye perceived as a series of episodes, but Renaissance painters made it possible to see the whole simultaneously. They discovered the landscape, created the illusion of distance, and focused on the physical loveliness of the world.

The Renaissance first came to flower in Italy, the nation that stood closest to the classical Roman culture; as a result, the great names we associate with its painting and sculpture are predominantly Italian: Donatello (c. 1386–1466), Botticelli (1444–1510), Leonardo da Vinci (1452–1519), Michelangelo (1475–1564), Raphael (1483–1520), and Titian (c. 1488–1576). With masters who lived in the second half of the sixteenth century, such as Tintoretto (1518–1594) and Veronese (1528–1588), we approach the world of the early Baroque.

From the colorful tapestry of Renaissance life emerges a galaxy of great names. The list includes the Dutch scholar-philosopher Erasmus (c. 1466–1536), the German religious reformer Martin Luther (1483–1546), the Italian statesman Machiavelli (1469–1527) and his compatriot the scientist Galileo (1564–1642), the French writer Rabelais (c. 1494–c. 1553), the Spanish author Cervantes (1547–1616), and the English playwrights Marlowe (1564–1593) and Shakespeare (1564–1616).

The Renaissance marks the birth of the modern European spirit and of Western society as we have come to know it. That turbulent time shaped the moral and cultural climate we live in today.

The human form, denied for centuries, was revealed in the Renaissance as an object of beauty. *David,* by **Michelangelo** (1475–1564). (Accademia, Florence)

Musicians in Renaissance Society

Musicians as professionals

Musicians of the fifteenth and sixteenth centuries were supported by the chief institutions of their society—the church, city, and state, as well as royal and aristocratic courts. Musicians could find employment as choirmasters, singers, organists, instrumentalists, copyists, composers, teachers, instrument builders, and music printers and publishers. There was a corresponding growth in a number of supporting musical institutions: church choirs and schools, publishing houses, civic wind bands. And there were increased opportunities for apprentices to study with master singers, players, and instrument builders. A few women can be identified as professional musicians in this era, earning their living as court instrumentalists and singers. In Chapter 16, we will learn more about a famous ensemble of vocalists known as the Concerto delle donne, or the Singing Ladies of Ferrara.

The rise of the merchant class brought with it a new group of music patrons. This development was paralleled by the emergence, among the cultivated middle and upper classes, of the amateur musician. When the system for printing from movable type was successfully adapted to music in the early sixteenth century, printed music books became available and affordable, making possible the rise of great publishing houses in Venice, Paris, and Antwerp. As a result, musical literacy spread dramatically.

Renaissance Musical Style

The vocal forms of the Renaissance were marked by smoothly gliding melodies conceived for the voice. In fact, the sixteenth century has come to be regarded as the golden age of the *a cappella* style (the term refers to a vocal work without instrumental accompaniment). Polyphony in such works was based on a principle called *continuous imitation.* In this procedure, the motives are exchanged between vocal lines, the voices imitating one another so that the same theme or motive is heard now in the soprano or alto, now in the tenor or bass, resulting in a close-knit musical fabric capable of the most subtle and varied effects. (See Listening Guide 5 for examples.)

A cappella music

Continuous imitation

Most church music was written in *a cappella* style. Secular music, on the other hand, was divided between purely vocal works and those in which the singers were supported by instruments. The period also saw the growth of solo instrumental music, especially for lute and for keyboard instruments. In the matter of harmony, composers of the Renaissance leaned toward fuller chords. They turned away from the parallel fifths and octaves preferred in medieval times to the more pleasing thirds and sixths. The expressive device of *word painting*—that is, making the music reflect the meaning of the words—was much favored in secular music. An unexpected, harsh dissonance might coincide with the word "death," or an ascending line might lead up to the word "heavens" or "stars." (The use of dissonance in sacred music was more carefully controlled.)

Word painting

Polyphonic writing offered the composer many possibilities, such as the use of a *cantus firmus* (fixed melody) as the basis for elaborate ornamentation in the other voices. As we have seen, triple meter had been especially attractive to the medieval mind because it symbolized the perfection of the Trinity. The new era, much less preoccupied with religious symbolism, showed a greater interest in duple meter.

Cantus firmus

The composers of the Burgundian, or Franco-Flemish, School were preeminent in European music from around 1450 to the end of the sixteenth

In the sixteenth century, women played an active role in music making in the bourgeois home. *Family Portrait,* credited to **Frans Floris,** 1561. (Stedelijk Museum Wuyts–Van Campen en Baron Caroly, Lier)

When the Old World Meets the New World

Can you imagine the reaction of European explorers to the Native American peoples and cultures they encountered on first reaching the New World? And vice versa? Christopher Columbus recorded his impressions in his diary, remarking that the first locals he met were "so peaceful . . . they love their neighbors as themselves; and their discourse is ever sweet and gentle, and accompanied by a smile."

Europeans found the music of the Native Americans quite foreign to their ears, noting the highly repetitive nature of the songs, the use of vocables (sung syllables that lack literal meaning), and the sometimes high, piercing vocal quality (sung by males in falsetto, a technique by which they can sing above their normal vocal range). The English explorer Captain John Smith (1580–1631) described the instruments he saw among the locals of eastern Virginia.

> For their musicke, they use a thicke cane, on which they pipe as on a Recorder. For their warres, they have a great deepe platter of wood. They cover the mouth thereof with a skin . . . that they may beat upon it as upon a drumme. But their chiefe instruments are Rattels made of small gourds or Pumpion [pumpkin] shels. Of these they have Base, Tenor, Countertenor, Meane and Trible.

Thus this particular tribe had flute- or whistle-like instruments (of the aerophone category) fashioned from cane, drums made from hollowed trees over which animal skins were stretched (membranophones), and rattles of widely varying sizes made from gourds or animal horns (idiophones). The use of the latter two categories of instruments typified the musics of many Native American nations.

There were frequent occasions for music making among the Native Americans. Their songs told of love and war, the harvest and the hunt, deities, birth, marriage, and death. For example, the music of the Iroquoian tribes (of southeastern Canada and the northeastern United States) was organized around their agricultural year; one song, the *Corn Dance*, was sung to the female corn spirit to encour-

Powatans of Virginia in ceremonial dance, as depicted by the English artist **John White** in 1585. (The British Museum, London)

Dancers from Cherokee Nation, at a modern-day powwow.

age the growth of their most important crop. The Plains tribes welcomed the summer crops with the Sun Dance, while the Pacific Coast tribes performed a Mystery Dance to honor the regeneration of nature in spring.

Smith had the opportunity to observe ceremonial rituals of one tribe in Virginia: "Their devotion was most in songs in which the chiefe Priest beginneth and the rest followed him." This call-and-response exchange, much like the responsorial singing we have noted in early church music, is a style that has developed in the musics of many world cultures.

Unlike some encounters we will observe, relatively little cross influence of styles took place between Native Americans and Europeans during the seventeenth century, perhaps because the two cultures were so profoundly different. The music of Native Americans has been preserved largely through oral tradition within their individual cultures. In our own century, there has been a lot of stylistic cross-fertilization. Young Native Americans listen to the same rock and country/western music as youths of European, African, or Asian heritage, while a few Native Americans have brought their music to a wider audience. For example, flutist R. Carlos Nakai (of Navaho-Ute heritage) has combined his native musical traditions with those of European art music and has made haunting recordings that have captured the imagination of many listeners.

TERMS TO NOTE:

vocable	idiophone
falsetto	call and response
aerophone	responsorial singing
membranophone	oral tradition

SUGGESTED LISTENING:

Native American ceremonial music
Modern Native American music
 (R. Carlos Nakai)

century. They came from the southern Lowlands (present-day Belgium) and from the adjoining provinces of northern France and Burgundy. Paramount among them was Josquin who created some of the masterpieces of the epoch.

15

Renaissance Sacred Music

"We know by experience that song has great force and vigor to move and inflame the hearts of men to invoke and praise God with a more vehement and ardent zeal."

—JOHN CALVIN

KEY POINTS

- Renaissance composers focused their polyphonic Mass settings on texts from the Ordinary of the Mass (Kyrie, Gloria, Credo, Sanctus, Agnus Dei).
- Important composers of Renaissance sacred music (Masses, motets, hymns) include Guillaume Du Fay, Josquin des Prez, and Giovanni Pierluigi da Palestrina.
- Du Fay uses a popular tune as a *cantus firmus* (fixed song) for his *L'homme armé* Mass.
- *Ave Maria . . . virgo serena,* by Josquin des Prez, is a motet to the Virgin Mary set in varied textural styles *(imitative, homorhythmic).*
- Palestrina's *Pope Marcellus* Mass is a Counter-Reformation work that meets the musical demands made by the Council of Trent for *a cappella* singing with clearly declaimed text.

Music played a prominent part in the ritual of the church. In addition to the monophonic Gregorian chant, music for church services included polyphonic settings of the Mass, motets, and hymns. These were normally contrapuntal and, especially in the early sixteenth century, based on preexistent music. Such works were sung by professional singers, trained from childhood in the various cathedral choir schools.

The Motet in the Renaissance

In the Renaissance, the motet became a sacred form with a single Latin text, for use in the Mass and other religious services. Motets in praise of the Virgin Mary were extremely popular because of the many religious groups all over Europe devoted to Marian worship. These works, written for three, four, or more voices, were sometimes based on a chant or other cantus firmus.

One of the greatest masters of the Renaissance motet was the northern French composer Josquin des Prez (c. 1450–1521). With him, the transition is complete from the anonymous composer of the Middle Ages and the shadowy figures of the late Gothic to the highly individual artist of the Renaissance.

Josquin des Prez and the Motet

Josquin des Prez

"He is the master of the notes. They have to do as he bids them; other composers have to do as the notes will."

—MARTIN LUTHER

Josquin (as he is known) exerted a powerful influence on generations of composers to follow. After spending his youth in the north, his varied career led him to Italy, where he served at several courts—especially those of Cardinal Ascanio Sforza of Milan and Ercole d'Este, duke of Ferrara—and in the papal choir in Rome. During his stay in Italy, his northern style absorbed the classical virtues of balance and moderation, the sense of harmonious proportion and clear form, that found their model in the radiant art of Andrea Mantegna. Toward the end of his life, Josquin returned to his native France, where he served as a provost at the collegiate church of Condé; he was buried in the choir of the church.

The older generation of musicians had been preoccupied with solving the technical problems of counterpoint, an interest that fit the intellectual climate of the late Middle Ages. Josquin appeared at a time when the humanizing influences of the Renaissance were being felt throughout Europe; he was able to harness contrapuntal ingenuity to a higher end: the expression of emotion. His music is rich in feeling, in serenely beautiful melody, and in expressive harmony.

Josquin composed more than one hundred motets, at least seventeen Masses, and numerous secular pieces, making use of a variety of techniques. Some works were based on preexistent monophonic or polyphonic models, others were original throughout.

Ave Maria . . . virgo serena is a prime example of how Josquin used the motet to experiment with different combinations of voices and textures (see Listening Guide 5). In this four-voice composition, which sets a rhymed poem to the Virgin Mary, high voices are set in dialogue with low ones and imitative textures alternate with *homorhythmic* settings (a texture in which all voices move together rhythmically). Josquin opens the piece with a musical reference to a chant for the Virgin, but soon drops this melody in favor of a freely composed form that is highly sensitive to the text. The final couplet, a personal plea to the Virgin ("O Mother of God, remember me"), is set in a simple texture that emphasizes the words, proclaiming the emotional and humanistic spirit of a new age.

Homorhythm

Listening Guide 5

CD: CHR/STD 1/32–38, SH 1/11–17

Josquin: *Ave Maria . . . virgo serena (Hail Mary . . . gentle virgin)* (4:38)

DATE OF WORK:	1480s?
GENRE:	4-voice motet
BASIS:	Chant to Virgin Mary (opening only)
POEM:	Rhymed poem (a couplet, 5 quatrains, and a closing couplet)

Opening of soprano line, based on Gregorian chant:

		TEXT	TRANSLATION	DESCRIPTION
11	0:00	Ave Maria, gratia plena, Dominus tecum, virgo serena.	Hail Mary, full of grace, The Lord is with you, gentle Virgin.	4 voices in imitation (SATB); chant used; duple meter.
12	0:45	Ave cujus conceptio Solemni plena gaudio Caelestia, terrestria, Nova replet laetitia.	Hail, whose conception, Full of solemn joy, Fills the heaven, the earth, With new rejoicing.	2 and 3 voices, later 4 voices; more homorhythmic texture.
13	1:21	Ave cujus nativitas Nostra fuit solemnitas,	Hail, whose birth Was our festival,	Voice pairs (SA/TB) in close imitation, then 4 voices in imitation.
		Ut lucifer lux oriens, Verum solem praeveniens.	As our luminous rising light Coming before the true sun.	
14	1:59	Ave pia humilitas, Sine viro fecunditas, Cujus annuntiatio, Nostra fuit salvatio.	Hail, pious humility, Fertility without a man, Whose annunciation Was our salvation.	Voice pairs (SA/TB); a more homorhythmic texture.
15	2:27	Ave vera virginitas, Immaculata castitas, Cujus purificatio Nostra fuit purgatio.	Hail, true virginity, Unspotted chastity, Whose purification Was our cleansing.	Triple meter; clear text declamation; homorhythmic texture.
16	3:04	Ave praeclara omnibus Angelicis virtutibus, Cujus fuit assumptio Nostra glorificatio.	Hail, famous with all Angelic virtues, Whose assumption was Our glorification.	Imitative voice pairs; return to duple meter.
17	3:59	O Mater Dei, Memento mei. Amen.	O Mother of God, Remember me. Amen.	Completely homorhythmic; text declamation in long notes, separated by simultaneous rests.

Continuous imitation, with voice entries at regular intervals:

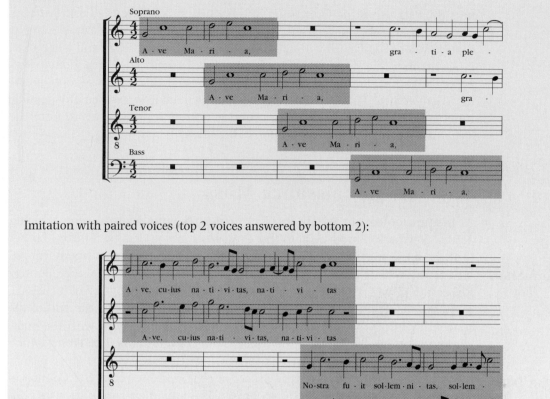

Imitation with paired voices (top 2 voices answered by bottom 2):

The Renaissance Mass

With the rise of Renaissance polyphony, composers concentrated their musical settings on the Ordinary, the fixed portion of the Mass that was sung daily. This practice brought into prominence the five main sections of the Mass: Kyrie, Gloria, Credo, Sanctus, and Agnus Dei. (Today, these sections of the Mass are recited or sung in the *vernacular,* that is, the language of the country.) The first of these sections, the Kyrie, is a prayer for mercy that dates from the early centuries of Christianity, as its Greek text attests. It takes an **A-B-A** form that consists of nine invocations: three of "Kyrie eleison" (Lord, have mercy), three of "Christe eleison" (Christ, have mercy), and again three of "Kyrie eleison." The Kyrie is followed by the Gloria ("Glory be to God on high"), a joyful hymn of praise that is omitted in the penitential seasons of Advent and Lent.

The third movement, the Credo ("I believe in one God, the Father Almighty"), is the confession of faith and the longest of the Mass texts. Fourth is the Sanctus ("Holy, holy, holy"), which concludes with the "Hosanna" ("Hosanna in the highest"). The fifth and last part, the Agnus Dei ("Lamb of God, Who takes away the sins of the world"), is sung three times. Twice it concludes with "miserere nobis" (have mercy on us), and the third time with the prayer "dona nobis pacem" (grant us peace). A summary of the order of the Mass, with its Proper and Ordinary movements, may be found on page 104. (Remember that we studied an Alleluia from the Proper of the Mass in Chapter 12.)

Sections of the Mass

Vernacular

Early polyphonic settings of the Mass were usually based on a fragment of Gregorian chant, which became the *cantus firmus* (fixed melody). The cantus firmus thus served as the foundation of the work, supporting the florid patterns that the other voices wove around it. It provided composers with a fixed element that they could embellish with all the resources of their artistry, and when used in all the movements, it helped unify the Mass as well. The Burgundian composer Guillaume Du Fay (c. 1397–1474) used the cantus-firmus technique in his *L'homme armé* Mass (*The Armed Man* Mass), which features a catchy popular tune as its basis. The Tenor voice sounds the tune in long notes to form the structural framework for each section of the Mass.

The Late Renaissance Mass

At the time of Josquin's death in 1521, major religious reforms were sweeping across Northern Europe. After the Protestant revolt led by Martin Luther (1483–1546), the Catholic Church responded with a reform movement focused on a return to true Christian piety. This movement became part of the Counter-Reformation, whereby the church strove to recapture the loyalty of its people. The Counter-Reformation, which extended from the 1530s to the end of the sixteenth century, witnessed various changes, including work with the poor, efforts to combat heresy, and the deliberations of the Council of Trent, which extended—with some interruptions—from 1545 to 1563.

Counter-Reformation

Council of Trent

In its desire to regulate every aspect of religious discipline, the Council of Trent took up the matter of church music. The attending cardinals were concerned about corruption of the traditional chant by the singers, who added extravagant embellishments to the Gregorian melodies. The council members

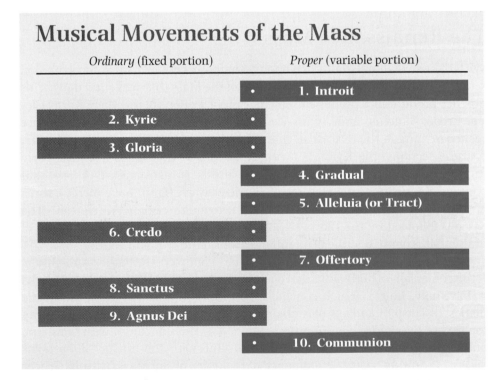

Musical Movements of the Mass

Ordinary (fixed portion)	*Proper* (variable portion)
	• 1. Introit
2. Kyrie •	
3. Gloria •	
	• 4. Gradual
	• 5. Alleluia (or Tract)
6. Credo •	
	• 7. Offertory
8. Sanctus •	
9. Agnus Dei •	
	• 10. Communion

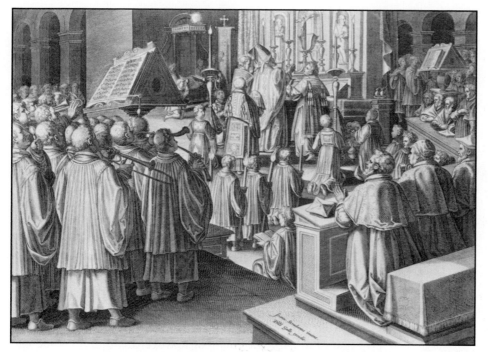

A choir and instruments participate in the celebration of Mass in this engraving by **Philip Galle,** after **J. Stradanus,** from *Encomium musices* of 1595.

objected to the use of certain instruments in religious services, to the practice of incorporating popular songs in Masses, to the secular spirit that had invaded sacred music, and to the generally irreverent attitude of church musicians. In polyphonic settings of the Mass, the cardinals claimed, the sacred text was made unintelligible by the overelaborate contrapuntal texture.

The committee assigned to deal with the problem contented itself with issuing general recommendations in favor of a pure vocal style that would respect the integrity of the sacred texts, that would avoid virtuosity and encourage piety. One composer who answered the demands for a reformed church music was Giovanni Pierluigi da Palestrina.

Palestrina and the *Pope Marcellus* Mass

"I have held nothing more desirable than what is sung throughout the year, according to the season, should be more agreeable to the ear by virtue of its vocal beauty."

Giovanni Pierluigi da Palestrina (c. 1525–1594), called Palestrina after his birthplace, worked as an organist and choirmaster at various churches, including St. Peter's in Rome. His patron, Pope Julius III (r. 1550–55), appointed him to the Sistine Chapel Choir even though, as a married man, he was ineligible for the semi-ecclesiastical post. He was dismissed by a later pope but ultimately returned to direct another choir at St. Peter's, where he spent the last twenty-three years of his life.

Palestrina wrote over a hundred Masses, of which the most famous is the Mass for Pope Marcellus, successor to Julius III. It is popularly believed that this Mass was written to satisfy the new, strict demands placed on polyphonic

in his own words

Our wisest mortals have decided that music should give zest to divine worship. If people take great pains to compose beautiful music for profane [secular] songs, they should devote at least as much thought to sacred song, nay, even more than to mere worldly matters.

Palestrina presents his earliest printed work to Pope Julius III, in this sixteenth-century engraving.

church music by the Council of Trent. Since the papal choir at the time sang without instrumental accompaniment, the *Pope Marcellus* Mass was probably performed *a cappella.* It was written for six voice parts—soprano, alto, two tenors, and two basses, a typical setting for the all-male church choirs of the era. The highest voice was sung by boy sopranos or male falsettists, the alto part by male altos, or countertenors (tenors with very high voices), and the lower parts were distributed among the normal ranges of the male voice.

The Gloria from the *Pope Marcellus* Mass exhibits Palestrina's conservative style. The work begins with a monophonic intonation of the opening line, "Gloria in excelsis Deo" (Glory be to God on high), which, according to church practice, is chanted by the celebrant (or officiating priest). Palestrina carefully constructed a polyphonic setting for the remaining text, balancing the harmonic and polyphonic elements of his art so that the words of the sacred text are clear and audible, an effect desired by the Council of Trent. Changes in register and in the number of voices singing at any one time vary the musical texture throughout. (See Listening Guide 6 for the text and analysis.)

Palestrina's music is representative of the pure *a cappella* style of vocal polyphony. This was his ideal sound—restrained, serene, and celestial.

Listening Guide 6

CD: CHR/STD 1/44–45, SH 1/18–19

Palestrina: *Pope Marcellus* Mass, Gloria   (6:19)

DATE OF WORK:	Published 1567
GENRE:	Mass; Gloria, from a setting of the Ordinary
VOICES:	6 (SATTBB)
CHARACTERISTICS:	Frequent textural changes, reduction of voices

WHAT TO LISTEN FOR:	Monophonic chant opening *(Gloria in excelsis Deo).* Changes of density and texture (SATTBB), set in various registers (high vs. low voices). *A cappella* performance (choral, with no accompaniment). Clearly audible text set syllabically, often sung nearly homorhythmically. Alternation of homorhythmic and polyphonic textures. Full, consonant harmony.

Opening of Gloria, showing 6 voice parts (4 singing at one time), in clear word declamation:

	TEXT	NO. OF VOICES	TRANSLATION
18 0:00	Gloria in excelsis Deo	1	Glory be to God on high,
	et in terra pax hominibus	4	and on earth peace to men
	bonae voluntatis.	4	of good will.
	Laudamus te. Benedicimus te.	4	We praise Thee. We bless Thee.
	Adoramus te.	3	We adore Thee.
	Glorificamus te.	4	We glorify Thee.
	Gratias agimus tibi propter	5/4	We give Thee thanks for
	magnam gloriam tuam.	3/4	Thy great glory.
	Domine Deus, Rex caelestis,	4	Lord God, heavenly King,
	Deus Pater omnipotens.	3	God, the Father Almighty.
	Domine Fili	4	O Lord, the only-begotten Son,
	unigenite, Jesu Christe.	6/5	Jesus Christ.
	Domine Deus, Agnus Dei,	3/4	Lord God, Lamb of God,
	Filius Patris.	6	Son of the Father.
19 2:43	Qui tollis peccata mundi,	4	Thou that takest away the sins of the world,
	miserere nobis.	4	have mercy on us.
	Qui tollis peccata mundi,	4/5	Thou that takest away the sins of the world,
	suscipe deprecationem nostram.	6/4	receive our prayer.
	Qui sedes ad dexteram Patris,	3	Thou that sittest at the right hand of the Father,
	miserere nobis.	3	have mercy on us.
	Quoniam tu solus sanctus.	4	For Thou alone art holy.
	Tu solus Dominus.	4	Thou only art the Lord.
	Tu solus Altissimus.	4	Thou alone art most high.
	Jesu Christe, cum Sancto Spiritu	6/3/4	Jesus Christ, along with the Holy Spirit
	in gloria Dei Patris.	4/5	in the glory of God the Father.
	Amen.	6	Amen.

16

Renaissance Secular Music

"Come sing to me a bawdy song, make me merry."
—FALSTAFF, IN WILLIAM SHAKESPEARE'S *HENRY IV, PART 1*

KEY POINTS

- The Renaissance saw a rise in amateur music-making, providing a new audience for the main secular genres of the French *chanson* and the *Italian* and *English madrigals.*
- Instrumental *dance music,* played by professional as well as amateur musicians, flourished during the Renaissance.
- The *madrigal* originated in Italy as a form of aristocratic entertainment; it was later adopted as a favored English secular genre.
- Monteverdi was a master of the Italian madrigal and of expressive devices such as *word painting.*
- The *English madrigal* was often simpler and lighter in style than its Italian counterpart.

Music in Court and City Life

In the Renaissance, both professionals and amateurs took part in music making. Professionals entertained noble guests at court and civic festivities, and with the rise of the merchant class, music making in the home became increasingly popular. Most prosperous homes had a lute (a plucked string instrument with a rounded body) or a keyboard instrument, and the study of music was considered part of the proper upbringing for a young girl or, to a lesser degree, boy. Women began to play a prominent part in the performance of music both in the home and at court. During the later sixteenth century in Italy, a number of professional women singers achieved great fame (see p. 110). From the union of poetry and music arose two important secular genres: the chanson and the madrigal.

The Chanson

In the fifteenth century, the chanson was the favored genre at the courts of the dukes of Burgundy and the kings of France, all great patrons of the arts. Chansons were usually written for three or four voices. They were set to the courtly love verses of the French Renaissance poets. We saw in the case of a Machaut chanson that the text, in a fixed form (rondeau), established the type of setting and the musical repetition of sections. By the early sixteenth century, poetic structures were freer, without set repetition patterns. This trend is exemplified in Josquin's poignant chanson *Mille regretz (A thousand regrets),* set in a four-voice texture.

The Renaissance chanson continued to be a favorite secular form throughout the sixteenth century, culminating in the works of the towering figure of Roland de Lassus (c. 1532–1594). This North European master wrote about 150 chansons on texts that express a wide range of emotions, from amorous to lusting to religious.

Instrumental Dance Music

The sixteenth century witnessed a remarkable blossoming of instrumental dance music. With the advent of music publishing, printed dance music became readily available for solo instruments as well as for small ensembles. The dances were often fashioned from vocal works such as madrigals and chansons, which were published in simplified versions that were played instead of sung.

A number of dance types became popular during the sixteenth century. The stately court dance known as the *pavane* often served as the first number of a set that included one or more quicker dances, especially the Italian *saltarello* (jumping dance) and the French *galliard* (a more vigorous version of the saltarello). The *allemande*, or German dance, in moderate duple time, retained its popularity throughout the time of Bach and was adapted into the Baroque dance suite. Less courtly was the *ronde*, or round dance, a lively romp associated with the outdoors and performed in a circle.

It was through dance music that Renaissance composers began to explore the possibilities of purely instrumental forms. These eventually gave way to the imposing structures of Western instrumental music.

Musicians perform a polyphonic chanson with voice, flute, and lute in this detail from *The Prodigal Son Among the Courtesans* (sixteenth century, artist unknown). (Musée Carnavalet, Paris)

The Italian Madrigal

"By shallow rivers to whose falls
melodious birds sing madrigals."
        —CHRISTOPHER MARLOWE

In the madrigal, Renaissance composers found one of their chief forms for secular music. The sixteenth-century *madrigal* was an aristocratic form of poetry-and-music that flourished at the Italian courts, where it was a favorite diversion of cultivated amateurs. The text consisted of a short poem of lyric or reflective character, often including the emotional words for weeping, sighing, trembling, and dying, which the Italian madrigalists set with a wealth of expression. Love and unsatisfied desire were popular topics of the madrigal but by no means the only ones. Included too were humor and satire, political themes, and scenes and incidents of city and country life, with the result that the Italian madrigal literature of the sixteenth century presents a vivid panorama of Renaissance thought and feeling.

Instruments participated in the performance of madrigals, duplicating or even substituting for the voices. Sometimes only the top part was sung while

A stylized sixteenth-century painting of four singers performing from music part books. The couple in back are beating time. *Concert in the Open Air,* Anonymous (Italian School). (Musée de Berry, Bourges)

the other lines were played on instruments. During the first period of the Renaissance madrigal—the second quarter of the sixteenth century—the composer's chief concern was to give pleasure to the performers, often amateurs, without much thought to virtuosic display. In the middle phase (c. 1550–80), the madrigal became an art form in which words and music were clearly linked.

The final phase of the Italian madrigal (1580–1620) extended beyond the late Renaissance into the world of the Baroque. The form became the direct expression of the composer's personality and feelings. Certain traits were carried to an extreme: rich chromatic harmony, dramatic declamation, vocal virtuosity, and vivid depiction of emotional words in music.

Monteverdi and the Madrigal

The late Renaissance madrigal came to full flower in the music of Claudio Monteverdi (1567–1643) who, between 1587 and 1643, published eight books of madrigals that span the transition from Renaissance to Baroque styles. Monteverdi's five-voice *A un giro sol,* from the *Fourth Book of Madrigals* (1603), represents a superb example of the composer's style. The poem, by Giovanni Guarini, is written in the courtly manner of much madrigal poetry, with exaggerated contrasts of delight and despair and rich examples of word painting.

Concerto delle donne

Monteverdi had intended to present some of the madrigals in this collection to the duke of Ferrara (in northern Italy), but the duke died before they were published. *A un giro sol* exhibits the passagework typical of a new singing style developed at Ferrara, which featured a famous ensemble of professional women singers known as the Concerto delle donne (Ensemble of the Ladies). The theorist Vincenzo Giustiniani, a frequent visitor to Ferrara, described their brilliant florid singing in some detail:

> The ladies vied with each other . . . in the design of exquisite passages. . . . They moderated their voices, loud or soft, heavy or light, according to the demands of the piece they were singing; now slow, breaking off sometimes with a gentle sigh, now singing long passages legato or detached, now turns, now leaps, now with long trills, now short, or again with sweet running passages sung softly to which one sometimes heard an echo answer unexpectedly. They accompanied the music and the sentiment with appropriate facial expressions, glances, and gesture. . . . They made the words clear in such a way that one could hear even the last syllable of every word.

Monteverdi was one of many composers who wrote music for these famous singers in a unique style that intermingled their high voices in sweet dissonance and elaborate ornamentation, accompanied by a bass instrument and a harpsichord or lute. The contrast of high and low, without the middle range filled in with polyphonic writing, sounded the beginnings of the new Baroque style. (We will consider Monteverdei's dramatic music in connection with early Baroque opera.)

The English Madrigal

Just as Shakespeare and other English poets adapted the Italian sonnet, so the composers of England took the Italian madrigal and developed it into a native art form. All the brilliance of the Elizabethan age is reflected in the school of madrigalists who flourished in the late sixteenth century during the reigns of Elizabeth I (1558–1603) and James I (1603–25).

This sixteenth-century Venetian painting may have been an homage to the famous women singers from Ferrara. Anonymous, *A Concert.*

In the first collection of Italian madrigals published in England, *Musica transalpina* (Music from beyond the Alps, 1588), the songs were "Englished"—that is, the texts were translated. In their own madrigals, the English composers preferred simpler texts. New, humorous madrigal types were cultivated, some with refrain syllables such as "fa la la."

John Farmer's Fair Phyllis

Born around 1570, John Farmer (fl. 1591–1601) was active in the 1590s in Dublin, where he was organist and master of the choirboys at Christ Church. In 1599, he moved to London and published his only collection of four-part madrigals. One of these, *Fair Phyllis*, attained great popularity that lasts to this day.

The pastoral text and cheerful mood of *Fair Phyllis* make it a typical English madrigal. Also typical are the sectional repetitions, the fragments of contrapuntal imitation that overlap and obscure the underlying meter, the changes

In this woodcut from **Edmund Spenser's** *The Shepheardes Calendar*, Queen Elizabeth is shown in a pastoral setting, surrounded by her musical ladies-in-waiting.

Farmer: *Fair Phyllis*

(1:21)

DATE OF WORK:	Published 1599
GENRE:	English madrigal, 4 voices
POEM:	6 lines (*a-b-a-b-c-c*), 10 or 11 syllables each
MUSICAL STYLE:	Polyphonic, with varied textures

WHAT TO LISTEN FOR: Lighthearted, pastoral English text.
4 voices (SATB), in varied textures (monophonic at opening, later polyphonic, then homorhythmic).
Change from duple or triple meter ("oh, then they fell a-kissing").
Obvious word painting as expressive device.

TEXT

20 0:00 Fair Phyllis I saw sitting all alone,
Feeding her flock near to the mountain side.
The shepherds knew not whither she was gone,
But after her [her] lover Amyntas hied.
Up and down he wandered, whilst she was missing;
When he found her, oh, then they fell a-kissing.

Examples of word painting

"Fair Phyllis I saw sitting all alone"—sung by soprano alone:

"Up and down"—descending line, repeated in all parts imitatively; shown in soprano and alto (overlapping in same register):

from homorhythmic to polyphonic texture, and the cadences on the weaker pulse of the measure. The last line of the poem is set to homorhythmic chords, with a change to triple meter.

The English composers also adopted the Italian practice of word painting. For example, the opening line, "Fair Phyllis I saw sitting all alone," is sung by a single voice (see Listening Guide 7 for the text). Note too that the statement that Phyllis's lover wandered "up and down" is rendered musically by a downward movement of the notes, which is repeated at various pitch levels and imitated in all the parts.

The Renaissance madrigal inspired composers to develop new techniques of combining music and poetry. In doing so, it prepared the way for one of the most influential forms of Western music—opera.

From Renaissance to Baroque

"The [Venetian] church of St. Mark was . . . so full of people that one could not move a step . . . a new platform was built for the singers, adjoining . . . there was a portable organ, in addition to the two famous organs of the church, and the other instruments made the most excellent music, in which the best singers and players that can be found in this region took part."

—FRANCESCO SANSOVINO

KEY POINTS

- Music at St. Mark's, in Venice, featured the use of multiple choirs *(polychoral)* singing together and in alternation *(antiphonal)*.
- Giovanni Gabrieli, choirmaster at St. Mark's, was the first composer to specify instruments and dynamics in music.

The stylistic changes that mark the shift from the Renaissance to the Baroque are dramatic; indeed, the new era that dawned at the onset of the seventeenth century can be viewed as a revolution in music. We have already seen that the madrigal, as a favored musical form of the late Renaissance, gave rise to a new style, one that focused more and more on the emotional content of the text.

The highly polyphonic style of the late Renaissance did not die away suddenly. In Venice, famous for its magnificent Basilica of St. Mark's and the impressive line of choirmasters and organists who worked there, a new grandiose style evolved. The chief characteristic of the Venetian school was *poly-*

Polychoral singing *choral singing,* involving the use of two or three choirs that either answered each other antiphonally, making possible all kinds of echo effects, or sang together.

Antiphonal performance (*Antiphonal* performance suggests groups singing in alternation and then together.) This Venetian tradition reached its high point in the works of Giovanni

Venetian painters captured the splendid pageantry of their city on canvas. Above, singers and instrumentalists take part in a religious ceremony. **Gentile Bellini** (c. 1429–1507), *Procession in Piazza San Marco.*

Gabrieli (c. 1557–1612), who fully exploited the possibilities of multiple choirs. The polychoral motet *O quam suavis* (published in 1615) is in Gabrieli's grandest manner. The use of such large forces drew him away from the subtle complexities of the old contrapuntal tradition to a broad, homorhythmic style.

This music, belonging as it does to the final decades of the sixteenth century, leaves the world of the Renaissance behind. The splendor of its sound brings us into the next great style period—the Baroque.

A Comparison of Renaissance and Baroque Styles

	RENAISSANCE (1450–1600)	BAROQUE (1600–1750)
COMPOSERS	Du Fay, Josquin, Palestrina, Monteverdi (early works)	Monteverdi (late works), Strozzi, Purcell, Vivaldi, Handel, Bach
HARMONY	Modal harmony	Major and minor tonality
TEXTURE	Imitative polyphony	New monodic or solo style; polyphony in late Baroque
MEDIUM	*A cappella* vocal music	Concerted music (voices and instruments)
SACRED VOCAL GENRES	Mass and motet dominant	Oratorio, Lutheran cantata
SECULAR VOCAL GENRES	Chanson, madrigal	Opera, cantata
INSTRUMENTAL GENRES	Derived from vocal forms: dance music (instruments not specified)	Sonata, concerto grosso, sinfonia, suite (instruments specified)
USE OF PREEXISTENT WORKS	Some works built on cantus firmus	Works are freely composed
PERFORMANCE SITES	Church and court	Public theaters

Romare Bearden
(1912–1988), *Mary Lou Williams: The Piano Lesson,* lithograph, c. 1984. (Hampton University Museum, Virginia; ©Romare Bearden Foundation/ licensed by VAGA, New York)

More Materials
of Music

unit **V**

The Organization of Musical Sounds

17

Musical Systems

"Composing is like driving down a foggy road toward a house. Slowly you see more details of the house, the color and slates and bricks, the shape of the windows. The notes are the bricks and mortar of the house."

—BENJAMIN BRITTEN

KEY POINTS

- An *octave* is the interval between two tones with the same name that are seven diatonic pitches apart (C to C).
- In Western music, the octave is divided into twelve *half steps.*
- The *chromatic scale* is made up of these twelve half steps in descending or ascending order, while a *diatonic scale* is built on patterns of seven whole and half steps that make up *major* and *minor scales.*
- A *sharp* is a symbol that raises a pitch by a half step; a *flat* lowers a tone by a half step.
- Other scale types used around the world include *tritonic* (three-note patterns), *pentatonic* (five-note patterns), and *heptatonic* (seven-note patterns other than major or minor).
- Some world cultures use intervals smaller than half steps, known as *microtones;* some scales from other cultures—for example, Indian *ragas*—have extra-musical associations.

At the beginning of this book, we learned the various elements, or building blocks, of music. Now that we have heard how these are combined in a number of works, we are ready to consider the materials of music on a more advanced level: specifically, how musical systems are built—in the West and elsewhere.

The Miracle of the Octave

To understand the concept of an octave, we need to review some basic principles of physics. A string that is set in motion vibrates at a certain rate per second and produces a certain pitch. Given the same conditions, a string half as long will vibrate twice as fast and sound an octave higher. A string twice as long will vibrate half as fast and sound an octave lower. When we sound two tones other than the octave simultaneously, such as C-D or C-F, we hear two distinctly different tones. But when we strike an octave—two notes with the same name, such as a C and another C—we recognize a very strong similarity between the two tones. Indeed, if we were not listening carefully, we might believe that a single tone was being sounded. This "miracle of the octave" was observed thousands of years ago in many musical cultures, with the result that the octave became the basic interval in music. (An interval, remember, is the distance and relationship between two tones.)

One important variable in the different languages of music around the world is the way the octave is divided. In Western music, it is divided into twelve equal semitones, or *half steps;* from these are built the major and minor scales (each with seven notes), which have constituted the basis of this musical language for nearly four hundred years.

Half steps

The Formation of Major and Minor Scales

The twelve semitones described above constitute what is known as the *chromatic scale.* (You can see these twelve half steps on the piano keyboard, counting all the white and black keys from any tone to its octave.) No matter how vast and intricate a musical work, it is made up of the same twelve tones and their higher and lower duplications. The composer Paul Hindemith once reminded his fellow musicians: "There are only twelve tones. You must treat them carefully."

Chromatic scale

Just as in fractions two halves make a whole, so do two half steps equal a whole step. The chart on page 118 gives the names of the notes on a piano keyboard. (By the way, we use the word "key" to describe the actual physical mechanism—the white or black note—on a piano or other keyboard instrument.) You can see that the black keys are named in relation to their white-key neighbors. When the black key between C and D is thought of as a half step higher than C, it is know as C-sharp (♯). When the same key is thought of as a half step lower than D, it is called D-flat (♭). Thus, a *sharp* raises a tone by a half step, and a *flat* lowers a tone a half step. Note that the distance between C and D is a whole step, made up of two half steps. Similarly, D-sharp is the same tone as E-flat, F-sharp is the same tone as G-flat, and G-sharp is the same tone as A-flat. Which of these names is used depends on the scale and key in which a sharp or flat appears.

Sharp
Flat

Both major and minor scales function within *tonality,* a principle of organization whereby we hear a piece of music in relation to a central tone, the tonic.

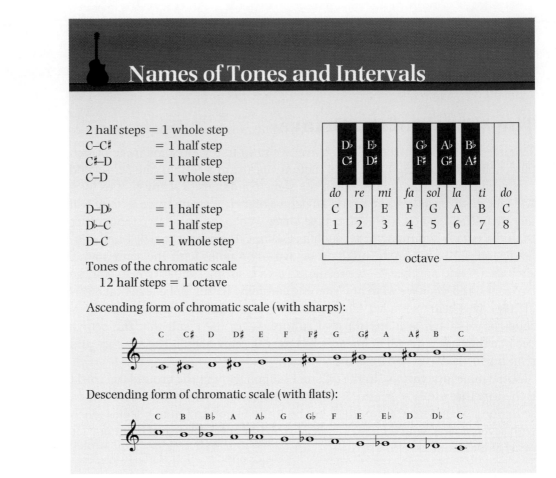

Names of Tones and Intervals

2 half steps = 1 whole step
C–C♯ = 1 half step
C♯–D = 1 half step
C–D = 1 whole step

D–D♭ = 1 half step
D♭–C = 1 half step
D–C = 1 whole step

Tones of the chromatic scale
12 half steps = 1 octave

Ascending form of chromatic scale (with sharps):

Descending form of chromatic scale (with flats):

When we listen to a composition in the key of C major, we hear a piece built around the central tone C, using the harmonies formed from the C-major scale. Tonality is the basic harmonic principle at work in most Western music written from around 1600 to 1900.

Key   By a *key,* then, we mean a group of related tones that revolve around the central tone, the tonic, or keynote, to which they ultimately gravitate. This perceived "loyalty to the tonic" is fostered by much of the music we hear. It underlies our whole system of relationships between the tones that form scales, harmonies, and keys.

The Major Scale

The major scale is probably very familiar to your ears. If you play the white keys on the piano from C to C (the C-major scale), you will hear the *do-re-mi-fa-sol-la-ti-do* pattern already mentioned. Let us examine it a little more closely.

Looking at the piano keyboard illustrated above, we notice that there is no black key on the piano between E and F *(mi-fa)* or between B and C *(ti-do).* These tones, therefore, are a half step apart, while the other white keys are a whole step apart. Consequently, when we sing the *do-re-mi-fa-sol-la-ti-do* sequence, we are measuring off a pattern of eight tones that are each a whole step apart except tones 3-4 *(mi-fa)* and 7-8 *(ti-do).* (The succession of intervals that form a major scale is summarized in the table on page 120.) You may find it helpful to sing this scale, trying to distinguish between the half- and whole-step distances as you sing.

Whether the major scale begins on C, D, E-flat, or any other tone, it follows the same pattern of whole and half steps. Such a pattern is known as a *mode*. Thus all the major scales have the same arrangement of whole and half steps and are in the major mode.

Mode

Within each major scale are certain relationships based on tension and resolution. One of the most important is the thrust of the seventh tone to the eighth (*ti* seeking to be resolved to *do*). Similarly, if we sing *do-re*, we are left with a sense of incompleteness that is resolved when *re* moves back to *do*; *fa* gravitates to *mi*; and *la* descends to *sol*.

Most important of all, the major scale defines two poles of traditional harmony: the tonic (*do*), the point of ultimate rest; and the fifth note, the dominant (*sol*), which represents the active harmony. Tonic going to dominant and returning to tonic is a basic progression of harmony in Western music. It also serves, we will find, as a basic principle of form.

The Minor Scale

The minor scale complements and serves as a contrast to the major. It differs from the major primarily in that its third degree is lowered a half step—hence the name "minor" (Latin for "smaller"). For example, the scale of C minor has an E-flat where the scale of C major has an E-natural (white key E); the interval C to E-flat is smaller than the interval C to E in the major ("larger") scale. The minor scale is pronouncedly different from the major in mood and coloring.

Like the major, the pattern of the minor scale (or mode), given in the table on page 120, may begin on any of the twelve tones of the octave. Each of the twelve major and minor scales is made up of its own particular group of seven tones; that is, each scale includes a different number of sharps or flats. The scales thus generate twelve keys in the major mode and twelve keys in the minor mode.

Chromaticism

In order for a piece to sound firmly rooted in a key, the seven notes of its scale should prevail. If the five additional foreign tones become too prominent in the melody and harmony, the relationship to the key center is weakened, and the key feeling becomes ambiguous. The distinction between the tones that do not belong within the key area and those that do is expressed in the contrasting terms "chromatic" and "diatonic." *Chromatic*, we have noted, refers to the twelve-tone scale, including all the semitones of the octave, whereas *diatonic* refers to music based on the seven tones of a major or minor scale, and to harmonies that are firmly rooted in the corresponding key. Romantic-era composers such as Liszt and Wagner explored the possibilities of chromaticism to charge their music with emotion. In contrast, music of the Baroque and Classical eras tended to be largely diatonic, centering more closely around a keynote and its related harmonies.

Chromatic
Diatonic

Other Scale Types

Pentatonic scale

The Western musical system is only one way to structure music. The musical languages of other cultures often divide the octave differently, producing different scale patterns. Among the most common is the *pentatonic*, or five-note, scale, used in some African, Far Eastern, and Native American musics. Pentatonic scales can be formed in a number of patterns, each with its own unique quality of sound. Thus the scales heard in Japan and China, although both pentatonic, sound quite different from each other. (Later we will hear a pentatonic scale in a traditional Chinese work.) Other scale types include *tritonic*, a three-note pattern found in the music of some African cultures, and a number of other seven-note, or *heptatonic*, scales fashioned from interval combinations other than those found in major and minor scales.

Tritonic and heptatonic scales

Microtones

Some scales are not easily playable on Western instruments because they employ intervals smaller than our half step. Such intervals, known as *microtones*, may sound "off-key" to Western ears. One way of producing microtonal music is by *inflecting* a pitch, or making a brief microtonal dip or rise from the original pitch; this technique, similar to that of the "blue note" in jazz (see Chapter 67), makes possible a host of subtle pitch changes. Microtonal inflections

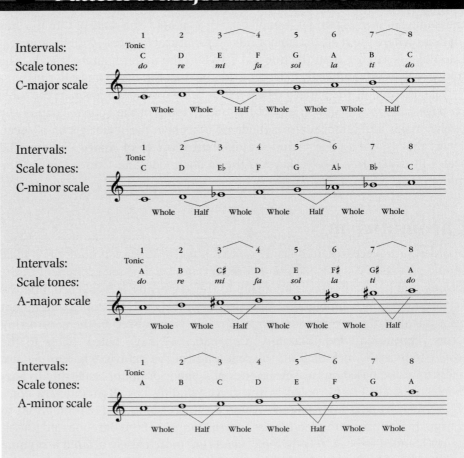

Pattern of Major and Minor Scales

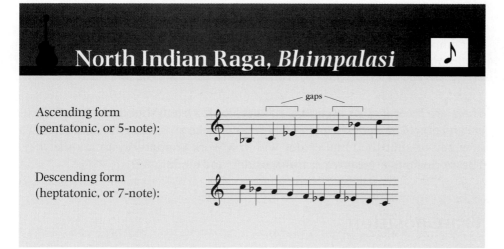

North Indian Raga, *Bhimpalasi*

Ascending form
(pentatonic, or 5-note):

Descending form
(heptatonic, or 7-note):

can be sung and played on a wide variety of string and wind instruments. We
will hear inflected pitches played and sung in several jazz selections (*Billie's
Blues* and *A Night in Tunisia*) and in a traditional Chinese piece played on string
instruments as well as in a Cajun dance tune (*Think of Me*).

In some cultures, the ascending and descending orders of a scale are more
complex, and melodic formulas can even be built into scales. In music of India,
for example, the scale formations—called *ragas*—contain certain pitches that
are heard in only one direction (see example above). These "scales" also have
extra-musical associations connected with certain emotions, colors, seasons,
times of day, or magical properties. The example above, entitled *Bhimpalasi*, is
pentatonic (B♭-C-E♭-F-G) as it ascends (with gaps between its notes) and heptatonic (seven-note) as it descends—its downward pattern also turns back up for
one note. This raga, performed in the afternoon, is meant to evoke a mood of
tenderness and longing in the listener.

Thus it is the musical system and the tones chosen in that system that determine the sound and character of each work, whether classical, popular, or traditional. They are what make Western music sound familiar to us and musics of
some cultures sound foreign.

Ragas

18

Aspects of the Major-Minor System

*"All music is nothing more than a succession of impulses that con-
verge towards a definite point of repose."*

—IGOR STRAVINSKY

KEY POINTS

■ Composers can shift the pitch level of an entire work (*transposition*), or
change the center, or key, during a work (*modulation*).

- The *tonic chord*, built on the first scale tone, is the home base to which *active chords* (*dominant*, on V; *subdominant*, on IV) need to resolve.
- Composers change the *key*, or modulate, during a piece to create tension and drama.

There are several other aspects of the harmonic system that make it both flexible and practical. For example, composers can take an entire work and set it in a new key or shift the tonal center within a work temporarily to another key. These principles are known as transposition and modulation.

Transposition

Suppose a certain melody usually begins on the pitch G. If you felt that the song lay a little too high for your voice, you might begin on F instead of G and shift all the tones of the melody one step lower. Someone else, who found the song too low, could begin on A and sing each tone of the melody one step higher. The act of shifting all the tones of a musical composition a uniform distance to a different pitch level is called *transposition*.

Choice of key   When we transpose a piece, we shift it to another key. We change the keynote and the corresponding notes of the scale. But the melody line remains the same because the pattern of its whole and half steps does not change in the new key. That is why the same song can be published in various keys for soprano, alto, tenor, or bass.

Why does a composer choose one key rather than another? In former times, external factors strongly influenced this choice. Up to around the year 1815, for example, brass instruments were not able to change keys as readily as they are now, since they had no valves. In writing for string instruments, composers considered the fact that certain effects, such as playing on the open strings, could be achieved in one key but not in another. Composers have even associated an emotional atmosphere or a color with certain keys, a concept not too far removed from the extra-musical meaning found in the ragas of India.

Modulation

The contrast between keys and the movement from one key to another is an essential element of musical structure. We have seen that the pitches belonging to a key form a group of seven out of twelve, which provides coherence and focus to the music. But this closed group may be opened up, in which case we are shifted, either gently or abruptly, to another area centering on another keynote. The process of passing from one key to another is known as *modulation*. There is no way to describe in words something that can only be heard. Suffice it to say that composers can "lift" us from one tonal area to another. As the composer Arnold Schoenberg put it, "Modulation is like a change of scenery."

The twelve major and twelve minor keys may be compared to rooms in a house, with the modulations equivalent to corridors leading from one to the other. (See illustration on p. 133 of the terraced levels in the Residenz, home of the Prince-Bishop of Würzburg.) We shall see that modulation was a common practice of the Baroque period and was refined as a formal procedure in the

Classical era. The eighteenth-century composer as a rule established the home key, shaped the passage of modulation—the "corridor"—in a clear-cut manner, and usually passed to a key area that was not too far away from the starting point. These procedures resulted in a spaciousness of structure that can be thought of as the musical counterpart to the balanced facades of eighteenth-century architecture.

Nineteenth-century Romanticism, on the other hand, demanded a whipping-up of emotions, an intensifying of all musical processes. In the Romantic era, modulations were more frequent and abrupt, leading to an emotion-charged music that wandered restlessly from key to key and fulfilled the Romantic artist's need for excitement.

Active and Rest Chords

Just as melodies have inherent active and rest notes, so do the harmonies supporting these tones. The three-note chord, or *triad*, built on the first scale tone is known as the I chord, or the *tonic*, and serves as a point of rest. But rest only has meaning in relation to activity. The chord of rest is counterposed to other chords, which are active. The active chords in turn seek to be completed, or resolved, in the rest chord. This striving for resolution is the dynamic force in Western music, providing a forward direction and goal.

Triad
Tonic

The fifth scale step, the *dominant*, is the chief active chord, which seeks to resolve to the tonic. The triad built on the fourth scale step *(fa)* is known as the *subdominant*. The movement from the subdominant to the tonic (IV to I) is familiar from the chords accompanying the "Amen" sung at the close of many hymns.

Dominant

Subdominant

These three triads, the basic ones of our system, suffice to harmonize many a tune. The Civil War song *The Battle Hymn of the Republic* (also known as *John Brown's Body*) is a good example.

♪

Mine	eyes	have	seen	the	glory	of	the	coming	of	the	Lord,
I											

He	is	trampling	out	the	vintage	where	the	grapes	of	wrath	are	stored;
I	IV					I						

He has	loosed	the	fateful	lightning	of	His	terrible	swift	sword,
I									

His	truth	is	marching	on.
I	IV	V	I	

Glory,	glory!	Hallelujah!	Glory,	glory! Halle- lujah!
I			IV	I

Glory,	glory!	Hallelujah!	His	truth	is	marching	on.
I			IV	V	I		

The Key as a Form-Building Element

The three main chords of a musical work—tonic (I), dominant (V), and sub-dominant (IV)—are the focal points over which melodies and harmonic progressions unfold. Thus the key becomes a prime factor for musical unity.

Key contrast   At the same time, the contrast between keys adds welcome variety. Composers can pit one key against another, thereby achieving a dramatic opposition between them. They begin by establishing the home key, then modulate to a related key, generally that of the dominant (for example, from C major to G major, or from G major to D major). In so doing, they create a tension, since the domi-

---

Listening Activity: Musical Key

CD: CHR/STD 2/55–61, SH 2/1–7

Haydn: Symphony No. 94 in G major (*Surprise*)

In Chapter 3, we listened to the second movement from this Haydn Symphony to distinguish the sounds of major and minor harmonies (see p. 26). Let's return to the work again to enrich your understanding of these important musical principles. Sing the opening melody, using the scale syllables shown below:

Do do mi mi sol sol mi	*fa fa re re*	*ti ti sol*
I (tonic)	**IV (subdom.)**	**V (dom.)**

do do mi mi sol sol mi	*do do fa($\sharp$)fa($\sharp$)*	*sol*
I (tonic)	**II^7 (new)**	**V (dom.)**

WHAT TO LISTEN FOR

- Opening key of C major, with melody and chords centered on the pitch C.
- First chord—the tonic (I), on C *(do)*—recurs often as a place of rest.
- Other important chords—the dominant (V), on G *(sol)*, and the subdominant (IV), on F *(fa)*—are active chords that need resolution to the tonic, on C.
- Each part of the melody suggests a chord: first the tonic (I), then subdominant (IV), then dominant (V), then tonic (I) again, followed by a new chord on II, then dominant (V). At this point, *sol* (V) needs resolution to tonic.
- Try to keep the pitch C, the tonic, in mind.
- The key change from C major to C minor (at 2 minutes and 20 seconds).

MORE LISTENING REVIEW (FROM CD SET)

- Major tonality—Mozart: *Eine kleine Nachtmusik*, first movement
- Minor tonality—Bach: Prelude and Fugue in C minor
- Major/minor tonality—Smetana: *The Moldau*
- Chromaticism—Purcell: Dido's Lament, from *Dido and Aeneas*
- Modulation—Mozart: *Eine kleine Nachtmusik*, first movement (during first minute, modulates from G major to D major)

nant key is unstable compared to the tonic. This tension requires resolution, which is provided by the return to the home key.

The progression, or movement, from home key to contrasting key and back outlines the basic musical pattern of statement-departure-return. The home key is the anchor, the safe harbor; the foreign key represents adventure. The home key provides unity; the foreign key ensures variety and contrast.

Hendrik Terbrugghen (1588–1629),
Duet. (The Louvre, Paris)

The Baroque Era

El Greco (1541–1614), Spanish painter

Giulio Caccini (1551–1618)

Jacopo Peri (1561–1633)

William Shakespeare (1564–1616), English dramatist

Galileo Galilei (1564–1642), Italian astronomer

Claudio Monteverdi (1567–1643)

Peter Paul Rubens (1577–1640), Flemish painter

Francesca Caccini (1587–1630)

Hendrik Terbrugghen (1588–1629), Dutch painter

René Descartes (1596–1650), French mathematician/philosopher

● Shakespeare's *Hamlet* (1601)

Rembrandt von Rijn (1606–1669), Dutch painter

First European settlement in America founded at Jamestown, Virginia (1607) ●

John Milton (1608–1674), English poet

Judith Leyster (1609–1660), Dutch painter

● King James version of Bible (1611)

Barbara Strozzi (1619–c. 1677)

Mayflower; Plymouth settled (1620) ●

William Harvey publishes treatise on the circulation of the blood (1628) ●

Jan Vermeer (1632–1675), Dutch painter

The Bay Psalm Book, first printed in the American colonies (1640) ●

Puritan Revolution begins in England (1642) ●

Reign of Louis XIV begins (1643) ●

Period of the Commonwealth begins in England (1649) ●

Milton's *Paradise Lost* (1665) ●

Baroque (1600–1750)

| 1680 | 1690 | 1700 | 1710 | 1720 | 1730 | 1740 | 1750 | 1760 | 1770 | 1780 | 1790 | 1800 |

● World Events
▬ Composers
▬ Principal Figures

Jean-Baptiste Lully (1632–1687)

Antonio Stradivarius (c. 1644–1737), Italian violin maker

John Blow (1649–1708)

Arcangelo Corelli (1653–1713)

Henry Purcell (1659–1695)

Elisabeth-Claude Jacquet de la Guerre (c. 1666–1729)

Johann Christophe Pepusch (1667–1752)

François Couperin (1668–1733)

Antonio Vivaldi (1678–1741)

Georg Phillip Telemann (1681–1767)

● Reign of Peter the Great (Russia) begins (1682)

Jean-Philippe Rameau (1683–1764)

Jean-Antoine Watteau (1684–1721), French painter

● Sir Issac Newton's theory of gravitation (1684)

John Gay (1685–1732)

Johann Sebastian Bach (1685–1750)

Domenico Scarlatti (1685–1757)

George Frideric Handel (1685–1759)

Jean-Jacques Rousseau (1712–1778), Swiss-born French philosopher/composer

Christoph Willibald Gluck (1714–1787)

Carl Phillip Emanuel Bach (1714–1788)

● Queen Anne succeeded by George I, Handel's patron (1714)

● Reign of Louis XV begins (1715)

| 1680 | 1690 | 1700 | 1710 | 1720 | 1730 | 1740 | 1750 | 1760 | 1770 | 1780 | 1790 | 1800 |

unit **VI**

The Baroque and the Arts

19

The Baroque Spirit

"I do not know what I may appear to the world; but to myself I seem to have been only like a boy playing on the seashore . . . whilst the great ocean of truth lay all undiscovered before me."

—SIR ISAAC NEWTON

KEY POINTS

- The Baroque era (1600–1750) was a time of turbulent change in politics, science, and the arts.
- It was also a time of religious wars (Protestants vs. Catholics) and of exploring the New World.
- The era saw the rise of middle-class culture, with music making centered in the home, church, and at the universities (in a group called the *collegium musicum*); art portrayed scenes of bourgeois life.
- In the New World, music served religion through the singing of psalms, important to both Protestants and Catholics (CP 7).

The Baroque period stretched across a stormy century and a half of European history. It began shortly before the year 1600, a convenient signpost that need not be taken too literally, and may be regarded as having come to a close with the death of Bach in 1750.

The term "baroque" was probably derived from the Portuguese *barroco,* a pearl of irregular shape much used in the jewelry of the time. The years 1600–1750 encompassed a period of change and adventure. The conquest of the New World stirred the imagination and filled the coffers of western Europe. The middle classes acquired wealth and power in their struggle against the aristocracy. Empires clashed for mastery of the world. Appalling poverty and wasteful luxury, magnificent idealism and savage oppression—against contradictions such as these evolved the pomp and splendor of Baroque art, in all its vigor, elaborate decoration, and grandeur.

The transition from the classically minded Renaissance to the Baroque was foreshadowed in the art of Michelangelo (1475–1564). His turbulent figures, their bodies twisted in struggle, reflect the Baroque love of the dramatic. In like fashion, the Venetian school of painters—Titian, Tintoretto, Caravaggio—captured the dynamic spirit of the new age: their crowded canvases are ablaze with color and movement.

The Baroque was an era of absolute monarchy. Rulers throughout Europe took as their model the splendor of the French court at Versailles, on the outskirts of Paris. Louis XIV's famous "I am the State" summed up a way of life in which all art and culture served the ruler. Courts large and small maintained elaborate musical establishments, including opera troupes, chapel choirs, and orchestras. Baroque opera, the favorite diversion of the aristocracy, told stories of the gods and heroes of antiquity, in whom the occupants of the royal box and their courtiers saw flattering likenesses of themselves.

The middle classes, excluded from the salons of the aristocracy, created a culture of their own. Their music making centered in the home, the church, and the university group known as *collegium musicum* (which functions once again on many campuses today). It was for them that the comic opera and the prose novel, both of which were filled with keen and witty observations of life, came into being. For them, painting abandoned its grandiose themes and turned to intimate scenes of bourgeois life. The Dutch School, embodying the vitality of a new burgher art, reached its high point in

The bold and vigorous Baroque style was foreshadowed in this dramatic drawing by **Michelangelo** (1474–1564), *Studies for the Libyan Sibyl.* (Metropolitan Museum of Art, New York)

The Flemish painter **Peter Paul Rubens** (1577–1640) instills his tribute to the pleasures of life with energy and drama. *The Garden of Love.* (The Prado, Madrid)

Music and the Religious Spirit in the New World

Throughout history, music has helped people express and disseminate their beliefs. What role, then, did music play in the establishment of various religions in the Americas? European settlers in the New World brought their faiths with them and, with the aid of music, converted some of the indigenous population. As a result, many people of modern-day Mexico, colonized by the Spanish, and of northeastern Canada, settled by the French, are Roman Catholics.

In the early seventeenth century, the Eastern Seaboard of the present United States and parts of coastal Canada were occupied by various Protestant groups from England, Germany, France, and the Netherlands. Music, largely the singing of psalms from the Old Testament, played a major part in the religious and social lives of these early colonists. (We learned of the importance of the psalms to Christianity in CP 4.) Some settlers brought psalm books with them from Europe, and in 1640, in Cambridge, Massachusetts, the North American colonies produced their first printed book: *The Whole Booke of Psalms* (commonly known as the *Bay Psalm Book*).

The choir sings with organ (upper right) in this service at the Old Lutheran Church, Reading, Pennsylvania, ca. 1800. From a drawing by **Lewis Miller.**

Gospel singer Yolanda performs at the 7th annual Essence Music Festival, held at the Louisiana Super Dome in New Orleans, on July 5, 2001.

Even though psalm books became increasingly available, not everyone had one, nor were all colonists even literate. Hence, a singing style known as lining out came into practice, characterized by a slow, drawn-out tempo, with a minister or member of the congregation chanting out the text line by line before it was sung by the congregation. Various people embellished the tune, resulting in dissonant heterophony—two or more decorated versions of the melody sung simultaneously—a practice typical of many music cultures around the world.

The lining out style eventually gave way to more sophisticated polyphonic settings of the psalms. The foremost American composer in this genre was the Boston music teacher William Billings (1746–1800), who is remembered today for his fuging tunes— polyphonic settings of psalms or hymns in an over-lapping, imitative setting (related to the fugue but not as strict in form). Billings's works were intended for use not in church services but as sacred or devotional music, performed in the singing schools that had sprung up in New England and in the maritime provinces of Canada.

Folklike devotional music was cultivated by African Americans and whites alike in the nineteenth and twentieth centuries in the form of spirituals and gospel hymns, religious songs sung at revivals and prayer meetings. (Later in this book, we will hear a contemporary art-song arrangement of the spiritual *Sometimes I Feel Like a Motherless Child*; see Listening Guide 44.) In the twentieth century, gospel music has become an eclectic style of Protestant African-American sacred music, which has supplanted spirituals in popularity for worship and entertainment. In this modern style, vocalists (like Mahalia Jackson), often accompanied by dancing and clapping, embellish simple melodies with complex rhythms, pitch alterations, and added phrases. Yet another devotional style popular among youth today is contemporary Christian music, a kind of sacred country rock exemplified in performances by Amy Grant and Michael W. Smith, among many others.

TERMS TO NOTE:

lining out	spiritual
heterophony	gospel music
fuging tune	

SUGGESTED LISTENING:

Early American hymn
Fuging tune (William Billings)
Spiritual (African-American or white)
Gospel music (Mahalia Jackson)
Contemporary Christian music (Amy Grant or Michael W. Smith)

(Above): *The Flute Player*, by the Dutch painter **Judith Leyster** (1609–1660), presents a bourgeois, or middle-class, music scene.

(Right): the rapturous mysticism of the Counter-Reformation found expression in this eerie landscape of **El Greco** (1541–1614), *View of Toledo*. (Metropolitan Museum of Art, New York)

Terbrugghen (1588–1629) and Rembrandt (1606–1669), masters whose insights penetrated the regions of the soul.

Under the leadership of merchant princes and financiers, the culture of the city came to rival that of the palace. These new art lovers vied with the court in their devotion to splendor; they responded to the beauty of brocade and velvet, marble and jewels. This aspect of the Baroque finds expression in the painting of Peter Paul Rubens (1577–1640), whose canvases exude a driving energy, a celebration of life. His voluptuous nudes established the seventeenth-century ideal of feminine beauty.

Scientific frontiers

The Baroque was an age of reason. The ideas of Kepler, Galileo, and Copernicus in physics and astronomy, of Descartes in mathematics and Spinoza in philosophy, were milestones in the intellectual history of Europe. The English physician William Harvey explained the circulation of the blood, and Sir Isaac Newton formulated the theory of gravity.

Religion

The Baroque was also an intensely devout period, and religion was a rallying cry on some of the bloodiest battlefields in history. The Protestants were centered in England, Scandinavia, Holland, and the north German cities, all strongholds of the rising middle class. On the Catholic side were two powerful dynasties, the French Bourbons and the Austrian-Spanish Hapsburgs, who fought one another as fiercely as they did their Protestant foes. After decades of struggle, the great Hapsburg empire was broken in the 1790s, and France emerged as the leading state on the Continent. Germany lay in ruins, England rose to world power, and Europe was ready to advance to the stage of a modern industrial society.

At the same time, religion (as well as basic survival) was an important part of life in the American colonies. Settled largely by Protestant refugees who emigrated from northern Europe during the seventeenth century, the colonies based their new society on religious principle, which some zealots carried to an extreme. (See CP 7.)

With *Paradise Lost*, England's John Milton (1608–1674) produced the poetic epic of Protestantism, as Dante three and a half centuries earlier had expressed the Catholic point of view in *The Divine Comedy*. The Catholic world answered Martin Luther's reforms with the Counter-Reformation, whose rapturous mysticism found expression in the canvases of El Greco (1541–1614). These paintings are the creations of a visionary mind that distorts the real in its search for a reality beyond.

Creative artists played a variety of roles in Baroque society. Peter Paul Rubens and Anthony Van Dyck were not only famous painters but also ambassadors and friends of princes. The composer Antonio Vivaldi was also a priest, John Milton a political leader, and George Frideric Handel an opera impresario. Artists usually functioned under royal or princely patronage, or, like Johann Sebastian Bach, they might be employed by a church or city administration. In all cases, artists were in direct contact with their public. Many musical works were created for specific occasions—an opera for a royal wedding, a cantata for a religious service—and for immediate use.

The role of the artist

20

Main Currents in Baroque Music

"The end of all good music is to affect the soul."

—CLAUDIO MONTEVERDI

KEY POINTS

- The Baroque era marks the introduction of a new style of music—*monody*, featuring solo song with instrumental accompaniment.
- Monody was developed by groups of writers and musicians (such as the Florentine Camerata) in order to resurrect the musical-dramatic art of ancient Greece; this new vocal style focused on the text and its emotional power.
- Harmony was notated with *figured bass*, a shorthand that allowed the performer to supply the chords through *improvisation*. The bass part, or *basso continuo*, was often played by two instruments (harpsichord and cello, for example).
- The *major-minor tonality* system was established in the Baroque era.
- While early Baroque music moved more freely, later Baroque style is characterized by a vigorous, regular rhythm and continuous melodic expansion.
- Subtle dynamic changes contributed to the expression of emotions.
- As musical instruments developed technically, the level of virtuosity rose, demanding more advanced playing techniques.
- The union of text and music was expressed in the Baroque *doctine of the affections*.

■ Women musicians figured among the professional singers and instrumentalists of the Baroque era.

Origins of the Monodic Style

Monody

The transition from Renaissance to Baroque brought with it a great change: the shift of interest from a texture of several independent parts to one in which a single melody stood out—that is, from polyphonic music to homophonic. The new style, which originated in vocal music around the year 1600, was named *monody*—literally, "one song"—or solo song with instrumental accompaniment. (Monody is not to be confused with monophony, which is an unaccompanied vocal line; see p. 27.)

The Camerata

Stile rappresentativo

The monodic style was first cultivated by a group of Florentine writers, artists, and musicians known as the Camerata, a name derived from the Italian word for "salon." Among the members of this group and the one that succeeded it were Vincenzo Galilei, father of the astronomer Galileo Galilei, and the composers Giulio Caccini (1551–1618) and Jacopo Peri (1561–1633). The members of the Camerata were aristocratic humanists who aimed to resurrect the musical-dramatic art of ancient Greece. Although little was known of ancient music, the Camerata deduced that music must heighten the emotional power of the text. Thus came into being what its inventors regarded as the *stile rappresentativo* (representational style), consisting of a melody that moved freely over a foundation of simple chords.

Origins of the opera

The Camerata appeared at a time when music had to free itself from the complexities of counterpoint. The year 1600 bristled with discussions about *le nuove musiche,* "the new music," and what its adherents proudly named "the expressive style." They soon realized that this representational style could be applied not only to a short text, like a poem, but also to an entire drama. In this way, they were led to what many regard as the single most important achievement of Baroque music: the invention of opera.

New Harmonic Structures

The melody-and-chords of the new music was far removed from the intricate interweaving of voices in the older Renaissance style. Since musicians were familiar with the basic harmonies, it was unnecessary to write the chords out in full. Instead, the composer put a numeral above or below the bass note, indicating the chord required (this kind of notation was called *figured bass*), and the performer filled in the necessary harmony. This system, known as *basso continuo,* often employed two instrumentalists for the accompaniment. One played the bass line on a cello or bassoon, and another filled in the harmonies on a chordal instrument, generally harpsichord or organ. Musicians of this period were able to "think with their fingers"; that is, they could read and improvise on these figures with ease, much like a jazz musician in the twentieth century. The resulting continuo provided a scaffolding over which a vocal or instrumental melody could unfold.

Figured bass

Basso continuo

As interest shifted from counterpoint to a simpler style based on a single-line melody, the harmonic system grew simpler too, leading to one of the most significant changes in music history: the establishment of major-minor tonality. With this development, the thrust to the keynote, or tonic, became the most powerful force in music, and each chord could assume its function in relation to the key center. Baroque composers soon learned to exploit the opposition between the chord of rest, the I (tonic), and the active chord, the V (dominant). So too the movement, or modulation, from home key to contrasting key and back became an important element in shaping musical structure. Composers developed forms of instrumental music larger than had ever before been known.

Major-minor tonality

Tonic and dominant

This transition to major-minor tonality was marked by a significant technical advance. Because of a curious quirk of nature, keyboard instruments tuned according to the scientific laws of acoustics (first discovered by the ancient Greek philosopher Pythagoras) give a pure sound in some keys but increasingly out-of-tune intervals in others. As instrumental music acquired greater prominence, it became more and more important to be able to play in any key. Attempts to achieve this goal resulted in a variety of tuning systems. In the seventeenth century, a discovery was made: by slightly adjusting, or tempering, the mathematically "pure" intervals within the octave to equalize the distance between adjacent tones, it became possible to play in every major and minor key without experiencing unpleasant sounds. This tuning adjustment, known as *equal temperament*, greatly increased the range of harmonic possibilities that were available to the composer.

Equal temperament

Although we are uncertain which of the many temperaments, or tuning systems, was preferred by Johann Sebastian Bach, this composer demonstrated that he could write in every one of the twelve major and twelve minor keys. The result, *The Well-Tempered Clavier*, is a two-volume collection, each containing twenty-four preludes and fugues, or one in every possible key. Equal temperament eventually transformed the major-minor system, making it a completely flexible medium of expression.

The grand staircase of the Residenz, home of the Prince-Bishop of Würzburg, is a superb example of Baroque interior design, with its sculptural ornaments and elaborate decorations.

Baroque Musical Style

During the Baroque era, the rhythmic freedom of the monodic style eventually gave way to a vigorous rhythm based on regular accent. Once under way, the steady pulsation never slackens, giving Baroque music its unflagging drive—the same effect of restless but controlled motion that we find in Baroque painting, sculpture, and architecture. Rhythm helped capture the drive and movement of a dynamic age.

The elaborate scrollwork of Baroque architecture found its musical equivalent in the principle of continuous expansion of melody. A movement may start with a striking musical figure that then spins out ceaselessly. In vocal music, wide leaps and the use of chromatic tones helped create melodies that were highly expressive of the text.

Baroque musicians used dissonant chords more and more freely, for emotional intensity and color. In setting poetry, for example, a composer might use a dissonant chord to heighten the impact of a particularly expressive word.

Dynamic contrasts The dynamic contrasts achieved in Renaissance music through varied imitative voicings and in polychoral works gave way to more subtle, nuanced treatment in the Baroque. While few dynamic markings occur in music of the seventeenth century, theoretical and musical sources demonstrate that subtle dynamic shadings were very much a feature of Baroque performance and contributed to the expression of emotions, especially of the text. On the other hand, Baroque keyboard instruments, such as harpsichord and organ, inherently produced a kind of graduated, or terraced, dynamics by the use of different registrations, and *forte/piano* contrasts and echo effects were also typical of the era.

It follows that Baroque composers were much more sparing of expression marks than those who came later. The music of the period carries little else than an occasional *forte* or *piano*, leaving it to the player to supply whatever else may be necessary.

The Rise of the Virtuoso Musician

The heightened interest in instruments during the Baroque era went hand in hand with the need to master their technique. A dramatic rise in the standards of playing paralleled the improvements introduced by the great builders of instruments in Italy and Germany. Composers in turn wrote works that demanded a more advanced playing technique. Out of these developments came the challenging harpsichord sonatas of Domenico Scarlatti and the virtuosic violin works of Antonio Vivaldi, to name only two masters of the period.

The emergence of instrumental virtuosity had its counterpart in the vocal sphere. The rise of opera saw the development of a phenomenal vocal technique, exemplified in the early eighteenth century by the *castrato*, a male singer castrated during boyhood in order to preserve the soprano or alto register of his voice for the rest of his life. What resulted, after years of training, was an incredibly agile voice of enormous range, powered by breath control unrivalled by most singers today. The castrato's voice combined the lung power of the male with the brilliance of the female upper register. Strange as it may seem to us, Baroque audiences associated this voice with heroic male roles. (The most famous of Baroque castratos was Farinelli, whose career was depicted in 1994 in the exquisite Belgian movie *Farinelli.*) After the French Revolution, this custom, so offensive to human dignity, was almost universally abolished. When castrato roles are performed today, they are usually sung in lower register by a tenor or baritone, or in the original register by a countertenor, a falsettist, or a woman singer in male costume.

Caricature of the famous castrato Farinelli, by **Pier Leone Ghezzi** (1674–1755).

Improvisation played a significant role in Baroque music. Singers and players alike added their own embellishments to what was written down (a custom found today in jazz and pop music) as their creative contribution to the work. The practice was so widespread that Baroque music sounded quite different in performance from what was notated on the page.

A performance at the Teatro Argentina in Rome, 1729, as portrayed by **Giovanni Paolo Pannini** (1697–1765).

The Doctrine of the Affections

The Baroque inherited from the Renaissance an impressive technique of text painting, in which the music vividly mirrored the words. It was generally accepted that music ought to arouse the emotions, or affections—joy, anger, love, fear, or exaltation. By the late seventeenth century, an entire piece or movement, even of instrumental music, was normally built on a single affection, applying what was known as the *doctrine of the affections*. The opening motive established the mood of the piece, which prevailed until the work's end. The procedure differs markedly from the practice of the Classical and Romantic eras, when music was based on two or more contrasting emotions.

Women in Baroque Music

Women continued to play an active and expanded role in the music of the Baroque. Two Italian musicians from the early decades of the era stand out for their talents as singers and composers. Francesca Caccini (1587–1638), daughter of Giulio Caccini, one of the creators of the "new music," was immersed in the musical culture of her time; she sang roles in several of the earliest operas written and is the first woman known to have composed an opera (1625). Barbara Strozzi (1619–1677), a prolific composer of secular and sacred vocal music, also received some notoriety as a singer. She was active as well in the famous literary academies of Venice. We will consider one of her vocal compositions in a later chapter.

With the establishment of opera houses throughout Europe, the opportunity for women to enter the ranks of professional musicians greatly increased. Some reached the level of superstars, such as the Italian sopranos Faustina Bordoni and Francesca Cuzzoni, who engaged in a bitter, notorious rivalry. One French musician who enjoyed the patronage of King Louis XIV was Elisabeth-Claude Jacquet de la Guerre (c. 1666–1729), renowned for her harpsichord music and her Biblical cantatas. Women also continued their important role as patrons of the arts and as hostesses at the salons where music was actively cultivated.

Internationalism

The Baroque was a culturally international period in which national styles existed—but without nationalism. Jean-Baptiste Lully, an Italian, created the French lyric tragedy. Handel, a German, wrote Italian operas for English audiences and gave England the oratorio. There was free interchange among national cultures. The sensuous beauty of Italian melody, the pointed precision of French dance rhythm, the luxuriance of German polyphony, the freshness of English choral song—these nourished an all-European art that absorbed the best of each national style.

Exoticism The great voyages of exploration during the Renaissance had opened up hitherto unknown regions of the globe, sparking a vivid interest among Europeans in remote cultures and far-off locales. As a result, exoticism became a discernible element of Baroque music. A number of operas looked to faraway lands for their settings—Persia, India, Turkey, the Near East, Peru, and the Americas. These operas offered picturesque scenes, interesting local color, and dances that may not have been authentic but that delighted audiences through their appeal to the imagination. Thus an international spirit combined with an interest in the exotic to produce music that flowed easily across national boundaries.

unit **VII**

Vocal Music
of the Baroque

Baroque Opera

"Opera is the delight of Princes."

　　　　　　　　　　—MARCO DA GAGLIANO

KEY POINTS

■ The most important new genre of the Baroque era was the *opera*, a large-scale music drama that combines poetry, acting, scenery, and costumes with singing and instrumental music.

■ The principal components of opera include the orchestra (playing the *overture*), solo *arias* (lyrical songs), and *recitatives* (speechlike declamations of the text), as well as ensemble numbers, including choruses. The opera composer works with a *librettist,* who writes the text.

■ The early Baroque master Claudio Monteverdi wrote operas based on mythology and Roman history, and helped establish the love duet as a central component of opera.

■ The English composer Henry Purcell wrote *Dido and Aeneas,* whose story is drawn from *The Aeneid,* a Roman epic by Virgil.

The Components of Opera

An opera is a large-scale drama that is sung. It combines the resources of vocal and instrumental music—soloists, ensembles, chorus, orchestra, and sometimes ballet—with poetry and drama, acting and pantomime, scenery and costumes. To weld the diverse elements into a unity is a challenge that has attracted some of the most creative minds in the history of music.

Recitative

Explanations necessary to advance the plot and action are generally presented in a kind of musical declamation, or speech, known as *recitative.* This vocal style, which grew out of the earliest monodies of the Florentine Camerata, imitates the natural inflections of speech; its rhythm is shaped to the rhythm of the language. Rarely presenting a purely musical line, recitative is often characterized by a fast-paced patter and "talky" repetition of the same note, as well as rapid question-and-answer dialogue that builds tension. In time, two styles of recitative became standard: *secco* (Italian for "dry"), which is accompanied only by continuo instruments and moves with great freedom, and *accompagnato,* which is accompanied by the orchestra and thus moves more evenly.

Aria

Recitative gives way at lyric moments to the *aria* (Italian for "air"), which releases through melody the emotional tension accumulated in the course of the action. The aria is a song, usually of a highly emotional kind. It is what audiences wait for, what they cheer, what they remember. An aria, because of its tunefulness, can be effective even when sung out of context—for example, in a concert or on a CD. Indeed, many arias are familiar to people who have never heard the operas from which they are excerpted. One formal convention that developed early in the genre's history is the *da capo aria,* a ternary, or **A-B-A,** form that brings back the first section with embellishments improvised by the soloist.

Ensemble

An opera may contain ensemble numbers—duets, trios, quartets, and so on—in which the characters pour out their respective feelings. The chorus may be used to back up the solo voices, or it may function independently. It may comment and reflect on the action like the chorus in Greek tragedy, or it may be integrated into the action.

Overture

The orchestra supports the action of the opera as well, setting the appropriate mood for the different scenes. The orchestra also performs the *overture,* an instrumental number heard at the beginning of most operas, which may introduce melodies from the arias. Each act of the opera normally opens with an orchestral introduction, and between scenes we may find interludes, or *sinfonias,* as they were called in Baroque opera.

Libretto

The opera composer works with a *librettist,* who writes the text of the work, using dramatic insight to create characters and plot and to fashion situations that justify the use of music. The *libretto,* the text or script of the opera, must be devised so as to give the composer an opportunity to write music for the diverse numbers—recitatives and arias, ensembles, choruses, interludes—that have become the traditional features of this art form.

Early Opera in Italy

An outgrowth of Renaissance theatrical traditions and the musical experiments of the Florentine Camerata, early opera lent itself to the lavish spectacles and scenic displays that graced royal weddings and similar ceremonial occasions. Two such operas, *Orfeo* (1607) and *Arianna* (1608), were composed by the first

Claudio Monteverdi

great master of the new genre, Claudio Monteverdi (1567–1643). In Monteverdi's operas, the innovations of the Florentine Camerata reached artistic maturity, and the dramatic spirit of the Baroque found its true representative.

Although his earliest operas derived their plots from Greek mythology, for *The Coronation of Poppea* (1642), a late work from his Venetian period, Monteverdi turned to history. By this time, the first public opera houses had opened in Venice; opera was moving out of the palace and becoming a popular entertainment. In his early court operas, Monteverdi used an orchestra of diverse instruments. But in writing *Poppea* (his last opera) for a theater that would include works by other composers, he developed a more standardized ensemble with strings at its core.

Monteverdi's late operas have powerful emotions that find expression in recitatives, arias, choruses, and passages in *arioso style* (between aria and recitative). With Monteverdi, Italian opera took on the basic shape it would maintain for the next several hundred years. The love duet, established in *The Coronation of Poppea*, became an essential operatic feature, and his powerful musical portrayal of human passions is echoed in the soaring melodies of Giuseppe Verdi's Romantic masterworks, as we will see later.

Opera in France

By the turn of the eighteenth century, Italian opera had gained wide popularity in the rest of western Europe. Only in France was the Italian genre rejected, as French composers set out to fashion a national style, drawn from their strong traditions of court ballet and classical tragedy. The result was the *tragédie lyrique*, which combined colorful, sumptuous dance scenes and spectacular choruses in tales of courtly love and heroic adventure. The most important composer of the tragédie lyrique was Jean-Baptiste Lully (1632–1687), whose operas won him favor with the French royal court under King Louis XIV. Lully was the first to succeed in adapting recitative to the inflections of the French language, and he exerted a major influence in shaping the French overture (see p. 171).

Tragédie lyrique

Jean-Baptiste Lully

Opera in England

During the reigns of the first two Stuart kings, James I (r. 1603–25) and Charles I (r. 1625–49), the English *masque*, a type of entertainment that combined vocal

In this richly colored painting *The Death of Dido*, by **Giovanni Barbieri**, called Guercino (1591–1666), Dido has stabbed herself with Aeneas's sword and thrown herself on the funeral pyre. Her sister and handmaidens look on in horror; in the background, Aeneas's ships leave the harbor.

Henry Purcell

and instrumental music with poetry and dance, became popular among the aristocracy. Many masques were presented privately in the homes of the nobility.

In the period of the Commonwealth that followed (1649–60), stage plays were forbidden, because the Puritans regarded the theater as an invention of the devil. A play set to music, though, could be passed off as a "concert." The "semi-operas" that flourished during the rule of Oliver Cromwell (1653–58) were essentially plays with a liberal mixture of solo songs, ensembles, and choral numbers interspersed with instrumental pieces. Since the dramatic tradition in England was much stronger than the operatic, the spoken word inevitably took precedence over the sung. However, in the 1680s, an important step toward opera was taken when John Blow (1649–1708) presented his *Venus and Adonis,* which was sung throughout; this work paved the way for the first great English opera, *Dido and Aeneas,* by Blow's pupil Henry Purcell.

Henry Purcell: His Life and Music

"As Poetry is the harmony of Words, so Musick is that of Notes; and as Poetry is a Rise above Prose and Oratory, so is Musick the exaltation of Poetry."

Henry Purcell (1659–1695) occupies a special niche in the musical history of his country. He won England a leading position in the world of music. Purcell's brief career spanned the reign of several monarchs, at whose courts he held various posts as singer, organist, and composer.

Purcell assimilated the achievements of the Continent—the dynamic instrumental style, the movement toward major-minor tonality, the recitative and aria of Italian opera, and the accentuated rhythms of the French—and acclimated these to his native land.

Purcell's court odes and religious anthems are solemn and ceremonial, with great breadth and power. His instrumental music ranks among the finest achievements of the middle Baroque. His songs display the charm of his lyricism as well as his gift for setting the English language. And in the domain of the theater, Purcell produced much incidental music for plays, including *Abdelazar* (*The Moor's Revenge,* 1695), from which Britten borrowed a dance as the basis for his *Young Person's Guide.* He also composed *Dido and Aeneas,* one of the gems of English opera.

in his own words

Poetry and painting have arrived to their perfection in our own country: music is yet but in its nonage [immaturity], a forward Child, which gives hope of what it may be hereafter in England, when the masters of it shall find more Encouragement.

Dido and Aeneas

First presented in 1689 "at Mr. Josias Priest's boarding school at Chelsy by young Gentlewomen . . . to a select audience of their parents and friends," *Dido and Aeneas* achieved a level of musical expression for which there was no precedent in England. A school production imposed obvious limitations, to which Purcell's genius adapted itself in extraordinary fashion. Each character in the opera is projected in a few telling strokes. Likewise, the mood of each scene is established with the utmost economy (the opera takes only an hour to perform).

Dido and Aeneas is based on an episode in Virgil's *Aeneid,* the ancient Roman epic that traces the adventures of the hero Aeneas after the fall of Troy. Both Purcell and his librettist, Nahum Tate, could assume that their audience was

🎺 Principal Works

Dramatic music, including *Dido and Aeneas* (1689) and *The Fairy Queen* (1692); incidental music for plays, including *Abdelazar* or *The Moor's Revenge* (1695)

Sacred vocal music, including a Magnificat, Te Deum, and anthems

Secular vocal music, including court odes

Instrumental music, including fantasias, sonatas, marches, overtures, and harpsichord suites and dances

thoroughly familiar with Virgil's classic; they could therefore compress the plot and suggest rather than fill in the details. Aeneas and his men are shipwrecked at Carthage on the northern shore of Africa. Dido, the Carthaginian queen, falls in love with him, and he returns her affection. But Aeneas cannot forget that the gods have commanded him to continue his journey until he reaches Italy, as he is destined to be the founder of Rome. Much as he hates to hurt the queen, he knows that he must depart.

In her grief, Dido decides her fate—death—in the moving recitative "Thy hand, Belinda," and the heartrending lament that is the culminating point of the opera, "When I am laid in earth." (For the text, see Listening Guide 8.) In Virgil's poem, Dido mounts the funeral pyre, whose flames light the way for Aeneas's ships as they sail out of the harbor. Dido's Lament unfolds over a five-measure *ground bass*, or ostinato (a repeated idea), that descends along the chromatic scale, always symbolic of grief in Baroque music. The opera closes with an emotional chorus mourning Dido's fate. In this work, Purcell discovered the true tone of lyric drama.

🎧 Listening Guide 8

CD: CHR/STD 1/66–68, SH 1/21–23

Purcell: *Dido and Aeneas*, Act III, Dido's Lament   (4:00)

DATE OF WORK:	1689
GENRE:	Opera, English
BASIS:	*Aeneid*, by Virgil
CHARACTERS:	Dido, queen of Carthage (soprano)
	Aeneas, adventuring hero (baritone)
	Belinda, Dido's serving maid (soprano)
	Sorceress, Spirit, Witches

WHAT TO LISTEN FOR: Free-flowing recitative ("Thy hand, Belinda"), with much chromaticism and half-step movement (sigh motive).

Descending chromatic line as a repeated *ground bass* in triple meter, heard before aria begins and throughout aria (11 statements).

Emotional, slow-moving aria in 2 sections, each repeated **(A-A-B-B); B** section begins "Remember me."

Silvery, transparent sounds of Baroque-period string instruments.

Recitative: "Thy hand, Belinda," sung by Dido

Introduces lament aria; accompanied by continuo only

TEXT

21 0:00   Thy hand, Belinda; darkness shades me.
On thy bosom let me rest;
More I would, but Death invades me;
Death is now a welcome guest.

Aria: "When I am laid in earth," Dido's Lament

Basis: Ground bass, 5-measure pattern in slow triple meter, descending chromatic scale, repeated 11 times

Opening of aria, with 2 statements of the ground bass (first statement shaded):

	TEXT	GROUND BASS STATEMENT NO.
22 0:00	Instrumental introduction	1
0:57	When I am laid in earth, may my wrongs create	2
	no trouble in thy breast.	3
	When I am laid . . .	4
	no trouble . . .	5

23	2:17	Remember me, remember me, but ah, forget	6
		my fate, remember me, but ah, forget my fate.	7
		Remember me . . .	8
		forget my fate . . .	9
		Instrumental closing	10
		Instrumental closing	11

Handel and Late Baroque Opera

Opera in the late Baroque was dominated by George Frideric Handel (1685–1759), who worked in London during the first decades of the eighteenth century. A German by birth, Handel was in every sense an international figure. His music united the beautiful vocal melody of the Italian style with the stately gestures of French music and the contrapuntal genius of the Germans. To these elements he added the majestic choral tradition of the English. The result was perfectly suited to the London scene.

Handel's dramatic works were in the vein of *opera seria*, or serious Italian opera, which projected heroic or tragic subjects. His opera about Julius Caesar (*Giulio Cesare*, 1724) is one of his finest. When opera seria declined in popularity, Handel turned his talents toward the *oratorio*, a music drama based on a religious subject, producing his famous masterwork *Messiah* in 1742. (Handel's life and works are discussed in Chapter 24.)

Julius Caesar

22

Barbara Strozzi and the Italian Secular Cantata

"Had she been born in another era she would certainly have usurped or enlarged the place of the muses."

—G. F. LOREDANO, OF BARBARA STROZZI

KEY POINTS:

- The Italian *cantata* was a vocal genre for solo singers and instrumental accompaniment based on *lyric, dramatic,* or *narrative poetry;* the earliest examples were short, secular works that alternated recitative and aria-like passages.
- Barbara Strozzi was a noted singer and composer of cantatas, madrigals, and solo motets in the virtuosic new style *(monody).*

We have seen that the Baroque inherited the great vocal polyphony of the sixteenth century, while, at the same time, composers pursued a new interest in

Barbara Strozzi

monody—solo song in dramatic declamation accompanied by instruments. Out of the fusion of these styles came opera and yet another new Baroque form, the cantata.

The *cantata* (from the Italian *cantare*, "to sing") is a work for one or more solo vocalists with instrumental accompaniment (chorus was later added to the genre) based on one of three poetic genres: *lyric*, which expresses personal emotion and allows the music to dominate the story; *dramatic*, which is written for performance in a play (a comedy or tragedy, for example); or *narrative*, which tells a story, following characters through a plot.

The earliest cantatas were short and intimate, and usually based on a secular text; they generally consisted of several sections set as recitatives and arias. Among the important proponents of this genre is the singer Barbara Strozzi.

Barbara Strozzi: Her Life and Music

Barbara Strozzi (1619–1677) is a unique figure in the early Baroque era. She was the adopted (and probably illegitimate) daughter of the Venetian poet and playwright Giulio Strozzi; her mother, Isabella Garzoni, was his servant. Giulio oversaw Barbara's education and introduction to the intellectual elite of Venice through an academy (not unlike the Florentine Camerata) that he founded. The records of the Accademia degli Unisoni demonstrate her activity as a singer, as a participant in debates, and as a hostess or mistress of ceremonies—all highly unusual, since the meetings of such academies were generally open to men only. We know of one instance where Barbara proposed a topic for debate at the academy—the relative power of tears and song. After both sides had presented their arguments, Barbara concluded the deliberations with a persuasive vote for music: "I do not question your decision, gentlemen, in favor of song, for well do I know that I would not have received the honor of your presence at our last session had I invited you to see me cry rather than to hear me sing."

It has been suggested that Barbara Strozzi was a courtesan, and while it is true she possessed the artistic skills of this profession—singing, playing the lute, and writing poetry—this remains yet a theory. The provocative portrait shown here (by Bernardo Strozzi) is generally believed to be of Barbara. Her musical talents were praised by her contemporaries, one noting her "bold and graceful singing," and another comparing her voice to the harmonies of the spheres.

Although Barbara did not hold any official musical posts at court, in churches, or at the theater, she did publish many of her compositions. In 1644,

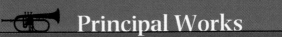

Principal Works

Secular vocal music, including a book of madrigals (1644) and 6 collections of arias and cantatas (1651–64)

Sacred solo motet collection (1655)

she issued a volume of madrigals on texts by her father; this collection was dedicated to a prominent noblewoman, Vittoria della Rovere, grand duchess of Tuscany.

A prolific composer of high-quality music, Strozzi's wrote seven secular collections, including madrigals, arias, and cantatas, as well as one book of sacred motets for solo voice. Her works show mastery of the new virtuosic solo style, for which Strozzi wrote out the desired ornamentation, and of *stile concitato* (agitated style), first introduced by Monteverdi. Our selection is *Begli occhi (Beautiful Eyes)*, a short cantata on a lyric poem for two sopranos and continuo from her 1654 collection. This work is characterized by many shifts between unmeasured and measured rhythms, and abrupt tempo and mood changes. The sinuous dialogue between the two voices tells of the bitterness of unrequited love, which we hear through poignant dissonances and expressive half-step movement, in alternation with lighter, dancelike sections.

in her own words

These harmonic notes are the language of the soul and the instruments of the heart.

Listening Guide 9

CD: CHR/STD 1/57–62, SH 1/24–29

Strozzi: *Begli occhi (Beautiful Eyes)*   (4:36)

DATE OF WORK:	Published in 1654 collection (Opus 3)
GENRE:	Italian secular cantata
MEDIUM:	Vocal duet (soprano and mezzo-soprano) and basso continuo
TEXT:	Love poem (lines of 7 or 11 syllables)
RHYME SCHEME:	*a-b-b-c-c-d-d-c-c-e-e*

WHAT TO LISTEN FOR: Shifts between unmeasured, slow sections and fast, dancelike sections.
Expressive chromaticism and dissonance.
Word painting (dissonance and half steps) on "langue" (languishing), and "mardaci" (biting).
Sighing motive on "oh."
Long melisma on "aspetta" (awaits) stretches out final idea.
Accompaniment by harpsichord (early keyboard instrument) and bass lute.

		TEXT	TRANSLATION	DESCRIPTION
24	0:00	Mi ferite oh begli occhi	You wound me, oh beautiful eyes	Slow, free opening, then short imitative exchanges.
25	0:32	Pensate che farebbono quei baci Si cocenti e mardaci.	Imagine what these kisses could do So burning and biting.	Quicker, dancelike compound meter; imitation between voices.

26	0:59	Langue l'anima e il cor vien meno Ahi ch'io vi moro in seno!	My soul languishes and my heart faints: Oh that I die there in my breast!	Slower; chromatic and dissonant; movement by half steps.
27	1:57	Pensate che farebbono gli strali; Si pungente e mortali.	Imagine what arrows could do; So sharp and deadly.	Return to quick, dancelike music, then fanfare-like motive.
28	2:23	Langue l'anima e il cor vien meno Ahi ch'io vi moro in seno!	My soul languishes and my heart faints; Oh that I die there in my breast!	Repeated text and music; chromatic and dissonant.
29	3:19	Ma forse non morrò senza vendetta; Ch'al fin chi morte da, la morte aspetta!	But perhaps I will not die without revenge; For he who deals death, awaits it in the end!	Fast, triple meter, in imitation; then the voices coming together; long melisma on "aspetta" (awaits).

Examples of word painting

Descending "sigh" motive on "oh," alternating between 2 voices:

Chromaticism and half-step movement on "Langue l'anima" (my soul languishes):

Melisma at end to signify the long wait for death ("aspetta"):

146

23

Bach and the Sacred Cantata

"Singing is a noble art and a good exercise. It has nothing to do with worldly affairs, with the strife of the marketplace, or the rivalries of the court."

—MARTIN LUTHER

KEY POINTS

- The *sacred cantatas* of north German composer Johann Sebastian Bach were written for the Lutheran church service; they are multimovement works with solo arias, recitatives, and choruses, all with orchestral accompaniment.
- Lutheran cantatas are generally unified by a *chorale*, or hymn tune, sung in four-part harmony.
- J. S. Bach was better known in his lifetime as a virtuoso organist than as a composer.
- In addition to his many cantatas and one Mass, Bach wrote orchestral suites, concertos, and much keyboard music (*chorale preludes*, *preludes*, and *fugues*) for organ and harpsichord.
- The cantata, *A Mighty Fortress Is Our God*, is an eight-movement work based on a familiar Protestant chorale tune, probably written by Martin Luther. The opening movement is an elaborate choral *fugue* (a form based on imitation).

Baroque cantatas could be based on either secular or sacred themes. The late-Baroque master J. S. Bach wrote both types, but it is his sacred Lutheran cantatas that are his enduring legacy. In the Lutheran tradition, to which Bach belonged, the sacred cantata was an integral part of the church service, related, along with the sermon and prayers that followed it, to the Gospel for the day. Most Sundays of the church year required its own cantata. With extra works for holidays and special occasions, an annual cycle came to about sixty cantatas. Bach composed four or five such cycles, from which only two hundred works have come down to us. By the second quarter of the eighteenth century, the German cantata had absorbed the recitative, aria, and duet of the opera, the pomp of the French operatic overture, and the dynamic instrumental style of the Italians. These elements were unified by the all-embracing presence of the Lutheran chorale.

The Lutheran Chorale

A *chorale* is a hymn tune, specifically one associated with German Protestantism. The chorales served as the battle hymns of the Reformation. As one of his reforms, Martin Luther required that the congregation participate in the service. To this end, he inaugurated services in German rather than Latin, and allotted an important role to congregational singing. "I wish," he wrote, "to

Chorale

Martin Luther

Johann Sebastian Bach

make German psalms for the people, that is to say sacred hymns, so that the word of God may dwell among the people also by means of song."

Luther and his fellow reformers created the first chorales by adapting melodies from Gregorian chant, from popular tunes, and from secular art music. Originally sung in unison, these hymns soon were written in four-part harmony to be sung by the choir. The melody was put in the soprano, where all could hear it and join in the singing. In this way, the chorales greatly strengthened the trend to clear-cut melody supported by chords (homophonic texture).

In the elaborate cantatas that were sung in the Protestant church service, the chorale served as a unifying thread. When at the close of an extended work the chorale sounded in simple four-part harmony, its granitic strength reflected the faith of a nation. The chorale nourished centuries of German music and came to full flower in the art of Bach.

Johann Sebastian Bach

"The aim and final reason of all music should be nothing else but the Glory of God and the refreshment of the spirit."

Johann Sebastian Bach (1685–1750) was heir to the polyphonic art of the past. He is the culminating figure of the Baroque style and one of the giants in the history of music.

His Life

Bach was born in Eisenach, Germany, of a family that had supplied musicians to the churches and town bands of the region for several generations. Left an orphan at the age of ten, he was raised by an older brother, an organist who prepared him for the family vocation. From the first, Bach displayed inexhaustible curiosity concerning every aspect of his art. "I had to work hard," he reported in later years, adding with considerably less accuracy, "Anyone who works as hard will get just as far."

At the age of twenty-three, Bach was appointed to his first important position: court organist and chamber musician to the duke of Weimar. The Weimar period (1708–17) saw the rise of his fame as an organ virtuoso and the composition of many of his most important works for that instrument. His first six children were born in this period. Bach's two marriages produced at least nineteen offspring, many of whom did not survive infancy. Four of his sons became leading composers of the next generation.

Disappointed because the duke of Weimar had failed to promote him, Bach decided to accept an offer from the prince of Anhalt-Cöthen, who happened to be partial to chamber music. In his five years at Cöthen (1717–23), Bach produced suites, concertos, sonatas for various instruments, and a wealth of keyboard music; also the six concerti

An eighteenth-century engraving of St. Thomas's Church in Leipzig, where Bach worked from 1723 until he died, in 1750.

Principal Works

Sacred vocal works, including over 200 church cantatas; 7 motets; Magnificat (1723), *St. John Passion* (1724), *St. Matthew Passion* (1727), *Christmas Oratorio* (1734), Mass in B minor (1749)

Secular vocal works, including over 20 cantatas

Orchestral music, including 4 orchestral suites, 6 *Brandenburg Concertos*, concertos for 1 and 2 violins, and for 1, 2, 3, and 4 harpsichords

Chamber music, including 6 sonatas and partitas for unaccompanied violin, 6 sonatas for violin and harpsichord, 6 suites for cello, *Musical Offering* (1747), flute sonatas, and viola da gamba sonatas

Keyboard music, including 2 volumes of *Das wohltemperirte Clavier (The Well-Tempered Clavier,* 1722, 1742), 6 *English Suites* (c. 1722), 6 *French Suites* (c. 1722), *Chromatic Fantasy and Fugue* (c. 1720), *Italian Concerto* (1735), *Goldberg Variations* (1741–42), and *Die Kunst der Fuge (The Art of Fugue,* c. 1745–50); suites, fugues, capriccios, concertos, inventions, sinfonias

Organ music, including over 150 chorale preludes, toccatas, fantasias, preludes, fugues, and passacaglias

grossi dedicated to the Margrave of Brandenburg. During this period, Bach's wife died, and in late 1721, he married Anna Magdalena Wilcke, a young singer at court.

Bach was thirty-eight when he was appointed to one of the most important music positions in Germany, that of cantor at St. Thomas's Church in Leipzig. His duties at St. Thomas's were formidable. He supervised the music for the city's four main churches, selected and trained their choristers, and wrote music for the church services as well as for special occasions such as weddings and funerals. In 1729, he was appointed to an additional post in Leipzig: director of the collegium musicum, a group of university students and musicians that gave regular concerts. In the midst of all this activity, Bach managed to produce truly magnificent works during his twenty-seven years in Leipzig (1723–50).

The routine of his life was enlivened by frequent professional journeys, when he was asked to test and inaugurate new organs. His last expedition, in 1747, was to the court of Frederick the Great at Potsdam, where Bach's son Carl Philipp Emanuel served as accompanist to the flute-playing monarch. Frederick announced to his courtiers with some excitement, "Gentlemen, old Bach has arrived," then led the composer through the palace, showing him the new pianos that were beginning to replace harpsichords as the preferred keyboard instruments. At Bach's invitation, the king suggested a theme, on which the composer improvised one of his astonishing fugues. After his return to Leipzig, Bach further elaborated on the royal theme, added a trio sonata based on the same theme, and dispatched the *Musical Offering* to Frederick.

The labors of a lifetime took their toll; after an apoplectic stroke and several operations for cataracts, Bach was stricken with blindness. Nevertheless, he

in his own words

Whereas the Honorable and Most Wise Council of this Town of Leipzig have engaged me as Cantor of the St. Thomas School. . . I shall set the boys a shining example . . . , serve the school industriously, . . . bring the music in both the principal churches of this town into good estate, . . . faithfully instruct the boys not only in vocal but also in instrumental music . . . arrange the music so that it shall not last too long, and shall . . . not make an operatic impression, but rather incite the listeners to devotion . . . treat the boys in a friendly manner and with caution, but, in case they do not wish to obey, chastise them with moderation or report them to the proper place.

persisted in his final task, the revising of eighteen chorale preludes for the organ. The dying master dictated to a son-in-law the last of these, *Before Thy Throne, My God, I Stand.*

His Music

Organ music
Chorale prelude

Bach was one of the greatest religious artists in history. He believed that music must serve "the glory of God." The prime medium for Bach's talents was the organ, and during his life he was known primarily as a virtuoso organist. Since he was a devout Lutheran, the *chorale prelude* (a short organ piece based on the embellishment of a chorale tune) was central to his output. One of his most famous organ works is the extended chorale prelude on the well-known hymn tune *A Mighty Fortress Is Our God.*

Solo and chamber music

In the field of keyboard music, Bach's most important work is *The Well-Tempered Clavier.* The forty-eight preludes and fugues in these two volumes have been called the pianist's Old Testament (the New Testament being Beethoven's thirty-two piano sonatas). Of the sonatas for various instruments, the six for unaccompanied violin are central to the repertory. The six *Brandenburg Concertos* present various instrumental combinations pitted against one another, and the lyricism of the four orchestral suites have made them immensely popular.

The two hundred or so church cantatas that have reached us form the centerpiece of Bach's religious music. They constitute a personal document of spirituality, projecting the composer's vision of life and death. The monumental Mass in B minor, which occupied Bach for a good part of the Leipzig period, was inappropriate for the Catholic service because of its length, but it found its eventual home in the concert hall. Bach's last works reveal the master at the height of his contrapuntal wizardry; these include the *Musical Offering* and *The Art of Fugue,* which was left unfinished at his death.

Bach's position in history is that of one who raised existing forms to the highest level rather than one who originated new forms. His sheer mastery of contrapuntal composition has never been equaled.

A German cantata performance with orchestra and organ, as depicted in **J. G. Walther's** *Dictionary* (1732).

Cantata No. 80: A Mighty Fortress Is Our God

Bach's cantatas typically have five to eight movements, of which the first, last, and usually one middle movement are choral numbers—normally fashioned from a chorale tune—ranging from simple hymnlike settings to elaborate choral fugues. Interspersed with the choruses are solo arias and recitatives, some of which may also be based on a chorale melody or its text.

In the cantata *A Mighty Fortress Is Our God,* Bach set Martin Luther's chorale of that name, for which Luther probably composed the music as well as the words. Luther's words and chorale melody are used in the first, second, fifth, and last movements of this cantata; the rest of the text is by Bach's favorite librettist, Salomo Franck.

Bach could take it for granted that the devout congregation of St. Thomas's knew Luther's chorale by heart. A majestic and inspiring melody, it is today a familiar Protestant hymn tune. Except for an occasional leap, the melody moves stepwise along the scale and is presented in nine phrases that parallel the nine lines of each stanza of Luther's poem (the first two phrases are repeated for lines three and four of the poem; see Listening Guide 10).

The cantata opens with an extended choral movement in D major, in which each line of text receives its own fugal treatment. (A *fugue* is a polyphonic composition based on imitation; the form will be discussed in detail in Chapter 26.) In this movement, each musical phrase is announced by one voice part of the choir, then imitated in turn by the other three. Each phrase is an embellished version of the original chorale tune. The trumpets and drums we hear in this movement were added after Bach's death by his son Wilhelm Friedemann, who strove to enhance the pomp and splendor of the sound.

First movement

The middle movements of the cantata feature freely composed recitatives and arias grouped around an energetic chorus based on Luther's chorale. In each movement, Bach captures a single affection, a practice typical of the era.

Middle movements

The final number rounds off the cantata, with the chorale sung in D major by full chorus and orchestra. We now hear Luther's melody in a hymnlike, four-part harmonization, with each vocal line doubled by instruments. In this homorhythmic texture, the great melody of the chorale is sounded in all its simplicity and grandeur.

Final movement

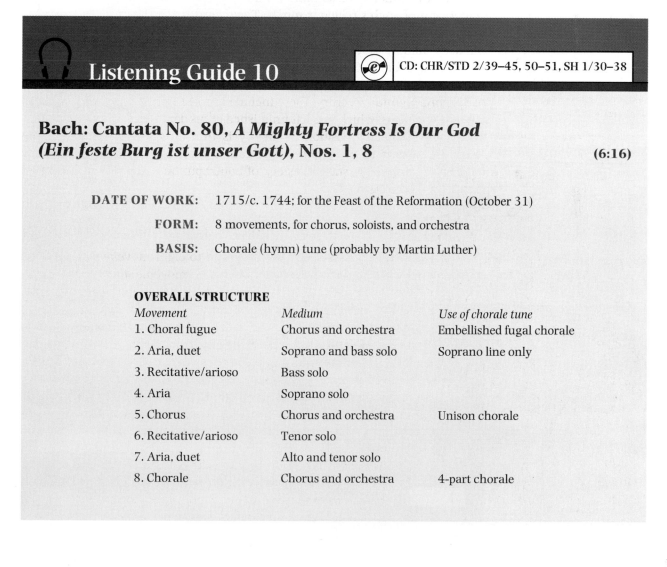

Listening Guide 10

CD: CHR/STD 2/39–45, 50–51, SH 1/30–38

Bach: Cantata No. 80, *A Mighty Fortress Is Our God (Ein feste Burg ist unser Gott)*, Nos. 1, 8

(6:16)

DATE OF WORK: 1715/c. 1744; for the Feast of the Reformation (October 31)

FORM: 8 movements, for chorus, soloists, and orchestra

BASIS: Chorale (hymn) tune (probably by Martin Luther)

OVERALL STRUCTURE

Movement	Medium	Use of chorale tune
1. Choral fugue	Chorus and orchestra	Embellished fugal chorale
2. Aria, duet	Soprano and bass solo	Soprano line only
3. Recitative/arioso	Bass solo	
4. Aria	Soprano solo	
5. Chorus	Chorus and orchestra	Unison chorale
6. Recitative/arioso	Tenor solo	
7. Aria, duet	Alto and tenor solo	
8. Chorale	Chorus and orchestra	4-part chorale

Original chorale tune:

1. Choral fugue, D major, 4/4 meter (Chorus and orchestra)

(4:54)

WHAT TO LISTEN FOR: Elaborate, imitative treatment of the familiar tune in all voice parts and in the trumpets.

Dense polyphonic texture created between chorus and orchestra for each line of text.

Canon (in strict imitation) on chorale tune heard in the instruments (trumpets and oboes vs. cellos), played in augmentation (long note-values).

		TEXT	TRANSLATION	FIRST SUNG BY
30	0:00	Ein feste Burg ist unser Gott,	A mighty fortress is our God,	Tenors
		ein' gute Wehr und Waffen;	a good defense and weapon:	Sopranos
31	1:15	er hilft uns frei aus aller Not,	He helps free us from all the troubles	Tenors
		die uns jetzt hat betroffen.	that have now befallen us.	Sopranos
32	2:29	Der alte böse Feind,	Our ever evil foe,	Basses
33	2:59	mit Ernst er's jetzt meint,	in earnest plots against us,	Altos
34	3:24	gross Macht und viel List	with great strength and cunning	Tenors
35	3:45	sein grausam Rüstung ist;	he prepares his dreadful plans.	Sopranos
36	4:09	auf Erd' ist nicht seinsgleichen.	Earth holds none like him.	Tenors

Opening fugal melody in tenors (notes of chorale marked with x's):

Instrumental canon, based on chorale tune in augmentation:

8. Chorale, D major, 4/4 meter, full chorus and orchestra   (1:22)

| WHAT TO LISTEN FOR: | 4-part hymn setting with the tune clearly heard in the top voice. All voices moving together (in homorhythmic texture). |

37	0:00	Das Wort sie sollen lassen stahn und kein Dank dazu haben. Er ist bei uns wohl auf dem Plan mit seinem Geist und Gaben.	Now let the Word of God abide without further thought. He is firmly on our side with His spirit and strength.
38	0:35	Nehmen sie uns den Leib, Gut, Ehr', Kind, und Weib, lass fahren dahin, sie haben's kein Gewinn; das Reich muss uns doch bleiben.	Though they deprive us of life, wealth, honor, child, and wife, we will not complain, it will avail them nothing; for God's kingdom must prevail.

Opening of hymnlike setting of chorale, in 4 voices (instruments doubling voices) and continuo:

George Frideric Handel

24

Handel and the Oratorio

KEY POINTS

- The Baroque *oratorio* is a large-scale dramatic genre with a religious or Biblical text performed by solo voices, chorus, and orchestra; it is not staged or costumed.
- George Frideric Handel was known for his Italian operas and, later in life, his English-texted oratorios (including *Messiah*).
- *Messiah* is set in three parts: the Christmas section, which opens with a French overture and features recitatives (*secco* and *accompagnato*), lyrical arias, and majestic choruses; the Easter section, which closes with the famous "Hallelujah Chorus"; and the final Redemption section.
- The text for *Messiah* is drawn from a compilation of Old and New Testament verses.

The Oratorio

The *oratorio*, one of the great Baroque vocal forms, descended from the religious play-with-music of the Counter-Reformation. It took its name from the Italian word for "a place of prayer." Although the first oratorios were sacred operas, toward the middle of the seventeenth century the genre shed the trappings of the stage and developed its own characteristics as a large-scale musical work for solo voices, chorus, and orchestra. It was generally based on a biblical story and performed in a church or hall without scenery, costumes, or acting. The action was usually depicted with the help of a narrator, in a series of recitatives and arias, ensemble numbers such as duets and trios, and choruses. The role of the chorus was often emphasized. The oratorios of George Frideric Handel make him the consummate master of this vocal form.

George Frideric Handel

"Milord, I should be sorry if I only entertained them. I wished to make them better."

If Bach represents the spirituality of the late Baroque, Handel (1685–1759) embodies its worldliness. Though born in the same year, the two giants of the age never met. As cantor of Leipzig, Bach had little point of contact with a composer who from the first was cut out for an international career.

His Life

Handel was born in Halle, Germany, the son of a prosperous barber-surgeon who did not regard music as a suitable profession for a young man of the middle class. After spending a year at the University of Halle, the ambitious youth moved to the German city of Hamburg, where he gravitated to the opera house and entered the orchestra as a second violinist. Handel absorbed the Italian operatic style popular in Hamburg so well that his first opera, *Almira*, written when he was twenty, created a sensation. He spent the next three years in Italy, where his operas were received just as enthusiastically.

At the age of twenty-five, Handel was appointed conductor to the Elector of Hanover; in this position, he received the equivalent of fifteen hundred dollars a year (Bach at Weimar was being paid only eighty). A visit to London in the autumn of 1710 brought him to the city that was to be his home for nearly fifty years.

His great opportunity came with the founding in 1720 of the Royal Academy of Music, launched for the purpose of presenting Italian opera. Handel was appointed one of the musical directors and at thirty-five found himself occupying a key position in the artistic life of England. For the next eight years, he was active in producing and directing his operas as well as writing them. His pace was feverish; he worked in bursts of inspiration, turning out a new opera in two to three weeks. To this period belongs *Julius Caesar*, one of his finest works in the new genre of *opera seria*, or serious opera.

Despite Handel's productivity, the Royal Academy failed. The final blow came in 1728 with the sensational success of John Gay's *The Beggar's Opera*. Sung in English and with tunes familiar to the audience, this humorous *ballad*, or *dialogue*, *opera* was the answer of middle-class England to the gods and heroes of the aristocratic opera seria.

Rather than accept failure, Handel turned from opera to oratorio, quickly realizing the advantages offered by a type of entertainment that dispensed with costly foreign singers and lavish scenery. Among his greatest achievements in this new genre were *Israel in Egypt*, *Messiah*, *Judas Maccabaeus*, and *Jephtha*. The

Principal Works

Operas (over 40), including *Almira* (1705), *Rinaldo* (1711), *Giulio Cesare* (*Julius Caesar*, 1724), and *Orlando* (1733)

Oratorios, including *Esther* (1718), *Alexander's Feast* (1736), *Israel in Egypt* (1739), *Messiah* (1742), *Samson* (1743), *Belshazzar* (1745), *Judas Maccabaeus* (1747), *Solomon* (1749), and *Jephtha* (1752); other sacred vocal music, including *Ode for the Birthday of Queen Anne* (c. 1713), *Acis and Galatea* (masque, 1718), *Ode for St. Cecilia's Day* (1739), *Utrecht Te Deum* (1713), anthems, and Latin church music

Secular vocal music, including solo and duo cantatas; arias

Orchestral music, including *Water Music* (1717) and *Music for the Royal Fireworks* (1749); concertos for oboe, organ, horn

Chamber music, including solo and trio sonatas

Keyboard music, including harpsichord suites, fugues, preludes, airs, and dances

British public could not help but respond to the imagery of the Old Testament as set forth in Handel's heroic music.

Handel suffered the same affliction as Bach—loss of eyesight from cataracts. Like Bach and the English poet John Milton, he dictated his last works, which were mainly revisions of earlier ones. But he continued to appear in public, conducting his oratorios and performing on the organ.

In 1759, shortly after his seventy-fourth birthday, Handel began his usual oratorio season, conducting ten major works in little over a month to packed houses. His most famous oratorio, *Messiah*, closed the series. He collapsed in the theater at the end of the performance and died some days later. The nation he had served for half a century accorded him its highest honor, as a London paper recounted: "Last night about Eight O'clock the remains of the late great Mr. Handel were deposited . . . in Westminster Abbey. . . . There was almost the greatest Concourse of People of all Ranks ever seen upon such, or indeed upon any other Occasion."

His Music

Handel's rhythm has the powerful drive of the late Baroque. You need only hear a Handel chorus to realize what momentum can be achieved with simple 4/4 time. Unlike Bach, who favored chromatic harmony, Handel leaned toward the diatonic. His melodies, rich in expression, rise and fall in great majestic arches. His works are based on massive pillars of sound—the chords—within which the voices interweave. And with his roots in the world of the theater, Handel knew how to use tone color for atmosphere and dramatic expression.

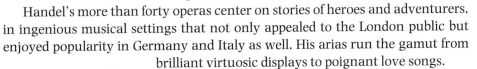

Handel's more than forty operas center on stories of heroes and adventurers, in ingenious musical settings that not only appealed to the London public but enjoyed popularity in Germany and Italy as well. His arias run the gamut from brilliant virtuosic displays to poignant love songs.

The oratorios are choral dramas that embody the splendor of the Baroque, with their soaring arias, dramatic recitatives, grandiose fugues, and majestic choruses.

Handel made the oratorio chorus—the people—the center of the drama. Freed from the rapid pace imposed by stage action, he expanded the chorus's role in each scene. The chorus at times touches off the action and at other times reflects on it. As in Greek tragedy, it serves as both protagonist and spectator.

Handel was prolific as well in composing instrumental music; his most important works are his concertos and his two memorable orchestral suites, the *Water Music* (1717) and *Music for the Royal Fireworks* (1749). (We will consider a movement from the *Water Music* in Chapter 26.)

Messiah

In the spring of 1742, the city of Dublin witnessed the premiere of one of the world's best-loved works, Handel's *Messiah*. Writing down the oratorio in only

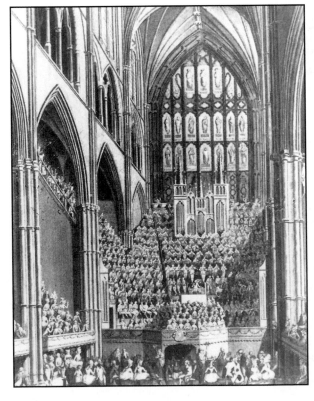

A performance of Handel's *Messiah* in 1784, from an eighteenth-century engraving.

Listening Guide 11

CD: CHR/STD 2/13–18, SH 1/39–44

Handel: *Messiah*, Nos. 18, 44 (7:39)

DATE OF WORK:	1742
GENRE:	Oratorio, in 3 parts
PARTS:	I—Christmas Section
	II—Easter Section
	III—Redemption Section

WHAT TO LISTEN FOR: Lyrical soprano aria ("Rejoice greatly"), with long melismas on "re-**joice**"; set in 3-part form **(A-B-A′)**, with shortened last section.
Famous chorus ("Hallelujah"), set in contrasting textures with interjections of "Hallelujah."

PART I: CHRISTMAS SECTION

		TEXT	DESCRIPTION
		18. Soprano aria (A-B-A′)	(4:16)
39	0:00		Instrumental introduction, vocal theme presented in violins in B♭ major.
		A	
		Rejoice greatly, O daughter of Zion shout, O daughter of Jerusalem,	Disjunct rising line, melismas on "rejoice"; melody exchanged between soprano and violin.
		behold, thy King cometh unto thee.	Syncopated, choppy melody, ends in F major. Instrumental ritornello.
		B	
40	1:29	He is the righteous Saviour and he shall speak peace unto the heathen.	Begins in G minor, slower and lyrical; modulates to B♭ major.
		A′	
41	2:43	Rejoice greatly . . .	Abridged instrumental ritornello; new melodic elaborations; longer melismas on "rejoice."

Extended melisma on "rejoice" from last section:

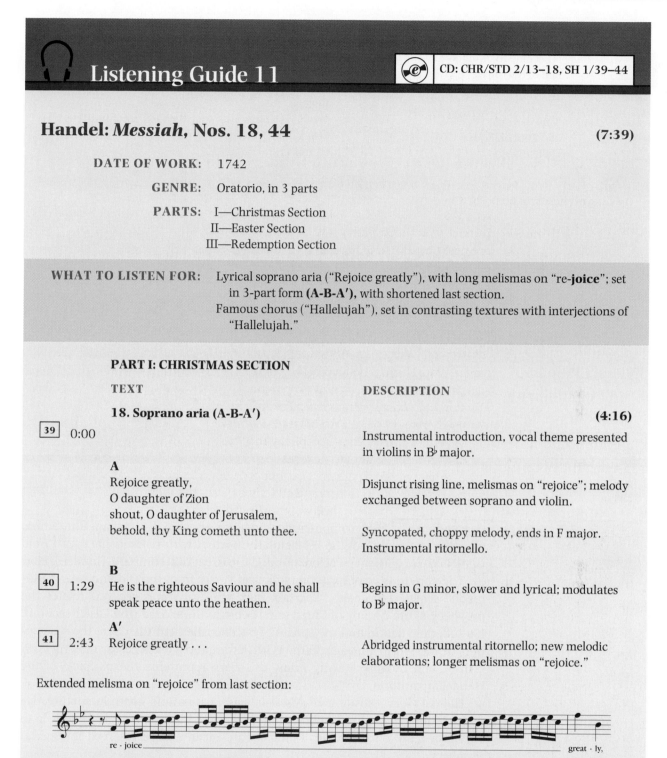

PART II: EASTER SECTION

		44. Chorus	(3:23)
42	0:00		Short instrumental introduction.
43	0:23	Hallelujah!	4 voices, homorhythmic at opening.
		For the Lord God omnipotent reigneth.	Textural reductions, leading to imitation and overlapping of text, builds in complexity.

	1:07	The kingdom of this world is become the Kingdom of our Lord and of His Christ;	Homorhythmic treatment, simple accompaniment.
44	1:23	and He shall reign for ever and ever.	Imitative polyphony, voices build from lowest to highest.
	1:43	King of Kings and Lord of Lords. Hallelujah!	Women's voices introduce the text, punctuated by "Hallelujah"; closes in homorhythmic setting with trumpets and timpani.

Opening of chorus, in homorhythmic style:

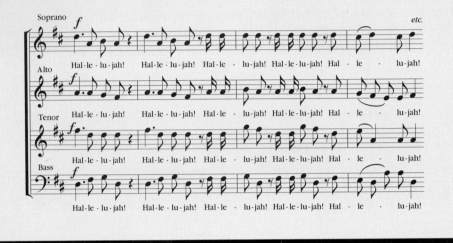

twenty-four days, the composer worked as if possessed. His servant found him, after the completion of the "Hallelujah Chorus," with tears in his eyes. "I did think I did see all Heaven before me, and the Great God Himself!" Handel said.

The libretto is a compilation of biblical verses from the Old and New Testaments, set in three parts. The first part (the Christmas section) relates the prophecy of the coming of Christ and his birth; the second (the Easter section), his suffering, death, and the spread of his doctrine; and the third, the redemption of the world through faith. With its impressive choruses, moving recitatives, and broadly flowing arias, the work represents the pinnacle of the Handelian oratorio.

Handel's orchestration of *Messiah* was modest and clear in texture. He wrote mainly for strings and continuo; oboes and bassoons were employed to strengthen the choral parts. Trumpets and drums were reserved for special numbers.

Part I
French overture The work opens with a *French overture*, which consists of two sections: a slow, somber introduction with dotted rhythms, followed by an Allegro imitative style. (The two-part French overture had been developed a century earlier by the master of Baroque opera in France, Jean-Baptiste Lully.) The first part of the oratorio proceeds with a series of arias, recitatives, and choruses.

Typical of Handel's jubilant style is the chorus "Glory to God," which is followed by the soprano aria "Rejoice greatly, O daughter of Zion," in three part, or **A-B-A′,** form. In this type of aria, the composer usually did not write out the third part, since it duplicated the first. Instead we find the words *da capo* at the end of the second section, indicating that the performer was to repeat the first section, freely elaborating it with ornamentation. (*Da capo* is Italian for "from the head," that is, from the beginning.) This kind of structure therefore came to be known as a *da capo aria*. For "Rejoice greatly," Handel did write out the last section, varying it considerably from the first.

Da capo aria

At the beginning of this aria, violins introduce an energetic figure that will soon be taken up by the voice. Notable are the melismatic passages on the word "rejoice." Throughout, the instruments exchange motives with the voice and help provide an element of unity with the ritornellos, or instrumental refrains, that brings back certain passages.

The climax of *Messiah* comes at the close of the second part, the Easter section, with the familiar "Hallelujah Chorus." In this movement, we hear shifting textures that alternate between overlapping imitative entries of the voice parts and homorhythmic sections in which all the voices clearly declaim the text together. The musical emphasis given the key word "Hallelujah" is one of those strokes of genius that resound through the ages.

Part II

Instrumental Music of the Baroque

25

The Baroque Sonata and Concerto

KEY POINTS

- Instrumental music claimed a new position of importance in the Baroque. Instruments were perfected, and new large-scale instrumental forms emerged (*sonata, concerto*).
- The *trio sonata* and *solo sonata* were the most popular forms of Baroque chamber music.
- Two types of *concertos* were popular during the Baroque: the *solo concerto*, with one instrument set against the orchestra; and the *concerto grosso*, with a small group of soloists set against the orchestra.
- Antonio Vivaldi, a virtuoso violinist, was the composer of *The Four Seasons*, a well-known set of solo violin concertos.
- J. S. Bach's 6 *Brandenburg Concertos* are excellent examples of the concerto grosso.

The Rise of Instrumental Music

The Baroque was the first period in history in which instrumental music became as important as vocal. New instruments were developed while old instruments were perfected. Great virtuosos such as Bach and Handel at the organ, Corelli and Vivaldi on the violin, and Scarlatti and Couperin on the harpsichord raised the technique of playing to new heights.

On the whole, composers still thought in terms of line rather than instrumental color, so that the same line of music might be played by a string, a woodwind, or a brass instrument. (Later, in the Classical and Romantic periods, instrumental color was changed frequently.) In the early Baroque, music was often performed by whatever instruments were available. Late Baroque composers tended to choose specific instruments according to their timbre. They also wrote more idiomatically for particular instruments, asking them to do what they could do best. As specifications became more precise, the art of orchestration was born.

Baroque Instruments

The seventeenth century saw a dramatic improvement in the construction of string instruments. Some of the finest violins ever built came from the workshops of Stradivarius, Guarneri, and Amati. The best of these now fetch sums unimagined even a generation ago. The young American violinist Joshua Bell has owned several valuable Stradivarius violins, including the "Tom Taylor" (built in 1732), which he played on the soundtrack for *The Red Violin*—a recent art film that tells a fictional account of a violin, from its creation to the present.

Strings   The strings of Baroque instruments were made of gut rather than the steel used today. Gut, produced from animal intestines, yielded a softer yet more penetrating sound. In general, the string instruments of the Baroque resemble their modern descendants except for certain details of construction. Playing techniques, though, have changed somewhat, especially bowing.

Woodwinds   The woodwind instruments were used increasingly for color in the late Baroque orchestra. The recorder, flute, and oboe, all made of wood at the time, were especially effective in suggesting pastoral scenes, while the bassoon cast a somber tone. Great improvements in the fingering mechanisms of these instruments were still to come.

Brass   The trumpet developed from an instrument used for military signals to one with a solo role in the orchestra. It was still a "natural instrument"—that is, without the valves that would enable it to play in all keys—demanding real virtuosity on the part of the player. Trumpets contributed a bright sonority to the

The Los Angeles Baroque Orchestra, led from the first violin stand by founder/director Gregory Maldonado, is one of a growing number of period-instrument ensembles. The Baroque bows the players use are shorter and lighter than their modern counterparts and produce crisp, articulate strokes on gut strings.

An evening outdoor concert in 1744 by the Collegium Musicum of Jena, Germany, featuring an orchestra of strings, woodwinds, trumpets, and drums gathered around a harpsichord.

orchestral palette, to which the horns, also natural instruments, added their gentler, outdoor sound. Timpani were occasionally added to the orchestra, furnishing a bass to the trumpets.

Keyboard instruments

The three important keyboard instruments of the Baroque were the organ, the harpsichord, and the clavichord. In ensemble music, these provided the continuo (continuous bass), and they were used extensively for solo performance as well. The Baroque *organ,* used both in church and in the home (see p. 172), had a pure, transparent timbre. The colors produced by the various sets of pipes contrasted sharply, so that the ear could pick out the separate lines of counterpoint. And the use of multiple keyboards made it possible to achieve terraced levels of soft and loud.

A French-style, two-manual harpsichord, made in 1769.

The *harpsichord* differed from the modern piano in two important respects. First, its strings were plucked by quills instead of being struck with hammers, and its tone could not be sustained like that of the piano, a product of the early Classical era. Second, the pressure of the fingers on the keys varied the tone only slightly, producing subtle dynamic nuances but not the piano's extremes of loud and soft. Rather, in order to obtain different sonorities and levels of sound on the harpsichord, makers often added another set or two of strings, usually with a second keyboard.

The *clavichord* was a favorite instrument for the home. Its very soft, gentle tone was produced by the action of a metal tangent, or lever, that exerted pressure on the string, allowing for some delicate effects not available on the harpsichord. By the end of the eighteenth century, both the harpsichord and the clavichord had been supplanted by the piano.

In recent years, a new drive for authenticity has made the sounds of eighteenth-century instruments familiar to us. Recorders and wooden flutes, restored violins with gut strings, and mellow-toned, valveless brass instruments are being played again, so that the Baroque orchestra has recovered not only its smaller scale but also its transparent tone quality. Our recordings of the instrumental selections that follow feature the silvery sound of period string instruments, supported by the colorful timbre of historical woodwinds and the bright sonority of early trumpets and horns.

Sonata Types

The sonata was the most widely cultivated form of chamber music in the Baroque. In its early stages, the sonata consisted of either a movement in several sections or several movements that contrasted in tempo and texture. A distinction was drawn between the *sonata da camera*, or *chamber sonata*, which was usually a group of stylized dances, and the *sonata da chiesa*, or *church sonata*, which was more serious in tone and more contrapuntal in texture, its four movements arranged in the sequence slow-fast-slow-fast. The prolific output of the Italian composer Arcangelo Corelli (1653–1713) emphasized the distinction between these two types.

Chamber sonata
Church sonata

Sonatas were written for one to six or even eight instruments. The favorite combination in the Baroque was two violins and continuo. Because of the three printed staves in the music, such compositions came to be known as *trio sonatas;* yet the title is misleading, because it refers to the number of parts rather than to the number of players. As we saw, the basso continuo often employed two performers—a cellist (or bassoonist) to play the bass line and a harpsichordist or organist to realize the harmonies indicated by the figures.

Trio sonata

Some Baroque composers wrote sonatas for single, unaccompanied instruments. Notable among these was Bach, whose sonatas for unaccompanied violin are centerpieces of the repertory. Domenico Scarlatti (1685–1757) is known for some 550 sonatas for solo harpsichord, characterized by brilliant passagework, hand crossing, and other virtuoso techniques that helped lay the foundation for modern piano technique. Set in one-movement binary form, Scarlatti's works bear the seed that was to develop into the Classical sonata.

Concerto Types

Contrast was as basic an element of Baroque music as unity. This twofold principle found expression in the *concerto*, an instrumental form based on the opposition between two dissimilar bodies of sound. (The Latin verb *concertare* means "to contend with," or "to vie with.")

Baroque composers produced two types: the *solo concerto* and the *concerto grosso*. The first type, the concerto for solo instrument and an accompanying instrumental group, lent itself to experiments in sonority and virtuoso playing, especially in the hands of the Italian master Antonio Vivaldi. The violin was the instrument featured most frequently in the solo concerto, which usually consisted of three movements, in the sequence Allegro-Adagio-Allegro. This flexible form prepared the way for the solo concerto of the Classical and Romantic periods.

Solo concerto

The *concerto grosso* was based on the opposition between a small group of instruments, the *concertino*, and a larger group, the *tutti*, or *ripieno* (Italian for "full"). Bach captured the spirit of the concerto grosso in his six *Brandenburg Concertos*, written for presentation to the Margrave Christian of Brandenburg. The second of the set, in F major, has long been a favorite, probably because of

Concerto grosso

its brillliant trumpet part. The solo group consists of trumpet, oboe, recorder (or flute), and violin, all of them instruments that play in the high register. The accompanying, or ripieno, group includes a string ensemble with basso continuo.

The concerto embodied what one writer of the time called "the fire and fury of the Italian style." This Italian style spread all over Europe and strongly influenced the German masters Bach and Handel, among others. Of the many Italian concerto composers, Vivaldi was the most famous and the most prolific.

Antonio Vivaldi: His Life and Music

"Above all, he was possessed by music."

—MARC PINCHERLE

Antonio Vivaldi

Antonio Vivaldi (1678–1741), the son of a violinist, grew up in his native Venice. He was ordained in the church while in his twenties and came to be known as "the red priest," a reference to the color of his hair. For the greater part of his career, Vivaldi was *maestro de' concerti*, or music master, at the most important of the four music schools for which Venice was famous, the Conservatorio del'Ospedale della Pietà. These schools were attached to charitable institutions established for the upbringing of orphaned girls, and they played a vital role in the musical life of Venetians. Much of Vivaldi's output was written for concerts at the school, which attracted visitors from all over Europe. One visitor, a French diplomat, recorded his impressions of Vivaldi's all-girl orchestra in 1739:

> The girls are educated at the expense of the state, and they are trained exclusively with the purpose of excelling in music. Thus, they sing like angels and play violin, flute, organ, oboe, cello, and bassoon; in short, no instrument, regardless of its size, frightens them. They live like nuns in a convent. All they do is perform concerts, generally in groups of about forty girls. I swear that there is nothing as pleasant as seeing a young and pretty nun, dressed all in white, with a flower over her ear, conducting the orchestra with all the gracefulness and precision imaginable.

Principal Works

Orchestral music, including over 239 violin concertos, including *Le quattro stagioni* (*The Four Seasons*, Op. 8, Nos. 1–4, c. 1725); other solo concertos (bassoon, cello, oboe, flute, recorder), double concertos, multiple concertos, sinfonias

Chamber music, including sonatas for violin, cello, and flute; trio sonatas

Vocal music, including oratorios (*Juditha triumphans*, 1716), Mass movements (Gloria), Magnificat, psalms, hymns, and motets; secular vocal music, including solo cantatas and operas

In *Concert in a Girls' School,*
Francesco Guardi
(1712–1793) depicts a
Venetian concert by an
orchestra of young women
(upper left) similar to the one
directed by Vivaldi. (Alte
Pinakothek, Munich)

While maintaining his position in Venice, Vivaldi traveled widely, compos-ing operas for other cities and building his reputation as a virtuoso performer. His life came to a mysterious end: a contemporary Venetian account notes that the composer, who had once earned 50,000 ducats in his day, died in poverty as a result of his extravagance.

Vivaldi is remembered for his more than 500 concertos—some 230 of which are for solo violin. Many of these have descriptive titles, such as *The Four Seasons,* a group of violin concertos that we will study. One of the most prolific composers of his era, he also wrote much chamber music and numerous operas, as well as cantatas, an oratorio, and an extended setting of the Gloria, which is today one of his most-performed works.

Vivaldi was active during a period that was crucially important to the explo-ration of a new style in which instruments were liberated from their earlier dependence on vocal music. His novel use of rapid scale passages, extended arpeggios, and contrasting registers contributed decisively to the development of violin style and technique. And he played a leading part in the history of the concerto, effectively exploiting the contrast in sonority between large and small groups of players.

The Four Seasons

Vivaldi's best-known work is *The Four Seasons,* a group of four violin concertos. Here Vivaldi applies the principle of word painting (where the music is meant to portray the action and emotion described by the words) to instrumental music. Each concerto is accompanied by a poem, presumably written by the composer, describing the joys of that particular season. Each line of the poem is printed above a certain passage in the score; the music at that point mirrors, as graphi-cally as possible, the action described.

In *Spring (La primavera),* the mood and atmosphere as well as the specific actions, are evoked. The solo violin is accompanied by an orchestra consisting of strings—first and second violins, violas, and cellos—with the basso continuo

First movement

realized (improvised from the figured bass) on harpsichord or organ. The poem is a sonnet whose first two quatrains (making eight lines of text) are distributed throughout the first movement, an Allegro in E major. (See Listening Guide 12 for the text.)

Both poem and music evoke the birds' joyous welcome to spring and the gentle murmur of streams, followed by thunder and lightning. The image of birdcalls takes shape in staccato notes, trills, and running scales; the storm is portrayed by agitated repeated notes answered by quickly ascending minor-key

Ritornello

scales. Throughout, an orchestral *ritornello*, or refrain, returns again and again (representing the general mood of spring) in alternation with the episodes, which often feature the solo violin. Ultimately, "the little birds take up again their melodious song" as we return to the home key of E. A florid passage for the soloist leads to the final ritornello.

Second and third movements

In the second movement, a Largo in 3/4, Vivaldi evokes an image from the poem of the goatherd who sleeps "in a pleasant, flowery meadow" with his faithful dog by his side. Over the bass line played by the violas, which sound an ostinato rhythm, he wrote, "The dog who barks." This dog clearly has a sense of rhythm. The solo violin unfolds a tender, melancholy melody in the most lyrical Baroque style. In the finale, an Allegro marked "Rustic Dance," we can visualize nymphs and shepherds cavorting in the fields as the music suggests the drone of bagpipes. Ritornellos and solo passages alternate in bringing the work to a happy conclusion.

Like Bach, Vivaldi was renowned in his day as a performer rather than a composer. Today, he is recognized both as the "father of the concerto," having established ritornello form as its basic procedure, and as a herald of musical Romanticism in his use of pictorial imagery.

Listening Guide 12

CD: CHR/STD 1/69–74, SH 1/45–50

Vivaldi: *Spring*, from *The Four Seasons* (*La primavera*, from *Le quattro stagioni*), Op. 8, No. 1, First Movement (3:33)

DATE OF WORK: Published 1725

GENRE: Programmatic concerto for solo violin, Op. 8 (*The Contest Between Harmony and Inspiration*), Nos. 1–4, each based on an Italian sonnet, with 3 movements each:

No. 1: *Spring (La primavera)*   No. 3: *Autumn (L'autunno)*
No. 2: *Summer (L'estate)*   No. 4: *Winter (L'inverno)*

I. Allegro

Joyful spring has arrived,
the birds greet it with their cheerful song,
and the brooks in the gentle breezes
flow with a sweet murmur.

The sky is covered with a black mantle,
and thunder and lightning announce a storm.
When they fall silent, the little birds
take up again their melodious song.

II. Largo

And in the pleasant, flowery meadow,
to the gentle murmur of bushes and trees,
the goatherd sleeps, his faithful dog at his side.

III. Allegro
(*Rustic Dance*)

To the festive sounds of a rustic bagpipe
nymphs and shepherds dance in their favorite spot
when spring appears in its brilliance.

First Movement: Allegro; in ritornello form, E major

WHAT TO LISTEN FOR: Distinctive timbre of Baroque-period string instruments.
Musical pictorialization of images of spring, based on the poem (birds, babbling brooks, gentle breezes, thunder and lightning).
Virtuosity of solo violin part, with fast-running scales and trills.
Recurring theme (ritornello, representing spring) that unifies the movement.

Ritornello theme:

		DESCRIPTION	PROGRAM
45	0:00	Ritornello 1, in E major.	Spring
	0:32	Episode 1; solo violin with birdlike trills and high running scales, accompanied by violins	Birds
46	1:07	Ritornello 2.	Spring
47	1:15	Episode 2; whispering figures like water flowing, played by orchestra.	Murmuring brooks
48	1:39	Ritornello 3.	Spring
	1:47	Episode 3 modulates; solo violin with repeated notes, fast ascending minor-key scales, accompanied by orchestra.	Thunder, lightning
49	2:15	Ritornello 4, in relative minor (C-sharp).	Spring
	2:24	Episode 4; trills and repeated notes in solo violin.	Birds
	2:43	Ritornello 5, returns to E major; brief solo passage interrupts.	
50	3:12	Closing tutti.	

26

The Baroque Suite and Other Instrumental Forms

KEY POINTS

■ The Baroque *suite* is a group of dances, usually in the same key, with each piece in binary form **(A-A-B-B)** or ternary form **(A-B-A)**. The standard dances in the suite are the *allemande, courante, sarabande,* and *gigue.*

■ Handel's best-known orchestral suites are the *Water Music* and *Music for the Royal Fireworks.*

■ J. S. Bach's *Well-Tempered Clavier* is his most famous collection of keyboard music and contains *preludes and fugues* (a free form followed by a strict imitative form).

■ The French Rococo and the German "sentimental" styles ushered in the new Classical era.

Dance types

The suite of the Baroque era was a natural outgrowth of earlier traditions that paired dances of contrasting tempos and character. The suite presented an international galaxy of dance types, all in the same key: the German *allemande,* in quadruple meter at a moderate tempo; the French *courante,* in triple meter at a moderate tempo; the Spanish *sarabande,* a stately dance in triple meter; and the English *jig (gigue),* in a lively 6/8 or 6/4. These had begun as popular dances, but by the late Baroque, they had left the ballroom far behind and become abstract types of art music. Between the slow sarabande and fast gigue composers could insert a variety of optional dances of peasant origin that introduced a refreshing earthiness into their more formal surroundings. The suite sometimes opened with an *overture* (see p. 171) and might include other brief pieces with descriptive titles.

Binary and ternary structure

A standard dance form of each piece in the suite was a highly developed binary structure (**A-B**) consisting of two sections of approximately equal length, each rounded off by a cadence and each repeated (**A-A-B-B**). Also common was a ternary structure (**A-B-A**), which we will hear in a hornpipe from Handel's *Water Music.* In both structures, the first part usually moved from the home key (tonic) to a contrasting key (dominant), while the **B** part made the corresponding move back. The two parts often used closely related melodic material. The form is easy to hear because of the modulation and the full stop at the end of each part.

The principle of combining dances into a suite could be applied to chamber, orchestral, and solo instrumental music as well. In the genre of chamber music, the Italian composer Arcangelo Corelli was noted for his sonatas in suite form, known as *sonatas da camera,* or *chamber sonatas.* (These were distinguished from *sonatas da chiesa,* or *church sonatas,* which were more serious, contrapuntal chamber works.) Bach's French and English suites for harpsichord are splendid examples of solo keyboard suites. Among the composers of solo keyboard suites

Standard Order of the Baroque Dance Suite

1. Overture (optional)
2. Allemande
3. Courante
4. Sarabande
5. Other dances (optional)
6. Gigue (jig)

was François Couperin (1668–1733), the central figure of the French harpsichord school, and Elisabeth-Claude Jacquet de la Guerre (c. 1666–1729), an extraordinary harpsichordist and composer at the French Royal Court, who published several collections of keyboard suites.

The four orchestral suites of J. S. Bach are indebted to seventeenth-century French ballet music. Bach's contemporary Georg Philipp Telemann (1681–1767) was amazingly prolific in this genre, contributing over 125 orchestral suites to the repertory, thereby establishing the French-style orchestral suite in Germany. Telemann's suites from his *Tafelmusik* collection (Table or Dinner Music, 1733) begin with a French overture—a work with a slow and stately introduction followed by a quick, fugal section—and then a series of contrasting dances that include both binary and ternary forms. These dances often bear fanciful or descriptive titles but have the character of one of the standard dances (for example, *Flaterie,* or flattery, is a sarabande in typical binary structure).

Handel and the Orchestral Suite

The two orchestral suites by Handel, the *Water Music* and *Music for the Royal Fireworks,* are memorable contributions to the genre. The *Water Music* was surely played (although probably not first composed) for a royal party on the Thames River in London on July 17, 1717. Two days later, the *Daily Courant* reported:

> On Wednesday Evening, at about 8, the King took Water at Whitehall in an open Barge, . . . and went up the River towards Chelsea. Many other Barges with Persons of Quality attended, and so great a Number of Boats, that the whole River in a manner was cover'd; a City Company's Barge was employ'd for the Musick, wherein were 50 Instruments of all sorts, who play'd all the Way from Lambeth (while the Barges drove with the Tide without Rowing, as far as Chelsea) the finest Symphonies, compos'd express for this Occasion, by Mr. Handel; which his Majesty liked so well, that he caus'd it to be plaid over three times in going and returning.

Water Music

The twenty-two numbers of the *Water Music* were performed without continuo instruments, as it was not possible to bring a harpsichord aboard the barge. The conditions of an outdoor performance, in which the music would have to contend with the breeze on the river, birdcalls, and similar noises, prompted

In this imaginary depiction of Handel's *Water Music*, the composer is seen perched on the edge of the front barge, with King George I to the right; in the second barge, musicians seem to be playing Handel's work.

Handel to create music that was marked by lively rhythms and catchy melodies.

The *Water Music* opens with a French overture (see p. 171) and includes a variety of dance numbers (not in the standard order of the suite), among them minuets in graceful 3/4 time, bourrées in fast 4/4, and hornpipes (an English country dance) in lively triple meter. In these varied numbers, Handel combined the Italian string style of Corelli with the songfulness of Purcell and the rhythmic vivacity of French music to produce a style that was imprinted with his own robust personality and was perfectly suited to the taste of an English audience.

The work is divided into three suites. In the opening Allegro of the D-major suite, a fanfare-like theme is sounded by trumpets, then answered by French horns and strings. The lively hornpipe that follows features decorative trills as part of its main theme and a reflective, minor-key middle section. (See Listening Guide 13.)

More than two and a half centuries after it was written, Handel's *Water Music* is still a favorite with the public, indoors or out. We need to hear only a few measures of the work to understand why.

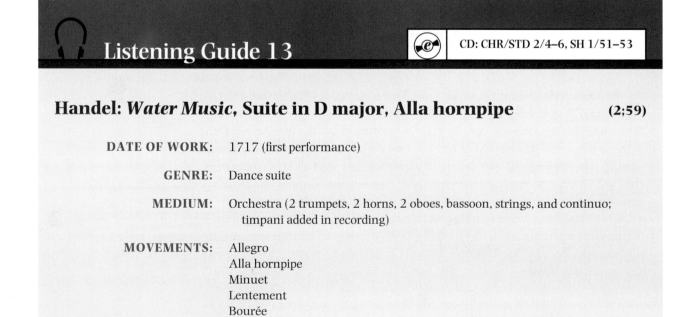

Listening Guide 13

CD: CHR/STD 2/4–6, SH 1/51–53

Handel: *Water Music*, Suite in D major, Alla hornpipe (2;59)

DATE OF WORK:	1717 (first performance)
GENRE:	Dance suite
MEDIUM:	Orchestra (2 trumpets, 2 horns, 2 oboes, bassoon, strings, and continuo; timpani added in recording)
MOVEMENTS:	Allegro
	Alla hornpipe
	Minuet
	Lentement
	Bourée

Second Movement: Alla hornpipe; A-B-A form, 3/2 meter, D major

WHAT TO LISTEN FOR: Alternation between strings/woodwinds and brass (trumpets and French horns) in first section.

Ascending melody with leaps and trills.

B section for strings and woodwinds only (no brass); descending melody in minor key.

Return of opening (3-part structure **A-B-A**), in major key.

| 51 | 0:00 | **A** SECTION
Disjunct theme in strings and double reeds, with trills, later answered by trumpets and French horns; in D major, at a moderate, spritely tempo: |

Continued alternation of motives between brass and strings.

| 52 | 1:00 | **B** SECTION
Strings and woodwinds only (no brass); fast-moving string part with syncopated winds; in B minor: |

| 53 | 1:55 | **A** SECTION
Repeat of entire first section; ends at close of section in D major. |

Passacaglia and Overture

One of the most majestic forms of Baroque music is the *passacaglia*, which draws on the principle of the ground bass. In this form, a melody, usually four or eight bars long and in a stately triple meter, is introduced alone in the bass. The theme is repeated again and again in the bass, serving as the foundation for a set of continuous variations that exploit all the resources of polyphonic music. (We heard a similar procedure earlier in Dido's Lament from Purcell's *Dido and Aeneas.*) A related structure is the *chaconne*, in which the variations are based not on a melody but on a succession of harmonies repeated over and over.

Passacaglia

Chaconne

Another important orchestral genre was the operatic overture, of which two types were popular during this period. The *French overture* generally followed the pattern slow-fast, its fast section in the loosely fugal style known as *fugato*. The *Italian overture* consisted of three short, simple sections: fast-slow-fast, with a vivacious, dancelike finale. This pattern, expanded into three separate movements, was later adopted by the concerto grosso and the solo concerto. In addition, as we will see, the opera overture of the Baroque was one of the ancestors of the symphony of later eras.

Overtures: French and Italian

Keyboard Forms

The keyboard forms of the Baroque fall into two categories: free forms based on harmony, with a strong element of improvisation, such as the prelude and chorale prelude; and stricter forms based on counterpoint, such as the fugue. Bach's keyboard music shows his mastery of both types.

A *prelude* is a fairly short piece based on the continuous expansion of a melodic or rhythmic figure. It originated in improvisations performed on the lute and keyboard instruments. In the late Baroque, the prelude was used to introduce a group of dance pieces or a fugue. Since its texture was for the most part homophonic, it made an effective contrast with the contrapuntal texture of the fugue that followed. Later in this chapter, we will study an example of a prelude and fugue from Bach's *Well-Tempered Clavier*.

Church organists, in introducing the chorale to be sung by the congregation, adopted the practice of embellishing the traditional melodies. A body of instrumental works—*chorale preludes* and *chorale variations*—was developed in which organ virtuosity of the highest level was combined with inspired improvisation. Bach wrote more than 140 organ chorale preludes, including one on *A Mighty Fortress Is Our God,* the chorale tune heard in Cantata No. 80 (see Chapter 23).

The Fugue and Its Devices

A spectacular Baroque organ (1738) in St. Bavo's Basilica, Haarlem, The Netherlands.

From the art and science of counterpoint came one of the most exciting forms of Baroque music, the fugue. The name is derived from *fuga,* the Latin word for "flight," implying a flight of fancy, or possibly the flight of the theme from one voice to the other. A *fugue* is a contrapuntal composition in which a theme of strongly marked character pervades the entire fabric, entering in one voice and then in another. The fugue, then, is based on the principle of imitation. Its main theme, the *subject,* constitutes the unifying idea, the focal point of interest in the contrapuntal web.

We have already encountered the fugue or fugal style in a number of works: at the beginning of the book, in Britten's *Young Person's Guide to the Orchestra (Variations and Fugue on a Theme of Purcell);* in Handel's "Hallelujah Chorus" from *Messiah;* and in the opening movement of Bach's cantata *A Mighty Fortress Is Our God.* Thus a fugue may be written for a group of instruments, for a solo instrument, or for full chorus. Whether the fugue is vocal or instrumental, its several lines are called voices. In vocal and orchestral fugues, each voice is sounded by a different performer or group of performers. In fugues for keyboard instruments, the ten fingers—and the feet, on the organ, playing the pedals—manage the complex interweaving of the voices.

The *subject,* or theme, is stated alone at the beginning in one of the voices—soprano, alto, tenor, or bass. It is then imitated in another voice—this is the

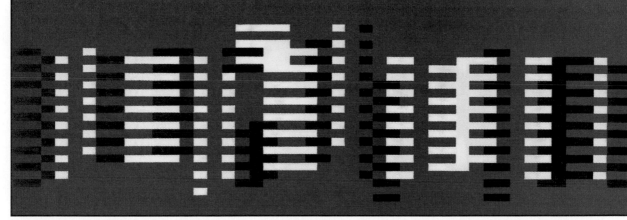

answer—while the first continues with a *countersubject*, or countertheme. Depending on the number of voices in the fugue, the subject will then appear in a third voice and be answered in the fourth (if any), while the other voices weave a free contrapuntal texture against these. When the theme has been presented in each voice once, the first section of the fugue, the *exposition*, is at an end. From then on, the fugue alternates between sections that feature entrances of the subject and *episodes*—interludes that serve as areas of relaxation—until it reaches its home key.

Episodes

The subject of the fugue is stated in the home key, the tonic. The answer is given in a related key, the dominant, which lies five tones above the tonic. There may be modulation to foreign keys in the course of the fugue, which builds up tension before the return home. The Baroque fugue thus embodied the opposition between home and contrasting keys, which was one of the basic principles of the new major-minor system.

The Baroque fugue, then, was a form based on imitative counterpoint that combined the composer's technical skill with imagination, feeling, and exuberant ornamentation to produce one of the supreme achievements of the era. Fugal composition reached unsurpassed heights at the hands of Bach.

Bach's Prelude and Fugue in C minor

The Well-Tempered Clavier was based on a new system of equal temperament for tuning keyboard instruments. It was this system that made it possible to play in all the keys. The first volume of the collection, completed in 1722 during the years Bach worked in Cöthen, contains a prelude and fugue in each of the twelve major and twelve minor keys. The second volume, also containing twenty-four preludes and fugues, appeared twenty years later. The whole collection is thus made up of forty-eight preludes and fugues.

Prelude

The Prelude and Fugue in C minor is No. 2 in the first volume of *The Well-Tempered Clavier*. The prelude is a "perpetual motion" type of piece based on running sixteenth notes in both hands that seem never to let up, outlining a single chord in each measure. Finally, one hand pauses just long enough to echo the other in strict imitation in a swift *Presto*, which leads into a free, cadenza-like passage. (A *cadenza* is a solo passage performed in the manner of an improvisation.) The final cadence, in C major, soon follows.

Listening Guide 14

CD: CHR/STD 2/33–38, SH 1/54–59

Bach: Prelude and Fugue in C minor, from *The Well-Tempered Clavier*, Book I

(3:27)

DATE OF WORK: 1722

MEDIUM: Solo harpsichord

Prelude (free, improvisatory movement)

(1:47)

WHAT TO LISTEN FOR: Free, improvisatory style.
Harpsichord timbre of plucked strings.
Fast-paced rhythmic movement without clear melody line, in minor mode.
Momentum eases, as one line drops out.
Slower, free-moving passage near end, played like a cadenza, then closing on a major chord.

54   0:00   Opening of prelude, showing 2 sixteenth-note patterns in top line (in C minor, then F minor), each repeated:

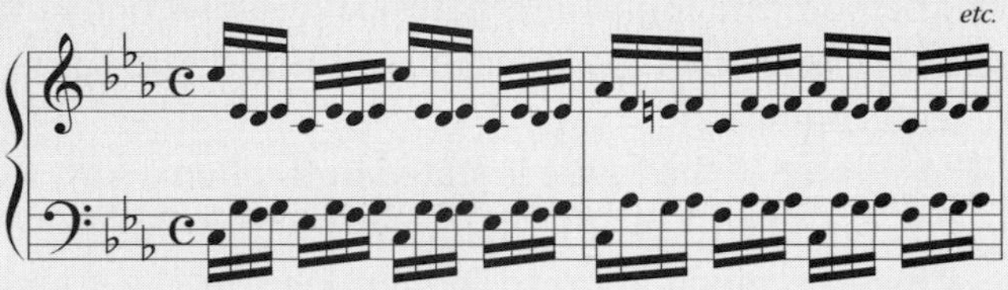

55   1:02   Presto, with left hand in strict imitation of right hand, one measure behind:

56   1:16   Free, cadenza-like passage near end:

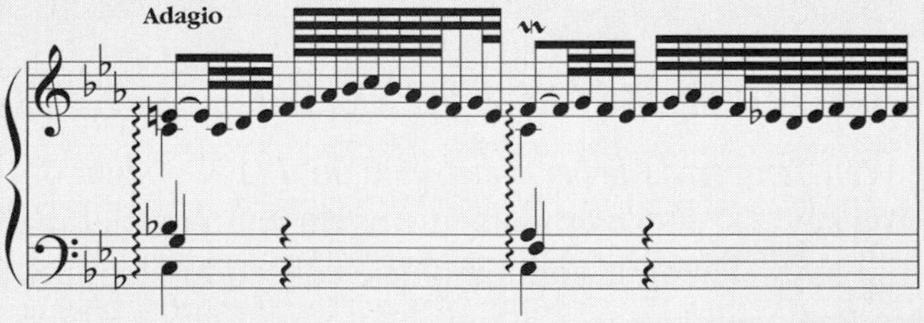

Fugue (3-voice imitative movement)

(1:40)

WHAT TO LISTEN FOR: 3 voices, or lines (SAB).
Opening disjunct theme (two-measure subject), stated alone, then with quick-moving polyphonic lines surrounding it.
Statements of the subject in various ranges of the instrument, separated by short episodes where the subject is not heard.
Final statement, in high range, against sustained bass note.

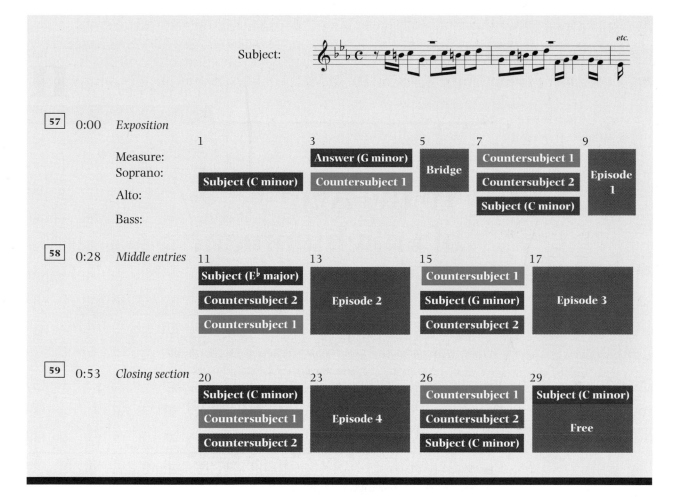

This prelude shows how deeply moving a series of harmonies can be. The music modulates from C minor to the relative major, E-flat major, then returns to the home key. Notable is the unity of mood, the "single affection" that gives this piece its unflagging momentum.

Fugue

The fugue, in three voices, is based on one of those short, incisive themes for which Bach had a special gift. Presented first by the alto voice in the home key of C minor, it is answered by the soprano in G minor, the dominant. The last statement of the subject in the bass line closes the exposition.

There are two countersubjects that play against the subject, whose successive entries are separated by episodes woven out of the basic idea (see Listening Guide 14). As in the prelude, the music is characterized by a relentless drive. When the piece finally reaches the C-major chord at the end, we are left with the sense of a journey completed.

To the Age of Enlightenment

"The Italian style and the French style have long divided the Republic of Music in France. . . . I have always valued those works which have merit, without regard for their composer or country of origin."

—FRANÇOIS COUPERIN

KEY POINTS

- Two pre-Classical styles prevailed in the early eighteenth century: the decorative *Rococo*, in France, and the sensitive style (*Empfindsamkeit*), in Germany.
- Several pre-Classical musicians wrote important music treatises on theoretical and pedagogical topics (instruction manuals for keyboard and violin).
- Taste in opera changed radically during this era; some preferred Italian comic opera over French court, and others were drawn to the more popular *ballad opera* (*The Beggar's Opera*), with its familiar songs and spoken text.
- The lyric drama of Christoph Willibald Gluck brought about new operatic reforms in the later eighteenth century.

The Rococo and the Age of Sensibility

The word "Rococo" derives from the French *rocaille*, "a shell," suggesting the decorative scroll- and shellwork characteristic of the style. The Rococo took shape as a reaction against the grandiose gesture of the Baroque. Out of the disintegrating world of the Baroque came a miniature, ornate art aimed at the enchantment of the senses and asserting a doctrine whose first law was "enjoy yourself."

The greatest painter of the French Rococo was Jean Antoine Watteau (1684–1721). To the dream world of love and gallantry that furnished the themes of his art, Watteau brought the techniques of the Dutch school of Rubens. Watteau's intimate, pastoral scenes reflected the shift in French society.

François Couperin

The musical counterpart to Watteau was François Couperin (1668–1733). Couperin came from a family of distinguished musicians. His works, along with

176

Jean Antoine Watteau (1684–1721), with his dream world of love and gallantry, was the artistic counterpart of François Couperin. *La gamme d'amour (The Gamut of Love).* (National Gallery, London)

those of Elisabeth-Claude Jacquet de la Guerre, crystallized the miniature world of the Rococo. Their goal was to charm, to delight, to entertain.

The coming era, known as the Age of Enlightenment, was characterized by the desire to systematize all knowledge, and this impulse also made itself felt on the musical scene. Jean-Philippe Rameau (1683–1764), the foremost French composer of the era, tried to establish a rational foundation for the harmonic practice of his time. His *Treatise on Harmony* (1722) set forth concepts that served as the point of departure for modern music theory.

Jean-Philippe Rameau

The Rococo witnessed as profound a change in taste as any that has ever occurred in the history of music. In turning to a polished entertainment music, composers adopted a new ideal of beauty. Elaborate polyphonic textures yielded to a single melody line with a simple chordal accompaniment (homophony), in much the same way that the contrapuntal complexities of late Renaissance music gave way to the early Baroque ideal of monody (it is surely true that history repeats itself). This era desired its music above all to be simple and expressive of natural feeling. Thus was born the "sensitive," or "sentimental," style of the *Empfindsamkeit* and the Age of Sensibility—an age that saw the first stirrings of that direct and natural expression that was to flower fully with Romanticism.

Empfindsamkeit

This musical revolution saw the expansion of the sonata and concerto, and the enrichment of symphonic styles with elements drawn from the operatic aria and overture and with the tunes and rhythms of Italian comic opera. From these developments was born something new—the Classical multimovement cycle, which will be described in Chapter 28.

One of the outstanding figures of the pre-Classical era was Carl Philipp Emanuel Bach (1714–1788), the second son of Johann Sebastian. He deepened the emotional content of the abstract instrumental forms and played a decisive role in the creation of the modern piano idiom. His theoretical treatise *Essay on*

C. P. E. Bach

the True Art of Playing Keyboard Instruments (1753–62) casts much light on the musical practices of the mid–eighteenth century.

The Changing Opera

The vast social changes taking shape in the eighteenth century were bound to be reflected in the lyric theater. Grandiose Baroque opera, geared to an era of absolute monarchy, had no place in the shifting societal structure. Increasingly its pretensions were satirized all over Europe. In 1728, *The Beggar's Opera*, by John Gay (1685–1732), a satirical play with folk songs and popular tunes arranged by Johann Christoph Pepusch (1667–1752), sounded the death knell of opera seria in England, and ushered in a vogue of racy pieces with popular songs and dances.

"War of the Buffoons"

In 1752, a troupe of Italian singers in Paris brought about a similar revolution with a performance of Giovanni Battista Pergolesi's comedy with music *La serva padrona* (*The Maid as Mistress.*) The so-called War of the Buffoons ensued, between those who favored the traditional French court opera and those who saw in the rising Italian comic opera, called *opera buffa,* a new, realistic art. In the larger sense, the War of the Buffoons was a contest between the rising bourgeois music and a dying aristocratic art.

Gluck and Opera Reform

Christoph Willibald Gluck

It fell to a German-born composer trained in Italy to liberate serious opera from some of its outmoded conventions. Christoph Willibald Gluck (1714–1787) found his way to a style that met the new need for dramatic truth and expressiveness. "Simplicity, truth, and naturalness are the great principles of beauty in all forms of art," he said.

in his own words

There is no musical rule I have not willingly sacrificed to dramatic effect.

This conviction was embodied in the works Gluck wrote for the Imperial Court Theater at Vienna, notably *Orpheus and Eurydice* (1762) and *Alceste* (1767). In these works, Gluck successfully fused a number of elements: the monumental choral scenes and dances that had always been a feature of French lyric tragedy, the animated ensembles of comic opera, the vigor of the new instrumental style in Italy and Germany, and the broadly arching vocal line that was part of Europe's operatic heritage. The result was a music drama whose dramatic truth and expressiveness profoundly affected the course of operatic history.

A Comparison of Baroque and Classical Styles

	BAROQUE (C. 1600–1750)	CLASSICAL (C. 1750–1825)
COMPOSERS	Monteverdi, Purcell, Barbara Strozzi, Corelli, Vivaldi, Handel, Bach	Haydn, Mozart, Beethoven, Schubert
MELODY	Continuous melody with wide leaps, chromatic tones for emotional effect	Symmetrical melody in balanced phrases and cadences; tuneful, diatonic, with narrow leaps
RHYTHM	Single rhythm predominant; steady, energetic pulse; freer in vocal music	Dance rhythms favored; regularly recurring accents
HARMONY	Chromatic harmony for expressive effect; major-minor system established with brief excursions to other keys	Diatonic harmony favored; tonic-dominant relationship expanded, becomes basis for large-scale form
TEXTURE	Monodic texture (early Baroque); polyphonic texture (late Baroque); linear-horizontal dimension	Homophonic texture; chordal-vertical dimension
INSTRUMENTAL GENRES	Fugue, concerto grosso, trio sonata, suite, chaconne, prelude, passacaglia	Symphony, solo concerto, solo sonata, string quartet, other chamber music genres
VOCAL GENRES	Opera, Mass, oratorio, cantata	Opera, Mass, oratorio
FORM	Binary form predominant	Ternary form becomes important, sonata-allegro form developed
DYNAMICS	Subtle dynamic nuances; *forte/piano* contrasts; echo effects	Continuously changing dynamics through *crescendo* and *decrescendo*
TIMBRE	Continuous tone color throughout one movement	Changing tone colors from one section to the next
PERFORMING FORCES	String orchestra, with added woodwinds; organ and harpsichord in use	Orchestra standardized into four choirs; introduction of clarinet, trombone; rise of piano to prominence
IMPROVISATION	Improvisation expected; harmonies realized from figured bass	Improvisation largely limited to cadenzas in concertos
EMOTION	Single affection; emotional exuberance and theatricality	Emotional balance and restraint

Georges Braque (1892–1963), *Guéridon,* oil on canvas, 1911. (Musée National d'Art Moderne, Centre Georges Pompidou, Paris)

More Materials of Form

unit **IX**

Focus on Form

27

The Development of Musical Ideas

"I alter some things, eliminate and try again until I am satisfied. Then begins the mental working out of this material in its breadth, its narrowness, its height and depth."

—LUDWIG VAN BEETHOVEN

KEY POINTS

- Melodic ideas, or *themes*, are used as building blocks in a composition; these melodies are made up of short melodic or rhythmic fragments known as *motives*.
- Themes can be expanded by varying the melody, rhythm, or harmony through *thematic development*; this usually happens in large-scale pieces.
- Repeated short patterns, or *ostinatos*, can also be used to build compositions.

Thinking, whether in words or music, demands continuity and sequence. Every thought should flow from the one before and lead logically into the next. In this way, we feel a sense of steady progression toward a goal. Uniting the first phrase of one melody and the second phrase of another would not make any more sense than joining the beginning of one sentence to the end of another. On the contrary, an impression of cause and effect, of natural flow, must pervade an entire musical work.

This desired impression is achieved in a variety of ways, depending on the piece's style. In Western music, as we saw, a musical idea that is used as a building block in the construction of a composition is called a *theme*, and its expansion is known as *thematic development,* achieved by varying its melodic outline, rhythm, or harmony. Conversely, a theme can be fragmented by dividing it into its constituent motives, a *motive* being its smallest melodic or rhythmic unit. A motive can grow, as a germ cell multiplies, into an expansive melody, or it can be treated in sequence, that is, repeated at a higher or lower level. A short, repeated musical pattern—called an *ostinato*—can also be an important organizing feature of a work.

Thematic development

Ostinato

Thematic development is generally too complex a technique to use in short pieces; in these, a simple contrast between sections and a modest expansion of material supply the necessary continuity. But thematic development is necessary in larger forms of music, where it provides clarity, coherence, and logic.

All the ways of developing thematic material—extension, contraction, repetition—are as typical of musics around the world as they are of Western art music. We have already seen that some music is improvised, or created spontaneously, by performers. Although it might seem that structure and logic would be alien to this process, this is rarely the case. In jazz, for example, musicians organize their improvised melodies within a highly structured, preestablished harmonic pattern, time frame, and melodic outline that is understood by all the performers. In India and the Middle East, improvisation is a refined and classical art, where the seemingly free and rhapsodic spinning out of the music is tied to a prescribed musical process that results in a lacework of variations.

Let's compare the way themes are developed in music from two very different cultures. The example below, from the opening of Beethoven's Symphony No. 5, which we will study later, illustrates the thematic development of a four-note motive that is repeated in sequence one step lower and then grows into a theme. Here the composer has developed and expanded his short idea to realize all its possibilities.

CD: CHR/STD 4/32–37, SH 2/8–13

Beethoven: Symphony No. 5 in C minor

Opening of first movement:

Theme based on repetitions of motive:

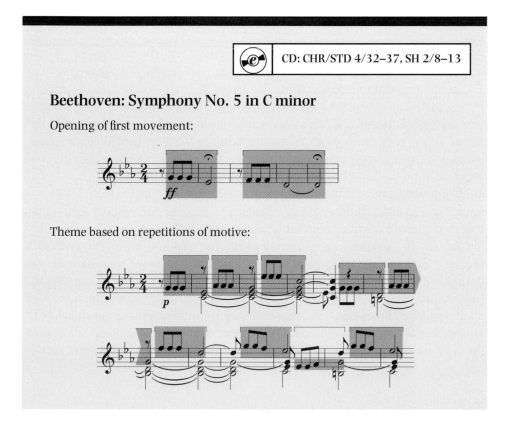

Theme based on extension of motive:

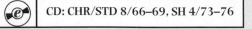

CD: CHR/STD 8/66–69, SH 4/73–76

The Moon Reflected on the Second Springs, Chinese traditional piece

Original melody:

3 transformations of the melodic idea:

Pitch inflections

The above example comes from *The Moon Reflected on the Second Springs,* a Chinese traditional work we will study in detail later in the book. Played on an *erhu* (a bowed two-string fiddle) accompanied by a *yangqin* (a hammered dulcimer; see p. 482), this piece evolves gradually from a short melodic phrase (shown in the chart) through a kind of variation proccess that continuously spins out new ideas with changing pitches and rhythms. Here, instead of sequence and repetition, there is a metamorphosis of the melody, much like we might hear in a jazz improvisation; but also like jazz, the tune is always recognizable and comes back at established intervals that make its appearance feel comfortable to the listener. We have already observed the variation process in Britten's *Variations and Fugue on the Theme by Purcell (Young Person's Guide to the Orchestra),* and we will study it as a major structural procedure in the Classical era (see pp. 186 and 215). Characteristic of this Chinese piece are the use of bent pitches, glissandos, slides, trills, and inflections—an embellishment style known as "adding flowers." Thus musical processes from distant cultures can sometimes be compared, even when their contexts and resulting sounds differ greatly.

Listening Activity: Thematic Development

CD: CHR/STD 4/32–37, SH 2/8–13

Beethoven: Symphony No. 5 in C minor, first movement

The familiar opening of Beethoven's Fifth Symphony allows us to hear how a small musical idea, a *motive*, grows and develops into a full-blown *theme*, one of the building blocks of large musical works.

WHAT TO LISTEN FOR

- Familiar opening, with its 4-note idea, or motive (dah-dah-dah-DAH).
- Repetition and variation of this motive at different pitch levels, in sequence.
- Insistent nature of the rhythmic pattern: short-short-short-long.
- Eventual growth of motive through thematic development to a full-blown melody, or theme.
- Return of motivic idea in other movements of his symphony.

MORE LISTENING REVIEW (FROM CD SET)

- Thematic development (variation)—Haydn: Symphony No. 94 in G major *(Surprise)*, second movement
- Improvisation—Gillespie/Parker: *A Night in Tunisia*
      Think of Me, by BeauSoleil
- Ostinato—Purcell: Dido's Lament, from *Dido and Aeneas*
      Billie's Blues, by Billie Holiday

28

Classical Forms

"Great art likes chains. The greater artists have created art within bounds. Or else they created their own chains."

—NADIA BOULANGER

KEY POINTS

■ Form is the most important organizing element in *absolute music*, which has no specific pictorial or literary program.

■ Many of the great masterworks of instrumental music are in the standard *multimovement cycle* of three or four movements; these include the Classic-era symphony, sonata, string quartet (and other chamber music), and the concerto.

■ The first movement of the cycle is usually in a fast tempo and in *sonata-allegro form*; this form has three main sections: *exposition, development,* and *recapitulation.*

■ The second movement of the cycle is ususaly slow and can be in various forms, including *theme and variations* or *ternary* **(A-B-A).**

- The third movement of the cycle is a triple-meter dance—either a *minuet and trio,* or a *scherzo and trio;* this dance movement is not present in all multi-movement cycles.
- The fourth movement is fast and lively, often in *rondo* or *sonata-allegro* form.
- *Cyclical structure* is a nineteenth-century device that links movements, and occurs when a theme from an earlier movement reappears in a later one.

Every musical work has a certain form; sometimes it is simple, other times complex. In some cases, the form is dictated by considerations outside music, such as a text or an accompanying program, as we observed in Vivaldi's *The Four Seasons.*

Absolute music   In *absolute* (or *pure*) *music,* however, form is especially important, since there is no prescribed story or text to hold the music together. The story is the music itself, so its shape is of primary concern for the composer, the performer, and the listener. Large-scale works have an overall form that determines the relations between the several movements and the tempos at which they proceed. In addition, each movement has an internal form that binds its different sections into one artistic whole. We have already learned two of the simplest forms: two-part, or binary **(A-B),** and three-part, or ternary **(A-B-A).**

Multimovement cycle   Now we will examine an important structural procedure in Western instrumental music—the standard *multimovement cycle* that was used from around 1750 through the Romantic era. This cycle generally consists of three or four movements in prescribed forms and tempos, and is employed in various genres, including the symphony, the sonata, the string quartet (and many other chamber works as well), and the concerto. The following discussion describes the standard form for each of these large-scale works.

The First Movement

The most highly organized and characteristic movement in this cycle is the opening one, which is usually in a fast tempo such as Allegro and is written in **Sonata-allegro form**   *sonata-allegro form* (also known as *first-movement form,* or simply *sonata form*). A movement in sonata-allegro form is based on two assumptions. The first is that the music establishes a home key, moves or modulates to another key, and ultimately returns to the home key. We may therefore regard sonata-allegro form as a drama between two contrasting key areas. The "plot"—that is, the action and the tension—derives from this contrast.

The second assumption is that each key area is associated with a theme, which has the potential for development (we saw an example in the previous chapter). Most useful for this purpose is a brief, incisive theme, one that has momentum and tension and lends itself well to creative manipulation. The themes are stated, or "exposed," in the first section; developed in the second; and restated, or "recapitulated," in the third.

Exposition   The opening section of sonata-allegro form, the *exposition,* or statement, generally presents the two opposing keys and their respective themes. (A theme may consist of several related ideas, in which case we speak of a *theme group.*) The first theme and its expansion establish the home key, or tonic. A *bridge,* or transitional passage, leads into a contrasting key; in other words, the function of the bridge is to modulate. The second theme and its expansion establish the contrasting key. A closing section—sometimes with a new closing theme—rounds off the exposition in the contrasting key. In eighteenth-century sonata-allegro form, the exposition is repeated to establish the themes.

Development

Conflict and action, the essence of drama, find their place in the *development,* where the conflict erupts, and the action reaches maximum intensity. This section may wander further through a series of foreign keys, building up tension against the inevitable return home. The frequent modulations contribute to a sense of activity and restlessness. At the same time, the composer seeks to reveal the potential of the themes by varying, expanding, or contracting them, breaking them into their component motives, or combining them with other motives or with new material. If the work is written for orchestra, a fragment of the theme may be presented by one group of instruments and imitated by another, thereby changing register and timbre.

Recapitulation

When the development has run its course, the tension lets up. A bridge passage leads back to the key of the tonic. The beginning of the third section, the *recapitulation,* or restatement, is in a sense the psychological climax of sonata-allegro form. The first theme appears as we first heard it, in the tonic, satisfying the listener's need for unity.

The recapitulation follows the general path of the exposition, restating the first and second themes more or less in their original form, but with new and varied twists. The third section differs in one important detail from the exposition: it now remains in the tonic for the second theme, which was originally

Summary of Sonata-Allegro Form

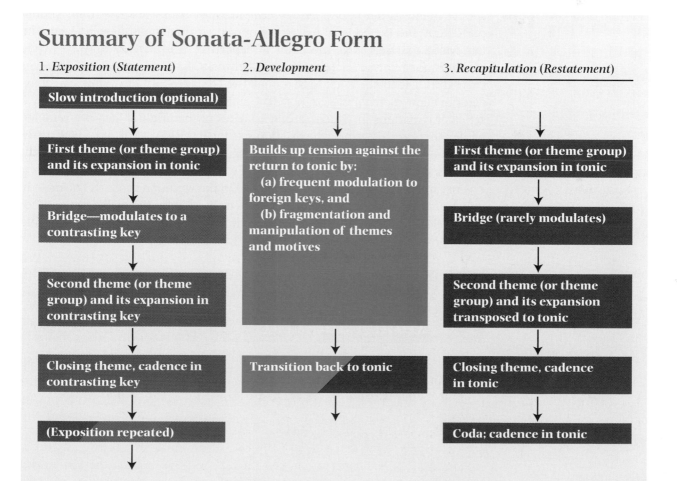

1. *Exposition (Statement)*   **2.** *Development*   **3.** *Recapitulation (Restatement)*

1. Exposition (Statement)	2. Development	3. Recapitulation (Restatement)
Slow introduction (optional)		
First theme (or theme group) and its expansion in tonic	Builds up tension against the return to tonic by: (a) frequent modulation to foreign keys, and (b) fragmentation and manipulation of themes and motives	First theme (or theme group) and its expansion in tonic
Bridge—modulates to a contrasting key		Bridge (rarely modulates)
Second theme (or theme group) and its expansion in contrasting key		Second theme (or theme group) and its expansion transposed to tonic
Closing theme, cadence in contrasting key	Transition back to tonic	Closing theme, cadence in tonic
(Exposition repeated)		Coda; cadence in tonic

Coda

heard in a contrasting key. In other words, although the second theme and its expansion play out in substantially the same way as before, we now hear this material transposed into the tonic. Most important of all, in the recapitulation the opposing elements are reconciled, the home key is triumphant.

The movement often ends with a *coda*, fashioned from material previously heard in the recapitulation's closing section. New matter is sometimes added to the coda, which leads us to the final cadence in the home key.

The features of sonata-allegro form, summed up in the chart on page 185 (which is color-coded to show keys), are present in one shape or another in many movements, yet no two are exactly alike. Each movement exhibits a unique character, mood, and relation of forces. Thus what looks on paper like a fixed plan followed by the composer becomes, when transformed into living sound, a supple framework for infinite variety.

The Second Movement

The second is usually the slow movement of the cycle, offering a contrast to the Allegro that preceded it; typically, it was an Andante or Adagio in **A-B-A** form, a shortened sonata form, a theme and variations, or, as in the case of several of our examples, a slow rondo. Here, composers can give prominence to lyrical, songful melody.

Theme and variations

We have seen that variation is an important procedure found in every species of music, but in one form—*theme and variations*—it is the ruling principle. There, the theme is stated at the outset, so that the audience learns the basic idea that serves as the point of departure. The melody may be newly invented or borrowed (like the theme in Britten's *The Young Person's Guide to the Orchestra*). The theme is apt to be a small two- or three-part idea, simple in character to allow room for elaboration. The statement of the theme is followed by a series of variations in which certain features of the original idea are retained while others are altered. Each variation sets forth the idea with some new modification—one might say in a new disguise—through which the listener glimpses something of the original theme.

Melodic variation

Any musical element may be developed in the variation process. The melody may be varied by adding or omitting notes or by shifting the melody to another key. *Melodic variation* is a favorite procedure in a jazz group, where the solo

Minuet and Trio

Minuet **(A)**	Trio **(B)**	Minuet **(A)**
‖ : **a** : ‖ : **b-a** : ‖	‖ : **c** : ‖ : **d-c** : ‖	**a-b-a**
or	or	or
‖ : **a** : ‖ : **b** : ‖	‖ : **c** : ‖ : **d** : ‖	**a-b**

player embellishes a popular tune with a series of decorative flourishes. In *harmonic variation*, the chords that accompany a melody are replaced by others, perhaps shifting from major to minor mode. The type of accompaniment may be changed, or the melody may be shifted to a lower register with new harmonies sounding above it. So too the rhythm, meter, and tempo may be varied—*rhythmic variation*—leading to interesting changes in the nature of the tune. The texture may be enriched by interweaving the melody with new themes or counter-melodies. By combining these methods with changes in dynamics and tone color, composers can also alter the expressive content of the theme; this type of character variation was especially favored in the nineteenth century.

Harmonic variation

Rhythmic variation

The Third Movement

In the Classical symphony, the third movement is almost invariably a *minuet and trio.* The minuet was actually a Baroque court dance whose stately triple (3/4) meter embodied the ideal of an aristocratic age. In the eighteenth century, the minuet was taken over into absolute music, where it served as the third movement of some large-scale instrumental works. (Note that this dance movement does not figure in all multimovement instrumental cycles.)

Minuet and trio

Since dance music lends itself to symmetrical construction, we often find in a minuet a clear-cut structure based on phrases of four and eight measures. (All the same, we will see that the minuets of Haydn and Mozart reveal an abundance of nonsymmetrical phrases.) In tempo, the minuet ranges from stateliness to a lively pace and whimsical character. Indeed, certain of Haydn's minuets are closer in spirit to folk dance than to the palace ballroom.

It was customary to present two dances as a group, the first repeated at the end of the second (resulting in **A-B-A).** The dance in the middle was originally arranged for only three instruments; hence the name "trio," which persisted even after the customary setting for three had long been abandoned. The trio as a rule is thinner in texture and more subdued in mood. Frequently in a symphony, woodwinds figure prominently in this section, creating an out-of-doors atmosphere that lends it a special charm. At the end of the trio, we find the words *da capo* ("from the beginning," often abbreviated *D.C.*), signifying that the first section is to be played over again.

Minuet-trio-minuet is a symmetrical three-part structure in which each part in turn is a small two-part, or binary, form. The second section of the minuet or trio may bring back the theme of the first at its close, making a *rounded binary form.* (See chart on facing page.) The composer indicates the repetition of the subsections within repeat signs (‖ : : ‖). However, when the minuet returns after the trio, it is customarily played straight through, without repeats. A *codetta* may round off each section.

Rounded binary form

In the nineteenth-century symphony, the minuet was replaced by the *scherzo*, generally the third movement but occasionally appearing as the second; it is usually in 3/4 meter. Like the minuet, it is a three-part form (scherzo-trio-scherzo), the first section being repeated after the middle part. But it differs from the minuet in its faster pace and vigorous rhythm. The scherzo—Italian for "jest"—is marked by abrupt changes of mood, from the humorous or the whimsical to the mysterious and even demonic. In Beethoven's hands, the scherzo became a movement of great rhythmic drive.

Scherzo

Multimovement Cycle: General Scheme

MOVEMENT	CHARACTER	FORM	TEMPO
FIRST	Long and dramatic	Sonata-allegro	Allegro
SECOND	Slow and lyrical	Theme and variations, sonata form, **A-B-A,** or rondo	Andante, Adagio, Largo
THIRD (optional)	Dancelike Minuet (18th century) Scherzo (19th century)	Minuet and trio Scherzo and trio	Allegretto Allegro
FOURTH	Lively, "happy ending" (18th century) Epic-dramatic with triumphal ending (19th century)	Sonata-allegro Sonata-rondo Theme and variations	Allegro, Vivace, Presto

The Fourth Movement

Rondo The Classical sonata and symphony often ended with a *rondo*—here, a lively movement filled with the spirit of the dance. Its distinguishing characteristic is the recurrence of a musical idea, the rondo theme, or refrain, in alternation with contrasting episodes much like the ritornello procedure of the Baroque era. Its symmetrical sections create a balanced architecture that is satisfying aesthetically and easy to hear. In its simplest form, **A-B-A-B-A,** the rondo is an extension of three-part form. If there are two contrasting themes, the sections may follow an **A-B-A-C-A** or similar pattern.

The rondo as developed by the Classical masters was more ambitious in scope, typically taking the arched form **A-B-A-C-A-B-A.** As the last movement, it featured a catchy theme that lent itself to being heard over and over again. The rondo figured in eighteenth- and nineteenth-century music both as an independent piece and as a member of the multimovement instrumental cycle. We will see, however, that symphonists in the nineteenth century frequently set the finale as a sonata-allegro, whose spacious dimensions served to balance the first movement.

The Multimovement Cycle as a Whole

The multimovement cycle of the Classical masters, as found in their symphonies, sonatas, string quartets, concertos, and other types of chamber music, became the vehicle for their most important instrumental music. The outline opposite sums up the common practice of the Classical-Romantic era. The outline will be helpful provided you remember that it is no more than a general scheme and does not necessarily apply to all works of this kind.

Eighteenth-century composers thought of the movements of the cycle as self-contained entities connected by key. First, third, and fourth movements were in the home key, the second movement in a contrasting key. The nineteenth century sought a more obvious connection between movements—a thematic link. This need was met by a *cyclical structure*, in which a theme from earlier movements reappears in the later ones as a kind of motto or unifying thread. We will see that Beethoven's famous Fifth Symphony displays elements of cyclical structure, with each movement making reference to the famous opening idea.

Cyclical structure

This large-scale structure satisfied composers' need for an extended instrumental work of an abstract nature, and showcased the contrasts of key and mode inherent in the major-minor system. With its fusion of emotional and intellectual elements, its intermingling of lyricism and action, the multimovement cycle may justly claim to be one of the most ingenious art forms ever devised.

Listening Activity: Hearing Larger Forms

CD: CHR/STD 3/59–61, SH 1/71–73

Mozart: *Eine kleine Nachtmusik,* third movement

The third-movement triple-meter dance, a *minuet and trio*, from Mozart's charming *Eine kleine Nachtmusik* will help us practice hearing on two levels: the big picture of its overall structure, and the detailed view of smaller sections.

WHAT TO LISTEN FOR

- Overall 3-part structure of the movement: minuet-trio-minuet.
- Minuet is rhythmic and strongly accented; trio is more lyrical and flowing.
- Listen again for smaller sections within movement.
- Minuet has 2 short sections, each repeated.
- Trio also has 2 short sections, each repeated.
- Music of the minuet returns, this time without the repeats.
- This is the third, or dance, movement of standard multimovement cycle.

MORE LISTENING REVIEW (FROM CD SET)

- Sonata-allegro form—Mozart: *Eine kleine Nachtmusik,* first movement
  Beethoven: Symphony No. 5 in C minor, first movement
- Theme and variations—Haydn: Symphony No. 94 in G major *(Surprise),* second movement
- Scherzo and trio—Beethoven: Symphony No. 5 in C minor, third movement
- Rondo—Beethoven: Piano Sonata in C minor *(Pathétique),* second movement
- Multimovement cycle—Mozart: *Eine kleine Nachtmusik* (4 movements)
  Beethoven: Symphony No. 5 in C minor (4 movements)

Jacques Louis David (1748–1825), *Mars Disarmed by Venus and the Graces,* 1824. (Musée Royaux des Beaux-Arts, Brussels)

Eighteenth-Century Classicism

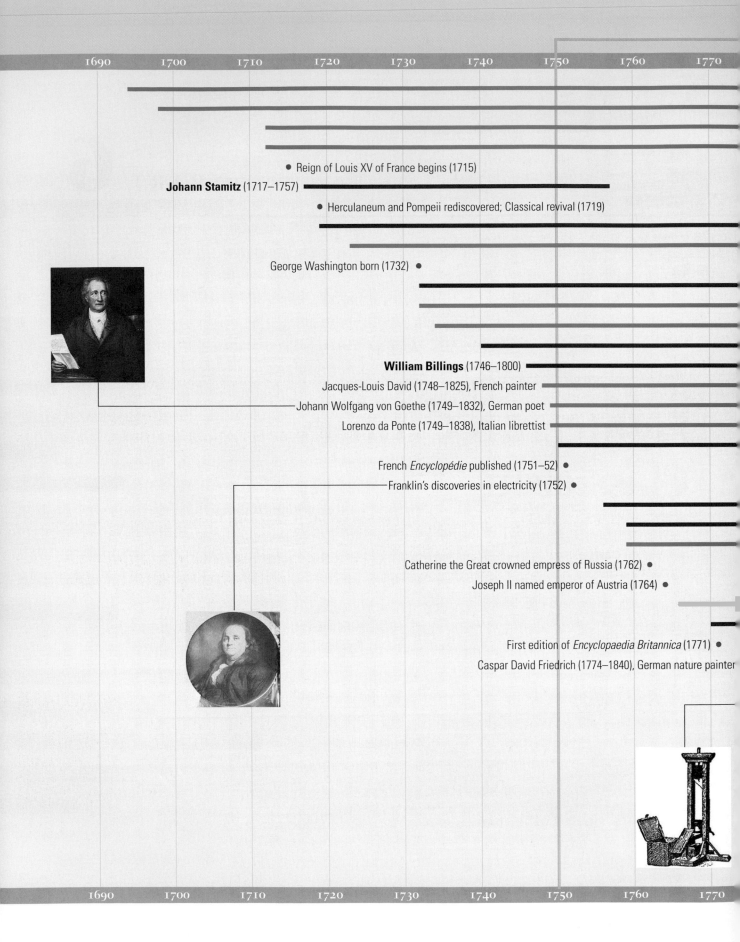

● Reign of Louis XV of France begins (1715)

Johann Stamitz (1717–1757)

● Herculaneum and Pompeii rediscovered; Classical revival (1719)

George Washington born (1732) ●

William Billings (1746–1800)

Jacques-Louis David (1748–1825), French painter

Johann Wolfgang von Goethe (1749–1832), German poet

Lorenzo da Ponte (1749–1838), Italian librettist

French *Encyclopédie* published (1751–52) ●

Franklin's discoveries in electricity (1752) ●

Catherine the Great crowned empress of Russia (1762) ●

Joseph II named emperor of Austria (1764) ●

First edition of *Encyclopaedia Britannica* (1771) ●

Caspar David Friedrich (1774–1840), German nature painter

Classical (1750–1825)

1780	1790	1800	1810	1820	1830	1840	1850	1860

Voltaire (1694–1778), French poet and philosopher

Pietro Metastasio (1698–1782), Italian poet and librettist

Jean-Jacques Rousseau (1712–1778), Swiss-born French philosopher and composer

Francesco Guardi (1712–1793), Italian painter

- World Events
- Composers
- Principal Figures

Leopold Mozart (1719–1787)

Joshua Reynolds (1723–1792), English portrait painter

Joseph Haydn (1732–1809)

Pierre-Augustin Caron de Beaumarchais (1732–1799), French playwright

Joseph Wright (1734–1797), English painter

Giovanni Paisiello (1740–1816)

Antonio Salieri (1750–1825)

Wolfgang Amadeus Mozart (1756–1791)

Maria Theresa von Paradis (1759–1824)

Friedrich von Schiller (1759–1805), German dramatist

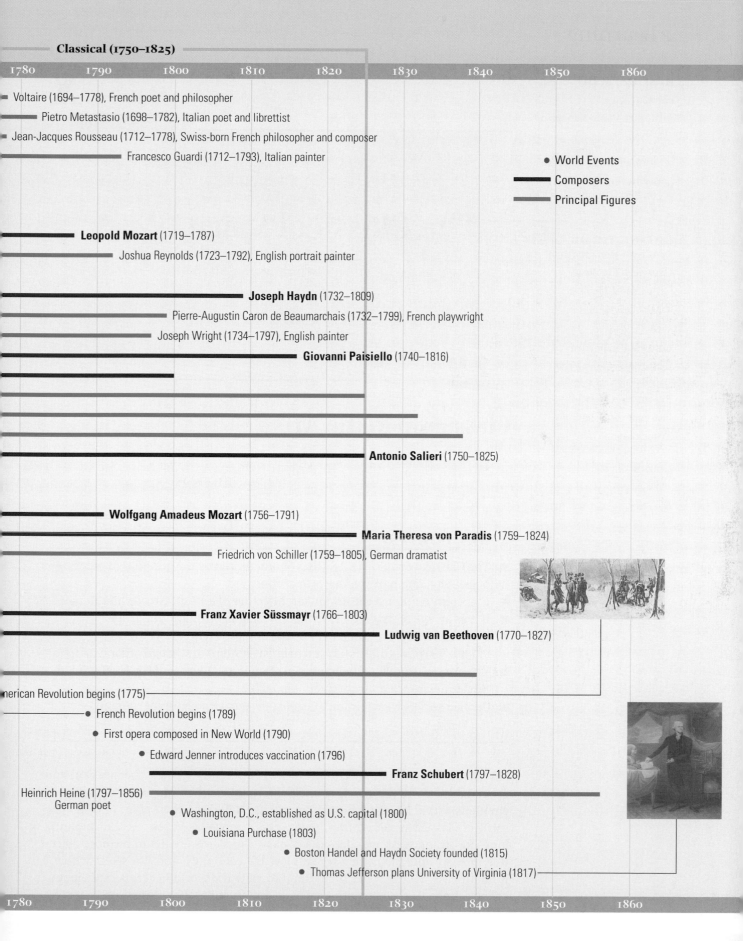

Franz Xavier Süssmayr (1766–1803)

Ludwig van Beethoven (1770–1827)

American Revolution begins (1775)

- French Revolution begins (1789)
- First opera composed in New World (1790)
- Edward Jenner introduces vaccination (1796)

Franz Schubert (1797–1828)

Heinrich Heine (1797–1856)
German poet

- Washington, D.C., established as U.S. capital (1800)
- Louisiana Purchase (1803)
- Boston Handel and Haydn Society founded (1815)
- Thomas Jefferson plans University of Virginia (1817)

1780	1790	1800	1810	1820	1830	1840	1850	1860

unit **X**

The Classical Spirit

29

Classicism in the Arts

"Music [is] the favorite passion of my soul."

—THOMAS JEFFERSON

KEY POINTS

- The Classical era (1750–1825) is characterized by the qualities of order, objectivity, and harmonious proportion.
- Classicists emulated the art and architecture of ancient Greece and Rome.
- It was an age of strong aristocratic sovereigns throughout Europe.
- The American Revolution (1775–83) and the French Revolution (1789–99) profoundly changed political systems and social order.
- The era saw significant advances in science and ideas and the Industrial Revolution made mass production possible.
- German writers were the first to signal interest in a concurrent romantic view of the world.

Historians observe that style in art moves between two poles, the classical and the romantic. Both the classicist and the romanticist strive to express significant emotions within beautiful forms. Where they differ is in their point of view. The spirit of classicism seeks order, poise, and serenity as surely as the romantic longs for strangeness, wonder, and ecstasy. Classicists are apt to be more objective in their approach; they try to view life rationally and "to see it whole." Romanticists, on the other hand, tend to view the world in terms of their personal feelings. The nineteenth-century German philosopher Friedrich Nietzsche dramatized the contrast between the two through the symbols of Apollo, Greek god of light and measure, and Dionysus, god of passion and intoxication. Classical and romantic ideals have alternated and even existed side by side from the beginning of time, for they correspond to two basic impulses in human nature: the need for moderation and the desire for uninhibited emotional expression.

The "Classical" and "Romantic" labels are also attached to two important periods in European art. We will deal with the Classical era first. It held the stage in the last half of the eighteenth century and the early decades of the nineteenth, when the literature and art of the ancient Greeks and Romans were considered as models of excellence to be emulated.

Classicists stress the power of their art as a means of communication rather than as a means of self-expression. For them, a work exists in its own right, not as an extension of their own egos. This disciplined view encourages the qualities of order, stability, and harmonious proportion that we have come to associate with the Classical style.

European rulers

The art of the eighteenth century bears the imprint of the spacious palaces and formal gardens—with their balanced proportions and finely wrought detail—that formed the setting for the era's great courts. In the middle of the century, Louis XV presided over extravagant celebrations in Versailles, Frederick the Great ruled in Prussia, Maria Theresa in Austria, and Catherine the Great in Russia. In such societies, the ruling class enjoyed its power through hereditary right. The past was revered and tradition was prized, no matter what the cost.

French Revolution

Before the end of the eighteenth century, Europe was convulsed by the French Revolution (1789–99). The Classical era therefore witnessed both the twilight of the old regime and the dawn of a new political-economic alignment in Europe—specifically, the transfer of power from the aristocracy to the middle class, whose wealth was based on a rapidly expanding capitalism. Such a drastic shift was made possible by the Industrial Revolution, which gathered momentum in the mid–eighteenth century with a series of important inventions, from James Watt's steam engine and James Hargreaves's spinning jenny in the 1760s to Eli Whitney's cotton gin in the 1790s.

Industrial Revolution

These decades saw significant advances in science. Benjamin Franklin harnessed electricity, Joseph Priestley discovered oxygen, and Edward Jenner perfected vaccination. There were important events in intellectual life as well, such

The Parthenon, Athens (448–432 B.C.E.). The architecture of ancient Greece embodied the ideals of order and harmonious proportions.

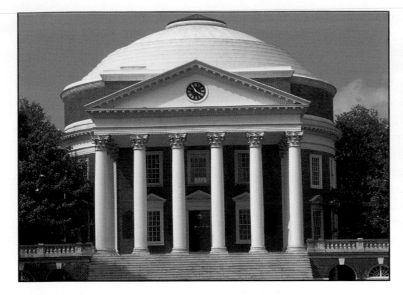

(Above): Thomas Jefferson's design for the Rotunda of the University of Virginia at Charlottesville reflects his admiration for classical architecture.

(Right): **Sir Joshua Reynolds** (1723–1792) captured the era's idealization of antiquity in his portrait *Mrs. Siddons as the Tragic Muse.* (Henry E. Huntington Library and Art Gallery, San Marino, California)

as the publication of the French *Encyclopédie* (1751–52) and the first edition of the *Encyclopaedia Britannica* (1771).

The American Revolution (1775–83) broke out more than fourteen years before the French. Its immediate cause was the anger of the colonists at the economic injustices imposed on them by King George III. Beyond that, however, was a larger vision of human equality and freedom, a vision that impelled Thomas Jefferson, principal author of the Declaration of Independence, to incorporate into that epoch-making document the idea that all people have the right to life, liberty, and the pursuit of happiness. These words became fundamental to the democratic faith that has resonated throughout the course of American history.

Intellectual climate

The intellectual climate of the Classical era, then, was nourished by two opposing streams. While Classical art captured the exquisite refinement of a way of life that was drawing to a close, it also caught the first intimations of a new social structure that was struggling to be born. The eighteenth century has been called the Age of Reason; but the philosophers who created the French *Encyclopédie* and the Enlightenment—Voltaire, Rousseau, and others—also invoked reason to attack the existing order. Thus these advocates for the rising middle class became prophets of the approaching upheaval.

Classical ideals

Eighteenth-century thinkers idealized the civilization of ancient Greece and Rome. They viewed the Greek temple as a thing of beauty, unity, proportion, and grace. And to the leaders of the middle class, Greece and Rome represented city-states that had rebelled against tyrants and absolute power. It was in this spirit that the foremost painter of revolutionary France, Jacques-Louis David, filled his canvases with symbols of Greek and Roman democracy. In this spirit too, Thomas Jefferson patterned the nation's Capitol, the University of Virginia, and his home at Monticello after Greek and Roman temples. His example gave strength to the classical revival in the United States, which made Ionic, Doric, and Corinthian columns indispensable features of public buildings well into the twentieth century.

By the 1760s, though, a number of works had already appeared that clearly indicated the new interest in a romantic point of view. In the same decade, the French philospher Jean-Jacques Rousseau (1712–1778), the "father of Romanticism," produced some of his most significant writings. His celebrated declaration "Man is born free, and everywhere he is in chains" epitomizes the temper of the time. The first manifestation of the Romantic spirit in Germany, the movement known as *Sturm und Drang* (storm and stress), took shape in the 1770s, when it produced two characteristic works by its most significant young writers: the *Sorrows of Young Werther*, by Johann Wolfgang von Goethe, and *The Robbers*, by Friedrich von Schiller. (Goethe, we shall see, became the favorite lyric poet of the Romantic composers.) By the end of the century, the atmosphere had completely changed.

Eighteenth-century Classicism, then, mirrored the unique moment in history when the old world was dying and the new was in the process of being born. From the meeting of two historic forces emerged an art of noble simplicity that constitutes one of the pinnacles of Western culture.

Literature

30

Classicism in Music

"Passions, whether violent or not, must never be expressed in such a way as to disgust, and [music] must never offend the ear."

W. A. MOZART

KEY POINTS

- The masters of the Classical musical style (Haydn, Mozart, Beethoven, Schubert—all members of the Viennese school), composed large-scale musical forms (symphony, concerto, sonata).
- Classical music is characterized by a singable, lyrical melody; diatonic harmony; regular rhythms and meters; homophonic texture; and the frequent use of folk elements.
- Music centered around the court, with composers (especially Haydn)—and women musicians—employed under the patronage system.
- Concert life in the early Americas was focused on the performance of European music (CP 8).

The Classical period in music (c. 1750–1825) is characterized best by the achievements of the masters of the Viennese School—Haydn, Mozart, Beethoven, and their successor Franz Schubert. These composers practiced their art in a time of great musical experimentation and discovery, when musicians took on three challenges: first, to explore fully the possibilities offered by the major-minor system; second, to perfect a large-scale form of absolute

The Viennese School

Map of Europe, 1763–1789, showing major musical centers.

instrumental music that would mobilize those possibilities to the fullest degree; and third, having found this ideal form, to differentiate between its various types—the solo and duo sonata, trio, quartet, other kinds of chamber music, the concerto, and the symphony.

If by "Classicism" we mean strict adherence to traditional forms, we certainly cannot apply the term to the composers of the Viennese School, who experimented boldly and ceaselessly with the materials at their disposal. It should not surprise us to find that Romantic elements abound in the music of Haydn, Mozart, and Beethoven, especially their late works. These composers dealt with musical challenges so brilliantly that their symphonies and concertos, piano sonatas, duo sonatas, trios, string quartets, and similar works remained unsurpassable as models for all who came after.

Elements of Classical Style

Lyrical melody   The music of the Viennese masters is notable for its elegant, lyrical melodies. Classical melodies "sing," even those intended for instruments. They are usually based on symmetrical four-bar phrases marked off by clear-cut cadences, and they move stepwise or by narrow leaps within a narrow range. Clarity is further provided by repetition and the frequent use of sequence (the repetition of a pattern at a higher or lower pitch). These devices make for balanced structures that are readily accessible to the listener.

Equally clear are the harmonies that sustain these melodies. The chords are firmly rooted in the key and do not change so rapidly as to be confusing. They underline the balanced symmetry of phrases and cadences, and they form vertical columns of sound over which the melody unfolds freely and easily, generally

Homophonic texture   in a *homophonic* texture (a melody with accompanying harmony). Note that this is somewhat different from the *homorhythmic* textures we heard in earlier eras, in which all voices moved together.

The harmony of the Classical period is based on the seven tones of the major or minor scale; in other words, it is largely *diatonic*. This diatonic harmony gives the music of Haydn, Mozart, and Beethoven its directness and its feeling of being rooted in the key.

Diatonic harmony

Melody and harmony are powered by strong rhythms that move at a steady tempo. Much of the music is in one of the four basic meters—2/4, 3/4, 4/4, or 6/8. If a piece or movement begins in a certain meter, it is apt to stay there until the end. Classical rhythm works closely with melody and harmony to make clear the symmetrical phrase-and-cadence structure of the piece. Clearly shaped sections establish the home key, move to contrasting but closely related keys, and return to the home key. The result is the beautifully molded architectural forms of the Classical style, fulfilling the listener's need for both unity and variety.

Rhythmic regularity

Despite its aristocratic elegance, music of the Classical era absorbed a variety of folk and popular elements. This influence made itself felt not only in the German dances and waltzes of the Viennese masters but also in their songs, symphonies, concertos, string quartets, and sonatas.

Folk elements

The Patronage System

The culture of the eighteenth century thrived under the patronage of an aristocracy that adopted the arts as a necessary adornment of life. Music was part of the elaborate ritual surrounding the nobility, and the center of musical life was the palace.

Aristocratic women musicians, in a Meissen ceramic, ca. 1760. (Scala/Art Resource, NY)

The social events at court created a steady demand for new works that composers had to supply. While musicians ranked little better than servants, their situation was not quite as depressing as it sounds, for in that society virtually everybody was a servant of the ruler. The patronage system actually gave musicians economic security and provided a social framework within which they could function. It offered important advantages to the great masters who successfully adjusted to its requirements, as the career of Haydn clearly shows. On the other hand, Mozart's tragic end, as we will see, illustrates how heavy the penalty could be for those unable to make that adjustment.

Women too found a place as musicians under the patronage system. In Italy and France, professional female singers achieved prominence in opera and in court ballets. Others found a place within aristocratic circles as court instrumentalists and music teachers, offering private lessons to members of the nobility. As we will see, a number of women pianists and violinists also made their mark as solo performers. With the growth of the music trades, especially music printing and publishing, women found more professional opportunities open to them. And as more amateurs participated in music making, women of the middle as well as upper classes found an outlet for their talents.

Concert Life in the Americas: Then and Now

What kind of music did people hear in eighteenth-century America and Canada? It should not surprise us that British musical tastes and traditions were highly influential. By the 1760s, European-style benefit and subscription concert series were flourishing in major Eastern cities, notably Boston, Charleston, and New York. Typically, a concert was a long affair, lasting three hours or more and featuring a wide variety of music and performers—quite different from modern events focused on a soloist, an orchestra, or a string quartet. Concerts were organized into acts, as we have in theatrical works, and frequently closed with a ball at which the latest fashionable dances were played. The concert repertory centered on English composers and others popular in England (such as Handel and Haydn).

Other types of entertainment aimed at a wider audience. In eighteenth-century America, opera was immensely popular. But an evening at the theater differed from what it is today: the performance of an English stage work might well include spoken drama, dance, mime, and even acrobatics. Songs were sometimes borrowed from other operas, and requests might be shouted from the audience, resulting in inserted numbers and encores. (An encore, from the French word for "again," is an extra piece or the repetition of a piece performed in response to audience applause.) The theater public sometimes became rowdy—in the gallery, the section farthest from the stage, there was even drunkenness, gambling, and prostitution going on during the performance—which caused some controversy over the morality of theatrical productions.

Public concert life slackened during the years of the American Revolution (1775–83), but music making continued in the home. Many of America's great patriots were amateur musicians: George Washington played the flute, Thomas Jefferson and Patrick Henry were both violinists, and Benjamin Franklin performed on the guitar, harp, and an instrument of his own invention called the glass harmonica (not a harmonica as we know it, but a set of glass bowls played by running a wet finger around the rim). This instrument became fashionable in Europe as well as America in the late eighteenth century. The literature even includes a quintet for flute, oboe, viola, cello, and glass harmonica composed by none other than Mozart.

A scene from an American performance of the dialogue opera *The Padlock* (1768), by the British composer Charles Dibdin (1745–1814). (New York Public Library)

Women too were active in amateur music making. The diary of Philip Fithian, an eighteenth-century teacher, describes talents then considered desirable in the educated woman: "She plays well on the Harpsichord, & Spinet; understands the principles of Musick, & therefore performs her Tunes in perfect time . . . she sings likewise to her instrument, has a full, strong voice, & a well-judging Ear."

After the revolution, musical societies, which sponsored professional and amateur concerts alike, sprang up around the country. Typical among these was the Boston Handel and Haydn Society, founded in 1815 and one of the earliest still in existence. As more North American composers were trained, their works were eventually included in the concert repertory along with those of the European masters. Theatrical spectacles with music were especially popular in the eastern Canadian provinces, and it was Montreal that saw the premiere of Joseph Quesnel's *Colas et Colinette* (1790), possibly the first opera written in North America.

The United States and Canada have sustained a vibrant musical life throughout their history, thanks to such major institutions as the Philharmonic Society of New York (established 1842), the Metropolitan Opera Company (1883), the Chicago Symphony Orchestra (1891), the Toronto Symphony Orchestra (1906), and the San Francisco Symphony Orchestra (1911). Today, symphony concerts and opera performances abound in large and small cities alike, on college campuses and in community forums, alongside rock concerts, Broadway musicals, and a myriad of other programs. Our musical palette continually widens, beckoning new audiences to sample its varied sounds.

A watercolor of a performance at New York's Park Theater (1822), by **John Searle,** showing the orchestra pit and tiered seating.

TERMS TO NOTE:

encore
subscription concert
glass harmonica

Concert venues At this time, musical performances were beginning to move from the palace to the concert hall. The rise of the public concert gave composers a new venue (site) in which to perform their works. Haydn and Beethoven conducted their own symphonies at concerts, and Mozart and Beethoven played their own piano concertos. The public flocked to hear the latest works—unlike modern concertgoers, who are interested mainly in the music of the past. The eagerness of eighteenth-century audiences for new music surely stimulated composers to greater productivity.

unit XI

Classical Chamber Music

31

Eighteenth-Century Chamber Music Style

"No other form of music can delight our senses with such exquisite beauty of sound, or display so clearly to our intelligence the intricacies and adventures of its design."

—SIR WILLIAM HENRY HADOW

KEY POINTS

- The Classical era is considered the golden age of chamber music (ensemble music for two to about ten performers, with one player per part).
- The string quartet was the most important chamber music genre of the era; duos, trios, quintets, serenades, and divertimentos were also cultivated.
- The form of a string quartet generally follows a standard four-movement structure of fast-slow-moderate dance-fast.
- Haydn's string quartets, characterized by dense textures and the use of folk elements, are central to the literature for this genre.

Chamber music, as we have seen, is music for a small ensemble—two to about ten players—with one player to a part. In this intimate genre, each instrument is expected to assert itself fully, but the style of playing differs from that of the solo virtuoso. Virtuosos are encouraged to display their own personalities; chamber music players function as part of a team.

The Classical era was the golden age of chamber music. Haydn and Mozart, Beethoven and Schubert established the true chamber music style, which is in the nature of a friendly conversation among equals. The central position in Classical chamber music was held by the string quartet, which, we have seen, consists of two violins (a first and a second), viola, and cello. Other favored combinations were the duo sonata—violin and piano, or cello and piano; the trio—violin, cello, and piano; and the quintet, usually a combination of string or wind instruments, or a string quartet and solo instrument such as the piano or clarinet. (See chart on p. 57.) Composers of the era also produced some memorable examples of chamber music for larger groups—sextets, septets, and octets.

Divertimento and serenade

Some types of compositions stood midway between chamber music and the symphony, their chief purpose being entertainment. Most popular among these were the *divertimento* and the *serenade*.

The String Quartet

The movements

The string quartet soon became the most influential chamber music genre of the Classical period. Although its four-line texture was viewed as ideal by composers, its focused string timbre posed a special challenge to both composer and listener. In its general structure, the string quartet follows the four-movement scheme of the standard multimovement cycle described in Chapter 28.

The musical texture is woven out of the movements' themes and motives, which the composer distributes among the four instruments. Haydn favored a dense musical texture based on the continual expansion and development of motives, while Mozart was more lyrical and melodic. Beethoven and Schubert further expanded the architecture of the quartet, the former through motivic

This eighteenth-century representation depicts a performance of a string quartet, the most influential chamber music genre of the era.

development and the latter through song, which was his special gift. Folk elements abound in Haydn's quartets (the last movement of his Op. 76, No. 2, smacks of a Hungarian dance), while Mozart's exude the elegance of court dances. Beethoven's rousing scherzos replaced the graceful minuet movement.

Because the string quartet was addressed to a small group of cultivated music lovers, composers did not need expansive gestures here. They could present in the quartet their most private thoughts, and indeed, the final string quartets of Haydn, Mozart, and Beethoven contain some of their most profound expressions.

32

Mozart and Chamber Music

"People make a mistake who think that my art has come easily to me. Nobody has devoted so much time and thought to composition as I. There is not a famous master whose music I have not studied over and over."

Wolfgang Amadeus Mozart

KEY POINTS

- The Austrian composer Wolfgang Amadeus Mozart was a child prodigy who started to write music before the age of five.
- Although he lived only to age thirty-five, Mozart made significant contributions to nearly all musical genres, including the symphony, sonata, concerto, chamber music, sacred music, and various types of opera (*buffa*, or comic; *seria*, or serious; and *Singspiel*, or with spoken dialogue).
- Mozart's music is notable for its lyrical melodic lines, colorful orchestration, and dramatic content.
- One of Mozart's best-known works is *Eine kleine Nachtmusik* (*A Little Night Music*), a serenade for strings.

Something of the miraculous hovers about the music of Mozart. His masterful melodic writing, his elegance of style, and his rich orchestral colors sound effortless. This deceptive simplicity is indeed the art that conceals art.

His Life

Wolfgang Amadeus Mozart (1756–1791) was born in Salzburg, Austria, the son of Leopold Mozart, an esteemed composer-violinist at the court of the Archbishop of Salzburg. Wolfgang began his career as the most extraordinarily gifted child in the history of music. He first started to compose before he was five, and, with his sister Nannerl, performed at the court of Empress Maria Theresa at the age of six. The following year, his ambitious father organized a concert tour that included Paris, London, and Munich. By the time he was thirteen, the boy had written sonatas, concertos, symphonies, religious works, and several operas.

Mozart Family Portrait (1780–81), by **Johann Nepomuk della Croce.** Child prodigies Wolfgang and his sister Nannerl are at the keyboard, while Leopold observes them, violin in hand. (Mozarteum, Salzburg)

Mozart reached adulthood having attained a mastery of all musical forms. The speed and sureness of his creative power, unrivaled by any other composer, is best described by Mozart himself: "Though it be long, the work is complete and finished in my mind. I take out of the bag of my memory what has previously been collected into it. For this reason the committing to paper is done quickly enough."

From patronage to free artist

The high-spirited young artist rebelled against the social restrictions imposed by the patronage system, and relations with his patron, the Archbishop of Salzburg, were strained. Mozart was finally dismissed after quarreling with the archbishop and at twenty-five established himself in Vienna to pursue the career of a freelance musician. His remaining ten years were spent in a struggle to achieve financial security, which meant winning the backing of the court. But Emperor Joseph II either passed him by in favor of lesser composers such as Antonio Salieri or assigned him to tasks unworthy of his genius, such as composing dances for the court balls.

Marriage to Constanze

In 1782, he married Constanze Weber, against his father's wishes. This step signaled Mozart's liberation from the very close ties that had bound him to his father, a domineering man who strove to ensure his son's success.

The da Ponte operas

With the opera *The Marriage of Figaro*, written in 1786 on a libretto by Lorenzo da Ponte, Mozart reached the peak of his career. The following year, he was commissioned to do another work for the Prague Opera; the result, with da Ponte again as librettist, was *Don Giovanni*. A success in Prague, this opera baffled the Viennese public.

Final years

Though his final years were spent in poor health, in the last year of his life he still managed to produce the Clarinet Concerto and, for the Viennese theater, his opera *The Magic Flute*. With a kind of fevered desperation, he then turned to the Requiem Mass. Mozart became obsessed with the notion that this Mass for the Dead was intended for himself and that he would not live to finish it. A tragic race with time began.

Mozart was cheered in his last days by the growing popularity of *The Magic Flute.* One afternoon, singers from the theater visited the gravely ill composer to sing through a completed movement of his Requiem. He died that same night, December 4, 1791, shortly before his thirty-sixth birthday. His favorite pupil, Franz Xavier Süssmayr, completed the work from the master's sketches, making some additions of his own.

The cause of Mozart's death has spurred many scientific theories over the years, including rheumatic fever, heart disease, and most recently, trichinosis from eating undercooked pork. None can be proven definitively, for, unlike the case of Beethoven (see page 219), no remains of the composer are extant for modern testing.

(see page 219)

in his own words

I learned from Haydn how to write quartets. No one else can do everything—be flirtatious and be unsettling, move to laughter and move to tears—as well as Joseph Haydn.

His Music

Mozart is preeminent among composers for the inexhaustible wealth of his simple, elegant, and songful melodies. His fondness for moderately chromatic harmonies is revealed especially in the development sections of his sonata forms. In all his instrumental music, Mozart infused a sense of drama, with contrasts of mood ranging from lively and playful to solemn and tragic. His orchestration is richly colorful, his part writing notable for its careful interweaving of the lines.

He wrote a large quantity of social music—divertimentos and serenades of great variety, the most famous of which is *Eine kleine Nachtmusik* (1787), the work we will study. In chamber music, Mozart, like Haydn, favored the string quartet. His last ten quartets are some of the finest in the literature, among them the set of six dedicated to Haydn, his "most celebrated and very dear friend."

One of the outstanding pianists of his time, Mozart wrote many works for his favorite instrument. The Fantasia in C minor, K. 475, and the Sonata in C minor, K. 457, are among his finest solo piano works. (The K followed by a number refers to the catalogue of Mozart's works by Ludwig Köchel, who numbered them all in what he determined to be the order of their composition.) And his twenty-seven concertos for piano and orchestra elevated this genre to one of the most important positions in the Classical era.

Mozart's symphonies, which extended across his career, are characterized by a richness of orchestration, a freedom in part writing, and a remarkable depth of emotion. The exact number of them is difficult to determine. Although four of the forty-one numbered symphonies are probably not by Mozart, newly discovered and reworked compositions still bring the number to over fifty. The most important are the six written in the final decade of his life. With these works, the symphony achieved its position as the most significant form of abstract music in this period.

A Classical orchestra, with the leader at a large rectangular harpsichord and the string players and singers distributed on both sides of the garden. *Open-Air Orchestra,* c. 1790. Engraving by **Giuseppe Servellini.**

🎺 Principal Works

Orchestral music, including some 40 symphonies (late symphonies: No. 35, *Haffner*, 1782; No. 36, *Linz*, 1783; No. 38, *Prague*, 1786; No. 39, No. 40, and No. 41, *Jupiter*, all from 1788); cassations, divertimentos, serenades, marches, dances

Concertos, including 27 for piano and 5 for violin; concertos for clarinet, oboe, French horn, bassoon, flute, and flute and harp

Operas, including *Idomeneo* (1781), *Die Entführung aus dem Serail* (*The Abduction from the Seraglio*, 1782), *Le nozze di Figaro* (*The Marriage of Figaro*, 1786), *Don Giovanni* (1787), *Cosí fan tutte* (*Women Are Like That*, 1790), and *Die Zauberflöte* (*The Magic Flute*, 1791)

Choral music, including 18 Masses, the Requiem, K. 626 (incomplete, 1791), and other liturgical music

Chamber music, including 23 string quartets; string quintets; clarinet quintet; oboe quartet; flute quartet; piano trios and quartets; violin and piano sonatas; and divertimentos and serenades (*Eine kleine Nachtmusik*, K. 525, 1787)

Keyboard music, including 17 piano sonatas and Fantasia in C minor (K. 475, 1785)

Secular vocal music

Operas   But the genre most central to Mozart's art was opera. He wrote in the three dramatic styles of his day: *opera buffa*, or Italian comic opera (including *The Marriage of Figaro* and *Don Giovanni); opera seria*, or Italian serious opera (including *Idomeneo*); and *Singspiel*, a lighter form of German opera with spoken dialogue (*The Magic Flute*). No one has ever surpassed his power to delineate character in music or his lyric gift, so delicately molded to the human voice. His orchestra, never obtruding upon the voice, becomes the magical framework within which the action takes place.

Eine kleine Nachtmusik

Mozartean elegance is embodied in *Eine kleine Nachtmusik,* a serenade for strings whose title means *A Little Night Music.* Probably the work was written for a string quartet supported by a bass and was meant for public entertainment, in outdoor performance. The four movements of the version we know (originally there were five) are compact, intimate, and beautifully proportioned.

First movement   The first movement, a sonata-allegro form in 4/4 time in G major, opens in a marchlike manner. The first theme ascends rapidly to its peak (this is sometimes called a *rocket theme*), then turns downward at the same rate. The second theme, with the downward curve of its opening measure, presents a graceful contrast to the upward-leaping character of the first. A delightful closing theme then rounds off the exposition. As befits the character of a serenade, which is less serious than a symphony or a concerto, the development section is brief. The recapitulation follows the course of the exposition but expands the closing theme into a vigorous coda. (See Listening Guide 15 for themes and an analysis of all four movements.)

Second is the Romanza, an eighteenth-century Andante that maintains the balance between lyricism and restraint. In this movement, symmetrical sections are arranged in a rondo-like structure. The main theme (**A**) is gracious, a quality that is maintained by the faster-moving **B** section. The **C** section, darker in tone, centers about C minor and is heard against a restless background of quick notes. The movement is brought to a close with a return to the **A** section.

Second movement

The minuet and trio is an Allegretto in G major, marked by regular four-bar phrases set in a rounded binary form. The minuet opens brightly and decisively. The trio, with its soaring Mozartian melody, presents a lyrical contrast. The opening music then returns, satisfying the Classical desire for balance and symmetry.

Third movement

The last movement, a sprightly Allegro in the home key of G, alternates with an idea in the key of the dominant, D major. We have here a prime example of the Classical sonata-rondo finale, bright, jovial, and stamped with an aristocratic refinement.

Fourth movement

Listening Guide 15

CD: CHR/STD 3/48–67, SH 1/60–79

Mozart: *Eine kleine Nachtmusik (A Little Night Music)*, K. 525 (17:35)

DATE OF WORK:	1787
MEDIUM:	String quartet with double bass, or chamber orchestra
MOVEMENTS:	I. Allegro; sonata-allegro form, G major
	II. Romanza, Andante; sectional rondo form, C major
	III. Allegretto; minuet and trio, G major
	IV. Allegro; sonata-rondo form, G major

First Movement: Allegro; sonata-allegro form, 4/4 meter, G major (5:30)

WHAT TO LISTEN FOR:	Intimate string chamber music style.
	Quick-paced movement with 3 themes and short development (sonata-allegro form).
	Overall homophonic texture.
	First theme is disjunct, marchlike, and ascends quickly (rocket theme); second theme graceful and conjunct.

60	0:00	EXPOSITION Theme 1—aggressive, ascending "rocket" theme, symmetrical phrasing, in G major:	

Transitional passage, modulating.

61	0:46	Theme 2—graceful, contrasting theme, less hurried, in key of dominant, D major:

	0:58	Closing theme—insistent, repetitive, ends in D major:

Repeat of exposition.

DEVELOPMENT

62	3:07	Short, begins in D major, manipulates theme 1 and closing theme; modulates, and prepares for recapitulation in G major.

RECAPITULATION

63	3:40	Theme 1, in G major.
64	4:22	Theme 2, in G major.
	4:34	Closing theme, in G major.
	5:05	Coda—extends closing, in G major.

Second Movement: Romanza, Andante; sectional rondo form, duple meter, C major

(5:50)

WHAT TO LISTEN FOR: Gentle, lyrical melodies in slow tempo.
Rondo-like structure, with opening section (**A**) recurring.

65	0:00	**A** section—lyrical, serene melody in 2 parts, each repeated (‖: **a** :‖ **b a** :‖):

66	0:55	First violin with faster movement at beginning of second part of **A**:

67	1:54	**B** section—more rhythmic movement, varies idea of **a**, brings **a** back at end; in 2 sections, each repeated (‖: **c** :‖ **d a** :‖):
68	2:55	Return of **a** theme (first time).

69	3:23	**C** section—in C minor, active rhythmic accompaniment; exchanges between violins and cellos; in 2 sections (‖: **e** :‖ **f**).
70	4:13	**A** section—return of first section in tonic, without repeats (**a-b-a**).
		Coda—3 loud chords extend the idea of **a**.

Third Movement: Allegretto; minuet and trio form, 3/4 meter, regular 4-measure phrases, G major

(2:09)

WHAT TO LISTEN FOR: Strongly rhythmic dance, in triple meter.
Lyrical, expressive trio.
Marked contrast between minuet and trio.
Balanced, regular form (minuet returns at end).
Homophonic texture.

71	0:00	Minuet theme—in accented triple meter, decisive character, in 2 sections (8 measures each), both repeated:
72	0:44	Trio theme—more lyrical and connected, in 2 sections (8 + 12 measures), both repeated:
73	1:41	Minuet returns, without repeats.

Fourth Movement: Allegro; sonata-rondo form, two main themes in alternation, 4/4 meter, G major

(4:06)

WHAT TO LISTEN FOR: Light and graceful finale, in homophonic texture.
Rocket theme, quick and spirited.
Form combines principles of rondo and sonata-allegro.

| 74 | 0:00 | EXPOSITION
Theme 1—merry, quick-paced rocket theme, symmetrical, 4-measure phrases, each repeated, in G major:

Transition. |
| 75 | 0:24 | Theme 2—begins with downward leap, opposite in character to theme 1, in D major: |
| | 0:40 | Theme 1—returns in varied setting as closing.

Exposition repeated. |

76	2:10	DEVELOPMENT Theme 1—modulates through various keys, ends up in G minor.
77	2:39	RECAPITULATION Theme 2—returns in tonic.
78	2:55	Theme 1—in tonic, as closing and extension of cadence.
79	3:26	Coda—theme 1 returns as in exposition, in G major.

unit **XII**

The Classical Symphony

e Learning

RESOURCE CD

*e*Music

Beethoven, Symphony No. 9 in D minor, IV (*Ode to Joy*)

*e*LGs

16 Haydn, Symphony No. 94 in G major (*Surprise*)

17 Beethoven, Symphony No. 5 in C minor, Op. 67

ONLINE TUTOR
www.wwnorton.com/enjoy

Composers: Classical

Wolfgang Amadeus Mozart

Joseph Haydn

Ludwig van Beethoven

Cultural Perspective:

9. The Composer Heard 'round the World

Resources: Classical

Listening: Classical

Quizzes: Classical

Reviewing 11, 12

Listening 11

Glossary

33

The Nature of the Symphony

"I frequently compare a symphony with a novel in which the themes are characters. After we have made their acquaintance, we follow their evolution, the unfolding of their psychology."

—ARTHUR HONEGGER

KEY POINTS

- The symphony was one of the principal instrumental forms of the Classical era.
- The heart of the Classical orchestra (about thirty to forty players) was the strings, assisted by woodwinds, brass, and percussion.
- The Classical symphony was generally set in the standard four-movement structure: I) fast, II) slow, III) moderate dance, and IV) fast.

Historical Background

The central place in Classical instrumental music was held by the symphony, which grew in dimension and significance. With the final works of Mozart and Haydn, it became the most important type of absolute music of the era.

The symphony as it developed in the Classical period had its roots in the Italian opera overture of the early eighteenth century. As we have already noted, the overture was a piece for orchestra in three sections: fast-slow-fast. First played to introduce an opera, these sections eventually became separate movements, to which the early German symphonists added a number of effects that were later taken over by Haydn and Mozart. One innovation was the use of a quick, aggressively rhythmic theme rising from low to high register with such speed that it came to be known as a *rocket theme* (as in the opening of Mozart's *Eine kleine Nachtmusik*). Equally important was the use of drawn-out *crescendos* (sometimes referred to as a *steamroller effect*) slowly gathering force as they rose to a climax. Both these effects are generally credited to composers active at Mannheim, a German city along the Rhine River. With the addition of the minuet and trio, also a Mannheim contribution, the symphony paralleled the string quartet in following the four-movement multimovement cycle.

The Classical Orchestra

The Classical masters established the orchestra as we know it today: an ensemble of the four instrumental families. The heart of the orchestra was the string choir. Woodwinds, used with great imagination, ably assisted the strings. The brass sustained the harmonies and contributed body to the sound mass, while the timpani supplied rhythmic life and vitality. The eighteenth-century orchestra numbered from thirty to forty players; thus the volume of sound was still more appropriate for the salon than the concert hall. (We will hear a movement from Haydn's Symphony No. 94 played on eighteenth-century period instruments.) It was only near the end of the Classical period that musical life began its move toward the public concert.

Haydn and Mozart created a dynamic style of orchestral writing in which all the instruments participated actively and each timbre could be heard. The interchange and imitation of themes among the various instrumental groups assumed the excitement of a witty conversation. The Classical orchestra also

Natural horns (without valves) and woodwinds are clearly visible in this painting of a small Classical orchestra performing in a Venetian palace (18th century, artist unknown). (Casa Goldoni, Venice)

The Classical Orchestra (30–40 players)

	HAYDN'S ORCHESTRA (Symphony No. 94, 1792)	BEETHOVEN'S ORCHESTRA (Symphony No. 5, 1807–08)
STRINGS	Violins 1 Violins 2 Violas Cellos and Double basses	Violins 1 Violins 2 Violas Cellos Double basses
WOODWINDS	2 Flutes 2 Oboes	1 Piccolo (4th movement only) 2 Flutes 2 Oboes 2 Clarinets 2 Bassoons 1 Contrabassoon (4th movement only)
BRASS	2 French horns 2 Trumpets	2 French horns 2 Trumpets 3 Trombones (4th movement only)
PERCUSSION	Timpani	Timpani

brought effects to absolute music that had long been familiar in the opera house, such as abrupt alternations of soft and loud, sudden accents, dramatic pauses, and the use of tremolo and pizzicato, all of which added drama and tension.

The Movements of the Symphony

The first movement of a Classical symphony is an Allegro in sonata-allegro form, sometimes preceded by a slow introduction. Sonata-allegro form, we saw, is based on the opposition of two keys, made clearly audible by the contrast between two themes. However, Haydn sometimes based a sonata-allegro movement on a single theme, which was first heard in the tonic key and then in the contrasting key. Such a movement is referred to as *monothematic*. Mozart, on the other hand, preferred two themes with maximum contrast between them, which was frequently achieved through varied instrumentation; for example, the first theme might be played by the strings and the lyrical second theme by the woodwinds.

First movement

The slow movement of a symphony is often a three-part form (**A-B-A**), a theme and variations, or a modified sonata-allegro (without a development

Second movement

section). Generally a Largo, Adagio, or Andante, this movement is in a key other than the tonic, with colorful orchestration that often emphasizes the woodwinds. The mood is essentially lyrical, and there is less development of themes here than in the opening movement.

Third movement

Third is the minuet and trio in triple meter, a graceful **A-B-A** form in the tonic key; as in the string quartet, its tempo is moderate. The trio is gentler in mood, with a moderately flowing melody and a prominent wind timbre. Beethoven's scherzo (a replacement for the minuet and trio), also in 3/4 time, is taken at a swifter pace.

Fourth movement

The fourth movement (finale), normally a vivacious Allegro molto or Presto in rondo or sonata-allegro form, is not only faster but also lighter than the first movement, and brings the cycle to a spirited ending. It often features themes with a folk-dance character, especially in Haydn's works. We will see that with Beethoven's Fifth Symphony, however, the fourth movement was transformed into a triumphant finale in sonata-allegro form.

34

Haydn and the Symphony

"Can you see the notes behave like waves? Up and down they go! Look, you can also see the mountains. You have to amuse yourself sometimes after being serious so long."

KEY POINTS

- The Austrian composer Joseph Haydn worked under the patronage of the Esterházy court.
- Haydn is remembered for his contributions to the development of Classical instrumental music, especially the symphony and the string quartet.
- One of Haydn's best-known symphonies, No. 94, the Surprise, was commissioned for a London concert series; its second movement is a theme and variations based on a simple yet memorable theme.

The long career of Haydn spanned the decades when the Classical style was being formed. The contribution he made to his art—especially to the symphony and string quartet—was second to none.

His Life

Joseph Haydn (1732–1809) was born in Rohrau, a village in lower Austria, the son of a wheelwright. Folk song and dance were his natural heritage. The beauty of his voice secured him a place as a choirboy at St. Stephen's Cathedral in Vienna, where he remained until he was sixteen and his voice had broken (the natural change that occurs at puberty in an adolescent boy's

Joseph Haydn

A modern-day photograph of the Eszterháza Palace in Fertöd, Hungary.

voice). Haydn then settled himself in Vienna, where he made his living through teaching and accompanying, and often joined the bands of musicians who performed in the streets. In this way, the popular Viennese idiom entered his style along with the folk music he had absorbed in childhood.

Before long, Haydn attracted the notice of the music-loving aristocracy of Vienna. In 1761, when he was twenty-nine, he entered the service of the Esterházys, a family of enormously wealthy Hungarian princes famous for their patronage of the arts. He remained with this family for almost thirty years, the greater part of his creative career. Eszterháza, the palace of the Esterházys, was one of the most splendid in Europe, even boasting its own opera house, and music played a central part in the constant round of festivities there. The musical establishment under the composer's direction included an orchestra, an opera company, a marionette theater, and a chapel. Haydn's life exemplifies the patronage system at its best.

By the time Haydn reached middle age, his music had brought him much fame. After the prince's death, he made two visits to England (1791–92 and 1794–95), where he conducted his works with phenomenal success. He died in 1809, revered by his countrymen and acknowledged throughout Europe as the premier musician of his time.

His Music

It was Haydn's historic role to help perfect the new instrumental music of the late eighteenth century. His terse, angular themes lent themselves readily to motivic development. Significant too, in his late symphonies, was his expansion of the orchestra's size and resources through greater emphasis on the brass,

Principal Works

Orchestral music, including over 100 symphonies (6 *Paris* Symphonies, Nos. 82–87, 1785–86; 12 *London*, or *Salomon*, Symphonies, Nos. 93–104, 1791–95); concertos for violin, cello, harpsichord, and trumpet; divertimentos

Chamber music, including some 68 string quartets, piano trios, and divertimentos

Sacred vocal music, including 14 Masses (*Mass in Time of War*, 1796; *Lord Nelson Mass*, 1798); oratorios, including *Die sieben letzten Worte* (*The Seven Last Words of Christ*, 1796), *Die Schöpfung* (*The Creation*, 1798), and *Die Jahreszeiten* (*The Seasons*, 1801)

Dramatic music, including 14 operas

Keyboard music, including about 40 sonatas; songs, including folk-song arrangements; secular choral music

clarinets (new to the orchestra), and percussion (on the new percussion instruments, see CP 10). In his expressive harmony, structural logic, and endlessly varied moods, the mature Classical style seemed to be fully realized for the first time.

Symphonies

The string quartet occupied a central position in Haydn's output; his works in that genre are today among the best loved and most frequently performed in the repertory. Like the quartets, the symphonies—over a hundred in number—extend across Haydn's entire career. Especially popular are the twelve written in the 1790s for his appearances in England. Known as the *London* Symphonies (or *Salomon* Symphonies, after the London impresario who commissioned them), they abound in effects generally associated with later composers: syncopation, sudden *crescendos* and accents, dramatic contrasts of soft and loud, daring modulations, and an imaginative plan in which each choir of instruments plays its allotted part. Haydn's symphonies, like his quartets, are the spiritual birthplace of Beethoven's style.

Haydn was also a prolific composer of church music; fourteen Masses form the core of his output in this repertory. His two oratorios, *The Creation* (1798) and *The Seasons* (1801), follow in the grand tradition of Handel.

in his own words

My Prince was always satisfied with my works. I not only had the encouragement of constant approval but as conductor of an orchestra I could make experiments, observe what produced an effect and what weakened it, and . . . improve, alter, make additions, or omissions, and be as bold as I pleased.

Symphony No. 94 (Surprise)

The best-known of Haydn's symphonies, the Surprise, in G major, is one of the twelve works composed for his concerts in London. The orchestra that presented these compositions to the world consisted of about forty members (see chart on p. 211). The work is subtitled *Surprise* because of a sudden *fortissimo* crashing chord in the slow movement, purposely intended to startle a dozing audience.

The work opens with a reflective slow introduction, followed by a forceful Vivace assai (very fast) in sonata-allegro form. The abrupt changes from *piano* to *forte* impart a dramatic quality to the movement and look ahead to Beethoven's emotion-charged style.

First movement

The second movement, a great favorite in the symphonic literature, presents a theme and four variations. This memorable theme, with all the allure of a folk song, is set in two repeated sections of eight measures each (or a binary structure). The opening melody, in C major, is announced by the violins playing staccato (short, detached notes); the phrase is repeated *pianissimo* and ends abruptly in a loud crash—the "surprise" chord of the work's nickname.

Second movement

The variations that follow display Haydn's workmanship and wit. The first variation opens at a *forte* level, then retreats to *piano*, with violin arabesques and flutes entering in dialogue with the tune. The second variation, with its dramatic shift to C minor, is played *fortissimo* by all the woodwinds and strings. A solo violin leads into the third variation, which presents the melody in quick, repeated sixteenth notes. The final variation is marked by changes in dynamics (now at *fortissimo*); in register (a shift to high range); in orchestration (woodwinds, brass, and timpani take the melody); and in Haydn's employment of a new triplet rhythm in the first violins, heard against offbeat chords in the other strings. The **B** section introduces a new version of the melody based on an uneven, dotted rhythm. The coda brings a return to the opening theme with new harmonies below, quietly summing up the movement.

The third movement, a minuet in G major, is a rollicking Allegro molto that leaves the elegant, courtly dance far behind in favor of a high-spirited, folklike romp. The finale, an energetic Allegro molto in sonata-allegro form, captures for its aristocratic listeners all the charm and humor of a traditional peasant dance. This work radiates the precise qualities that made the London symphonies so successful—innocent, appealing melodies within a masterful treatment of forms.

Third and fourth movements

Listening Guide 16

CD: CHR/STD 2/55–61, SH 2/1–7

Haydn: Symphony No. 94 in G major (*Surprise*), Second Movement

(6:39)

DATE OF WORK: First performed 1792

MEDIUM: Orchestra, with pairs of flutes, oboes, bassoons, French horns, and trumpets, along with strings and timpani

MOVEMENTS:
I. Adagio cantabile; Vivace assai; sonata-allegro form with slow introduction, G major
II. Andante; theme and variations form, C major
III. Menuetto: Allegro molto; minuet and trio form, G major
IV. Allegro molto; sonata-allegro form, G major

Folklike theme in 2 regular phrases, each repeated (binary structure).

Loud, crashing chord (the "surprise") at the end of the first theme.

4 variations on the theme, with changes in dynamics and texture (Var. 1); shift in key center, from major to minor (Var. 2); quick-paced rhythmic treatment (Var. 3); and varied orchestration and dynamics (Var. 4).

Eighteenth-century period string, wind, and percussion instruments.

Second Movement: Andante; theme and variations form, 2/4 meter, C major

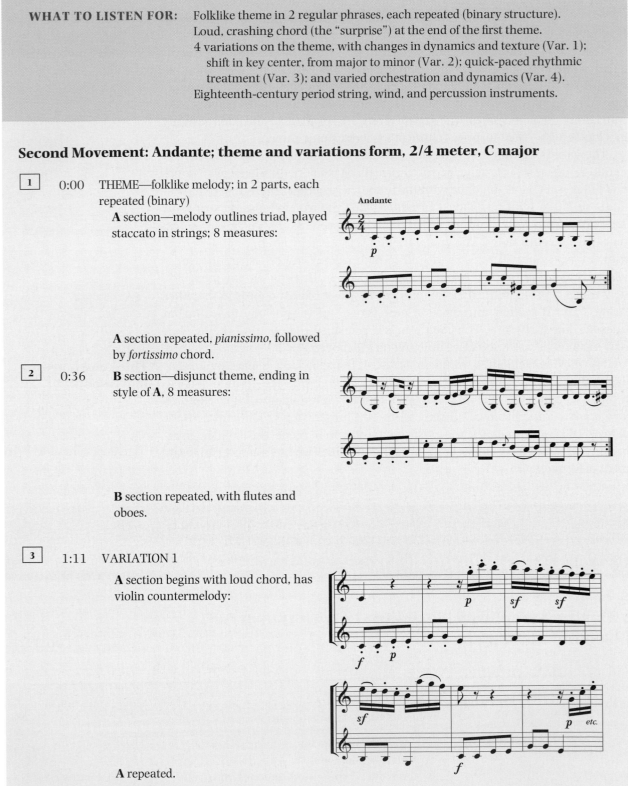

1　0:00　THEME—folklike melody; in 2 parts, each repeated (binary)

A section—melody outlines triad, played staccato in strings; 8 measures:

A section repeated, *pianissimo*, followed by *fortissimo* chord.

2　0:36　B section—disjunct theme, ending in style of A, 8 measures:

B section repeated, with flutes and oboes.

3　1:11　VARIATION 1

A section begins with loud chord, has violin countermelody:

A repeated.

B, with decorated violin line.

B repeated.

| 4 | 2:20 | VARIATION 2 |

A heard *fortissimo*, in C minor (later shifts to major):
A repeated.

Development of **A**, with fast passages in strings, remains in minor.

Solo violins lead into Variation 3.

| 5 | 3:35 | VARIATION 3 |

A in fast rhythm, heard in oboes:

A repeated in violins, with woodwind countermelody; low strings drop out:

B continues with violins and woodwinds alone.

B repeated.

| 6 | 4:43 | VARIATION 4 |

A heard in full orchestra, loud statement, includes trumpets and timpani; violins with fast passagework; accents on offbeats:

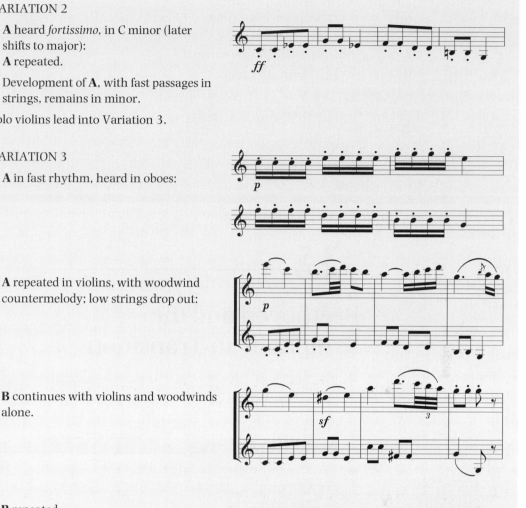

217

A heard in violins in uneven, dotted rhythm, with accompaniment playing offbeats.

B continues in uneven rhythms in strings.

B repeated in loud statement by full orchestra.

5:51 Bridge to coda; staccato pattern, followed by sustained chord.

7 6:05 Coda returns to **A** melody, with varied harmony underneath; ends quietly in C major.

35

Beethoven and the Symphony in Transition

"Freedom above all!"

KEY POINTS

- The Viennese master Ludwig van Beethoven is viewed as a transitional figure whose music—divided into three style periods—straddles the Classical and Romantic eras.
- Beethoven's nine symphonies are monumental works intended for the concert hall rather than the aristocratic salon; his Fifth Symphony, his best-known composition, is built on a now-famous four-note motive that permeates all four movements.
- Beethoven is probably the most influential—and revered—composer of art music (CP 9).

Beethoven belonged to the generation that felt the full impact of the French Revolution. He created the music of a heroic age and, in sounds never to be forgotten, proclaimed a faith in the power of people to shape their own destinies.

Ludwig van Beethoven

His Life

Ludwig van Beethoven (1770–1827) was born in Bonn, Germany, where his father and grandfather were singers at the court of the local prince, the elector Max Friedrich. The family situation was unhappy; his father was an alcoholic, and Ludwig at an early age was forced to support his mother and two younger brothers. At eleven and a half, he was assistant organist in the court chapel, and a year later he became harpsichordist in the court orchestra. A visit to Vienna in his seventeenth year provided him with an opportunity to play for Mozart. The youth improvised so brilliantly on a theme given to him that Mozart remarked to his friends, "Keep an eye on him—he will make a noise in the world some day."

Beethoven's talents as a pianist took the music-loving aristocracy by storm. He functioned under a modified form of the patronage system. Though he was not attached to the court of a prince, the music-loving aristocrats of Vienna helped him in various ways—by paying him handsomely for lessons or presenting him with gifts. He was also aided by the emergence of a middle-class public and the growth of concert life and music publishing. A youthful exuberance pervades the first decade of his career, an almost arrogant consciousness of his strength.

Early years in Vienna

Then, fate struck in a vulnerable spot: Beethoven began to lose his hearing. His helplessness in the face of this affliction dealt a shattering blow to his pride: "Ah, how could I possibly admit an infirmity in the one sense that should have been more perfect in me than in others. A sense I once possessed in highest perfection. Oh, I cannot do it!" As deafness closed in on him—the first symptoms appeared when he was in his late twenties—it brought a sense of apartness from other people. On the advice of his doctors, he retired in 1802 to a summer resort outside Vienna called Heiligenstadt. There he was torn between the destructive forces in his soul and his desire to live and create: "But little more and I would have put an end to my life. Only art . . . withheld me." Beethoven slowly realized that art must give him the happiness that life withheld. The will to struggle reasserted itself; he fought his way back to health, although he never regained his hearing. The remainder of his career was spent in ceaseless effort to achieve his artistic goals. Biographers and painters have made familiar the image of the squat, sturdy figure (he was five foot four, the same height as that other conqueror of the age, Napoleon) walking hatless through Vienna, the bulging brow wrinkled in thought, stopping to jot down an idea in his sketchbook—an idea that, because he could not hear its sonorous beauty, he envisioned all the more vividly in his mind. A ride in an open carriage during severe weather brought on an attack of edema that proved fatal. Beethoven died in his fifty-seventh year, famous and revered.

The onset of deafness

Modern science has offered a theory on the reason for Beethoven's deafness and the internal disorders he suffered in later life. DNA analysis of a lock of the composer's hair, cut off at his death and preserved through the years, has revealed a massive lead content, possibly from his china, pots, or the wine he drank—all potential sources of lead. We know today that lead toxicity can cause serious health problems, many of which match Beethoven's symptoms. A fascinating book, *Beethoven's Hair*, by Russell Martin (2000), traces the history of this remarkable relic.

His Music

Beethoven is the supreme architect in music. His genius found expression in the structural type of thinking embodied in the sonata and the symphony. The sketchbooks in which he worked out his ideas show how they gradually reached their final shape.

in his own words

I carry my thoughts about with me for a long time . . . before writing them down. . . . once I have grasped a theme, I shall not forget it even years later. I change many things, discard others, and try again and again until I am satisfied; then, in my head . . . [the work] rises, it grows, I hear and see the image in front of me from every angle . . . and only the labor of writing it down remains. . . . I turn my ideas into tones that resound, roar, and rage until at last they stand before me in the form of notes.

The Composer Heard 'round the World

Ludwig van Beethoven stands today as the most popular composer of art music in the world. What accounts for the universality of this master? Clearly, his wide acceptance results from more than the powerful influence that Western culture has exerted globally.

Beethoven's Fifth Symphony was recognized in its day as a masterpiece. Premiered in Vienna (December 2, 1808) at a four-hour concert of his music, the work was immediately hailed by one reviewer, the German composer Johann Friedrich Reichardt, as "a great symphony"—not a typical critic's reaction to new music. Although the general public might not have fully understood the master's works, they revered him nevertheless—some twenty thousand people turned out for his funeral in Vienna!

Beethoven on his deathbed. A lithograph by **Joseph Danhauser** (1827).

Beethoven represented the newly emerging "free artist," who lived from the sale of his works rather than the bounty of a single prince. In his lifetime, his music was published widely, from Russia to the United States, and emerging music societies around the globe performed his orchestral and choral compositions. The Philharmonic Society of New York (the oldest continuing orchestra in the United States, founded in 1842) opened its first public program with the "Grand Symphony in C minor (the 5th)" by Beethoven. The nineteenth-century composer Hector Berlioz, on first hearing the master's symphonies in 1828, claimed that "Beethoven opened before me a new world of music, as Shakespeare had revealed a new universe of poetry." Berlioz then convinced his teacher, Jean-François Lesueur, to attend a performance of the Fifth Symphony at the Paris Conservatory. Lesueur's reaction was immediate: "Let me get out. I must have some air. It's amazing! Wonderful! I was so moved and disturbed that when I emerged from the box and attempted to put on my hat, I couldn't find my head."

The famous opening motive of the Fifth Symphony—three shorts and a long—has inspired a variety of interpretations, the most popular being "fate knocking at the door." During the Second World War, the rhythm was associated with its Morse code meaning of "V" for victory, and transmitted via radio waves over thousands of miles.

Perhaps even more popular is Beethoven's great Ninth Symphony, with its famous choral finale—commonly known as the *Ode to Joy*—set to inspirational words of unity among peoples by the German

Compositional periods Beethoven's compositional activity fell into three periods. The first reflected the Classical elements he had inherited from Haydn and Mozart. The middle period saw the appearance of characteristics more closely associated with the nineteenth century: strong dynamic contrasts, explosive accents, and longer movements. Beethoven expanded the dimensions of the first movement, especially the coda, and like Haydn and Mozart, he made the development section the dynamic center of sonata-allegro form. In his hands, the slow movement

Beethoven's death, unlike Haydn's and Mozart's, did not pass unnoticed. Thousands of people from all walks of life followed his funeral procession to the cemetery. A watercolor by **Franz Stöber.** (Beethoven-Haus, Bonn)

poet Friedrich von Schiller. This musical work has exerted such strong appeal that it has been used as a rallying cry for widely divergent philosophies, including democracy, totalitarianism, and fascism. In Japan, the piece is traditionally performed each December 31 with a colossal choir, to bring the year to a close.

The youth of the early rock-and-roll era rejected this style of art music, as Chuck Berry's 1956 hit *Roll Over, Beethoven* demonstrated, but even this vernacular music has succumbed to the timelessness of Beethoven: several disco settings of the Fifth Symphony have been produced, including the popular *Hooked on Classics*, and a karaoke version of the Ninth Symphony finale is now available in Japan. (The Japanese term *karaoke* means "empty orchestra.") Today, Beethoven's music can be heard in commercials and movie soundtracks, including the classic animated films *Fantasia* (1941) and *Fantasia* (2000), the entertaining video *Beethoven Lives Upstairs* (1992), the art film *Immortal Beloved* (1994), and the new, comic children's CD, *Beethoven's Wig* (2002). These are further testament to the continued popularity of this ageless musician.

TERMS TO NOTE:

Philharmonic
karaoke

SUGGESTED LISTENING:

Beethoven: Symphony No. 9, Fourth Movement
Hooked on Classics

acquired a hymnlike character, the essence of Beethovenian pathos. The scherzo became a movement of rhythmic energy spanning many moods; his goal here was powerful expression rather than elegance. And he enlarged the finale into a movement comparable in size and scope to the first, ending the symphony on a triumphant note. In his third period—the years of the final piano sonatas and string quartets as well as the Ninth Symphony—Beethoven used more chromatic harmonies and developed a skeletal language from which all nonessentials were rigidly pared away. It was a language that transcended his time.

Symphonies

Beethoven's nine symphonies are conceived on a scale too large for the aristocratic salon; they demand the concert hall. The first two symphonies stand closest to the two Classical masters who preceded him, but with his Third Symphony, the *Eroica*, Beethoven achieved his own mature style. The Fifth Symphony is popularly viewed as the archetype of the genre, and the Seventh rivals it in universal appeal. The finale of the Ninth, or *Choral* Symphony, in which vocal soloists and chorus join the orchestra, is a setting of Schiller's *Ode to Joy*, a ringing prophecy of the time when "all people will be brothers."

Concertos and piano sonatas

The concerto offered Beethoven an ideal form in which to combine virtuosity with symphonic structure. His Violin Concerto displays the technical abilities of the soloist within a much enlarged form, and his five piano concertos both coincided with and encouraged the rising popularity of the instrument. The piano itself occupied a central position in Beethoven's art. His thirty-two sonatas form an indispensable part of its literature, whether for the amateur pianist or the concert artist. They are often considered the pianist's New Testament (the Old being *The Well-Tempered Clavier* of Bach).

String quartets

Beethoven wrote a great deal of chamber music, the string quartet lying closest to his heart. The six quartets of Opus 18 are the first in a series that extended throughout his entire career. His supreme achievements in this genre are the last five quartets, which, together with the Grand Fugue, Op. 133, occupied the final years of his life.

Vocal music

Beethoven also made significant contributions to vocal music. His one opera, *Fidelio*, centers on wifely devotion, human freedom, and the defeat of those who would destroy that freedom. The *Missa solemnis* (*Solemn Mass*), which transcends the limits of any specific creed or faith, ranks in importance with the Ninth Symphony and the final quartets. In his manuscript for the

Principal Works

Orchestral music, including 9 symphonies: No. 1 (1800); No. 2 (1802); No. 3, *Eroica* (1803); No. 4 (1806); No. 5 (1808); No. 6, *Pastoral* (1808); No. 7 (1812); No. 8 (1812); No. 9, *Choral* (1824); overtures, including *Leonore* (Nos. 1, 2, 3) and *Egmont*; incidental music

Concertos, including 5 for piano, 1 for violin (1806), and 1 triple concerto (piano, violin, and cello, 1804)

Chamber music, including string quartets, piano trios, quartets, 1 quintet, 1 septet, violin and cello sonatas, serenades and wind chamber music

32 piano sonatas, including Op. 13, *Pathétique* (1806); Op. 27, No. 2, *Moonlight* (1801); Op. 53, *Waldstein* (1804); and Op. 57, *Appassionata* (1805)

1 opera, *Fidelio* (1805)

Choral music, including *Missa solemnis* (1823)

Songs, including song cycle *An die ferne Geliebte* (*To the Distant Beloved*, 1816)

Autograph manuscript of the opening to Beethoven's Fifth Symphony.

Kyrie of the Mass, the composer wrote a sentence that applies to the whole of his music: "From the heart . . . may it find its way to the heart."

The Fifth Symphony

Perhaps the best-known of all symphonies, Beethoven's Symphony No. 5 in C minor, Op. 67, is also the most concentrated expression of what we have come to call Beethovenian. The first movement, in a sonata-allegro form marked Allegro con brio (lively, with vigor), springs out of the rhythmic idea of "three shorts and a long" that dominates the entire symphony. This idea, the most compact and commanding gesture in the whole symphonic literature, is pursued with an almost terrifying single-mindedness in this dramatic movement. In an extended coda, the basic rhythm reveals yet a new fund of explosive energy. (See Listening Guide 17.)

First movement

The second movement is a serene theme and variations, with two melodic ideas. In the course of the movement, Beethoven exploits his two themes with all the procedures of variation—changes in melodic outline, harmony, rhythm, tempo, dynamics, register, key, mode, and timbre.

Second movement

Third in the cycle of movements is the scherzo, which opens with a rocket theme introduced by cellos and double basses. After the gruff, humorous trio in C major, the scherzo returns in a modified version, followed by a transitional passage to the final movement in which the memorable four-note motive of the first movement is sounded by the timpani.

Third movement

In the monumental fourth movement, composed in sonata-allegro form, Beethoven once again brings back three shorts and a long, making this symphony an example of cyclical form. At the end of the extended coda, the tonic chord is proclaimed triumphantly by the orchestra again and again.

Fourth movement

Beethoven's career bridged the transition from the old society to the new. His music is the expression of a titanic force, the affirmation of an all-conquering will.

Listening Guide 17

CD: CHR/STD 4/32–56, SH 2/8–32

Beethoven: Symphony No. 5 in C minor, Op. 67 (32:02)

DATE OF WORK: 1807–8

MOVEMENTS:
I. Allegro con brio; sonata-allegro form, C minor
II. Andante con moto; theme and variations form (2 themes), A-flat major
III. Allegro; scherzo and trio form, C minor
IV. Allegro; sonata-allegro form, C major

First Movement: Allegro con brio; sonata-allegro form, 2/4 meter, C minor (7:31)

WHAT TO LISTEN FOR: Famous motive (short-short-short-long) is basis for entire movement; heard in sequence, extended beyond 4 notes, and turned upside down.
Sonata-allegro form, with fiery opening theme and sweet 2nd theme.
Dramatic tonal shifts between major and minor.

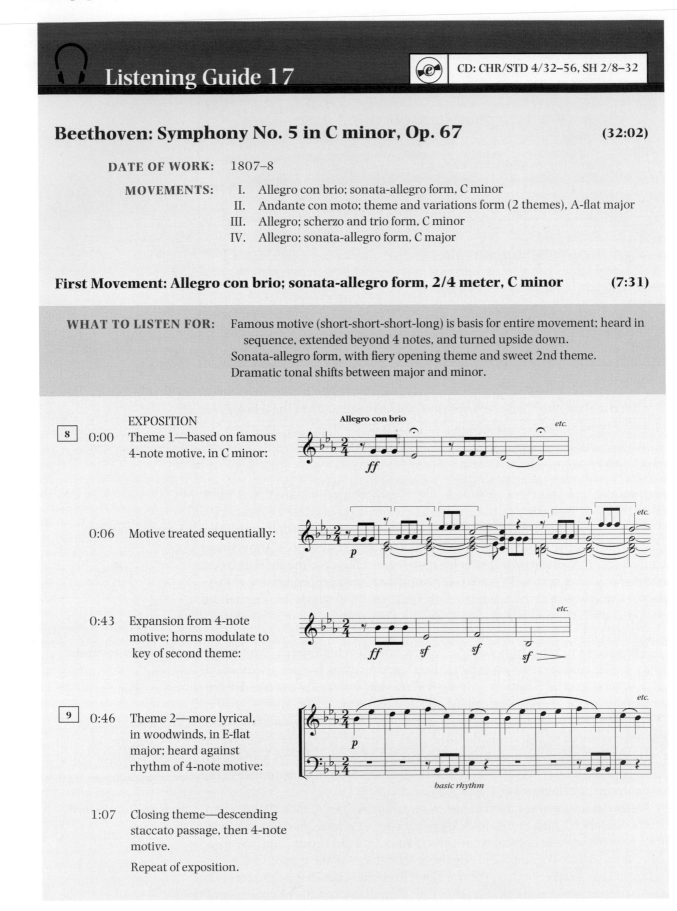

8 0:00	EXPOSITION Theme 1—based on famous 4-note motive, in C minor:	
0:06	Motive treated sequentially:	
0:43	Expansion from 4-note motive; horns modulate to key of second theme:	
9 0:46	Theme 2—more lyrical, in woodwinds, in E-flat major; heard against rhythm of 4-note motive:	
1:07	Closing theme—descending staccato passage, then 4-note motive. Repeat of exposition.	

DEVELOPMENT

10 2:54 Beginning of development, announced by horns.

3:05 Manipulation of 4-note motive through a descending sequence:

3:16 Melodic variation, interval filled in and inverted:

4:13 Expansion through repetition; leads into recapitulation:

RECAPITULATION

11 4:18 Theme 1—in C minor, followed by brief oboe solo in cadenza style.

12 5:15 Theme 2—returns in C major.

5:51 Closing theme.

13 5:58 Coda—extended treatment of 4-note motive; ends in C minor.

Second Movement: Andante con moto; theme and variations form, with two themes, 3/8, meter, A-flat major

(10:13)

WHAT TO LISTEN FOR: Movement based on 2 contrasting themes, both subjected to variation procedure.

Varied melodies, harmonies (major/minor), rhythms, tempo, and accompaniment.

Orchestra sections featured as groups: warm strings, brilliant woodwinds, and powerful brass.

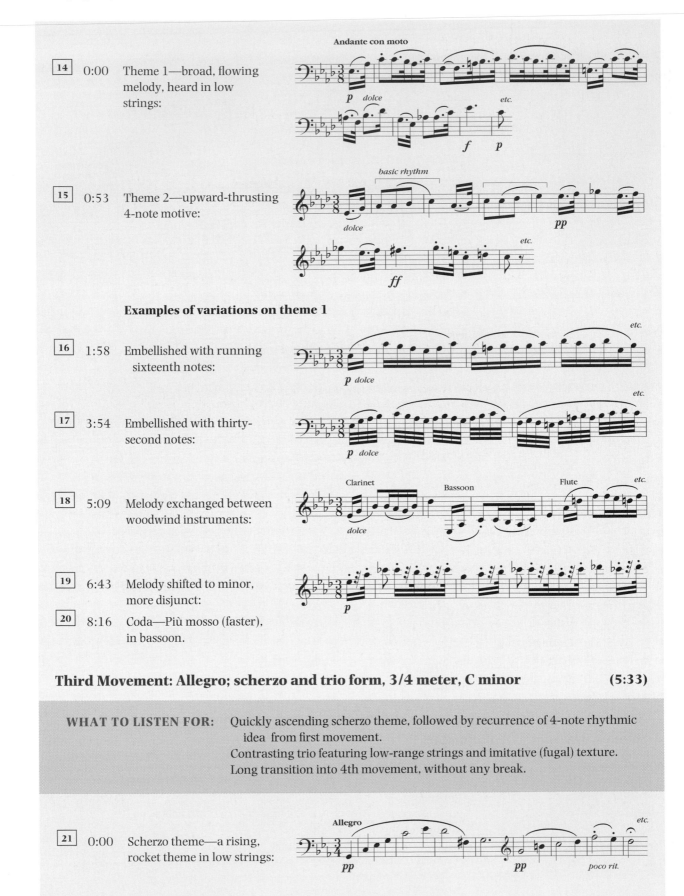

14	0:00	Theme 1—broad, flowing melody, heard in low strings:
15	0:53	Theme 2—upward-thrusting 4-note motive:

Examples of variations on theme 1

16	1:58	Embellished with running sixteenth notes:
17	3:54	Embellished with thirty-second notes:
18	5:09	Melody exchanged between woodwind instruments:
19	6:43	Melody shifted to minor, more disjunct:
20	8:16	Coda—Più mosso (faster), in bassoon.

Third Movement: Allegro; scherzo and trio form, 3/4 meter, C minor   (5:33)

WHAT TO LISTEN FOR: Quickly ascending scherzo theme, followed by recurrence of 4-note rhythmic idea from first movement.
Contrasting trio featuring low-range strings and imitative (fugal) texture.
Long transition into 4th movement, without any break.

21	0:00	Scherzo theme—a rising, rocket theme in low strings:

	0:18	Recurrent rhythmic motive (from opening of first movement):
22	1:58	Trio theme—in C major, in double basses, set fugally:
	2:29	Trio theme is broken up and expanded through sequences:
23	3:29	Scherzo returns, with varied orchestration.
24	4:49	Transition to next movement with timpani rhythm from opening 4-note motive:

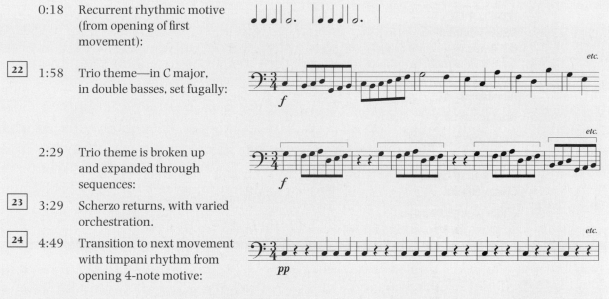

Fourth Movement: Allegro; sonata-allegro form, 4/4 meter, C major   (8:45)

WHAT TO LISTEN FOR: Triumphant theme in trumpets brilliantly proclaiming C-major tonality.
4-note motive recurs as unifying device for entire symphony.
Long coda affirms victorious C-major tonality (over C minor, the opening key of the entire symphony).

25	5:33	EXPOSITION Theme 1—in C major, a powerful melody whose opening outlines a C-major chord:
26	6:06	Lyrical transition theme, modulating from C to G major:
27	6:32	Theme 2—in G major, vigorous melody with triplets:
	6:58	Closing theme—featuring clarinet and violas, decisive:

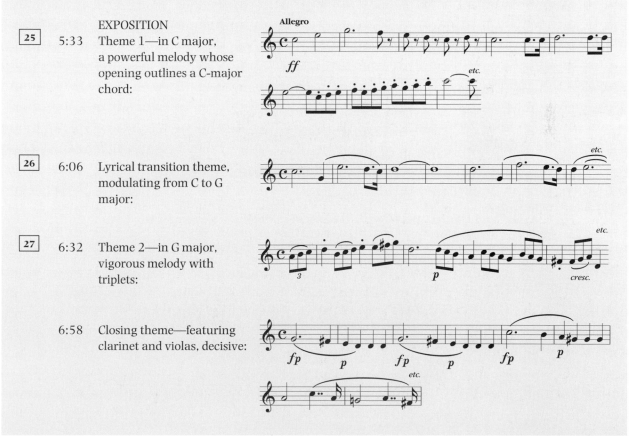

28	7:29	DEVELOPMENT Much modulation and free rhythmic treatment; brings back 4-note motive (3 short and a long) from first movement.
29	9:10	Brief recurrence of scherzo.
30	9:43	RECAPITULATION Theme 1, in C major.
31	10:50	Theme 2, in C major. Closing theme.
32	11:47	Coda—long extension.

unit XIII

The Eighteenth-Century Concerto and Sonata

36

The Classical Concerto

"Give me the best instrument in Europe, but listeners who understand nothing or do not wish to understand and who do not feel with me in what I am playing, and all my pleasure is spoilt."

—W. A. MOZART

KEY POINTS

■ The Classical concerto form has three movements, alternating fast-slow-fast.

■ The first movement is the longest and most complex, combining elements of Baroque ritornello procedure and *sonata-allegro form*, resulting in *first-movement concerto form* (or simply *concerto form*).

■ Mozart's Piano Concerto in G major, K. 453—with its graceful melodies, brilliant piano passagework, and virtuosic *cadenzas* (improvised solo passages)—is a notable example of the genre.

The Movements of the Concerto

We saw that in the Baroque era, the word "concerto" implied a mixing together of contrasting forces, and could refer to a solo group and orchestra or to a solo instrument and orchestra. The Classical era shifted the emphasis to the latter combination, with the piano and violin the most common solo instruments.

The three movements of the Classical concerto follow the established fast-slow-fast pattern. One characteristic feature of the concerto is the *cadenza*, a fanciful solo passage in the manner of an improvisation that interrupts the

Cadenza

Mozart's fortepiano, now housed in the Mozarteum in Salzburg. Notice how the white and black keys are reversed in color.

movement toward the end. The cadenza came out of a time when improvisation was an important element in art music, as it still is in jazz. In the solo concerto, the cadenza has a dramatic effect: the orchestra falls silent, and the soloist launches into a free play of fantasy on one or more themes of the movement.

The Classical concerto begins with a first-movement form that adapts the principles of the Baroque concerto's ritornello procedure (based on a recurring theme) to those of sonata-allegro form. First-movement concerto form is sometimes described as a sonata-allegro form with a double exposition. The movement usually opens with an orchestral exposition, or ritornello, in the tonic key, often presenting several themes. A second exposition, for the solo instrument and orchestra, now makes the necessary key change to the dominant (or the relative major). The soloist often plays elaborated versions of the themes first heard in the orchestra, and can add new material as well. The development section offers ample opportunity for solo virtuosic display, in dialogue with the orchestra. In the recapitulation, the soloist and orchestra bring back the themes in the tonic. The solo cadenza, a brilliant improvisation, appears near the end of the movement, and a coda brings the movement to a close with a strong affirmation of the home key.

The slow and lyrical second movement, generally an Andante, Adagio, or Largo, features the soloist in songlike melody. This movement is often composed in a key that lies close to the tonic. Thus, if the first movement is in C major, the second might well be in F major (the subdominant), four steps above.

A typical finale is an Allegro molto or Presto (very fast) that is shorter than the first movement and in rondo form, which could be modified to adopt some developmental features of sonata-allegro form. This movement may contain its own cadenza that calls for virtuoso playing and brings the piece to an exciting end.

Mozart's Piano Concerto in G major, K. 453

Mozart played a crucial role in the development of the piano concerto. His concertos, written primarily as display pieces for his own public performances, abound in the brilliant flourishes and ceremonious gestures characteristic of eighteenth-century music.

First movement The first movement, marked Allegro, opens with an orchestral ritornello; the piano then ushers in its own exposition, which includes a new theme. An orchestral tutti leads to the development section, and the ritornello is heard again in the recapitulation. This concerto, notable for its graceful writing for piano and woodwinds, is usually performed today with a cadenza that Mozart wrote for this work. (For analysis, see Listening Guide 18.)

The ensuing slow movement features a kind of double exposition format that is more typical of concerto first movements. The closing movement, an Allegretto in 2/2, or cut time, is in theme and variations form. The theme is a graceful, dancelike tune made up of two short phrases, each of which is repeated. The five variations that follow set the piano and orchestra in a dialogue of melodic, rhythmic, and harmonic elaborations on the highly appealing theme. (Mozart was so fond of this tune that he taught it to his pet starling, who consistently missed one note and got the rhythm wrong.)

Second and third movements

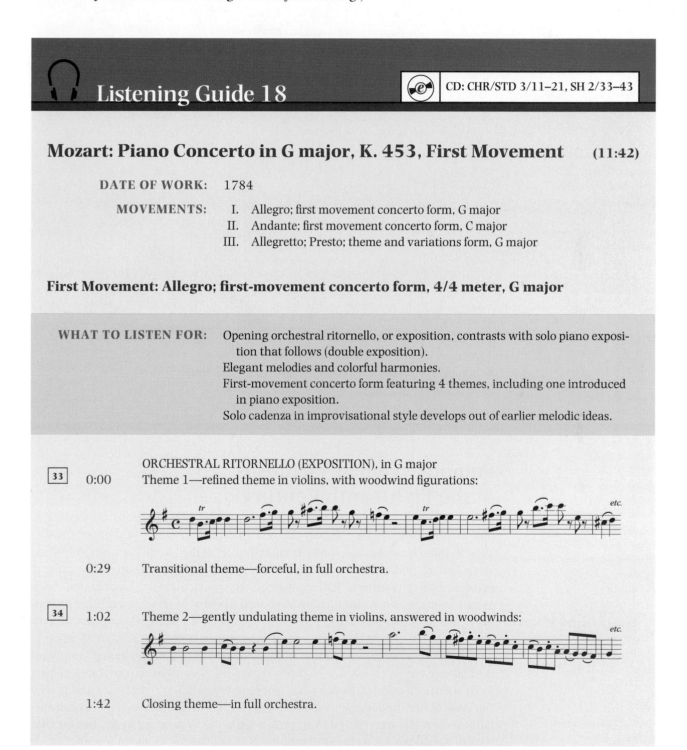

Listening Guide 18

CD: CHR/STD 3/11–21, SH 2/33–43

Mozart: Piano Concerto in G major, K. 453, First Movement   (11:42)

DATE OF WORK: 1784

MOVEMENTS:
 I. Allegro; first movement concerto form, G major
 II. Andante; first movement concerto form, C major
 III. Allegretto; Presto; theme and variations form, G major

First Movement: Allegro; first-movement concerto form, 4/4 meter, G major

WHAT TO LISTEN FOR: Opening orchestral ritornello, or exposition, contrasts with solo piano exposition that follows (double exposition).
Elegant melodies and colorful harmonies.
First-movement concerto form featuring 4 themes, including one introduced in piano exposition.
Solo cadenza in improvisational style develops out of earlier melodic ideas.

| 33 | 0:00 | ORCHESTRAL RITORNELLO (EXPOSITION), in G major
Theme 1—refined theme in violins, with woodwind figurations: |

| | 0:29 | Transitional theme—forceful, in full orchestra. |

| 34 | 1:02 | Theme 2—gently undulating theme in violins, answered in woodwinds: |

| | 1:42 | Closing theme—in full orchestra. |

35   2:13   SOLO EXPOSITION
Theme 1—piano enters with sweep into main theme, decorated, in G major; woodwind accompaniment; scales and arpeggio figurations in piano.

     2:50   Transitional theme—orchestral ritornello; piano with decorative part; modulates to key of dominant.

36   3:17   Piano theme—introduced by piano alone in D major, then presented in woodwinds:

37   4:07   Theme 2—in piano, with string accompaniment.

     5:03   Closing—decisive, in D major.

38   5:23   DEVELOPMENT
Virtuosic piano part, references to piano theme, runs and arpeggios against woodwinds; various modulations, leading back to tonic.

39   6:42   RECAPITULATION
Theme 1—returns in strings, with woodwind accompaniment; piano joins in with decorated version of theme.

     7:14   Transition theme—forceful, in full orchestra.

40   7:43   Piano theme, solo, in G major, more decorated, with light orchestral accompaniment.

41   8:33   Theme 2—in piano, then in woodwinds, now in G major.

42   9:41   Cadenza—solo piano, variations on earlier themes; ends on dominant.

43   10:58   Closing—final ritornello, in G major.

Famous Women Virtuosos of the Eighteenth Century

Maria Anna Mozart

Since eighteenth-century society deemed it proper that noble and upper-middle-class women study music, many became highly skilled amateurs. Some women were able to make a living as music teachers, and a few attained the status of professional performers. Three women in particular—all associated with Mozart—stand out as impressive keyboard players of the late eighteenth century. Maria Anna Mozart (1751–1829), known as Nannerl, was an accomplished pianist who as a child toured extensively with her brother Wolfgang, performing concertos and four-hand piano works. Her father noted that Nannerl, at age twelve, was "one of the most skillful players in Europe," able to perform the most difficult works with "incredible precision," and that she played "so beautifully that everyone is talking about her and admiring her execution." Later, when she had retired from professional life to raise a family, her brother wrote several works for her and sent his piano cadenzas to her to try out.

The career of the blind musician Maria Theresa von Paradis (1759–1824) parallels that of her friend Mozart. An excellent pianist and organist, she was renowned for her remarkable musical memory, which was able to retain some sixty different concertos that she prepared for an extended European tour (1783–86). Paradis was a composer herself, but many of her works, including two concertos, a piano trio, and a number of sonatas, have been lost.

The third gifted pianist was Barbara von Ployer, a young student of Mozart's for whom he wrote two concertos, including the G-major work we just studied. Mozart was so proud of his talented student that he invited the composer Giovanni Paisiello (1740–1816) to the premiere of the concerto. He wrote to his father, "I am fetching Paisiello in my carriage, as I want him to hear both my pupil and my compositions."

The public prominence achieved by these women performers was unusual for the era. However, the many engravings and paintings of the time illustrating music-making scenes make it clear that women participated frequently in performances at home, in aristocratic salons, and at court.

The pianist Maria Anna Mozart, sister of the composer.

37

The Classical Sonata

KEY POINTS

- The Classical sonata was set either for a solo instrument (piano) or for a duo (violin and piano, for example).
- Haydn, Mozart, and Beethoven all wrote music influenced by the Turkish Janissary, or military, band (CP 10).
- The *Pathétique* Sonata is one of Beethoven's best-known piano works; it evokes the new Romantic style.

The Movements of the Sonata

We saw in an earlier chapter that the sonata, as Haydn, Mozart, and their successors understood the term, was an instrumental work for one or two instruments, consisting of three or four contrasting movements. The movements followed the basic multimovement cycle described earlier in the discussions of string quartet, symphony, and concerto.

In the Classical era, the sonata—for piano solo or for two instruments—became an important genre for amateurs in the home, as well as for composers performing their own music at concerts. In duo sonatas for violin or cello and piano, the piano initially took the leading role, with the string instrument acting as accompaniment. Mozart and Beethoven, however, began to treat the two instruments as equal partners. And the solo piano sonatas of these two composers are the most significant in the literature.

East Meets West: Turkish Influences on the Viennese Classics

We are all attracted and excited by the new and the mysterious. The public of eighteenth-century Vienna turned to the East to satisfy its appetite for the unusual. Over the centuries, there had been ample opportunities, most of them military, for cultural interaction between the Austrian Hapsburg Empire and the large and powerful Ottoman Empire, of which Turkey was a part. When the dust from their hostile skirmishes had settled, more civil relations were established. Viennese cuisine smacked increasingly of Eastern spices, fashions hinted at an Eastern look, and the city's music took on a distinctly martial sound, derived from the Turkish Janissary, or military, bands.

The Janissary band originated in Turkey in the fourteenth century as an elite corps of mounted musicians composed of players of the shawm and bass drum. (We have already noted the introduction of these instruments into western Europe as a result of the Crusades and the establishment of early trade routes.) In the seventeenth century, the trumpet, small kettledrums, cymbals, and bell trees were added to this ceremonial ensemble, producing a loud and highly percussive effect. The Turkish sound captured the imagination of the Viennese masters, who attempted to re-create it in their orchestral and theatrical works. Haydn wrote three "military" symphonies, Beethoven composed three orchestral works with Turkish percussion (including his monumental Symphony No. 9), and Mozart and Haydn, among others, used this military sound in their operas. Mozart noted that "Music must never offend the ear, but must please the listener, or in other words must never cease to be music. . . . The Janissary chorus [from *Die Entführung*] . . . is all that can be desired, that is, short, lively, and written to please the Viennese." The influence was felt even in piano music—notably in Mozart's appealing Rondo alla turca from his Sonata in A major, which we studied. So popular was this style that

A Turkish Janissary band featuring mounted players of trumpets *(boru)*, cymbals *(zil)*, cylindrical drums *(davul)*, and kettledrums *(kös)*. Miniature from *The Festival Book of Vehbi*, written and illuminated for Ahmed III (r. 1703–30). (Topkapi Sarayi Museum, Istanbul)

Whirling dervishes dancing, from the Mevlevi sect ceremony in Konya, Turkey.

some nineteenth-century pianos featured a "Janissary pedal" to add percussive effects.

Although the fascination with Turkish music proved to be a passing fancy, it nevertheless affected the makeup of the Western orchestra by leading to the establishment of percussion instruments of Turkish origin (bass drum, cymbals, bells) as permanent members of the ensemble. It's hard to imagine an orchestra today without them! The Turkish Janissary ensemble also had a significant impact on the development of the military band in the West and is the direct antecedent of the modern Shriners' band (Ancient Arabic Order of Nobles of the Mystic Shrine), frequently seen in parades today.

Beethoven was fascinated by another Turkish musical tradition—this one a mystical religious ceremony to which he alluded in his incidental music for the stage work *The Ruins of Athens* (1811). The ceremony derives from one of the sects of Islam, that of the Mevlevis, who were famous for their whirling dervish ritual: dancing in a circle with a slow, controlled spinning motion as a part of their religious experience. This ceremony was sung to the accompaniment of flute, lute, and percussion, including kettledrum and cymbals. Beethoven's *Chorus of*

Whirling Dervishes, a pale imitation of the original, is an example of exoticism that has been filtered through Western culture. Both the Janissary band and the whirling dervish ceremony are obsolete in modern-day Turkey, except as tourist attractions. The term "whirling dervish"—implying one who twists and turns, like a restless child—has, however, endured in the West.

TERMS TO NOTE:

Janissary band
whirling dervish

SUGGESTED LISTENING:

Turkish music (Janissary ensemble)
Mozart: Rondo alla turca, from Piano Sonata
   in A, K. 331
Haydn: Symphony No. 100, *Military*, Second
   Movement
Beethoven: Symphony No. 9, Fourth Movement ♪
Mozart: *The Abduction from the Seraglio*, Overture
Beethoven: *The Ruins of Athens*, "Turkish March" ♪

An eighteenth-century engraving dated 1773 showing a typical violin-piano duo. (Bibliothèque Nationale, Paris)

One of Mozart's most delightful piano works is his Sonata in A major, K. 331, which closes with a rondo labeled "alla turca" that evokes the percussive sound of the Turkish Janissary bands then popular in Vienna. This quick-time march in A minor has many effects meant to suggest the jangling of bell trees, cymbals, and triangles that accompanied Turkish soldiers on parade. (See CP 10 for a discussion of Turkish influences on Western music.)

It is the piano sonatas of Beethoven, however, that are the most significant in the solo literature for that instrument. They truly epitomize the genre in the Classical era.

Beethoven's Pathétique *Sonata*

Beethoven himself dubbed the Piano Sonata in C minor, Op. 13, the *Pathétique.* Certainly the Beethovenian pathos is apparent from the first chords of the slow introduction (see Listening Guide 19). Marked Grave (solemn), this opening has something fantasylike about it, as if Beethoven had captured here the passionate intensity of his own keyboard improvisations.

In the movement proper, marked Allegro di molto e con brio (very fast and with vigor), Beethoven uses the resources of the piano most imaginatively: there are contrasts in dynamics and register, brilliant scale passages, and exciting uses of tremolo and a slowly gathering *crescendo.*

Second movement

The second movement is a famous Adagio cantabile (Slow and songful), which shows off the piano's ability to sing. The opening theme of this melodious rondo (in **A-B-A-C-A** form) is stated in A-flat major, then repeated an octave higher. After a brief contrasting episode, the opening theme returns, followed by a new section in which insistent triplets increase the tension in a dialogue between the pianist's right and left hands. The animation continues through the last statement of the memorable theme and a short coda. This hymnlike Adagio combines an introspective character with the quality of strength that Beethoven made his own.

Third movement

The final movement is also a rondo, whose principal theme is darkened by the C-minor tonality, setting it apart from the usually cheerful rondo finales of Haydn and Mozart. Within its spacious structure, lyric episodes alternate with dramatic ones. The *Pathétique* has been a favorite for generations. In the hands of a great performing artist, it stands as one of Beethoven's most personal sonatas.

Listening Guide 19

CD:CHR/STD 4/12–16, SH 2/44–48

Beethoven: Piano Sonata in C minor, Op. 13 (*Pathétique*), Second Movement

(4:32)

DATE OF WORK:	1798
MOVEMENTS:	I. Grave, Allegro di molto e con brio; sonata-allegro form, C minor
	II. Adagio cantabile; 5-part rondo form, A-flat major
	III. Allegro; 7-part rondo form, C minor

Second Movement: Adagio cantabile; 5-part rondo form (A-B-A-C-A), 2/4 meter, A-flat major

WHAT TO LISTEN FOR: Balanced proportions of 5-part rondo form, unified by recurring refrain—
a memorable, songful melody.
Lyrical melodies throughout, in contrast to outer movements of sonata.

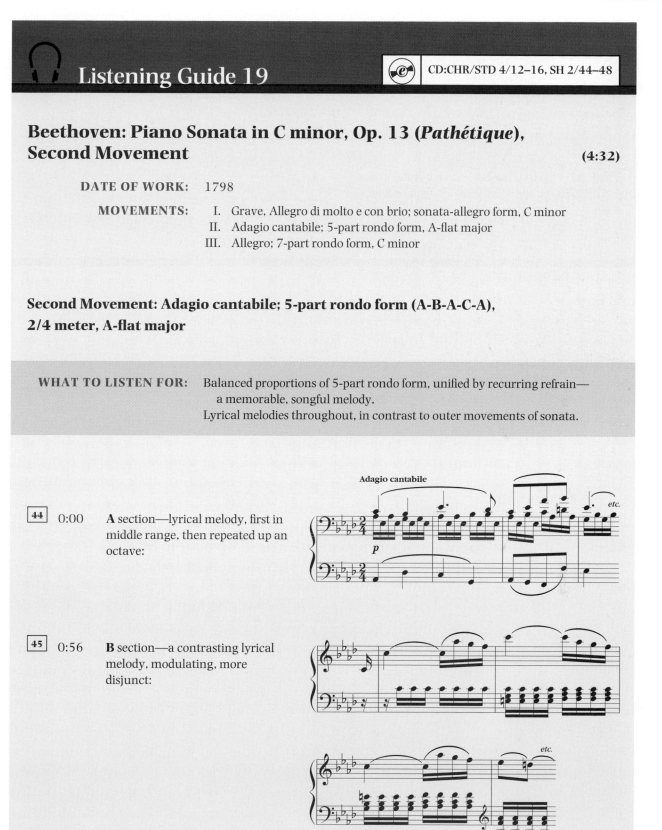

44	0:00	**A** section—lyrical melody, first in middle range, then repeated up an octave:
45	0:56	**B** section—a contrasting lyrical melody, modulating, more disjunct:
46	1:44	**A** section—returns in A-flat major.

| 47 | 2:13 | **C** section—more dramatic episode, with triplet figures, accents, and arpeggios: |

| 48 | 2:56 | **A** section—returns in A-flat major, more rhythmically animated, in triplets. |

Coda

Choral Music and Opera in the Classical Era

e Learning

RESOURCE CD

*e*Music

Beethoven, Symphony No. 9 in D minor, IV *(Ode to Joy)*

*e*LGs

20 Mozart, Opera: *The Marriage of Figaro*

ONLINE TUTOR
www.wwnorton.com/enjoy

Composers: Classical

Joseph Haydn

Wolfgang Amadeus Mozart

Franz Schubert

Resources: Classical

Listening: Classical

Transitions: Classical to Romantic

Quizzes: Classical

Reviewing 14

Listening 13

38

Sacred Choral Music and Opera

"Make a joyful noise to the Lord, all the earth; break forth into joyous song and sing praises."

—PSALM 98

KEY POINTS

- The Mass, Requiem Mass, and the oratorio were the dominant sacred choral forms of the Classical era.
- Haydn wrote two oratorios, including *The Creation,* based on the book of Genesis and on John Milton's *Paradise Lost.*
- In the Classical era, *opera buffa* (Italian comic opera) and *opera seria* (Italian serious opera) prevailed. In addition, there were nationalistic styles (*opéra comique, Singspiel, ballad opera*), sung in the vernacular (language of the people).
- *The Marriage of Figaro* is one of Mozart's most popular comic operas; it is based on a play by Beaumarchais, with a libretto by Lorenzo da Ponte.
- In *The Marriage of Figaro,* the aristocracy is satirized, and the servants (Figaro, Susannah, and Cherubino) outsmart the nobility (the Count).
- In opera, each *aria* allows for emotional expression, while the *recitative* moves the action forward.

Choral Forms

The late eighteenth century inherited a rich tradition of choral music from the Baroque. Among the principal genres were the Mass and Requiem. A *Mass,* you

An opera performance at Eszterháza. The musician at the harpsichord (far left, bottom) is thought to be Haydn. Anonymous eighteenth-century watercolor. (Deutsches Theatermuseum, Munich)

will recall, is a musical setting of the most solemn service of the Roman Catholic Church, and a *Requiem* is a musical setting of the Mass for the Dead. Both types were originally intended to be performed in church. By the nineteenth century, they had found a much larger audience in the concert hall.

The blending of many voices in a large space such as a church or cathedral could not fail to be an uplifting experience. For this reason, both the Catholic and Protestant churches were patrons of choral music throughout the ages. Haydn and Mozart made significant contributions to the Mass repertory. Haydn's Mass in D minor (*Lord Nelson*) remains one of his most frequently performed works, and Mozart's Requiem, his last composition, quickly established itself as one of the masterpieces of the Classical Viennese School.

Another important genre was the oratorio, made popular by Handel in such works as *Messiah*. Haydn wrote two oratorios—*The Creation* and *The Seasons*, which attained enormous popularity and helped build a new audience for these genres.

Classical Opera

The opera house was a center of experimentation in the Classical era. Opera was the most important branch of musical entertainment, the one that reached the widest public. The point of departure was the music, which imposed its forms on the drama.

The opera of the early eighteenth century accurately reflected the society out of which it sprang. The prevalent form was *opera seria*, "serious," or tragic, Italian opera, a highly formalized genre inherited from the Baroque consisting mainly of recitatives and arias specifically designed to display the virtuosity of star singers to the aristocracy. Its rigid conventions were shaped largely by the poet Pietro Metastasio (1698–1782), whose librettos, featuring stories of kings and heroes drawn from the legends of antiquity, were set again and again throughout the century.

Opera seria

I like an aria to fit a singer as perfectly as a well-tailored suit of clothes.
—W.A. Mozart

Increasingly, however, the need was felt for simplicity and naturalness, for a style of opera that reflected human emotions more realistically. One impulse toward reform came from the operas of Christoph Willibald Gluck, whose achievement in this regard was recounted earlier (see p. 176). Another resulted in the popular comic opera that flourished in every country of Europe. Known in England as *ballad*, or *dialogue*, *opera*, in Germany as *Singspiel*, in France as *opéra comique*, and in Italy as *opera buffa*, this lighter genre was the response of the rising middle class to the aristocratic form it would inevitably supplant.

Comic opera

Comic opera differed from opera seria in several basic ways. It was sung in the language of the audience rather than in Italian, which was the standard language of international opera. It presented lively, down-to-earth plots rather than dealing with the remote concerns of gods and mythological heroes. It featured an exciting ensemble at the end of each act in which all the characters participated, instead of an unbroken succession of solo arias, as the older style did. And it abounded in farcical situations, humorous dialogue, popular tunes, and the impertinent remarks of the *buffo*, the traditional character derived from the theater of buffoons, who spoke to the audience in a bass voice, with a wink and a nod—a new sound in theaters previously dominated by the artificial soprano voice of the castrato.

As the Age of Revolution approached, comic opera became an important social force whose lively wit delighted even the aristocrats it satirized. Classical opera buffa spread quickly, steadily expanding its scope until it culminated in the works of Mozart, the greatest dramatist of the eighteenth century.

Mozart's Comic Opera The Marriage of Figaro

Mozart found his ideal librettist in Lorenzo da Ponte (1749–1838), an Italian-Jewish adventurer and poet whose dramatic vitality matched the composer's own. Their collaboration produced three great operas: *The Marriage of Figaro*, *Don Giovanni*, and *Cosí fan tutte* (*Women Are Like That*).

Da Ponte adapted his libretto for *The Marriage of Figaro* from a play by Pierre-Augustin Caron de Beaumarchais (1732–1799), a truly revolutionary work in that it satirized the upper classes and allowed a servant—Figaro, the clever and cocky valet of Count Almaviva—to outwit his master. Vienna was even more conservative than Paris: the play was forbidden there. But what could not be spoken could be sung. Mozart's opera was produced at Vienna's Imperial Court Theater in May 1786, and brought him the greatest success of his life.

Although *The Marriage of Figaro* came out of the rich tradition of popular comic opera, Mozart's genius lifted the genre to another dimension. In place of the stereotyped characters of opera buffa, he created real human beings who come alive through his music. The Count is a likable ladies' man; the Countess is noble in her suffering. Her maid, Susanna, is pert and endlessly resourceful in resisting the advances of her master. Figaro is equally resourceful in foiling the schemes of the Count. And the Countess's page, Cherubino, is irresistible in his boyish innocence and ardor.

The action weaves a complex web: the Count has designs on Figaro's bride, Susanna; the housekeeper is interested in Figaro; and Cherubino is smitten with the Countess. We first hear Cherubino's aria from Act I, "Non so più," which establishes his character as a young man in love with love. "I no longer know who I am or what I'm doing," he sings. "Every woman I see makes me blush and tremble." In Classical opera, the part of a young man was often sung by a

in his own words

In an opera the poetry must be altogether the obedient daughter. . . . An opera is sure of success when the plot is well worked out, and when the words are written solely for the music, not shoved in here and there to suit some miserable rhyme. . . . The best of all is when a good composer, who understands the stage and is talented enough to make sound suggestions, meets a true phoenix, an able poet.

Act I

"The Count discovers the Page." Detail of an illustration from the first Paris edition of Beaumarchais's comedy *Le Mariage de Figaro*, engraved by **Jean-Baptiste Liénard,** 1785.

soprano or alto wearing trousers. In Mozart's opera, the mezzo-soprano voice is ideally suited to Cherubino's romantic idealism. (For the Italian and English text and an analysis of the aria, see Listening Guide 20.)

Cherubino's aria

Cherubino's aria is followed by recitative, the rapid-fire, talky kind of singing whose main function is to advance the plot. Eighteenth-century audiences accepted this change of texture and orchestration just as today we accept, in a Broadway musical, the change from song to spoken dialogue.

The action moves rapidly, with overtones of farce. Cherubino has sung his love song to the Countess in Susanna's room. When the Count arrives to ask Susanna to meet him that night in the garden, Cherubino hides behind a huge armchair. At this point, the music master Basilio, a gossip if ever there was one, arrives looking for the Count, who also tries to hide behind the chair. Susanna cleverly places herself between the Count and Cherubino, so that the page is able to slip in front of the chair and curl up in it, where she covers him with a throw. With both the front and back of the armchair occupied, Susanna scolds Basilio as a busybody. At this point, the Count reveals his presence (see illustration above).

Susanna is aghast that the Count has been discovered in her room. The Count, having overheard Basilio say that Cherubino adores the Countess, is angry with the young man. And Basilio thoroughly enjoys the rumpus he has stirred up. The action stops as Susanna, the Count, and Basilio join in a trio in which they express their individual emotions, with quick exchanges between the three voices and much repetition of text. No one has ever equaled Mozart's ability to reconcile the demands of a dramatic situation with the requirements

The trio

of absolute musical form, and this trio ("Cosa sento! Tosto andate"), which is related to sonata form, is a good example.

When the Count finally pulls the cloth from the chair and discovers Cherubino, he vows to banish him from the estate. At this point, Figaro arrives with a group of peasants. He has told them that the Count has decided to abolish the "right of the first night," the hated feudal privilege that gave the lord of the manor the right to deflower every young woman in his domain. In their gratitude, the peasants have come to serenade their master, singing, "His great kindness preserves the purity of a bride for the one she loves." Figaro, delighted to have forced the Count's hand, announces his impending marriage to Susanna, and the Count plays along by accepting the tributes of the crowd.

Figaro then intercedes for Cherubino with his master, whereupon the Count relents, appoints the page to a captain's post in his regiment, and leaves with Basilio. The complications in the next three acts (and there are many) lead to a happy ending: the Count is reconciled with his wife, and Figaro wins his beloved Susanna.

Two centuries have passed since Mozart's characters first strutted across the stage. They live on today in every major opera house in the world, lifted above time and fashion by the genius of their creator.

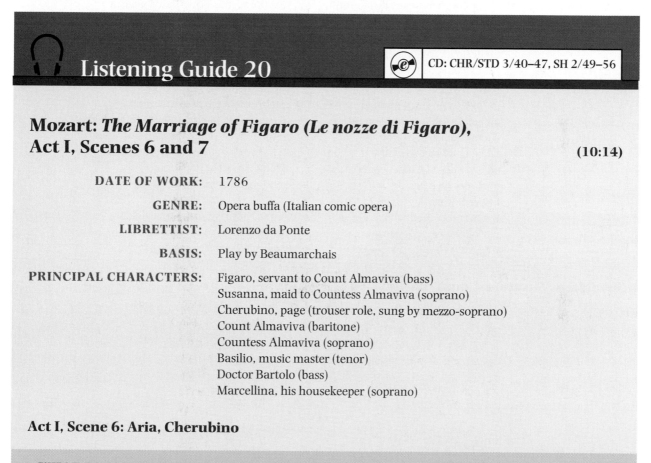

Listening Guide 20

CD: CHR/STD 3/40–47, SH 2/49–56

Mozart: *The Marriage of Figaro (Le nozze di Figaro),* Act I, Scenes 6 and 7

(10:14)

DATE OF WORK:	1786
GENRE:	Opera buffa (Italian comic opera)
LIBRETTIST:	Lorenzo da Ponte
BASIS:	Play by Beaumarchais
PRINCIPAL CHARACTERS:	Figaro, servant to Count Almaviva (bass)
	Susanna, maid to Countess Almaviva (soprano)
	Cherubino, page (trouser role, sung by mezzo-soprano)
	Count Almaviva (baritone)
	Countess Almaviva (soprano)
	Basilio, music master (tenor)
	Doctor Bartolo (bass)
	Marcellina, his housekeeper (soprano)

Act I, Scene 6: Aria, Cherubino

WHAT TO LISTEN FOR: Breathless and quick opening of love song, reflecting the character's emotional state.
Return of opening (**A**) unifies the 4-part structure (**A-B-A-C**).

Form: **A-B-A-C,** followed by recitative
A—quick rhythms (in E-flat):

B—more lyrical (in B-flat):

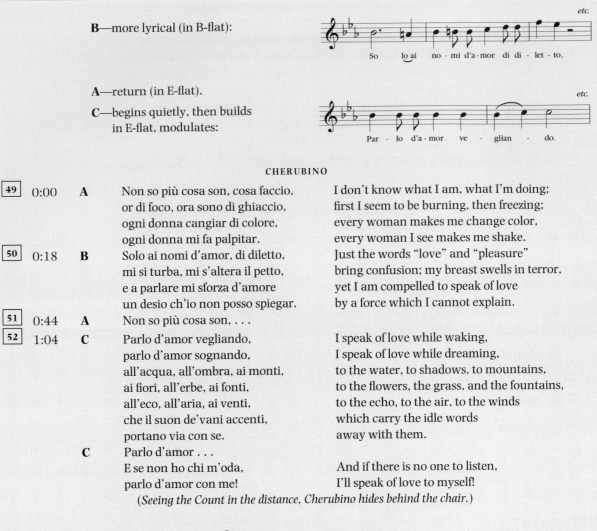

etc.

So lo ai no · mi d'a · mor di di · let · to,

A—return (in E-flat).

C—begins quietly, then builds in E-flat, modulates:

etc.

Par · lo d'a · mor ve · glian · do.

CHERUBINO

49	0:00	**A**	Non so più cosa son, cosa faccio,	I don't know what I am, what I'm doing;
			or di foco, ora sono di ghiaccio,	first I seem to be burning, then freezing;
			ogni donna cangiar di colore,	every woman makes me change color,
			ogni donna mi fa palpitar.	every woman I see makes me shake.
50	0:18	**B**	Solo ai nomi d'amor, di diletto,	Just the words "love" and "pleasure"
			mi si turba, mi s'altera il petto,	bring confusion; my breast swells in terror,
			e a parlare mi sforza d'amore	yet I am compelled to speak of love
			un desio ch'io non posso spiegar.	by a force which I cannot explain.
51	0:44	**A**	Non so più cosa son, . . .	
52	1:04	**C**	Parlo d'amor vegliando,	I speak of love while waking,
			parlo d'amor sognando,	I speak of love while dreaming,
			all'acqua, all'ombra, ai monti,	to the water, to shadows, to mountains,
			ai fiori, all'erbe, ai fonti,	to the flowers, the grass, and the fountains,
			all'eco, all'aria, ai venti,	to the echo, to the air, to the winds
			che il suon de'vani accenti,	which carry the idle words
			portano via con se.	away with them.
	C		Parlo d'amor . . .	
			E se non ho chi m'oda,	And if there is no one to listen,
			parlo d'amor con me!	I'll speak of love to myself!

(Seeing the Count in the distance, Cherubino hides behind the chair.)

Recitative: Susanna, Count, Basilio

WHAT TO LISTEN FOR: Rapid, conversational style that moves action ahead.

CHERUBINO

| 53 | 2:50 | Ah! Son perduto! | I'm done for! |

SUSANNA

Che timor . . . il Conte! Misera me!   I'm afraid . . . the Count! Poor me!

(tries to conceal Cherubino)

COUNT ALMAVIVA (ENTERING)

Susanna, tu mi sembri agitata e confusa.   Susanna, you seem to be agitated and confused.

SUSANNA

Signor, io chiedo scusa,   My lord, I beg your pardon,
ma, se mai, qui sorpresa,   but . . . indeed . . . the surprise . . .
par carità, partite.   I implore you, please go.

COUNT

(sits down on the chair and takes Susanna's hand; she draws it forcibly away)

Un momento, e ti lascio. Odi.   One moment, then I'll leave. Listen.

SUSANNA

Non odo nulla.   I don't want to hear anything.

COUNT

Due parole: tu sai che ambasciatore   Just a word; you know that the king
a Londra il Re mi dichiarò;   has named me ambassador to London;
di condur meco Figaro destinai.   I had intended to take Figaro with me.

SUSANNA

Signor, se osassi—   My lord, if I dare—

COUNT *(rising)*

Parla, parla, mia cara,   Speak, speak, my dear,
e con quel dritto ch'oggi prendi su me,   and with that right you have of me today,
finchè tu vivi chiedi, imponi, prescrivi.   as long as you live, you may ask, demand,
                                             prescribe.

SUSANNA

Lasciatemi, signor,   Let go of me, my lord,
dritti non prendo,   I have no rights,
non ne vò, non ne intendo.   I do not want them, nor claim them.
Oh me infelice!   Oh, what misery!

COUNT

Ah no, Susanna, io ti vò far felice!   Ah no, Susanna, I want to make you happy!
Tu ben sai quanto io t'amo;   You well know how much I love you;
a te Basilio tutto già disse.   Basilio has told you that already.
Or senti, se per pochi momenti meco   Now listen, if you would meet me
in giardin, sull'imbrunir del giorno,   briefly in the garden at dusk,
ah, per questo favore io pagherei . . .   ah, for this favor I would pay . . .

BASILIO *(outside the door)*

E uscito poco fa.   He went out just now.

COUNT

Chi parla?   Whose voice is that?

SUSANNA

O Dei!   Oh, heavens!

COUNT

Esci, ed alcun non entri.   Go, and let no one come in.

SUSANNA

Ch'io vi lasci qui solo?   And leave you here alone?

BASILIO *(outside)*

Da madama sarà, vado a cercarlo.   He'll be with my lady, I'll go and find him.

COUNT

Qui dietro mi porrò.	I'll get behind here.

(points to the chair)

SUSANNA

Non vi celate.	No, don't hide.

COUNT

Taci, e cerca ch'ei parta.	Hush, and try to make him go.

SUSANNA

Ohimè! che fate?	Oh dear! What are you doing?

(The Count is about to hide behind the chair; Susanna steps between him and the page. The count pushes her gently away. She draws back; meanwhile the page slips round to the front of the chair and hops in with his feet drawn up. Susanna rearranges the dress to cover him.)

BASILIO

Susanna, il ciel vi salvi!	Heaven bless you, Susanna!
Avreste a caso veduto il Conte?	Have you seen his lordship by any chance?

SUSANNA

E cosa deve far meco il Conte?	And what should his lordship be doing here
Animo, uscite.	with me? Come now, be gone!

BASILIO

Aspettate, sentite, Figaro di lui cerca.	But listen, Figaro is looking for him.

SUSANNA *(aside)*

Oh cielo!	Oh dear! Then he's looking for the one
Ei cerca chi, dopo voi, più l'odia.	man who, after you, hates him most!

COUNT *(aside)*

Vediam come mi serve.	Now we'll see how he serves me.

BASILIO

Io non ho mai nella moral sentito	I have never heard it preached that
ch'uno ch'ama la moglie odi il marito,	one who loves the wife should hate the husband;
per dir che il Conte v'ama.	that's a way of saying the Count loves you.

SUSANNA

Sortite, vil ministro dell'altrui sfrenatezza:	Get out, vile minister of others' lechery!
io non ho d'uopo della vostra morale,	I have no need of your preaching
del Conte, del suo amor!	nor of the Count or his lovemaking!

BASILIO

Non c'è alcun male.	No offense meant.
Ha ciascun i suoi gusti.	Everyone to their own taste.
Io mi credea che preferir	I thought you would have preferred
doveste per amante,	as your lover,
come fan tutte quante,	as all other women would,
un signor liberal, prudente, e saggio,	a lord who's liberal, prudent, and wise,
a un giovinastro, a un paggio.	to a raw youth, a mere page.

SUSANNA

A Cherubino?	To Cherubino?

BASILIO

A Cherubino! Cherubin d'amore,	To Cherubino! Love's little cherub
ch'oggi sul far del giorno	who early today
passeggiava qui intorno per entrar.	was hanging about here waiting to come in.

SUSANNA

Uom maligno, un'impostura è questa.	You insinuating wretch, that's a lie.

BASILIO

E un maligno con voi	Do you call it an insinuation
chi ha gli occhi in testa?	to have eyes in one's head?
E quella canzonetta,	And that little ditty,
ditemi in confidenza,	tell me confidentially
io sono amico,	as a friend,
ed altrui nulla dico,	and I will tell no one else,
è per voi, per madama?	was it written for you or my lady?

SUSANNA (aside)

Chi diavol gliel'ha detto?	Who the devil told him about that?

BASILIO

A proposito, figlia, istruitelo meglio.	By the way, my child, you must teach him
Egli la guarda a tavola sí spesso,	better. At table he gazes at her so often
e con tale immodestia,	and so wantonly,
che s'il Conte s'accorge—	that if the Count noticed it—
e sul tal punto sapete, egli è una bestia—	on that subject, as you know, he's quite wild—

SUSANNA

Scellerato! e perchè andate voi	You wretch! Why do you go around
tai menzogne spargendo?	spreading such lies?

BASILIO

Io! che ingiustizia!	I! How unfair!
Quel che compro io vendo,	That which I buy I sell,
a quel che tutti dicono,	and to what is common knowledge
io non ci aggiungo un pelo.	I add not a tittle.

COUNT (emerging from his hiding place)

Come! che dicon tutti?	Indeed! And what is common knowledge?

BASILIO (aside)

Oh bella!	How wonderful!

SUSANNA

Oh cielo!	Oh heavens!

Act I, Scene 7: Terzetto (Trio), Count, Basilio, Susanna

WHAT TO LISTEN FOR: Lively exchanges between 3 characters, each with different emotional reaction to the situation.
Structure reminiscent of a 3-part sonata-allegro form (with development and recapitulation).

Form: Sonata-type structure, with development and recapitulation
Style: Quick exchange between voices; much text repetition; each character with own emotional commentary

The Count—angry:

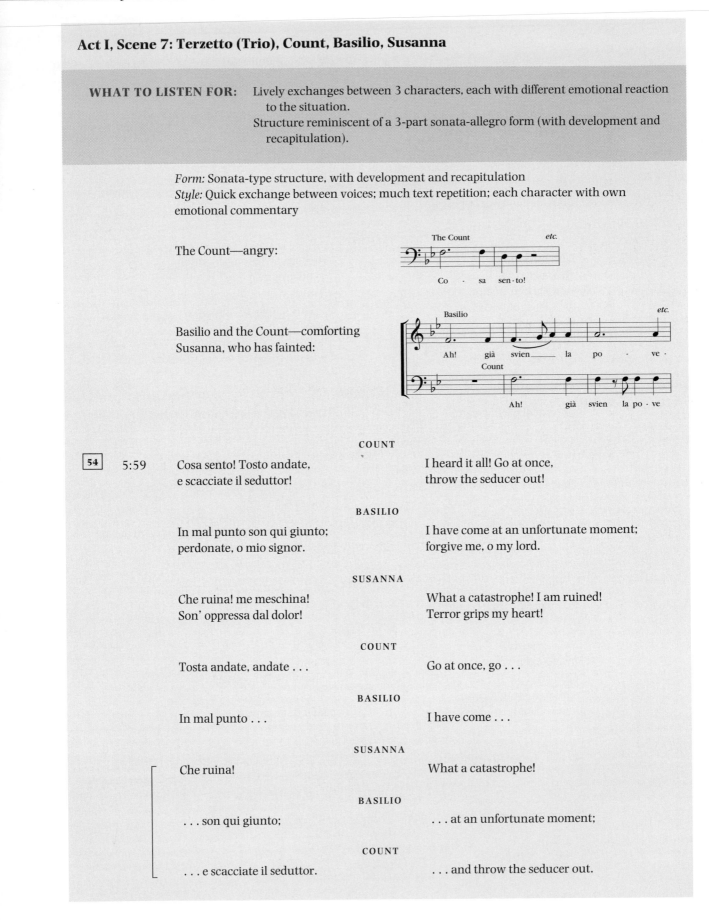

Basilio and the Count—comforting Susanna, who has fainted:

54	5:59	**COUNT**
		Cosa sento! Tosto andate, e scacciate il seduttor!	I heard it all! Go at once, throw the seducer out!

COUNT

Cosa sento! Tosto andate,
e scacciate il seduttor!

I heard it all! Go at once,
throw the seducer out!

BASILIO

In mal punto son qui giunto;
perdonate, o mio signor.

I have come at an unfortunate moment;
forgive me, o my lord.

SUSANNA

Che ruina! me meschina!
Son' oppressa dal dolor!

What a catastrophe! I am ruined!
Terror grips my heart!

COUNT

Tosta andate, andate . . .

Go at once, go . . .

BASILIO

In mal punto . . .

I have come . . .

SUSANNA

Che ruina!

What a catastrophe!

BASILIO

. . . son qui giunto;

. . . at an unfortunate moment;

COUNT

. . . e scacciate il seduttor.

. . . and throw the seducer out.

248

BASILIO

. . . perdonate, o mio signor.   . . . forgive me, o my lord.

SUSANNA

Me meschina!   I am ruined!
Me meschina!   I am ruined!
Son' oppressa dal dolor.   Terror grips my heart.

BASILIO, COUNT *(supporting Susanna)*

Ah! già svien la poverina!   Ah! The poor girl's fainted!
Come, oh Dio! le batte il cor.   O God, how her heart is beating.

BASILIO

Pian, pianin, su questo seggio—   Gently, gently on to the chair—
                (taking her to the chair)

SUSANNA *(coming to)*

Dove sono? Cosa veggio?   Where am I? What's this I see?
Che insolenza! andate fuor.   What insolence! Leave this room.

BASILIO, COUNT

Siamo qui per aiutarvi, . . .   We're here to help you, . . .

BASILIO

. . . è sicuro il vostro onor.   . . . your virtue is safe.

COUNT

. . . non turbarti, o mio tesor.   . . . do not worry, sweetheart.

BASILIO

Ah, del paggio, quel che ho detto,   What I was saying about the page
era solo un mio sospetto.   was only my own suspicion.

SUSANNA

E un'insidia, una perfidia,   It was a nasty insinuation,
non credete all'impostor.   do not believe the liar.

COUNT

55   7:48   Parta, parta il damerino, . . .   The young fop must go, . . .

SUSANNA, BASILIO

Poverino!   Poor boy!

COUNT

. . . parta, parta il damerino.   . . . the young fop must go.

SUSANNA, BASILIO

Poverino!   Poor boy!

COUNT

Poverino! poverino!   Poor boy! Poor boy!
ma da me sorpreso ancor!   But I caught him yet again!

SUSANNA

Come? | How?

BASILIO

Che? | What?

SUSANNA

Che? | What?

BASILIO

Come? | How?

SUSANNA, BASILIO

Come? che? | How? What?

COUNT

Da tua cugina,	At your cousin's house
l'uscio jer trovai rinchiuso,	I found the door shut yesterday.
picchio, m'apre Barbarina	I knocked and Barbarina opened it
paurosa fuor dell'uso.	much more timidly than usual.
Io, dal muso insospettito,	My suspicions aroused by her expression,
guardo, cerco in ogni sito,	I had a good look around,
ed alzando pian, pianino,	and very gently lifting
il tappeto al tavolino,	the cloth upon the table,
vedo il paggio.	I found the page.

(imitating his own action with the dress over the chair, he reveals the page)

Ah, cosa veggio? | Ah, what do I see?

SUSANNA

Ah! crude stelle! | Ah! wicked fate!

BASILIO

Ah! meglio ancora! | Ah! better still!

COUNT

56	8:54	Onestissima signora, . . .	Most virtuous lady, . . .

SUSANNA

Accader non può di peggio. | Nothing worse could happen!

COUNT

. . . or capisco come va! | . . . now I see what's happening!

SUSANNA

Giusti Dei, che mai sarà! | Merciful heaven, whatever will happen?

BASILIO

Cosí fan tutte . . . | They're all the same . . .

SUSANNA

Giusti Dei! che mai sarà	Merciful heaven! Whatever will happen?
Accader non può di peggio,	Nothing worse could happen!
ah no! ah no!	ah no! ah no!

BASILIO

. . . le belle,
non c'è alcuna novità,
cosí fan tutte.

. . . the fair sex,
there's nothing new about it,
they're all the same.

COUNT

Or capisco come va,
onestissima signora!
or capisco, *ecc.*

Now I see what's happening,
most virtuous lady!
Now I see, *etc.*

BASILIO

Ah, del paggio, quel che ho detto,
era solo un mio sospetto.

What I was saying about the page
was only my own suspicion.

SUSANNA

Accader non può di peggio, *ecc.*

Nothing worse could happen, *etc.*

COUNT

Onestissima signora, *ecc.*

Most virtuous lady, *etc.*

BASILIO

Cosí fan tutte, *ecc.*

They're all the same, *etc.*

From Classicism to Romanticism

"I am in the world only for the purpose of composing. What I feel in my heart, I give to the world."

—FRANZ SCHUBERT

KEY POINTS

- Like Beethoven, Viennese composer Franz Schubert is a transitional figure between eighteenth-century Classicism and the new spirit of Romanticism.
- Schubert's symphonies and chamber music follow in the Classical tradition of Haydn, Mozart, and Beethoven; his songs, however, reflect Romantic elements.

We have studied three great masters of the Viennese Classical School: Haydn, Mozart, and Beethoven. Certain characteristics of Beethoven's music—his striking dynamic contrasts, his explosive accents, his expansion of strict Classical forms, his hymnlike slow movements, and the overall dramatic intensity of his music—clearly foreshadow the Romantic style.

The music of another Viennese master, Franz Schubert (1797–1828), reveals him to be heir to the Classical tradition. In his approach to chamber music and the symphony, Schubert followed in a direct line of development from Haydn, Mozart, and Beethoven. But Schubert's life coincided with the first upsurge of Romanticism, and in his songs we can hear many of the prime interests of this new Romanticism, especially a fascination with nature. One song that beautifully captures the imagery of the subject is *The Trout (Die Forelle)*, with its folklike melody and bubbling accompaniment. Two years after he wrote this song, Schubert used the tune in the fourth movement of his popular Piano Quintet in A major (known as the *Trout*). This chamber music movement, a theme and variations, and the song that forms its basis, reveal in Schubert the happy marriage of Classical forms and Romantic content. (We will consider Schubert's life and works later.)

A Comparison of Classical and Romantic Styles

	CLASSICAL (C. 1750–1825)	ROMANTIC (C. 1820–1900)
COMPOSERS	Haydn, Mozart, Beethoven, Schubert	Beethoven, Schubert, Fanny Mendelssohn Hensel, Felix Mendelssohn, Clara Schumann, Robert Schumann, Chopin, Liszt, Berlioz, Brahms, Tchaikovsky, Verdi, Wagner
MELODY	Symmetrical melody in balanced phrases and cadences; tuneful; diatonic, with narrow leaps	Expansive, singing melodies; wide ranging; more varied, with chromatic inflections
RHYTHM	Clear rhythmically, with regularly recurring accents; dance rhythms favored	Rhythmic diversity and elasticity; tempo rubato
HARMONY	Diatonic harmony favored; tonic-dominant relationships expanded, became basis for large-scale forms	Increasing chromaticism; expanded concepts of tonality
TEXTURE	Homophonic textures; horizontal perspective	Homophony, turning to increased polyphony in later years of era
INSTRUMENTAL GENRES	Symphony, solo concerto, solo sonata, string quartet	Same large genres, adding one-movement symphonic poem; solo piano works
VOCAL GENRES	Opera, Mass, solo song	Same vocal forms, adding works for solo voice and piano/orchestra
FORM	Ternary form predominant; sonata-allegro form developed; absolute forms preferred	Expansion of forms and interest in continuous as well as miniature programmatic forms
AUDIENCE	Secular music predominant; aristocratic audience	Secular music predominant; middle-class audience
DYNAMICS	Continuously changing dynamics through *crescendo* and *decrescendo*	Widely ranging dynamics for expressive purposes
TIMBRE	Changing tone colors between sections of works	Continual change and blend of tone colors; experiments with new instruments and unusual ranges
PERFORMING FORCES	String orchestra with woodwinds and some brass; 30-to-40-member orchestra; rise of piano to prominence	Introduction of new instruments (tuba, Englishhorn, valved brass, harp, piccolo); much larger orchestras; piano predominant as solo instrument
VIRTUOSITY	Improvisation largely limited to cadenzas in concertos	Increased virtuosity; composers specified more in scores
EXPRESSION	Emotional restraint and balance	Emotions, mood, atmosphere emphasized; interest in the bizarre and macabre

Caspar David Friedrich (1774–1840), *The Chalk Cliffs of Rugen*.

PART 7

The Nineteenth Century

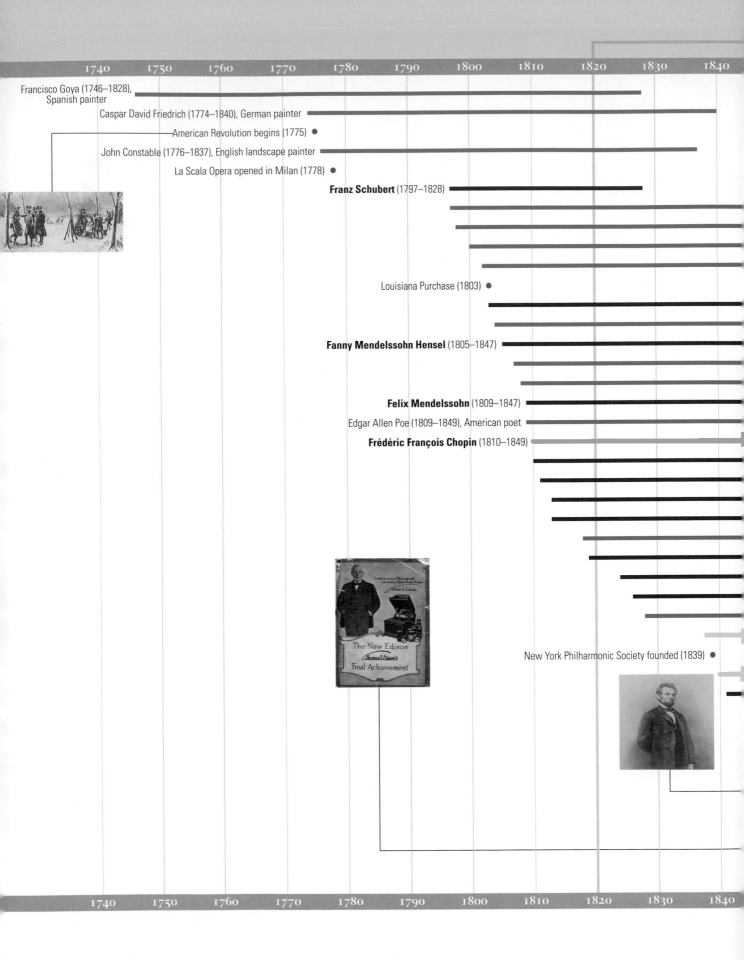

1740　1750　1760　1770　1780　1790　1800　1810　1820　1830　1840

Francisco Goya (1746–1828), Spanish painter

Caspar David Friedrich (1774–1840), German painter

American Revolution begins (1775)

John Constable (1776–1837), English landscape painter

La Scala Opera opened in Milan (1778)

Franz Schubert (1797–1828)

Louisiana Purchase (1803)

Fanny Mendelssohn Hensel (1805–1847)

Felix Mendelssohn (1809–1847)

Edgar Allen Poe (1809–1849), American poet

Frédéric François Chopin (1810–1849)

New York Philharmonic Society founded (1839)

1740　1750　1760　1770　1780　1790　1800　1810　1820　1830　1840

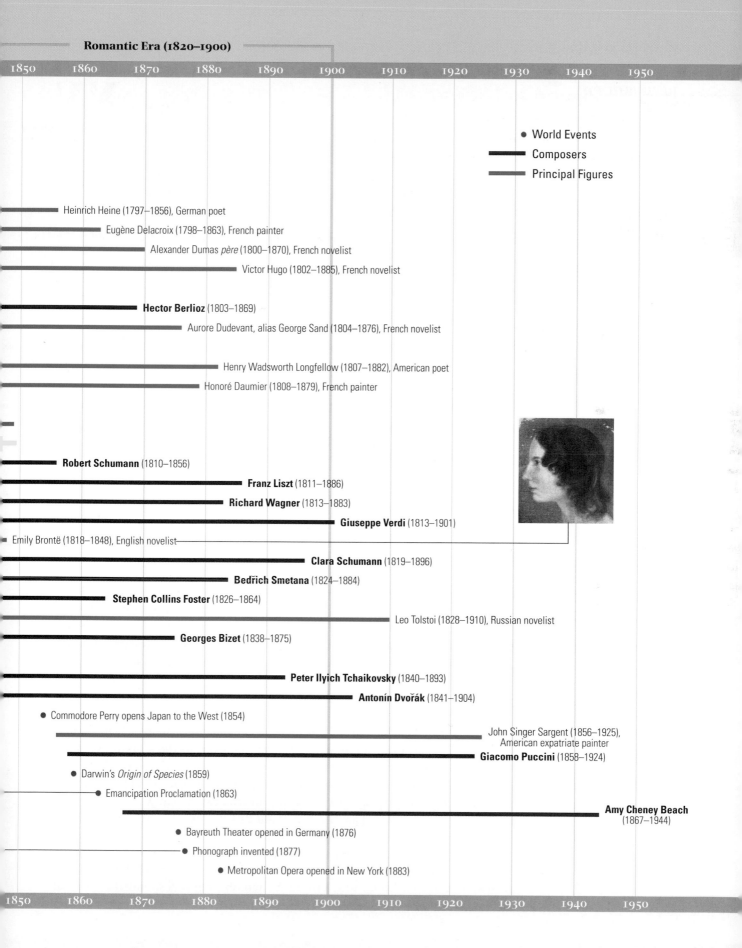

Romantic Era (1820–1900)

| 1850 | 1860 | 1870 | 1880 | 1890 | 1900 | 1910 | 1920 | 1930 | 1940 | 1950 |

- World Events
- Composers
- Principal Figures

Heinrich Heine (1797–1856), German poet

Eugène Delacroix (1798–1863), French painter

Alexander Dumas *père* (1800–1870), French novelist

Victor Hugo (1802–1885), French novelist

Hector Berlioz (1803–1869)

Aurore Dudevant, alias George Sand (1804–1876), French novelist

Henry Wadsworth Longfellow (1807–1882), American poet

Honoré Daumier (1808–1879), French painter

Robert Schumann (1810–1856)

Franz Liszt (1811–1886)

Richard Wagner (1813–1883)

Giuseppe Verdi (1813–1901)

Emily Brontë (1818–1848), English novelist

Clara Schumann (1819–1896)

Bedřich Smetana (1824–1884)

Stephen Collins Foster (1826–1864)

Leo Tolstoi (1828–1910), Russian novelist

Georges Bizet (1838–1875)

Peter Ilyich Tchaikovsky (1840–1893)

Antonín Dvořák (1841–1904)

- Commodore Perry opens Japan to the West (1854)

John Singer Sargent (1856–1925), American expatriate painter

Giacomo Puccini (1858–1924)

- Darwin's *Origin of Species* (1859)

- Emancipation Proclamation (1863)

Amy Cheney Beach (1867–1944)

- Bayreuth Theater opened in Germany (1876)

- Phonograph invented (1877)

- Metropolitan Opera opened in New York (1883)

| 1850 | 1860 | 1870 | 1880 | 1890 | 1900 | 1910 | 1920 | 1930 | 1940 | 1950 |

e Learning

RESOURCE CD

*e*Music

Beethoven, *Ruins of Athens,* "Turkish March"

Puccini, "O mio babbino caro," from *Gianni Schicchi*

ONLINE TUTOR
www.wwnorton.com/enjoy

Overview: Romantic

    Historical Themes

    Musical Context

    Style

Resources: Romantic

Listening: Romantic

Transitions:

    Classical to Romantic

Quizzes: Romantic

    Reviewing 15

Glossary

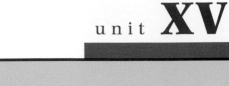

unit XV

The Romantic Movement

39

The Spirit of Romanticism

"Music, of all the liberal arts, has the greatest influence over the passions."

—NAPOLEON BONAPARTE

KEY POINTS

- The French Revolution resulted in the rise of a middle-class, or bourgeois, society.
- Romantic poets and artists abandoned traditional subjects, turning instead to the passionate and the fanciful; novels explored deep human conflicts and exotic settings.

French Revolution   The Romantic era, which grew out of the social and political upheavals that followed the French Revolution, came into full blossom in the second quarter of the nineteenth century. The French Revolution resulted from the inevitable clash between momentous social forces. It signaled the transfer of power from a hereditary landholding aristocracy to the middle class, firmly rooted in urban commerce and industry. Like the American Revolution, this upheaval ushered in a social order shaped by the technological advances of the Industrial Revolution. The new society, based on free enterprise, emphasized the individual as never before. The slogan of the French Revolution—"Liberty, Equality, Fraternity"—inspired hopes and visions to which artists responded with zeal. Sympathy for the oppressed, interest in simple folk and in children, faith in

254

The spirit of the French Revolution is captured in *Liberty Leading the People,* by **Eugène Delacroix** (1798–1863). (The Louvre, Paris)

humankind and its destiny, all formed part of the increasingly democratic character of the Romantic period.

The Romantic poets rebelled against the conventional concerns of their Classical predecessors; these poets were drawn to the fanciful, the picturesque, and the passionate. One of the prime traits of all Romantic artists was their emphasis on intensely emotional expression. Another was their sense of uniqueness, their heightened awareness of themselves as individuals apart from all others. "I am different from all the men I have seen," proclaimed Jean Jacques Rousseau. "If I am not better, at least I am different." In Germany, a group of young writers created a new kind of lyric poetry that culminated in the art of Heinrich Heine, who became a favorite poet of Romantic composers. A similar movement in France was led by Victor Hugo, its greatest prose writer, and Alphonse de Lamartine, its greatest poet. In England, the revolt against the formalism of the Classical age produced an outpouring of lyric poetry that reached its peak in the works of Byron, Shelley, and Keats.

The newly won freedom of the artist proved to be a mixed blessing. Confronted by a bourgeois world indifferent to artistic and cultural values, artists felt more and more cut off. A new type emerged—the artist as bohemian, the rejected dreamer who starved in an attic and through peculiarities of dress and behavior "shocked the bourgeois." Eternal longing, regret for the lost happiness of childhood, an indefinable discontent that gnawed at the soul—these were the ingredients of the Romantic mood. Yet the artist's pessimism had its basis in reality. It became apparent

Romantic writers

Sympathy for the oppressed underscored the essentially democratic character of the Romantic movement. **Honoré Daumier** (1808–1879), *The Third-Class Carriage.* (Metropolitan Museum of Art, New York)

The nineteenth-century longing for far-off lands inspired exotic scenes such as the painting *Femmes d'Alger*, by **Eugène Delacroix** (1798–1863). (The Louvre, Paris)

> *It is in music, perhaps, that the soul most nearly attains the great end for which, when inspired by the poetic sentiment, it struggles—the creation of supernal beauty.*
> —Edgar Allen Poe

that the high hopes fostered by the revolution were not to be realized overnight. Despite the brave slogans, all people were not yet equal or free. Inevitably optimism gave way to doubt and disenchantment—"the illness of the century."

This state of mind was reflected in the arts of the time. Hugo dedicated *Les misérables* "to the unhappy ones of the earth." The nineteenth-century novel found one of its great themes in the conflict between the individual and society. Jean Valjean, the hero of Hugo's novel, Heathcliff in Emily Brontë's *Wuthering Heights*, and Tolstoy's Anna Karenina are among the memorable characters who point up the frustrations and guilts of the nineteenth century.

Some writers sought escape by glamorizing the past, as did Sir Walter Scott in *Ivanhoe* and Alexandre Dumas *père* in *The Three Musketeers*. A longing for far-off lands inspired the exotic scenes that glow on the canvases of J. M. W. Turner and Eugène Delacroix. The Romantic world was one of "strangeness and wonder": the eerie landscape we meet in Coleridge's *Kubla Khan*, Hawthorne's *The Scarlet Letter*, and Poe's *The Raven*.

Romanticism dominated the artistic output of the nineteenth century. It gave its name to a movement and an era, and created a multitude of colorful works that still hold millions in thrall.

40

Romanticism in Music

"Music is the melody whose text is the world."
—ARTHUR SCHOPENHAUER

KEY POINTS

- The Industrial Revolution spurred many technical advances for instruments and made them more affordable.
- Educational opportunities in music started to broaden as conservatories were established across Europe and the Americas.
- The orchestra grew significantly in size and sound when new and improved instruments were introduced; accordingly, composers demanded new levels of expression.
- Romantic composers exploited nationalistic folklore and exotic subjects from far-away lands.
- Romantic music is characterized by memorable melodies, richly expressive harmony, and broad, expanded forms.
- The Romantic era saw the rise of the virtuoso soloist and of professional and amateur music making.
- Women musicians achieved an elevated status in society as performers, teachers, composers, and music patrons.

Art mirrors the great social forces of its time. Thus Romantic music reflected the profound changes that were taking place in the nineteenth century at every level of human existence.

Improved musical instruments

The Industrial Revolution brought with it the means to create cheaper and more responsive musical instruments, with technical improvements that strongly influenced the sound of Romantic music. For example, the addition of valves to brass instruments made them much more maneuverable, so that composers like Wagner and Tchaikovsky could write melodies for the horns and trumpets that would have been unplayable in the time of Haydn and Mozart. Several new wind instruments were developed as well, including the tuba and the saxophone. As a result of improved manufacturing techniques, the piano acquired a cast-iron frame and thicker strings, giving it a deeper and more brilliant tone. If a piano work by Liszt sounds different from a sonata by Mozart, it is not only because Liszt's era demanded a different kind of expression, but also because he was writing for a piano capable of effects that were impossible in the earlier period.

Increased educational opportunities

The gradual democratization of society resulted in a broadening of educational opportunities. New conservatories were established in the chief cities of Europe to train more and better musicians, so that nineteenth-century composers could count on performers whose skill was considerably more advanced than in former times.

Rehearsal of the Pasdeloup Orchestra at the Cirque d'Hiver, by **John Singer Sargeant** (1856–1925). (The Hayden Collection, Boston Museum of Fine Arts)

As music moved from palace and church to the public concert hall, orchestras increased in size, giving composers a more varied and colorful means of expression. This naturally had a direct influence on the sound. New instruments such as the piccolo, English horn, and contrabassoon added varied timbres and extended the extreme high and low ranges of the orchestra (see table below). The dynamic range also expanded. It was far greater than that of the eighteenth-century ensemble—sweeping contrasts of loud (*fff*) and soft (*ppp*) now lent new drama to the music of the Romantics. And as orchestral music developed, so did the technique of writing for instruments—individually and together. *Orchestration* became an art in itself. Composers now had a palette as broad as painters', and they used it to create mood and atmosphere, to suggest nature scenes, and to evoke profound emotional responses. With all these developments, it was no longer feasible to direct an orchestra from the keyboard or the first violin desk, as had been the tradition in the eighteenth century, and thus the practice of having a central figure—the conductor—guide the performance became widely accepted.

In order to communicate their intentions as precisely as possible, composers developed a vocabulary of highly expressive terms. Among the directions frequently encountered in nineteenth-century musical scores are *dolce* (sweetly), *cantabile* (songful), *dolente* (weeping), *mesto* (sad), *maestoso* (majestic), *gioioso* (joyous), *con amore* (with love, tenderly). These and similar terms suggest not only the character of the music but the frame of mind behind it.

Use of folklore

The interest in folklore and the rising tide of nationalism inspired Romantic musicians to make increased use of the folk songs and dances of their native lands. As a result, a number of national idioms—Hungarian, Polish, Russian, Bohemian, Scandinavian, and eventually American—flourished, greatly enriching the melodic, harmonic, and rhythmic language of music.

Exoticism

Nineteenth-century exoticism manifested itself first in the northern nations' longing for the warmth and color of the south, and second in the West's interest in the fairy-tale splendors of Asia and the Far East. The first impulse found expression in the works of German, French, and Russian composers who turned for inspiration to Italy and Spain.

The glamour of the East was brought to international attention by the Russian national school, whose music is pervaded by the fairy-tale background of Asia. Rimsky-Korsakov's orchestrally resplendent *Sheherazade* is but one example that found favor with Western audiences. A number of French and Italian opera composers also drew on exotic themes: Saint-Saëns in *Samson and Delilah*, Verdi in *Aida*, and Puccini in *Madame Butterfly*, which we will study.

Romantic Style Traits

The nineteenth century above all was the period when musicians tried to make their instruments "sing." It is no accident that themes from Romantic symphonies, concertos, and other instrumental works have been transformed into popular songs, for Romantic melody was marked by a lyricism that gave it an immediate emotional appeal. This is evidenced by the enduring popularity of the tunes of Schubert, Verdi, and Tchaikovsky, among others. Through innumerable songs and operas as well as instrumental pieces, Romantic melody appealed to a wider audience than music ever had before.

Nineteenth-century music strove for a harmony that was highly emotional and expressive. Composers such as Richard Wagner employed various combinations of pitches that were more chromatic and dissonant than those of their predecessors.

> *We have learned to express the more delicate nuances of feeling by penetrating more deeply into the mysteries of harmony.*
> —ROBERT SCHUMANN

The Romantic Orchestra

BERLIOZ'S ORCHESTRA (*Symphonie fantastique*, 1830)	**BRAHMS'S ORCHESTRA** (*Symphony No. 3*, 1883)	**TCHAIKOVSKY'S ORCHESTRA** (*The Nutcracker*, 1892)
STRINGS Violins 1 Violins 2 Violas Cellos Double basses 2 Harps	**STRINGS** Violins 1 Violins 2 Violas Cellos Double basses	**STRINGS** Violins 1 Violins 2 Violas Cellos Double basses 2 Harps
WOODWINDS 2 Flutes (1 on Piccolo) 2 Oboes 2 Clarinets (1 on E-flat Clarinet) 4 Bassoons	**WOODWINDS** 2 Flutes 2 Oboes 2 Clarinets 2 Bassoons, Contrabassoon	**WOODWINDS** 2 Flutes and Piccolo 2 Oboes, 1 English horn 2 Clarinets, Bass clarinet 2 Bassoons
BRASS 4 French horns 2 Cornets, 2 Valved trumpets 3 Trombones (1 Bass trombone) 2 Ophicleides	**BRASS** 4 French horns 2 Trumpets 3 Trombones	**BRASS** 4 French horns 2 Valved trumpets 2 Trombones, Bass trombone Tuba
PERCUSSION Timpani Cymbals Snare drum Bass drum Tubular bells (chimes)	**PERCUSSION** Timpani	**PERCUSSION** Timpani Cymbals, gong Tambourine, castanets Bass drum Tubular bells (chimes) Other special effects (including toy instruments)
		Keyboard Celesta

The Royal Pavilion at Brighton, England (1815–18), with its Islamic domes, minarets, and screens, reflects the nineteenth-century fascination with Eastern culture. Designed by **John Nash** (1752–1835).

Romantic composers gradually expanded the instrumental forms they had inherited from the eighteenth century, to give their ideas more time to play out. A symphony by Haydn or Mozart takes about twenty minutes to perform; one by Tchaikovsky, Brahms, or Dvořák lasts at least twice that long. As public concert life developed, the symphony became the most important genre of orchestral music, comparable to the novel in Romantic literature. New orchestral forms emerged as well, including the one-movement symphonic poem, the choral symphony, and works for solo voice with orchestra.

Music in the nineteenth century drew steadily closer to literature and painting—that is, to elements that lay outside the realm of sound. The connection with Romantic poetry and drama is most obvious in the case of music with words. However, even in their purely orchestral music, the Romantic composers responded to the mood of the time and captured with remarkable vividness the emotional atmosphere that surrounded nineteenth-century poetry and painting.

Nineteenth-century music was linked to dreams and passions, to profound meditations on life and death, human destiny, God and nature, pride in one's country, desire for freedom, the political struggles of the age, the ultimate triumph of good over evil. These intellectual and emotional associations, nurtured by the Romantic movement, brought music into a commanding position as a moral force, a vision of human greatness, and a direct link between the artist's inner life and the outside world.

The Musician in Society

The emergence of a new kind of democratic society strongly affected the lives of composers and performers. Musical life began to center on the public concert hall as well as the salons of the aristocracy and upper middle class. Where eighteenth-century musicians had functioned under the system of aristocratic patronage and had been dependent on the favor of royal courts or the nobility, nineteenth-century musicians were supported by the new middle-class audience, whom they met as equals. Indeed, as solo performers began to dominate the concert hall, whether as pianists, violinists, or conductors, they became "stars" who were idolized by the public. Mendelssohn, Liszt, and Paganini were welcomed into the great homes of their time as celebrities, unlike Haydn and Mozart half a century earlier.

Music thrived both in private homes and in the public life of most cities and towns. Permanent orchestras and singing societies abounded, printed music was readily available at a cost that many could afford, and music journals kept the public informed about musical activities and new works.

With this expansion of musical life, composers and performing artists were called on to assume

Ladies swoon at a performance by Liszt in Berlin.

new roles as educators. Felix Mendelssohn, active as composer, pianist, and conductor, used his immense prestige to found and direct the Leipzig Conservatory, whose curriculum became a model for music schools all over Europe and America. Robert Schumann became a widely read critic. Franz Liszt, a composer, conductor, and considered to be the greatest pianist of his time, taught extensively and trained a generation of great concert pianists. And Richard Wagner directed his own theater at Bayreuth, thus helping the newly interested public understand his music dramas.

Women in Music

We have already observed a handful of women who were recognized in their day as virtuoso performers. The society of the nineteenth century saw women make great strides in establishing careers as professional musicians. This path was now possible through the broadening of educational opportunities; in public conservatories, women could receive training as singers, instrumentalists, and even composers. Likewise, the rise of the piano as the favored chamber instrument—both solo and with voice or instruments—provided women of the middle and upper classes with a performance outlet that was socially acceptable. Women's talents received full expression on the stage, where as opera singers they performed major roles.

Although composition remained largely a man's province, some women broke away from tradition and overcame societal stereotypes to become successful composers: among them were Fanny Mendelssohn Hensel, known for her Lieder, piano music, and chamber works; Clara Schumann, a talented performer and composer of piano and chamber music, whom we will study; and the American Amy Cheney Beach, one of the first women composers to be recognized in the field of orchestral music. (The issues and attitudes surrounding nineteenth-century women composers are discussed further in CP 13 on p. 314.)

Women as patrons

Women also exerted a significant influence as patrons of music or through their friendships with composers. George Sand played an important part in the career of Chopin, while Nadezhda von Meck is remembered as the woman who supported Tchaikovsky in the early years of his career and made it possible for him to compose. Several women of the upper class presided over musical salons where composers could gather to perform and discuss their music. One such musical center was the home of the Mendelssohn family, where Fanny Mendelssohn organized concerts that featured works by her more famous brother, Felix.

All in all, women musicians made steady strides in the direction of professional equality throughout the nineteenth century, and thereby laid the foundation for their even greater achievements in the twentieth.

When [Liszt] sits at the piano and, having repeatedly pushed his hair back over his brow, begins to improvise, then he often rages all too madly upon the ivory keys and lets loose a deluge of heaven-storming ideas, with here and there a few sweet flowers to shed fragrance upon the whole. One feels both blessedness and anxiety, but rather more anxiety. . . .
—Heinrich Heine

e Learning

RESOURCE CD

*e*LGs

21 Schubert: Lied: *Erlking*

22 R. Schumann: Song
cycle: *A Poet's Love*

ONLINE TUTOR
www.wwnorton.com/enjoy

Composers: Romantic

  Franz Schubert

  Robert Schumann

  Fanny Mendelssohn
  Hensel

Resources: Romantic

Listening: Romantic

Quizzes: Romantic

  Reviewing 16

  Listening 14

Glossary

unit **XVI**

Nineteenth-Century Art Song

41

The Romantic Song

"Out of my great sorrows I make my little songs."

—HEINRICH HEINE

KEY POINTS

- The German art song, or *Lied*—for solo voice and piano—was one of the most favored genres of the Romantic era.
- Typical song structures include *strophic* and *through-composed* forms; some songs fall between the two, into a *modified strophic* form.
- Composers wrote *song cycles* that unified a group of songs by poem or theme.
- The poetry of the Lied exploited themes of love and nature; the favored poets were Goethe and Heine.

The art song met the nineteenth-century need for intimate personal expression. The form came into prominence in the early decades of the century and emerged as a favored example of the new lyricism.

Types of Song Structure

Strophic form

In the nineteenth century, two main types of song structure prevailed. One that is already familiar is *strophic form*, in which the same melody is repeated with every stanza, or strophe, of the poem—hymns, carols, and most folk and popular songs are strophic. Although the form permits no real closeness between words and music, it sets up a general atmosphere that accommodates itself equally well to all the stanzas. The first may tell of a lover's expectancy, the second of his joy at seeing his beloved, the third of her father's harshness in separating them, and the fourth of her sad death, all sung to the same tune.

The other song type, what the Germans call *durchkomponiert,* or *through-composed,* proceeds from beginning to end, without repetitions of whole sections. Here the music follows the story line, changing according to the text. This makes it possible for the composer to mirror every shade of meaning in the words.

Through-composed form

There is also an intermediate type that combines features of the other two. The same melody may be repeated for two or three stanzas, with new material introduced when the poem requires it, generally at the climax. This is a *modified strophic form,* of which Robert Schumann's "And if the flowers knew" (Listening Guide 22) is a fine example.

Modified strophic form

The Lied

Though songs have been sung throughout the ages, the art song as we know it today was a product of the Romantic era. Among the great Romantic masters of the art song were Franz Schubert, Robert Schumann, Johannes Brahms, Fanny Mendelssohn Hensel, and Clara Schumann. The *Lied* (plural, *Lieder*), as the new genre came to be known, is a German-texted solo vocal song with piano accompaniment. Some composers wrote groups of Lieder that were unified by a narrative thread or a descriptive theme. Such a group is known as a *song cycle;* an example is Robert Schumann's *A Poet's Love,* which we will study in Chapter 43.

Song cycle

The Lied depended for its flowering on the outpouring of lyric poetry that marked the rise of German Romanticism. Johann Wolfgang von Goethe

The immense popularity of the Romantic art song was due in part to the emergence of the piano as the universal household instrument. A lithograph by **Achille Devéria** (1800–1857), *In the Salon.* (Germänische National-museum, Nuremberg)

The beauty of nature provided rich artistic subjects for Romantic poets and artists alike. The English landscape painter **John Constable** (1776–1837) achieves striking contrasts of light and shade in *Branch Hill Pond, Hampstead Heath*. (The Cleveland Museum of Art)

When I compose a song, my concern is not to make music but, first and foremost, to do justice to the poet's intention. I have tried to let the poem reveal itself, and indeed to raise it to a higher power.
—EDVARD GRIEG

(1749–1832) and Heinrich Heine (1797–1856) are the two leading figures among a group of poets who, like Wordsworth, Byron, Shelley, and Keats in English literature, favored short, personal lyric poems. The texts of the Lied range from tender sentiment to dramatic balladry; its favorite themes are love, longing, and the beauty of nature. One representative Lied is *Mountain Yearning* (1847), by Fanny Mendelssohn Hensel (1805–1847), which projects the era's fascination with nature through a folk-inspired poem set with rich musical text painting.

Another circumstance that made the Romantic art song popular was the emergence of the piano as the universal household instrument of the nineteenth century. The piano accompaniment translated the poetic images into music. Voice and piano together infused the short lyric form with feeling, and made it suitable for amateurs and artists alike, for the home and the concert hall.

42

Schubert and the Lied

"When I wished to sing of love, it turned to sorrow. And when I wished to sing of sorrow, it was transformed for me into love."

KEY POINTS

■ The Viennese composer Franz Schubert was a gifted song writer who wrote more than six hundred Lieder and several famous song cycles.

- *Erlking*—a through-composed Lied based on German legend set in a dramatic poem by Goethe—is one of his most famous songs.
- Schubert died young and impoverished, in part because of his bohemian lifestyle.

Franz Schubert's life has become a romantic symbol of the artist's fate. He was not properly appreciated during his lifetime, and he died very young, leaving the world a musical legacy of some 900 works.

His Life

Franz Schubert (1797–1828) was born in a suburb of Vienna, the son of a schoolmaster. The boy learned the violin from his father and piano from an elder brother; his beautiful soprano voice gained him admittance to the imperial chapel (he was one of the Vienna Choir Boys) and school where the court singers were trained. His teachers were astonished at the musicality of the shy, dreamy lad. One of them remarked that Franz "had learned everything from God."

Franz Schubert

When his schooldays were over, young Schubert tried to follow in his father's footsteps, but he was not cut out for the routine of the classroom. He found escape by immersing himself in the lyric poets, the first voices of German Romanticism. As one of his friends said, "Everything he touched turned to song." The music came to him with miraculous spontaneity. *Erlking*, set to a poem by Goethe, was written when Schubert was still a teenager. The song, one of his greatest, drew him immediate public recognition yet, incredibly, he had difficulty finding a publisher.

Schubert was not as well-known as some composers of his era (the virtuoso Paganini, for example, received much critical attention), but he was appreciated by the Viennese public and his reputation grew steadily. Still, his musical world was centered in the home, in salon concerts amid a select circle of friends and acquaintances.

Later years

Schubert endured much suffering in his later years, largely owing to his progressive debilitation from syphilis. He was often pressed for money, and sold his

In his unfinished oil sketch, Romantic artist **Moritz von Schwind** (1804–1871) shows Schubert seated at the piano. Next to him is the singer Johann Michael Vogl, who introduced many of Schubert's songs to the Viennese public. (Schubert-Museum, Vienna)

265

Principal Works

More than 600 Lieder, including *Erlkönig (Erlking*, 1815) and 3 song cycles, among them *Die schöne Müllerin (The Lovely Maid of the Mill*, 1823) and *Winterreise (Winter's Journey*, 1827)

9 symphonies, including the *Unfinished* (No. 8, 1822)

Chamber music, including 15 string quartets; 1 string quintet; 2 piano trios and the *Trout* Quintet; 1 octet; various sonatas

Piano sonatas, dances, and character pieces

Choral music, including 7 Masses, other liturgical pieces, and part songs

Operas and incidental music for dramas

in his own words

No one understands another's grief, no one understands another's joy. . . . My music is the product of my talent and my misery. And that which I have written in my greatest distress is what the world seems to like best.

music for much less than it was worth. Gradually, his youthful exuberance gave way to the maturity of a deeply emotional Romantic artist. "It seems to me at times that I no longer belong to this world," he wrote. This emotional climate also pervades the magnificent song cycle *Winter's Journey,* in which the composer introduced a somber lyricism new to music. Overcoming his discouragement, he embarked on his last efforts. To the earlier masterpieces he added, in the final year of his life, a group of profound works that includes the Mass in E-flat, the String Quintet in C, the three posthumous piano sonatas, and thirteen of his finest songs.

Schubert was thirty-one years old when he died in 1828. His dying wish was to be buried near the master he worshipped above all others—Beethoven. His wish was granted.

His Music

Schubert's music marks the confluence of the Classical and Romantic eras. His symphonies are Classical in their clear form; but in his Lieder and piano pieces, he was wholly the Romantic. The melodies have a tenderness and a quality of longing that match the Romantic quality of the poetry they set.

Chamber music   In his chamber music, Schubert revealed himself as a direct descendant of Haydn and Mozart. His string quartets, the two piano trios, the String Quintet in C, and the *Trout* Quintet, all masterworks, end the line of Viennese Classi-

Piano works   cism. In the impromptus and other short piano pieces, the piano sings with a new lyricism.

Songs   Finally, there are the songs, more than six hundred of them. Many were written down at white heat, sometimes five, six, seven in a single morning. Of special interest are the accompaniments: a measure or two conjures up images of the rustling brook or a horse riding through the night (in *Erlking*). Certain of his melodies achieve the universality of folk song; their eloquence and fresh feeling have never been surpassed. The two superb song cycles, *The Lovely Maid of the Mill* and *Winter's Journey,* both on poems of Wilhelm Müller, convey the deepest feelings of love and despair.

Erlking

This masterpiece of Schubert's youth captures the Romantic "strangeness and wonder" of Goethe's celebrated ballad. *Erlking* is based on the legend that whoever is touched by the king of the elves must die.

The eerie atmosphere of the poem is immediately established by the piano. Galloping triplets are heard against a rumbling figure in the bass. This motive pervades the song, helping to unify it. The poem's four characters—the narrator, the father, the child, and the seductive elf—are vividly differentiated through changes in the melody, harmony, rhythm, and accompaniment. The child's terror is suggested by clashing dissonance and a high vocal range. The father, calming his son's fears, has a more rounded vocal line, sung in a low register. And the Erlking cajoles in suavely melodious phrases.

The song is through-composed; the music follows the action of the narrative with a steady rise in tension—and pitch—that builds almost to the end. The obsessive triplet rhythm slows down as horse and rider reach home, then drops out altogether on the last line: "In his arms the child"—a dramatic pause precedes the two final words—"was dead." The work of an eighteen-year-old, *Erlking* was a milestone in the history of Romanticism.

The Legend of *The Erlking* (c. 1860), as portrayed by Moritz von Schwind. (Schack-Galerie, Munich)

Listening Guide 21

CD: CHR/STD 5/1–8, SH 1/80–87

Schubert: *Erlking (Erlkönig)*

(4:06)

DATE OF WORK:	1815
FORM:	Through-composed Lied
TEXT:	Narrative poem by Johann Wolfgang von Goethe
MEDIUM:	Solo voice and piano
TEMPO:	Schnell (fast)
CHARACTERS	(performed by one vocalist):
	Narrator: middle register, minor mode
	Father: low register, minor mode; reassuring
	Son: high register, minor mode; frightened
	Erlking: medium range, major mode; coaxing, then insistent

WHAT TO LISTEN FOR:	Piano accompaniment establishes mood of urgency and drama for the Lied; piano's triplet rhythm continues until very last text line.
	Narrative text with 4 characters (narrator, father, son, Erlking), each expressed through differing vocal registers.
	Shifts from minor to major mode (for Erlking) and dissonance to project the boy's terror (each cry is a step higher).

Piano introduction—minor key and rapid repeated octaves in triplets set mood, simulating horse's hooves:

Melody of son's dissonant outcry on "My father, my father":

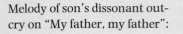

Mein Va - ter, mein Va - ter,

TEXT	TRANSLATION

NARRATOR *(minor mode, middle range)*

80   0:00

Wer reitet so spät durch Nacht und Wind?   Who rides so late through night and wind?
Es ist der Vater mit seinem Kind;   It is a father with his child;
Er hat den Knaben wohl in dem Arm,   he has the boy close in his arm,
Er fasst ihn sicher, er hält ihn warm.   he holds him tight, he keeps him warm.

FATHER *(low range)*

"Mein Sohn, was birgst du so bang   "My son, why do you hide your face in
    dein Gesicht?   "fear?"

SON *(high range)*

"Siehst, Vater, du den Erlkönig nicht?   "Father, don't you see the Erlking?
Den Erlenkönig mit Kron' und Schweif?"   The Erlking with his crown and train?"

FATHER *(low range)*

"Mein Sohn, es ist ein Nebelstreif."   "My son, it is a streak of mist."

ERLKING *(major mode, melodic)*

81   1:29

"Du liebes Kind, komm, geh mit mir!   "You dear child, come with me!
Gar schöne Spiele spiel' ich mit dir;   I'll play very lovely games with you.
Manch' bunte Blumen sind an dem Strand;   There are lots of colorful flowers by the
     shore;
Meine Mutter hat manch' gülden Gewand."   my mother has some golden robes."

SON *(high range, frightened)*

82   1:53

"Mein Vater, mein Vater, und hörest du nicht,   "My father, my father, don't you hear
Was Erlenkönig mir leise verspricht?"   the Erlking whispering promises to me?"

FATHER *(low range, calming)*

"Sei ruhig, bleibe ruhig, mein Kind;   "Be still, stay calm, my child;
In dürren Blättern säuselt der Wind."   it's the wind rustling in the dry leaves."

ERLKING *(major mode, cajoling)*

83   2:16

"Willst, feiner Knabe, du mit mir geh'n?   "My fine lad, do you want to come with me?
Meine Töchter sollen dich warten schön;   My daughters will take care of you;
Meine Töchter führen den nächtlichen Reih'n   my daughters lead the nightly dance,
Und wiegen und tanzen und singen dich ein."   and they'll rock and dance and sing you to
     sleep."

		SON *(high range, dissonant outcry)*	
84	2:33	"Mein Vater, mein Vater, und siehst du nicht dort, Erlkönigs Töchter am düstern Ort?"	"My father, my father, don't you see the Erlking's daughters over there in the shadows?"

FATHER *(low range, reassuring)*

		"Mein Sohn, mein Sohn, ich seh' es genau, Es scheinen die alten Weiden so grau."	"My son, my son, I see it clearly, it's the gray sheen of the old willows."

ERLKING *(loving, then insistent)*

85	3:02	"Ich liebe dich, mich reizt deine schöne Gestalt, Und bist du nicht willig, so brauch' ich Gewalt."	"I love you, your beautiful form delights me! And if you're not willing, then I'll use force."

SON *(high range, terrified)*

86	3:14	"Mein Vater, mein Vater, jetzt fasst er mich an! Erlkönig hat mir ein Leids gethan!"	"My father, my father, now he's grasping me! The Erlking has hurt me!"

NARRATOR *(middle register, speechlike)*

87	3:27	Dem Vater grauset's, er reitet geschwind, Er hält in Armen das ächzende Kind, Erreicht den Hof mit Müh und Noth: In seinen Armen das Kind war todt.	The father shudders, he rides swiftly, he holds the moaning child in his arms; with effort and urgency he reaches the courtyard: in his arms the child was dead.

43

Robert Schumann and the Song Cycle

"Music is to me the perfect expression of the soul."

KEY POINTS

- The German composer Robert Schumann is known for his symphonies, piano music, chamber music, and Lieder; he also established an important literary magazine for music criticism.
- Many of Schumann's Lieder were written for his fiancé, the pianist and composer Clara Wieck. These include *A Poet's Love*, a song cycle set to the poetry of Heinrich Heine.

The turbulence of German Romanticism, its fantasy and subjective emotion, found its voice in Robert Schumann. His music is German to the core, yet transcends national styles to belong to the world.

Principal Works

More than 300 Lieder, including song cycles *Frauenliebe und Leben (A Woman's Love and Life*, 1840) and *Dichterliebe (A Poet's Love*, 1840)

Orchestral music, including 4 symphonies and 1 piano concerto (A minor, 1841–45)

Chamber music, including 3 string quartets, 1 piano quintet, 1 piano quartet, piano trios, and sonatas

Piano music, including 3 sonatas; numerous miniatures and collections, among them *Papillons (Butterflies*, 1831), *Carnaval* (1835), and *Kinderszenen (Scenes from Childhood*, 1838); large works, including *Symphonic Etudes* (1835–37) and *Fantasy in C* (1836–38)

1 opera; incidental music; choral music

His Life

Robert Schumann

Marriage to Clara

Robert Schumann (1810–1856) was born in Zwickau, a town in southeastern Germany, the son of a bookseller whose love of literature was passed on to the boy. At his mother's insistence, he undertook the study of law, first at the University of Leipzig, then at Heidelberg. More and more he surrendered to his passion for music; it was his ambition to become a pianist. At last he won his mother's consent and returned to Leipzig to study with Friedrich Wieck, one of the foremost teachers of the day.

The young man practiced intensively to make up for his late start. Unfortunately, physical difficulties with the fingers of his right hand ended his hopes as a pianist. He then turned his interest to composing, and in a burst of creative energy produced, while still in his twenties, his most important works for piano. At the same time, Schumann's literary bent found expression in an important publication, *Neue Zeitschrift für Musik* (The New Journal for Music), which he established and which, under his direction, became one of the most important journals of music criticism in Europe.

The hectic quality of the 1830s was intensified by Schumann's courtship of the gifted pianist and composer Clara Wieck (see Chapter 46). When he first came to study with her father, Clara was an eleven-year-old prodigy. Five years later, Robert realized he loved her, but her father opposed their marriage, with a vehemence that bordered on the psychopathic. At length, since she was not yet of age, the couple were forced to appeal to the courts against Wieck. The marriage took place in 1840, when Clara was twenty-one and Robert thirty. This was his "year of song," when he produced over a hundred of the Lieder that represent his lyric gift at its purest.

The two musicians settled in Leipzig, pursuing their careers side by side. Clara became the foremost interpreter of Robert's piano works and in the ensuing decade contributed substantially to the spread of his fame. Yet neither her love nor that of their children could ward off an increasing withdrawal from the world that plagued her husband. Moodiness and nervous exhaustion culminated, in 1844, in a severe breakdown. The couple moved to Dresden, where Robert seemed to recover, but the periods of depression returned ever more frequently. In 1850, Schumann was appointed music director at Düsseldorf. But he was ill-suited for public life and was forced to relinquish the post.

Schumann continued to experience auditory hallucinations. Once he rose in the middle of the night to write down a theme that he imagined had been brought him by the spirits of Schubert and Mendelssohn. It was his last melody. A week later, in a fit of depression, he threw himself into the Rhine River. He was rescued by fishermen, and Clara had no choice then but to place him in a private asylum near Bonn. He died two years later at the age of forty-six.

His Music

In the emotional exuberance of his music, Schumann is the true Romantic. His piano pieces brim over with impassioned melody, novel changes of harmony, and driving rhythms. The titles are characteristic: *Fantasiestücke* (*Fantasy Pieces*), *Romances, Scenes from Childhood*. He often attached literary meanings to his music, and was especially fond of cycles of short pieces connected by a literary theme or musical motto.

Piano pieces

As a composer of Lieder, Schumann ranks second only to Schubert. A common theme in his songs is love, particularly from a woman's point of view. His favored poet was Heine, for whom he had an affinity like Schubert's for Goethe. Especially notable are his several song cycles, the best-known of which are *A Poet's Love*, on poems of Heine, and *A Woman's Love and Life*, on poems of Chamisso.

Lieder

The four symphonies are thoroughly Romantic in feeling. These works, especially the first and fourth, communicate a lyric freshness that has preserved their appeal.

Symphonies

A Poet's Love

Schumann wrote his great song cycle *A Poet's Love* (*Dichterliebe*) in 1840, his "year of song," at lightning-fast speed. For the texts, he chose sixteen poems from the *Lyriches Intermezzo* of Heinrich Heine, who wrote some of the Romantic era's most poignant works. The songs tell no real story; rather, they follow a psychological progression that spirals downward from the freshness of love through a growing disappointment to complete despair.

In the eighth song in the cycle, "And if the flowers knew," the first three verses offer comfort—through the flowers, the nightingales, and the stars—to the poet's lovesick grief, while the last verse echoes the hopelessness of his suffering: only she who has broken his heart knows its depths. The melody, in quick-paced, declamatory style, is delivered in four short phrases for each verse. Schumann sets the first three verses to the same music, which he then reshapes for the emotional climax in the closing verse. The piano's active accompaniment suits the breathless character of the voice, and its closing measures confirm the angry frustration heard in the last lines of the poem.

Clearly, Schumann was able to achieve the desired unity of expression in this perfect fusion of dramatic and lyric elements. *A Poet's Love* is universally regarded as a masterpiece of Romanticism.

in his own words

The singing voice is hardly sufficient in itself; it cannot carry the whole task of interpretation un-aided. In addition to its overall expression, the finer shadings of the poem must be represented as well—provided that the melody does not suffer in the process.

Listening Guide 22

CD: CHR/STD 5/49–52, SH 2/57–60

Robert Schumann: "And if the flowers knew," from *A Poet's Love (Dichterliebe)*, No. 8

(1:14)

DATE OF WORK:	1840
GENRE:	Lied, from a song cycle
FORM:	Modified strophic form
TEXT:	Lyric poem by Heinrich Heine 4 verses (rhyme: *a-b-a-b c-d-c-d e-f-e-f g-b-g-b*)
MEDIUM:	Solo voice and piano

WHAT TO LISTEN FOR: Fast and breathless melody, with homophonic accompaniment.
Hurried tempo, in quick, uneven rhythms.
Dramatic, emotional mood turns to anger in piano postlude.
3 stanzas sung to the same music; 4th stanza varied for drama.

Opening vocal line, showing rushed, uneven rhythms:

Und wüs - sten's die Blu - men, die klei - nen, wie tief ver - wun - det mein Herz,

		TEXT	TRANSLATION
57	0:00	Und wüssten's die Blumen, die kleinen, Wie tief verwundet mein Herz, Sie würden mit mir weinen, Zu heilen meinen Schmerz.	And if the flowers, the little ones, knew how deeply my heart is wounded, they would weep with me to heal my pain.
58	0:15	Und wüssten's die Nachtigallen, Wie ich so traurig und krank, Sie liessen fröhlich erschallen Erquickenden Gesang.	And if the nightingales knew how sad and sick I am, they would happily sound out their life-affirming song.
59	0:30	Und wüssten sie mein Wehe, Die goldenen Sternelein, Sie kämen aus ihrer Höhe, Und sprächen Trost mir ein.	And if the little golden stars knew my hurt, they would descend from their heights and speak words of comfort to me.
60	0:45	Sie alle können's nicht wissen, Nur Eine kennt meinen Schmerz; Sie hat ja selbst zerrissen, Zerrissen mir das Herz.	All of these cannot know, only one understands my pain; because she herself has torn— has torn my heart in two.
	1:00	Piano postlude	

unit **XVII**

The Nineteenth-Century Piano Piece

e Learning

RESOURCE CD

***e*LG**

23 Chopin, Nocturne in C minor, Op. 48, No. 1

24 C. Schumann, Scherzo, Op. 10

ONLINE TUTOR

www.wwnorton.com/enjoy

Composers: Romantic

Frédéric François Chopin

Franz Liszt

Clara Schumann

Resources: Romantic

Listening: Romantic

Quizzes: Romantic

Reviewing 17

Listening 15

Glossary

44

The Piano and Its Literature

"I have called my piano pieces after the names of my favorite haunts . . . they will form a delightful souvenir, a kind of second diary."

—FANNY MENDELSSOHN HENSEL

KEY POINTS

- In the Romantic era, the piano was both a popular instrument for home use as well as the favored solo instrument for virtuosos such as Liszt and Chopin.
- Technical improvements to the nineteenth-century piano led to the development of the modern concert grand piano.
- The short lyric piano piece, often with a fanciful title, was a favorite Romantic genre.

The rise in popularity of the piano helped shape the musical culture of the Romantic era. All over Europe and America, the instrument became a mainstay of music in the home. It proved especially attractive to amateurs because, unlike the string and wind instruments, it enabled them to play melody and harmony together. Also popular was *four-hand piano music,* a chamber music form for two performers at one piano or occasionally at two; many works were arranged for this genre, which allowed for home and salon performances of orchestral and other large-ensemble music. The piano thus played a crucial role in the taste and experience of the new mass public.

Four-hand piano music

This beautiful, ornate grand piano was made for the Baroness of Kidderminster by Erard, c 1840. (Metropolitan Museum of Art, New York)

The modern piano

Hardly less important was the rise of the virtuoso pianist. At first the performer was, as a rule, also the composer; Mozart and Beethoven introduced their own piano concertos to the public. With the developing concert industry, however, a class of virtuoso performers arose whose only function was to dazzle audiences by playing music others had written. Yet there are important exceptions to this trend, among them the Hungarian composer and teacher Franz Liszt (1811–1886), who was one of the greatest pianists—and showmen—of his day. Liszt, along with Chopin, contributed to modern piano technique. His *Transcendental Etudes after Paganini* transform the study piece into imaginative and appealing works that press the limitations of the keyboard. Clara Schumann was another highly acclaimed musician and composer. (We will study a virtuoso piano work by her in Chapter 46.)

The nineteenth century saw a series of crucial technical improvements that led to the development of the modern concert grand piano. Romantic composers' quest for greater power and dynamic range mandated increased string diameter and tension, which in turn required more bracing within the wooden piano case. Piano manufacturing eventually moved from the craft shop to the factory, allowing a huge increase in production at a significantly reduced cost. National building styles gave way to a more standardized instrument that had a metal frame supporting the increased string tension, as well as an improved mechanical action and extended range of notes—from five octaves to seven or more. At the Paris Exhibition of 1867, two American manufacturers took the top awards, among them Steinway, maker of some of today's finest pianos. By the early twentieth century, the piano had become a universal fixture in the homes of many middle-class, as well as upper-class, families.

German artist **Ludwig Richter** (1802–1884) portrays a typical family music-making scene in his woodcut *Hausmusik* (1851).

The Short Lyric Piano Piece

The song found an instrumental equivalent in the short lyric piano piece, with its ability to project melodious and dramatic moods within a compact form. Composers adopted new and sometimes fanciful terms for such works. Some titles—"Prelude," "Intermezzo" (interlude), "Impromptu" (on the spur of the moment), for example—suggest free, almost improvisational forms. Many composers turned to dance music, and produced keyboard versions of the Polish mazurka and polonaise, the Viennese waltz, and the lively scherzo. Composers sometimes chose more descriptive titles, such as *Wild Hunt*, *The Little Bell*, and *Forest Murmurs* (all by Franz Liszt).

The nineteenth-century masters of the short piano piece—Schubert, Chopin, Liszt, Felix Mendelssohn, Fanny Mendelssohn Hensel, Robert and Clara Schumann, Brahms—showed inexhaustible ingenuity in exploring the technical resources of the instrument and its potential for expression.

> *The pianoforte is the most important of all musical instruments; its invention was to music what the invention of printing was to poetry*
>
> —GEORGE BERNARD SHAW

45

Chopin and Piano Music

"My life [is] an episode without a beginning and with a sad end."

KEY POINTS

- The composer Frédéric Chopin dedicated his entire compositional output to works centered around the piano; he is said to have originated the modern piano style.
- Chopin lived and worked in Paris among the leading intellectuals and artists of France.
- His output includes études—highly virtuosic and technical study pieces—meditative nocturnes, preludes, and dances (including Polish folk dance types) as well as sonatas and concertos for piano.

Frédéric François Chopin (1810–1849) has been called the "poet of the piano." The title is a valid one. His music, rooted in the heart of Romanticism, made this era the piano's golden age.

His Life

Chopin, considered the national composer of Poland, was half French. His father had emigrated to Warsaw, where he married a lady-in-waiting to a countess and taught French to the sons of the nobility. Frédéric, who proved to be musically gifted as a child, was educated at the newly founded Conservatory of Warsaw. At the age of twenty-one, he left for Paris, where he spent the rest of his career. Paris in the 1830s was the center of the new Romanticism. The circle in which Chopin moved included musicians such as Liszt and Berlioz, and

Frédéric Chopin

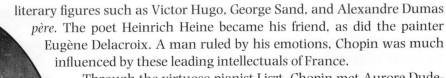

literary figures such as Victor Hugo, George Sand, and Alexandre Dumas *père*. The poet Heinrich Heine became his friend, as did the painter Eugène Delacroix. A man ruled by his emotions, Chopin was much influenced by these leading intellectuals of France.

Through the virtuoso pianist Liszt, Chopin met Aurore Dudevant, "the lady with the somber eye," known to the world as the novelist George Sand. She was thirty-four, he twenty-eight when their famous friendship began. Madame Sand was brilliant and domineering; her need to dominate found its counterpart in Chopin's need to be ruled. She left a memorable account of the composer at work:

His creative power was spontaneous, miraculous. It came to him without effort or warning.... But then began the most heartrending labor I have ever witnessed. It was a series of attempts, of fits of irresolution and impatience to recover certain details. He would shut himself in his room for days, pacing up and down, breaking his pens, repeating and modifying one bar a hundred times.

George Sand (Aurore Dudevant)

For the next eight years, Chopin spent his summers at Sand's estate at Nohant, where she entertained many of France's prominent artists and writers. These were productive years for the composer, although his health grew progressively worse and his relationship with Sand ran its course from love to conflict, from jealousy to hostility. They parted in bitterness.

Chopin died of tuberculosis in Paris at the age of thirty-nine. Thousands joined together at his funeral to pay him homage. The artistic world bid its farewell to the strains of the composer's own funeral march, from his B-flat-minor Piano Sonata.

His Music

in his own words

One needs only to study a certain positioning of the hand in relation to the keys to obtain with ease the most beautiful sound, to know how to play long notes and short notes and to [attain] certain unlimited dexterity. . . . A well-formed technique, it seems to me, [is one] that can control and vary a beautiful sound quality.

Chopin was one of the most original artists of the nineteenth century. His style is so entirely his own that there is no mistaking it for any other. He was the only master of the first rank whose creative life centered about the piano, and he is credited with originating the modern piano style. It is remarkable that so many of Chopin's works have remained in the standard repertory. His nocturnes—night songs, as the name implies—are melancholic and meditative. The preludes are visionary fragments; some are only a page in length, several consist of two or three lines. In the études, which crown the literature of the study piece, piano technique is transformed into poetry. The impromptus are fanciful and capricious, and the waltzes capture the brilliance and coquetry of the salon. The mazurkas, derived from a Polish peasant dance, evoke the idealized landscape of his youth.

Among the larger forms are the four ballades, epic works of spacious proportions. The polonaises revive the stately processional dance in which Poland's nobles hailed their kings. The Fantasy in F minor and the dramatic scherzos reveal the composer at the peak of his art. The Sonatas in B minor and in B-flat minor are thoroughly Romantic in spirit, as are the Piano Concertos in E minor and F minor.

Principal Works

Works for piano and orchestra, including 2 piano concertos

Piano music, including 4 ballades, Fantasy in F minor (1841), *Berceuse* (1844), *Barcarolle* (1846), 3 sonatas (including B minor, Op. 58, 1844), preludes, études, mazurkas, nocturnes, waltzes, polonaises, impromptus, scherzos, rondos, marches, and variations

Chamber music, all including piano; songs

Nocturne in C minor, Op. 48, No. 1

Chopin adopted the name and the character of the nocturne from the Irish composer and pianist John Field, who first used the term in 1812 for his lyrical and contemplative "night" pieces. Most of Chopin's works in this genre are sentimental, introspective, and nonvirtuosic—expressive poetic statements meant to move the emotions. His Nocturne in C minor, Op. 48, No. 1, written in 1841, surpasses the others in its breadth, virtuosity, and eloquence. The first theme of this ternary form is both calm and majestic—a C-minor melody that spins out ever so slowly over a soft chordal accompaniment. It follows beautifully shaped arches while meandering through various key centers. The middle section, in C major, moves even slower, in a hymnlike, chordal setting. Rolled, or arpeggiated, chords and an active triplet-figure accompaniment intrude on the solemnity of the mood as the section grows to a colossal climax. The third section returns to the opening melody (**A′**), now played twice as fast and accompanied by a restless triplet rhythm; this builds to a second climax that resolves in the poignantly expressive coda in which the melody gradually fades like a dying flame.

Important in this piece, as in all of Chopin's music, is the *tempo rubato*—the "robbed time," or "borrowed time," that is so characteristic of Romantic style. In tempo rubato, certain liberties are taken with the rhythm without upsetting the basic beat. As Chopin taught it, the accompaniment—usually the left hand—was played in strict time, while above it the right-hand melody might hesitate a little here or hurry forward there. In either case, the borrowing had to be repaid before the end of the phrase. Rubato remains an essential ingredient of Chopin's style.

Chopin giving a piano lesson to the renowned opera singer Pauline Viardot (see p. 325). A caricature (1844) by **Maurice Sand.**

Listening Guide 23

CD: CHR/STD 5/46–48, SH 2/61–63

Chopin: Nocturne in C minor, Op. 48, No. 1 (6:23)

DATE OF WORK:	1841
GENRE:	Nocturne (lyrical, contemplative work)
FORM:	Ternary (**A-B-A'** + coda)
MEDIUM:	Solo piano
TEMPO:	Lento (slow)

WHAT TO LISTEN FOR: Meditative melody, with block-chord accompaniment.
Use of tempo rubato and chromaticism for emotional intensity.
Shifts of tonality between sections of the 3-part form (minor-major-minor).
Dramatic middle section with triplet accompaniment; bursts into lavish
climax, and then returns to opening melody.

61 0:00 **A** section—tranquil C-minor melody
spun out against soft chords in left hand:

0:23 4-measure melody restated in major,
with varied melodic passagework.

0:46 Decorative, arched melodic line, played
with expressive rubato.

1:33 Return to opening melody, followed by
descending chromatic passage leading
into a strong cadence in new key
(C major).

62 2:21 **B** section—hymnlike setting in C major,
played softly; moves a little slower
(*poco più lento*):

2:44 Chords played in harplike arpeggiations

3:39 Triplet-figure rhythm introduced as
accompaniment; figure becomes insistent
and grows to huge climax.

	4:17	Descending chromatic passage, played *fortissimo*, serves as a transition to **A'** section.
63	4:27	**A'** section—return of opening melody in quicker movement (*doppio movimento*) and with agitated triplet-figure accompaniment.
	5:38	Brief coda, with simple, chromatic melody; ascending melody trails off and a brief silence is broken by the final 3 *pianissimo* chords.

46

Clara Schumann: Pianist and Composer

"The practice of [music] is . . . a great part of my inner self. To me, it is the very air I breathe."

KEY POINTS

- Clara Wieck Schumann was a virtuoso pianist, composer, and leading interpreter of the music of Brahms, Chopin, and Robert Schumann, her husband.
- She is known for her songs, piano music, and chamber music.
- Her works are technically difficult and also deeply introspective.

Clara Schumann (1819–1896) is universally regarded as one of the most distinguished musicians of the nineteenth century. She was admired throughout Europe as a leading pianist of the era, but the world in which she lived was not prepared to acknowledge that a woman could be an outstanding composer. Hence her considerable creative gifts were not recognized or encouraged during her lifetime.

Her Life

Clara Schumann's close association with two great composers—her husband, Robert Schumann (see Chapter 43), and her lifelong friend Johannes Brahms (see Chapter 51)—put her at the center of musical life in her time. From her earliest years, she had the clearest possible conception of her goals as an artist and the strength of character to realize them. She studied piano from age five, made her first public appearance as a concert artist in Leipzig at age nine, and undertook her first extended concert tour several years later.

A great crisis in her life came with the violent opposition of Friedrich Wieck, her father and teacher, to her marrying Robert Schumann, but she had the courage to defy him. She then faced the problems of a woman torn between the

Clara Schumann

demands of an exacting career and her responsibilities as a wife and mother. She and Robert had seven children (an eighth died in infancy), yet she managed throughout those years to maintain her position as one of the outstanding concert artists of Europe. Liszt admired her playing for its "complete technical mastery, depth, and sincerity of feeling." Her situation was made more difficult by her being much more famous than her husband during their life together. The disparity in their reputations might have led to serious strains between them, had she not from the first dedicated her talents to advancing Robert's music. She gave first performances of all his important works, also becoming known as a leading interpreter of Brahms and Chopin.

Although Clara enjoyed a loving relationship with her husband, life became increasingly difficult. Robert suffered from shifting moods and frequent depressions that eventually led to a complete breakdown. After his death, she concertized in order to support herself and her children. Now she in turn was sustained by Brahms's devotion.

Societal attitudes　　Clara had the talent, training, and background that many composers would envy, but from the beginning of her career she accepted the nineteenth-century attitude toward women composers. At twenty, she confided to her diary, "I once believed that I possessed creative talent, but I have given up this idea; a woman must not desire to compose—there has never yet been one able to do it. Should I expect to be the one? To believe this would be arrogant, something that my father once, in former days, induced me to do." (See CP 13 on women and music.)

Robert also accepted the prevailing attitudes. "Clara has composed a series of small pieces," he wrote in their joint diary, "which show a musical and tender ingenuity such as she never attained before. But to have children, and a husband who is always living in the realm of imagination, does not go together

Clara Schumann playing with the virtuoso violinist Joseph Joachim. A chalk drawing by **Adolf von Menzel** (1854).

Principal Works

Solo piano music, including dances, caprices, romances, scherzos (including Op. 10, 1838), impromptus, character pieces (*Quatre pièces fugitives*, Op. 15, 1845), variations (including one set on a theme by Robert Schumann, 1854), and cadenzas for Mozart and Beethoven piano concertos

1 piano concerto with orchestra or quintet (1837)

Chamber music, including 1 piano trio (1846) and 3 romances for violin and piano (1855–56)

Lieder, with texts by Burns, Rückert, Heine, and other poets

with composing. She cannot work at it regularly, and I am often disturbed to think how many profound ideas are lost because she cannot work them out."

Clara Schumann gave her last public concert at the age of seventy-two, and succumbed to a stroke five years later, in 1896. Her dying wish was to hear her husband's music once more.

Her Music

Clara's output includes many small, intimate works such as songs and piano pieces. There are also two large-scale works, a piano concerto and a trio for piano and strings; a number of virtuoso pieces; and, as a gesture of homage to her husband, a set of *Variations on a Theme by Robert Schumann.* While her early works leaned toward technical display, which showed off her phenomenal talent, the later ones were more serious and introspective pieces typical of the era in which she lived.

Scherzo, Opus 10

Composed in 1838 when Clara was nineteen, the Scherzo in D minor, Opus 10, exemplifies her virtuoso style. Marked Con passione (with passion), a performance indication typical of the Romantic period, the piece is the kind that allows pianists to dazzle their public. Clara wrote to Robert from Paris, "It is extraordinary to me that my Scherzo is so well liked here. I always have to repeat it."

The structure is altogether clear-cut: an impetuous scherzo expanded to include two trios, or contrasting sections, more relaxed in character. (See Listening Guide 24.) Sudden dissonances and *sforzandos* (accents) add to the drama; trills and extended arpeggio figures keep the pianist's fingers busy. The main theme, an exuberant rising figure, builds steadily to the *fortissimo* ending, while the two trios, with their flowing melodic lines, offer the necessary release of tension.

This scherzo displays Clara's creative gift in a most attractive way. It further attests to her extraordinary talents as a virtuoso performer. Forgotten for decades, Clara Schumann is finally receiving the world recognition long due her.

in her own words

Composing gives me great pleasure . . . there is nothing that surpasses the joy of creation, if only because through it one wins hours of self-forgetfulness, when one lives in a world of sound.

Listening Guide 24

CD: CHR/STD 6/20–27, SH 3/1–8

Clara Schumann: Scherzo, Op. 10

(4:57)

DATE OF WORK:	c. 1838
FORM:	Scherzo with 2 trios
MEDIUM:	Solo piano
TEMPO:	Presto, Scherzo con passione, in 3/4 meter
KEY:	D minor

WHAT TO LISTEN FOR: Effusive, passionate, and highly virtuosic style.
Contrast between the dramatic scherzo sections (heard at beginning, middle, and end) that alternate with 2 lyrical trios.
Overall rondo-like form (**A-B-A-C-A**).

1 0:00 Introduction—14 measures; trill-like, arpeggiated figures lead to main theme:

2 0:08 Scherzo—very rhythmic, unison rising line; soft, punctuated by *sf* chord, alternates with arpeggiated figure, key of D minor:

Opening theme restated in G minor; return of trill-like figure from introduction followed by loud, dissonant chords.

3 0:36 Scherzo repeated in D minor.

4 1:04 Scherzo varied, opens in D minor; trill figures in left hand, then both hands; becomes more chromatic—*diminuendo* into trio.

5   1:30   Trio I—marked *doloroso* (sorrowful), slower; smooth descending melodic lines:

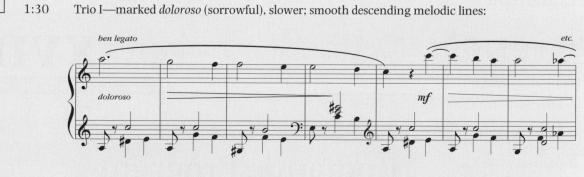

Alternates with rhythmic, accented theme from opening scherzo (4-note rhythm); returns to conjunct line, more chromatic; *crescendo* into opening tempo, based on 4-note rhythm.

6   2:12   Scherzo returns—*fortissimo*, arpeggiated figures increasingly chromatic and slower, leading to 2nd trio.

7   2:41   Trio 2—arched *marcato* (stressed) melody—begins in E-flat major:

Lower-pitched melody played rubato, then in middle range with rolled chord and 4-note rhythm accompaniment; trill and arpeggio figures lead back to scherzo.

8   4:13   Scherzo returns in D minor, builds to loud, fiery close with descending arpeggio and 2 *fortissimo* chords.

unit **XVIII**

Romantic Program Music

47

The Nature of Program Music

"The painter turns a poem into a painting; the musician sets a picture to music."

—ROBERT SCHUMANN

KEY POINTS

- Romantic composers cultivated *program music*—instrumental music with a literary or pictorial association supplied by the composer—over *absolute music.*
- The four main types of program music include the *concert overture, incidental music* to a play, the *program symphony* (a multimovement work), and the *symphonic poem* (a one-movement work).

Program music is instrumental music that has literary or pictorial associations; the nature of these associations is indicated by the title of the piece or by an explanatory note—the "program"—supplied by the composer. A title such as *King Lear* (by Berlioz) suggests specific characters and events, while the title *Pièces fugitives* (*Fleeting Pieces,* by Clara Schumann) merely labels the mood or character of the work. Program music, we saw earlier, is distinguished from absolute, or pure, music, which consists of musical patterns that have no literary or pictorial meanings.

This genre was of special importance in the nineteenth century, when musicians became sharply conscious of the connection between their art and the world about them. It helped them to bring music closer to poetry and painting, and to relate their work to the moral and political issues of their time.

Varieties of Program Music

One impulse toward program music came from the opera house, where the overture was a rousing orchestral piece in one movement designed to serve as an introduction to an opera (or a play). Many operatic overtures achieved independent popularity as separate concert pieces. This pointed the way to a new type of overture not associated with an opera: a single-movement concert piece for orchestra based on a literary idea, such as Tchaikovsky's *Romeo and Juliet*. Such a composition, the *concert overture*, might evoke a land- or seascape or embody a poetic or patriotic idea.

Another species of program music, *incidental music,* usually consists of an overture and a series of pieces to be performed between the acts of a play and during important scenes. The most successful pieces of incidental music were arranged into suites (such as Mendelssohn's music for Shakespeare's *A Midsummer Night's Dream* and Beethoven's music for the play *The Ruins of Athens*). Incidental music is still important today, in the form of film music and background music for television.

The passion for program music was so strong that it invaded even the most hallowed form of absolute music, the symphony. Thus came into being the *program symphony,* a multimovement orchestral work. We will consider one of the most important examples of a program symphony—Berlioz's *Symphonie fantastique.*

Eventually, the need was felt for a large form of orchestral music that would serve the Romantic era as well as the symphony had served the Classical. Franz

The concert overture

Incidental music

♪

Program symphony

I have grown accustomed to composing in our garden . . . today or tomorrow I am going to dream there the Midsummer Night's Dream.
—Felix Mendelssohn

Shakespeare's play *A Midsummer Night's Dream* inspired Felix Mendelssohn's incidental music as well as this fanciful canvas by **Henry Fuseli,** *Titania and Bottom* (c. 1790). (Tate Gallery, London)

Liszt filled this need with the creation of the *symphonic poem* (he first used the term in 1848), the nineteenth century's one original contribution to the large forms. Liszt's *Les préludes* is among the best-known examples of this genre.

Symphonic poem

A symphonic poem is a piece of program music for orchestra, in one movement, which in the course of contrasting sections develops a poetic idea, suggests a scene, or creates a mood. It differs from the concert overture, which usually retains one of the traditional Classical forms, by being much freer in its structure. The symphonic poem (also called *tone poem*) gave composers the flexibility they needed for a big single-movement form. It became the most widely cultivated type of orchestral program music through the second half of the century. We will study two examples: *The Moldau*, by the Bohemian composer Bedřich Smetana, and *Prelude to "The Afternoon of a Faun,"* by Claude Debussy.

Program music is one of the most striking manifestations of nineteenth-century Romanticism. This new, descriptive genre impelled composers to express specific feelings; it proclaimed the direct relationship of music to life.

48

Berlioz and the Program Symphony

"To render my works properly requires a combination of extreme precision and irresistible verve, a regulated vehemence, a dreamy tenderness, and an almost morbid melancholy."

KEY POINTS

- French composer and conductor Hector Berlioz won a coveted composition award for *Symphonie fantastique*, a five-movement program symphony.
- The program for the work drew on his personal life and on his infatuation and courtship with the actress Harriet Smithson; his other symphonic works drew from Romantic literary sources.
- Berlioz was an innovative writer for orchestra, introducing new colors and instrumental techniques to the ensemble; he also wrote a treatise on orchestration.
- The five movements of *Symphonie fantastique* are unified by a recurring theme (*idée fixe*) representing his beloved.

The flamboyance of Victor Hugo's poetry and the dramatic intensity of Eugène Delacroix's painting found their counterpart in the works of Hector Berlioz, the first great exponent of musical Romanticism in France.

His Life

Hector Berlioz (1803–1869) was born in France in a small town near Grenoble. His father, a well-to-do physician, expected the boy to follow in his footsteps,

Hector Berlioz

and at eighteen Hector was sent away to attend medical school in Paris. The conservatory and the opera, however, intrigued Berlioz much more than the dissecting room. The following year, the fiery youth made a decision that horrified his upper-middle-class family: he gave up medicine for music.

The Romantic revolution was brewing in Paris, and Berlioz, along with Hugo and Delacroix, found himself in the camp of "young France." Having been cut off by his parents, he gave music lessons and sang in a theater chorus to make ends meet. He became a huge fan of Beethoven and of Shakespeare, to whose plays he was introduced by a visiting English troupe. Berlioz fell madly in love with an actress in this troupe, whose portrayals of Ophelia and Juliet excited the admiration of the Parisians. In his *Memoirs*, which read like a Romantic novel, he describes his infatuation with Harriet Smithson: "I became obsessed by an intense, overpowering sense of sadness. I could not sleep, I could not work, and I spent my time wandering aimlessly about Paris and its environs."

In 1830, Berlioz was awarded the coveted Prix de Rome, which gave him an opportunity to live and work in Italy. That same year he composed the *Symphonie fantastique*, to this day his most celebrated work. Upon his return from Rome, he commenced a hectic courtship of Harriet Smithson. There were strenuous objections from both their families, and violent scenes, during one of which the excitable Hector attempted suicide. But he recovered, and the two were married.

Now that the unattainable ideal had become his wife, Berlioz's passion cooled. It was Shakespeare he had loved rather than Harriet, and in time he sought the ideal elsewhere. All the same, the first years of his marriage were the most fruitful of his life. By age forty, he had produced most of the works on which his fame would rest.

In the latter part of his life, Berlioz conducted his music in all the capitals of Europe. Paris, however, resisted him to the end. For his last major work, the opera *Béatrice et Bénédict,* he wrote his own libretto after Shakespeare's *Much Ado About Nothing.* Following this effort, the embittered composer wrote no more. He died seven years later, at sixty-six.

Harriet Smithson

in his own words

Generally speaking, my style is very bold . . . the prevaling characteristics of my music are passionate expression, intense ardor, rhythmical animations, and unexpected turns.

His Music

Berlioz was one of the boldest innovators of the nineteenth century. His approach to music was wholly individual, his sense of sound unique. From the start, he had an affinity in his orchestral music for the vividly dramatic or pictorial program.

Orchestral works

His works show the favorite literary influences of the Romantic period. *The Damnation of Faust,* for example, was inspired by Goethe; *Harold in Italy* (a program symphony with viola solo) and *The Corsair* (an overture) are based on works by the English poet Byron. Shakespeare is the source for the overture *King Lear* and for the dramatic symphony *Romeo and Juliet.*

Vocal works

Berlioz's most important opera, *The Trojans,* on his own libretto after the ancient Roman poet Virgil, has been successfully revived in recent years. His sacred vocal works, including the Requiem and the Te Deum, are conceived on a similarly grandiose scale.

Principal Works

Orchestral music, including overtures *Waverley* (1828), *Rob Roy* (1831), *Le roi Lear* (*King Lear*, 1831); and program symphonies *Symphonie fantastique* (1830), *Harold en Italie* (*Harold in Italy*, 1834), *Romeo et Juliette* (1839)

Choral music, including a Requiem Mass (1837), Te Deum (Hymn of Praise, 1849), *La damnation de Faust* (*The Damnation of Faust*, 1846), and the oratorio *L'enfance du Christ* (*The Childhood of Christ*, 1854)

3 operas, including *Les Troyens* (*The Trojans*, 1858) and *Béatrice et Bénédict* (1862)

9 solo vocal works with orchestra

Writings on music, including an orchestration treatise (1843/55)

It was in the domain of orchestration that Berlioz's genius asserted itself most fully. His daring originality in handling the instruments opened up a new world of Romantic sound. His scores, calling for the largest orchestra that had ever been used, abound in novel effects and discoveries that would serve as models for all who came after him. Indeed, the conductor Felix Weingartner called Berlioz "the creator of the modern orchestra."

Symphonie fantastique

Berlioz wrote his best-known program symphony when he was twenty-seven years old, drawing its story from his personal life. "A young musician of morbid sensibility and ardent imagination, in . . . lovesick despair, has poisoned himself with opium. The drug, too weak to kill, plunges him into a heavy sleep accompanied by strange visions. . . . The beloved one herself becomes for him a melody, a recurrent theme that haunts him everywhere."

Idée fixe

The symphony's recurrent theme, called an *idée fixe* (fixed idea), symbolizes the beloved; it becomes a musical thread unifying the five diverse movements, though its appearances are varied in harmony, rhythm, meter, tempo, dynamics, register, and instrumental color. (See Listening Guide 25 for theme and analysis.) These transformations take on literary as well as musical significance, as the following description by Berlioz shows.

The program

I. *Reveries, Passions.* "[The musician] remembers the weariness of soul, the indefinable yearning he knew before meeting his beloved. Then, the volcanic love with which she at once inspired him, his delirious suffering . . . his religious consolation." The Allegro section introduces a soaring melody—the fixed idea.

II. *A Ball.* "Amid the tumult and excitement of a brilliant ball he glimpses the loved one again." This dance movement is in ternary, or three-part, form. In the middle section, the fixed idea reappears in waltz time.

III. *Scene in the Fields.* "On a summer evening in the country he hears two shepherds piping. The pastoral duet, the quiet surroundings . . . all unite to fill his heart with a long absent calm. But she appears again. His heart contracts. Painful forebodings fill his soul." The composer said that his aim in this pastoral movement was to establish a mood "of sorrowful loneliness."

IV. *March to the Scaffold.* "He dreams that he has killed his beloved, that he has been condemned to die and is being led to the scaffold. . . . At the very end the fixed idea reappears for an instant, like a last thought of love interrupted by the fall of the blade."

V. *Dream of a Witches' Sabbath.* "He sees himself at a witches' sabbath surrounded by a host of fearsome spirits who have gathered for his funeral. Unearthly sounds, groans, shrieks of laughter. The melody of his beloved is heard, but it has lost its noble and reserved character. It has become a vulgar tune, trivial and grotesque. It is she who comes to the infernal orgy. A howl of joy greets her arrival. She joins the diabolical dance. Bells toll for the dead. A burlesque of the *Dies irae.* Dance of the witches. The dance and the *Dies irae* combined."

Francisco Goya (1746–1828) anticipated the passionate intensity of Berlioz's music in this painting of the *Witches' Sabbath,* c. 1819–23. (Museo del Prado, Madrid)

The fourth movement, a diabolical march in minor, exemplifies the nineteenth-century love of the fantastic. The theme of the beloved appears at the very end, on the clarinet, and is cut off by a grim *fortissimo* chord. In this vivid portrayal of the story, one clearly hears the final blow of the blade, the head rolling, and the resounding cheers of the crowd. In the final movement, Berlioz enters into a kind of infernal spirit that nourished a century of satanic operas, ballets, and symphonic poems. The mood is heightened with the introduction of the traditional religious chant *Dies irae* (Day of Wrath) from the ancient Mass for the Dead.

Fourth movement

Fifth movement

There is a grandeur of line and gesture in the music of Berlioz, and an abundance of vitality and invention. He is one of the major prophets of the era.

Listening Guide 25

CD: CHR/STD 5/19–24, SH 3/9–14

Berlioz: *Symphonie fantastique,* Fourth Movement   (6:34)

DATE OF WORK:	1830
GENRE:	Program symphony, 5 movements
PROGRAM:	A lovesick artist in an opium trance is haunted by a vision of his beloved, which becomes an *idée fixe* (fixed idea).

I. *Reveries, Passions*

Largo, Allegro agitato e appassionato assai (lively, agitated, and very impassioned); introduces the main theme, the fixed idea:

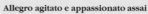

II. *A Ball*

Valse, Allegro non troppo (Waltz, not too fast); **A-B-A** form, triple-meter dance.

III. *Scene in the Fields*

Adagio; **A-B-A** form, 6/8 meter.

IV. *March to the Scaffold*

Allegretto non troppo; duple-meter march, in minor mode.

V. *Dream of a Witches' Sabbath*

Largo-Allegro; diabolical dance with *Dies irae.*

IV. *March to the Scaffold*

WHAT TO LISTEN FOR: Diabolical march with 2 themes, played by large orchestra.
Recurring melody (*idée fixe*) heard at closing, in clarinet.
Vivid musical portrayal of the beheading.

9	0:00	Opening motive: muted horns, timpani, and pizzicato low strings, forecasts syncopated rhythm of march (theme **B**):
10	0:26	Theme **A**—an energetic, downward minor scale, played by low strings, then violins:
11	1:35	Theme **B**—diabolical march tune, played by brass and woodwinds:
		Opening section repeated.
12	3:55	Developmental section:
		Theme **B**—in brass, accompanied by strings and woodwinds.
		Theme **A**—soft, with pizzicato strings.

Theme **B**—brass, with woodwinds added.
Theme **A**—soft, pizzicato strings, then
     loud in brass.

13   5:03   Theme **A**—full orchestra statement in original
               form, then inverted (now an ascending scale).

14   6:04   *Idée fixe* (fixed idea) melody in clarinet
               ("a last thought of love"), marked "dolce
               assai e appassionato" (as sweetly and
               passionately as possible), followed by loud
               chord that cuts off melody ("the fall of the
               blade"):

        Loud forceful chords close movement.

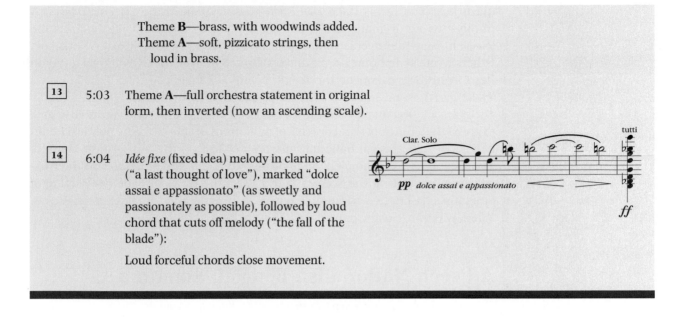

49

Musical Nationalism

*"I grew up in a quiet spot and was saturated from earliest childhood
with the wonderful beauty of Russian popular song. I am therefore
passionately devoted to every expression of the Russian spirit. In
short, I am a Russian through and through!"*

—PETER ILYICH TCHAIKOVSKY

KEY POINTS

- Political unrest throughout Europe stimulated nationalism, which in music
  took many forms (use of folklore, for example, or works written to celebrate
  national heros, events, or places).
- Prominent national schools of composers arose in Russia, Scandinavia,
  Spain, England, and Bohemia, among other locales.
- The Bohemian master Bedřich Smetana wrote nationalistic music about his
  homeland, including a set of six symphonic poems entitled *My Country;* the
  most famous of these is *The Moldau.*

In nineteenth-century Europe, political conditions encouraged the growth of
nationalism to such a degree that it became a decisive force within the Romantic movement. The pride of conquering nations and the struggle for freedom of
suppressed ones gave rise to strong emotions that inspired the works of many
creative artists.

The Romantic composers expressed their nationalism in a number of ways.
Some based their music on the songs and dances of their people: Chopin in his

mazurkas, Liszt in his *Hungarian Rhapsodies,* Dvořák in the *Slavonic Dances.* A number wrote dramatic works based on folklore or peasant life, such as the Russian fairy-tale operas and ballets of Tchaikovsky and Rimsky-Korsakov. Others wrote symphonic poems and operas celebrating the exploits of a national hero, a historic event, or the scenic beauty of their country; Tchaikovsky's *1812 Overture* and Smetana's *The Moldau* exemplify this trend.

In associating music with the love of homeland, composers were able to give expression to the hopes and dreams of millions of people. And the political implications of this musical nationalism were not lost on the authorities. Many of Verdi's operas, for example, had to be altered again and again to suit the Austrian censor. During the Second World War, the Nazis forbade the playing of Smetana's descriptive symphonic poems in Prague and Chopin's polonaises in Warsaw because of the powerful symbolism behind these works.

A Czech Nationalist: Bedřich Smetana

"My compositions do not belong to the realm of absolute music, where one can get along well enough with musical signs and a metronome."

Bedřich Smetana

Bedřich Smetana (1824–1884) was the first Bohemian composer to achieve international prominence. He was born in a small village in eastern Bohemia (now the Czech Republic), the son of a master brewer. In his teens, he was sent to school in Prague, where his love for music was kindled by the city's active cultural life. Smetana's career, like those of other nationalist composers, played out against a background of political agitation. Bohemia stirred restlessly under Austrian rule, caught up in a surge of nationalist fervor that culminated in a series of uprisings in 1848. The young Smetana joined the patriotic cause. After the revolution was crushed, the atmosphere in Prague was oppressive for those suspected of sympathy with the nationalists, so in 1856, he accepted a conducting position in Sweden.

On his return to Prague several years later, Smetana resumed his musical career by writing operas for the National Theater, where performances were given in his native tongue. Of his eight operas, *The Bartered Bride* won him worldwide fame. Today he is best-known for *My Country (Má vlast),* a vast cycle

Principal Works

8 operas, including *The Bartered Bride* (1866)

Orchestral music, including *Má vlast (My Country),* cycle of 6 symphonic poems (No. 2 is *The Moldau,* 1874–79)

Chamber and keyboard works, choral music, and songs

The Moldau River flows in majestic peace through the Czech capital city of Prague.

of six symphonic poems whose composition occupied his time from 1874 to 1879. These works were inspired by the beauty of Bohemia's countryside, the rhythm of its folk songs and dances, and the pomp and pageantry of its legends. While writing the cycle, Smetana's health declined as a result of advanced syphilis, and, like Beethoven, he grew deaf. His diary reveals his deep suffering: "If my illness is incurable," he wrote, "then I should prefer to be delivered from this miserable existence."

The Moldau

The Moldau, the second of the programmatic poems from *My Country,* represents Smetana's finest achievement in the field of orchestral music. In this work, the Bohemian river Moldau (Vltava in Czech) becomes a poetic symbol of the beloved homeland. (For the text of Smetana's program, see Listening Guide 26.) The music suggests first the rippling streams that flow through the forest to form the mighty river. Smetana then evokes a hunting scene with French horns and trumpets, followed by a peasant wedding in a lilting folk dance. The mood changes to one of enchantment as nymphs emerge from their fairy-tale haunts to hold their nightly revels under the moonlight; here, the melody is heard in muted strings over a bubbling accompaniment. The portrayal of the St. John Rapids musters all the brass and percussion, which announce the broad river theme in major mode. Finally, as the Moldau approaches the capital city of Prague, it flows past castles and fortresses that remind the composer of his country's proud history. The river then flows out to sea, as the music fades to a *pianissimo,* closing a work that has captured the imagination of listeners for over a century.

The program

Other Nationalists

Antonín Dvořák (1841–1904) stands alongside Smetana as a founder of the Czech national school. His music drew inspiration not only from the songs and

Music, Folklore, and Nationalism

We have noted that musical nationalism can take a number of different forms: it can conjure up images of a particular scene, it can portray a folk hero, or it can retell a legend from folklore. In *My Country,* a cycle of six symphonic poems, Bedřich Smetana aims to present images of the scenery, the history, and the folk legends of his native land.

Each culture has a value system that lies at the heart of its folklore: children learn right from wrong and prepare for adulthood through folktales, which are transmitted, like folk music, through oral tradition. The characters we find in these folk legends are often rascals whose wrongdoings prove the moral of the story. Such is the case with Peer Gynt, a peasant figure from Norwegian history whose adventures are recounted musically by Edvard Grieg in incidental music to a drama by Henrik Ibsen. Peer Gynt abandons his wife to seek other pleasures, then returns to her forty years later to find her still faithful to him. His wanderings take him to Africa, where he incurs the wrath of the Mountain King for seducing a local maiden. Another famous musical rogue, this one from medieval German legend, is portrayed in Richard Strauss's popular tone poem *Till Eulenspiegel's Merry Pranks* (1895). Till's adventures include riding through a marketplace and upsetting all the goods, disguising himself as a priest, mocking a group of professors, and finally paying the penalty for his pranks: he is tried and hanged, though his spirit cannot be suppressed.

Bernadette Peters as the witch and Pamela Winslow as Rapunzel in the 1987 Broadway production of Stephen Sondheim's musical *Into the Woods.*

Folk material also inspired the Russian composer Modest Musorgsky in composing his programmatic suite *Pictures at an Exhibition*, written for piano and made famous in an orchestral version by Maurice Ravel. The suite is based on an art show commemorating the life and works of Victor Hartmann. One movement, *The Hut on Fowl's Legs*, describes Hartmann's design for a clock shaped like the house of the witch Baba-Yaga. According to Russian legend, Baba-Yaga lured small children to her hut in the woods, where she ate them and ground their bones in her giant mortar. An equally frightening episode occurs in the famous tale of "Hansel and Gretel," collected and retold by Jakob and Wilhelm Grimm; here, the witch's hut is a gingerbread house to which the children are attracted, only to be fattened up for her to eat. This German legend inspired an opera by the nineteenth-century composer Engelbert Humperdinck (whose name was adopted by a twentieth-century pop singer) and was later included as one of a pastiche of tales in the popular Stephen Sondheim musical *Into the Woods* (1988).

In addition to Musorgsky, other Russian composers have turned to their native folk traditions for inspiration: the early-twentieth-century master Igor Stravinsky brought life to the Russian fable of *The Firebird* in an exquisite ballet (1910); and his contemporary Sergei Prokofiev immortalized the well-known story of *Peter and the Wolf* in a symphonic fairy tale of the same name (1936).

Folklore often transcends national boundaries. The French tales "Sleeping Beauty" and "Cinderella" (both from the 1697 collection of Charles Perrault) were set as Russian ballets (*The Sleeping Beauty* by Tchaikovsky in 1890 and *Cinderella* by Prokofiev in 1945); and a fanciful story by the German writer E. T. A. Hoffmann, in an expanded version by French writer Alexandre Dumas, served as the basis for Tchaikovsky's most famous ballet, *The Nutcracker* (1892), which we will study in a later chapter.

The characters Beauty and the Beast at the Disney film premiere (1991).

The theater has traditionally offered an enjoyable means through which to retell these stories, in the form of operas and musicals, as well as ballets. Today, Perrault's "Sleeping Beauty," the Grimms' "Beauty and the Beast," Hans Christian Andersen's "The Little Mermaid," the ancient Greek myth of "Hercules," the Arabian folktale of "Aladdin" from *The Thousand and One Nights*, and *Mulan*, based on a Chinese tale, are brought to life in Disney animated films, whose images and songs keep these cultural expressions alive for a younger generation.

SUGGESTED LISTENING:

Grieg: Incidental music from *Peer Gynt*
Musorgsky: *The Hut on Fowl's Legs*, from *Pictures at an Exhibition*
Tchaikovsky: *The Sleeping Beauty* or *The Nutcracker*
Prokofiev: *Peter and the Wolf*
Sondheim: *Into the Woods*

Colorful, exotic costumes by Russian designer **Léon Bakst** (1866–1924) for the ballet *Sheherazade* (1910), based on music by Rimsky-Korsakov.

dances of his native land but also from America, as we will see in a later chapter.

Edvard Grieg

To the international music public, Edvard Grieg (1843–1907) came to represent "the voice of Norway." The nationalist movement was especially resonant in Norway, owing to the country's struggle for independence from Sweden. It was a cause to which Grieg was devoted and which succeeded shortly before his death. To the concertgoing public, he is known best for his Piano Concerto and the incidental music for *Peer Gynt.*

Jean Sibelius

In the final decades of the nineteenth century, Finland tried to free itself from czarist Russia. Out of this turmoil flowered the art of Jean Sibelius (1865–1957), which announced to the world that his country had come of age musically. During the 1890s, Sibelius produced a series of symphonic poems that captured the spirit of Finnish legends and myths. The most popular of these is *Finlandia* (1899), which occupies the same position in Finland as *The Moldau* does in the Czech Republic.

Russian national school

A Russian national school was represented by a group of young musicians who were called "The Mighty Five" or "The Mighty Handful." Their leader was Mily Balakirev (1837–1910), a self-taught composer who persuaded his four disciples—Alexander Borodin (1833–1887), César Cui (1835–1918), Nikolai Rimsky-Korsakov (1844–1908), and Modest Musorgsky (1839–1881)—that they would have to free themselves from the influence of the German symphony, Italian opera, and French ballet if they wanted to express the Russian soul. Their colleague Peter Ilyich Tchaikovsky (1840–1893) was more receptive to European influences. Of these musicians, Musorgsky and Tchaikovsky are now recognized as Russia's greatest composers.

Late in the century, musical nationalism came to England in the works of Edward Elgar (1857–1934) and Frederick Delius (1862–1934). Spain produced three important nationalists in Isaac Albéniz (1860–1909), Enrique Granados (1867–1916), and Manuel de Falla (1876–1946). America's musical nationalism, relatively late in flowering, will be discussed in Chapter 53.

Listening Guide 26

CD: CHR/STD 6/28–35, SH 3/15–22

Smetana: *The Moldau*

(11:36)

DATE:	1874–79
GENRE:	Symphonic poem, from cycle *My Country* (*Má vlast*)
TEMPO:	Allegro commodo non agitato (fast, not agitated)
PROGRAM:	Scenes along the river Moldau in Bohemia

WHAT TO LISTEN FOR: Musical images of scenes along the river Moldau, each scene marked by different instrumentation (flutes for the bubbling spring; horns for the hunt; staccato strings for peasant dance; double reeds for nymphs in moonlight.
Wide-ranging river theme, which recurs to unify the work.
Shifts between minor and major mode (river theme heard in both major and minor).

Smetana's program: "Two springs pour forth in the shade of the Bohemian forest, one warm and gushing, the other cold and peaceful. Coming through Bohemia's valleys, they grow into a mighty stream. Through the thick woods it flows as the merry sounds of a hunt and the notes of the hunter's horn are heard ever closer. It flows through grass-grown pastures and lowlands where a wedding feast is being celebrated with song and dance. At night, wood and water nymphs revel in its sparkling waves. Reflected on its surface are fortresses and castles—witnesses of bygone days of knightly splendor and the vanished glory of martial times. The Moldau swirls through the St. John Rapids, finally flowing on in majestic peace toward Prague to be welcomed by historic Vyšehrad. Then it vanishes far beyond the poet's gaze."

		PROGRAM	DESCRIPTION
15	0:00	Source of river, two springs	Rippling figures in flute, then added clarinets; plucked string accompaniment.
		Stream broadens	Rippling figure moves to low strings.
16	1:11	River theme	Stepwise melody in violins, minor mode, rippling in low strings; repeated:

17	3:01	Hunting scene	Fanfare in French horns and trumpets:

Rippling continues (in strings); dies down to gently rocking motion.

| 18 | 3:58 | Peasant dance | Repeated notes in strings lead to rustic folk tune, staccato in strings and woodwinds: |

L'istesso tempo, ma moderato

mf

Closes with repeated single note in strings.

| 19 | 5:39 | Nymphs in moonlight | Mysterious, long notes in double reeds: |

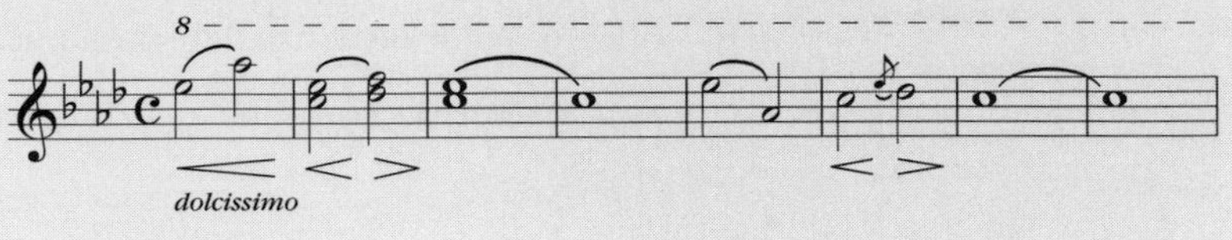

dolcissimo

Rippling figures in flutes; muted string theme with harp, punctuated by French horn; brass *crescendo*, fanfare.

20	8:01	River theme	Like beginning, strings in minor, then shift to major (raised 3rd scale step).
21	8:41	St. John Rapids	Brass and woodwinds exchange an agitated dialogue, build to climax, then die out.
	9:57	River theme	Full orchestra, loudest statement.
22	10:22	Ancient castle (near river mouth)	Hymnlike tune in brass, slow, then accelerates:

ff *sf*   *ff* *sf*   *sf*   *sf*

| | 11:06 | River dies away | Strings slow down, lose momentum; 2 forceful closing chords. |

e Learning

RESOURCE CD

*e*LGs

27 Brahms, Symphony No. 3 in F major

ONLINE TUTOR
www.wwnorton.com/enjoy/

Composers: Romantic
  Johannes Brahms
  Antonín Dvořák
  Felix Mendelssohn
  Amy Beach

Cultural Perspectives
  12. Dvořák's Influence on African-American Art Music
  13. Women and Music: A Feminist Perspective

Resources: Romantic

Listening: Romantic

Quizzes: Romantic
  Reviewing 19, 20
  Listening 16

Glossary

unit **XIX**

Absolute Forms in the Nineteenth Century

50

The Romantic Symphony

"A great symphony is a man-made Mississippi down which we irresistibly flow from the instant of our leave-taking to a long foreseen destination."

—AARON COPLAND

KEY POINTS

- The symphony continued as a favored genre throughout the Romantic era, alongside new programmatic forms (symphonic poem, program symphony).
- The Romantic orchestra increased in size, as many new instruments were added.
- The Romantic symphony was characterized by lyrical themes, colorful harmonies, and expanded proportions.
- The first movement of the Romantic symphony usually remained in sonata-allegro form, and the third movement was most often a spirited scherzo.
- The Bohemian composer Antonín Dvořák found inspiration in nationalist themes and traditional music from his homeland and from the United States, where he lived for several years.
- While in the United States, Dvořák studied the traditional music of African Americans, and incorporated musical elements of spirituals in his music (CP 12).
- The *New World* Symphony, Dvořák's most popular work today, is Classical in its structure but Romantic in its orchestral and harmonic color.
- The *New World* Symphony is loosely programmatic, inspired by Longfellow's poem *The Song of Hiawatha* and by the composer's impressions of the New World.

A symphony must be like the world; it must embrace everything.
—GUSTAV MAHLER

During the Classical period, the symphony became the most exalted form of absolute orchestral music. The three Viennese masters—Haydn, Mozart, and Beethoven—carried it to its highest level of significance and formal beauty. They passed on to composers of the Romantic era a flexible art form that could be adapted to meet the emotional needs of the new age.

In the course of its development, the symphony gained greater weight and importance. Nineteenth-century composers found the symphony a suitable framework for their lyrical themes, harmonic experiments, and individual expressions. By the Romantic era, music had moved from palace to public concert hall, the orchestra had vastly increased in size (see Table on p. 259), and the symphonic structure was growing steadily longer and more expansive. As noted earlier, the nineteenth-century symphonists were thus not as prolific as their predecessors had been. Felix Mendelssohn, Robert Schumann, Brahms, and Tchaikovsky each wrote fewer than seven symphonies. These were in the domain of absolute music, while Liszt and Berlioz cultivated the program symphony.

The Nature of the Symphony

In the hands of Romantic composers, the standard four-movement Classical symphony took on new proportions. For example, the usual number and tempo scheme of the movements was not religiously followed; Tchaikovsky closed his *Pathétique* Symphony with a long, expressive slow movement, and Beethoven pushed the cycle to five movements in his *Pastoral* Symphony.

First movement
The first movement, the most dramatic of the Romantic symphony, generally exhibits the basic elements of sonata-allegro form. It might draw out the

The nineteenth-century orchestra offered the composer new instruments and a larger ensemble. Engraving of an orchestral concert at the Covent Garden Theatre, London, 1846.

A Typical Romantic Symphony

FIRST MOVEMENT	**Sonata-allegro form** **Home key**	**Allegro; optional slow** **introduction**
	Exposition —Theme 1 (home key) —Theme 2 (contrasting key) —Closing theme (same contrasting key)	Rhythmic character Lyrical character
	Development (free modulation)	Fragmentation or expansion of themes
	Recapitulation —Theme 1 (home key) —Theme 2 (home key) —Closing theme (home key)	
SECOND MOVEMENT	**Sonata-allegro form, A-B-A form,** **or theme and variations** **Different key**	**Slow, lyrical**
THIRD MOVEMENT	**Minuet and trio or scherzo and trio,** **A-B-A** **Home key** Minuet or scherzo, 2 sections Trio, 2 sections Minuet or scherzo returns	**Triple meter** Sections repeated
FOURTH MOVEMENT	**Sonata-allegro form, rondo form, or** **some other form** **Home key**	**Allegro or presto; shorter and** **lighter than first movement**

slow introduction, and it often features a long and expressive development section that ventures into distant keys and transforms themes into something the ear perceives as entirely new.

Second movement

The second movement of the Romantic symphony may retain its slow and lyrical nature, but also range in mood from whimsical and playful to tragic and passionate. This movement frequently takes a loose three-part form, but may also fall into the theme and variations mold.

Third movement

Third in the cycle is a strongly rhythmic and exciting scherzo, with overtones of humor, surprise, caprice, or folk dance. In mood, it may be anything from elfin lightness to demonic energy. The tempo marking—usually Allegro, Allegro molto, or Vivace—indicates a lively pace. Scherzo form generally follows the **A-B-A** structure of the minuet and trio. In some symphonies, such as Beethoven's Ninth, the scherzo is second in the cycle. We will see that Brahms wrote a melancholy waltz for the third movement of his Symphony No. 3.

Dvořák's Influence on African-American Art Music

The Bohemian composer Antonín Dvořák was inspired by traditional music of America (as well as of his native Bohemia)—specifically, spirituals, Creole tunes and dances, and what he perceived as music of Native Americans. Yet there is little in the *New World* Symphony that is reminiscent of actual Native American music, although, as we have learned, the two middle movements can be linked with Henry Wadsworth Longfellow's epic poem *The Song of Hiawatha.*

What, then, of Dvořák's professed interest in the traditional music of African Americans? We know that the composer came to love the spirituals sung to him by his student Henry T. Burleigh (1866–1949), and he supposedly had a particular fondness for *Swing Low, Sweet Chariot* (a variant of this spiritual is evoked—perhaps coincidentally— in the first movement of the symphony). The rhythmic syncopations and the particular scale formations used in the *New World* Symphony (the minor mode with a lowered, or flatted, seventh degree) have often been cited as evidence of borrowings from African-American musical styles.

But Dvořák gave much more to American music than he took from it. As a respected teacher, he issued a challenge to American composers to throw

(Left): William Grant Still, composer of the *Afro-American* Symphony.

(Above): Henry T. Burleigh, one of Dvořák's students, noted for his collections of spirituals in art-music style.

Fourth movement The fourth and final movement of the Romantic symphony has a dimension and character designed to balance the first. Often, this movement is a spirited Allegro in sonata-allegro form, and may close the symphony on a note of triumph or pathos. Some composers experimented with the form: in his Fourth Symphony, for example, Brahms turned to the noble Baroque passacaglia (a variation form based on a melodic or harmonic ostinato) for its closing movement, while the finale of Mendelssohn's *Italian* Symphony is based on a popular Italian "jumping dance" known as the saltarello. The chart on page 301 reviews the standard form of the symphony.

off the domination of European music and forge a path of their own, using the "beautiful and varied themes . . . the folk songs of America." Some followed his suggestion, including two of his African-American students. Burleigh published a landmark collection of spirituals arranged in an art music style (*Jubilee Songs of the U.S.A.*, 1916, which included *Deep River*); his goal was to bring the genre to the concert stage. Will Marion Cook (1869–1944), while a student in Dvořák's composition class, began an opera on *Uncle Tom's Cabin* (Harriet Beecher Stowe's novel about life under slavery), but then turned his efforts to musical theater.

Florence Price (1888–1953), the first African-American woman to be recognized as a distinguished composer, is believed to have drawn inspiration for her Symphony in E minor (1932) directly from Dvořák's *New World* Symphony. Price's work parallels Dvořák's in a number of ways, including original themes that allude to characteristic African-American rhythms and melodies.

The composer who best rose to Dvořák's challenge was William Grant Still (1895–1978), whose output exceeds one hundred concert works in a wide variety of genres—symphonies, symphonic poems, suites, operas, ballets, chamber music, choral music, and songs. A nationalist, Still drew musical inspiration from African-American work songs, spirituals, ragtime, blues, and jazz. For his *Afro-American* Symphony (1930), his best-known work today, Still stated his goal clearly: "I knew I wanted to write a symphony, I knew that it had to be an American work; and I wanted to demonstrate how the blues, so often considered a lowly expression, could be elevated to the highest musical level." Although not the first symphonic work written in a jazz or blues style (George Gershwin's *Rhapsody in Blue* was premiered in 1924; on Gershwin, see Chapter 68), Still's symphony was firmly rooted in the music of his African-American heritage.

Dvořák would surely have welcomed these examples of musical nationalism, which were products of an early-twentieth-century movement often referred to as the Black, or Harlem, Renaissance. This movement also saw the rise of great black performers, including Marian Anderson, perhaps the leading contralto soloist in the twentieth century. Anderson broke with tradition in a memorable 1935 art song recital in Salzburg, Austria, in which she closed with a set of black spirituals. One writer noted that what Anderson had done was "outside the limits of classical or romantic music . . . she frightened us with the conception . . . of a mighty suffering." Today, the "validation" of a vernacular music by art music standards described by William Grant Still is no longer necessary, since all musics are coming to be accepted as valuable products of the culture and people who created them.

SUGGESTED LISTENING:

Dvořák: *New World* Symphony, Second Movement
Still: *Afro-American* Symphony, First Movement
Spirituals (*Swing Low, Sweet Chariot; Sometimes I Feel Like a Motherless Child*) ♪

Dvořák as a Symphonist

Antonín Dvořák (1841–1904) is one of numerous late-Romantic composers who found inspiration in the traditional music of their native land. He was born in Bohemia (now part of the Czech Republic) and grew up in a village near Prague, where his father kept an inn. For a time, poverty threatened to rule out a musical career. However, at sixteen the boy managed to get to Prague, where he mastered his craft and secured a position playing the viola in the Czech National Theater under the baton of Smetana. In 1874, the Austrian government

Dvořák's family shortly after their arrival in America in 1892.

awarded him a stipend that allowed him to resign his orchestra post and devote himself to composing. By the time he was forty, Dvořák was a professor of composition at the Conservatory of Prague, a post in which he was able to exert an important influence on the musical life of his country.

The spontaneity and melodious character of his music assured its popularity; by the last decade of the century, Dvořák was known throughout Europe and the United States. In 1891, Jeannette Thurber, who ran the National Conservatory of Music in New York City, invited him to become its director. There he received $15,000 a year (a fabulous sum in those days), as compared with the annual $600 he had earned in Prague. His stay in the United States was eminently fruitful, resulting in what has remained his most successful symphony, *From the New World*, a number of chamber music works, including the *American* Quartet, and the highly lyrical Cello Concerto. Mrs. Thurber wanted him to write an opera on *The Song of Hiawatha;* but although Dvořák already knew and admired Longfellow's poem, the project never materialized. The operas he did complete—fourteen in all—were based on European themes.

Armed with an established reputation as a nationalist composer, Dvořák tried to steer his American pupils toward their native heritage. One of his students was Henry T. Burleigh, an African-American baritone and arranger of spirituals. The melodies Dvořák heard from Burleigh appealed to the folk poet in him, and strengthened his conviction that American composers would find their true path only when they had thrown off the influence of Europe and sought their inspiration in the Native American, African-American, and traditional folk songs of their own country. This doctrine helped prepare the way for the rich harvest of American works by composers of the next generations. The composer eventually returned to his beloved Bohemia, where he died at the age of sixty-three, revered as a national artist.

Dvořák had a great gift for melody, a love of native folk tunes, and a solid craftsmanship, which enabled him to shape musical ideas into large forms notable for their clarity. He wrote his Symphony No. 9, subtitled *From the New World*, during his stay in the United States, and it received its first performance in New York in 1893. The whole symphony may be seen as a descriptive landscape, evoking the openness of the American prairie as well as the composer's longing for his homeland. It is set in a standard four-movement framework, the middle movements of which can be directly linked to the influence of Longfellow's *Song of Hiawatha*. The clearest association is in the third movement, a scherzo, which portrays *Hiawatha's Wedding Feast* (beginning with the *Dance of the Pa-Puk-Keewis*); the trio depicts a group of natives who are turned into birds. The deeply felt English-horn tune that opens the second movement, a Largo, was made famous when sung as a kind of spiritual, set to the words "Goin' Home."

in his own words

In the Negro melodies of America I discover all that is needed for a great and noble school of music. These beautiful and varied themes are the product of the soil. . . . They are the folk songs of America, and your composers must turn to them.

51

Brahms and the Late Romantic Symphony

"It is not hard to compose, but it is wonderfully hard to let the super-fluous notes fall under the table."

KEY POINTS

- The German composer Johannes Brahms continued the Classical traditions of the Viennese masters; in particular, he revered the works of Beethoven.
- Brahms studied with Robert Schumann, and after Schumann's death, remained a close friend of his wife, Clara.
- Brahms is known for his four symphonies, his solo piano and chamber music, and his Lieder, which follow in the tradition of Schubert and Schumann.
- Brahms's Third Symphony is Classical in its structures and proportions, but highly Romantic in its tone.

Johannes Brahms created a Romantic art in the purest Classical style. His veneration for the past and his mastery of musical architecture brought him closer to the spirit of Beethoven than any of his contemporaries.

His Life

Johannes Brahms (1833–1897) was born in Hamburg, the son of a double-bass player. At the age of ten, Johannes helped increase the family income by playing the piano in the dance halls of the slum district where he grew up.

His first compositions greatly impressed Joseph Joachim, the leading violinist of the day, who arranged for Brahms to visit Robert Schumann at Düsseldorf and study with him. Schumann recognized in the shy young composer a future leader of the circle dedicated to absolute music. Robert and Clara Schumann took the fair-haired youth into their home, and their friendship opened up new horizons for him. But then came the tragedy of Schumann's mental collapse. With tenderness and strength, Brahms supported Clara through the ordeal of Robert's illness. (On Robert Schumann as a composer, see Chapter 43.)

Robert Schumann lingered for two years while Brahms was shaken by the great love of his life. Fourteen years his senior and the mother of seven children, Clara Schumann, herself a fine pianist and composer, appeared to young Brahms as the ideal of womanly and artistic achievement. (On Clara Schumann, see Chapter 46.) What began as filial devotion ripened into romantic passion. At the same time, he was torn by feelings of guilt, for he loved and revered Robert Schumann, his friend and benefactor, above all others.

Johannes Brahms

Principal Works

Orchestral music, including 4 symphonies (1876, 1877, 1883, 1884–85); *Variations on a Theme by Haydn* (1873); 2 overtures (*Academic Festival*, 1880; *Tragic*, 1886); 4 concertos (2 for piano, 1858, 1881; 1 for violin, 1878; 1 double concerto for violin and cello, 1887)

Chamber music, including string quartets, quintets, sextets; piano trios, quartets, and 1 quintet; 1 clarinet quintet; sonatas (violin, cello, clarinet/viola)

Piano music, including sonatas, character pieces, dances, and variation sets (on a theme by Handel, 1861; on a theme by Paganini, 1862–63)

Choral music, including *A German Requiem* (1868), *Alto Rhapsody* (1869), and part songs

Lieder, including *Vergebliches Ständchen* (*Futile Serenade*, 1881), *Four Serious Songs* (1896), and folk song arrangements

This conflict was resolved the following year by Robert's death, but another conflict took its place. Brahms was faced with the choice between love and freedom. Time and again in the course of his life, he was torn between the two, with the decision always going to freedom. His ardor subsided into a lifelong friendship, although two decades later he could still write her, "I love you more than myself and more than anybody and anything on earth."

Ultimately, Brahms settled in Vienna, where he remained for the next thirty-five years. During this time, he became enormously successful, the acknowledged heir of the Viennese masters.

In early manhood, his mother's death had led him to write *A German Requiem*. In 1896, Clara Schumann's declining health gave rise to the *Four Serious Songs*. Her death profoundly affected the composer, already ill with cancer. He died ten months later, at the age of sixty-four, and was buried in Vienna not far from Beethoven and Schubert.

His Music

Brahms was a traditionalist; his aim was to show that new and important things could still be said in the tradition of the Classical masters. His four symphonies are unsurpassed in the late Romantic period in breadth of conception and design, yet their forms draw upon those of earlier eras. Among his other orchestral works, the *Variations on a Theme by Haydn* and his two concert overtures are often heard today. In his two piano concertos and his violin concerto, the solo instrument is integrated into a full-scale symphonic structure.

Orchestral music

Chamber and solo music

To a greater degree than any of his contemporaries, Brahms captured the tone of intimacy that is the essence of chamber music style. He is an important figure in piano music as well. His two variation sets, on themes by Handel and Paganini, represent his top achievement in that field. The Romantic in Brahms

Brahms: Symphony No. 3 in F major, Third Movement (6:24)

DATE OF WORK:	1883
GENRE:	Symphony
MEDIUM:	Orchestra (strings and woodwinds only in this movement)
MOVEMENTS:	I. Allegro con brio; sonata-allegro, F major
	II. Andante; modified sonata form, C major
	III. Poco allegretto; **A-B-A'** form, C minor
	IV. Allegro; sonata-allegro; F major

WHAT TO LISTEN FOR: Melancholy minor-key melody in cellos, then violins, woodwinds, and French horns.

Regular, symmetrical phrases set in moderate triple meter.

3-part structure with modal shifts (minor-major-minor).

Rhythmic complexity through "three-against-two" patterns; syncopated rhythms that lean over the barline.

Third Movement: Poco allegretto; 3/8 meter, C minor, A-B-A' form

23 0:00 **A** section—yearning cello melody, accompanied by rustling string figures; symmetrical phrasing:

0:27 Violins repeat the cello theme, extending the range and dynamics.

0:52 New, 2nd theme, played by violins, "leans" over the barline over moving cello line; violins and cellos join in brief duet:

1:27 Return of opening theme in flutes and oboes, with broader accompaniment.

24 1:57 **B** section—connected 3-note figure in woodwinds, in A-flat major, accompanied by offbeat sixteenth notes in the cellos:

3:27 Woodwinds hint at return to main theme, accompanied by sustained strings.

25 3:46 **A′ section**—French horns announce the opening theme in C minor, with richer orchestration.

4:14 Oboes take up the haunting melody as accompaniment builds.

4:41 Theme 2, now heard in the clarinets and bassoons.

5:17 Violins and cellos take up the main theme, played in octaves for greater intensity; generally thicker and more contrapuntal accompaniment.

5:44 Brief coda; reminiscent of **B** section; last chord is punctuated by pizzicato strings.

Vocal music

also found expression in short lyric piano pieces: the rhapsodies, ballades, capriccios, and intermezzi are among the treasures of the literature, but his *Hungarian Dances* and the set of sixteen waltzes for piano duet are more popular.

As a song writer, Brahms stands in the direct line of succession to Schubert and Robert Schumann. His output includes about two hundred solo songs and an almost equal number for two, three, or four voices. The favorite themes are love, nature, and death. His *German Requiem,* written to biblical texts that he selected himself, made him more famous during his lifetime than any of his other works (see Chapter 54).

Symphony No. 3 in F Major

Brahms did not attempt to write a symphony until he was past forty. He was fond of saying that it was no laughing matter to compose a symphony after Beethoven. "You have no idea," he told a friend, "how the likes of us feel when we hear the tramp of a giant like him behind us."

The Third Symphony, written in 1883 when Brahms was fifty years old, is the shortest of his four symphonies and the most Romantic in tone. In form, however, the work looks back to the Classical structures of the eighteenth century. The first movement, a conventional sonata-allegro, opens with a dramatic figure: a three-note motive (F-A♭-F) that is often related to the composer's personal motto, "Frei aber froh" (Free but happy). This motive permeates the entire symphony. The slow movement, a haunting Andante in sonata-allegro form, evokes the peacefulness of nature with its simple, hymnlike theme in the woodwinds.

Rather than following with a scherzo, Brahms writes a melancholy waltz in C minor, set in ternary form (see Listening Guide 27). The opening theme, a yearning cello melody, is heard throughout this impassioned orchestral "song without words," accompanied by restless string figures. First the violins, then the woodwinds take up the poignant melody, whose arched rise and fall suggests a huge orchestral sigh. The middle section, now in a major key, presents two themes set against an expressive, chromatic accompaniment. The return of the opening theme is newly orchestrated, heard first in the French horns and oboes, then in an emotional statement by the violins and cellos playing in octaves. A short coda brings back the mood of the middle section, and then closes quietly, with two soft pizzicato chords.

A famous caricature of Brahms in his later years; the composer was a familiar sight in Vienna as he made his way to The Red Hedgehog, his favorite tavern.

The finale, a dramatic sonata-allegro, features concise themes and abrupt changes of mood that challenge the listener and affirm the technical command and the creative invention of a great Romantic master.

52

The Romantic Concerto

"We are so made that we can derive intense enjoyment only from a contrast."

—SIGMUND FREUD

KEY POINTS

- The Romantic concerto preserves the Classical three-movement structure, but uses standard forms (e.g., sonata-allegro and first-movement concerto form) more freely.
- The concerto was a vehicle for brilliant virtuosic display by the soloist.
- Many concertos were written with a specific soloist in mind, and thus tailored to the technical abilities of that musician.
- Felix Mendelssohn preserves many Classical elements in his compositions, including his Violin Concerto in E minor.

The Nature of the Concerto

The Romantic concerto retains the Classical three-movement form, opening with a dramatic Allegro, usually in sonata form, which is followed by a lyrical slow movement and a brilliant finale. The first movement, though, is usually freer than its Classical counterpart: the solo instrument may not wait for an orchestral exposition to make its first statement, and the cadenza, normally played at the close of the recapitulation and before the coda, may occur earlier, as part of the development. The second movement continues to present songful melodies, often in a loosely structured three-part form. And the finale, which brings the dramatic tension between soloist and orchestra to a head, often features another cadenza, bringing the work to an exciting close.

Virtuosity and the Concerto

The origins of the Romantic concerto reach back to the late eighteenth century. Mozart and Beethoven, both formidable pianists, performed their concertos in public, delighting and dazzling their audiences. This element of virtuosic display, combined with appealing melodies, helped make the concerto one of the most widely appreciated types of concert music. As the concert industry developed, technical brilliance became a more and more important element of concerto style. We have seen that nineteenth-century composer-performers

The demonic is that which cannot be explained in a cerebral and a rational manner. . . . Paganini is imbued with it to a remarkable degree, and it is through this that he produces such a great effect.
—JOHANN WILHELM VON GOETHE

such as Paganini and Liszt carried virtuosity to new heights. This development kept pace with the increase in the size and resources of the symphony orchestra. The Romantic concerto became one of the most favored genres of the age. Felix Mendelssohn, Chopin, Liszt, Robert and Clara Schumann, Brahms, Tchaikovsky, and Dvořák all contributed to its literature.

Composers of the concerto often write with particular artists in mind, and may even consult them about what is possible given their own technique and that of their instrument. We have already seen that Mozart wrote piano concertos not only for himself but for several women performers of his time, including one of his students. The Violin Concerto of Felix Mendelssohn was written for the virtuoso Ferdinand David, concertmaster of the Leipzig Gewandhaus Orchestra, which the composer conducted. Brahms consulted Joseph Joachim, the leading violinist of the day, when he wrote his Violin Concerto. And Tchaikovsky wrote his with the virtuoso Leopold Auer in mind; when Auer found the work unplayable, the composer turned to another extraordinary violinist, Adolf Brodsky, who gave the premiere performance.

Felix Mendelssohn and the Concerto

Felix Mendelssohn (1809–1847), whose music is a blend of meticulous craftsmanship and serene, elegant expression, represents the classicist trend within the Romantic movement. The works of this man of culture, education, and creative gifts hold a prominent place in the repertory. The Mendelssohn home was a meeting place for Berlin intellectuals, their garden house the scene of memorable concerts. Here an orchestra under the direction of the seventeen-year-old Felix performed his Overture to *A Midsummer Night's Dream* for a captivated audience. Felix was not the only musician in the household. His sister Fanny was a gifted pianist and composer as well. (Some of her works were published under her brother's name.)

Mendelssohn excelled in a number of roles—as pianist, conductor, organizer of music festivals, and educator. At twenty-six, he was named conductor of the

Felix Mendelssohn

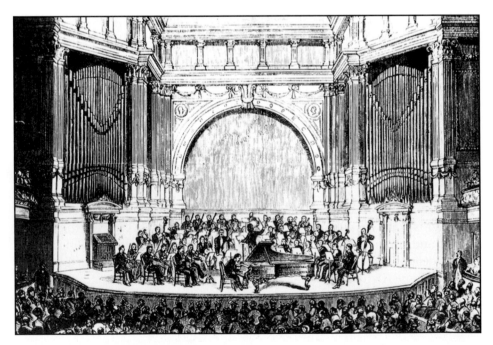

In this woodcut from the 1870s, the noted virtuoso Hans von Bülow performs a piano concerto with orchestra in New York City.

A Typical Romantic Concerto

FIRST MOVEMENT	Concerto form (double exposition) Home key	Allegro
	Orchestral exposition —Several themes Solo exposition —Same themes and others Development Recapitulation Cadenza (solo instrument alone) Coda, or closing	
SECOND MOVEMENT	A-B-A form Contrasting key	Slow, lyrical
THIRD MOVEMENT	Rondo form or sonata-allegro form Home key	Allegro or presto

Gewandhaus Orchestra in Leipzig and went on to transform the orchestra into the finest in Europe. Later he founded the Conservatory of Leipzig, which raised the standards for the training of musicians. Mendelssohn's happy life was shattered in 1847 by the death of his sister Fanny, to whom he was deeply attached. This blow, along with his very demanding musical career, brought on a stroke, from which he died at age thirty-eight.

Mendelssohn was dedicated to preserving the tradition of the Classical forms in an age that was turning from them. But it should not be supposed that he was untouched by Romanticism. Of his symphonies, the best-known are the Third (the *Scottish*) and the Fourth (the *Italian*)—mementos of his youthful travels. Mendelssohn was also a prolific writer for the voice; the oratorio *Elijah*, one of his best-loved works, represents the peak of his achievement in this category.

The Violin Concerto in E minor (1844), written three years before the composer's death, was Mendelssohn's last orchestral work and is one of the most popular violin concertos of all time. This work reveals the composer's special gifts: clarify of form, subtlety of orchestration, and a reserved, sentimental expression. The concerto's three-movement structure conforms to the classical ideals, although new ideas of unity have been imposed. For example, the three movements are to be played without pause, and a reference back to the first movement occurs in the second, hinting at cyclical form. Also, the first movement, an Allegro molto appassionato (Very fast and impassioned), does away with the customary orchestral introduction in concerto form; rather, the solo violin announces the main theme almost immediately in a dramatic and expansive melody that forms a broad arch with balanced, symmetrical phrases. The work gives the soloist plenty of opportunity for brilliant display and, with its appealing melodies and formal clarity, displays the tender sentiment and classical moderation that are so typical of Mendelssohn's music.

Violin Concerto in E minor

53

The Rise of Classical Composition in America

"I hear America singing, the varied carols I hear."
—WALT WHITMAN

KEY POINTS

- The European musical tradition was dominant in the United States throughout much of the nineteenth century, and most American musicians studied in Europe.
- The late-nineteenth-century New England School of composition, which included Amy Beach, was the first to make its original mark on musical styles in America.
- Amy Beach was active as a pianist, composer, and music educator.
- Her Symphony in E minor was inspired by Dvořák's *New World* Symphony; her Violin Sonata in A minor shows the influence of Brahms, with its major-minor tonal shifts.
- Women musicians of the Romantic era were discouraged from pursuing professional careers as composers (CP 13).

We have already explored various aspects of early American music and concert life in Cultural Perspectives (pp. 128, 196), noting several styles that were unique to North America. By 1850, a vibrant musical life had grown up in major U.S. and Canadian cities, dominated by European composers and musicians. Young Americans who were attracted to careers as performers or composers went abroad to complete their studies. When they returned home, they brought the European traditions with them. Virtuosity was admired by American audiences, who thronged to hear the "Swedish nightingale" Jenny Lind on her extended concert tour. One of America's first native virtuoso musicians was Louis Moreau Gottschalk (1829–1869), a charismatic pianist and composer of mixed racial heritage who was born in New Orleans and trained in Paris. Gottschalk pioneered the use of American song and dance in his works; his original keyboard compositions, such as *The Banjo* and *Bamboula*, incorporated elements from African-American and Creole music idioms that he had absorbed growing up in New Orleans.

The European musical tradition prevailed in the Americas for several more generations. The German-born conductor Theodore Thomas devoted his energies to cultivating a public taste for orchestral music in America by setting up a concert series across the continent and establishing, in 1864, New York City's second professional orchestra (the Philharmonic Society had been formed in 1842). Among American educators, Lowell Mason (1792–1872) was single-handedly responsible for establishing music as a part of the public school curriculum, a contribution still valued today.

Melody . . . may be classed as the gift of folk song to music, and harmony is its shadow language.
—EDWARD MACDOWELL

Among the first American composers to write music comparable in quality to that of European musicians was the New Englander John Knowles Paine (1839–1906), whose Mass in D, modeled on Beethoven's *Missa solemnis,* was the first large-scale classical work by an American to be performed in Europe. From 1876 until his death thirty years later, Paine held the country's first professorship in music, at Harvard University.

George Whitefield Chadwick (1854–1931) was influential in giving an American flavor to music based on European models. His symphonic works, most of which were premiered by the Boston Symphony Orchestra, and his five string quartets were well received. Chadwick left his mark on students both as a teacher and as director of the New England Conservatory in Boston.

Another composer who made important strides in turning the national path away from the Germanic style was Edward MacDowell (1860–1908), a New Yorker who studied piano and composition in Europe. His very popular *Woodland Sketches,* for piano, and his Second Orchestral Suite both incorporate Native American tunes. In 1896, MacDowell became the first professor of music at Columbia University. Amy Cheney Beach, a contemporary of all these influential musicians, was widely recognized in her lifetime as the leading American woman composer. Renewed interest in her work has shown her to be in the forefront of the so-called New England School of composition.

Amy Cheney Beach and Music in New England

Amy Cheney (1867–1944) was born in Henniker, New Hampshire, the only child of a wealthy industrialist and a gifted amateur singer and pianist. A child prodigy, Amy had a keen ear for music. She studied piano with her mother and later piano and composition in Boston. She published her first composition, a song set to a Longfellow poem, in 1883.

Amy concertized regularly and in 1885 performed Chopin's F-minor Piano Concerto in the first of several concerts she played with the Boston Symphony Orchestra. In the same year, she married Henry Harris Aubrey Beach, a forty-three-year-old physician and amateur singer.

Between 1885 and 1910, Amy Cheney Beach (or Mrs. H. H. A. Beach, as she chose to be known) produced a number of her major works. These include the Mass in E-flat, the concert aria *Racing Clouds,* the *Gaelic* Symphony, and the Piano Concerto in C-sharp minor—all performed by prestigious musical groups such as the Boston Symphony Orchestra, the Symphony Society of New York, and the Handel and Haydn Society of Boston. Her *Festival Jubilate,* commissioned for the dedication of the Women's Building of the Chicago World Exposition of 1893, provided her with the international venue she needed to gain wide visibility and recognition as a composer.

In her later years, Beach helped shape the careers of many young musicians. She held leadership positions in the Music Educators National Conference and the Music Teachers National Association; she also served as co-founder and first president of the Society of American Women Composers. At her death in 1944, she left her royalties to the MacDowell Colony, a retreat for artists, writers, and composers in Peterborough, New Hampshire, where she spent a portion of each summer from 1921 on.

Beach's Symphony in E minor, the first symphony composed by an American woman, is a masterpiece that is thought to have been inspired by Dvořák's *New World* Symphony, also in E minor. Aware of Dvořák suggestion that

in her own words

The women composers of today have advanced in technique, resourcefulness, and force, and even the younger composers have achieved some effects which the great masters themselves would never have dared to attempt. The present composers are getting away more and more from the idea that they must cater to the popular taste, and in expressing their individual ideas, are giving us music of real worth and beauty.

Amy Cheney Beach

Women and Music: A Feminist Perspective

Have you wondered why we study so few works by women composers? We have seen that in earlier eras, upper-class women frequently studied music, especially keyboard playing and singing—indeed, such study was a near necessity in proper society. Some, like the medieval abbess Hildegard of Bingen, were inspired to compose music, but exclusively for the needs of the church; others, like Barbara Strozzi, performed and composed within the elite world of the Italian intellectual academies. One Baroque-era musician, Lavinia della Pietà, composed in secret; as she confided to her diary, "I could not do otherwise. They would not take me seriously, they would never let me compose. The music of others is like words addressed to me; I must answer and hear the sound of my own voice. . . . Woe betide me should they find out."

Although the gender barrier began to break down in the later nineteenth century, many still held the view that women lacked creativity in the arts. This attitude drove some women to pursue literary careers under male pseudonyms: George Eliot (alias Mary Ann Evans), George Sand (alias Baronne Aurore Dudevant), and Daniel Stern (alias Comtesse Marie d'Agoult), to name just three. Despite the social attitudes of the era, Clara Schumann and Fanny Mendelssohn Hensel, among others, saw their compositions published and critically acclaimed. But the odds were against them in this endeavor. George Upton, writing in 1880, claimed, "Not only are women too emotional and lacking in stamina to write music, but a woman's mind simply cannot grasp the scientific logic of music making," and even Clara Schumann herself remarked that "women always betray themselves in their compositions." Still, women made their musical mark, especially in songs, piano music, and chamber works.

Repression of women became an important social issue at the beginning of the twentieth century. A women's movement arose to bring about social reform: some worked against societal problems such as alcoholism, some fought for improved education, and many rallied for suffrage, or the right to vote. (It was not until 1920, with the passage of the Twentieth Amendment to the Constitution, that women won legal equality in the political arena.) By the turn of the century, some female musicians had adopted militant feminist perspectives.

One such activist was the English composer Ethel Smyth, a prominent suffragist who fought against sexual discrimination in music. Her *March of the Women* became the anthem of a feminist organization called the Women's Social and Political Union. It was sung at meetings, in the streets, and even in prison. (Smyth herself was imprisoned for two months, for breaking the windows of a cabinet minister.) She also led a campaign to secure positions in all professional orchestras for women performers. (This crusade was not altogether successful in her lifetime—the Vienna Philharmonic Orchestra reluctantly admitted its first permanent woman member, a harpist, in 1997!) In her later years, Smyth was viewed as somewhat eccentric when she began wearing manly tweed suits and smoking a pipe.

Not all women composers followed her courageous path. As we have seen, the American composer Amy Beach was more conservative, choosing to be known professionally as Mrs. H. H. A. Beach in

The title page to English composer Ethel Smyth's *March of the Women*, a work that became the rallying cry of the early feminist movement.

deference to her married status; however, in later life, she headed several important educational organizations that reached out to both sexes.

Feminists today have posed some interesting questions regarding women composers. For example, do women and men speak differently through music? Is there a woman's "voice" in music, and if so, what characterizes it? More scientifically, does biology play a role in the creative process? Reviewers, mostly male, have criticized musical works by nineteenth-century women that failed to conform to traditional structural procedures (such as the symphony cycle or sonata-allegro form). Did women base their choice of forms on their concert settings (which were mostly salons instead of public halls), on the makeup of their audiences, or on their musical training, which usually occurred at home? Or did they avoid the common procedures of composition because of the "masculine" implications of the forms—which were, after all, designed and defined exclusively by men? Critics have not always applied the same standards to compositions by both sexes: while a woman might be criticized for writing music that was too "feminine," a man who writes music considered "feminine" (Chopin, for example) is credited with having a full range of emotional expression.

Society has clearly come a long way in accepting women and their creative musical expressions. And while we have not fully resolved the intriguing questions raised above, differences between the sexes include the ideas men and women express through music. One of the major contributions of the feminist perspective in modern times has been the recognition of women's own experiences, as distinct from men's perception of women's experiences. Thus, the multimedia artist Meredith Monk often composes works about women and their views of life. Her 1988 film *Book of Days*, for example, tells the tale of a fourteenth-century Jewish girl who is troubled with baffling visions of the future, and her operas *Education of the Girlchild* (1975) and *Atlas* (1991), the latter commissioned by the Houston Grand Opera, both focus on women and their lifetime quests. The contemporary composer Libby Larsen (b. 1950), frequently sets women's writings to music. Her *Songs from Letters: Calamity Jane to Her Daughter Janey* (1989) is a song cycle based on

The country pop group the Dixie Chicks, performing at a 1999 Lilith Fair concert in Hershey, Pennsylvania.

excerpts from the famous frontierwoman's diary and her opera *Frankenstein, the Modern Prometheus* (1990) reinterprets Mary Shelley's famous novel. We will study Joan Tower (b. 1938), whose six *Fanfares for the Uncommon Woman* pay homage to the well-known *Fanfare for the Common Man* by Aaron Copland while making a tongue-in-cheek feminist statement.

Popular music has opened up to a new woman's voice and to improved perceptions of women. While many rock songs have made demeaning references to women and expressed violent attitudes toward them, modern artists such as Salt 'N Pepa, the first successful female rap group, hip-hop artists Queen Latifah, Missy Elliot, and Li'L Kim, and the all-female cast of the Lilith Fair tours, organized by Sarah MacLaughlin, have sounded a strong voice against female bashing through their own artistic creations. As society gradually moves not only to accept the creative contributions of women, but to welcome and understand them, there is no doubt that more female musicians and composers will achieve success and inspire others in their chosen professions.

SUGGESTED LISTENING:

Works by Hildegard, Clara Schumann, Fanny Mendelssohn Hensel, Ethel Smyth, Meredith Monk, Libby Larsen, Salt 'N Pepa, Queen Latifah *(All Hail the Queen)*, Alanis Morissette *(Under Rug Swept)*

American composers look to their own folk music for inspiration (see CP 12), Beach noted that New Englanders were likely to be of Irish, Scottish, or English ancestry, and thus drew on these musical traditions in her *Gaelic* Symphony. In the realm of chamber music, Beach contrinuted many works, including the Violin Sonata in A minor. This well-constructed, appealing work, along with the *Gaelic* Symphony, signaled the final strains of American Romanticism. It also marks Beach's significant contribution to classical composition in North America.

Choral and Dramatic Music in the Nineteenth Century

Romantic Choral Music

"God sent his singers upon earth with songs of sadness and of mirth."

—HENRY WADSWORTH LONGFELLOW

KEY POINTS

- Choral music grew in popularity during the Romantic era and was an artistic outlet for the middle classes.
- Favored genres in the nineteenth century include *part songs* (unaccompanied secular songs in three or four parts), the oratorio, the Mass, and the Requiem Mass.
- Brahms's *German Requiem,* set to biblical texts chosen by the composer, is one of the masterworks of the romantic choral repertory.

The nineteenth century witnessed a spreading of the democratic ideal and an enormous expansion of the audience for music. This climate was uniquely favorable to choral singing, a group activity enjoyed by increasing numbers of amateur music lovers that played an important role in the musical life of the Romantic era.

Since singing in a chorus required a different skill than playing in an orchestra, it attracted many people who had never learned to play an instrument or who could not afford to buy one. With a modest amount of rehearsal (and modest vocal quality), they could take part in the performance of great choral works. The members of the chorus not only enjoyed a pleasant social evening

Amateur choral groups

In the nineteenth century, enormous choral and orchestral forces were a common sight, as in this engraving depicting the opening concert at St. Martin's Hall, London, 1850.

The oldest, truest, most beautiful organ of music, the origin to which our music owes its being, is the human voice.
—RICHARD WAGNER

once or twice a week but also, if their group was good enough, became a source of pride to their community.

Choral music offered the masses an ideal outlet for their artistic energies. The repertory centered about the great choral heritage of the past. Nevertheless, if choral music was to remain a vital force, its literature had to be enriched by new works that would reflect the spirit of the time. The list of composers active in this area includes some of the most important names of the nineteenth century: Schubert, Berlioz, Felix and Fanny Mendelssohn, Clara and Robert Schumann, Liszt, Verdi, Brahms, Dvořák. These composers produced a body of choral music that represents some of the best creative efforts of the Romantic period.

Choral forms
Among the large-scale genres of choral music in the nineteenth century were the Mass, the Requiem Mass, and the oratorio. We have seen that all three were originally intended to be performed in church, but by the nineteenth century they had found a wider audience in the concert hall. In addition, a vast literature of secular choral pieces appeared. These works, settings for chorus of **Part songs** lyric poems in a variety of moods and styles, were known as *part songs*—that is, songs with three or four voice parts. Most of them were short melodious works, easy enough for amateurs. They gave pleasure both to the singers and to their listeners, and played an important role in developing the new audience of the nineteenth century.

Brahms's A German Requiem

A German Requiem was rooted in the Protestant tradition into which Johannes Brahms was born. Its aim was to console the living and lead them to a serene acceptance of death as an inevitable part of life, hence its gentle lyricism. Brahms chose his text from the Old and New Testaments: from the Psalms, Proverbs, Isaiah, and Ecclesiastes as well as from Paul, Matthew, Peter, John, and Revelation. Brahms was not religious in the conventional sense, nor was he affiliated with any particular church. He was moved to compose his Requiem by the death first of his teacher and friend Robert Schumann, then of his mother, whom he idolized; but the piece transcends personal emotions and endures as a song of mourning for all humanity.

Written for soloists, four-part chorus, and orchestra, *A German Requiem* is in seven movements arranged in a formation resembling an arch. There are connections between the first and last movements, between the second and sixth, and between the third and fifth; that leaves the fourth movement, the widely sung chorus *How Lovely Is Thy Dwelling Place*, as the centerpiece.

This movement is based on a verse from Psalm 84 (see Listening Guide 28). The first two lines of the psalm are heard three times, separated by two contrasting sections that present the other lines. The form, therefore, is **A-B-A′-C-A′**. The first two sections for the most part move in quarter notes, but the third section (**C**) moves more quickly in a vigorous rhythm, better suiting the line "die loben dich immerdar" (that praise Thee evermore), with much expansion on *immerdar* (evermore). With the final reappearance of the **A** section, the slower tempo returns. Marked *piano* and *dolce* (soft and sweet), this passage serves as a coda that brings the piece to its gentle and serene close.

Listening Guide 28

CD: CHR/STD 5/58–62, SH 3/26–30

Brahms: *A German Requiem*, Fourth Movement   (5:46)

DATE OF WORK:	1868
GENRE:	Protestant Requiem
MEDIUM:	4-part chorus, soloists, and orchestra
MOVEMENTS:	7

WHAT TO LISTEN FOR: Lyrically beautiful choral melody at opening unifies the 5-part rondo structure.
Changes in mode (major-minor) and texture (homorhythmic/polyphonic).
Use of word painting—quicker in **C** section, and drawn out at end, according to text.
Emotional expressions of loss and acceptance of death.

Fourth Movement: Mässig bewegt (moderately agitated)

Text: Psalm 84
Form: Rondo (**A-B-A′-C-A′**)
Character: Lilting triple meter, marked *dolce* (sweetly)

Opening melody—clarinets and flutes begin with inversion of first phrase in chorus:

		TEXT	TRANSLATION	DESCRIPTION
26	0:00	Wie lieblich sind deine Wohnungen, Herr Zebaoth!	How lovely is Thy dwelling place, O Lord of Hosts!	**A**—a flowing, arched melody, SATB homophonic setting, answers orchestral opening, in E-flat major; text repeated in tenors, joined by other voices.
27	1:26	Meine Seele verlanget und sehnet sich nach den Vorhöfen des Herrn; mein Leib und Seele freuen sich in dem lebendigen Gott.	My soul longs and even faints for the courts of the Lord; my flesh and soul rejoice in the living God.	**B**—shift to minor, builds fugally with word repetition from lowest to highest voices; sudden accents on first beat of measures, with plucked strings; text is repeated, climax on "lebendigen."
28	2:39	Wie lieblich . . . Wohl denen, die in deinem Hause wohnen,	How lovely . . . Blessed are they that live in Thy house,	**A′**—opening returns in E-flat major, with new text and varied setting.
29	3:51	die loben dich immerdar!	that praise Thee evermore!	**C**—martial quality, faster movement in polyphonic setting.
30	4:44	Wie lieblich . . .	How lovely . . .	**A′**—coda-like return, reminiscent of opening; soft orchestral closing, in E-flat major.

55

Romantic Opera

"Opera is free from any servile imitation of nature. By the power of music it attunes the soul to a beautiful receptiveness."

—FRIEDRICH VON SCHILLER

KEY POINTS

- Romantic opera developed into distinct national styles in France, Germany, and Italy.
- In France, *lyric opera* represented a merger between *grand opera* (serious historical dramas with spectacular effects) and *opéra comique* (comic opera with spoken dialogue).
- In Germany, the earlier genre of *Singspiel* (light, comic drama with spoken dialogue) gave way to more serious works, including Richard Wagner's *music drama,* a genre that integrated all elements of opera.

- Both *opera seria* (serious opera) and *opera buffa* (comic opera) were favored in Italy; they marked the pinnacle of the *bel canto* (beautiful singing) style.
- Many Romantic composers turned to exotic plots for their operas, looking to far-away lands or cultures for inspiration. The lyric opera *Carmen*, by French composer Georges Bizet, exemplifies this trend by romanticizing Roma, or Gypsy, culture in Spain (see CP 14).

For well over three hundred years, opera has been one of the most alluring forms of musical entertainment. A special glamour is attached to everything connected with it—its superstar performers, extravagant scenic designs, even the glitter and excitement of opening nights.

At first glance, opera seems to demand that the spectator believe the unbelievable. It presents us with human beings caught up in dramatic situations, who sing to each other instead of speaking, even after they've been strangled or stabbed or shot. True enough, people in real life do not sing to each other. Neither do they converse in blank verse, as Shakespeare's characters do, nor live in rooms of which one wall is conveniently missing so that the audience may look in. All the arts employ conventions that are accepted by both the artist and the audience. The conventions of opera are just, perhaps, more evident. In any case, the fundamental goal of art is not to copy nature but to heighten our awareness of it.

Opera uses the human voice to project basic emotions—love, hate, jealousy, joy, grief—with an elemental force. The logic of reality gives way on the operatic stage to the power of music and the imagination.

> *I have never encountered anything more false and foolish than the effort to get truth into opera. In opera everything is based upon the untrue.*
> —PETER ILYICH TCHAIKOVSKY

The Development of National Styles

As one of the most important and best-loved theatrical genres of the nineteenth century, opera fostered different national styles in three of Europe's leading musical countries—France, Germany, and Italy.

In Paris, the opera center of all Europe in the late eighteenth and early nineteenth centuries, *grand opera* was all the rage. This new genre, which focused on serious, historical themes and was nourished by the propagandist purposes of France's new leaders, suited the bourgeoisie's taste for the big and the spectacular very well. Complete with huge choruses, crowd scenes, ornate costumes and scenery, and elaborate dance episodes, grand opera was as much a spectacle as a musical event. Giacomo Meyerbeer (1791–1864), a German composer who studied in Italy, was primarily responsible for bringing grand opera to Paris. His best-known works in the style are *Robert le diable* (*Robert the Devil*, 1831) and *Les Huguenots* (1836), both of which reveal careful attention to the drama as a

Margrave's Opera House in Bayreuth, 1879. A painting by **Gustav Bauernfeind.** (Deutsches Theatermuseum, Munich)

The Lure of Spain

The French composer Georges Bizet's opera *Carmen* is one of many examples of exoticism. But what exactly did Bizet find exotic about this story (based on a tale by French writer Prosper Mérimée) and its Spanish setting? And how does his music for this opera fire the listener's imagination with thoughts of far-off lands?

In *Carmen*, Bizet romanticized Gypsy (or Roma) culture, which he presents through a title character whose moral values—or lack of them—shocked nineteenth-century audiences. The libretto echoes the theme of naturalism, a movement led by the French novelist Émile Zola (1840–1902) that fo-

cused on the life of the lower classes and their suffering. Carmen and her friends, a band of Gypsy smugglers, fall far short of the standards of middle-class virtue. But they are seen against the exotic allure of Spain, and Bizet's music invests them with a certain human dignity. The music for *Carmen* imitates the songs and dances of the Spanish Gypsies, a style often referred to as flamenco. Typical of southern Spain, flamenco music is actually a variety of different dance songs, most performed to the accompaniment of a strummed guitar, with hand clapping, foot stomping, and finger snapping. One type of flamenco music heard in *Carmen* is the seguidilla,

The American expatriate painter **John Singer Sargent** (1856–1925) was drawn to the exoticism of Spain, as illustrated here in *El Jaleo: Spanish Dancer with Guitarists.* (Isabella Stewart Gardner Museum, Boston)

whole—a blend of social statement, history, and spectacle with memorable melodies and rich orchestration.

Opéra comique   Less pretentious than French grand opera was *opéra comique*, which required smaller performance forces, featured a simpler compositional style, and included spoken dialogue rather than recitatives. One of the lighter works that delighted Parisian audiences was Jacques Offenbach's (1819–1880) *Orphée aux enfers* (*Orpheus in the Underworld,* 1858), which blended wit and satire into the popular model. Eventually the spectacle of grand opera and the simplicity of **Lyric opera**   opéra comique merged, to produce *lyric opera.* This hybrid type featured appeal-a dance in moderate triple meter that is sung to a fixed poetic verse form. Flamenco performances often begin with shouts of encouragement from the audience, followed by a rhapsodic guitar introduction that sets the mood for the dancers. Distinctive features include a hoarse, nasal vocal quality and a freely melismatic style of singing, both influences of Arab music in southern Spain. Some styles of flamenco also make use of castanets, a percussion instrument consisting of two shell-shaped pieces of wood clapped together in one hand. Today, flamenco remains a vibrant and spectacular entertainment that reflects the interpenetration of other folk and popular genres.

But Bizet also looked to a more distant locale in his music. Carmen's famous aria—the *Habanera*, which we will study—is based on a Cuban dance form. A habanera is a slow dance in duple meter whose name reflects its origin in Havana. It gained popularity in nineteenth-century Europe and Latin America, and greatly influenced the Argentine tango, a dance with sudden rhythmic movements performed by couples in a tight embrace. The tango has enjoyed popularity for some years as a ballroom dance. Today, the *Tangos nuevos* (new tangos) of the Argentinian composer and virtuoso bandoneon (accordion) player Astor Piazzolla (1921–1992) are

Tango dancers in a dramatic pose.

heard throughout the world. A merger of various musical styles, these eclectic pieces are bold, dramatic, and passionate. The history of this colorful dance has also been chronicled in a popular Broadway show *Forever Tango* (1997).

TERMS TO NOTE:

flamenco	habanera
seguidilla	tango
castanets	bandoneon

SUGGESTED LISTENING:

Bizet: *Habanera,* from *Carmen*
Spanish dance music (flamenco)
Tango music (Astor Piazzolla)

ing melodies and romantic drama, and found its greatest proponent in Georges Bizet, whose *Carmen* is a masterpiece of the French lyric stage.

Nineteenth-century Germany had no long-established opera tradition, as France and Italy did. The immediate predecessor of German Romantic opera was the *Singspiel,* a light or comic drama with spoken dialogue. The first composer to express the German Romantic spirit in opera was Carl Maria von Weber (1786–1826), whose best-known work is *Der Freischütz (The Freeshooter,* 1821). In this opera, supernatural beings and mysterious forces of nature intertwine with heros and heroines to produce drama featuring simple and direct melodies

Germany

Singspiel

that are almost folklike, accompanied by expressive timbres and harmonies. The greatest figure in German opera—and one of the most significant in the history of the Romantic era—was Richard Wagner, who created the *music drama,* a genre that integrated theater and music completely (see Chapter 57).

Italy   Italy in the early nineteenth century still recognized the opposing genres of *opera seria* (serious opera) and *opera buffa* (the Italian version of comic opera), legacies of an earlier period. Important composers of these styles include Gioachino Rossini (1792–1868), whose masterpiece was *Il barbiere di Siviglia* (*The Barber of Seville,* 1816); Gaetano Donizetti (1797–1848), composer of some seventy operas, including *Lucia di Lammermoor* (*Lucy of Lammermore,* 1835); and Vincenzo Bellini (1801–1835), whose *Norma* (1831) is preeminent for its **Bel canto style**   lovely melodies. These operas marked the high point of a *bel canto* (beautiful singing) style, characterized by florid melodic lines and delivered by voices of great agility and purity of tone. The consummate master of nineteenth-century Italian opera was Giuseppe Verdi, who sought to develop a uniquely national style (see Chapter 56).

Exoticism in Opera

We saw that a yearning for far-off lands was an important component of the Romantic imagination. This tendency found a perfect outlet in opera, whose action could take place anywhere in the world. Composers of such works were not terribly interested in authenticity; their primary concern was to create a picturesque atmosphere that would appeal to audiences. In other words, an exotic setting reflected the imagination of the composer rather than first-hand knowledge of a culture. If the action took place in Asia or Africa, the work was still in the musical language of the West, but that language was flavored with melodies, harmonies, and rhythms suggestive of the faraway locale.

A prime example is Verdi's *Aida,* which manages within the traditional idiom of Italian opera to evoke ancient Egypt under the pharaohs. The French composer Camille Saint-Saëns (1835–1921) turned to the Bible for the story of *Samson and Delilah.* Another biblical story inspired the German composer Richard Strauss to write *Salome;* although the opera is set in ancient Judea, Salome's *Dance of the Seven Veils* centers around a tune reminiscent of a langorous Viennese waltz. The turn-of-the-century Italian master Giacomo Puccini (1858–1924) produced two well-known operas with Asian settings: *Turandot,* based on a legend of ancient China, and *Madame Butterfly,* a romantic drama set in late-nineteenth-century Japan, which we will study in Chapter 58.

Women in Opera

Opera was one medium that allowed women musicians a good deal of visibility. Only a few tried their hand at composing full-scale operas, but those who did **Louise Bertin**   were able to see a number of their works produced. The French composer Louise Bertin (1805–1877) had several produced at the exclusive Opéra-Comique in Paris, including *La Esmeralda* (1836), on a libretto based on Victor Hugo's well-known novel about the hunchback of Notre Dame.

Women opera singers were among the most prominent performers of their day, idolized and in demand throughout Europe and the Americas. One such

The famous singer Jenny Lind during a recital at Exeter Hall, London, 1855.

Jenny Lind

international star was Jenny Lind (1820–1887), known as the "Swedish nightingale" and famous for her roles in operas by Meyerbeer, Donizetti, Weber, and Bellini. A concert artist as well, Lind made her American debut in 1850 in a tour managed with immense hoopla by circus impresario P. T. Barnum.

Professional singing was often a family tradition: the offspring of the celebrated Spanish tenor Manuel Garcia provide a case in point. A brilliant teacher, Garcia coached two of his daughters to stardom. His eldest, Maria Malibran (1808–1836), became renowned as an interpreter of Rossini, whose works she sang in London, Paris, Milan, Naples, and New York. A riding accident brought her very successful career to a tragic close. Her youngest sister, Pauline Viardot (1821–1910), was highly acclaimed for her great musical and dramatic gifts. Viardot did much to further the careers of Charles Gounod, Jules Massenet, and Gabriel Fauré (French composers of operas and songs), and sang the premieres of vocal works by Brahms, Robert Schumann, and Berlioz. In 1849, her Paris performance in Meyerbeer's *Le prophète (The Prophet)*, in a role created specially for her, prompted Berlioz to write: "Madame Viardot is one of the greatest artists . . . in the past and present history of music." A composer herself, Viardot's intellectual approach to her art did much to raise the status of women singers (see illustration on p. 277).

Maria Malibran

Pauline Viardot

56

Verdi and Italian Opera

"Success is impossible for me if I cannot write as my heart dictates!"

KEY POINTS

- The Italian nationalist composer Giuseppe Verdi is best known for his twenty-eight operas; they embody the spirit of Romantic drama and passion.
- *Rigoletto*, Verdi's opera based on a play by Victor Hugo, is one of the most performed works in the repertory today.

In the case of Giuseppe Verdi, the most widely loved of operatic composers, time, place, and personality were happily merged. He inherited a rich musical tradition, his capacity for growth was matched by extraordinary energy and will, and he was granted a long life in which to exploit fully his creative gift.

His Life

Born in a small town in northern Italy where his father kept an inn, Giuseppe Verdi (1813–1901) grew up amid the poverty of village life. His talent attracted the attention of a prosperous merchant and music lover in the neighboring town of Busseto who made it possible for the youth to pursue his studies. After two years in Milan, Verdi returned to Busseto to take a position as an organist. When he fell in love with his benefactor's daughter, the merchant in wholly untraditional fashion accepted the penniless young musician as his son-in-law. Verdi was twenty-three, Margherita sixteen.

Three years later, he returned to Milan with the manuscript of an opera, which was produced at the opera house of La Scala in 1839. The work brought him a commission to write three others. At this time, Verdi faced a string of crises in his life. His first child, a daughter, had died before he left for Milan. The second, a baby boy, was carried off by fever in 1839, a catastrophe followed several months later by the death of his young wife. "In a sudden moment of despondency I despaired of finding any comfort in my art and resolved to give up composing," he wrote.

As the months passed, the distraught young composer held to his decision. Then one night he happened to meet the director of La Scala, who insisted that he take home a libretto about Nebuchadnezzar, King of Babylon. Verdi returned to work, and the resulting opera, *Nabucco*, presented at La Scala in 1842, was a triumph for the twenty-nine-year-old composer and launched him on a spectacular career.

Italy at the time was liberating itself from Austrian Hapsburg rule. Verdi identified himself with the national cause from the beginning: "I am first of all an Italian!" he declared. In this charged atmosphere, his works took on special

Giuseppe Verdi

meaning for his compatriots. Whatever the time or place in which an opera was set, it was interpreted as a symbol of their cause. The chorus of exiled Jews from *Nabucco* became an Italian patriotic song that is still sung today.

Although he became a world-renowned figure, Verdi retained the simplicity that was at the core of both the artist and the man. He returned to his roots, to Busseto, where he settled with his second wife, the singer Giuseppina Strepponi. She was a sensitive and intelligent woman who had created the leading roles in his early operas and who was his devoted companion for half a century. After Italy won independence, Verdi was urged to run for a seat in parliament because of the prestige his name would bring the new state. Although the task conformed to neither his talents nor his inclinations, he accepted and sat in the Chamber of Deputies for some years.

During his time in public life, he was somehow able to produce one masterpiece after another. He was fifty-seven when he wrote *Aida.* At seventy-three, he completed *Otello,* his greatest lyric tragedy. And in 1893, on the threshold of eighty, he astonished the world with *Falstaff.* In all, he wrote twenty-eight operas.

Verdi's death at eighty-seven was mourned throughout the world. He left the bulk of his fortune to a home for aged musicians that he had founded in Milan (still in operation today). Italy accorded him the rites reserved for a national hero. From the voices of thousands who marched in his funeral procession there arose the haunting melody of "Va pensiero sull' ali dorate" (Go, thought, on gilded wings), the chorus from *Nabucco,* with which he had inspired his fellow Italians sixty years earlier.

The singer Giuseppina Strepponi, Verdi's second wife, with a score of his opera *Nabucco.* (Museo Teatrale alla Scala, Milan)

His Music

Verdi's music stands as the epitome of Romantic drama and passion. Endowed with an imagination that saw all emotion in terms of action and conflict, Verdi was able to communicate a dramatic situation with shattering expressiveness. True Italian that he was, he prized melody above all; to him this was the most immediate expression of human feeling. "Art without spontaneity, naturalness, and simplicity," he maintained, "is no art."

Of his fifteen early operas, the most important is *Macbeth,* his first work based on story material from Shakespeare. Following in close succession came *Rigoletto* (which we will study), on a play by Victor Hugo; *Il trovatore* (*The Troubador*), derived from a fanciful Spanish play; and *La traviata,* based on *La dame aux camélias* (*The Lady of the Camellias*), by the younger Alexandre Dumas. In these works, the mature musical dramatist was revealed.

The operas of the middle period show Verdi writing on a more ambitious scale and incorporating elements of the French grand opera. The three most important are *A Masked Ball, The Force of Destiny,* and *Don Carlos.* His artistic aims were carried even further in *Aida,* the work that ushers in his final period (1870–93). *Aida* was commissioned in 1870 by the ruler of Egypt to mark the opening of the Suez Canal. (You may know *Aida* as the recent Broadway show by Elton John and Tim Rice, which is based on Verdi's masterpiece.) In 1874, the composer completed his Requiem, dedicated to the memory of Alessandro

in his own words

It seems to me that the best material I have yet put to music is Rigoletto. *It has the most powerful situations, it has variety, vitality, pathos; all the dramatic developments result from the frivolous, licentious character of the Duke. Hence Rigoletto's fears, Gilda's passion, etc., which give rise to many dramatic situations, including the scene of the quartet.*

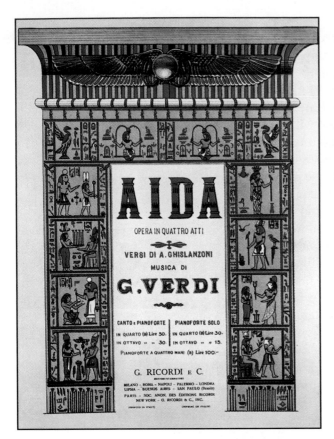

The Egyptian theme of Verdi's opera *Aida* is graphically illustrated on the cover of the score published by G. Ricordi in Milan.

Manzoni, a novelist and patriot whom Verdi had revered.

For his last two operas, Verdi found an ideal librettist in Arrigo Boito (1842–1918), who brilliantly adapted two plays by Shakespeare. *Otello*, their first collaboration, is the high point of three hundred years of Italian lyric tragedy. Six years later (1893), Verdi completed *Falstaff*, based on Shakespeare's *Merry Wives of Windsor*. Fitting crown to the labors of a lifetime, this luminous work ranks with the greatest comic operas.

Rigoletto

The writer Victor Hugo, an acknowledged leader of French Romanticism, was Verdi's source of inspiration for *Rigoletto*. Hugo's play *Le roi s'amuse* (*The King Is Amused*, 1832) was banned in France but achieved universal popularity through its adaptation in Verdi's opera. The plot, featuring lechery, deformity, irony, and assassination, revolves around a hunchbacked jester, Rigoletto, who is a fascinating study in opposites. (You will remember that Hugo wrote of another hunchback, in his historical novel *Notre-Dame de Paris*, or *The Hunchback of Notre Dame*; the intriguing bell-ringer Quasimodo has inspired several well-known movies, including the Disney animated musical.) With a libretto by Francesco Piave, *Rigoletto* was Verdi's first great success.

The story is set in the Renaissance era at the ducal court of Mantua, a small city in northern Italy (Monteverdi wrote his early operas there). The first scene takes place in a great hall of the ducal palace, where a ball is in progress. The Duke, a notorious womanizer, woos the wife of one of his courtiers, the Count of Ceprano. The court jester, Rigoletto, mocks the unlucky husband to all who will listen, and then suggests to the Duke that the Count of Ceprano be disposed of. Meanwhile, gossiping courtiers spread a rumor that the hunchbacked jester has a mistress. An elderly nobleman, Monterone, interrupts the scene and accuses the Duke of having seduced his daughter. The Duke promptly has the aging father arrested; Rigoletto taunts the man, who returns his gibes with a curse.

Principal Works

28 operas, including *Macbeth* (1847), *Rigoletto* (1851), *Il trovatore* (*The Troubadour*, 1853), *La traviata* (*The Lost One*, 1853), *Un ballo in maschera* (*A Masked Ball*, 1859), *La forza del destino* (*The Force of Destiny*, 1862), *Don Carlos* (1867), *Aida* (1871), *Otello* (1887), and *Falstaff* (1893)

Vocal music, including a Requiem Mass (1874)

In a dark alley, Rigoletto meets up with the assassin Sparafucile, who warns the jester that he has enemies and offers him his services. Arriving home, Rigoletto warns Gilda and her nurse to stay in the house and not admit anyone. As Rigoletto leaves, the Duke enters the garden, realizing then that the beautiful young woman he had noticed in church is the jester's daughter. The Duke, claiming to be a poor student, professes his love to Gilda. As courtiers approach the house, he escapes. Believing that Gilda is the deformed jester's mistress, the courtiers plan to abduct her in retribution for Rigoletto's cruel taunting. When the father returns, he is tricked into being blindfolded, and Gilda is carried off as Rigoletto recalls Monterone's curse.

In Act II, Rigoletto strives to convince everyone that Gilda is indeed his daughter. She is brought out and throws herself in her father's arms, ashamed of her behavior with the Duke. Rigoletto vows vengeance on the abductors.

Costumes for the first production of Verdi's *Rigoletto* at Teatro la Fenice, Venice, March 11, 1851.

The final act takes place on a stormy night at a tavern near the river. Sparafucile's sister, Maddalena, has lured the Duke to the lonely tavern, and Rigoletto forces Gilda to watch through a window as the Duke pursues Maddalena. Planning to send her away, Rigoletto then instructs his daughter to dress as a man for her escape. Meanwhile, it has been arranged that Sparafucile will kill the Duke and return his body to Rigoletto in a bag to be thrown in the river. However, Maddalena succumbs to the Duke's charms and begs her brother to spare the handsome nobleman. Sparafucile agrees, only if a substitute shows up at the tavern. Gilda, now in male attire, overhears the plan, and enters the tavern to sacrifice herself for the unworthy man she loves. Sparafucile returns the sack to Rigoletto, as arranged, but just as the hunchback is about to dispose of the body, he hears the Duke singing from an upstairs window. Horrified, he opens the sack to find a dying Gilda, who begs forgiveness for herself and the Duke. Rigoletto recalls the curse one last time, as Gilda dies in his arms.

Two of the most popular operatic moments of all time occur in Act III. The Duke sings the best-known of Verdi's tunes, "La donna è mobile" (Woman is fickle), a simple but rousing song accompanied by a guitar-like orchestral strumming. The orchestra previews the catchy melody, which is heard numerous times as a ritornello in a strophic setting that brings back the opening text as a refrain.

The quartet that follows shortly is a masterpiece of operatic ensemble writing, as Verdi himself noted in the quote above. Each of the four characters presents a different point of view: the Duke woos Maddalena in a lovely bel canto–style melody, calling her "beautiful daughter of love"; Maddalena answers with a laughing line in short notes, "Ha! Ha! I laugh heartily"; Gilda, watching from outside, is heartbroken as she laments her lost love; and Rigoletto hushes her, swearing vengeance for such treatment of his beloved daughter. Although the text

The quartet scene from Verdi's *Rigoletto* in the London premiere (1853) at Covent Garden. Rigoletto and his daughter, Gilda (on the right), are watching the Duke and Maddalena inside the tavern.

becomes increasingly more difficult to follow as the characters sing together, the emotions of each soar through clearly (see Listening Guide 29 for text and form).

These two show-stopping numbers ensured the immediate success of *Rigoletto*. It remains one of the most frequently performed operas of the international repertory.

Listening Guide 29

CD: CHR/STD 6/14–19, SH 3/31–36

Verdi: *Rigoletto*, Act III, excerpts

(8:13)

FIRST PERFORMANCE:	1851, Venice
LIBRETTIST:	Francesco Maria Piave
BASIS:	Play, *Le roi s'amuse*, by Victor Hugo
MAJOR CHARACTERS:	The Duke of Mantua (tenor)
	Rigoletto, the Duke's jester, a hunchback (baritone)
	Gilda, Rigoletto's daughter (soprano)
	Sparafucile, an assassin (bass)
	Maddalena, Sparafucile's sister (contralto)

WHAT TO LISTEN FOR: Opening orchestral ritornello that returns in the middle and end to unify the aria.
Memorable aria in a lilting triple meter, with 2 verses sung strophically.
Quartet reflects the emotions and points of view of each character: the Duke, Maddalena, Gilda, and Rigoletto.

Aria: "La donna è mobile" (Duke)

Form: Strophic, with refrain

Orchestral introduction previews the Duke's solo, also appears in middle and at the closing; opening melody of aria:

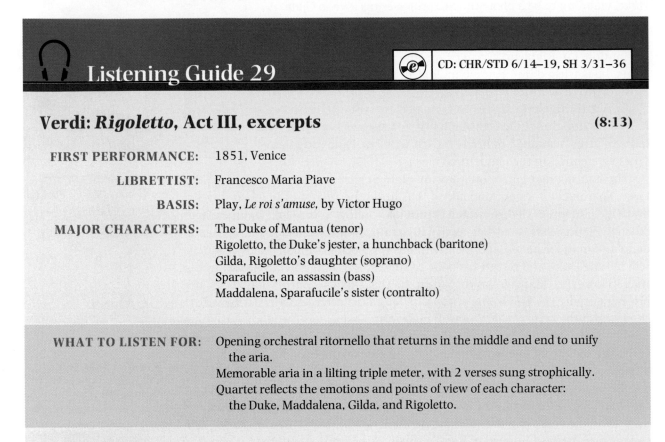

La don - na è   mo - bi - le   qual pium - a al   ven - to,   mut - a d'ac - cen - to

The Duke, in a simple cavalry officer's uniform, sings in the inn;
Sparafucile,
Gilda, and Rigoletto listen outside.

DUKE

31	0:00	La donna è mobile	Woman is fickle
		Qual piuma al vento,	like a feather in the wind,
		Muta d'accento,	she changes her words
		E di pensiero.	and her thoughts.

Sempre un amabile	Always lovable,
Leggiadro viso,	and a lovely face,
In pianto o in riso,	weeping or laughing,
È menzognero.	is lying.

32 1:10

La donna è mobile, etc.	Woman is fickle, etc.
È sempre misero	The man's always wretched
Chi a le s'affida,	who believes in her,
Chi lei confida	who recklessly entrusts
Mal cauto il core!	his heart to her!
Pur mai non sentesi	And yet one who never
Felice appieno	drinks love on that breast
Chi su quel seno	never feels
Non liba amore!	entirely happy!
La donna è mobile, etc.	Woman is fickle, etc.

Sparafucile comes back in with a bottle of wine and two glasses, which he sets on the table; then he strikes the ceiling twice with the hilt of his long sword. At this signal, a laughing young woman in gypsy dress leaps down the stairs: the Duke runs to embrace her, but she escapes him. Meanwhile Sparafucile has gone into the street, where he speaks softly to Rigoletto.

SPARAFUCILE

È là il vostr'uomo . . .	Your man is there . . .
Viver dee o morire?	Must he live or die?

RIGOLETTO

Più tardi tornerò l'opra a compire.	I'll return later to complete the deed.

Sparafucile goes off behind the house toward the river. Gilda and Rigoletto remain in the street, the Duke and Maddalena on the ground floor.

Quartet: "Un dì" (Duke, Maddalena, Gilda, Rigoletto)

DUKE

33 2:44

Un dì, se ben rammentomi,	One day, if I remember right,
O bella, t'incontrai . . .	I met you, O beauty . . .
Mi piacque di te chiedere,	I was pleased to ask about you,
E intesi che qui stai.	and I learned that you live here.
Or sappi, che d'allora	Know then, that since that time
Sol te quest'alma adora!	my soul adores only you!

GILDA

Iniquo!	Villain!

MADDALENA

Ah, ah! . . . e vent'altre appresso	Ha, ha! . . . And does it now perhaps
Le scorda forse adesso?	forget twenty others?
Ha un'aria il signorino	The young gentleman looks like
Da vero libertino . . .	a true libertine . . .

DUKE *(starting to embrace her)*

Sí . . . un mostro son . . .	Yes . . . I'm a monster . . .

GILDA

Ah padre mio!	Ah, Father!

MADDALENA

Lasciatemi, stordito.	Let me go, foolish man!

DUKE

Ih che fracasso!	Ah, what a fuss!

MADDALENA

Stia saggio.	Be good.

DUKE

E tu sii docile,	And you, be yielding,
Non fare tanto chiasso.	don't make so much noise.
Ogni saggezza chiudesi	All wisdom concludes
Nel gaudio e nell'amore.	in pleasure and in love.

(He takes her hand.)

La bella mano candida!	What a lovely, white hand!

MADDALENA

Scherzate voi, signore.	You're joking, sir.

DUKE

No, no.	No, no.

MADDALENA

Son brutta.	I'm ugly.

DUKE

Abbracciami.	Embrace me.

GILDA

Iniquo!	Villain!

MADDALENA

Ebro!	You're drunk!

DUKE

D'amor ardente.	With ardent love.

MADDALENA

Signor l'indifferente,	My indifferent sir,
Vi piace canzonar?	would you like to sing?

DUKE

No, no, ti vo' sposar.	No, no, I want to marry you.

MADDALENA

Ne voglio la parola.   I want your word.

DUKE *(ironic)*

Amabile figliuola!   Lovable maiden!

RIGOLETTO *(to Gilda, who has seen and heard all)*

È non ti basta ancor?   Isn't that enough for you yet?

GILDA

Iniquo traditor!   Villainous betrayer!

MADDALENA

Ne voglio la parola.   I want your word.

DUKE

Amabile figliuola!   Lovable maiden!

RIGOLETTO

È non ti basta ancor?   Isn't that enough for you yet?

Quartet (2nd part): "Bella figlia" (Duke, Maddalena, Gilda, Rigoletto)

Overall form: **A-B-A′-C**

Diagram showing how characters interact in the ensemble and how they fit into the musical structure:

Section:	**A**	**B**	**A′**	**C**	**Coda**
soprano:		Gilda		all characters	all characters
alto:		Maddalena			
tenor:	Duke	Duke			
baritone:		Rigoletto			

Opening melody of "Bella figlia," sung by Duke:

Bel - la fi - glia dell' a - mo - re, schia - vo son de' vez - zi tuo - i,

DUKE

34	4:15	Bella figlia dell'amore,	Beautiful daughter of love,	A
		Schiavo son de' vezzi tuoi;	I am the slave of your charms;	
		Con un detto sol tu puoi	with a single word you can	(Many lines of text
		Le mie pene consolar.	console my sufferings.	throughout the
		Vieni, e senti del mio core	Come, and feel the quick beating	quartet are repeated.)

Il frequente palpitar . . .   of my heart . . .
Con un detto sol tuo puoi   With a single word you can
Le mie pene consolar.   console my sufferings.

MADDALENA

35   5:19   Ah! ah! rido ben di core,   Ha! Ha! I laugh heartily,   **B**
Chè tai baie costan poco.   for such tales cost little.

GILDA

Ah! cosí parlar d'amore . . .   Ah! To speak thus of love . . .

MADDALENA

Quanto valga il vostro gioco,   Believe me, I can judge
Mel credete, sò apprezzar.   how much your game is worth.

GILDA

. . . a me pur l'infame ho udito!   . . . I too have heard the villain so!

RIGOLETTO *(to Gilda)*

Taci, il piangere non vale.   Hush, weeping is of no avail.

GILDA

Infelice cor tradito,   Unhappy, betrayed heart,
Per angoscia non scoppiar. No, no!   do not burst with anguish. Ah, no!

MADDALENA

Son avvezza, bel signore,   I'm accustomed, handsome sir,
Ad un simile scherzare.   to similar joking.
Mio bel signor!   My handsome sir!

DUKE

36   7:01   Bella figlia dell'amore, etc.   Beautiful daughter of love, etc.   **A′**
Vieni!   Come!

RIGOLETTO

Ch'ei mentiva sei sicura.   You are sure that he was lying.
Taci, e mia sarà la cura   Hush, and I will take care
La vendetta d'affrettar.   to hasten vengeance.
Sì, pronta fia, sarà fatale,   Yes, it will be swift and fatal,
Io saprollo fulminar.   I will know how to strike him down.
Taci, taci . . .   Hush, hush . . .

Text repeated   **C and Coda**

57

Wagner and the Music Drama

"The error in the art genre of opera consists in the fact that a means of expression—music—has been made the object, while the object of expression—the drama—has been made the means."

KEY POINTS

- The German composer Richard Wagner revolutionized opera with his idea of the *Gesamtkunstwerk*—a total work of art unifying all elements.
- Wagner's operas—called *music dramas*—are not sectional (in arias, ensembles, and the like), but are continuous; they are unifed by *leitmotifs*, or recurring themes, that represent a person, place, or idea.
- The emotional quality of Wagner's music is heightened by his extensive use of chromatic dissonance.
- Wagner's most famous work is his four-opera cycle, *The Ring of the Nibelung.*

Richard Wagner

Richard Wagner looms as the single most important phenomenon in the artistic life of the later nineteenth century. Historians often divide the period into "before" and "after" Wagner. The course of post-Romantic music is unimaginable without the impact of this complex and fascinating figure.

His Life

Richard Wagner (1813–1883) was born in Leipzig, the son of a minor police official who died when Richard was still an infant. The future composer was almost entirely self-taught; he received in all about six months of instruction in music theory. At twenty, he abandoned his academic studies at the University of Leipzig and obtained a position as chorus master in a small opera house.

Early years

Wagner was thirty when his grand opera *Rienzi* won a huge success in Dresden. As a result, he found himself appointed conductor to the king of Saxony. With his next three works, *The Flying Dutchman, Tannhäuser,* and *Lohengrin,* Wagner took an important step from the drama of historical intrigue to the idealized folk legend. He chose subjects derived from medieval German epics, displayed a profound feeling for nature, employed the supernatural as an element of the drama, and glorified the German land and people. But the Dresden public was not prepared for *Tannhäuser.* They had come to see another *Rienzi* and were disappointed.

A revolution broke out in Dresden in 1849. Wagner not only sympathized openly with the revolutionaries but took part in their activities. When the revolt failed, he fled to Weimar, where his friend Liszt helped him cross the border into Switzerland. In Zurich, he commenced the most productive period of his career. First, Wagner produced his most important literary works, *Art and Revolution, The Art Work of the Future,* and the two-volume *Opera and Drama,* which sets forth his theories of the *music drama,* as he named his concept of opera that

Wagner the revolutionary

Music drama

Richard Wagner at Home in Bayreuth: a painting by **W. Beckmann**, 1882. To Wagner's left is his wife, Cosima; to his right, Franz Liszt and Hans von Wolzogen.

integrated theater and music completely. He next proceeded to put theory into practice in the cycle of four music dramas called *The Ring of the Nibelung*. But when he reached the second act of *Siegfried* (the third opera in the cycle), he grew tired and laid aside the gigantic task. He turned to writing two of his finest works—*Tristan and Isolde* and *Die Meistersinger von Nürnberg*.

The years following the completion of *Tristan* were the darkest of his life. The musical scores accumulated in his drawer without hope of performance; Europe contained neither singers nor a theater capable of presenting them. At this point, a miraculous turn of events intervened. In 1864, an eighteen-year-old boy who was a passionate admirer of Wagner's music ascended the throne of Bavaria as Ludwig II. In one of his most artistically important acts, the young monarch summoned the composer to Munich, where *Tristan* and *Die Meistersinger* were performed at last. The king then commissioned him to complete the *Ring*, and Wagner took up where he had left off a number of years earlier.

Bayreuth A theater was planned specifically for the presentation of Wagner's music dramas, which ultimately resulted in the Festival Theater at Bayreuth. And to crown his happiness, the composer found a woman he considered his equal in will and courage—Cosima, the daughter of his old friend Liszt. She left her husband and children in order to join Wagner; they were married some years later, after the death of his first wife.

One task remained: to make good the financial deficit of the festival, Wagner undertook *Parsifal* (1877–82), a "consecrational festival drama" based on the legend of the Holy Grail. He finished the opera as he reached seventy. In every sense a conqueror, Wagner died shortly thereafter and was buried at Bayreuth.

His Music

Wagner did away with the old "number" opera with its separate arias, duets, ensembles, choruses, and ballets. His aim was to create a continuous fabric of melody that would never allow the emotions to cool. He therefore evolved an "endless melody" that was molded to the natural inflections of the German language, more melodious than the traditional recitative, more flexible and free than the traditional aria. Wagner's concept of opera, or music drama as his later works were known, was that of a total artwork (in German, *Gesamtkunstwerk*), in which all the arts—music, poetry, drama, visual spectacle—were fused.

Endless melody

The orchestra is in fact the focal point and unifying element in Wagnerian music drama. It floods the characters and the audience in a torrent of sound that embodies the sensuous ideal of the Romantic era. The orchestral tissue is fashioned out of concise themes, the *leitmotifs*, or "leading motives"—Wagner called them basic themes—that recur throughout a work, undergoing variation and development as do the themes and motives of a symphony. The leitmotifs carry specific meanings, like the "fixed idea" of Berlioz's *Symphonie fantastique*. They have an uncanny power to suggest in a few notes a person, an emotion, an idea, an object (the gold, the ring, the sword) or a landscape (the Rhine, Valhalla, the lonely shore of Tristan's home). Through a process of continual transformation, the leitmotifs trace the course of the drama, the changes in the characters, their experiences and memories, their thoughts and hidden desires.

Role of orchestra

Leitmotifs

Wagner based his musical language on chromatic harmony, which he pushed to its then farthermost limits. Chromatic dissonance gives Wagner's music its restless, intensely emotional quality. Never before had unstable pitch combinations been used so eloquently to portray states of soul.

Chromatic harmony

Die Walküre

The story of *The Ring of the Nibelung* centers on the treasure of gold that lies hidden in the depths of the Rhine River, guarded by three Rhine Maidens. From this treasure is fashioned a ring that brings unlimited power to its owner. But there is a terrible curse on the ring: it will destroy the peace of mind of all who gain possession of it, and bring them misfortune and death.

Thus begins the cycle of four dramas that ends only when the curse-bearing ring is returned to the Rhine Maidens. Gods and heroes, mortals and Nibelungs,

Principal Works

13 operas (or music dramas), including *Rienzi* (1842); *Der fliegende Holländer* (*The Flying Dutchman*, 1843); *Tannhäuser* (1845); *Lohengrin* (1850); *Tristan und Isolde* (1865); *Die Meistersinger von Nürnberg* (*The Mastersingers of Nuremberg*, 1868); *Der Ring des Nibelungen* (*The Ring of the Nibelung*), consisting of *Das Rheingold* (*The Rhine Gold*, 1869), *Die Walküre* (*The Valkyrie*, 1870), *Siegfried* (1876), and *Götterdämmerung* (*The Twilight of the Gods*, 1876); and *Parsifal* (1882)

Orchestral music, including *Siegfried Idyll* (1870)

Piano music; vocal music; choral music

The Ride of the Valkyries, from Wagners' opera *Die Walküre,* in a design by **Carl Emil Doepler** (c. 1876). (Richard Wagner Museum, Bayreuth)

intermingle freely in this tale of betrayed love, broken promises, magic spells, and general corruption brought on by the lust for power. Wagner freely adapted the story from the myths of the Norse sagas and the legends associated with a medieval German epic poem, the *Nibelungenlied.* (Norse mythology was also the inspiration for J. R. R. Tolkien's epic *Lord of the Rings* and for the popular recent movies of that literary work.)

He wrote the four librettos in reverse order. First came his poem on the death of the hero Siegfried. This became the final opera, *Götterdämmerung,* in the course of which Siegfried, now possessor of the ring, betrays Brünnhilde, to whom he has sworn his love, and is in turn betrayed by her. Wagner then realized that the events in Siegfried's life resulted from what had happened to him in his youth; the poem of *Siegfried* explains the forces that shaped the young hero. Aware that these in turn were determined by events set in motion before the hero was born, Wagner next wrote the poem about Siegfried's parents, Siegmund and Sieglinde, that became *Die Walküre.* Finally, this trilogy was prefaced by *Das Rheingold,* the drama that unleashes the workings of fate and the curse of gold out of which the entire action stems.

First performed in Munich in 1870, *Die Walküre* revolves around the twin brother and sister who are the offspring of Wotan by a mortal. (In Norse as in Greek and Roman mythology, kings and heroes were the children of gods.) The ill-fated love of Siegmund and Sieglinde is not only incestuous but also adulterous, for she has been forced into a loveless marriage with the grim chieftain Hunding, who challenges Siegmund to battle.

Act II The second act opens with a scene between Wotan and Brünnhilde. She is one of the Valkyries, the nine daughters of Wotan, whose perpetual task is to circle the battlefield on their winged horses and swoop down to gather up the fallen heroes, whom they bear away to Valhalla, where they will sit forever feasting with the gods. Wotan first tells Brünnhilde, his favorite daughter, that in the ensuing combat between Siegmund and Hunding, she must see to it that Siegmund is the victor. But Wotan's wife, Fricka, the goddess of marriage, insists that Siegmund has violated the holiest law of the universe, and that he must die. Although he argues with her, Wotan sadly realizes that even he must obey the law. When Brünnhilde comes to Siegmund to tell him of his fate, she yields to pity and decides to disobey her father. The two heroes fight, and Brünnhilde tries to shield Siegmund. At the decisive moment, Wotan appears and holds out his spear, upon which Siegmund's sword is shattered. Hunding then buries his own spear in Siegmund's breast. Wotan, overcome by his son's death, turns a ferocious look upon Hunding, who falls dead. Then the god rouses himself and hurries off in pursuit of the daughter who dared to defy his command.

Act III The prelude to Act III is the famous *Ride of the Valkyries,* a vivid orchestral image of the Amazon-like goddesses whirling through a storm on their chargers.

Brünnhilde rushes in to carry off Siegmund's body from the scene of battle. His lover, Sieglinde, wants to die, but Brünnhilde hands her the two fragments of Siegmund's sword and tells her she must live to bear his son, who will become the world's mightiest hero. Sieglinde takes refuge in the forest, while Brünnhilde remains to face her father's wrath. Her punishment is severe. She is to be deprived of her godhood, Wotan tells her, to become a mortal woman. No more will she sit with the gods, nor will she carry heroes to Valhalla. He will put her to sleep on a rock, and she will fall prey to the first mortal who finds her. Brünnhilde defends herself. In trying to protect Siegmund, was she not carrying out her father's innermost desire? She begs him to soften her punishment: let him at least surround the rock with flames, so that only a fearless hero will be able to penetrate the wall of fire. Wotan relents and grants her request. He kisses her on both eyes, which close at once.

Striking the rock three times, he invokes Loge, the god of fire. Flames spring up around the rock—and in the music, through the use of lietmotif—as the tall figure of the god in his black cloak is silhouetted against the red sky. "Whoso-ever fears the tip of my spear shall never pass through the fire," he sings, as the orchestra announces the theme of Siegfried, the fearless hero who in the next music drama will force his way through the flames and awaken Brünnhilde with a kiss. (See Listening Guide 30 for text and an analysis.) The curtain falls on a version of the Sleeping Beauty legend as poetic as any artist ever created.

in his own words

True drama can be conceived only as resulting from the collective impulse of all the arts to communicate in the most immediate way with a collective public. . . . Thus especially the art of tone, developed with such singular diversity in instrumental music, will realize in the collective artwork its richest potential. . . . For in its isolation music has formed itself an organ capable of the most immeasurable expression—the orchestra.

Listening Guide 30

CD: CHR/STD 5/55–57, SH 3/37–39

Wagner: *Die Walküre (The Valkyrie)*, Act III, Finale   (4:21)

DATE OF WORK:	1856; first performed 1870, Munich
GENRE:	Music drama, second in a cycle of 4, *The Ring of the Nibelung*
CHARACTERS:	Wotan, father of the gods (bass-baritone)
	Brünnhilde, one of the Valkyries, the favorite of the 9 daughters of Wotan (soprano)

WHAT TO LISTEN FOR:	Sense of endless melody and continuous orchestral sound.
	Richly chromatic harmony for heightened emotional effect.
	Use of 4 recurring themes (leitmotifs)—slumber, magic sleep, magic fire, and Siegfried—to unify drama.

37	0:00	Forceful trombone passage precedes invocation to Loge:

TEXT	TRANSLATION

WOTAN

Loge, hör'! Lausche hieher!	Loge, listen! Harken here!
Wie zuerst ich dich fand, als feurige Gluth,	As I found you first, a fiery blaze,
wie dann einst du mir schwandest,	as once you vanished from me,
als schweifende Lohe;	a random fire;
wie ich dich band, bann' ich dich heut'!	as I allied with you, so today I conjure you!
Herauf, wabernde Lohe,	Arise, magic flame,
umlod're mir feurig den Fels!	girdle the rock with fire for me!

(He strikes the rock thrice with his spear.)

Loge! Loge! Hieher!	Loge! Loge! Come here!

(A flash of flames issue from the rock, which swell to an ever-brightening fiery glow. Bright shooting flames surround Wotan. With his spear he directs the sea of fire to encircle the rock; it presently spreads toward the background, where it encloses the mountain in flames.)

38 1:01   "Magic fire" music is heard in full orchestra:

"Magic sleep" music is heard, followed by "slumber" motive in orchestra.

WOTAN

39 2:00

Wer meines Speeres Spitze fürchtet,	Whosoever fears the tip of my spear
durchschreite das Feuer nie!	shall never pass through the fire!

(He stretches out the spear as a spell. He gazes sorrowfully back on Brünnhilde. Slowly he turns to depart. He turns his head again and looks back. He disappears through the fire.)

Wotan sings "Siegfried" motive to text above, followed by brass, announcing the hero to come:

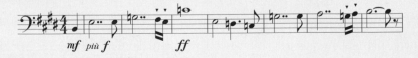

Orchestral closing with "magic fire" music and "slumber" motive.

58

Puccini and Late Romantic Opera

"God touched me with His little finger and said, "Write for the theater, only for the theater." And I obeyed the supreme command."

KEY POINTS

- The post-Romantic composer Giacomo Puccini wrote some of the best-loved operas of all time, including *La bohème* and *Madame Butterfly*.
- In *Madame Butterfly*, Puccini combines end-of-the-century *verismo* (realism) and exoticism (Japanese music and culture).
- The libretto for *Madame Butterfly* reflects end-of-the-century European-American interest in geisha culture.

Giacomo Puccini

The Italian operatic tradition was carried on in the post-Romantic era by a group of composers that included Pietro Mascagni (1863–1945), Ruggero Leoncavallo (1857–1919), and Giacomo Puccini, whom we will study. These Italians were associated with a movement known as *verismo* (realism), whose advocates tried to bring into the lyric theater the naturalism of writers such as Émile Zola, Henrik Ibsen, and their contemporaries. Instead of choosing historical or mythological themes, they picked subjects from everyday life and treated them in down-to-earth fashion. Two of the most famous operas in this tradition are by Puccini: *La bohème* (*Bohemian Life*, 1896) and *Tosca* (1900). Although it was a short-lived movement, verismo had counterparts in Germany and France and produced some of the best-loved works in the operatic repertory.

Verismo

His Life and Music

Giacomo Puccini was born in 1858 in Lucca, Italy, the son of a church organist in whose footsteps he expected to follow. But Puccini decided to compose opera instead, and in 1880 he traveled to Milan, where he studied at the Conservatory. Within five years, he had scored his first operatic success, and his third opera, *Manon Lescaut* (1893), established him as the most promising among the rising generation of Italian composers. For this work, he collaborated with librettists Luigi Illica and Giuseppe Giacosa, both of whom collaborated with him on the three most successful operas of the early twentieth century: *La bohème* (1896), *Tosca* (1900), and *Madame Butterfly* (1904), which we will study.

Prosperity and misfortune followed Puccini's early successes. His travels to oversee the international premieres of several of his works were demanding. In 1903, a serious car crash left him bedridden for six months, and in 1908 his wife accused him of having an affair with a live-in assistant, thus causing a public scandal. Handsome and magnetic, Puccini evidently gave his wife reason to doubt his fidelity: "I am always falling in love," he once declared. "When I no longer am, make my funeral." In 1910, his *The Girl of the Golden West* received

Later years

341

Principal Works

12 operas, including *La bohème* (1896), *Tosca* (1900), *Madame Butterfly* (1904), *La Fanciulla del West* (*The Girl of the Golden West*, 1910), *Turandot* (1926), and three one-act works (including *Gianni Schicchi*, 1918)

Vocal works, including motets, cantatas, and a Mass in A-flat (1880); solo songs

Instrumental music, including orchestral, chamber, and solo piano works

its world premiere at the Metropolitan Opera House in New York; this was followed by a trio of three one-act works that included *Gianni Schicchi* (1918), one of his best-loved masterpieces.

Puccini's last opera, *Turandot*, exemplifies his far-reaching search for new material. After considering texts by many authors, he settled on *Turandot*, a Chinese fairy tale about a beautiful but cruel princess. Ill with cancer, Puccini pushed on to complete the project, but he died in 1924 from a heart attack, before finishing the final scene. His friend Franco Alfano completed the opera, using Puccini's sketches. The first performance occurred in 1926 at La Scala, and was conducted by Arturo Toscanini, Puccini's greatest interpreter. The opera ended as Puccini had requested, without the final scene—Toscanini laid down his baton during the lament over the body of Li, turned to the audience and said in a choking voice, "Here ends the master's work."

Madame Butterfly

Puccini's inspiration for the opera came in 1900 during a visit to London, where he attended a performance of David Belasco's play *Madame Butterfly*, a dramatization of a short story by John Luther Long, which was in turn taken from Pierre Loti's tale *Madame Chrysanthème*. The composer immediately applied for rights to Belasco's work, acquired Long's story for his librettists Illica and Giacosa, and set to work on the piece. The libretto was completed in 1902, but Puccini insisted on further revisions and thus did not complete *Madame Butterfly* until 1904.

Although the composer was well-established in the opera world, his new work suffered a disas-

Cover of the earliest English vocal score of *Madame Butterfly*, published by Ricordi. Design by **Leopold Metlicovitz.**

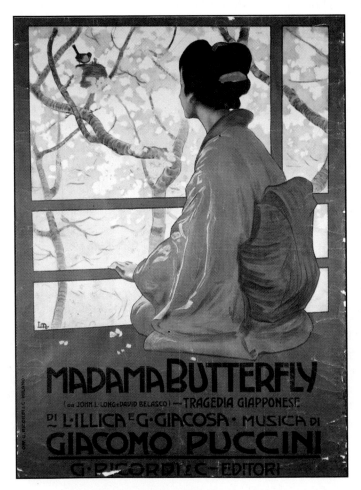

Interior of Teatro alla Scala (La Scala), in Milan, Italy's most famous opera house.

Premier

trous premiere—rivaled only by the famous riot at the first performance of Stravinsky's ballet *Rite of Spring* (discussed in Chapter 63). Undaunted, the composer reworked the opera. When the revised *Madame Butterfly* was performed in Brescia three months after its premiere, it became an instant success.

Like his other operas, *Madame Butterfly* focuses on a tragic-heroic female protagonist—here, a young geisha named Cio-Cio-San (Madame Butterfly) from Nagasaki who renounces her profession and religion in order to marry an American naval officer named Pinkerton. (A *geisha* is most closely equivalent to a courtesan in Western culture.) The two, who have never met before, get married in a house promised to the couple by the marriage broker. Pinkerton departs soon thereafter. When he returns several years later—with his new American wife in tow—Pinkerton learns that Butterfly has given birth to their son, and decides to take the child to America. Butterfly accepts his decision with dignity, but rather than return to her life as a geisha, she commits suicide (the samurai warrior's ritual known as *hara-kiri*). Despite its elements of *verismo* (or realism), Butterfly herself is not a believable character—yet it is her naivety and vulnerability that makes her a beloved heroine.

Madame Butterfly marks a turn-of-the-century interest in exoticism. The entire score is tinged with Japanese color: traditional Japanese melodies are juxtaposed with pentatonic and whole-tone passages, and instrument combinations evoking the timbres of a Japanese *gagaku* orchestra (harp, flute and piccolo, and bells) are exploited. Simple moments in the score—a single, unaccompanied melody, for example—have their equivalents in the clear lines of Japanese prints. Here too Puccini captures the ritualistic aspect of Japanese life.

Act I opens with a brief reference to *The Star-Spangled Banner* (another exotic reference for Puccini), after which some of the main characters are introduced: Goro, the marriage broker; Sharpless, the American consul at Nagasaki; Suzuki, Butterfly's maid; and Pinkerton himself. All are busily preparing Butterfly's new house and awaiting her arrival. Meanwhile, Pinkerton sings about his carefree

in his own words

I have had a visit today from Mme. Ohyama, wife of the Japanese ambassador. She told me a great many interesting things and sang some native songs to me. She has promised to send me native Japanese music. I sketched the story of the libretto for her, and she liked it, especially as just such a story as Butterfly's is known to her as having happened in real life.

A geisha committing suicide in the samurai *jigai* manner. Drawing by **Yoshitoshi Taiso** (1839–1892).

view on love; all too quickly we learn that this marriage will not have a happy ending. Butterfly soon arrives with a group of friends, and she meets Pinkerton for the first time. Butterfly's family appears, only to be interrupted by her Uncle Bonze, who announces that his niece has renounced her faith. Her shocked relatives quickly depart, and Pinkerton consoles his young wife.

Act II, Part 1, takes place three years after the marriage. Butterfly has heard nothing from her husband, which leads Suzuki to doubt that Pinkerton will ever return. She is quickly rebuked, however, in Butterfly's soaring aria, "Un bel dì" (One beautiful day), in which the young bride pictures their happy reunion and recalls Pinkerton's promise to return "when the robins build their nests" (see Listening Guide 31).

Sharpless then arrives with a letter from Pinkerton, who has asked him to seek out Butterfly. They are interrupted by a visit from the marriage broker and Prince Yamadori, who proposes to Butterfly. Sharpless urges her to accept but she refuses, stating that she is already married and that she would rather die by her own hand than to return to her former life as a geisha. She also reveals to Sharpless that she has had Pinkerton's child.

The harbor cannon signals the arrival of a ship that Butterfly identifies immediately as Pinkerton's—the *Abraham Lincoln*. Butterfly dresses in her wedding gown in anticipation of their meeting. The scene closes with an orchestral interlude that leads to the final scene.

Dawn is breaking in Part 2 of Act II, and Butterfly struggles to stay awake after a sleepness night. Sharpless and Pinkerton arrive, along with Kate, Pinkerton's new wife; they are greeted by Suzuki, who informs them that Butterfly is resting. Pinkerton announces his intention to take the child to give him a good American upbringing and then leaves. When Butterfly awakens, she learns about Pinkerton and his American wife, and the fate of her young son. She accepts the situation with dignity but asks that Pinkerton return in half an hour for the boy. She says a final farewell to her son, and then stabs herself with her father's samurai dagger, which bears the inscription "He dies with honor who can no longer live with honor." In the distance, Pinkerton is heard desperately calling out her name.

Un bel dì The aria "Un bel dì" is one of the most memorable in all opera literature. At first, Butterfly sings with a distant, ethereal quality, accompanied by solo violin, as she dreams of Pinkerton's return. The intensity rises as she envisons seeing his ship in the harbor. She relates the vision and her reaction in a speechlike melody which peaks on the word "morire" (die), as she explains she will playfully hide from him at first in order not to die at their reunion. The emotional

Listening Guide 31

CD: CHR/STD 7/1–2, SH 3/40–41

Puccini: "Un bel dì," from *Madame Butterfly*, Act II   (4:35)

DATE OF WORK:	1904
LIBRETTIST:	Giuseppe Giacosa and Luigi IIica
BASIS:	Play by David Belasco, from short story by John Luther Long, derived from Pierre Loti's tale *Madame Chrysanthème*
SETTING:	Nagasaki, Japan, at the beginning of the 20th century
PRINCIPAL CHARACTERS:	Cio-Cio-San, or Madame Butterfly (soprano)
	Suzuki, her maid (mezzo-soprano)
	B. F. Pinkerton, lieutenant in the U.S. Navy (tenor)
	Sharpless, U.S. consul at Nagasaki (baritone)
	Goro, marriage broker (tenor)
	Prince Yamadori (tenor)
	Kate Pinkerton, American wife of Pinkerton (mezzo-soprano)
	Relatives and friends of Cio-Cio-San

WHAT TO LISTEN FOR: Dreamlike quality of opening vocal line, with sparse, solo violin accompaniment.

Excited, speechlike singing as the emotional and dynamic levels rise.

Passionate, soaring climaxes on key words ("die," "await"), with rich, unison string writing.

Opening, ethereal vocal line:

Final climactic moment on "l'aspetto" (I will wait for him):

TEXT	**TRANSLATION**
40 0:00 Un bel dì, vedremo	One lovely day we'll see
Levarsi un fil di fumo	a thread of smoke rise
dall'estremo confin del mare.	At the distant edge of the sea.
E poi la nave appare—	And then the ship appears—
Poi la nave bianca entra nel porto,	then the white ship enters the harbor,

		Romba il suo saluto.	Thunders its salute.
		Vedi? E venuto!	You see? He's come!
		Io non gli scendo incontro. Io no.	I don't go down to meet him. Not I.
		Mi metto là sul cieglio del colle	I place myself at the brow of the hill
		E aspetto gran tempo e non mi pesa,	and wait a long time, but the long
		La lunga attesa.	Wait doesn't oppress me.
		E uscito dalla folla cittadina	And coming out of the city's crowd
		Un uomo, un picciol punto	A man, a tiny speck
		S'avvia per la collina.	Starts toward the hill.

41 2:14

Chi sarà? Chi sarà?
E come sarà giunto
Che dirà? Che dirà?
Chiamerà Butterfly dalla lontana.
Io senza dar risposta me ne starò nascosta
Un po' per celia
E un po' per non morire al primo incontro,
Ed egli alquanto in pena chiamerà:
Piccina mogliettina olezzo di verbena,
I nomi che mi dava al suo venire
Tutto questo avverrà, te lo prometto.
Tienti la tua paura,
Io con sicura fede l'aspetto.

Who will it be? Who?
And when he arrives
What will he say? What?
He'll call Butterfly from the distance.
I'll stay hidden, partly to tease him
and partly not to die
at our first meeting,
And a little worried he'll call
Little wife, verbena blossom,
the names he gave me when he came here.
All this will happen, I promise you.
Keep your fear to yourself,
With certain faith I am waiting for him.

level builds—along with the dynamics—as Butterfly swears that "all this will happen." Her final soaring line climaxes on "l'aspetto" (I will wait for him), with the orchestra now playing the heartrending music at *fff*.

The geisha song *A White Fan* in block-form calligraphy, by master calligrapher **Kaieda Shumpo** (Miyaji Harumi). The characters are read from right to left.

みて浪風立たぬ水の面うら
やましいではないかいな

みどり立ち寄る庭の池塘
に移が故の景色もまさる深き

て固き契りの銀盤撫く髪
白扇の末広がりの末かけ

Looking East to Japanese Culture

The musical traditions of Japan are rich and varied, in both art and folk music. We have already mentioned *gagaku*, the ancient court music of Japan, and *Noh drama*, a genre of theater music. Here we will consider a more popular genre: the *kouta*, or short song, which dates to the nineteenth century. The *geisha*—a kind of courtesan who entertained men in tea houses—was central to the development of this popular genre.

The first geisha emerged in the so-called pleasure quarters during the 1600s and were, in fact, men. It was not until the middle of the eighteenth century that a female geisha appeared but by the 1800s all geisha were women. At that time, a geisha was literally an "arts person" who was carefully trained in her trade, like courtesans in Western culture. She entertained men with her dancing, singing, and playing on *shamisen* (a three-string, long-necked, Japanese lute) or *koto* (a long, wooden zither with thirteen strings); engaged them in stimulating or flattering conversation; or challenged them to *go* (an ancient board game of strategy and skill). She was easily recognized by her elaborate hairdo (piled high in black lacquered coils and decorated with pins and combs), distinctive makeup (white-painted face and crimson lips), ornate silk kimono and obi (a wide, stiff sash), and high, wooden clogs. There has recently been a resurgence of interest in geisha culture in the West, with the publication of *Memoirs of a Geisha,* by Arthur Golden (1997), and the writings of anthropologist Liza Dalby (*Geisha,* 1983; *Kimono: Fashioning Culture,* 1993), who was the first Western woman to live among geisha and become a geisha.

The Japanese Kouta

The term *kouta* applies both to a specific poetic form and to a type of music for voice and shamisen. The shamisen plays sharp rhythmic attacks with the fingers or a *plectrum* (a piece of wood, ivory, or another substance used to sound the strings), while the voice sings more freely, often articulating syllables on the offbeat.

A geisha plays shamisen while seated on a low chest decorated with a view of Mount Fuji. The inscription refers to a bad playing habit. Woodblock by **Keisai Eisen** (1791–1848).

The kouta is often associated with *kabuki theater,* a type of traditional entertainment characterized by brilliant costumes and spectacular drama. A kouta text is highly structured, full of symbolism, and often suggestive, evoking images that appeal to the senses. There are songs for every occasion and mood, each work making its point in only a few words; this is similar to the Japanese poetic form of *haiku.* A geisha would generally learn each song by ear—that is, memorizing it through repetition—rather than through notation. Our selection, *Hakusen no (A White Fan),* is set to a love poem with five-and seven-syllable lines and rich imagery (see Listening Guide 32). This sentimental text might be appropriate for a wedding or a private entertainment; in it, the pine tree symbolizes longevity, and the clear pond an image of the lovers' future. The poem turns on the words "kagayaku kage ni," referring both to the shimmering of the fan and to the pine tree, thus unifying the textual imagery. The shamisen plays an introduction and a closing sequence and, with the voice, weaves a linear, heterophonic texture. The singer determines the tempo and register for the performance. The short melodic motives seem to repeat but are varied each time, often with embellishments. The vocalist's rhythmic delivery is very flexible against the metric playing of the shamisen. Our recording, sung by a geisha in the 1960s, also features shakuhachi (an end-blown flute) and drum.

Listening Guide 32

CD: CHR/STD 8/77, SH 3/42

Japanese Kouta: *Hakusen no (A White Fan)* (3:22)

DATE OF WORK: Mid- to late-19th century

GENRE: *Kouta* (short song)

MEDIUM: Female voice, shamisen (3-stringed lute), shakuhachi (flute), drum

WHAT TO LISTEN FOR: Instrumental introduction and interludes on shamisen.
Free rhythmic treatment.
Heterophonic texture among voice, shamisen, and shakuhachi.
Bent, or inflected, pitches by voice and instruments.
Short melodic phrases with some varied repetitions.
Percussive effects plucked on shamisen.

42   0:00   Solo shamisen introduction; slow moving
chords and disjunct intervals, played rhythmically.

Opening vocal line, sung freely
(notated nonmetrically):

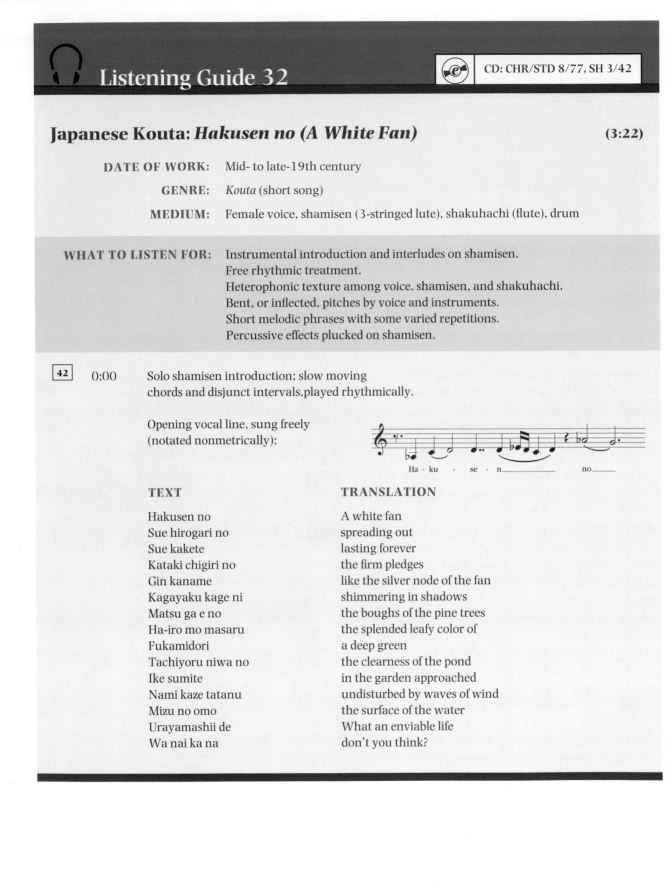

Ha - ku - se - n   no

TEXT	TRANSLATION
Hakusen no	A white fan
Sue hirogari no	spreading out
Sue kakete	lasting forever
Kataki chigiri no	the firm pledges
Gin kaname	like the silver node of the fan
Kagayaku kage ni	shimmering in shadows
Matsu ga e no	the boughs of the pine trees
Ha-iro mo masaru	the splended leafy color of
Fukamidori	a deep green
Tachiyoru niwa no	the clearness of the pond
Ike sumite	in the garden approached
Nami kaze tatanu	undisturbed by waves of wind
Mizu no omo	the surface of the water
Urayamashii de	What an enviable life
Wa nai ka na	don't you think?

59

Tchaikovsky and the Ballet

"Dance is the hidden language of the soul."

—MARTHA GRAHAM

KEY POINTS

■ Previously part of lavish entertainments, ballet was established as an independent art form in the eighteenth century, particularly in France and Russia.

■ The Russian choreographer Marius Petipa created the *pas de deux* (dance for two), which became central to classical ballet.

■ The three ballets of Russian composer Peter Ilyich Tchaikovsky—*Swan Lake*, *Sleeping Beauty*, and *The Nutcracker*—remain favorites today.

Ballet—Past and Present

Ballet has been an adornment of European culture for centuries. Ever since the Renaissance, it has been central to lavish festivals and theatrical entertainments presented at the courts of kings and dukes.

The eighteenth century saw the rise of ballet as an independent art form. French ballet achieved preeminence in the early nineteenth century. Then Russian ballet came into its own, fostered by the patronage of the czar's court and helped along considerably by the arrival in 1847 of Marius Petipa, the great choreographer at St. Petersburg. Petipa created the dances for more than a hundred works, invented the structure of the classic *pas de deux* (dance for two), and brought the art of staging ballets to unprecedented heights.

Marius Petipa

The history of early-twentieth-century ballet is closely identified with the career of Serge Diaghilev (1872–1929) whose dance company, the Ballets Russes in Paris in the years before the First World War, opened up a new chapter in the cultural life of Europe. He surrounded his dancers—the greatest were Vaslav Nijinsky and Tamara Karsavina—with productions worthy of their talents. He invited artists such as Picasso and Braque to paint the scenery, and commissioned the three ballets—*The Firebird*, *Petrushka*, and *The Rite of Spring*—that catapulted the composer Igor Stravinsky to fame. (We will study Stravinsky's ballet *The Rite of Spring* in Chapter 63.) His ballets have served as models for the composers and choreographers who followed.

Serge Diaghilev

Ballet is the most physical of the arts, depending as it does on the leaps and turns of the human body. Out of these movements it weaves an enchantment all its own. A special glamour attaches to the great dancers—Nureyev, Baryshnikov, and their peers—yet theirs is an art based on an inhumanly demanding discipline. Their bodies are their instruments, which they must keep in excellent shape in order to perform the gymnastics required of them. They create moments of elusive beauty, made possible only by total control of their muscles. It is this combination of physical and emotional factors that marks the distinctive power of ballet.

O body swayed to music,
O brightening glance,
How can we know the
*   dancer from the dance?*
*   —W. B. YEATS*

Peter Ilyich Tchaikovsky

Peter Ilyich Tchaikovsky: His Life and Music

"Truly there would be reason to go mad were it not for music."

Few composers typify the end-of-the-century mood as does Peter Ilyich Tchaikovsky (1840–1893), who belonged to a generation that saw its truths crumbling and found none to replace them. This composer expressed above all the pessimism that engulfed the late Romantic movement.

Tchaikovsky was born at Votinsk in a distant province of Russia, the son of a government official. His family intended him for a career in the government; he graduated at nineteen from the aristocratic School of Jurisprudence in St. Petersburg and obtained a minor post in the Ministry of Justice. But at age twenty-three, he decided to resign his position and enter the newly founded Conservatory of St. Petersburg. He completed the music course there in three years and was immediately recommended by Anton Rubinstein, director of the school, for a teaching post in the new Moscow Conservatory. His twelve years in Moscow saw the production of some of his most successful works.

Extremely sensitive by nature, Tchaikovsky was subject to attacks of depression aggravated by guilt over his homosexuality. In the hope of achieving some degree of stability, he married a student of the conservatory, Antonina Milyukova, who was hopelessly in love with him. But his sympathy for her soon turned into uncontrollable revulsion, and, on the verge of a serious breakdown, he fled to his brothers in St. Petersburg.

In this desperate hour, Nadezhda von Meck, the wealthy widow of an industrialist, sent him money to go abroad and recover his health, and launched him on the most productive period of his career. Her passion was music, especially Tchaikovsky's. Bound by the rigid conventions of her time and her class, she had to be certain that her enthusiasm was for the artist, not the man; hence she stipulated that she was never to meet the recipient of her patronage.

The following years saw the spread of Tchaikovsky's fame. He was the first Russian whose music appealed to Western tastes, and in 1891 he was invited to participate in the ceremonies for the opening of Carnegie Hall in New York. In

in his own words

How can one express the indefinable sensations that one experiences while writing an instrumental composition that has no definite subject? It is a purely lyrical process. It is a musical confession of the soul, which unburdens itself through sounds just as a lyric poet expresses himself through poetry. . . . As the poet Heine said, "Where words leave off, music begins."

Principal Works

8 operas, including *Eugene Onegin* (1879) and *Pique Dame* (*The Queen of Spades,* 1890)

3 ballets: *Swan Lake* (1877), *The Sleeping Beauty* (1890), and *The Nutcracker* (1892)

Orchestral music, including 7 symphonies (No. 1, 1866; No. 2, 1872; No. 3, 1875; No. 4, 1878; No. 5, 1888; No. 6, *Pathétique,* 1893; *Manfred,* 1885); 3 piano concertos, 1 violin concerto; and symphonic poems and overtures (*Romeo and Juliet,* 1870; 1812 Overture, 1880)

Chamber and keyboard music; choral music and songs

Mikhail Baryshnikov in an American Ballet Theater production of *The Nutcracker*.

1893, immediately after finishing his Sixth Symphony, the *Pathétique*, he went to St. Petersburg to conduct it. The work met with a lukewarm reception, in part because Tchaikovsky, painfully shy in public, conducted his music without conviction. He died within several weeks, at the age of fifty-three. The suddenness of his death and the tragic tone of his last work led to rumors that he had committed suicide.

Final year

In the eyes of Russians, Tchaikovsky is a national artist. He himself laid great weight on the national element in his music: "I am Russian through and through!" At the same time, Tchaikovsky was a cosmopolitan who came under the spell of Italian opera, French ballet, German symphony and song. These he joined to the strain of folk melody that was his heritage as a Russian, imposing on this mixture his sharply defined personality.

The Nutcracker

Tchaikovsky had a natural affinity for the ballet. Dances, especially waltzes, are scattered throughout his works. His three ballets—*Swan Lake, The Sleeping Beauty,* and *The Nutcracker*—were not immediately popular with the dancers, who complained that the rhythms were too complicated to be danced to. Within a few years, however, they had changed their view, and these three ballets established themselves as basic works of the Russian repertory.

The Nutcracker was based on a fanciful story by E. T. A. Hoffmann. An expanded version by Alexandre Dumas served as the basis for choreographer Petipa's scenario, which was offered to Tchaikovsky when he returned from his visit to the United States in 1891.

Act I takes place at a Christmas party during which two children, Clara and Fritz, help decorate the tree. Their godfather arrives with gifts, among them a nutcracker. The children go to bed but Clara returns to gaze at her gift, falls asleep, and begins to dream. (Russian nutcrackers are often shaped like a human head or a whole person, which makes it quite logical for Clara to dream, as she does, that this one was transformed into a handsome prince.) First, she is

Act I

351

terrified to see mice scampering around the tree. Then the dolls she has received come alive and fight a battle with the mice, which reaches a climax in the combat between the Nutcracker and the Mouse King. Clara helps her beloved Nutcracker by throwing a slipper at the Mouse King, who is vanquished. The Nutcracker then becomes the Prince, who takes Clara away with him.

Act II   Act II takes place in Confiturembourg, the land of sweets, which is ruled by the Sugar Plum Fairy. The Prince presents Clara to his family, and a celebration follows, with a series of dances that reveal all the attractions of this magic realm.

The mood of the ballet is set by the Overture, whose light, airy effect Tchaikovsky achieved by omitting most of the brass instruments. The peppy _March_ is played as the guests arrive for the party (see Listening Guide 33). "I have discovered a new instrument in Paris," Tchaikovsky wrote his publisher, "something between a piano and a glockenspiel, with a divinely beautiful tone, and I want to introduce it into the ballet." The instrument was the _celesta_, whose timbre perfectly suits the Sugar Plum Fairy and her veils. In the _Trepak_ (Russian Dance, with the famous Cossack squat-kick), the orchestral sound is enlivened by a tambourine. The muted _Arab Dance_ is followed by the _Chinese Dance_, in which bassoons set up an ostinato that bobs up and down against the shrill melody of flute and piccolo. _The Dance of the Toy Flutes_ is extraordinarily graceful. Finally, the climax of the ballet comes with the _Waltz of the Flowers_, which has delighted audiences for more than a century. With its suggestion of swirling ballerinas, this finale conjures up everything we have come to associate with the Romantic ballet.

Listening Guide 33

CD: CHR/STD 6/44–46, SH 3/43–45

Tchaikovsky: *The Nutcracker, March*   (2:13)

DATE OF WORK:	1892
GENRE:	Ballet (from which an orchestral suite was made)
BASIS:	E. T. A. Hoffmann story, expanded by Alexandre Dumas
CHOREOGRAPHER:	Marius Petipa

SEQUENCE OF DANCES:

March	_Chinese Dance_
Dance of the Sugar Plum Fairy	_Dance of the Toy Flutes_
Trepak	_Waltz of the Flowers_
Arab Dance	

March: **Tempo di marcia viva (lively march); A-B-A form, 4/4 meter, G major**

WHAT TO LISTEN FOR: Sprightly march tune in trumpets, answered by strings.
Shift from major to minor tonality in march.
Brief contrasing middle section, with staccato runs in woodwinds.

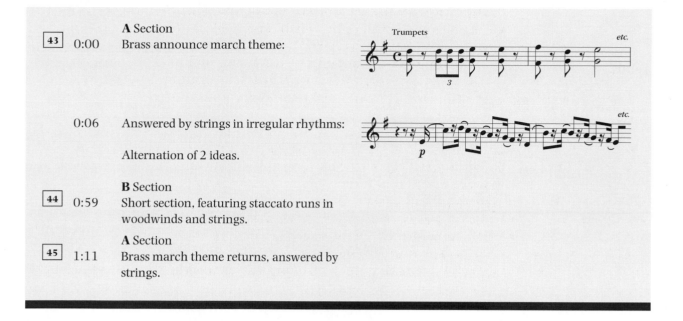

43   0:00   **A** Section
Brass announce march theme:

0:06   Answered by strings in irregular rhythms:

Alternation of 2 ideas.

44   0:59   **B** Section
Short section, featuring staccato runs in
woodwinds and strings.

45   1:11   **A** Section
Brass march theme returns, answered by
strings.

Pablo Picasso (1881–1973), *Three Dancers*, canvas, 1925. (The Tate Gallery, London)

The Twentieth Century

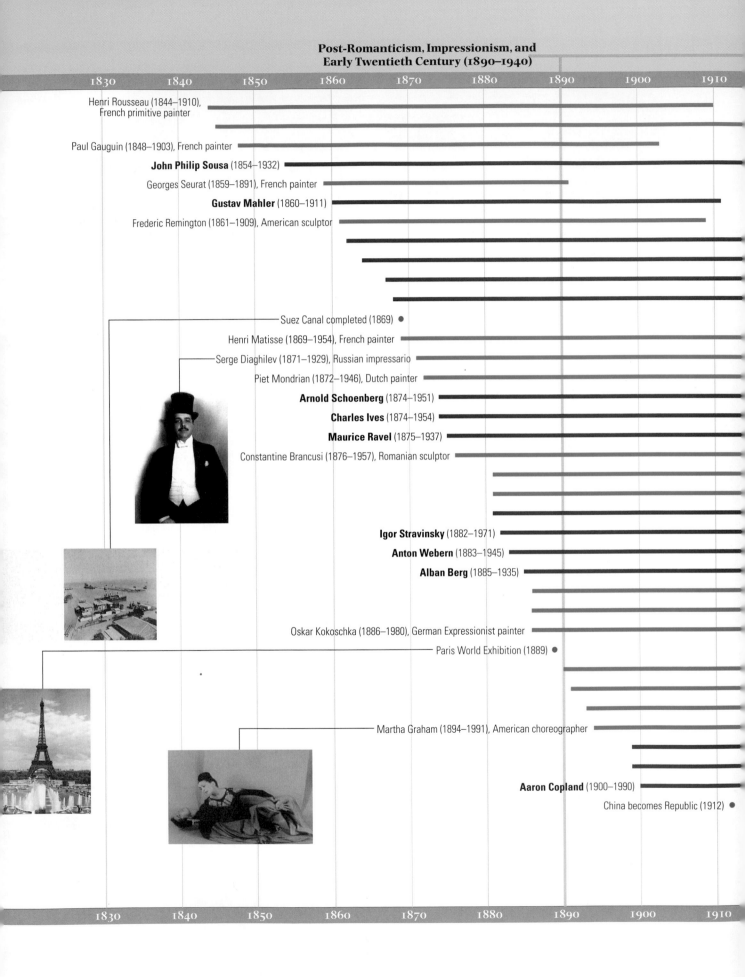

1830   1840   1850   1860   1870   1880   1890   1900   1910

Henri Rousseau (1844–1910), French primitive painter

Paul Gauguin (1848–1903), French painter

John Philip Sousa (1854–1932)

Georges Seurat (1859–1891), French painter

Gustav Mahler (1860–1911)

Frederic Remington (1861–1909), American sculptor

Suez Canal completed (1869) ●

Henri Matisse (1869–1954), French painter

Serge Diaghilev (1871–1929), Russian impressario

Piet Mondrian (1872–1946), Dutch painter

Arnold Schoenberg (1874–1951)

Charles Ives (1874–1954)

Maurice Ravel (1875–1937)

Constantine Brancusi (1876–1957), Romanian sculptor

Igor Stravinsky (1882–1971)

Anton Webern (1883–1945)

Alban Berg (1885–1935)

Oskar Kokoschka (1886–1980), German Expressionist painter

Paris World Exhibition (1889) ●

Martha Graham (1894–1991), American choreographer

Aaron Copland (1900–1990)

China becomes Republic (1912) ●

POST-ROMANTICISM, IMPRESSIONISM, AND EARLY TWENTIETH CENTURY

1920 1930 1940 1950 1960 1970 1980 1990 2000

Mary Cassatt (1845–1926), American painter

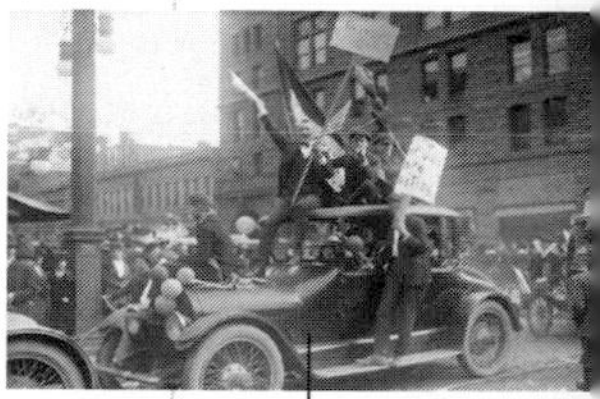

Claude Debussy (1862–1918)

Richard Strauss (1864–1949)

Amy Cheney Beach (1867–1944)

Scott Joplin (1868–1917)

Natalia Goncharova (1881–1962), Russian painter

Pablo Picasso (1881–1973), Spanish artist

Béla Bartók (1881–1945)

Wassily Kandinsky (1886–1944), Russian-born French painter

Diego Rivera (1886–1951), Mexican painter

Vaslav Nijinsky, dancer (1890–1950)

Grant Wood (1891–1942), American painter

Joan Miró (1893–1983), Spanish painter

Silvestre Revueltas (1899–1940)

Carlos Chávez (1899–1978)

- World Events
- Composers
- Principal Figures

- U.S. enters World War I (1917)
- Women's suffrage: Nineteenth Amendment passed (1920)
- USSR established (1923)
- Spanish Civil War (1936)

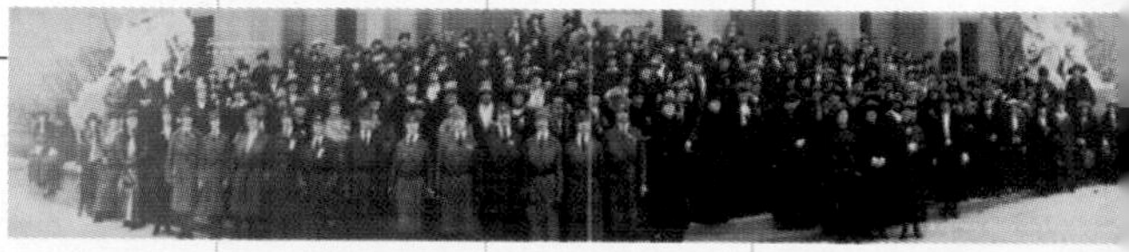

1920 1930 1940 1950 1960 1970 1980 1990 2000

e Learning

transition **IV**

The Post-Romantic Era

"I came into a very young world in a very old time."

—ERIK SATIE

KEY POINTS

- Two important movements surfaced at the turn of the twentieth century: Post-Romanticism, in Germany and Austria; and Impressionism, in France.
- Viennese composer Gustav Mahler is remembered for his symphonies and song cycles with orchestral accompaniment.
- The arts in Vienna felt the influence of Far Eastern culture; Mahler's *The Song of the Earth* exemplifies this trend.

It became apparent toward the end of the nineteenth century that the Romantic impulse had run its course. It fell to the composers who reached artistic maturity in the final years of the century to bridge the gap between a dying Romanticism and the twentieth century.

Some composers of this period, from about 1890 to 1910, continued on the traditional path; others struck out in new directions; and still others tried to steer a middle course between the old and the new; all were influenced in one way or another by Wagner's chromatic language.

Two important movements ushered in the twentieth century: Impressionism, heralded by the French composers Claude Debussy and Maurice Ravel, and post-Romanticism, exemplified in Italy by Giacomo Puccini (whose opera *Madame Butterfly* we studied) and in Germany and Austria by Richard Strauss and Gustav Mahler.

Germanic Post-Romanticism

The German composer Richard Strauss (1864–1949) was a beacon of post-Romanticism. Well-known for his vividly programmatic symphonic poems (*Don Juan* and *Till Eulenspiegel's Merry Pranks,* among others), Strauss conquered the operatic stage in the early years of the twentieth century with *Salome* (1905, from Oscar Wilde's play), *Elektra* (1909, from a version of the Greek tragedy), and *Der Rosenkavalier* (*The Cavalier of the Rose,* 1911). The last work is notable for its sensuous lyricism and entrancing waltzes.

The Viennese symphonic tradition extended into the twentieth century through the works of Gustav Mahler (1860–1911), following in the illustrious line from Haydn, Mozart, Beethoven, and Schubert. In his symphonic works, Mahler's tonal imagery is permeated by the jovial spirit of Austrian popular song and dance. His nine symphonies abound with lyricism, with long, flowing melodies and richly expressive harmonies. (The Tenth Symphony, complete in a draft at his death, has now been edited and made available for performance.) Mahler's sense of color ranks with the great masters of orchestration; he contrasts solo instruments in the manner of chamber music, achieving his color effects through clarity of line rather than massed sonorities. He never abandoned the principle of tonality; he needed the key as a framework for his vast designs.

The spirit of song permeates Mahler's art. He followed Schubert and Robert Schumann in cultivating the song cycle. Among this best efforts is *The Song of the Earth* (*Das Lied von der Erde,* 1908), six songs with orchestra that mark the peak of his achievement in this genre. Mahler's text for *The Song of the Earth* was drawn from Hans Bethge's *Chinese Flute,* a translation—more accurately, stylization—of poems, including some by the great Chinese poet Li-Tai-Po. The images of China—"a pavillion of green and of white porcelain," "a bridge of jade"—are evoked through pentatonic scale patterns and the use of the triangle and haunting woodwind instruments. Mahler held several prominent conducting posts during his career, including director of the New York Philharmonic Orchestra from 1909 to 1911.

These masters felt strongly the influence of Wagner. Alongside them, however, was a new generation that reacted vigorously against the extremes of Romantic harmony. And with this group of composers emerged the movement that more than any other ushered in the twentieth century—Impressionism.

> *I know that so long as I can sum up my experience in words, I can certainly not create music about it. My need to express myself in music symphonically begins precisely where dark feelings hold sway, at the gate that leads into the "other world," the world in which things no longer are divided by time and space.*
>
> —GUSTAV MAHLER

The Song of the Earth

In the early 1900s, Viennese artists like **Gustav Klimt** (1862–1918) responded to the vogue for Eastern effects. *Expectation* (1905–9). (Österreichisches Museum für angewandte Kunst, Vienna)

e Learning

unit **XXI**

The Impressionist and Post-Impressionist Eras

60

Debussy and Impressionism

"For we desire above all—nuance,
Not color but half-shades!
Ah! nuance alone unites
Dream with dream and flute with horn."

—PAUL VERLAINE

KEY POINTS

- *Impressionism* was a French movement developed by painters who tried to capture their "first impression" of a subject through use of light and color.
- The literary response to Impressionism was *Symbolism,* in which writings are suggestive of images and ideas rather than literally descriptive.
- Impressionism in music is characterized by exotic scales *(chromatic, whole tone),* unresolved dissonances, parallel chords, rich orchestral color, and free rhythm, all generally cast in small-scale programmatic forms.
- The most important French Impressionist composer was Claude Debussy. His orchestral work, *Prelude to "The Afternoon of a Faun,"* was inspired by a Symbolist poem.
- Debussy, along with other late Romantic composers, was highly influenced by new sounds of non-Western and traditional music styles heard at the Paris World Exhibition of 1889.

The Impressionist Painters

In 1867, the artist Claude Monet (1840–1926), rebuffed by the academic salons, nevertheless found a place to exhibit his painting *Impression: Sun Rising*. Before long, "Impressionism" had become a term of derision to describe the hazy, luminous paintings of Monet and his followers. A distinctly Parisian style, Impressionism counted among its exponents Camille Pissarro (1830–1903), Edouard Manet (1832–1883), Edgar Degas (1834–1917), and Auguste Renoir (1841–1919). These artists strove to retain on canvas the freshness of their first impressions. What fascinated them was the continuous change in the appearance of things. They ventured out of the studio into the open air to paint water lilies, a haystack, or a cathedral again and again at different hours of the day. Instead of mixing their pigments on the palette, they juxtaposed brush strokes of pure color on the canvas, leaving it to the eye of the viewer to do the mixing. An iridescent sheen bathes each painting as outlines shimmer and melt in a luminous haze.

The Impressionists abandoned the grandiose subjects of Romanticism. Their focus shifted from the human form to light itself. They showed little interest in the drama-packed themes that had inspired centuries of European art, preferring "unimportant" material: still lifes, dancing girls, nudes; everyday scenes of middle-class life, picnics, boating and café scenes; nature in all its beauty, Paris in all its moods.

The Symbolist Poets

A parallel revolt against tradition took place in poetry under the leadership of the Symbolists, who strove for direct poetic experience unspoiled by intellectual

The Impressionists took painting out of the studio and into the open air; their subject was light. **Claude Monet** (1840–1926), *Impression: Sun Rising*. (Musée Marmottan, Paris)

elements. They sought to suggest rather than describe, to present the symbol rather than state the thing. Symbolism as a literary movement gained prominence in the work of French writers Stéphane Mallarmé (1842–1898) and Paul Verlaine (1844–1896), both of whom were strongly influenced by the American poet Edgar Allan Poe (1809–1849). They were sensitive to the sound of a word as well as its meaning, and tried to evoke poetic images that affected all the senses. Through their experiments in free verse forms, the Symbolists were able to achieve in language an abstract quality that had once belonged to music alone.

Impressionism in Music

Impressionism surfaced in France at a crucial moment in the history of European music. The major-minor system had served the art since the seventeenth century, but composers were beginning to feel that its possibilities had been exhausted. Debussy and his followers were attracted to other scales, such as the church modes of the Middle Ages, which gave their music an archaic sound. They began to emphasize the primary intervals—octaves, fourths, fifths—and the parallel movement of chords in the manner of medieval organum. They also explored scale structures introduced by nationalist composers, and they responded especially to non-Western music: the Moorish strain in the songs and dances of Spain, and the Javanese and Chinese orchestras that performed in Paris during the World Exposition of 1889. Here they found rhythms, scales, and colors that offered a bewitching contrast to the traditional sounds of Western music.

While classical harmony looked upon dissonance as a momentary disturbance that found its resolution in the consonance, composers now began to use dissonance as a value in itself, freeing it from the need to resolve. They taught their contemporaries to accept tone combinations that had formerly been regarded as inadmissible, even as the Impressionist painters taught people to see colors in sky, grass, and water that had never been seen there before.

Impressionist composers made use of the entire spectrum of pitches in the *chromatic scale,* and explored the *whole-tone scale,* derived from non-Western sources. This latter pattern is built entirely of whole-tone intervals: for example, C-D-E-F♯-G♯-A♯-C. The result is a fluid sequence of pitches that lacks the pull toward a tonic, or point of rest.

Several other procedures came to be associated with musical Impressionism as well. One of the most important is the use of parallel, or "gliding," chords, in which a chord built on one tone is duplicated immediately on a higher or lower tone. Such parallel motion was prohibited in the Classical system of harmony, but it was precisely these forbidden progressions that Impressionist composers found fascinating.

The harmonic innovations identified with Impressionism led to the formation of daring new tone

Music and ballet provided **Edgar Degas** (1834–1917) with many subjects, as in this painting, *The Dance Class.* (Metropolitan Museum of Art, New York)

In *The Boating Party*, by American painter **Mary Cassatt** (1845–1926), the eye is drawn toward the relaxed mother and child figures. Inspired by a Monet painting, this work features the strong lines and dramatic colors typical of second-generation Impressionists. (National Gallery of Art, Washington, D.C.)

combinations. Characteristic was the use of the five-note combinations known as *ninth chords* (in which the interval between the lowest and highest tones was a ninth). As a result of all these procedures, Impressionist music wavers between major and minor without adhering to either. It hovers in a border-land between keys, creating elusive effects that might be compared to the misty outlines of Impressionist painting.

Ninth chords

These floating harmonies demanded the most subtle colors. There was no room here for the lush, full sonority of the Romantic orchestra. Instead, we hear a veiled blending of timbres: flutes and clarinets in their dark lower registers, violins in their lustrous upper range, trumpets and horns discreetly muted; and over the whole, a shimmering gossamer of harp, celesta, triangle, glockenspiel, muffled drum, and cymbal brushed with a drumstick. One instrumental color flows into another close by, as from oboe to clarinet to flute, in the same way that Impressionist painting moves from one color to another in the spectrum, as from yellow to green to blue.

Orchestral color

Impressionist rhythm too shows the influence of non-Western music. The metrical patterns of the Classical-Romantic era were marked by a recurrent accent on the first beat of the measure. Such emphasis was hardly appropriate for the new dreamlike style. In many works of the Impressionist School, the music glides across the bar line from one measure to the next in a floating rhythm that discreetly obscures the pulse.

Rhythm

The Impressionists turned away from the large forms of the Austro-German tradition, such as symphonies and concertos. They preferred short lyric forms—preludes, nocturnes, arabesques—whose titles suggested intimate lyricism or painting, such as Debussy's *Clair de lune (Moonlight)*, *Nuages (Clouds)*, and *Jardins sous la pluie (Gardens in the Rain)*. Without a doubt, Debussy and his followers rebelled against certain aspects of Romanticism, especially the symphonic tradition of Beethoven and the music drama of Wagner. Yet in a number of ways, Impressionism continued the fundamental tendencies of the Romantic

Small forms

movement in its love of beautiful sound; emphasis on program music, tone painting, and nature worship; addiction to lyricism; attempt to unite music, painting, and poetry; and emphasis on mood and atmosphere. In effect, the Impressionists substituted a thoroughly French brand of Romanticism for the Austro-German variety.

Claude Debussy: His Life and Music

"I love music passionately. And because I love it, I try to free it from barren traditions that stifle it. It is a free art gushing forth, an open-air art boundless as the elements, the wind, the sky, the sea. It must never be shut in and become an academic art."

Claude Debussy

The most important French composer of the early twentieth century, Claude Debussy (1862–1918) was born near Paris in the town of St. Germain-en-Laye, where his parents kept a china shop. He entered the Paris Conservatory when he was eleven. Within a few years, he shocked his professors with bizarre harmonies that defied the rules.

"What rules, then, do you observe?" inquired one of his teachers.

"None—only my own pleasure!"

"That's all very well," retorted the professor, "provided you're a genius." It became increasingly apparent that the daring young man was one indeed.

Early years

Pelléas and Mélisande

Debussy was only twenty-two when his cantata *The Prodigal Son* won the coveted Prix de Rome. The 1890s, the most productive decade of Debussy's career, culminated in the opera *Pelléas and Mélisande*, based on the symbolist drama by the Belgian poet Maurice Maeterlinck. The quiet intensity and subtlety of nuance had a profound impact on the musical public, and the work became an international success. After *Pelléas*, Debussy was famous.

Principal Works

Orchestral music, including *Prélude à "L'après-midi d'un faune"* (*Prelude to "The Afternoon of a Faun,"* 1894), *Nocturnes* (1899), *La mer* (*The Sea*, 1905), *Images* (1912), incidental music

Dramatic works, including the opera *Pelléas et Mélisande* (1902) and the ballet *Jeux* (*Games*, 1913)

Chamber music, including a string quartet (1893) and various sonatas (cello, 1915; violin, 1917; flute, viola, and harp, 1915)

Piano music, including *Pour le piano* (*For the Piano*, 1901), *Estampes* (*Prints*, 1903), 2 books of preludes (1909–10, 1912–13)

Songs and choral music; cantatas, including *L'enfant prodigue* (*The Prodigal Son*, 1884)

in his own words

I am more and more convinced that music is not, in essence, a thing which can be cast into a traditional and fixed form. It is made up of color and rhythms.

His energies sapped by the ravages of cancer, Debussy worked on with remarkable fortitude. The outbreak of war in 1914 robbed him of all interest in music. But after a year of silence, he realized that he had to contribute to the struggle in the only way he could, "by creating to the best of my ability a little of the beauty that the enemy is attacking with such fury." Debussy died in March 1918 during the bombardment of Paris. The funeral procession made its way through deserted streets as the shells of the German guns ripped into his beloved city just eight months before victory was celebrated in France. And French culture has ever since celebrated Debussy as one of its most distinguished representatives.

Like the artist Monet and the writer Verlaine, Debussy considered art to be primarily a sensuous experience. The epic themes of Romanticism offended his temperament as both a man and an artist. "French music," he declared, "is clearness, elegance, simple and natural declamation. French music aims first of all to give pleasure."

Debussy turned against sonata-allegro form, the grand structure that the Germans counted as a supreme achievement. He regarded exposition-development-recapitulation as an outmoded formula. (At a concert once, he whispered to a friend, "Let's go—he's beginning to develop!")

From the Romantic grandeur that left nothing unsaid, Debussy turned toward an art of indirection, subtle and discreet, expressed in short, flexible forms. These mood pieces evoke the favorite images of Impressionist painting: gardens in the rain, sunlight through the leaves, clouds, moonlight, sea, mist.

Orchestral works

Because Debussy worked slowly, his fame rests on a comparatively small output; *Pelléas and Mélisande* is viewed by many as his greatest achievement. Among the orchestral compositions, the *Prelude to "The Afternoon of a Faun"* became a favorite with the public early on, as did the three nocturnes (*Clouds, Festivals, Sirens*) and *La mer (The Sea)*. His handling of the orchestra is thoroughly French, allowing individual instruments to stand out against the ensemble. In his scores, the melodic lines are widely spaced, the texture light and airy.

Piano works

Debussy was one of the important piano composers; he created a distinctive new style of writing for the instrument and composed works that form an essential part of the modern repertory. Among his best-known works are *Clair de lune* (*Moonlight*, the most popular piece he ever wrote), *Evening in Granada*, *Reflections in the Water*, and *The Sunken Cathedral*. Many of his piano pieces demonstrate an interest in non-Western scales and instruments, which he first heard at the Paris Exhibition in 1889 (discussed in CP 15).

Vocal and chamber music

Debussy helped establish the French song as a national art form independent of the German Lied. In chamber music, he achieved an unqualified success with his String Quartet in G minor. The three sonatas of his last years—for cello and piano; violin and piano; and flute, viola, and harp—reveal him moving toward a more abstract and concentrated style.

Debussy chose this Japanese print, *The Hollow of the Wave off Kanagawa*, by **Katsushika Hokusai** (1760–1849), for the front cover of his orchestral work *La mer* (*The Sea*). (Metropolitan Museum of Art, New York)

The Paris World Exhibition of 1889: A Cultural Awakening

How and when did people from distant regions of the world interact before the era of jet travel and electronic communications? One kind of event that has long brought people from various cultures together is a world exposition.

In 1889, France hosted an exposition marking the centenary of the French Revolution. The Eiffel Tower was the French showcase for this world's fair. Musicians from around the world performed for a receptive European public. One of the most popular of the exhibits, from the Indonesian island of Java, featured dancers and gamelan. (A gamelan is an ensemble of mainly percussion instruments—including gongs, chimes, and drums, among others.) Many classical composers, including Claude Debussy and Maurice Ravel, heard this gamelan for the first time. Debussy wrote of its unique sound to a friend: "Do you not remember the Javanese music able to express every nuance of meaning, even

unmentionable shades, and which makes our tonic and dominant seem like empty phantoms for the use of unwise infants?" He attempted to capture something of this sound—its pentatonic scale, unusual timbre, and texture—in a number of his compositions, including the famous symphonic poem *La mer* (*The Sea,* 1905), the piano work *Pagodas* (from *Estampes,* 1903), and several piano preludes. Twentieth-century composers continued to explore the unique timbre of the gamelan, including the bold innovator John Cage, discussed on p. 472.

Other events sparked the imagination of visitors to the Paris Exhibition. Evening festivities included a parade of musicians esreprenting the African nations of Algeria, Senegal, and the Congo, as well as Java, Anam (now Vietnam), and New Caledonia (a Pacific island off the Australian coast). Performances included belly dancers and whirling

A Javanese gamelan orchestra plays various metallophones as accompaniment for a dance. In front, two dancers hold bow and arrow as part of the work they are performing.

dervishes from the Middle East (see p. 235); African-American cakewalk dancers from the southern United States (a cakewalk was a nineteenth-century dance that featured rhythmic strutting and prancing arm in arm in a parody of white plantation owners' behavior); and dancing women from Cambodia.

Folk and popular musics traversed cultural boundaries at the Paris Exhibition. It was there that Debussy was introduced to traditional Russian songs in settings by Rimsky-Korsakov as well as the music of Hungarian and Spanish Gypsies. Like Bizet, Debussy attempted to capture the rhythms of the habanera and the strumming style of flamenco guitars in several of his piano works (*The Interrupted Serenade* and *Evening in Granada*).

The French composer Maurice Ravel (1875–1937) was even more profoundly influenced by this new world of music. Born in the Basque region of France (where the Pyrénées separate France from Spain), Ravel imbued his *Spanish Rhapsody* with rich Iberian color, his violin work *Tzigane* (*Gypsy*, 1924) with showy, exotic effects, and his song cycle *Don Quixote to Dulcinea* (1933, based on the writings of Miguel de Cervantes) with authentic Spanish dance rhythms. Likewise, his most famous work, the hypnotic *Boléro* for orchestra, is accompanied by the insistent rhythm of a popular Spanish dance form. Nor did the mysteries of Asia escape Ravel: his orchestral song cycle *Sheherazade* (1903) was inspired by the Arabian folktales of *The Thousand and One Nights* (sometimes called *Arabian Nights* and the source for the stories of Aladdin and Ali Baba) and includes what he believed was a Persian melody. A movement from the charming *Mother Goose Suite* (originally for piano), called *Empress of the Pagodas,* is based on a fairy tale about an empress who is serenaded during her bath by whimsical creatures playing fantastic instruments.

Ravel's broad-ranging interests drew him to folk songs from around the world (he arranged Greek, Hebrew, Italian, and French tunes, among others), to the newly popular African-American styles of ragtime, blues, and jazz (the second movement of his Violin Sonata is entitled *Blues*), and to the music of Madagascar (an African island and the subject

This watercolor of a *Cambodian Dancer* (1906), by **Auguste Rodin** (1840–1917), reflects the artistic interest in exotic subjects.

of his intense song cycle *Songs of Madagascar,* 1925–26).

Today, we do not have to wait for a world exposition to experience music from around the world. We have only to tune in a PBS (Public Broadcasting System) special on Mexican mariachi bands, rent a library video of Japanese Noh drama, or locate a Web site on Irish step dancing to stimulate our eyes, ears, and imagination.

TERMS TO NOTE:

gamelan
cakewalk

SUGGESTED LISTENING:

Debussy: *La mer, Pagodas* (from *Estampes*), or
  Evening in Grenada
Ravel: *Songs of Madagascar, Boléro, Tzigane,*
  Sheherazade, or *Blues* (from Violin Sonata)
Javanese music (gamelan orchestra)

Prelude to "The Afternoon of a Faun"

Debussy's best-known orchestral work was inspired by a pastoral poem of Stéphane Mallarmé that evokes a landscape of antiquity. The text centers on the faun, a mythological creature of the forest that is half man, half goat. This "simple sensuous passionate being" awakes in the woods and tries to remember: was he visited by three lovely nymphs, or was this but a dream? He will never know. The sun is warm, the earth fragrant. He curls himself up and falls into a wine-drugged sleep.

The work is in sections that follow the familiar pattern of statement-departure-return **(A-B-A').** Yet the movement is fluid and rhapsodic, with almost every fragment of melody repeated immediately. The relaxed rhythm flows across the bar line in a continuous stream. By weakening and even wiping out the accent, Debussy achieved that dreamlike fluidity that is a prime trait of Impressionist music.

We first hear a flute solo in the velvety lower register. The melody glides along the chromatic scale, narrow in range and languorous. (See Listening Guide 34 for themes and an excerpt from the poem.) Glissandos on the harp usher in a brief dialogue in the horns. Such a mixture of colors had never been heard before.

Next, a more decisive motive emerges, marked *en animant* (growing lively). This is followed by a third theme, marked *même movement et très soutenu* (same tempo and very sustained)—an impassioned melody that carries the composition to an emotional climax. The first theme then returns in an altered guise. At the close, antique cymbals play *pianissimo.* (*Antique cymbals* are small disks of brass; the rims are struck together gently and allowed to vibrate.) "Blue" chords (with lowered thirds and sevenths) are heard on the muted horns and violins, sounding infinitely remote. The work finally dissolves into silence, having taken nine minutes to play. Rarely has so much been said in so brief a time.

The great Russian dancer Vaslav Nijinsky as the Faun in the ballet *L'après-midi d'un faune.* Design by **Léon Bakst** (1866–1924).

Listening Guide 34

CD: CHR/STD 6/62–66, SH 3/46–50

Debussy: *Prelude to "The Afternoon of a Faun"* (*Prélude à "L'après-midi d'un faune"*)   (9:45)

DATE OF WORK:	1894
GENRE:	Symphonic poem
ORCHESTRA:	Strings (with 2 harps), flute, oboes, English horn, clarinets, French horns, and antique cymbals
BASIS:	Symbolist poem by Stéphane Mallarmé
FORM:	Free ternary **(A-B-A')**

WHAT TO LISTEN FOR: Lyrical, sinuous melodies (opening is chromatic), that repeat.

Rich instrumental color, with individual timbres that stand out against the orchestra; free-flowing rhythm gives a sense of floating.

Loose 3-part (ternary, or **A-B-A′**) structure.

Evocative mood that expresses the poem's sensuality.

Emotional climax in middle section that peaks in range, dynamics, and textural density.

Opening of poem:

TEXT

Ces nymphes, je les veux perpétuer.
          Si clair
Leur incarnat léger, qu'il voltige dans l'air
Assoupi de sommeils touffus.
                  Amais-je un rêve?
Mon doute, amas de nuit ancienne, s'achève
En maint rameau subtil, qui, de meuré les vrais
Bois mèmes, prouve, hélas! que bien seul je
    m'offrais
Pour triomphe la faute idéale de roses.

Réfléchissons . . . ou si les femmes dont tu
    gloses
Figurent un souhait de tes sens fabuleux!

TRANSLATION

These nymphs I would perpetuate.
          So light
their gossamer embodiment, floating on the air
inert with heavy slumber.
                  Was it a dream I loved?
My doubting harvest of the bygone night ends
in countless tiny branches; together remaining
a whole forest, they prove, alas, that since I am
    alone,
my fancied triumph was but the ideal
imperfection of roses.

Let us reflect . . . or suppose those women that
    you idolize
were but imaginings of your fantastic lust!

46	0:00	**A** SECTION

Opening chromatic melody in flute; passes from one instrument to another, accompanied by muted strings and vague beat:

47	2:48	**B** SECTION

Clarinet introduces more animated idea, answered by rhythmic figure in cellos.

48	3:16

New theme, more animated rhythmically in solo oboe, builds in *crescendo*:

49	4:34

Contrasting theme in woodwinds, then strings, with syncopated rhythms, builds to climax:

50	6:22	**A′** SECTION

Abridged return, in varied setting.

365

unit **XXII**

The Early Twentieth Century

61

Main Currents in Early-Twentieth-Century Music

"The entire history of modern music may be said to be a history of the gradual pull-away from the German musical tradition of the past century."

—AARON COPLAND

KEY POINTS

- The diverse artistic trends of the early twentieth century were a reaction against Romanticism.
- Early-twentieth-century artistic trends explored simplicity and abstraction (non-Western arts, Dadaism, Cubism) and the world of dreams and the inner soul (Surrealism, Expressionism).
- Expressionism was the German response to French Impressionism; in music, composers such as Schoenberg and Webern explored new harmonic systems and the extreme registers of instruments.
- The Neoclassical movement sought to revive balance and objectivity in the arts by returning to formal structures of the past.

The Reaction against Romanticism

Early-twentieth-century composers had to fight not only the Romantic past but the Romanticism in themselves. The new attitudes took hold just before the outbreak of the First World War. European arts sought to escape their over-refinement and tried to capture the spontaneity and the freedom from inhibition that was associated with primitive life. The fine arts discovered the abstraction of African sculpture, while Paul Gauguin and Henri Rousseau created exotic paintings of monumental simplicity. Some composers turned to the dynamism of non-Western rhythm, seeking fresh concepts in the musics of Africa, Asia, and eastern Europe.

New Trends in the Arts

We have seen that changing currents in art and literature nearly always find parallels in music. In the years around the First World War, an influential art movement appeared: Dadaism, founded in Switzerland after 1918. The Dadaists, principally writers and artists who reacted to the horrors of the bloodbath that had engulfed Europe, rejected the concept of Art with a capital "A"—that is, something to be put on a pedestal and reverently admired. To make their point, they produced works of absolute absurdity. They also reacted against the excessive complexity of Western art by trying to recapture the simplicity of a child's worldview.

Following their example, the French composer Erik Satie led the way toward a simple, "everyday" music, and exerted an important influence—along with the writer Jean Cocteau—on the group called *Les Six* (see p. 387). Several decades later, this influence was clearly apparent in the works of the American composer John Cage, who will be discussed in Chapter 72.

The Dada group, which included artists like Hans Arp and Marcel Duchamp, soon merged into the school of Surrealism, as exemplified by Salvador Dali and Joan Miró, who exploited the world of dreams. Other styles of modern art included Cubism, the Paris-based style of painting embodied in the works of Pablo Picasso, Georges Braque, and Juan Gris, which encouraged the painter to construct a visual world in terms of geometric patterns; and Expressionism,

The powerful abstraction of African sculpture helped European art resist its overrefinement. A bronze musician from Nigeria.

French painter **Henri Rousseau** (1844–1910) found his subject matter in the images of distant places, just as composers of the era sought inspiration in primitive elements of world musics. *The Sleeping Gypsy* (1897). (Museum of Modern Art, New York)

Spanish artist **Joan Miró** (1893–1983) explores the surrealist world of dreams through the distortion of all the shapes within the composition. *Dutch Interior I.* (Museum of Modern Art, New York)

which we will see had a significant impact on music of the early twentieth century.

Expressionism

Expressionism was the German answer to French Impressionism. Whereas the French genius rejoiced in radiant impressions of the outer world, the Germanic temperament preferred digging down to the depths of the soul. As with Impressionism, the impulse for the movement came from painting. Wassily Kandinsky (1866–1944), Paul Klee (1879–1940), Oskar Kokoschka (1886–1980), and Edvard Munch (1863–1944)—famous for *The Scream*—influenced the composer Arnold Schoenberg and his followers even as the Impressionist painters influenced Debussy. Expressionism is familiar not only through the paintings of these artists, but also in the writings of Franz Kafka (1883–1924). Expressionism in music triumphed first in central Europe, especially Germany, and reached its full tide in the dramatic works of the *Second Viennese School* (a term referring to Arnold Schoenberg and his disciples Alban Berg and Anton Webern).

The musical language of Expressionism favored a hyperexpressive harmonic language marked by extraordinarily wide leaps in the melody and by the use of instruments in their extreme registers. Expressionist music soon reached the boundaries of what was possible within the major-minor system. Inevitably, it had to push beyond.

Neoclassicism

One way of rejecting the nineteenth century was to return to the eighteenth. Instead of revering Beethoven and Wagner, as the Romantics had done, composers of the 1920s began to emulate the great musicians of the early eighteenth century—Bach, Handel, and Vivaldi—and the detached, objective style that is often associated with their music.

The German Expressionist painter **Oskar Kokoschka** (1886–1980) reveals his feelings about the end of his love affair with Alma Mahler, the composer's widow, and his terror of war in *Knight Errant* (1915). (Solomon R. Guggenheim Museum, New York)

Neoclassicism tried to rid music of the story-and-picture meanings favored in the nineteenth century. Neoclassical composers turned away from the symphonic poem and the Romantic attempt to bring music closer to poetry and painting. They preferred absolute to program music, and they focused attention on craftsmanship and balance, a positive affirmation of the Classical virtues of objectivity and control.

Absolute music

62

New Elements of Musical Style

"To study music, we must learn the rules. To create music, we must break them."

—NADIA BOULANGER

KEY POINTS

- Early-twentieth-century composers revitalized rhythm by increasing its complexity—for example, using *polyrhythm, polymeter, changing meters,* or *irregular meters.*
- Melody was no longer the focus of a composition; the style was often more "instrumental" in character.
- New conceptions of harmony *(polychords, polytonality, atonality)* pressed music beyond the traditional systems of tonality.
- The *twelve-tone method* (or *serialism*), devised by Arnold Schoenberg, was an important and influential compositional technique.
- Linear movement replaced vertical, chordal conceptions, and extreme dissonance became part of the normal sound palette.
- The early-twentieth-century orchestra, which focused on winds, percussion, and piano rather than on strings, was generally smaller than its nineteenth-century predecessor.
- Composers absorbed influences from ragtime, jazz, and other popular styles, which invigorated their works.

The New Rhythmic Complexity

Twentieth-century music discarded the standard rhythmic patterns of duple, triple, and quadruple meter. Rather, composers explored the possibilities of non-symmetrical patterns based on odd numbers: five, seven, eleven, thirteen beats to the measure. In nineteenth-century music, a single meter customarily prevailed through an entire movement or section. Now the metrical flow shifted constantly *(changing meter)*, sometimes with each measure. Formerly, one rhythmic pattern was used at a time. Now composers turned to *polyrhythm*— the simultaneous use of several rhythmic patterns. As a result of these innovations, Western music achieved something of the complexity and suppleness of Asian and African rhythms.

Polymeter

Polyrhythm

The new generation of composers preferred freer rhythms of the highest flexibility that gave their works an almost physical power and drive. Indeed, the revitalization of rhythm is one of the major achievements of early-twentieth-century music.

The New Melody

Instrumental melody

Nineteenth-century melody is fundamentally vocal in character; composers tried then to make the instruments "sing." Early-twentieth-century melody is neither unvocal nor antivocal; it is simply not conceived in relation to the voice. It abounds in wide leaps and dissonant intervals. Besides, in much twentieth-century music, melody is not even a primary element. In any case, twentieth-century composers have greatly expanded our notion of what a melody is: many patterns are accepted as melodies today that would hardly have been considered as such a century ago.

The New Harmony

Polychords and polyharmony

No single factor sets off early-twentieth-century music from that of the past more decisively than the new conceptions of harmony. The triads of traditional harmony, we saw, were formed by combining three tones, on every other degree of the scale, or in thirds: 1-3-5 (for example, C-E-G), 2-4-6 (D-F-A), and so on. Traditional harmony also employed four-note combinations, with another third piled on top of the triad, known as seventh chords (1-3-5-7), and (in music of the Impressionists) five-note combinations known as ninth chords (1-3-5-7-9). Twentieth-century composers added more "stories" to such chords, forming highly dissonant *polychords* of six and seven notes. The emergence of these complex "skyscraper" chords brought increased tension to music and allowed the composer to play two or more streams of harmony against each other, creating *polyharmony*.

New Conceptions of Tonality

The new sounds of twentieth-century music necessarily burst the confines of traditional tonality and called for new means of organization, extending or replacing the major-minor system. These approaches, in general, followed four principal paths—expanded tonality, polytonality, atonality, and twelve-tone music.

The widespread use of chromatic harmony in late nineteenth century led, in the early twentieth, to the free use of all twelve tones around a center. Although this approach retained the basic principle of traditional tonality—gravitation to the tonic—it wiped out the distinction between diatonic and chromatic and between major and minor modes.

From the development of polyharmony, a further step followed logically: heightening the contrast of two keys by presenting them simultaneously, which resulted in *polytonality*. Confronting the ear with two keys at the same time meant a radical departure from the basic principle of traditional harmony: centering on a single key. Polytonal pieces still gave the impression of orderly progress

Every dissonance doesn't have to resolve if it doesn't happen to feel like it, any more than every horse should have its tail bobbed just because it's the prevailing fashion.
—GEORGE IVES, TO HIS SON CHARLES

toward a central point, though, by permitting one key to assert itself at the end. Polytonality came into prominence with the music of Stravinsky, in such works as *The Rite of Spring,* which we will study.

The idea of abandoning tonality altogether is associated with the composer Arnold Schoenberg, whom we will meet later. Schoenberg advocated doing away with the tonic by giving the twelve tones of the chromatic scale, in no set order, equal importance—thus creating *atonal* music. (We will study an example of atonality in his song cycle *Pierrot lunaire.*) Atonality was much more of an innovation than polytonality, because it entirely rejected the framework of key.

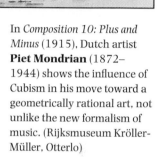

In *Composition 10: Plus and Minus* (1915), Dutch artist **Piet Mondrian** (1872–1944) shows the influence of Cubism in his move toward a geometrically rational art, not unlike the new formalism of music. (Rijksmuseum Kröller-Müller, Otterlo)

The Twelve-Tone Method

Having accepted the necessity of moving beyond the existing tonal system, Schoenberg sought a unifying principle that would take its place. He found this in a strict technique, worked out by the early 1920s, that he called "the method of composing with twelve tones"—that is, with twelve equal tones. Each composition that uses Schoenberg's method, also known as *serialism,* is based on a particular arrangement of the twelve chromatic tones called a *tone row.* This row is the unifying idea for that composition, and serves as the source of all the musical events that take place in it.

The tone row

Once established, a tone row is the basis from which a composer builds themes, harmonies, and counterpoint. Schoenberg provided flexibility and variety in this seemingly confining system through alternative forms of the tone row. A *transposed* row begins on a different note. In its *inversion,* the movement of the notes is in the opposite direction, up instead of down and vice versa, so that the row appears upside down. Its *retrograde* is an arrangement of the pitches in reverse order, so that the row comes out backward, and its *retrograde inversion* turns the row upside down and backward. (You will remember that the same techniques were used in earlier music, especially in the Baroque fugue; see diagram on p. 30)

Forms of the tone row

The Emancipation of Dissonance

The history of music, we have seen, has been the history of a steadily increasing tolerance on the part of listeners. Throughout this long evolution, one factor remained constant: a clear distinction was drawn between dissonance, the element of tension, and consonance, the element of rest. Consonance was the norm, dissonance the temporary disturbance. In many contemporary works, however, tension becomes the norm. Therefore, a dissonance can serve even as a final cadence, provided it is less dissonant than the chord that came before; in relation to the greater dissonance, it is judged to be consonant. Twentieth-century composers emancipated dissonance by freeing it from the obligation to resolve to consonance. Their music taught listeners to accept tone combinations whose like had never been heard before.

Texture: Dissonant Counterpoint

The nineteenth century was preoccupied with rich, lush harmony; the early twentieth emphasized linear movement, or counterpoint. The new style swept away the sounds of both the Romantic cloudburst and Impressionistic haze. In their place came a sparse linear texture that fit the New Classical ideal of craftsmanship, order, and detachment. Composers began to use dissonance to set off one line against another. Instead of basing their counterpoint on the agreeable intervals of the third and sixth, they turned to astringent seconds and sevenths. Or they might heighten the independence of the voices by putting them in different keys.

Orchestration

The rich sonorities of nineteenth-century orchestration gave way to a leaner sound, one that was hard and bright, played by a smaller orchestra. The decisive factor in the handling of the orchestra was the change to a linear texture. Color came to be used in the new music not so much for atmosphere as for bringing out the lines of counterpoint and of form. The string section lost its traditional role as the heart of the orchestra; its tone was felt to be too warm. Attention was focused on the more penetrating winds. Composers favored darker instruments—viola, bassoon, trombone. The emphasis on rhythm brought the percussion group into greater prominence than ever before, and the piano, which in the Romantic era was preeminently a solo instrument, found a place in the orchestral ensemble.

Romanian sculptor **Constantin Brancusi** (1876–1957) revolutionized the movement toward abstraction and reductive formalism in *The Kiss* (1908). (The Philadelphia Museum of Art, Louise and Walter Arensberg Collection)

New Conceptions of Form

The first quarter of the century saw the final expansion of traditional forms in the gigantic symphonies and symphonic poems of Mahler and Strauss. As music could hardly go further in this direction, composers began to move toward the Classical ideals of tight organization and succinctness. In addition, they revived a number of older forms such as toccata, fugue, passacaglia and chaconne, concerto grosso, theme and variations, and suite, while retaining the traditional symphony, sonata, and concerto. They tended to value the formal above the expressive, a principle known as *formalism.* The New Classicism, like the old, strove for purity of line and proportion.

Composers also vitalized their music through materials drawn from popular styles. Ragtime, with its sprightly syncopations, traveled across the Atlantic to Europe. The rhythmic freedom of jazz captured the ears of many composers, who strove to achieve something of the spontaneity that distinguished the popular style. (We will look into the origins of jazz and its influence on other styles in a later chapter.)

63

Stravinsky and the Revitalization of Rhythm

"I hold that it was a mistake to consider me a revolutionary. If one only need break habit in order to be labeled a revolutionary, then every artist who has something to say and who in order to say it steps outside the bounds of established convention could be considered revolutionary."

KEY POINTS

- Russian composer Igor Stravinsky was a bold experimenter with rhythm and with new instrumental combinations.
- Stravinsky's musical language also explores the percussive use of dissonance, as well as polyrhythms and polytonality.
- Stravinsky's early works, including his ballets *The Firebird, Petrushka,* and *The Rite of Spring,* are strongly nationalistic; the last of these re-creates rites of ancient Russia.
- Stravinsky's style evolved throughout his life; he explored Neoclassicism and serial (twelve-tone) techniques.

Igor Stravinsky

Certain artists embody the most significant impulses of their time and affect the cultural life in a most powerful fashion. One such artist was Igor Stravinsky, the Russian composer who for half a century reflected the main currents in twentieth-century music.

His Life

Igor Stravinsky (1882–1971) was born in Oranienbaum, a summer resort not far from St. Petersburg. He grew up in a musical environment: his father was the leading bass at the Imperial Opera. Although he was taught to play the piano, his musical education was kept on the amateur level because his parents wanted him to study law. Still, while enrolled at the University of St. Petersburg, he continued his musical studies. At twenty, he submitted his compositions to the Russian master Nicolai Rimsky-Korsakov, with whom he subsequently worked for three years.

Success came early to Stravinsky. His music attracted the notice of Serge Diaghilev, the legendary impresario of the Paris-based Russian Ballet, who commissioned Stravinsky to write a score for *The Firebird,* which was produced in 1910. *The Firebird* was followed a year later by the ballet *Petrushka.* With dancers Vaslav Nijinsky and Tamara Karsavina in the leading roles, the production secured Stravinsky's position in the forefront of the modern movement. The spring of 1913 saw the staging of the third and most spectacular of the

Serge Diaghilev

Principal Works

Orchestral music, including Symphonies of Wind Instruments (1920), Concerto for Piano and Winds (1924), *Dumbarton Oaks Concerto* (1938), Symphony in C (1940), Symphony in Three Movements (1945), and *Ebony Concerto* (1945)

Ballets, including *L'oiseau de feu* (*The Firebird*, 1910), *Petrushka* (1911), *Le sacre du printemps* (*The Rite of Spring*, 1913), *Les noces* (*The Wedding*, 1923), and *Agon* (1957)

Operas, including *The Rake's Progress* (1951); opera-oratorio *Oedipus Rex* (1927); other dramatic works, including *L'histoire du soldat* (*The Soldier's Tale*, 1918)

Choral music, including *Symphony of Psalms* (1930), *Canticum sacrum* (1955), *Threni* (1958), and *Requiem Canticles* (1966)

Chamber music; piano music (solo and for two pianos); songs

The Rite of Spring ballets Stravinsky wrote for Diaghilev, *The Rite of Spring.* On opening night, one of the most scandalous in modern music history, the revolutionary score touched off a near riot. People hooted and screamed, convinced that what they were hearing "constituted a blasphemous attempt to destroy music as an art." However, when the work was presented a year later at a symphony concert under conductor Pierre Monteux, it was received with enthusiasm and established itself as a masterpiece.

The outbreak of war in 1914 ended the way of life that had nurtured Diaghilev's sumptuous dance spectacles. Stravinsky and his family took refuge in Switzerland, their home for the next six years. In 1920, the Russian Revolution having severed Stravinsky's ties with his homeland, he settled in France, where he remained until 1939. During these years, Stravinsky concertized extensively throughout Europe, performing his own music as pianist and conductor. In 1939, he was invited to deliver a lecture series at Harvard Univer-

American years sity. When the Second World War broke out, he decided to settle in California, outside Los Angeles; in 1945, he became an American citizen. Stravinsky's later concert tours around the world made him the most celebrated figure in twentieth-century music. He died in New York on April 6, 1971, at the age of eighty-nine.

His Music

Stravinsky's style evolved continuously throughout his career, from the post-Impressionism of *The Firebird* and the primitivism of *The Rite of Spring* to the controlled classicism of his mature style and, finally, to the serialism of his late works.

Early works Stravinsky was a leader in the revitalization of rhythm in European art music. His first success came as a composer of ballet, where rhythm is allied with body movement and expressive gesture. His was a rhythm of unparalleled dynamic power, furious yet controlled. Stravinsky reacted against the restless chromaticism of the Romantic period, but no matter how daring his harmony, he retained a sense of key. His subtle sense of sound makes him one of the great orchestrators; his sonority is marked by a polished brightness and a texture so clear that, as Diaghilev remarked, "one can see through it with one's ears."

The national element predominates in such early works as *The Firebird*, *Petrushka*, and *The Rite of Spring*, the last of which re-creates sacrificial rites of ancient Russia. In the decade of the First World War, the composer turned to a more economic style; his *Soldier's Tale*, a dance-drama for four characters, is an intimate theater work accompanied by a seven-piece band. The most important work of the years that followed is *The Wedding*, a stylization of a Russian peasant wedding.

Stravinsky's Neoclassical period culminated in several major compositions. *Oedipus Rex* is an "opera-oratorio" whose text is a translation into Latin of Jean Cocteau's adaptation of the Greek tragedy by Sophocles. The *Symphony of Psalms*, for chorus and orchestra, regarded by many as the chief work of Stravinsky's maturity, was composed, according to the composer, "for the glory of God." Equally admired is *The Rake's Progress*, an opera on a libretto by W. H. Auden and Chester Kallman, after a celebrated series of engravings by William Hogarth. Written as the composer was approaching seventy, this radiantly melodious score, which uses the set forms of Mozartean opera, stands as the essence of Neoclassicism. In the works written after he was seventy, he showed an increasing receptiveness to the serial procedures of the twelve-tone style, including the ballet *Agon* and the choral work *Threni: Lamentations of the Prophet Jeremiah*, both written in the mid-1950s.

Neoclassical period

The Rite of Spring

The Rite of Spring, subtitled *Scenes of Pagan Russia*, not only embodies the cult of primitivism that so startled its first-night audience, but also sets forth a new musical language characterized by the percussive use of dissonance, as well as polyrhythms and polytonality.

Stravinsky described his "fleeting vision": "I saw in my imagination a solemn pagan rite: sage elders, seated in a circle, watching a young girl dance herself to death. They were sacrificing her to propitiate the God of Spring." In Part I of the ballet, celebrations for the arrival of spring include a lustful abduction of women, a rivalry between two tribes, and a round dance. At the climax of these activities, the oldest and wisest man of the village is brought out for the ritual kissing of the earth, and the tribes respond joyfully and energetically.

Part II is more solemn. The women of the tribe, conducting a mysterious game, select a young maiden whom they will sacrifice in order to save the fertility of the earth. The Chosen One begins her fatal dance in front of the elders, and her limp body is eventually carried off to the Sun God Yarilo. The plot is vague, the anthropology is dubious, but the visions are effectively theatrical.

As a ballet, *The Rite of Spring* had a brief life, but the music survived independently as a concert piece. Today, this work stands as one of the landmarks in twentieth-century symphonic literature. The size of the orchestra is monumental, even by the standards of late Romanticism. Stravinsky expands the ensemble to include eight French horns, five trumpets, five from each of the woodwind groups, and an extraordinary battery of percussion instruments. He often uses the full force of the brass and percussion to create a barbaric, primeval sound.

in his own words

Mild protests against the music could be heard from the very beginning of the performance [of Rite of Spring*]. Then, when the curtain opened on the group of knock-kneed and long-braided Lolitas jumping up and down (Danse des adolescents), the storm broke. Cries of "Ta gueule" [Shut up] came from behind me. I heard Florent Schmitt shout "Taisez-vous garces du seizième" [Be quiet, you bitches of the sixteenth]; the "garces" of the 16th arrondissement were, of course, the most elegant ladies in Paris. The uproar continued, however, and a few minutes later I left the hall in a rage. . . . I have never again been that angry. The music was so familiar to me; I loved it, and I could not understand why people who had not yet heard it wanted to protest in advance.*

The rhythmic arrangement of line and color in *The Dance* (1909–10) by **Henri Matisse** (1869–1954) is suggestive of the *Dance of the Youths and Maidens*, from Stravinsky's *Rite of Spring*.

Stravinsky ignores the natural lyric qualities of the string instruments, giving them percussive material such as pizzicato and successive down-bow strokes. The overall impact of the orchestration is harsh and loud, with constantly changing colors.

Melody and harmony

Stravinsky's melodies are modeled after Russian folk songs—in fact, a number of authentic tunes are quoted—and the remaining melodic material, often presented in short fragments, use limited ranges and extended repetition in a folk song–like manner. The harmonies are derived from an eclectic language, including whole-tone and octatonic (eight-tone) scales, polytonality, and dissonance.

Rhythm and meter

The energetic interaction between rhythm and meter is the most innovative and influential element of *The Rite of Spring*. In some scenes, a steady pulse is set up, only to serve as a backdrop for unpredictable accents or melodic entrances. In other passages, the concept of a regular metric pulse is abandoned altogether, and downbeats occur seemingly at random. With *The Rite of Spring*, Stravinsky liberated Western music from the traditional constraints of metric regularity.

Part I

In the Introduction to Part I, *Adoration of the Earth*, a writhing bassoon melody set in its uppermost range depicts the awakening of the Earth in spring. In *The Dance of the Youths and Maidens*, the strings play dissonant chords in their lower register—an elemental pounding heightened by the use of polytonal harmonies. The scenes that follow continue the pubescent rites, using modal harmonies to create an archaic atmosphere. Part I closes with the *Dance of the Earth*, which requires the utmost physicality from its players.

Part II

Glorification of the Chosen One

We will consider three scenes from Part II, *The Sacrifice*, which allow us to hear Stravinsky's primitive rhythmic treatment, eerie orchestration, and bitingly dissonant harmonic language at its finest. In the *Glorification of the Chosen One*, rhythm is dominant. The **A-B-A′** form is preceded by eleven pounding chords, which establish a metric pulse that is immediately contradicted by two 5/8 measures with accents on subbeats two and four. The continued juxtaposition of these 5/8 measures with passages of steady alternating eighth notes, swooping orchestral gestures, and a brief melodic fragment creates a chaotic, barbaric character.

The **B** section begins with a strong bass-drum downbeat that reinforces this mood by using intense dissonances, often marked *fff*. A contrasting melodic idea—a five-note motive first presented in the strings—briefly interrupts and then dominates the remainder of the **B** section. Set with an ostinato percussion accompaniment, the repetitive quality of the melodic idea momentarily restores a sense of metric regularity, which is then quickly disrupted by the return of **A**.

The *Evocation of the Ancestors* projects a statelier mood. A single theme is presented five times, in varying lengths, orchestration, and metric accents. Each entrance of a melodic phrase is preceded by a percussive downbeat in the timpani, contrabassoon, and low strings. During the melodic statements, the lower instruments reinforce the static quality by sustaining a pedal note.

Evocation of the Ancestors

The *Ritual Action of the Ancestors*, set in an arch form **(A-B-C-B′-A′)**, begins with quick melodic figures in the English horn and alto flute in simple quadruple pulse. The processional character continues into the **B** section, where the muted trumpets intone a folklike melody over an alto flute accompaniment. The mood is abruptly altered when the French horns enter *fff*, creating a more sinister character. Section **C** then tosses around several melodic motives, after which the horns reestablish the intensity of section **B′**. The movement closes quietly and ominously with the muted E-flat trumpet and woodwinds playing the quick melodic figures of the opening **(A′)**. Our selection closes just before the *Sacrificial Dance*, during which the young girl dances herself to death in a frenzied climax to the ballet.

Ritual Action of the Ancestors

Listening Guide 35

CD: CHR/STD 7/34–42, SH 3/51–59

Stravinsky: *The Rite of Spring (Le sacre du printemps)*, Part II, excerpts

(5:44)

DATE OF WORK:	1913
GENRE:	Ballet (often performed as a concert piece for orchestra)
BASIS:	Scenes of pagan Russia
SCENARIO:	Nikolai Roerich and Igor Stravinsky
CHOREOGRAPHY:	Vaslav Nijinsky

SECTIONS:

Part I: *Adoration of the Earth*
  Introduction
  Dance of the Youths and Maidens
  Game of Abduction
  Spring Rounds
  Games of the Rival Tribes
  Procession of the Sage
  Dance of the Earth

Part II: *The Sacrifice*
  Introduction
  Mystic Circle of the Chosen One
  Glorification of the Chosen One
  Evocation of the Ancestors
  Ritual Action of the Ancestors
  Sacrificial Dance

WHAT TO LISTEN FOR: Huge orchestral forces, with constantly changing timbral colors.
Violent rhythmic conflicts (polyrhythm, changing meters, shifting accents).
Short melodic motives exchanged among instruments.
Modern, dissonant harmonic palette.
Extreme dynamic contrasts.

Glorification of the Chosen One   (1:35)

Principal Instruments: Brass, percussion, and percussive strings
Tempo: *Vivo* (very fast)
Form: **A-B-A′**

51 0:00 **A** section—11 accented chords introduce loud and dissonant exchanges, swooping woodwind lines vs. strings, in shifting meters, with primitive accents alternating with steady eighth notes (reduced score, showing flutes, first violins, and double basses):

0:20 Strings have 4-note descending fragment, bowed, then pizzicato:

52 0:34 **B** section—bass drum downbeats, answered by dissonant brass.

0:42 Pizzicato strings introduce new idea, heard against thundering timpani:

1:01 Woodwinds join strings, alternating with brass motive:

Pace slows to prepare for return of **A** section.

53 1:16 **A′** section—return of opening material, abridged.

Evocation of the Ancestors   (0:40)

   Principal Instruments: Trumpets, bassoons, and percussion

   Tempo: Moderate

   Form: Repetitions of a single theme

54   0:00   Explosive attack, followed by accented rhythmic theme in block chords heard
             in trumpets and woodwinds; alternates betweeen 2/4 and 3/4 meter:

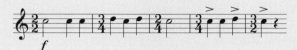

     0:08   Answered by soft and short statement in strings, followed by percussive attack.

     0:14   Extended statement of theme by trumpet and woodwinds, with string echo (*pp*), then
             percussive attack.

     0:25   Bassoon section states theme (*p*).

     0:34   Abbreviated statement (*ff*) by trumpets and woodwinds.

     0:38   Slow bassoon passage leads to next section.

Ritual Action of the Ancestors   (3:29)

   Principal Instruments: Woodwinds, brass, and percussion

   Tempo: Moderate

   Form: **A-B-C-B′-A′**

55   0:00   **A** section—begins with marchlike steady beat, pizzicato, with offbeats in timpani.

     0:12   Slow, chromatic melodic fragments and held notes in English horn (then other woodwinds):

            Steady marchlike beat fades out.

56   0:56   **B** section—flute, with wavering line, and bassoons set up accompaniment pattern.

     1:10   Folklike melody in muted trumpets:

            Violins play tremelos against steady accompaniment.

     1:44   French horns play folklike melody, with full orchestra, at fortissimo.

57   1:56   **C** section—alternation of short, chromatic melodic ideas in orchestral dialogue.

58   2:23   **B′** section—folklike theme, played fortissimo, in French horns, with tremelos in strings and
             woodwinds; very dissonant.

59   2:42   **A′** section—return to opening idea, played by bass trumpet, answered by alto flute.

     3:02   Clarinets have meandering line over steady, marchlike accompaniment leading to loud chord
             (beginning of *Sacrificial Dance*).

64

Schoenberg and the Second Viennese School

"I personally hate to be called a revolutionist, which I am not. What I did was neither revolution nor anarchy."

Arnold Schoenberg

KEY POINTS

- Arnold Schoenberg, along with his students Alban Berg and Anton Webern, constitute the *Second Viennese School*.
- Schoenberg was highly influenced by German *Expressionism*, and was himself an Expressionist painter and playwright.
- As a composer, Schoenberg experimented with abandoning the tonal system; his *twelve-tone*, or *serial*, method revolutionized twentieth-century composition.
- His song cycle, *Pierrot lunaire*, represents his atonal-Expressionist period (a transition between his tonal style and his twelve-tone period).
- In *Pierrot lunaire*, Schoenberg joins the text and music through the vocal technique of *Sprechstimme* (spoken voice), accompanied by highly disjunct instrumental lines (*Klangfarbenmelodie*).

The German Expressionist movement was manifested in the music of Arnold Schoenberg and his followers. Schoenberg's pioneering efforts in the breakdown of the traditional tonal system and his development of the twelve-tone method, described earlier, revolutionized musical composition. His innovations were taken further by his most gifted students, Alban Berg and Anton Webern. These three composers are often referred to as the *Second Viennese School* (the first being Haydn, Mozart, and Beethoven).

His Life

Arnold Schoenberg (1874–1951) was born in Vienna. He began to study the violin at the age of eight, and soon afterward made his initial attempts at composing. Having decided to devote his life to music, he left school while in his teens. Soon he became acquainted with a young musician, Alexander von Zemlinsky, who for a few months gave him lessons in counterpoint. This was the only musical instruction he ever had.

Through Zemlinsky, young Schoenberg was introduced to the advanced musical circles of Vienna, which at that time were under the spell of Wagner's operas. In 1899, when he was twenty-five, Schoenberg wrote the string sextet *Transfigured Night*. The following year, several of his songs were performed in Vienna and created a scene. "And ever since that day," he once remarked "the scandal has not ceased."

in his own words

Whether one calls oneself conservative or revolutionary, whether one composes in a conventional or progressive manner, whether one tries to imitate old styles or is destined to express new ideas—whether one is a good composer or not—one must be convinced of the infallibility of one's own fantasy and one must believe in one's own inspiration.

Schoenberg became active as a teacher and soon gathered about him a band of devoted disciples that included Alban Berg and Anton Webern. With each new work, Schoenberg moved closer to taking as bold a step as any composer has ever taken—the rejection of tonality.

The First World War interrupted Schoenberg's creative activity. Although he was past forty, he was called up for military duty in the Vienna garrison. An eight-year period of compositional silence (1915–23) allowed the development of a set of structural procedures to replace tonality. His "method of composing with twelve tones" caused much bewilderment in the musical world. All the same, he was now firmly established as a leader of contemporary musical thought.

With the coming to power of Hitler in 1933, Schoenberg emigrated to America. Like many Austrian-Jewish intellectuals of his generation, he had grown away from his Jewish origins. Schoenberg converted to Lutheranism, but after leaving Germany, he returned to his Hebrew faith. He arrived in the United States in the fall of 1933; shortly afterward, he joined the faculty of the University of Southern California, and was later appointed professor of composition at the University of California in Los Angeles. He became an American citizen in 1940, taught until his retirement at the age of seventy, and continued his musical activities until his death seven years later.

Arnold Schoenberg completed this Expressionist painting, *The Red Gaze* (1910), just two years before he wrote *Pierrot lunaire*. It is highly reminiscent of Edvard Munch's *The Scream*. (Arnold Schönberg Center, Vienna)

His Music

Schoenberg's early works are representative of post-Wagnerian Romanticism; they still used key signatures and remained within the boundaries of tonality. The best-known composition of this era is *Transfigured Night*. In Schoenberg's

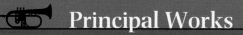

Principal Works

Orchestral music, including Five Pieces for Orchestra (1909), Variations for Orchestra (1928), and concertos for violin (1936) and piano (1942)

Operas, including *Die glückliche Hand* (*The Blessed Hand*, 1913) and *Moses und Aron* (incomplete, 1932)

Choral music, including *Gurrelieder* (1911), *Die Jakobsleiter* (*Jacob's Ladder*, 1922), and *A Survivor from Warsaw* (1947); smaller choral works, including *Friede auf Erden* (*Peace on Earth*, 1907)

Chamber music, including 4 string quartets, serenade, wind quintet, string trio, and string sextet *Verklärte Nacht* (*Transfigured Night*, 1899)

Vocal chamber music, including *Pierrot lunaire* (*Moonstruck Peter*, 1912)

Piano music, including Three Piano Pieces, Op. 11 (1909)

French Expressionist painter **Georges Rouault** (1871–1958) was highly influenced by medieval stained-glass technique in this dark portrayal of *Pierrot* (c. 1937).

second period, the atonal-Expressionist, he abolished the distinction between consonance and dissonance and did away with any sense of a home key. The high point of this period is *Pierrot lunaire*, which we will study. During this era, Schoenberg's interest in Expressionism was manifested not only in his music, but in his work as an artist (see p. 381) and writer.

Schoenberg's third style period, incorporating the twelve-tone method, reached its climax in the Variations for Orchestra, Opus 31, one of his most powerful works. In the fourth and last part of his career—the American phase—he carried the twelve-tone technique to further stages of refinement.

Pierrot lunaire

For his song cycle, *Pierrot lunaire*, Schoenberg drew on the stock characters of the *commedia dell'arte* (comedy of the arts), an Italian comic theatrical entertainment that originated in the mid-sixteenth century. One of the most parodied characters is the clown Pierrot (Pagliaccio in Italian; Petrushka in Russian), who has been the model for pantomime for centuries.

Schoenberg chose the texts for his song cycle from a collection of poems entitled *Pierrot lunaire* by the Belgian writer Albert Giraud, a disciple of the Symbolists. Giraud's Pierrot was the poet-rascal-clown whose chalk-white face, passing abruptly from laughter to tears, enlivened every puppet show and pantomime in Europe. The poems were liberally spiced with elements of the macabre and the bizarre; their abrupt changes of mood from guilt and depression to atonement and playfulness fired Schoenberg's imagination. He picked twenty-one texts (in German translation), arranged them in three groups of seven, and set them for a female reciter and a chamber music ensemble of five players using eight instruments: piano, flute/piccolo, clarinet/bass clarinet, violin/viola, and cello.

Sprechstimme

One of Schoenberg's goals was to bring spoken word and music as close together as possible; he achieved this aim through *Sprechstimme* (spoken voice), a new style in which the vocal melody is spoken rather than sung on exact pitches and in strict rhythm. As Schoenberg explained it, "the melody in the speaker's part is *not* meant to be sung." The result is a weird but strangely effective vocal line.

Klangfarbenmelodie

Sprechstimme serves as a unifying element in this series of miniatures. Schoenberg also experimented with what he called *Klangfarbenmelodie* (tone-color melody), in which each note of a melody is played by a different instrument, creating a shifting effect that evokes the moonbeams mentioned in the poems.

The Moonfleck

We will focus on No. 18, *The Moonfleck* (*Der Mondfleck;* see Listening Guide 36 for the text). Pierrot, out to have fun, is disturbed by a white spot—a patch of moonlight—on the collar of his jet-black jacket. He rubs and rubs but cannot get rid of it. His predicament inspired Schoenberg to contrapuntal complexities

Listening Guide 36

CD: CHR/STD 7/15–16, SH 4/1–2

Schoenberg: *Pierrot lunaire,* No. 18   (0:55)

DATE OF WORK:	1912
GENRE:	Song cycle
MEDIUM:	Solo voice (mezzo-soprano) and 5 instrumentalists (violin/viola, cello, flute/piccolo, clarinet/bass clarinet, piano)
TEXT:	21 poems from Albert Giraud's *Pierrot lunaire,* all in rondeau form; cycle organized in 3 parts

Part I: Pierrot, sad clown figure, is obsessed with the moon, having drunk moonwine; his loves, fantasies, and frenzies are exposed.

1. *Moondrunk*
2. *Columbine*
3. *The Dandy*
4. *Pale Washerwoman*
5. *Valse de Chopin*
6. *Madonna*
7. *The Sick Moon*

Part II: Pierrot becomes ridden with guilt and wants to make atonement.

8. *Night*
9. *Prayer to Pierrot*
10. *Theft*
11. *Red Mass*
12. *Gallows Ditty*
13. *Beheading*
14. *The Crosses*

Part III: Pierrot climbs from the depths of depression to a more playful mood, but with fleeting thoughts of guilt; then he becomes sober.

15. *Homesickness*
16. *Vulgar Horseplay*
17. *Parody*
18. *The Moonfleck*
19. *Serenade*
20. *Homeward Journey*
21. *O Scent of Fabled Yesteryear*

18. The Moonfleck (Der Mondfleck)

Medium: Voice, piccolo, clarinet in B♭, violin, cello, piano
Tempo: Sehr rasche (very quickly)

WHAT TO LISTEN FOR: Use of Sprechstimme against fast, dissonant accompaniment.
Complex contrapuntal texture, with canonic treatment.
Musical and poetical refrain (on words "Einen weissen Fleck").
Flickering effects created by instruments, playing independently from vocal part.

TEXT

1 0:00

Einen weissen Fleck des hellen Mondes
Auf dem Rücken seines schwarzen Rockes,
So spaziert Pierrot im lauen Abend,
Aufzusuchen Glück und Abenteuer.

Plötzlich stört ihn was an seinem Anzug,
Er beschaut sich rings und findet richtig—
Einen weissen Fleck des hellen Mondes

2 0:26

Auf dem Rücken seines schwarzen Rockes.

Warte! denkt er: das ist so ein Gipsfleck!
Wischt und wischt, doch—bringt ihn
nicht herunter!
Und so geht er, giftgeschwollen, weiter,
Reibt und reibt bis an den frühen Morgen—
Einen weissen Fleck des hellen Mondes.

TRANSLATION

With a fleck of white—from the bright moon—
on the back of his black jacket.
Pierrot strolls about in the mild evening
seeking his fortune and adventure.

Suddenly something strikes him as wrong,
he checks his clothes and sure enough finds
a fleck of white—from the bright moon—
on the back of his black jacket.

Damn! he thinks: that's a spot of plaster!
Wipes and wipes, but—he can't get it off.

And so goes on his way, his pleasure poisoned,
rubs and rubs till the early morning—
a fleck of white—from the bright moon.

Opening, for voice and instruments:

of a spectacular kind. The piano introduces a three-voice fugue, while the other instruments unfold devices such as strict canons in diminution (smaller note values) and retrograde (backward). It is, according to composer George Perle, "a work that one never 'gets used to.'"

Schoenberg's Students: Berg and Webern

Following in his teacher's footsteps, Alban Berg (1885–1935) wrote music that emanated from the world of German Romanticism. His most widely known composition is *Wozzeck* (1922), an opera based on a play by Georg Buchner and set in an atonal-Expressionist musical idiom. Here, Berg anticipated certain twelve-tone procedures, but also looked back to the tonal tradition and the leit-motif technique of Wagner. *Wozzeck* envelops the listener in a world of hallucinations, unveiled through Berg's great lyric imagination.

Anton Webern (1883–1945), on the other hand, carried the philosophy of brevity of statement to an extreme. He assigned each tone a specific function in the overall scheme using the device of Klangfarbenmelodie, or tone-color melody, described earlier. Webern often used instruments in their extreme registers as well. He employed Schoenberg's twelve-tone method with unprecedented strictness, moving toward complete control, or total serialism, thus establishing this compositional system as a major influence in twentieth-century music.

e Learning

unit **XXIII**

Twentieth-Century Nationalism

65

The European Tradition

"The art of music above all other arts is the expression of the soul of a nation. The composer must love the tunes of his country and they must become an integral part of him."

—RALPH VAUGHAN WILLIAMS

KEY POINTS

- Because of the ability to preserve traditional music more accurately, twentieth-century composers used more authentic folk and traditional elements in their nationalistic music than nineteenth-century composers had.
- National "schools" of composition developed across Europe in France, Russia, England, Germany, Spain, Scandinavia, and in various Eastern European countries.
- Hungarian composer Béla Bartók collected traditional music (songs and dances) from his native land, and incorporated many of these authentic elements into his compositions.
- Bartók's music displays new scales and rhythmic ideas and a modern, polytonal harmonic language, all set in Classical forms.
- His *Concerto for Orchestra* is a programmatic work that uses the whole ensemble as the "soloist."

Twentieth-century nationalism differed from its nineteenth-century counterpart in one important respect. Composers approached traditional music with a scientific spirit, prizing the ancient tunes precisely because they departed from the

386

Inspired by the German bombing of the Basque town of Guernica on April 28, 1937, this nationalistic painting was produced by **Pablo Picasso** for the Spanish Pavilion at the 1938 International Exhibition in Paris. *Guernica*. (Museo del Prado, Madrid)

conventional mold. By this time, the phonograph had been invented. The new students of folklore took recording equipment into the field in order to preserve the songs exactly as the village folk sang them, and the composers who used those songs in their works tried to retain the traditional flavor of the originals.

National Schools

French composers in the generation after Debussy and Ravel tried to capture the wit and spirit that are part of their national heritage. One group in particular, called *Les Six* (The Six), followed the example of Erik Satie (1866–1925) in their efforts to develop a style that combined objectivity and understatement with the Neoclassicism and the even newer concepts of harmony. Of this group, Darius Milhaud (1892–1974) is remembered today for his ballet *The Creation of the World* (1923) and for being a leader in the development of polytonality. Francis Poulenc (1899–1963) has emerged as the most significant figure of *Les Six*. One of the outstanding art song composers of his day, he also wrote thoroughly Parisian piano pieces and several operas that are performed frequently.

French school

Les Six

In the post-Romantic period, the Russian school produced two composers of international fame. The piano works of Sergei Rachmaninoff (1873–1943) are enormously popular with the concertgoing public, especially his Second Piano Concerto and his Variations on a Theme of Paganini. Alexander Scriabin (1872–1915), a visionary artist whose music is wreathed in a subtle lyricism, was one of the leaders in the twentieth-century search for new harmonies. In the next generation, two important figures emerged: Sergei Prokofiev (1891–1953), who sought to recapture the spirit of the Beethovenian symphony and brought the full power of his resources to film music in *Lieutenant Kije* (1933) and *Alexander Nevsky* (1938); and Dmitri Shostakovich (1906–1975), the first Russian composer of international repute who was wholly a product of the musical culture during the period of the Soviet Union (1917–91).

Russian school

Two figures were of prime importance in establishing the modern English school—Ralph Vaughan Williams (1872–1958) and Benjamin Britten (1913–1976). Britten's works for the stage have established his reputation as one of the foremost opera composers of the era. Among his operas are *Peter Grimes* (1945), about an English fishing village, and *Billy Budd* (1951), after Herman Melville's story. You will recall that Britten's *Variations and Fugue on a Theme of Purcell (The Young Person's Guide to the Orchestra)* was discussed earlier (see Chapter 9).

English school

German school

Among the composers who came into prominence in Germany in the years after the First World War, Paul Hindemith (1895–1963) was the most significant. He left Germany when Hitler came to power—his music was banned from the Third Reich as "cultural Bolshevism"—and spent two decades in the United States, during which he taught at Yale University and at Tanglewood, Massachusetts, where many young Americans came under his influence.

Carl Orff (1895–1982) took his point of departure from the clear-cut melodies and vigorous rhythms of Bavarian folk song. He is best-known in North America for his stirring cantata *Carmina burana* (1937), set to racy medieval lyrics. Kurt Weill (1900–1950) is remembered for *The Threepenny Opera* (1928), which he and the poet Bertolt Brecht adapted from *The Beggar's Opera* by John Gay. Frequent revivals have made this one of the century's most famous theater pieces (the best-known song is *Mack the Knife*).

Other nationalists

Hungarian nationalism found two major representatives in Béla Bartók, whom we will study, and Zoltán Kodály (1882–1967). Both composers collected and studied traditional songs, and made the folk element prominent in their music. The Czech national school is well represented by Leoš Janáček (1854–1928), whose operas have found great favor with the American public. The major figure of the modern Spanish school was Manuel de Falla (1876–1946), best-known for his ballet *The Three-Cornered Hat*.

Finland's Jean Sibelius (1865–1957) is enjoying a revival of his symphonies, his Violin Concerto, and the tone poem *Finlandia*. The Jewish composer Ernest Bloch (1880–1959) is known for *Schelomo*—the biblical name of King Solomon—a "Hebrew Rhapsody" for cello and orchestra that gave eloquent expression to his heritage, much as Arnold Schoenberg did a generation later in *A Survivor from Warsaw*.

Béla Bartók: His Life and Music

"What is the best way for a composer to reap the full benefits of his studies in peasant music? It is to assimilate the idiom of peasant music so completely that he is able to forget all about it and use it as his musical mother tongue."

Béla Bartók

Folk songs bind the nation, bind all nations and all people with one spirit, one happiness, one paradise.
—LEOS JANÁCEK

Béla Bartók (1881–1945) reconciled the traditional songs of his native Hungary with the main currents of European music, thus creating an entirely personal language.

Bartók was born in a small Hungarian town in which his father served as director of an agricultural school, and studied at the Royal Academy in Budapest. His interest in folklore led him to realize that what passed for Hungarian in the eyes of the world was really the music of the Roma, or Gypsies. The true Hungarian idiom, he decided, was found only among the peasants. With his fellow composer Zoltán Kodály, he toured the remote villages of the country, determined to collect the native songs before they died out forever. "Those days I spent in the villages among the peasants," he wrote later, "were among the happiest of my life. In order to feel the vitality of this music one must . . . [come] to know it by direct contact with the peasants."

With the performance at the Budapest Opera of his ballet *The Wooden Prince* (1917), Bartók came into his own. Then in 1918, the fall of the Hapsburg

Principal Works

Orchestral works, including *Music for Strings, Percussion, and Celesta* (1936), *Concerto for Orchestra* (1943), 2 violin concertos (1908, 1938), and 3 piano concertos (1926, 1931, 1945)

1 opera: *Bluebeard's Castle* (1918)

2 ballets: *The Wooden Prince* (1917) and *The Miraculous Mandarin* (1926)

Chamber music, including 6 string quartets (1908–39); *Contrasts* (for violin, clarinet, and piano, 1938); sonatas, duos

Piano music, including *Allegro barbaro* (1911) and *Mikrokosmos* (6 books, 1926–39)

Choral music, including *Cantata profana* (1930); folk-song arrangements

Songs, including folk song arrangements

monarchy released a surge of national sentiment that created a favorable climate for his music. In the following decade, Bartók became a leading figure in the musical life of his country.

Emigration to America

The alliance between the Hungarian government and Nazi Germany on the eve of the Second World War confronted the composer with issues that he faced squarely. He protested the performances of his music on the Berlin radio and at every opportunity took an anti-Fascist stand. To go into exile meant surrendering the position he enjoyed in Hungary, but he would not compromise. Bartók came to the United States in 1940 and settled in New York City.

Final years

The American years were not happy ones. Sensitive and retiring, he felt uprooted, isolated in his new surroundings. In his final years, Bartók suffered from leukemia and was no longer able to appear in public. A series of commissions from various sources spurred him to compose his last works, which rank among his finest. "The trouble is," he remarked to his doctor shortly before the end, "that I have to go with so much still to say." He died in New York City at the age of sixty-four.

Melody and harmony

Bartók found that Eastern European traditional music was based on ancient modes, unfamiliar scales, and nonsymmetrical rhythms. These features freed him in his composing from what he called "the tyrannical rule of the major and minor keys," and brought him to new concepts of melody, harmony, and rhythm. Bartók's harmony can be bitingly dissonant. Polytonality abounds in his work; but despite an occasional leaning toward atonality, he never wholly abandoned the principle of key.

Rhythm and meter

Bartók's is one of the great rhythmic innovators of modern times. His pounding, stabbing rhythms constitute the primitive aspect of his art. Like Stravinsky, Bartók sometimes changed the meter at almost every bar and frequently used syncopations and repeated patterns (ostinatos). He, along with Stravinsky, played a major role in the revitalization of European rhythm, infusing it with earthy vitality and tension.

Bartók—A Folk-Song Collector

What kinds of music did the Hungarian composer Béla Bartók hear in the Eastern European villages he visited? What are the essential ingredients of the traditional music of his native Hungary and neighboring regions? Bartók, along with fellow composer Zoltán Kodály (1882–1967), searched out and wrote down folk songs in an attempt to identify the national musics of various Eastern European cultures. The two took on this project not as composers but as folklorists who wanted to study traditional music scientifically. (Today, we would call them ethnomusicologists. The comparative study of musics of the world, focusing on the cultural context of performance, is known as ethnomusicology.) Their fieldwork, in the villages and countrysides of Eastern Europe, centered on the music of numerous distinct groups: Slovak, Romanian, Bulgarian, Serbian, Croatian, and Arab, as well as Hungarian. The many thousands of songs they collected reflect the very essence of these peoples—their social rituals (weddings, matchmaking, and dancing) and their religious ceremonies.

Bartók drew extensively in his compositions from the melodies, rhythms, and poetic structures of this rich body of traditional music. He was partial to modal scales, especially those typical of Slovak and Romanian melodies. But rhythm was the primary attraction of this body of folk music and dance. Bartók tried at times to imitate the vocal style of Hungarian music, which is based on free speech-rhythms and follows the natural inflection of the language. At other times, he used the irregular folk dance rhythms typical of Bulgarian music. These propelling rhythms were driven by additive meters built from unit groups of 2, 3, or 4. Thus instead of dividing a 9/8 meter into regular divisions of 3, he might build it from irregular groups of 2 and 3 (2 + 3 + 2 + 2, for example; see the discussion of additive meters on p. 22). From this folk legacy Bartók fashioned a unique musical style.

One type of music collected by Bartók was that of the Roma, or Gypsies, a word that conjures up Hollywood-style images of traveling caravans full of roguish and colorful entertainers. In reality, this little-understood and itinerant group has a long and esteemed musical history. Believed to have originated in northern India, Roma peoples eventually settled throughout Europe and America. One of the most important and well-documented groups is the Hungarian Romanies, who were especially famous for their dance music, played by violinists and bagpipers. Bartók soon understood that theirs was not the traditional music he sought to collect but rather an urban, commercial style cultivated by professional performers. Beginning in the late eighteenth century, Roma bands were usually made up of two violins, a cimbalom (a zither-like instrument whose strings were struck), and a double bass. The Hungarian composer Franz Liszt, who also drew inspiration and themes from this music, publicly

Form The composer was more traditional in his choices of form—his model was the Beethoven sonata, but more tightly structured. In his middle years, he came under the influence of Baroque music and turned increasingly from thinking harmonically to thinking linearly. The resulting complex texture is a masterly example of modern dissonant counterpoint.

Orchestration Bartók's orchestral sound derived from a palette of colors all his own. His orchestration ranges from brilliant mixtures to threads of pure color that bring out the intertwining melody lines; from a hard, bright glitter to a luminous haze. He is best-known to the public by the three major works of his last period: the *Music for Strings, Percussion, and Celesta*, regarded by many as his masterpiece; the *Concerto for Orchestra*, a favorite with American audiences (and the work we

Béla Bartók in 1907, recording Slovakian folk songs on an acoustic cylinder machine in the Hungarian village of Zobordarázs.

recognized the skill and musicianship of these performers in his book *The Gypsy in Music*. Roma ensembles remain popular in modern-day Hungary; they consist of professionally trained musicians playing all styles of music—art, traditional, and popular.

TERMS TO NOTE:

ethnomusicology
fieldwork
additive meter

SUGGESTED LISTENING:

Bartók: *Music for Strings, Percussion, and Celesta*, Fourth Movement
Liszt: *Hungarian Rhapsody* No. 2
Folk songs collected by Bartók
Gypsy (Roma) music

will study); and his final effort, the Third Piano Concerto, an impassioned and broadly conceived work.

Concerto for Orchestra

In the summer of 1943, two years before his death from leukemia, Bartók received a visit from the conductor Serge Koussevitzky, who offered him a commission of $1,000 and a premiere by the Boston Symphony Orchestra for a new work. The terminally ill composer rallied his strength and set to work on the *Concerto for Orchestra*, which he completed in October of the same year. Of symphonic dimension, the work is called a concerto because of its tendency, as

in his own words

Bartók explained, "to treat the single orchestral instruments in a concertante or soloistic manner." In other words, he used the term in its eighteenth-century meaning, although in this case, the virtuoso is the entire orchestra.

The concerto has five movements: the first, a spacious Introduction, is in sonata-allegro form and makes use of a folklike pentatonic scale; the second is a joking "game of pairs" with short sections, each of which features a different pair of wind instruments; the third, called *Elegia*, is a contemplative and rhapsodic nocturne, or "night music"; the fourth (which we will study) is a songful Intermezzo that separates the two serious movements surrounding it; and the fifth is a rhythmic and primitive-sounding folk dance set as a sonata allegro.

The fourth movement, titled *Interrupted Intermezzo*, opens with a plaintive tune in the oboe and flute whose pentatonic structure evokes a Hungarian folk song. The nonsymmetrical rhythm, alternating between 2/4 and 5/8 meter, gives the movement an unpredictable charm. A memorable broad theme is then heard in the strings, highly reminiscent of the song *You Are Lovely, You Are Beautiful, Hungary.* The mood is interrupted by a harsh clarinet melody borrowed from the Russian composer Dmitri Shostakovich's Symphony No. 7, a musical portrayal of the Nazi invasion of Russia in 1942. Bartók made an autobiographical statement in this movement: "The artist declares his love for his native land in a serenade, which is suddenly interrupted in a crude and violent manner; he is seized by rough, booted men who even break his instrument." The two opening themes eventually return in a sentimental declaration of the composer's love for his homeland.

Listening Guide 37

CD: CHR/STD 7/27–33, SH 4/3–9

Bartók: *Interrupted Intermezzo*, from *Concerto for Orchestra* (4:20)

DATE OF WORK:	1943
GENRE:	Orchestral concerto
MOVEMENTS:	1. Introduction, Allegro non troppo/Allegro vivace; sonata-allegro form
	2. *Game of Pairs*, Allegretto scherzando; **A-B-A′** form
	3. *Elegia*, Andante non troppo; in 3 episodes
	4. *Interrupted Intermezzo*, Allegretto; rondo-like form
	5. Pesante/Presto; sonata-allegro form

WHAT TO LISTEN FOR:	3 contrasting themes (1st is folklike and pentatonic; 2nd is broad and lyrical; 3rd interrupts with portrayal of a Nazi invasion that erupts in violence).
	Shifting meters and irregular rhythms.
	Polytonal and atonal harmonies.
	Rondo-like form, with recurrences of opening folk tune (**A-B-A′-C-B′-A″**).
	Sentimental mood representing composer's love for his homeland.

FOURTH MOVEMENT: *Interrupted Intermezzo*, **Allegretto; rondo-like form, shifting meter (2/4, 5/8, 3/4, 5/8)**

3	0:00	Dramatic 4-note introduction, unison in strings.
	0:05	**A** section—plaintive, folklike tune, played by oboe in changing meter with asymmetrical rhythms:

Theme heard in flute and clarinets; dialogue continues in woodwinds and French horn.

4	1:00	**B** section—sweeping lyrical melody in violas, in shifting meter:

Violins take up lyrical theme an octave higher, with countermelody in violas; marked "calmo" (calm).

5	1:44	**A′** section—dissonant woodwinds lead to varied statement of opening theme; more chromatic.
6	2:04	**C** section—tempo picks up; clarinet introduces new theme (from Shostakovich symphony):

	2:17	Dissonant punctuations in brass and woodwinds.
	2:31	Theme parodied in violins.
7	2:44	Theme of **C** section introduced by tubas with theme in its original form, then heard in inversion in strings:

8	2:57	**B′** section—flowing **B** section theme returns in muted strings.
9	3:31	**A″** section—woodwinds with fragments of open theme; flute cadenza; leads into gentle closing.

66

Music of the Americas

"Armies of men . . . have turned to a better life by first hearing the sounds of a Salvation Army band. The next time you hear a Salvation Army band, no matter how humble, take off your hat."

—JOHN PHILIP SOUSA

KEY POINTS

- Music publications in early America were largely devotional; some were written in a *shape-note* system designed for easy reading.
- The parlor and minstrel songs of nineteenth-century composer Stephen Foster were very popular during his lifetime and remain so today.
- The great bandmaster and composer John Philip Sousa promoted and fostered the American wind band tradition, which was an outgrowth of the British military band.
- Charles Ives was one of the most innovative and original composers of his time; he drew on the music of his New England childhood—hymns, patriotic songs, brass band marches, and dance tunes—which he set in a very modern style.
- American composer Aaron Copland was inspired by songs of the Old West and by Mexican dance music; his orchestral music and ballets (for example, *Billy the Kid*) established his popularity.
- The music of Mexican composer Silvestre Revueltas has a powerful nationalistic expression: it draws on colorful, folklike rhythms and melodies, which he set in a modern, dissonant idiom.

Unlike the composers of the New England School (see p. 312), who derived much of their inspiration and techniques from European models, certain twentieth-century American masters based their works on popular and traditional music of their native land. The nationalism of Charles Ives, one of America's most original spirits, and Aaron Copland, one of its most prolific and gifted, takes us back to campground revival meetings, minstrel shows, old-time band concerts, and scenes from our Western frontiers. It is to these musical traditions that we now turn our attention.

Popular Music in Late-Nineteenth-Century America

We have noted already the rise of devotional music—notably spirituals and gospel hymns—among African Americans and whites in the nineteenth century (see CP 7). Publishers reached out to the public by issuing books of folk hymns and so-called "white spirituals" with music printed in *shape-note* notation, a new, easy system designed for people lacking music literacy. The

M E A R. C. M. Sharp Key on G.

A shape-note hymn entitled *Mear*, from *The Easy Instructor* (1801). The different shapes represent the syllables *fa, sol, la,* and *mi* used in singing.

melodies of the shape-note hymns, which resemble those of the ballads and fiddle tunes of the era, are set in simple four-part harmonizations; some of these works remain popular even today in gospel and contemporary Christian music arrangements.

One prophet of indigenous American song remains a household name: Stephen Foster (1826–1864), who is known for his lyrical parlor ballads, minstrel show tunes, and poignant plantation songs. Foster strove to write a simpler music that could be understood by all. Among his most popular songs are *Oh! Susanna* (1848) and *Camptown Races* (1850), both minstrel-show songs that remain in the common tradition; the well-known and highly nostalgic plantation songs *Old Folks at Home* (1851; the official state song of Florida) and *My Old Kentucky Home* (1853; the state song of Kentucky); and the timeless ballads *Jeanie with the Light Brown Hair* (1854) and *Beautiful Dreamer* (1864), the first a lament on the lost happiness in his marriage and the second, his last song, written in the style of an Italian air.

Foster's songs gradually moved from the stereotypical depiction of African Americans in stock minstrel-show tradition to a more realistic image of a people experiencing pain, joy, and sorrow. *Oh! Boys, Carry Me 'Long* (1851) makes a request commonly heard in spirituals, for deliverance from pain through death. Stephen Foster, America's most beloved songwriter, died an alcoholic in 1864, alone and in poverty.

America's vernacular tradition included instrumental music as well, particularly performances by brass bands. An outgrowth of the British military band, wind groups thrived throughout the United States. One, the U.S. Marine Band (now called The President's Own), formed in 1798, comprised two oboes, two clarinets, two French horns, bassoon, and drums. The refinement of rotary-valved brass instruments by various makers, including the Belgian Adolphe Sax (inventor of the saxophone), revolutionized the makeup of civic bands; thus, by the Civil War era (1861–65), both Northern and Southern regiments marched to the sounds of brass groups. Many bands reorganized after the war as concert and dance ensembles.

The United States Marine Band marches in parade, with its director, John Philip Sousa (1854–1932), playing cornet (in right front). (Harry Ransom Humanities Research Center, University of Texas, Austin)

395

Music and the Patriotic Spirit

Have you ever been moved to tears by a patriotic song—perhaps your national anthem? Music has often fueled emotions, inciting acts of heroism and patriotism that are remembered for generations through song. We can hear some traditional songs of the Civil War echoing through the twentieth-century compositions of Charles Ives. Many tunes well-known to most of us had their origins in wartime as well. The colonial troops of the American Revolution marched to the fife-and-drum strains of *Yankee Doodle. Dixie* ("I wish I was in the land of cotton," written, ironically, by a Northerner) became a rallying cry of the Civil War's Confederacy sounded against the North's *Battle Hymn of the Republic* (a poem by author Julia Ward Howe, sung to the tune of *John Brown's Body*).

In the early twentieth century, songwriter George M. Cohan was so moved by the U.S. declaration of war against Germany in 1917 that he wrote *Over There* ("Send the word, over there, that the Yanks are coming"), a catchy song that caught on immediately with the American public and soldiers during the First World War. Likewise, songwriter Irving Berlin joined with singer Kate Smith in a 1938 radio broadcast on Armistice Day (now Veterans Day) to build patriotic support in the United States as the Second World War was looming. The song that captured the hearts of millions then was *God Bless America,* now considered by many the country's "second national anthem."

A new tide of patriotism has recently swept across the United States, a response to the unthink-

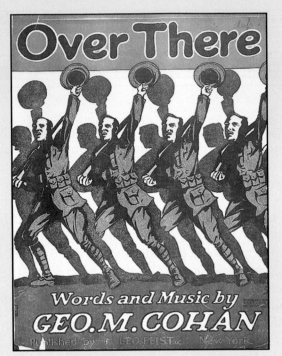

Sheet music for *Over There,* by George M. Cohan, written to inspire American troops fighting in the First World War. The cover design is by the famous American illustrator **Norman Rockwell.**

able events of September 11, 2001—the terrorist bombings of the World Trade Center and the Pentagon. And once again, the lyrics of *God Bless America* have resonated deeply in the hearts of all Americans, thanks to the outpouring of musical tributes that include many new renditions of this moving song.

The national anthems of many countries were

John Philip Sousa

America's greatest bandmaster was undoubtedly John Philip Sousa (1854–1932), who conducted the U.S. Marine Band from 1880 to 1892 and later formed the incomparable Sousa's Band. Known as "the march king," Sousa wrote over 130 marches for band, as well as dance music and operettas. He toured North America and Europe extensively with his group, delighting audiences with his *Semper Fidelis* (1888), *The Washington Post* (1889), the ever-popular *Stars and Stripes Forever* (1897), and band arrangements of ragtime, the newest rage (see p. 409). Almost single-handedly, Sousa created a national music for America that the direct result of wartime emotions. The lyrics of *The Star-Spangled Banner* were written in 1814 by a Baltimore attorney named Francis Scott Key during the English bombardment of Fort McHenry (a famous battle during the War of 1812). Key was aboard a small ship in the Chesapeake Bay, nervously watching the American flag over the fort and knowing that if it went down, so too would his beloved Baltimore. Thus the flag-inspired lyrics— "Oh, say, can you see, by the dawn's early light, what so proudly we hailed at the twilight's last gleaming? Whose broad stripes and bright stars through the perilous fight"—which he adapted to the disjunct tune of an English drinking song that now everyone finds difficult to sing. (The song was not adopted as the U.S. national anthem until 1931.) France's *La Marseillaise* is another example of a revolutionary anthem ("Allons, enfants de la patrie! Le jour de gloire est arrivé," or "Arise, children of the homeland! The day of glory has arrived"), as is Mexico's *Mexicanos, al grito de guerra (Mexicans, to the War Cry)*, a spirited song of independence.

Happily, the patriotic spirit is alive in peacetime as well. It has produced such notable anthems as Britain's *God Save the Queen* (or *King*)—the same tune to which we sing *America* ("My country, 'tis of thee") and the stately *Emperor's Hymn* by Haydn. The latter was originally adopted as the Austrian anthem but serves today as the national song of recently unified Germany, with the text "Einigkeit und Recht und Freiheit," or "Unity and right and liberty." Canada also recently adopted an anthem that draws together its multiethnic population—*O Canada*, written in 1880 by the French-Canadian Calixa Lavallée, was named the country's national hymn (in French and English) in 1980. The universality of music is illustrated in Israel's anthem, *Hatikvah (The Hope)*, a moving poem of the Jewish people returning to their ancient homeland in the late nineteenth century, set to the melody of a haunting Bohemian folk song. In times of national crisis or pride, whether responding to a war or an Olympic victory, these memorable songs resound deep in the soul of a people.

New York City policeman Daniel Rodriguez sings *God Bless America* at the opening ceremony of the 2002 Winter Olympic Games.

SUGGESTED LISTENING:

National anthems (of the United States, France, Mexico, Canada, Israel, Great Britain, Germany)

continues to resonate in its concert halls, on its streets, in its sports stadiums, and in the hearts of its people.

One New England musician born into this rich environment of inspirational hymns, patriotic songs, and especially brass bands—his father was a Civil War bandmaster—was Charles Ives, who never forgot his nineteenth-century vernacular heritage even while nurturing very modern tendencies. One of Ives's most nostalgic songs, *The Things Our Father's Loved*, reminisces on the music of bygone days in a medley of familiar tunes—some patriotic, some reli-

Charles Ives

Aaron Copland

gious, some from the popular tradition—tinged with his own bittersweet harmonies. Like the familiar melodies he cites in his music, Ives has become an American classic.

Aaron Copland: His Life and Music

"I no longer feel the need of seeking out conscious Americanism. Because we live here and work here, we can be certain that when our music is mature it will also be American in quality."

Few composers have been able to capture the spirit of the American experience as successfully as Aaron Copland (1900–1990)—his well-crafted and classically proportioned works have an immediate appeal. Copland was born "on a street in Brooklyn that can only be described as drab. . . . Music was the last thing anyone would have connected with it." During his early twenties, he studied in Paris with the famous teacher Nadia Boulanger; he was her first full-time American pupil.

In his growth as a composer, Copland mirrored the dominant trends of his **Jazz idiom** time. After his return from Paris, he turned to the jazz idiom, a phase that culminated in his brilliant Piano Concerto. Then followed a period during which **Neoclassical period** Copland the Neoclassicist experimented with the abstract and produced the Piano Variations, *Short Symphony*, and *Statements for Orchestra*. He realized that a new public for contemporary music was being created by the radio, phonograph, and film scores. "It made no sense to ignore them and to continue writing as if they did not exist. I felt that it was worth the effort to see if I couldn't say what I had to say in the simplest possible terms." In this fashion, Copland was led to what became a most significant development after the 1930s: his attempt to simplify the new music so that it would communicate to a large public.

The 1930s and 1940s saw the creation of works that established Copland's popularity. *El salón México* (1936) is an orchestral piece based on Mexican melodies and rhythms. The three ballets, *Billy the Kid*, *Rodeo*, and *Appalachian Spring*, continue to delight an international audience. Among his film scores are

🎺 Principal Works

Orchestral music, including 3 symphonies, Piano Concerto (1926), *Short Symphony* (1933), *Statements for Orchestra* (1933–35), *El salón México* (1936), *A Lincoln Portrait* (1942), *Fanfare for the Common Man* (1942), and *Connotations for Orchestra* (1962)

3 ballets: *Billy the Kid* (1938), *Rodeo* (1942), *Appalachian Spring* (1944)

Film scores, including *The City* (1939), *Of Mice and Men* 1939), *Our Town* (1940), *The Red Pony* (1948), and *The Heiress* (1948)

Piano music, including Piano Variations (1930)

Chamber music; choral music and songs

Listening Guide 38

CD: CHR/STD 7/70–74, SH 4/10–14

Copland: *Billy the Kid*, Scene 1, *Street in a Frontier Town*   (6:24)

DATE OF WORK: 1938 (ballet first performed); 1939 (orchestral suite)

GENRE: Orchestral suite from ballet

BASIS: Actual story of outlaw William Bonney (called Billy the Kid)

SECTIONS OF ORCHESTRAL SUITE:

The Open Prairie	*Gun Battle*
Street in a Frontier Town	*Celebration* (after Billy's capture)
Prairie Night (Card Game at Night)	*Billy's Death*

Copland's notes on the ballet: *The ballet begins and ends on the open prairie. The first scene is a street in a frontier town. Cowboys saunter into town, some on horseback, others on foot with their lassos; some Mexican women do a jarabe, which is interrupted by a fight between two drunks. Attracted by the gathering crowd, Billy is seen for the first time, a boy of twelve, with his mother. The brawl turns ugly, guns are drawn, and in some unaccountable way, Billy's mother is killed. Without an instant's hesitation, in cold fury, Billy draws a knife from a cowhand's sheath and stabs his mother's slayers. His short but famous career has begun. In swift succession we see episodes in Billy's later life—at night, under the stars, in a quiet card game with his outlaw friends, hunted by a posse led by his former friend Pat Garrett, in a gun battle. A drunken celebration takes place when he is captured. Billy makes one of his legendary escapes from prison. Tired and worn out in the desert, Billy rests with his girl. Finally the posse catches up with him.*

WHAT TO LISTEN FOR: Melodic paraphrases of a number of classic cowboy songs.
Shifting meters, including a dance in 5/8, and much syncopation.
Accented dissonance and polytonal harmonies.
Extensive use of percussion.
Dramatic and dissonant climax at end (death of Billy's mother).

Street in a Frontier Town; Moderato

10   0:00   Piccolo solo, with tune *Great Grand-Dad:*

Other woodwinds join in dialogue.

0:21   New tune (paraphrased from *Git Along, Little Dogies*) in oboe and trumpet, almost in unison, with dissonance on strong beat (x):

0:45   *Great Grand-Dad* heard in piccolo, while strings enter with dissonant tune from above.

0:57   Alternation of 2 tunes—the first in woodwinds and strings, second in trombones.

11 1:10 Trumpet, with new, shifting-meter tune (4 + 3 + 4 + 3), and accompaniment in opposite meter (3 + 4 + 3 + 4):

1:15 Strings take up shifting-meter tune; brass and strings return to dissonant tune, which dies out.

1:48 Large chords played _fortissimo_ in full orchestra, punctuated by bass drum; disjunct tune based on _The Old Chisolm Trail._

12 1:58 Quick dance tune in strings in 4/4 (loosely based on _The Old Chisolm Trail_), accompanied by syncopated woodblock:

2:19 Trombones enter with tune from _The Streets of Laredo_:

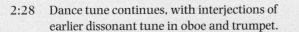

2:28 Dance tune continues, with interjections of earlier dissonant tune in oboe and trumpet.

2:57 Opening tune heard in piccolo and clarinet, more animated, with grace notes and harmonics in strings and sleigh bells, followed by slower, legato melody in low strings and brass (based on _The Streets of Laredo_).

13 3:27 Mexican dance (jarabe) and finale; trumpet, with melody in 5/8 meter _(based on Git Along, Little Dogies)_, accompanied by woodblock and gourd (accents shown with x's):

14 4:15 Violins enter with tune _Goodbye, Old Paint_ in legato, 3/4 meter; alternate with oboe playing verse of same cowboy song:

5:24 _Goodbye, Old Paint_ continues in fabric of complex polyphony; full orchestra plays tune, alternating chorus and verse; transformed as it builds to climax.

5:57 3 loud chords, followed by 2 low notes (gunshots), end section.

Quiet City, Of Mice and Men, Our Town, The Red Pony, and *The Heiress,* the last of which brought him an Academy Award. He wrote two important works during wartime: *A Lincoln Portrait,* for speaker and chorus, with texts drawn from Lincoln's own speeches, and the Third Symphony. In the 1960s, Copland clearly demonstrated that he could handle twelve-tone techniques when he wrote his powerful *Connotations for Orchestra.*

Billy the Kid

For the ballet based on the saga of Billy the Kid, Copland produced one of his freshest scores. Several classic cowboy tunes are used in this work as a point of departure for his own creations; they flavor his music but are assimilated into his personal style rather than quoted literally.

Billy the Kid—the Brooklyn-born William Bonney—had a brief but intense career as a desperado and soon became one of the legends of the Wild West. The ballet touches on the chief episodes of his life. We see him first as a boy of twelve; when his mother is killed by a stray bullet in a street brawl, he stabs the man responsible for her death. Later, during a card game, he is accused of cheating and kills the accuser. Captured after a gun battle, he is put in jail, but he murders his jailer and gets away. A romantic interlude ensues when Billy joins his Mexican sweetheart in the desert. But he is tracked down and killed by his childhood friend Sheriff Pat Garrett. At the close, we hear a lament on the death of the notorious outlaw.

The concert suite Copland put together of *Billy the Kid* contains about two-thirds of the ballet. *The Open Prairie,* which serves as a prologue, evokes a remote and spacious landscape, a poetic symbol of all that is vast and unchanging. We will hear the first scene, *Street in a Frontier Town,* in which, as Copland explained, he used tunes of the Wild West such as *Goodbye, Old Paint; The Old Chisholm Trail; Git Along, Little Dogies; The Streets of Laredo;* and *Great Grand-Dad.* (See Listening Guide 38 for details.) But the composer decked them out with polyrhythms, polytonal harmonies, and dissonances made more striking because they fall on accented beats. The result is a music of powerful rhythmic thrust and vigorous physical activity, bursting with energy and excitement as it mounts to a *fortissimo* climax.

Music has a glorious way of leaping over barriers of race, religion, and nationality. And so it was given to the son of Russian-Jewish immigrants growing up on the streets of Brooklyn to create a musical image of the American West, the prairie, and the cowboy that is heard and recognized worldwide.

Silvestre Revueltas and Art Music Traditions in Mexico

"From an early age I learned to love [the music of] Bach and Beethoven. . . . I can tolerate some of the classics and even some of my own works, but I prefer the music of my people that is heard in the provinces."

The modern musical traditions of Mexico are rich and varied, drawing from the indigenous Amerindian cultures as well as from the country's Hispanic culture.

in his own words

I would say that a composer writes music to express and communicate and put down in permanent form certain thoughts, emotions and states of being. . . . The resultant work of art should speak to men and women of the artist's own time with a directness and immediacy of communicative power that no previous art expression can give.

Copland Looks West and South of the Border

We have seen that composer Aaron Copland was inspired by songs of the Western frontier, although he was born and raised in Brooklyn, New York. There is a wide repertory of traditional tunes of the West that have come down to us today. Some tell of famous outlaws such as Billy the Kid and Jesse James or of high-stakes gamblers like Wild Bill Hickok; others are work songs (*Git Along, Little Dogies*) or laments of death on the trail or in gunfights (*The Streets of Laredo.*) In short, they narrate the way of life of the American cowboy. Traditional songs such as *Goodbye, Old Paint* suggest that a per-

son's horse was not only a tool of the trade, but a trusted companion as well. ("Old paint" refers to a pinto horse, *pinto* being Spanish for "spotted"; see p. 34 for the tune and words.)

The Hollywood image of the American cowboy, with John Wayne always winning the fights against the bad guys, is somewhat distorted. Many of those roving the American frontier were Southerners—whites and African Americans—who lost their homes and families in the Civil War. It is through an ex-slave named Charley Willis that the song *Goodbye, Old Paint* is preserved today; Willis taught it to a ranch hand who, in old age, recorded it for folk-song collector John Lomax. Other cowboys were Native Americans, and many were Chicanos (called *vaqueros*, the Spanish word for "cowboys"). Several commonly used words derive from the early days of Spanish colonization in the West: "lariat" (a rope) comes from *la reata*, and "chaps" (leather leg coverings) is short for *chaparreras.*

What of women in the West? Several were legendary: the expert markswoman Annie Oakley was originally from Cincinnati, at the edge of the frontier, and traveled as part of a Wild West show, while Calamity Jane came from the Dakota Territory (the Dakotas were not yet states) and reportedly could outshoot any man. (Annie Oakley inspired the well-known 1946 Broadway musical *Annie Get Your Gun*, by Irving Berlin, recently revived on Broadway with Reba McIntyre in the title role.) Another heroine of frontier days was Emily West, an African American woman who played a key role in the Battle of San Jacinto, in which the Texans defeated the Mexican army of General Antonio Lopez de Santa Ana. It is she, not a flower, who is the subject of *The*

Copland's music for *Billy the Kid* is as firmly rooted in uniquely American traditions as are the cowboy bronzes of **Frederic Remington** (1861–1909), like *Bronco Buster*. (Amon Carter Museum, Fort Worth)

European influence Mexico's ties to Spain began in 1519, when Spanish soldiers colonized the country, and continued until 1821, when Mexico achieved its independence. During this three-hundred-year period, the Catholic Church maintained a highly influential profile in Mexican musical life by using music to convert the native peoples. Thus Spanish polyphony—both sacred and secular—was practiced widely in early Mexico.

A dancer from the Fort Worth-Dallas Ballet's 2000–01 production of Copland's *Billy the Kid.*

Yellow Rose of Texas ("the yellow rose of Texas beats the belles of Tennessee"—the allusion to "yellow" refers to the fact that she was of mixed Caucasian and African American ancestry). Many more unnamed women braved the long and difficult trip west to establish a new life for their families. The familiar song *Sweet Betsy from Pike* praises one such courageous woman ("Oh, don't you remember Sweet Betsy from Pike, who crossed the big mountains with her lover Ike?").

These cowboy songs and other Western frontier tunes have been preserved through the efforts of folk-song collectors and the media, especially the singing cowboys who were popular in 1930s and 1940s movies (Gene Autry, Roy Rogers, and Tex Ritter).

The lore of the West intrigued visual artists as well, and several have left us vivid images of life of this earlier era. Most famous are the American painters Winslow Homer (1836–1910) and Frederic Remington (1861–1909), the latter well-known for his rough-and-tumble cowboys and cavalrymen and for his much-prized bronze sculptures like *Bronco Buster.*

Aaron Copland also looked to Latin America for traditional music. He toured Mexico and South America, visiting with such native composers as Carlos Chávez (1899–1978), Alberto Ginastera (1916–1983), and Silvestre Revueltas (1899–1940) whom we will study. All of them combined indigenous musics with European styles in their own compositions. Copland's orchestral work *El salón México* (1936) draws on the colorful sounds of Mexican dance music, as does his ballet suite *Billy the Kid.* This latter work incorporates the jarabe, a rural Mexican dance and musical form that has various sections in different tempos and meters. An exhibition dance, the jarabe is performed by a couple attired in gala dress—the man with wide-brimmed hat and chaps, the woman in a multi-colored, sequined skirt and shawl. Today, the jarabe is an urban form, accompanied by mariachi groups (with trumpets, violins, guitar, and guitarrón, or bass guitar). Mariachi bands, originally from western Mexico, can be heard today throughout that country and in parts of the United States as well.

TERMS TO NOTE:

jarabe
mariachi

SUGGESTED LISTENING:

Copland: *Street in a Frontier Town* from
  Billy the Kid, or *El salón México*
Traditional songs of the Old West
Mexican music (mariachi band, jarabe)
Works by Carlos Chávez, Alberto Ginastera, or
  Silvestre Revueltas

By the late nineteenth century, nationalistic stirrings lured musicians and artists alike to Amerindian and Mestizo cultures. (*Mestizo* refers to people of mixed Spanish and Amerindian ancestry; they are the majority in Latin-American countries.) The Mexican Revolution of 1910 further changed the artistic life of the country, conjuring strong feelings of patriotism. In the post–Revolutionary period composers did not wish to recreate the traditional

Rise of indigenous cultures

Silvestre Revueltas

music but only to evoke, or suggest, the character of this native music. Among those composers who have had a decisive influence on Mexican musical culture are Carlos Chávez (1899–1978), whose works are rich in Amerindian flavor; and Silvestre Revueltas (1899–1940), a Mexican composer of international acclaim. Revueltas is considered a representative of "mestizo realism," a movement that drew on elements from the popular culture of contemporary Mexico.

His Life and Music

Born in the mountain state of Durango, Silvestre Revueltas was a child prodigy on violin and later studied composition at the Conservatorio Nacional de Música in Mexico City. He continued his studies in the United States, where he took his first post as conductor of a theater orchestra in Texas. In 1929, Revueltas was called home by Carlos Chávez to serve as assistant conductor of the Orquesta Sinfónica de Mexico.

The 1930s were a high point in the development of music and art in Mexico, and it was in this environment that Revueltas produced some of his finest masterworks. His first orchestral piece, *Cuauhnahuac* (1930; the old name of the town of Cuernavaca), was Romantic in inspiration but modern in dissonant harmonies and chromaticism. This work displays the colorful orchestration and vigorous rhythmic energy that became his trademark.

Film music In 1935, Revueltas collaborated with Paul Strand on the powerful film *Redes* (Nets), focused on the struggle of the lower classes—in this case, the rights of fishermen. Like Copland and Prokofiev, Revueltas is recognized for his contributions to music in films.

Years in Spain With the onset of the Spanish Civil War in the late 1930s, the intensely political Revueltas went to Spain, where he participated in the cultural activities of the Loyalist government. One of the early tragedies of the Civil War was the execution in 1936 of the poet Federico García Lorca by a Fascist firing squad. The openly homosexual García Lorca had made anti-Fascist statements and had provoked Franco with his politically controversial plays. (In Chapter 72, we will study a piece by American composer George Crumb that sets texts

🎺 Principal Works

Chamber music, including 4 string quartets; works for violin and piano; *8 x Radio* (*Ocho por radio*, 1933); and *Homenaje a Federico García Lorca* (1937)

Orchestral music, including *Venetenas* (1931), *Janitzio* (1936), and *Sensemayá* (1938)

7 film scores, including *Redes* (1935) and *La noche de los mayas* (1939)

2 ballets, including *La Coronela* (1940)

Songs, including 7 *Canciones* (1938; on poems by García Lorca)

by García Lorca.) Revueltas' response to this event, his moving composition *Homenaje a Federico García Lorca (Homage to Federico García Lorca)*, premiered in Madrid in 1937 during a Fascist bombing of the city. The review in the *Heraldo de Madrid* accorded Revueltas's music a "revolutionary status."

Upon his return home in late 1937, Revueltas' life began to fall apart. Like his idol, the artist Vincent Van Gogh, the composer shifted between the highs of his creative powers and the lows of self-destruction. Despite his acute alcoholism, for which he was institutionalized on several occasions, Revueltas continued to produce masterworks, including his best-known orchestral piece, *Sensemayá* (1938). This work was inspired by the verses of Afro-Cuban poet Nicolás Guillén, which imitate onomatopoetically the sounds and rhythm of Afro-Cuban music and speak against colonial imperialism. His last work, left unfinished at his death but now completed and orchestrated, was a ballet entitled *La Coronela* about a girl colonel attempting to overthrow a dictatorship. The composer died at age forty of alcohol-induced pneumonia, a death his sister Rosaura called "senseless, incomprehensible, tragic."

The murals of the Mexican painter **Diego Rivera** (1886–1937) glorify his native culture and people in an elegant social and historical narrative. *Flower Festival* (1925). (Los Angeles County Museum of Art)

Revueltas instills his music with colorful, folkloric elements while never quoting actual traditional songs; rather, he recreates native melodies and strikingly dancelike rhythms. His love for Mexican provincial music is immediately obvious, voiced through lyrical, direct melodies that are driven by complex rhythms exploiting techniques such as polyrhythm and ostinatos. Despite a very modern harmonic language rich in dissonance and chromaticism, Revueltas's music is deeply emotional and Romantic in its inspiration. His skillful handling of the orchestral palette—often with unusual instrumental combinations—evokes the picturesque *orquestas típicas*—the traditional orchestras—of Mexico.

Homenaje a Federico García Lorca

Written in Spain in 1937, *Homenaje a Federico García Lorca* succeeds in erasing the boundaries between popular and classical music. The work is for a chamber ensemble that is heavily balanced toward winds—the string section has only two violins and one bass—and includes piano. The first movement, *Baile* (Dance), develops into a quick-paced, duple-meter dance with a bitingly dissonant tune. The movement closes as it began, with solo trumpet. The second movement, *Duelo* (Sorrow), also makes use of an ostinato heard against a soulful melody.

First and Second movements

The title of the last movement, *Son*, refers to a type of traditional Mexican dance. *Sones* (plural of *son*) are characterized by shifting meter, frequently moving between simple triple (3/4) to compound duple (6/8) meter. (We heard how Copland used shifting meter as well for the Mexican jarabe in *Billy the Kid*.) Revueltas's writing here is highly evocative of a Mexican *mariachi ensemble*, one of the most common groups that performs *sones*. The typical mariachi consists

Third movement

in his own words

of several trumpets, violins, and guitars (including a five-stringed vihuela and guitarrón, or bass guitar). Revueltas maintains the distinctive mariachi sound of paired trumpets and violins, while enriching the uppermost and lowest registers with high woodwinds and low brass and bass, and replacing the guitars with piano.

This movement, in a rondo-like form, begins explosively, tossing about fragmentary ideas with unrestrained energy. The strings and piano then establish a steady 6/8 pulse, over which the muted trumpet sounds a narrow-ranged theme built from whole tones (see Listening Guide 39). Rhythmic confusion and percussive accents lead to the principal theme—a syncopated Mexican dance tune (the *son*) in the trumpets and violins, played in parallel thirds typical of mariachi style. A rhythmic idea from this theme is then manipulated and developed by various instruments, after which the mariachi tune returns in a full orchestral statement, set in a new key. A final frenetic coda is unleashed after two dissonant cluster chords in the piano.

This carefree movement may seem like a strange homage to the slain poet. But the Mexican view of life (and death) is to experience each day to the fullest—as Revueltas did. In Mexico, the Day of the Dead is celebrated joyfully—houses are decorated with colorful skulls made from sugar, and tables are adorned with breads shaped like bones. The poet Rafael Alberti praised *Homenaje a Federico García Lorca*, noting that "what Manuel de Falla did with . . . with Spanish music . . . Silvestre Revueltas achieves with the accent of his own country—and in magisterial style."

Listening Guide 39

CD: CHR/STD 7/62–69, SH 4/15–22

Revueltas: *Homenaje a Federico García Lorca,* Third Movement, *Son*

(2:55)

DATE OF WORK:	1937
MEDIUM:	Chamber orchestra (piccolo, E-flat clarinet, 2 trumpets, trombone, tuba, piano, percussion, 2 violins, and bass)
FORM:	Sectional, rondo-like **(A-B-A-C-A-C-B-A-C-Coda)**
OVERVIEW:	I. *Baile* (Dance)
	II. *Duelo* (Sorrow)
	III. *Son*

WHAT TO LISTEN FOR: Unusual instrumentation, focused on winds along with 2 violins, piano, and bass.
Colorful, folklike character, with themes reminiscent of mariachi ensembles.
Strongly rhythmic and syncopated, with percussive accents; use of ostinatos.
Return of 3 thematic ideas in a rondo-like structure.

15 0:00 **A** section—rhythmic and highly syncopated, in shifting meter; 7-note melodic turns in piano and violins, with glissandos in violins (Violin I shown):

16 0:15 **B** section—piano and string ostinato introduces chromatic solo trumpet melody (accompanied by trombone):

0:29 **A** section—rhythmic punctuations, as in introduction.

17 0:35 **C** section—Mexican dance theme *(son,)* in alternating meter (6/8 and 2/4); muted trumpets playing in parallel thirds:

Trumpets answered by violins and woodwinds.

0:58 Development of rhythmic figure from above, in low brass (tuba), answered by woodwinds, then trumpets.

1:08 Brief return of **A**.

18 1:21 Return of Mexican tune (**C** section), in full orchestra.

1:37 Rhythmic figure from **C** developed.

19 1:55 **B** section—return of slow trumpet melody, with trombone countermelody.

20 2:05 **A** section—return of opening section.

21 2:20 **C** section—mariachi melody in violins, trumpet offbeats.
Grows dissonant.

22 2:34 **Coda**—cluster chord in piano, then fast, loud, frenetic.

Popular Styles

67

Ragtime, Blues, and Early Jazz

All riddles are blues,
And all blues are sad,
And I'm only mentioning
Some blues I've had.

—MAYA ANGELOU

KEY POINTS

- *Jazz* is an American musical style that arose in the early twentieth century and drew elements from African traditions as well as from popular and art music traditions of the West.

- Its roots are in West African music (including call-and-response singing) and in nineteenth-century African-American ceremonial and work songs (CP 19).

- *Ragtime* is a precursor to jazz that developed from an African-American piano style characterized by highly syncopated rhythms and sectional forms.

- Scott Joplin, often considered the "king of ragtime," is the first African-American composer to win international fame; he is remembered for his piano rags, especially *Maple Leaf Rag*.

- Louis Armstrong is one of the great early jazz performers (on trumpet); he also introduced *scat singing* (singing on syllables without literal meaning) and other jazz improvisational practices that became standard.

- Armstrong was first associated with *New Orleans–style jazz*, which is characterized by a small ensemble of players improvising simultaneously.

- *Blues* is an American genre of folk music based on a simple, repetitive, poetic-musical form; a typical *blues text* has three-line strophes set to a repeating harmonic pattern of twelve (or occasionally sixteen) bars.
- Billie Holiday is one of the leading female jazz singers; she broke racial barriers by performing live with white bands.

Scott Joplin

Ragtime, blues, and jazz are rooted in the music of African Americans. These musical styles are part and parcel of the great American melting pot, and have captured the imagination of the world.

Jazz refers to a music created mainly by African Americans around the turn of the twentieth century as they blended elements drawn from African musics with the popular and art traditions of the West. One of the most influential precursors of jazz was ragtime, which gained popularity in instrumental ensemble arrangements by Scott Joplin.

Scott Joplin and Ragtime

Known as "the king of ragtime," Scott Joplin (1868–1917) was one of the first black Americans to gain importance as a composer. He was born in Texarkana, Texas, to a musical family. His father, a former slave, played violin, and his mother sang and played banjo, as did his brothers. Joplin began his musical instruction on the guitar and bugle, but soon showed such a gift for improvisation that he was given free piano lessons. He left home when he was only four-teen, after the death of his mother, and traveled throughout the Mississippi Valley playing honky-tonks and piano bars, and absorbing the current styles of folk and popular music. In 1885, he arrived in St. Louis, then the center of a growing ragtime tradition.

Title page of *Maple Leaf Rag* (1899), by Scott Joplin. (Library of Congress)

Ragtime (or "ragged rhythm") was originally an African-American piano style marked by highly syncopated melodies. It first gained public notice as a form of instrumental ensemble music when Joplin and his small orchestra performed at the 1893 World Exposition in Chicago. Around this time, Joplin sought more formal musical training at the George R. Smith College in Sedalia, Missouri, where he studied music theory and composition. It was at a club in Sedalia that Joplin, surrounded by a circle of black entertainers, introduced his *Maple Leaf Rag.* Fame came to the composer in 1899, when the sheet music of the piece sold a million copies. Four years later, he wrote the first of his two operas, *A Guest of Honor,* but the work was never performed during his lifetime and is now lost. In 1906, Joplin moved from St. Louis to Chicago and ultimately to New York, where he was active as a teacher, composer, and performer. As an aid to amateur musicians, he published a series of piano exercises (1908) that offered drills for the tricky rhythmic patterns typical of the style.

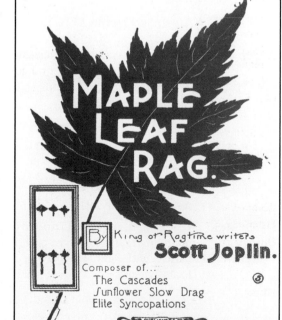

Joplin strove to elevate ragtime from a purely improvised style to a more serious art form that could stand on a level with European art music and possibly become the basis for

Listening Guide 40

CD: CHR/STD 7/10–14, SH 4/23–27

Joplin: *Maple Leaf Rag*

(3:21)

DATE OF WORK:	Published 1899
GENRE:	Piano rag
PERFORMANCE:	Piano roll of Joplin on 1910 Steinway player piano
FORM:	Sectional dance form; 4 sections, or strains (each of 16 measures), with repeats (**A-A-B-B-A-C-C-D-D**)
TEMPO:	Tempo di marcia; 2/4 meter

WHAT TO LISTEN FOR: Catchy, syncopated melodies (in right hand) accompanied by a steady, duple-meter rhythm (in left hand).
Sectional form, with four 16-measure phrases, each repeated (**A-A-B-B-A-C-C-D-D**).
Rolled, or arpeggiated, chords as decorative embellishments.
Change of key (to IV, or subdominant) in the trio (**C** section).

23 0:00 **A**—strain 1—syncopated middle-range ascending melody, accompanied by steady bass; begins with upbeat in bass; in A-flat major; performer adds ornamental flourishes in left hand:

0:22 **A**—strain 1 repeated.

24 0:44 **B**—strain 2—similar syncopated pattern in melody; begins in higher range and descends; steady bass accompaniment; in A-flat major:

1:06 **B**—strain 2 repeated.

25 1:28 **A**—return to strain 1.

26 1:50 **C**—strain 3, also called Trio—in D-flat major; more static melody; new rhythmic pattern with right hand playing on down-beats; bass accompaniment more disjunct:

2:12   **C**—strain 3 repeated.

27   2:34   **D**—strain 4—return to A-flat major, with contrasting theme; syncopated pattern related to strain 1:

D—strain 4 repeated.

larger forms such as opera or the symphony. Realizing that he must lead the way in this merger of styles, he began work on his opera *Treemonisha*, which he finished in 1911. But the opera, produced in a scaled-down performance, was not well received, and Joplin fell into a severe depression from which he never fully recovered; he died in New York City on April 1, 1917. *Treemonisha* remained virtually unknown until its extremely successful revival in 1972 by the Houston Grand Opera. In 1976, nearly sixty years after his death, Joplin was awarded a Pulitzer Prize for his masterpiece.

Scott Joplin is best remembered today for his piano rags, some of which were recorded by the composer himself and preserved on punched paper rolls made in 1910 on a Steinway player piano. The rags reflect Joplin's preoccupation with classical forms. They exhibit balanced phrasing and key structures, combined with catchy, imaginative melodies. Like earlier dance forms, they are built in clear-cut sections, their patterns of repetition reminiscent of those heard in the marches of John Philip Sousa, whose own band frequently played arrangements of Joplin rags.

The *Maple Leaf Rag*, perhaps the best-known rag ever composed, is typical in its regular, sectional form. Quite simply, the dance presents a series of sixteen-measure phrases, called *strains*, in a moderate duple meter; each strain is repeated before the next one begins. The *Maple Leaf Rag* established the form, with four strains; in this work, the opening idea returns once before a shift to the subdominant (IV) key area in the third strain (see Listening Guide 40). As in most rags, the listener's interest is focused throughout on the syncopated rhythms of the melodies, played by the right hand, which are supported by an easy, steady duple-rhythm accompaniment in the left hand.

Joplin's sophisticated piano rags brought him worldwide recognition. Their continued popularity nearly a century later confirms that they are the work of a master.

in his own words

What is scurrilously called ragtime is an invention that is here to stay. That is now conceded by all classes of musicians. . . . All publications masquerading under the name of ragtime are not the genuine article. . . . That real ragtime of the higher class is rather difficult to play is a painful truth which most pianists have discovered.

Blues and New Orleans Jazz

"There's only two ways to sum up music: either it's good or it's bad. If it's good, you don't mess with it; you just enjoy it."

—LOUIS ARMSTRONG

Blues is a truly American form of folk music based on a simple, repetitive, poetic-musical structure. The term refers to a mood as well as a harmonic progression,

Blues

The Roots of Jazz

Jazz has been viewed by many as a truly American art form, but in reality it draws together traditions from West Africa, Europe, and the Americas. The African origins of jazz evoke an earlier episode of American history: the slave trade from Africa. Many of the slaves brought to America came from the west coast of Africa, often called the Ivory or Gold Coast. It is not surprising, then, that studies comparing the musical traditions in sub-Saharan Africa with those in certain isolated regions of black America have confirmed many similarities. These include singing styles (call-and-response patterns and various vocal inflections) and storytelling techniques, traits that have remained alive for several centuries in both regions through oral tradition.

Black music in nineteenth-century America included dancing for ritual and ceremonial purposes and the singing of work songs (communal songs that synchronized the rhythm of group tasks; see illustration, p. 66) and spirituals (a kind of religious folk song, often with a refrain). West African religious traditions mingled freely with the Protestant Christianity adopted by some slaves. The art of storytelling through music, typical of many West African tribes, and praise singing (glorifying deities or royalty) were other traditions retained by slaves that would contribute to spirituals and blues. Although both men and women took part in praise singing—either could lead call-and-response ceremonial songs—the musical storyteller, called the

The *Bamboula*, danced in Congo Square, New Orleans, to the accompaniment of drums and singing, according to artist **E. V. Kemble** in 1885.

which is usually twelve (or occasionally sixteen) bars in length. Characteristic is the *blue note*, a slight drop in pitch on the third, fifth, or seventh tone of the scale. A blues text typically consists of a three-line stanza of which the first two lines are identical. Its vocal style was derived from the work songs of Southern blacks.

New Orleans jazz   Blues is a fundamental form in jazz. The music we call jazz was born in New Orleans through the fusion of African-American elements such as ragtime and

412

griot, was always a male, whose mission it was to preserve and transmit the history, stories, and poetry of the people.

The city of New Orleans fueled the early sounds of jazz. There, in Congo Square, slaves met in the pre–Civil War era to dance to the accompaniment of all sorts of instruments, including drums, gourds, mouth harps, and banjos. Their music featured a strong underlying pulse over which syncopations and polyrhythmic elaborations took place. Melodies incorporated African-derived techniques such as rhythmic interjections, vocal glides, and percussive sounds made with the tongue and throat, and were often set in a musical scale with blue notes (lowered scale degrees on the third, fifth, or seventh of a major scale).

In the years after the Civil War and the Emancipation Proclamation (1863), a new style of music arose in the South, especially in the Mississippi Delta—country, or rural, blues, performed by a raspy-voiced male singer and, by the turn of the century, accompanied by a steel-string guitar. This music voiced the difficulties of everyday life in a continuation of the storyteller, or griot, tradition. The vocal lines featured melodic pitch bending, or blue notes, sung over repeated bass patterns. One of the greatest early blues singers was Charlie Patton.

Dance music also flourished among Southern blacks, and one type in particular, ragtime, strongly influenced early jazz. Ragtime was the first African-American music to experience widespread popularity. This catchy style was soon heard across the country and in Europe, both as accompanied song and as solo piano music; we have already learned of Scott Joplin's important contribution to this genre. The rhythmic vitality of ragtime fascinated European and American composers alike. We will hear shortly how George Gershwin and David Baker

Blues singer Robert Johnson (1911–1938) is represented in this drawing of a makeshift recording studio set up in a San Antonio hotel room, November 1936.

infused their music with expressive elements of blues and jazz.

TERMS TO NOTE:

spiritual	blue note	griot
call and response	ragtime	

SUGGESTED LISTENING:

African-American spirituals (*Sometimes I Feel Like a Motherless Child*) ♪
Rural blues (Charlie Patton)
Hard Time Killing Floor Blues (from *O Brother, Where Art Thou?*)
Ragtime (Scott Joplin)
New Orleans jazz (Louis Armstrong's *West End Blues*) or *When the Saints Go Marchin' In*, by the Preservation Hall Jazz Band ♪

blues with other traditional styles—spirituals, work songs, and shouts. (For more on the roots of jazz, see CP 19.) In all of these styles, the art of improvisation was crucially important. Performers made up their parts as they went along, often with several musicians improvising at the same time. This seemingly chaotic practice worked because all the players knew the basic rules—the tempo, the form, the harmonic progression, and the order in which

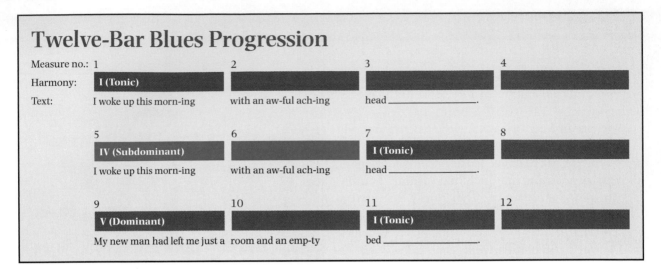

Twelve-Bar Blues Progression

Measure no.:	1	2	3	4
Harmony:	I (Tonic)			
Text:	I woke up this morn-ing	with an aw-ful ach-ing	head _____.	
	5	6	7	8
	IV (Subdominant)		I (Tonic)	
	I woke up this morn-ing	with an aw-ful ach-ing	head _____.	
	9	10	11	12
	V (Dominant)		I (Tonic)	
	My new man had left me just a	room and an emp-ty	bed _____.	

instruments were to be featured. A twelve-bar blues progression followed a standard harmonic pattern (see above).

New Orleans jazz actually depended on the players' multiple improvisation to create a polyphonic texture. The trumpet or cornet played the melody or an embellished version; the clarinet was often featured in a countermelody above the main tune; the trombone improvised below the trumpet and signaled the chord changes; and the rhythm section—consisting of string bass or tuba, guitar, banjo, or piano and drums—provided rhythmic and harmonic support. Among the greats of New Orleans jazz were Joseph "King" Oliver (cornet), Sidney Bechet (soprano saxophone), Ferdinand "Jelly Roll" Morton (piano), and Louis "Satchmo" Armstrong (trumpet).

Louis Armstrong (1901–1971) was unquestionably the most important single force in the development of early jazz styles. He was a great improviser who used a variety of mutes to expand the capacities of his trumpet in range and tone color. To distinguish his unique melodic-rhythmic style of performance, his admirers coined the term "swing," which became a standard description of jazz. His 1926 recording of *Heebie Jeebies* introduced *scat singing*, in which syllables without literal meaning (*vocables*) are set to an improvised vocal line. Singer Ella Fitzgerald (1918–1996) later brought this technique to a truly virtuosic level.

Scat singing

Chorus

In jazz, a *chorus* is a single statement of melodic-harmonic pattern, like a twelve-bar blues progression. Armstrong's style of jazz introduced a number of new features: stop-time choruses (solos accompanied by spaced staccato chords); double-time choruses, in which each beat of each measure was subdivided; a simple two- or four-beat meter based on evenly accented pulses; and solo rather than ensemble choruses. In his solos, only hints of the original tune are recognizable. Through these innovations, jazz was transformed into a solo art that presented improvised fantasias on chord changes rather than on a repeated melody. Armstrong's instrumental-like approach to singing, his distinctive inflections, and his improvisatory style were highly influential to jazz vocalists, paramount among them Billie Holiday, one of the leading female singers in jazz history.

The Jazz Singer Billie Holiday

"I can't stand to sing the same song the same way two nights in succession, let alone two years or ten years. If you can, then it ain't music; it's close-order drill or exercise or yodeling or something, not music."

Billie Holiday (1915–1959), known as Lady Day, was born in 1915 as Eleanora Fagan, daughter of a guitar player with the Fletcher Henderson Band. Abandoned by her father, Billie was raised by relatives who mistreated her. In 1928, with barely any formal education behind her, she went to join her mother in New York, where she probably worked as a prostitute. Around 1930, Billie began singing at clubs in Brooklyn and Harlem and was discovered in 1933 by a talent scout who arranged for her to record with the clarinetist Benny Goodman. This first break earned her thirty-five dollars.

By 1935, Billie was recording with some of the best jazz musicians of her day. As her popularity increased, she was featured with Count Basie's band, and in 1938, with Artie Shaw's group—making her one of the first black singers to break the color barrier and sing in public with a white orchestra. (At this time, there was a restriction barring whites and blacks from performing together on stage.) Billie recorded one of her most famous songs in 1939—*Strange Fruit*, about a Southern lynching. With its horrible images of blacks dangling from trees, the song resonated deeply with blacks and whites alike and became a powerful social commentary on black identity and equality. Billie's delivery of the macabre lyrics is cold and factual, but her voice is not.

By the 1940s, Billie's life had deteriorated, the result of alcohol and drug abuse and of ill-chosen relationships with abusive men. She began using opium and heroin, and was jailed on drug charges in 1947. Her health—and her voice—suffered greatly because of her addictions, although she still made a number of memorable recordings. In May 1959, she was diagnosed with cirrhosis of the liver and died several months later, at the age of forty-four.

Billie Holiday had a unique talent that was immediately recognized by other musicians. Although her voice was untrained and her range small, she had a remarkable sense of pitch and an unfaulting delivery—a style she learned from listening to her two idols, Bessie Smith and Louis Armstrong. Although she was best known for her romantic ballads, we will hear a blues that Billie wrote and recorded in 1936, with Artie Shaw (clarinet) and Bunny Berigan (trumpet), and which she performed regularly throughout her career. It is a twelve-bar blues, with a short introduction and six choruses, some of which are instrumental (see Listening Guide 41). The first text-verse is a typical three-line strophe (as shown in the chart above), but as the work progresses, the form becomes freer. In the vocal verses, Billie demonstrates her masterful rhythmic flexibility and jazz embellishments (scoops and dips on notes). In this performance, we also hear Artie Shaw's creative clarinet improvisations and Bunny Berigan's earthy, "gutbucket" trumpet playing (this refers to an unrestrained, raspy quality of tone). Shaw remembered this 1936 recording session some years later, saying that Billie was "already beginning to develop that distinctive style of hers which has been copied and imitated by so many singers of popular music that the average listener of today cannot realize how original she actually is."

Early years

Billie Holiday

in her own words

I don't think I'm singing. I feel like I'm playing a horn. I try to improvise like . . . Louis Armstrong . . . what comes out is what I feel. I hate straight singing. I have to change a tune to my own way of doing it.

Listening Guide 41

CD: CHR/STD 8/1–7, SH 4/28–34

Holiday: *Billie's Blues*

(2:38)

DATE OF WORK:	Recorded 1936
PERFORMERS:	Billie Holiday, vocal
	Bunny Berigan, trumpet
	Artie Shaw, clarinet
	Joe Bushkin, piano
	Dick McDonough, guitar
	Pete Peterson, string bass
	Cozy Cole, drums
FORM:	12-bar blues (introduction and 6 choruses)
TEMPO:	Slow blues; 4/4 meter

WHAT TO LISTEN FOR: Repeated harmonic progression (12 bars long), heard 6 times (after introduction).

Steady rhythm section keeps the beat under improvisations; slow, languid tempo with syncopated rhythms.

First vocal chorus (2) has typical blues text; others are more free.

Differing improvisational styles of 3 featured soloists: Holiday (voice), Shaw (clarinet) and Berigan (trumpet).

Pitch inflections (bent notes, blue notes, and scoops) typical of blues.

28	0:00	Introduction (4 bars), bass and piano.
29	0:07	Chorus 1, ensemble (12 bars).
30	0:32	Chorus 2, vocal (12 bars):

> Lord, I love my man, tell the world I do,
> I love my man, tell th' world I do,
> But when he mistreats me, makes me feel so blue.

Opening of first vocal chorus, showing syncopated line, with slide at the end:

31	0:56	Chorus 3, vocal (12 bars):

My man wouldn' gimme no breakfast,
Wouldn' gimme no dinner,
Squawked about my supper 'n put me outdoors,
Had the nerve to lay a matchbox on my clothes;
I didn't have so many but I had a long, long ways to go.

32   1:21   Chorus 4, solo clarinet improvisation (12 bars):

33   1:45   Chorus 5, solo trumpet improvisation (12 bars).

34   2:11   Chorus 6, vocal (12 bars):

Some men like me 'cause I'm happy,
Some 'cause I'm snappy,
Some call me honey, others think I've got money,
Some tell me, "Baby you're built for speed,"
Now if you put that all together,
Makes me ev'rything a good man needs.

68

The Swing Era and Beyond

"What's swinging in words? If a guy makes you pat your foot and if you feel it down your back, you don't have to ask anybody if that's good music or not. You can always feel it."

—MILES DAVIS

KEY POINTS

■ The highly improvisational style of New Orleans jazz led, in the 1930s, to the *swing era* (or *big band era*) and the brilliantly composed jazz of Duke Ellington.

■ Big band jazz gave way, in the late 1940s, to innovative styles featuring smaller groups, including *bebop, cool jazz*, and *West Coast jazz*.

■ Charlie Parker (alto saxophone) and Dizzy Gillespie (trumpet) were leaders in the bebop movement, and Miles Davis (trumpet) was influential in establishing the lyrical cool jazz style.

■ *Third stream jazz*, developed in the 1950s, combines elements of art music (classical instruments, forms, and tonal devices) and jazz to produce a new stream, or style.

■ More recent jazz trends include *fusion* (combining elements of jazz and rock), *Neoclassical style* (with expanded tonalities and modal improvisations), *free jazz*, and *new-age jazz*. Interactive technology (including MIDI) has been influential in modern jazz performance as well.

■ Known for his Tin Pan Alley songs and musical theater productions, Gershwin also sought to unite jazz and classical music in his instrumental works (*Rhapsody in Blue, An American in Paris*, and his *Three Piano Preludes*).

■ The African-American composer David Baker writes third stream music that combines elements of jazz and classical styles to produce his original "voice."

Duke Ellington and the Big Band Era

"Somehow I suspect that if Shakespeare were alive today, he might be a jazz fan himself."

The highly creative era of early jazz gave way to another great historical moment—the swing, or big band, era of the 1930s and 1940s. By this time, jazz had evolved into a musical style and aesthetic in its own right and was, without a doubt, America's voice in popular music. This was also the time of the Great Depression, the most severe economic slowdown in American history, which cost many musicians their livelihood but also provided an opening for new performers and jazz bands to gain a footing in the entertainment world. Jazz in particular provided new opportunities for black musicians to gain recognition and garner new levels of prosperity: among those who ascended to stardom in this era was Edward Kennedy "Duke" Ellington (1899–1974), whose group first went on the road in 1932 and remained popular until his death. His unique style of big-band composed jazz won over a wide audience—both black and white—who danced away their cares in clubs and hotel ballrooms across the country.

"Duke" Ellington was born in Washington, D.C., and was playing in New York jazz clubs by the 1920s. He became famous as a composer in the following decade. The advent of the big bands brought a greater need for arranged, or written-down, music, and Ellington played a major role in this development. A fine pianist himself, he was an even better orchestrator. As one of his collaborators remarked, "He plays piano, but his real instrument is the orchestra."

Duke Ellington (piano) and his band in a movie still from the Metro Goldwin Mayer musical *Cabin in the Sky* (1943).

Ellington's orchestral palette was much richer than that of the New Orleans band. It included two trumpets, one cornet, three trombones, four saxophones (some of the players doubling on clarinet), two string basses, guitar, drums, vibraphone, and piano. One of the theme songs for Ellington's orchestra was *Take the A Train*, written by composer/arranger Billy Strayhorn and first recorded in 1941. Like most jazz tunes, *Take the A Train* was built on the changes (the harmonic progression) of an earlier song but enhanced with a playful tune, complex harmonies, and rich orchestration.

Ellington's multifaceted contribution influenced the world of jazz profoundly. As a composer, he brought his art to new heights and a newfound legitimacy; as an arranger, he left a rich legacy of works for a wide range of jazz groups; as a band leader, he has served as teacher and model to several generations of jazz musicians. America's cultural heritage would have been far poorer without him.

Bebop and Later Jazz Styles

"It's taken me all my life to learn what not to play."

—DIZZY GILLESPIE

By the end of the 1940s, musicians had become disenchanted with big band jazz. Their rebellion resulted in the new styles known as bebop and cool jazz. *Bebop* (also known as *bop*) was an invented word mimicking the two-note phrase that is the trademark of this style. Trumpeter Dizzy Gillespie, saxophonist Charlie Parker, and pianists Bud Powell and Thelonious Monk were among the leaders of the bebop movement in the 1940s. Over the next two decades, the term "bebop" came to include a number of substyles such as *cool jazz* (the "cool" suggesting a restrained, unemotional manner), West Coast jazz, hard bop, and soul jazz. The principal exponent of cool jazz, a laid-back style characterized by lush harmonies, lowered levels of volume, moderate tempos, and a new lyricism, was trumpeter Miles Davis. *West Coast jazz* is essentially a small-group, cool-jazz style featuring mixed timbres (one instrument for each color, without piano) and contrapuntal improvisations. Among the important West Coast ensembles that sprang up in the 1950s are the Dave Brubeck Quartet (with Paul Desmond on saxophone) and the Gerry Mulligan Quartet (with Chet Baker on trumpet).

Bebop

Cool jazz

West Coast jazz

Latin American music has been highly influential in the development of jazz, chiefly its dance rhythms and percussion instruments (conga drum, bongos, and cowbells). In the 1930s and 1940s, Latin bandleaders such as Don Azpiazú and Xavier Cugat brought Latin dance music—especially the rumba—into the mainstream. Duke Ellington's band recorded two hit Latin numbers: *Caravan* (1937, featuring Puerto Rican trombonist Juan Tizol) and *Congo Brava* (1940). Latin elements were integral to the bebop style of the late 1940s as we will hear shortly in *A Night in Tunisia*, by Dizzy Gillespie. The next decades saw a strong Brazilian, as well as Cuban, influence on jazz (see CP 20).

We will consider a famous bebop work written by Dizzy Gillespie: the Latin-tinged *A Night in Tunisia*, which features two jazz legends—Charlie Parker (known as Bird), on alto saxophone, and a very young Miles Davis, on trumpet. It is performed by a six-person ensemble in the unique musical language of bebop, a somewhat frenetic style that Ellington likened to "playing Scrabble with all the vowels missing." Because bebop is so reliant on improvisation, the standard performance usually presents the entire tune first—here a thirty-two-bar song form (**A-A-B-A**, or chorus 1 with four eight-bar phrases)—followed by several improvised choruses over the same chord pattern, or changes (see Listening Guide 42). A nervous, syncopated ostinato is established in the introduction, after which the disjunct tune is played on muted trumpet by Miles Davis, with a brief alto saxophone solo (in the **B** section). After a unison saxophone interlude, Charlie Parker plays a highly virtuosic, and now famous, *break* (a solo passage that interrupts the accompaniment—in this case, a flurry of sixteenth notes that moves all over the horn) that leads into the second chorus, split

Charlie Parker was one of the most influential saxophonists of the 1940s.

419

Listening Guide 42

CD: CHR/STD 8/13–18, SH 4/35–40

Gillespie/Parker: *A Night in Tunisia* (3:01)

DATE: Recorded 1946

PERFORMERS: Charlie Parker Septet
Charlie Parker, alto saxophone
Miles Davis, trumpet
Lucky Thompson, tenor saxophone
Dodo Mamarosa, piano
Arv Garrison, guitar
Vic McMillan, bass
Roy Porter, drums

FORM: 32-bar song form (**A-A-B-A**), in 3 choruses

TEMPO: Moderate 4/4

KEY: D minor

WHAT TO LISTEN FOR: Short motivic ideas (riffs) that are repeated; underlying bass ostinato.
Soloistic style (often featuring a single player).
Statement of tune, played by muted trumpet (Miles Davis) and alto saxophone (Charlie Parker).
Frenetic improvisational style of Charlie Parker in chorus 2.
Choruses 2 and 3: solo improvisations on trumpet, tenor saxophone, and guitar, with short melodic ideas alternating between lyrical lines.
Recap of tune, and final ostinato.

Riff

between Parker's and Davis's creative improvisations. Parker is known for his alternation of short riff-like passages (a *riff* is a short melodic ostinato heard in jazz) with more flowing lines. The last chorus features solos by the tenor saxophone, guitar, and finally, the trumpet; the work closes as it began, with the bass ostinato fading out. Gillespie's *A Night in Tunisia* has been recorded many times since, and is an established jazz classic.

In a 1957 lecture, composer and jazz historian Gunther Schuller put forth the idea that art music could learn from jazz, and vice versa. He coined the term **Third stream jazz** *third stream*, holding that the first stream was classical music, the second jazz, and the third a combination of the other two. Although the designation referred mainly to the instruments used, it was soon extended to include other elements as well, such as the adoption by jazz performers of classical forms and tonal devices.

Schuller's idea was taken over by a number of jazz musicians, among them pianist John Lewis (b. 1920), who formed the Modern Jazz Quartet in answer to the growing demand for jazz on college campuses across the country. More

35   0:00   **Introduction**—8-bar ostinato (bass and percussion);
              4 bar saxophone ostinato.

Opening disjunct line of tune (**A**), with a short idea (9 notes) that is repeated (played first by muted trumpet):

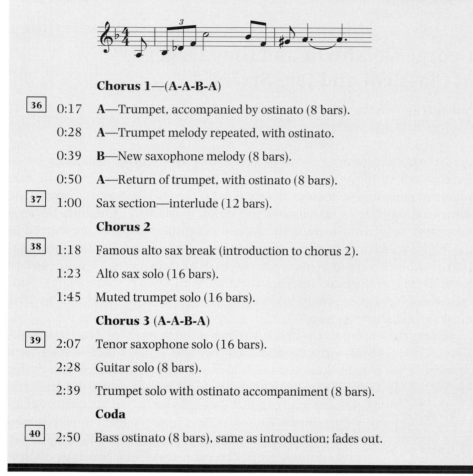

Chorus 1—(A-A-B-A)

36   0:17   **A**—Trumpet, accompanied by ostinato (8 bars).

     0:28   **A**—Trumpet melody repeated, with ostinato.

     0:39   **B**—New saxophone melody (8 bars).

     0:50   **A**—Return of trumpet, with ostinato (8 bars).

37   1:00   Sax section—interlude (12 bars).

Chorus 2

38   1:18   Famous alto sax break (introduction to chorus 2).

     1:23   Alto sax solo (16 bars).

     1:45   Muted trumpet solo (16 bars).

Chorus 3 (A-A-B-A)

39   2:07   Tenor saxophone solo (16 bars).

     2:28   Guitar solo (8 bars).

     2:39   Trumpet solo with ostinato accompaniment (8 bars).

Coda

40   2:50   Bass ostinato (8 bars), same as introduction; fades out.

recently, trumpeter Wynton Marsalis demonstrated his mastery of both jazz and classical styles in his Pulitzer-Prize-winning jazz oratorio *Blood on the Fields* (1996) and his Stravinsky-inspired *A Fiddler's Tale* (1998).

By the 1960s, new experiments were in the making. A free-style *avant-garde jazz* emerged, with tenor saxophonist John Coltrane as its leading proponent. Also heard for the first time was a hybrid style known as *fusion*, which combined jazz improvisation with amplified instruments and the rhythmic pulse of rock. Trumpeter Miles Davis was an important catalyst in the advent of this style, and performers such as guitarist Jerry Garcia (1942–1995, of the Grateful Dead) and vibraphone player Gary Burton are modern-day exponents of the fusion sound.

In the last several decades, jazz styles have taken conflicting turns. Modern bebop arose as a contemporary *Neoclassical style* of the 1980s, characterized by expanded tonalities, modal improvisation, and new forms merged with bebop's disjunct lines. Wynton Marsalis is one of the new voices of this Neoclassicism. *Free jazz*, founded by saxophonist Ornette Coleman in the 1960s, has developed

Avant-garde jazz

Fusion

Neoclassical style

Free jazz

New-age jazz   alongside the more mellow, contemplative strains of *new-age jazz*, the latter best exemplified by saxophonist Paul Winter. New technologies, including MIDI and interactive performance between musicians and computers, have opened a world of creative possibilities and sounds; meanwhile, other performers are looking back to the fundamentals of jazz, reinventing it for today's listeners.

George Gershwin and the Merger of Classical and Jazz Styles

"Jazz has contributed an enduring value to America in the sense that it has expressed ourselves."

We have noted a number of composers—European and American alike—who were drawn to the vernacular genres of ragtime, blues, and jazz, and who sought to integrate elements of these popular styles into their music. Among the American musicians who mastered this fusion were George Gershwin—whose appealing songs, Broadway musicals, and instrumental works are steeped in the new jazz idiom—and the contemporary jazz composer/educator David Baker—whose works span many genres but draw from jazz and blues as well as from classical influences, marking them as third stream compositions. Both composers have successfully bridged the gap between classical and popular music, each in his own way.

George Gershwin (1898–1937) was one of the most gifted American musicians of the twentieth century. His early musical studies were classically focused, but it was jazz that ultimately caught his fancy. "This is American music," he told one of his teachers. "This is the kind of music I want to write." In his youth, Gershwin worked as a Tin Pan Alley "song plugger" (a pianist who plays, or "plugs," a company's new tunes to sell sheet music). He became an accomplished pianist and song writer, working in collaboration with his brother Ira.

Gershwin's songs drew on elements of ragtime, blues, and jazz to create a distinctive sound characterized by rhythmic complexity, colorful chromaticism, and sudden modulations. Among his best-loved songs are *Love Me, Oh Lady Be Good, Fascinating Rhythm, The Man I Love, Someone to Watch Over Me,* and *'S Wonderful,* several of which came from successful Broadway shows. His brother Ira Gershwin proved to be the ideal lyricist; together, they brought a new level of sophistication to popular songs of the 1920s. George and Ira Gershwin's finest contribution to the stage was the American folk-opera *Porgy and Bess* (1935), based on the novel and play by DuBose and Dorothy Heyward about blacks living in Charleston, South Carolina's "Catfish Row," and featuring the memorable tunes *Summertime, I Got Plenty of Nuttin', It Ain't Necessarily So,* and *Bess, You Is My Woman Now.* (We will consider the origins and development of American musical theater in Chapter 69.)

It is in Gershwin's instrumental works, however, that he was able to merge the rhythmic vitality and harmonic language

The original 1924 poster advertising the premiere of George Gershwin's *Rhapsody in Blue* as "an experiment in modern music."

🎺 Principal Works

Orchestral works, including *Rhapsody in Blue* (1924, for piano and jazz orchestra), *Concerto in F* (1925), and a tone poem, *An American in Paris* (1928)

Piano music, including Three Preludes (1927)

More than 30 stage works, including *Lady, Be Good!* (1924), *Strike Up the Band* (1927), *Girl Crazy* (1930), *Of Thee I Sing* (1931), and *Porgy and Bess* (1935)

Songs for films, including *Shall We Dance* (1937) and *A Damsel In Distress* (1937); songs for shows by other composers; and other individually published songs

of jazz with classical forms. His first "classical" piece was *Rhapsody in Blue*, scored for piano and orchestra and premiered in 1924 with the Paul Whiteman band (with Gershwin on piano) in a concert billed as "An Experiment in Modern Music." The critical response was very positive, and the work catapulted Gershwin to fame. He followed *Rhapsody* with his *Concerto in F* (1925), for piano and orchestra, performed at New York's Carnegie Hall, and his tone poem *An American in Paris* (1928), with Gershwin himself conducting the New York Philharmonic Orchestra in an open-air concert for an audience of 15,000. With these works, he successfully had taken jazz into the concert hall and into the hearts of classical-music lovers.

George Gershwin

Piano Preludes

We will consider one of his three piano preludes, written in 1927 and transcribed for violin and piano by the great virtuoso violinist Jascha Heifetz (1901–1987). Gershwin had long intended to write a work for his close friend Heifetz, who, after the composer's untimely death, transcribed five songs from *Porgy and Bess* as well as these short preludes. The first of the preludes is a fine introduction to Gershwin's jazzy, rhythmic style. Marked *Allegro ben ritmato e deciso* (fast, rhythmic, and decisive), the work begins freely, with a brief motive whose repetition sounds a lowered seventh-scale tone (blue note). The piano then sets up a quick-paced, syncopated accompaniment with strong accents, over which the rhythmic, wide-ranging melody unfolds. The middle section features a more static tune in even rhythms that begins with a rising interval (a fourth, then a fifth), followed by repeated pitches, this still accompanied by a syncopated left-hand pattern that leads us through various key centers. The electrifying first theme returns, this time heard with sweeping scales and in high-ranging octaves. One last glissando leads to the closing fortissimo chord.

Gershwin's dream of uniting jazz and classical music was clearly a beacon for later generations of composers, for whom, Leonard Bernstein claimed, "jazz entered their bloodstream, became part of the air they breathed, so that it came out in their music. . . . [They] have written music that is American without even trying."

in his own words

The best music being written today . . . comes from folk sources. Jazz, ragtime, Negro spirituals and blues, Southern mountain songs, country fiddling, and cowboy songs can all be employed in the creation of American art-music, and are actually used by many composers now.

Gershwin: Piano Prelude No. 1

(1:40)

DATE OF WORK:	Published 1927 (in set of 3 Preludes)
FORM:	Loose ternary (**A-B-A′**)
TEMPO:	Allegro ben ritmato e deciso (Fast, rhythmic, and decisive)
ARRANGED:	By Jascha Heifetz for violin and piano, performed by Joshua Bell (violin) and John Williams (piano)

WHAT TO LISTEN FOR: Energetic, syncopated first theme, with expressive blue note.
Highly rhythmic and accented accompaniment.
Quick exchanges between violin and piano.
Overall 3-part structure (**A-B-A′**).
Sweeping high-range lines build to climax in last section.

41 0:00 **A** section
Short, free introduction in piano, then violin previews main theme, with lowered 7th-scale degree.
Quick tempo set in piano with syncopated chords and offbeats in violin;

0:17 Theme 1 introduced by violin; accented and syncopated:

42 0:29 **B** section
Begins softly with theme that rises a 4th (or sometimes a 5th), followed by repeated pitches played by violin then piano, over syncopated accompaniment:

Dynamic level and range builds.

43 1:03 **A′** section
Return of opening theme, with sweeping scalar lines leading to new statement up an octave; dynamics build and theme is heard in octaves and in high range of violin; sweeping glissando into final chords.

David Baker and the Spiritual as Art Song

*"My choice of materials is a reflection of my personal philosophy. . . .
I draw very heavily on jazz components in my writing—improvisation, jazz scales, African rhythms, gospel music, R&B, the blues, inflection."*

We mentioned earlier that Bohemian composer Antonín Dvořák had inspired several of his African-American students to draw on the music of their heritage, especially the spiritual, a genre of traditional religious song (see p. 302). You may recall that Henry Burleigh followed his teacher's advice and in 1916 published *Jubilee Songs of the U.S.A.*, a collection of spirituals arranged as art songs. Prior to this collection, black spirituals had been arranged as choral works, and widely performed with great success in the late nineteenth century by the Fisk Jubilee Singers, a famous African-American ensemble from Fisk University in Nashville, Tennesee. We will consider a contemporary setting of a well-known spiritual composed by the African-American composer David Baker, and see how this music continues to express the black experience.

David Baker (b. 1931) was born in Indianapolis, and studied music at Indiana University. A trombonist, Baker played professionally with vibraphonist Lionel Hampton and, on the West Coast, with the Stan Kenton band and trumpeter Maynard Ferguson. When an accident left Baker unable to play the trombone for some years, he took up the cello and, in doing so, pioneered the use of the cello in jazz. He returned in Indiana University in 1966 as a faculty

When we let freedom ring . . . from village and every hamlet, from every state and city, we will be able to speed up that day when all of God's children, black men and white men, Jews and Gentiles, Protestants and Catholics, will be able to join hands and sing in the words of the old Negro spiritual, "Free at last! Free at last! Thank God, Almighty, we are free at last!"
—MARTIN LUTHER KING, JR.

Principal Works

Music for orchestra, including concertos (*Levels*, for solo double bass, jazz band, winds, and strings, 1973)

Solo instrumental works (for violin, cello, clarinet, flute, and piano); string orchestra and instrumental ensembles, including 2 piano trios (*Roots*, 1976; *Roots II*, 1992), *Singers of Songs/Weavers of Dreams: Homage to My Friends* (1980), and *Homage à l'histoire* (for clarinet, bassoon, trumpet, percussion, violin, and double bass, 1994)

Music for voice and instrumental ensemble, including *Through This Vale of Tears* (1986)

Choral and dramatic music, including *Psalm 22* (1966); incidental music for television

Multimedia works, including *A Salute to Beethoven* (for solo winds, jazz ensemble, and tape, 1970)

Works (over 100) for varied jazz groups

Writings about music, including books on Miles Davis, John Coltrane, Cannonball Adderley, and textbooks on jazz composition and arranging

David Baker

member, and eventually became head of the jazz department there. Widely recognized as a jazz educator, he has written many books on jazz improvisation, composition, and pedagogy and has held positions as a music adviser to the National Endowment for the Arts and to the John F. Kennedy Center for the Performing Arts.

The Song Cycle Through This Vale of Tears

Baker has composed in a wide range of genres, drawing on influences from both popular and classical styles. He uses jazz rhythms, serial techniques, and sonata form, and sometimes combines jazz and classical ensembles in a style considered third stream (see p. 420). In 1973, his composition *Levels*, a concerto for double bass, jazz band, winds, and strings, received a Pulitzer Prize nomination. If his music has a recurring theme, it is paying homage to great musicians. Among the works in this category are the *Ellingtones: A Fantasy for Saxophone and Orchestra* (1987), commissioned by the New York Philharmonic Orchestra and honoring Duke Ellington, and *Homage à l'histoire* (1994), after Stravinsky's *A Soldier's Tale*.

Another theme in Baker's music is the black experience, as seen in *Roots II* (1992), a piano trio that weaves a history of blacks through "work songs, field hollers, blues, ragtime, boogie-woogie, rhythm & blues, spirituals, gospel songs, calypso, rock & roll, rap, and, of course, jazz." Baker's song cycle *Through This Vale of Tears* (1986), for tenor soloist, string quartet, and piano, is a moving commentary on the death of Martin Luther King, Jr.—what Baker called "one of the most significant events in my life and in the lives of most black people." The song cycle was commissioned by the African-American tenor William Brown, who performs the recording we will hear. The work is in seven movements, set to texts from the Bible (three are from Psalm 22) and by African-American writers. The first song, *Thou Dost Lay Me in the Dust of Death*, is reworked from a portion of an earlier composition by Baker entitled *Black America: To the Memory of Martin Luther King, Jr.*, and is vaguely reminiscent of Baroque vocal style with continuo. The third movement, *My God, Hast Thou Forsaken Me?* is cast as a spiritual, while the fifth song, *Deliver My Soul*, is a kind of gospel waltz. The last song of the set, *Now That He is Safely Dead*, is also recast from *Black America*, and sets what Baker calls "a devastatingly powerful poem" by Carl Hines.

We will hear the sixth song, *Sometimes I Feel Like a Motherless Child*, based on the traditional spiritual of the same name. Here, Baker sets the melancholy tune against a very modern, dissonant accompaniment that smacks of serial, or twelve-tone, treatment. The song begins with a solo *vocalise*—wordless singing—of the gently syncopated melody in which blue notes are heard; the first verse starts with an outcry—"Oh, my brother!"—answered by instruments whose harsh harmonies seem to comment on the sorrowful text. A brief instrumental interlude occurs, leading to the second verse—"Sometimes I feel like I'm almost gone"—and an expressive closing. Throughout, the extreme dissonances are resolved only on the word "home," which symbolizes eternity in many spirituals. Baker's song cycle is a poignant—and personal—musical tribute to the slain civil rights leader.

in his own words

I view music in a decidedly African way, as a total experience and not apart from other aspects of life. . . . I try to crystalize the black experience and maintain a link with the past to affect a kind of continuum that reflects where I come from, where I am, and where I'm going.

♪

Vocalise

Listening Guide 44

CD: CHR/STD 8/39–42, SH 4/44–47

Baker, *Sometimes I Feel Like a Motherless Child,* from *Through This Vale of Tears*

(3:51)

DATE: 1986

GENRE: Song cycle (7 songs)

FORM: Introduction, 2 verses, with interlude and coda

MEDIUM: Tenor voice, string quartet, and piano

SUBJECT: Tribute to Martin Luther King, Jr.

BASIS: Traditional spiritual

TEMPO: Very slow

OVERALL STRUCTURE (AND TEXT SOURCE):

   I. *Thou Dost Lay Me in the Dust of Death* (Psalm 22)
   II. *If There Be Sorrow* (Mari Evans)
   III. *My God, Why Hast Thou Forsaken Me?* (Psalm 22)
   IV. *Parades to Hell* (Solomon Edwards)
   V. *Deliver My Soul* (Psalm 22)
   VI. *Sometimes I Feel Like a Motherless Child* (traditional)
   VII. *Now That He is Safely Dead* (Carl Hines)

WHAT TO LISTEN FOR:
First statement of spiritual sung unaccompanied as *vocalise* (wordless).
Very slow tempo with gentle syncopations in undulating tune.
Extreme levels of dissonance in string and piano accompaniment.
Inflected, or blue, notes (sung slightly lower than pitch).
Call-and-response pattern between voice and instruments.
Resolution of dissonance at close of verses, on word "home."

44 0:00 Wordless vocal introduction, sung *ad libitum* (freely) and without accompaniment, introduces spiritual tune, with blue notes.

First statement of the tune, in vocalise, with inflected note marked (b♮):

45 0:38 **Verse 1**

Oh my brother,
Sometimes I feel like a motherless child,
Sometimes I feel like a motherless child,
Sometimes I feel like a motherless child,
A long way from home.

Dissonant string and piano
accompaniment; in
alternation with voice

Ends on unison A

| 46 | 1:57 | Instrumental interlude; brief change to triple meter; more animated. |

	2:10	**Verse 2**
		Sometimes I feel like I'm almost gone, Dissonant
		Sometimes I feel like I'm almost gone, accompaniment
		Sometimes I feel like I'm almost gone, continues;
		A long way from home. ends on unison A.

47	3:08	**Coda**
		Oh my brother, oh my brother Begins with *sforzando*; then
		A long way from home. very soft, with voice singing
		falsetto against more
		consonant accompaniment.

69

Musical Theater

"The hills are alive with the sound of music."

—OSCAR HAMMERSTEIN II

KEY POINTS

- American musical theater has roots in European *operetta*, which was brought to America by emigré composers.
- Musicals feature romantic plots (some taken from novels), comic moments, appealing melodies, and large ensemble and dance numbers.
- The great composer/lyricist teams include Rodgers and Hart (*Babes in Arms*), Rodgers and Hammerstein (*The Sound of Music*), Lerner and Lowe (*My Fair Lady*); other well-known composers of musicals are Stephen Sondheim (*Into the Woods*), Andrew Lloyd Webber (*Phantom of the Opera*), and Claude-Michel Schonberg (*Les Misérables*).
- Leonard Bernstein is remembered today as a conductor and composer of symphonic and choral music, film music, and musical theater works.
- Bernstein's *West Side Story*, a classic musical that updates the Romeo and Juliet legend, is set in New York City amid turf wars of rival street gangs.
- Dance music from Latin America and the Caribbean has enjoyed continued popularity and has influenced many musical genres, including Bernstein's *West Side Story* (CP 20).

The Development of American Musical Theater

The American musical theater of today developed from the comic opera, or *operetta*, tradition of Johann Strauss Jr., Jacques Offenbach, and the British team of Gilbert and Sullivan. The genre was revamped to the American taste by composers such as Victor Herbert, Sigmund Romberg, and Jerome Kern, known for his landmark *Show Boat* (1927), a tale of Mississippi River life that introduced the classic songs *Ol' Man River* and *Can't Help Lovin' Dat Man of Mine*. In the ensuing decades, the musical established itself as America's unique contribution to world theater.

Musical theater depended on romantic plots in picturesque settings enlivened by comedy, appealing melodies, choruses, and dances. Within the framework of a thoroughly commercial theater, a group of talented composers and writers created works that not only enchanted audiences of their time but lasted well beyond it. Among these were Burton Lane's *Finian's Rainbow* (1947), Cole Porter's *Kiss Me, Kate* (1948), Frank Loesser's *Guys and Dolls* (1950), Harold Rome's *Fanny* (1954), and Alan Jay Lerner and Frederick Loewe's *My Fair Lady* (1956).

Originally, the plots of musicals were contrived and silly, functioning mainly as scaffolding for the songs and dances. The emphasis gradually changed when composers began turning to sophisticated literary sources for their plots, which presented more convincing treatment of characters and situations. *Show Boat* was based on an Edna Ferber novel, *Kiss Me, Kate* on Shakespeare's *The Taming of the Shrew*, *Guys and Dolls* on the stories of Damon Runyon, *Fanny* on Marcel Pagnol's trilogy, and *My Fair Lady* on George Bernard Shaw's play *Pygmalion*. As the musicals' approach grew more serious, the genre outgrew its original limitations.

George Gershwin's masterpiece *Porgy and Bess* (see discussion on p. 422) was so far ahead of its time that, despite its focus on African-American folk idioms, it did not become a success until a revival toured Europe in the 1950s. The work paved the way for musicals such as Leonard Bernstein's *West Side Story* (1957), one of the first musical theater pieces to end tragically, and Jerry Bock's *Fiddler on the Roof* (1964), based on stories by the great Yiddish writer Sholem Aleichem. Both works earned worldwide success, and both would have been unthinkable twenty years earlier because of the serious elements in their plots.

The composer Richard Rodgers collaborated with two talented lyricists during his long career to produce some of the best-loved musicals of the twentieth century. Along with Lorenz Hart, he created a string of successful Broadway shows, including *Babes in Arms* (1937), which featured the now-classic ballad *My Funny Valentine*. After the death of Hart in 1943, Rodgers teamed up with Oscar Hammerstein II to write unforgettable musicals such as *Oklahoma!* (1943), *Carousel* (1945), *South Pacific* (1949), *The King and I* (1951), and *The Sound of Music* (1959). Here too the literary sources were of a high order. *Carousel* was based on Ferenc Molnár's *Liliom*, *Oklahoma!* on Lynn Riggs's *Green Grow the Lilacs*, *South Pacific* on the stories of James Michener, *The King and I* on *Anna and the King of Siam* by Margaret Landon, and *The Sound of Music* on the moving memoir of Baroness Maria von Trapp.

In the 1970s and 1980s, Stephen Sondheim brought the genre to new levels of sophistication in a series of works that included *A Little Night Music* (1973),

Sweeney Todd (1979), *Sunday in the Park with George* (1983), and *Into the Woods* (1988), which had a recent and successful revival on Broadway. His shows of the 1990s continued his original musical voice and dramatic expression. In *Passion* (1994), he dropped the typical numbered musical tunes of most shows, and wrote a symphonic score. Sondheim challenges his audiences with a dramatic style that is far more serious than his Broadway successors and peers. He uses complex musical language that shows an affinity to the classical masters Ravel and Copland.

Andrew Lloyd Webber

A new era opened with the advent of rock musicals such as Galt MacDermot's *Hair* (1968), The Who's *Tommy* (1969; music and lyrics by Peter Townshend), and Andrew Lloyd Webber's *Jesus Christ Superstar* (1971). Suddenly, the romantic show tunes to which millions of young Americans had learned to dance and flirt went completely out of fashion. After a while, however, melody returned. The British Lloyd Webber conquered the international stage with *Evita* (1978), *Cats* (1981), *Starlight Express* (1984), *The Phantom of the Opera* (1986), and *Sunset Boulevard* (1993)—works in which song and dance were combined with dazzling scenic effects, as in the court operas of the Baroque. Together with Frenchman Claude-Michel Schonberg's *Les Misérables* (1987), *Miss Saigon* (1988), and *Martin Guerre* (1996)—the last two in collaboration with Alain Boublil—these musicals represented a new phenomenon. What had been almost exclusively an American product was now taken over by Europeans.

Film-based musicals

Many "classic" musicals have enjoyed recent successful revivals on Broadway; among these are *Chicago*; *The Sound of Music*; *Annie Get Your Gun*; *The Music Man*; *Kiss Me, Kate*; *Cabaret*; *Into the Woods*; and *42nd Street*. A new category of musicals based on films has swept the Broadway stage, including the Disney studio's *Beauty and the Beast* (1994) and *The Lion King* (1997), both based on the animated films. These works have reversed the standard order of a hit musical generating a film and opened up a new world of source material. Three new shows have gone in this direction: Mel Brooks's award-winning comedy *The Producers* (2001), based on his 1967 film; *The Full Monty* (2001, with music and lyrics by David Yazbek), an Americanization of the risqué 1997

Kate (Marin Mazzie) and Petruchio (Brian Stokes Mitchell) in the final scene of the 1999 Broadway revival of Cole Porter's *Kiss Me, Kate*, based on Shakespeare's *Taming of the Shrew*.

British film; and, most recently, *Thoroughly Modern Millie* (2002 Tony Award–winner), adopted from the 1967 film of the same name.

Some musicals find their sources in older classics: Jonathan Larsen's hit show *Rent*, a modern rock opera inspired by Puccini's opera *La Bohème*, premiered on the hundredth anniversary of the Italian masterwork; and Elton John and Tim Rice's *Aida*, a Disney production, is based on Verdi's masterpiece of the same name about love and power in ancient Egypt. Dance has inspired a new type of musical in which choreography takes precedence over story line, as in *Bring in 'da Noise, Bring in 'da Funk* (1995), featuring tap star Savion Glover, and *Riverdance* (1994), with the sensational Irish step dancer Michael Flatley. This trend has diversified into staged shows featuring rhythmic percussion and dancing, as in *Stomp* (1994), and brilliant visuals and pageantry like *BLAST!* (2000; see illustration on p. 8).

Leonard Bernstein and the Broadway Musical

"Any composer's writing is the sum of himself, of all his roots and influences."

We have seen how jazz was merged with many styles of music. The composer-conductor Leonard Bernstein attempted another important union: jazz with musical theater. The result was *West Side Story*, a stage work that has achieved the status of a classic.

Leonard Bernstein

As a composer, conductor, educator, pianist, and television personality, Bernstein (1918–1990) enjoyed a spectacular career. He was born in Lawrence, Massachusetts, the son of Russian-Jewish immigrants. At thirteen, he was playing piano with a jazz band. He entered Harvard at seventeen, where he studied composition, attended the prestigious Curtis Institute in Philadelphia, and then became a disciple of the conductor Serge Koussevitzky. In 1943, when he was twenty-five, Bernstein was appointed assistant to Artur Rodzinski, conductor of the New York Philharmonic. A few weeks later, a guest conductor, Bruno Walter, was suddenly taken ill, and Rodzinski was out of town. With only a few hours' notice, Bernstein took over the Sunday afternoon concert, which was being broadcast coast to coast, and led a stunning performance. Overnight he became famous. Fifteen years later, he was himself named director of the New York Philharmonic, the first American-born conductor (and the youngest, at age forty) to occupy the post.

As a composer, Bernstein straddled the worlds of serious and popular music. He was thus able to bring to the Broadway musical a compositional technique and knowledge of music that few of its earlier practitioners had possessed. In his concert works, he spoke the language of contemporary music with enormous fluency. He possessed a genuine flair for orchestration—the balance and spacing of sonorities, the use of the brass in the high register, and the idiomatic writing that shows off each instrument to its best advantage all bespeak a master. His harmonic idiom is spicily dissonant, his jazzy rhythms have great vitality, and his melodies soar.

Bernstein's feeling for the urban scene—specifically that of New York City—is vividly projected in his theater music. In *On the Town* (a full-length version of

Dance Music from Latin America and the Caribbean

The energetic rhythms of Leonard Bernstein's *West Side Story* do not sound particularly foreign to us, yet they are based on dances from a variety of Latin-American countries. Some dances, like the Brazilian samba and the Cuban rumba, began as rural music that was later popularized by urban bands. In the 1950s and 1960s, Americans and Europeans alike were dancing to the distinctive rhythms of the Cuban cha cha cha and mambo and the Brazilian bossa nova (meaning "new wave"), all derived from earlier traditional styles. We noted previously that the Argentinian tango, a heated couple dance that had its origins in the poor neighborhoods of Buenos Aires, has remained popular through much of the twentieth century. The Afro-Cuban conga is a favorite Latin-American Carnival dance whose name is also applied to a long, single-headed drum used in much Latin-American popular music. The collective term "salsa" (Spanish for "sauce," as in "spicy") is sometimes used to label various contemporary styles loosely based on Afro-Cuban dance music.

Cuba remains one of the most influential sources of Latin American music. Recently, we have become reacquainted with the "golden era" of Cuban dance music through the 1999 documentary film *Buena Vista Social Club*. This rich film takes us back to the elegant dance club of 1950s Havana—before the 1959 Castro revolution—complete with its crooning singers (*soneros*) and the dancers moving sensually to the complex syncopated rhythms of the acoustic (unplugged) band. Cuba was, in the Prohibition era (1920–33), the playground of Americans looking for glitzy nightlife, gambling, prostitution, and alcohol. The movie gave birth to a Grammy-winning CD featuring, among others, the legendary Cuban pianist Ruben Gonzales and singer Ibrahim Ferrer; both of these music giants have since gone on to record their own albums. Producer/guitarist

Cuban *son* singer Ibrahim Ferrer, one of the stars of the Buena Vista Social Club, in concert at London's Royal Albert Hall, November 2001.

his ballet *Fancy Free)* and *West Side Story*, he created a sophisticated kind of musical theater that explodes with movement, energy, and sentiment. His death in October 1990 aroused universal mourning in the music world and beyond.

West Side Story

In *West Side Story*, Bernstein realized a dream: to create a musical based on the Romeo and Juliet story. This updated tale, with a book by playwright Arthur Laurents and lyrics by Stephen Sondheim (his first job as a lyricist), sets the saga

Jamaican reggae star Bunny Wailer (Livingston), who sang with the original Bob Marley and the Wailers, performing at Madison Square Garden in 1986.

Other dance music types have also achieved international prominence. In the 1960s, a Jamaican style called ska became popular; it was characterized by quick, off-the-beat rhythms and jazzy instrumentals; it was represented by artists such as the Skatalites. Ska led the way for reggae, a Jamaican style of music that slows down the quick beat of ska and emphasizes the role of the bass, placing it in a complex rhythmic relationship with the other parts (see p. 446). Bob Marley, one of the most important world music artists, remains the model for reggae musicians. Ska has recently undergone a revival; its feel-good mood and up-tempo rhythms have gained broad appeal. The Skatalites remain the masters of ska. Much of their music has been reissued in recent years—reinterpreted by a band madeup of some of the original members.

TERMS TO NOTE:

samba	bossa nova	ska
rumba	tango	reggae
cha cha cha	conga	global pop
mambo	salsa	son
soneros		

SUGGESTED LISTENING:

Bernstein: *West Side Story*
Latin-American dance music
ska or reggae
Bob Marley and the Wailers
Buena Vista Social Club (Ruben Gonzales, Ibrahim Ferrer)

Ry Cooder explains that "these are the greatest musicians alive on the planet today, hot-shot players and classic people. . . . In my experience Cuban musicians are unique. The organization of the musical group is perfectly understood, there is no ego, no jockeying for position so they have evolved the perfect ensemble concept." The typical dance song form—known as a *son*—generally features a singer with a choral refrain set against a complex polyrhythmic background. The Buena Vista Social Club lives on today in the film, in recordings, on the Internet, and on the dance floor.

amid turf wars of two rival street gangs in New York City. The hostility between the Jets (led by Riff) and their Puerto Rican rivals, the Sharks (led by Bernardo), is a modern-day counterpart of the feud between the Capulets and the Montagues in Shakespeare's play. In Bernstein's tragic tale, Tony, one of the Jets, and Maria, Bernardo's sister, meet at a dance and immediately fall in love. Riff and Bernardo bring their two gangs together for a fight. When Tony tries to stop them, Riff is stabbed by Bernardo, and Tony in turn kills Bernardo. Tony begs Maria for forgiveness, but the gang warfare mounts to a final rumble in which Tony is killed. This story of star-crossed lovers unfolds in scenes of great tenderness, with

Principal Works

Orchestral works, including the *Jeremiah* Symphony (1942); Symphony No. 2, *The Age of Anxiety* (piano and orchestra, 1949); *Serenade* (violin, strings, and percussion, 1954); and Symphony No. 3, *Kaddish* (1963)

Works for chorus and orchestra, including *Chichester Psalms* (1965) and *Songfest* (1977)

Operas, including *A Quiet Place* (1983)

Musicals, including *On the Town* (1944), *Wonderful Town* (1953), *Candide* (1956), and *West Side Story* (1957)

Other dramatic music, including the ballet *Fancy Free* (1944), the film score *On the Waterfront* (1954), and *Mass* (1971)

Chamber and instrumental music; solo vocal music

memorable songs such as *Maria, Tonight,* and *Somewhere* alternating with electrifying dance sequences choreographed by Jerome Robbins.

We will hear first the *Mambo*, a part of the dance scene where Tony meets Maria. When the lively Latin beat starts, the Jets and Sharks are on opposite sides of the hall. At the climax of the dance, Tony and Maria catch a glimpse of each other across the room. A *mambo* is an Afro-Cuban dance with a fast and highly syncopated beat; in Bernstein's dance, the bongos and cowbells keep the frenetic pulse under the shouts of the gang members and the jazzy riffs of the woodwinds and brass. The music dies away as Maria and Tony walk toward each other on the dance floor.

The *Tonight* Ensemble is set later the same evening, after a fire-escape version of Shakespeare's famous balcony scene, where Tony and Maria first sing their love duet. As darkness falls, the two gangs anxiously await the expected fight, each vowing to cut the other down to size. Underneath the gang music, an ominous three-note ostinato is heard throughout. Tony's thoughts are only of Maria as he sings the lyrical ballad *Tonight* (an **A-A'-B-A″** form we have seen in jazz compositions) over an animated Latin rhythmic accompaniment. The gang music returns briefly, after which Maria and later Tony repeat their love song, their voices soaring above the complex dialogue in an exciting climax to the first act.

West Side Story remains, more than forty-five years after its debut, a timeless masterpiece of musical theater; its dramatic content, stirring melodies, colorful orchestration, and vivacious dance scenes continue to delight audiences of today.

Richard Beymer and Natalie Wood in the "balcony scene" from the film *West Side Story*, directed by Robert Wise and Jerome Robbins.

Listening Guide 45

CD: CHR/STD 8/19–29, SH 4/48–58

Bernstein: *West Side Story*, excerpts

(5:26)

DATE OF WORK:	1957
GENRE:	Musical theater
CHARACTERS:	Maria, a Puerto Rican girl, sister of Bernardo
	Tony, member of the Jets
	Anita, Puerto Rican girlfriend of Bernardo
	Riff, leader of the Jets
	Bernardo, leader of the Sharks

Act I: The Dance at the Gym, Mambo

(1:48)

WHAT TO LISTEN FOR: Frenetic Afro-Cuban dance, with highly syncopated rhythms.
Rich orchestration featuring brass with Latin-American rhythm instruments
(bongo drums, cowbells).
Vocal interjections ("mambo") and rhythmic hand-clapping.

48   0:00   Percussion introduction, 8 bars, with bongos and cowbells; very fast and syncopated.

0:07   Brass, with accented chords; Sharks shout, "Mambo!"; followed by quieter string line, accompanied by snare drum rolls; accented brass chords return; Sharks shout, "Mambo!" again.

0:28   High dissonant woodwinds in dialogue with rhythmic brass.

49   0:33   Trumpets play riff over *fff* chords:

Woodwinds and brass alternate in highly polyphonic texture.

1:00   Rocking two-note woodwind line above syncopated low brass:

50   1:13   Solo trumpet enters in high range above complex rhythmic accompaniment:

Complex *fortissimo* polyphony until climax; rhythm slows as music dies away at close.

Act I: Tonight Ensemble (3:38)

WHAT TO LISTEN FOR:	Lively gang music in unison, with 3-note ostinato figure.
	Soaring love song, with Tony and Maria.
	Complex musical texture combines gang music with ballad (*Tonight*).
	Fast and rhythmic tempo.

Setting: The neighborhood, 6:00–9:00 p.m. Riff and the Jets, Bernardo and the Sharks, Anita, Maria, and Tony all wait expectantly for the coming of night.

51 0:00   Short, rhythmic orchestral introduction featuring brass and percussion; based on 3-note ostinato:

TEXT

RIFF AND THE JETS

The Jets are gonna have their day
Tonight.

BERNARDO AND THE SHARKS

The Sharks are gonna have their way
Tonight.

RIFF AND THE JETS

The Puerto Ricans grumble,
"Fair fight."
But if they start a rumble,
We'll rumble 'em right.

SHARKS

We're gonna hand 'em a surprise
Tonight.

JETS

We're gonna cut them down to size
Tonight.

SHARKS

We said, "OK, no rumpus,
No tricks."
But just in case they jump us,
We're ready to mix

52 0:42   Tonight!

BOTH

We're gonna rock it tonight,
We're gonna jazz it up and have us
    a ball!

DESCRIPTION

Gangs sing in alternation, in marked recitative style:

Unison chorus, more emphatic and accented; with accented brass interjections.

436

They're gonna get it tonight;
The more they turn it on, the harder
   they fall!

JETS

Well, they began it!

SHARKS

Well, they began it—

BOTH

And we're the ones to stop 'em once
   and for all,
Tonight.

ANITA

53   1:08   Anita's gonna get her kicks
Tonight.
We'll have our private little mix
Tonight.
He'll walk in hot and tired,
So what!
Don't matter if he's tired,
As long as he's hot,
Tonight!

Antiphonal exchange between gangs; punctuated
by sharp chords in orchestra.

Opening melody now in uneven triplet
rhythm; sung sexily:

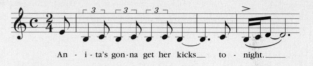

Reprise of song, in **A-A′-B-A″** form, lyrical vocal line
over syncopated accompaniment:

A section (8 bars):

TONY

54   1:25   Tonight, tonight,
Won't be just any night,
Tonight there will be no morning
   star.

Tonight, tonight,
I'll see my love tonight,
And for us, stars will stop where
   they are.

A′ section (8 bars); higher range, more emotional:

B section (8 bars); strings in canon with voice:

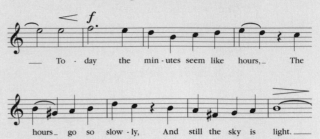

55 1:51 Today the minutes seem like
hours,
The hours go so slowly,
And still the sky is light . . .

A″ section (8 bars); reaches climax, then cuts off:

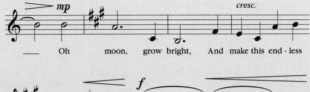

Oh moon, grow bright,
And make this endless day endless
night!

56 2:14   Instrumental interlude.

RIFF (to Tony)

I'm counting on you to be there   Return to opening idea, sung more vehemently.
Tonight!
When Diesel wins it fair and square
Tonight!
That Puerto Rican punk'll go down
And when he's hollered Uncle,
We'll tear up the town!

Ensemble finale: Maria sings *Tonight* in high range, against simultaneous dialogue and
interjections over the same syncopated dance rhythm that accompanied Tony's solo; dramatic
climax on last ensemble statement of "Tonight!"

MARIA (warmly)   *RIFF AND THE JETS*

57 2:39 [**A**] Tonight, tonight   So I can count on you boy?

                                           TONY (abstractedly)
                                           All right.

                                         RIFF AND THE JETS

Won't be just any night,   We're gonna have us a ball.

                                         TONY
                                           All right.

	RIFF
Tonight there will be no morning star.	Womb to tomb!

TONY
Sperm to worm!

RIFF
I'll see you there about eight.

TONY
Tonight.

JETS
We're gonna rock it tonight!

[**A'**] Tonight, tonight,

SHARKS
We're gonna jazz it tonight!

I'll see my love tonight,

ANITA
Tonight, tonight,
Late tonight. We're gonna mix it tonight.

And for us, stars will stop where they are.

SHARKS
They're gonna get it tonight!

TONY AND MARIA

58 3:05 [**B**] Today the minutes seem like hours,

ANITA
Anita's gonna have her day,
Bernardo's gonna have his way tonight.

The hours go so slowly,

SHARKS
They began it. And we're the ones to stop 'em once and for all!

And still the sky is light.

JETS
They began it. We'll stop 'em once and for all!

[**A''**] Oh moon, grow bright,

JETS AND SHARKS
The Sharks/Jets are gonna have their day, we're gonna rock it tonight, tonight!

ANITA
Tonight, this very night,
we're gonna rock it tonight, tonight!

And make this endless day endless night, endless night, tonight!

70

Rock and the Global Scene

"You know my temperature's risin',
The juke box's blowin' a fuse,
My heart's beatin' rhythm,
My soul keeps singin' the blues—
Roll over, Beethoven,
Tell Tchaikovsky the news."

—CHUCK BERRY

KEY POINTS

- The rise of *rock and roll* in the 1950s is one of the most significant phenomena in twentieth-century music history.
- Rock had its origins in rhythm and blues, country-western, pop music and gospel; early rock crossed racial lines, featuring both white and black performers.
- The Beatles, first heard in the United States in 1964, were highly influential because of their catchy melodies, hard-driving beats, and their expressive experiments in various musical styles (including non-Western).
- California groups also contributed to the expressiveness of rock, particularly to the emergence of *folk rock*.
- The 1960s and 1970s saw the rise of many eclectic musical styles, including *acid rock, jazz rock, art rock, Latin rock, punk rock, disco, reggae,* and *new wave*.
- Music videos and MTV were important media for the dissemination of rock in the 1980s; other technological developments led the way for the development of rap.
- *Rap*, or *hip hop*, is one of the most popular forms of African-American music; like earlier rock styles, it has crossed racial lines and been imitated by white performers.
- In the 1990s and beyond, *grunge rock, alternative rock* and *global pop* have captured the listening audience, along with numerous revivals by well-known artists and groups.
- The origins of *country-western music* are in Appalachian folk songs; through the Grand Ol' Opry and the Nashville recording industry, this style has developed commercially into one of the most widespread genres of popular music.
- The range of *global pop* styles and performers continues to grow, as music from all corners of the world is made available—some in "authentic" recordings and performances, others in a blend of contemporary and traditional styles (CP 21).

The rise of rock and roll and its offspring rock is the most important music phenomenon of the past half century. Economically, rock music has grown into a multibillion-dollar industry; socially, it has had a far-reaching impact on the way people live, dress, talk, and even think; musically, it has dominated the popular scene for some fifty years, and influenced virtually every other style of music—classical, jazz, country-western, and contemporary global pop. The Rock and Roll Hall of Fame opened in 1995 in Cleveland, Ohio, to honor the superstars of the genre.

Rock and roll, which first came on the scene in the 1950s, was born of a union of African-American rhythm and blues with country-western and swing music. *Rhythm and blues*, popular from the late 1940s through the early 1960s, is a predominantly vocal genre, featuring a solo singer accompanied by a small group including piano, guitar (acoustic or electric), acoustic bass, drums, and tenor saxophone. Its harmonies and structure are clearly drawn from twelve-bar blues and thirty-two-bar pop song form (both of which we heard in Chapter 68). As the name implies, the style is characterized by a strong, driving beat, usually in a quadruple meter. Of the great rhythm and blues performers, the majority were African-Americans such as Louis Jordan, Etta James, Bo Diddley, Joe Turner, and B. B. King.

Rhythm and blues

In the mid-1950s, rock and roll emerged as a form of rhythm and blues that crossed racial lines: white singers like Bill Haley (*Rock Around the Clock*, with the Comets, 1954), Elvis Presley (*Heartbreak Hotel, Hound Dog*, and *Don't Be Cruel*, all from 1956), and Jerry Lee Lewis (*Whole Lotta Shakin' Going On* and *Great Balls of Fire*, both from 1957) drew heavily from black music, creating a style known as *rockabilly*, featuring twelve-bar blues progression and boogie rhythms (in triplet patterns). At the same time, African-Americans like Chuck Berry (*Roll Over, Beethoven*, 1956; *Johnny B. Goode*, 1958), Fats Domino (*Blueberry Hill*, 1956), and Little Richard (*Tutti Frutti*, 1955–56; *Good Golly Miss Molly*, 1958) caught the attention of a white audience. The style of Little Richard clearly derived from gospel music, while Chuck Berry and Jerry Lee Lewis borrowed songs from the country-western repertory and played them with a rhythm-and-blues flair. The new sounds of rock and roll, belted out with a bluesy growl and always in a lively manner, revolutionized the music industry's concept of markets, appealing to wide audiences across racial lines.

Rock and roll

As hard driving rock and roll declined in popularity around 1960, a new generation of *teen idols* emerged with a gentler, more lyrical style, which drew

The irrepressible Chuck Berry, seen in three typical positions.

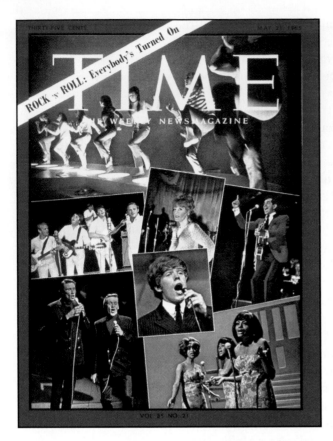

Cover of *Time* magazine (May 21, 1965), featuring rock and roll stars (top) the Shindig Dancers; (middle row) the Beach Boys, Petula Clark, Trini Lopez; (bottom row) the Righteous Brothers, Herman of Herman's Hermits, and the Supremes, with Diana Ross.

as much from Frank Sinatra as from Elvis Presley. The medium of radio furthered the crooning styles of white singers Bobby Darin (*Splish, Splash*, 1958), Neil Sedaka (*Calendar Girl*, 1960–61), and Paul Anka (*Puppy Love*, 1960). Meanwhile, black America was listening to the sound of *soul* and *Motown* (from Motortown, or Detroit—a fusion of gospel, pop, and rhythm and blues). Top recording artists included Diana Ross and the Supremes (*Where Did Our Love Go*, 1964), James Brown (*Papa's Got a Brand New Bag*, 1965), Martha Reeves and the Vandellas (*Dancing in the Street*, 1964), Smokey Robinson and the Miracles (*The Track of My Tears*, 1965; *I Second That Emotion*, 1967) and Aretha Franklin (*Respect*, 1967). Ray Charles (*I've Got a Woman*, 1965) is often considered to be the "father" of soul.

In the early 1960s, rock and roll was revitalized with the popularity of a new dance, the *twist*, and with the emergence of new groups, notably the Beach Boys in the United States and the Beatles, the Rolling Stones, and The Who in Britain. It was the Beatles who provided direction amid a variety of styles. In 1964, this group from Liverpool, England, took America by storm, performing at Carnegie Hall in New York, and on television's highly popular *Ed Sullivan Show*. In 1964, the Beatles starred in a hit movie (*A Hard Day's Night*) and held the top five spots on the *Billboard* chart with *Can't Buy Me Love, Twist and Shout, She Loves You, I Want to Hold Your Hand*, and *Please Please Me*. This foursome—Paul McCartney on electric bass, George Harrison on lead guitar, John Lennon on rhythm guitar and harmonica, and Ringo Starr on drums—featured a hard-driving beat and catchy melodies, with John, Paul, and George singing unison and two- and three-part vocals in a high range, almost a falsetto.

The Beatles' success story continued through the decade because they had the creativity to experiment with other types of music. In Paul McCartney's lyrical ballad *Yesterday* (1965), the Beatles moved from rock and roll to a sound that combined pop songwriting with a string quartet; and in the albums *Rubber Soul* (1965) and *Revolver* (1966), the group adopted a new style, with more expressive lyrics, complex harmonies, and sophisticated recording techniques. George Harrison took up the Indian sitar for the 1965 song *Norwegian Wood*, helping to spark a surge of interest in non-Western music in the pop marketplace. With these new sounds, the old rock and roll was gone, and the more **Rock** complex style known as *rock* emerged.

In 1966, tired of playing concerts that could not be heard over the din of screaming fans, the Beatles retired from the stage and devoted their energies to musical experimentation in the studio. *Hey Jude* (1968) was their biggest-selling single of all time; and the albums *Sgt. Pepper's Lonely Hearts Club Band* (1967) and *Abbey Road* (1969) were both stunning musical achievements that showcased their various songwriting abilities. Notable among the selections on these albums are John Lennon's *Lucy in the Sky with Diamonds*, Paul McCartney's *When I'm Sixty-Four*, and George Harrison's *Here Comes the Sun*. In 1970, the

442

group broke up, its members going on to establish successful solo careers. John Lennon was shot and killed in 1980, and George Harrison died of cancer in 2001, cutting short the creative lives of two of the group's members.

Many of the expressive features of rock were molded by California bands. The Beach Boys (*God Only Knows* and *Good Vibrations*, both 1966), led by Brian Wilson, introduced new harmonic and melodic possibilities to rock songwriting and raised the standard for studio production. Another important California group was the Byrds, whose music combined the folk style of protest singers Bob Dylan and Joan Baez with the new sounds of rock, thereby creating *folk rock.* Their first release was their biggest hit: *Mr. Tambourine Man* (1965), a rock setting of words and music by Bob Dylan. This was followed in the same year by *Turn, Turn, Turn*, a Pete Seeger song with lyrics from the biblical book of Ecclesiastes. Inspired by the success of this folk-rock hybrid, Bob Dylan introduced his own electric rock group at the 1966 Newport (Rhode Island) Folk Festival to the boos and catcalls of folk music purists. The fusion of folk protest songs with rock music proved to be a potent element in a growing political movement concerned with free speech, civil rights, and America's involvement in the Vietnam War (1957–75).

The Beach Boys

The Byrds

Folk rock

Meanwhile, the success of the Beatles in America had sparked a British invasion of rock groups—the Dave Clark Five (*Over and Over*, 1965), the Animals (*The House of the Rising Sun*, 1964), and especially the Rolling Stones (*I Can't Get No Satisfaction*, 1965). Drawing from the American blues style of Muddy Waters, the Stones became the "bad boys" of rock: their lyrics, most by Mick Jagger, and their public behavior condoned sexual freedom, drugs, and violence. Openly sexual innuendo (*Let's Spend the Night Together*) and tales of violence (*Gimme Shelter*) are subjects typical of their songs. Despite the negative image they acquired, more than any other group the Rolling Stones opened the

The British invasion

The Beatles (Paul, Ringo, John, George) on stage in November 1963.

path for several of the styles that would emerge the 1970s and 1980s: hard rock, punk rock, and heavy metal.

America's answer to this British invasion was *acid rock*—a style that focused on drugs, instrumental improvisations, and new sound technologies. The music represented a countercultural movement, with Utopian ideals, based in the Haight-Asbury district of San Francisco. The Jefferson Airplane (*White Rabbit*, 1967), featuring female lead singer Grace Slick, made no pretense about their psychedelic lyrics, and the Grateful Dead, with lead guitarist Jerry Garcia, performed lengthy instrumental improvisations enhanced by elaborate lighting and sound effects.

The Grateful Dead, with guitarist and pop culture idol Jerry Garcia, at RFK Stadium, in Washington, DC, in a 1993 concert.

Woodstock

The culminating event for rock music of the 1960s was the Woodstock Festival, held in upstate New York in August 1969, where over 300,000 music fans gathered for four days of "peace, love, and brotherhood." Important performances were given there by The Who (*My Generation*, with Peter Townshend's famous guitar-smashing routine), Joe Cocker (singing the Beatles' *With a Little Help from My Friends*), Sly and the Family Stone (*I Want to Take You Higher*), Country Joe and the Fish (with the antiwar song *Feel-Like-I'm-Fixin'-To-Die Rag*), Jimi Hendrix (remembered for his psychedelic rendition of *The Star-Spangled Banner*), Richie Havens (singing the spiritual *Motherless Child*), and a then unknown group named Santana (*Soul Sacrifice*), that went on to develop Latin rock. Other performers included the North Indian sitarist Ravi Shankar, raspy-voiced blues singer Janis Joplin, and folk singers Joan Baez and Arlo Guthrie. On the thirtieth anniversary of this festival a new generation of musicians played a concert dubbed Woodstock '99, which was, in stark contrast with the peacefulness of the original, marred by numerous episodes of crowd violence.

In 1970–71, the music world was shaken by the alcohol- and drug-related deaths of three superstars: the phenomenal blues guitarist Jimi Hendrix, the gravelly voiced Janis Joplin, and the lead singer of the Doors, Jim Morrison. Each was only twenty-seven years old. Acid rock seemed destined to become a short-lived style, but the Grateful Dead remained one of the world's top-grossing

The legendary guitarist/singer Jimi Hendrix at the Woodstock Festival (1969), flashing a peace sign to the audience.

concert acts until the death of Garcia in 1995. The British group Pink Floyd has also exhibited great longevity: their 1973 album *Dark Side of the Moon*, with its ageless themes of madness and death, remained on the Top 40 charts for a record 751 weeks. A later gem, the two-album set *The Wall* (1980), ensured their place in the annals of rock. Both Pink Floyd and the Grateful Dead helped to spawn a new generation of improvisational *jam bands* and psychedelic *trance music* in the 1990s.

Jam bands and trance music

The Eclecticism of the 1970s

Two eclectic styles of rock were developing in the early 1970s: *jazz rock* featuring traditional jazz-style instruments (trumpet, trombone, saxophone, and flute) playing long, improvised melodic lines; and *art rock*, which used large forms, complex harmonies, and occasional quotations from classical music. One of the most important jazz rock, or fusion, groups was Blood, Sweat, and Tears, whose 1969 album launched three hits—*You've Made Me So Very Happy, And When I Die*, and *Spinning Wheel*, the last of which epitomized the style with its complex chord progressions and improvised solos. The group Chicago (*Does Anybody Really Know What Time It Is?* 1971), which was more rock-oriented, was noted for its horn lines and vocal improvisations.

Jazz rock

Art rock

Art rock (sometimes called *progressive rock*) was largely a British style, pioneered by the Moody Blues with their 1968 album *Days of Future Passed*, recorded with the London Symphony Orchestra. The Who experimented with rock's narrative possibilities, and the result was the first rock opera, *Tommy*, written by Peter Townshend and premiered in 1969. Three years later, keyboardist Keith Emerson, together with Greg Lake and Carl Palmer, produced a major art rock work based on a well-known suite by the Russian composer Musorgsky—*Pictures at an Exhibition*. One American who experimented with art rock's large forms was Frank Zappa (1940–1993), leader of the Mothers of Invention. Zappa who counted the composers Bartók and Varèse among his influences, invited listeners to dissect his music: "These things are so carefully constructed that it breaks my heart when people don't dig into them and see all the levels that I put into them."

> When I'm onstage, I feel this incredible, almost spiritual experience . . . lost in a naturally induced high. Those great rock-'n'-roll experiences are getting harder and harder to come by, because they have to transcend a lot of drug-induced stupor. But when they occur, they are sacred.
> —PETER TOWNSHEND

Among the jazz-oriented rock bands that have remained popular is Santana, named after its leader/guitarist. The group started out as a California blues band to which Carlos Santana, the son of a Mexican mariachi musician, added Latin and African percussion instruments. The resulting style, called *Latin rock*, electrified the audience at Woodstock. Santana's unique sound came from their instrumentation—conga drums (of Afro-Cuban origin, played with bare hands), maracas (Latin-American rattles), and timbales (small kettledrums of Cuban origin)—their tight, Latin-style polyrhythms, and Carlos Santana's distinctive, and much-imitated, guitar tone. His band enjoyed international popularity in the early 1970s with hit songs such as *Evil Ways* (1969), *Black Magic Woman/ Gypsy Queen* and *Oyé Como Va* (both 1970). In 1999, with a new line-up of band members, Santana capitalized on the resurgence in popularity of Latin rock; his album *Supernatural* won the Grammys for Record of the Year, Album of the Year, and Song of the Year (*Smooth*, with Rob Thomas).

Latin rock

The 1970s and 1980s were characterized by a fragmentation of musical styles and a continual procession of new groups. Mainstream rock was represented by the groups America (*A Horse with No Name*, 1972), The Eagles (*Hotel*

Guitarist Carlos Santana, who has remained a popular Latin rock and jazz musician for some thirty years, performing in Mexico City, 1993.

California, 1972), and the Doobie Brothers (*Listen to the Music*, 1972), among others. The British once again invaded, this time with *heavy metal*, featuring simple, repetitive motives and loud, distorted instrumental solos. Led Zeppelin (*Stairway to Heaven*, 1971) and Black Sabbath (*Paranoid*, 1970) were the most important heavy metal bands of the 1970s. *Glitter rock* (also known as *glam rock*), a showy, theatrical style of performance, was represented by Britain's outrageous David Bowie (*The Rise and Fall of Ziggy Stardust and the Spiders from Mars*, 1972) and by America's Lou Reed (*Walk on the Wild Side*, 1972), formerly of the New York band the Velvet Underground. The outlandish costumes of glitter rock were quickly adopted by mainstream artists like the talented keyboardist Elton John (*Bennie and the Jets*, 1973).

The ultimate rebellion came in the form of *punk rock*, a return to the basics of rock and roll—simple, repetitive, and loud—coupled with offensive lyrics and shocking behavior. The Ramones (*Blitzkrieg Bop*, 1976), a group from New York with a street-tough attitude, was the first punk group to make an impact. After touring England in 1976, they inspired a great number of imitators, including the politically radical Sex Pistols (*Anarchy in the U.K.* and *God Save the Queen*, both from 1977), featuring lead singer Johnny Rotten. They were followed by other politically conscious groups like The Clash, who focused their music on the central issues of the punk rebellion: unemployment (*Career Opportunities*), violence (*Hate and War*), racism (*White Riot*), and police brutality (*Police and Thieves*). The

Cover last work is a *cover* (a recording that remakes an earlier recording by another singer or group) of a reggae hit.

Other reactions to the difficult times of the 1970s included the commercial

Disco and reggae dance music known as *disco*, and *reggae*. Fostered in gay dance clubs, disco was characterized by repetitive lyrics, often sung in a high range, and a thumping, mechanical beat, and is exemplified by acts such as the Bee Gees (*Stayin' Alive*, 1977). Reggae is a Jamaican style with offbeat rhythms and chanted vocals that reflected the beliefs of a Christian religious movement known as Rastafarianism. Representative reggae groups included Bob Marley and the Wailers (*Rastaman Vibrations*, 1977) and Black Uhuru. The style was especially popular in Britain, where Eric Clapton's cover of Bob Marley's *I Shot the Sheriff* (1974)

Soft rock met with great success. A new form of *soft rock*, yet another rejection of heavy metal and punk rock, was epitomized by artists such as the Carpenters (*We've Only Just Begun*, 1970) and Olivia Newton-John (*I Honestly Love You*, 1975), among others.

New wave *New wave*, a commercially accessible offshoot of punk rock, has been popular among British and American groups since the late 1970s, leading the way to a more melodic and danceable form of rock. In Britain, the new wave scene was set by Elvis Costello (backed up by the Attractions in *This Year's Model*, 1978) and The Police, with lead singer/bassist Sting (*Roxanne*, 1978; *Every Breath You Take*, 1986). The New York City scene developed around a number of clubs in lower Manhattan, most notably CBGB's (Country, Blue Grass, and Blues), where the group Blondie debuted in 1975. Featuring the attractive blond singer Deborah Harry, the group achieved commercial success with its album *Parallel Lines* (1978), and later turned to disco (*Heart of Glass*, 1980) and reggae styles (*The Tide Is High*, 1980). America's most influential new wave group was the Talking Heads who, like Blondie and the Ramones, played at CBGB's and whose lyrics (by songwriter-singer David Byrne) expressed the alienation and social consciousness of punk rock and whose style embraced various world musics.

The 1980s and Beyond

"Music allowed me to eat. But it also allowed me to express myself. I played because I had to play. I rid myself of bad dreams and rotten memories."

—PRINCE

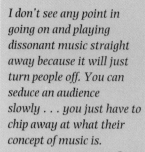

I don't see any point in going on and playing dissonant music straight away because it will just turn people off. You can seduce an audience slowly . . . you just have to chip away at what their concept of music is.

—STING

The single most important development in the 1980s was the music video. Now, instead of the radio, the visual medium (and especially MTV, or Music Television, which premiered in August 1981) was the principal means of presenting the latest music to the public. New and colorful performers like Duran Duran came on the scene, and an image- and fashion-conscious aesthetic soon dominated rock. One giant in the video arena was Michael Jackson, who had gained fame as lead singer of the Jackson Five (a group of brothers who carried on the Motown sound) and who then became a superstar in the 1980s. Jackson's album *Thriller* (1982–83) broke all previous sales figures; its hit songs included *The Girl Is Mine* (sung with Paul McCartney), *Billie Jean*, and *Beat It* (Jackson's version of the rumble scene from Bernstein's *West Side Story*). Jackson's fast dance style, together with his talent as a ballad singer, helps account for his worldwide popularity; his two-CD album *HIStory: Past, Present, and Future, Part 1*, topped the charts in 1995. Other superstars of the 1980s include Bruce Springsteen (*Born in the USA*, 1984), Prince (*Purple Rain*, 1984), and Madonna, who launched her first big hit with *Like a Virgin* (1984), which she followed with the eclectic album *True Blue* (1986). She has achieved great success, including a film career (*Evita*, 1996), based on her carefully developed image as a sex object.

Among the important groups in the late 1980s, two stand out. The Irish group U2 sounded a unified voice of political activism and personal spirituality in their collection *The Unforgettable Fire* (1984, see photo, p. 47). Following a series of concerts for Live Aid and Amnesty International, the group achieved stardom with the 1987 Grammy-winning album *The Joshua Tree*, which included two major hits: *With or Without You* and *I Still Haven't Found What I'm Looking For*. Los Angeles band Guns n' Roses, featuring outspoken lead singer Axl Rose and guitarist Slash, transcended their metal roots in *Appetite for Destruction* (1987) and *Use Your Illusion* (I and II, both from 1991), revealing an accessible style that is derivative of many of rock's greatest performers.

The technological developments of the late 1970s and early 1980s, including the use of synthesizers and stereo turntables that created

Music videos

The sultry and seductive blonde bombshell Madonna promoting her 1994 album *Bedtime Stories*.

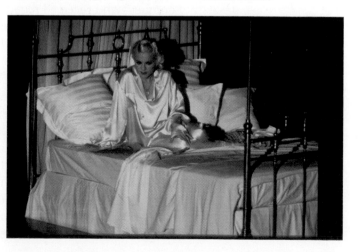

Hip-hop singers Run DMC with members of the Beastie Boys, at the Paramount Theater in 1987.

Rap

Gangsta rap

If you're really a rapper, you can't stop rapping. . . . The album [Return of the Real, 1996] is based around the words, not as much the music . . . it's based on the contexts and theories of life. . . . If you never get into the life, you wouldn't understand what I'm rapping about.

—ICE-T

collages of prerecorded sounds and rhythmic effects, paved the way for _rap_, a highly rhythmic style of musical patter that had been popular with New York audiences in the 1970s and later developed wider appeal. The group Run DMC (_Raising Hell_, 1986) was largely responsible for the commercialization of rap; their collaboration with Aerosmith on the cover recording of the 1977 hit song _Walk This Way_ introduced the style to white audiences. Public Enemy, a group from Long Island, New York, produced several highly influential rap albums (_It Takes a Nation of Millions to Hold Us Back_, 1988; _Apocalypse 91: The Enemy Strikes Black_, 1991), and female rapper Queen Latifah made a strong case against the genre's frequent female bashing in _All Hail the Queen_ (1989).

Rap (or _hip hop_) in its diversified forms has continued as one of the most popular types of African-American music and has been imitated by white performers such as the Beastie Boys and Eminem. _Gangsta rap_ of the 1990s has further disseminated the style through graphic descriptions of inner-city realities. Leaders in this style include N.W.A. (Niggas with Attitude)—whose 1991 album _Efil4zaggin_ ("Niggaz 4 Life" spelled backward) hit the top of the charts—and former N.W.A. member Dr. Dre (_The Chronic_, 1993) as well as his protégé Snoop Doggy Dogg (_Doggystyle_, 1993). The violent shooting deaths of two well-known gangsta rappers, Tupac Shakur in 1996 and Notorious B.I.G. in 1997, has highlighted the violence associated with this musical industry. B.I.G.'s last album, released after his murder, was appropriately titled _Life After Death_ (1997).

Gangsta rap is part of the much bigger hip-hop culture, the "urban alternative" rebellion of choice for many young people. The riveting rhythms of hip hop have transcended racial boundaries; its sounds, slang, and fashions are now commonly featured on prime-time television, in movies, and in advertising.

The more mellow sounds of soul and rhythm and blues also have a strong following today, especially the music of Whitney Houston (_I Will Always Love You_, from the movie _The Bodyguard_, 1992) and Mariah Carey (_Daydreams_, 1995), both of whom utilize a heavily melismatic singing style that has come to represent the new sound of R & B. One of the most important forces behind the success of these performers is songwriter/producer/artist Kenneth "Babyface" Edmonds, who received record numbers of Grammy nominations in 1997 and 1998, including recognition for the best collaboration (with Stevie Wonder, in _Gone Too Soon_, a cover of a Michael Jackson tune), for the album of the year (_The Day_, 1998), and for the best song in a motion picture (_A Song for Mama_, sung by Boyz II Men in _Soul Food_, 1997).

The late 1980s and early 1990s also saw the rise of a Seattle-based hybrid of punk and 1970s metal known as _grunge rock_ (so-called after the unkept appearance of the groups, in sharp contrast to the slick, theatrical costumes of hard rockers). Popular groups to come out of the grunge scene were Soundgarden, Nirvana, and Pearl Jam. Pearl Jam's _Ten_ and Nirvana's _Nevermind_ (both from 1991) were huge hits, attracting widely diverse audiences. In 1994, when Nirvana was at the height of its popularity, guitarist-songwriter Kurt Cobain committed suicide; his untimely death at twenty-seven—the same age that signaled the end for Jimi Hendrix, Janis Joplin, and Jim Morrison—promoted sales of their last album, *Unplugged in New York* (1994). Pearl Jam has maintained a strong following with its more recent releases—*Vitalogy* (1994), *Yield* (1998), and *Binaural* (2000).

Among the newer alternative bands who have captured the spotlight are the Smashing Pumpkins, whose 1995 album *Mellon Collie and the Infinite Sadness* exhibits a surprising breadth of styles. Another popular artist who draws from a wide range of sources is Beck (*Odelay*, 1996), who combined 1960s soul, 1930s country music, and even a bit of Schubert's *Unfinished* Symphony to create a fresh

Veteran rock star Neil Young performs with Pearl Jam in a benefit concert for pro-choice abortion rights.

and futuristic sound. Popular groups representing the British scene include Oasis (*Definitely Maybe*, 1994; *What's the Story/Morning Glory*, 1995), with well-crafted tunes by songwriter Noel Gallagher, and Radiohead (*Kid A*, 2000), which has been favorably compared with U2.

Women musicians have come a long way in recent years, as evinced by the success of singer/actresses such as Courtney Love (Kurt Cobain's widow, who had the hit album *Live through This*, 1994, with her band Hole), and the Icelandic singer Björk (*Post*, 1995), who won Best Actress honors at the Cannes Film Festival in 2000 for her role in the musical film *Dancer in the Dark*, for which she also composed the soundtrack. The 1990s also saw the first Canadian women to top the charts: Alanis Morissette (*Jagged Little Pill*, 1995), and Celine Dion, who won a 1996 Grammy for *Falling into You* and who sang the award-winning song *My Heart Will Go On* in the blockbuster movie *Titanic* (1997). As we enter the twenty-first century, we find successful women in all genres of popular music. Confessional piano-playing singers/songwriters, like Tori Amos (*Under the Pink*, 1994) and Fiona Apple (*When the Pawn. . . .* 1999) have garnered much critical praise for their complex compositions and introspective lyrics. Neo-folk singers like Jewel (*Pieces of You*, 1996) and Ani DiFranco (*Up Up Up Up Up Up*, 1999) have helped to redefine the role of the female acoustic guitar player in pop music. The country pop group the Dixie Chicks broke into the mainstream with their number one album *Fly* (2000). Even in the male-dominated world of rap, female artists like Missy "Misdemeanor" Elliot and Li'l Kim have claimed their share of the pop audience.

Recent years have seen a number of significant revivals as well. The Eagles regrouped for a tour (as well as a special performance at their induction into the Rock and Roll Hall of Fame) and for cutting the award-winning album *Hell Freezes Over* (1994); the Rolling Stones continue to make successful tours (including a new World Tour beginning September 2002) and the Beatles, without John Lennon (who was shot and killed in 1980), reconstructed an old demo to produce *Free as a Bird*, the opener to their chart-topping, three-volume album of studio outtakes, rarities, and remixes—*The Beatles Anthology* (1995). England's Elton John

Icelandic singer Björk caused a stir with her swan dress at the 2001 Academy Awards in Los Angeles.

has matured from his glitter rock days of the 1970s, writing memorable ballads for the soundtrack of Disney's delightful 1994 film *The Lion King* (*Can You Feel the Love Tonight?*) and for the Westminster Abbey funeral service of Diana, Princess of Wales (*Candle in the Wind*, 1997). American songwriter Bob Dylan has made a comeback as well, as a Kennedy Center honoree in the arts and compiler of a best-selling album, *Time out of Mind* (1997). The Dylan name promises to live on through his son, Jakob, guitarist with the group Wallflowers.

At the forefront of older musical styles that have been updated for twenty-first-century audiences is a punk-inspired ska, made popular by the southern California group No Doubt (*Return of Saturn*, 2000) with their charismatic lead singer Gwen Stefani. The late 1990s also saw a revival of *boy bands*, a combination of Motown formula that succeeded for groups like the Jackson Five and the ready-for-television image of pre-fab groups like the Monkees. Today's boy bands like N'Sync and the Backstreet Boys have been incredibly popular among hordes of screaming teenage fans.

This overview of rock has highlighted a mere handful of groups, those whose influence is difficult to challenge. Rock is unquestionably here to stay, but popularity in this genre is fleeting; only time will tell which current artists and styles will be remembered tomorrow.

Rock star Elton John performs in 1978 wearing an outlandish pink suit.

Country-Western Music

"When people hear that [country] music, they get a feeling that they belong to the music and the music belongs to them."

—COUSIN MINNIE PEARL

Hillbilly music

Singing cowboys

The music known today as *country-western* has its origins in the mountains of Appalachia. Although the songs of this region had been studied as folklore for some years, the recording industry did not discover this well-spring of traditional music until the 1920s. Labelled *hillbilly music*, these recordings became the Anglo-American counterpart to the "race records" that introduced the world to African-American blues. Two of the most important bands of this early genre were the Carter Family, known for their close harmonies and distinctive guitar style, and Jimmie Rodgers, who introduced the "blue yodel" and the steel guitar to popular music. Hollywood picked up on this rural sound and began producing movies featuring *singing cowboys* like Gene Autry (*Tumblin' Tumbleweeds*, 1936; see p. 403). Meanwhile, radio station WSM in Nashville, Tennessee, had begun broadcasting a weekly music showcase called *The Grand Ol' Opry*, which introduced many new acts to a national audience. One of the styles that debuted on the Grand Ol' Opry was *bluegrass*, featuring traditional folk melodies played at quick tempos with improvised instrumental solos and high vocal harmonies. Bluegrass was largely the invention of the Monroe brothers; they were followed by influential instrumentalists such as Lester Flatt (guitar) and Earl Scruggs (banjo). Typically, bluegrass was played by an acoustic string band made up of violin, mandolin, guitar, five-string banjo, and double bass, with some of the players also performing vocals. In recent years, the style has become commercial and "plugged in" (with electric instruments). The professionalism that radio performances brought to country music also resulted in a highly polished *Nashville sound*, with top-notch studio musicians backing singers like Patsy Cline (*Walkin' after Midnight*, 1957).

By the 1950s, this folk-derived music had been electrified, creating a sound called *honkytonk*, exemplified by Hank Williams (*Lovesick Blues*, 1949) and closely allied to early rock and roll. In fact, country star Johnny Cash (*I Walk the Line*, 1956) recorded at Sun Studios in Memphis, the same studio that gave the world Elvis Presley and Jerry Lee Lewis. By the end of the 1950s, country music was an established genre in its own right.

Over the next four decades, country music continued to grow and diversify. The 1960s and 1970s was a period of *classic country* music, with artists like Loretta Lynn (*Coal Miner's Daughter*, 1970) and Merle Haggard (*Mama Tried*, 1976; *Okie from Muskogee*, 1969) staying true to their roots in southern folk music. Other artists, like John Denver (*Country Roads*, 1971) and Glen Campbell (*Rhinestone Cowboy*, 1973), tried for a more *mainstream country* sound, and some, like the Allman Brothers (*Ramblin' Man*, 1971), experimented with the guitar-driven sounds of *country rock*. During the 1980s, the audience for country music increased even more, attracted to performers such as Dolly Parton (*9 to 5*, 1980) and Willie Nelson (*On the Road Again*, 1980), both of whom combined a traditional country sound with pop songwriting. Their success helped pave the way for the country music boom in the 1990s, featuring the very popular Garth Brooks (*No Fences*, 1990) and Shania Twain (*The Woman in Me*, 1995), among others. This genre, which began as humble folk music in the rural American South, is now a huge entertainment industry that is as popular in urban centers as in rural areas.

Country singer Shania Twain won the 1999 Entertainer of the Year award at the Country Music Awards in Nashville.

Global Pop

Today's most eclectic musical movement brings a new global perspective to the music listener. Not a single style, this movement promotes popular music of the third world, traditional music from all regions, and collaborations between Western and non-Western musicians. *Global pop* has been around for some time. In the 1950s, television fans heard Afro-Cuban music—including mambos and rhumbas—played by Desi Arnaz on the sitcom *I Love Lucy*, and enjoyed Harry Belafonte's vocal calypsos, a mixture of Jamaican and American styles. In the 1960s, the Brazilian bossa nova found favor (*The Girl from Ipanema*), and Ravi Shankar, along with the Beatles, brought Indian sitar music to the West. One style of global pop now enjoying widespread popularity is Cajun music.

BeauSoleil and the Revival of Cajun Music

"When I was growing up, the word Cajun was never used. People finally started to become a little more proud of their culture. Even if you weren't as educated as a Philadelphia lawyer, you had something to offer, to give—a way of life."

—MICHAEL DOUCET

Southwestern Louisiana developed its varied musical culture from two distinct groups—Creoles (people of mixed French, Spanish, and African or Afro-Caribbean

The International Sound

When you visit your nearest CD store and browse through the international or world section, you are likely to find an overwhelming selection from all corners of the earth—chants by Tibetan monks, Bolivian panpipe ensembles, Javanese gamelan orchestras, folk songs from Bosnia and Herzegovina, ceremonial drumming from Ghana, and Navajo dance music, to name only a few possibilities. It seems that America is as hungry for world music as it is for pizza and sushi.

Where did a listening audience with such international tastes come from? This global awakening began with the wars of the mid-twentieth century, in which thousands of Americans were transported to far-off places (South Pacific islands, Vietnam, Iraq), and the public at home was made increasingly aware of these locales through the media. Global communications brought us vivid, next-day images from Vietnam and, recently, live pictures from Afghanistan. Another factor was the raised sociopolitical consciousness of the 1960s and historical events such as Woodstock, where hundreds of thousands were moved by the performance of Indian sitarist Ravi Shankar playing a music to which they had had little prior exposure. The legendary sitarist has remained a force on the global scene for decades, continuing to popularize Indian classical music in the West through his many cross-cultural projects in film, dance, and theater. According to the late George Harrison, who studied with the north Indian musician, "Ravi Shankar is the godfather of world music" (see photo, p. 56).

Other artists have similarly "crossed-over" to create new sounds through a merger of musical styles. The popular Chinese-American cellist Yo-Yo Ma has won the hearts of many Americans with his series of Appalachian recordings (*Appalachian Waltz*, 1996; *Appalachian Journey*, 2000; and the recent compilation *Heartland: An Appalachian Anthology*, 2001) that emulate ancient Celtic fiddling, and with

The Gyütö monks from Tibet, famous for their extraordinary style of chanting Buddhist Tantras.

The eclectic style of songstress Cesaria Evora, from the island nation of Cape Verde, combines elements from traditional musics of West Africa, Portugal, and Brazil.

his Silk Road Project, which celebrates musical traditions of the Far East. "Throughout my travels," he explains, "I have thought about the culture, religions, and ideas that have been influential for centuries along the historical land and sea routes that compile the Silk Road, and have wondered how these complex interconnections occurred and how new musical voices were formed from the diversity of these traditions." Yo-Yo Ma has teamed up with many musicians, including composer Tan Dun (in the soundtrack for the film *Crouching Tiger, Hidden Dragon*, see p. 493) and the incomparable Béla Fleck (of the Flecktones; see photo, p. 48), who has applied his lightning-fast, finger-picking style to nearly every style of music, from bluegrass to jazz, fusion, world, and classical. His recent compilation *Live at the Quick* (2002) reflects this diversity, exploring African vocals and polyrhythmic drumming, the multiphonics of Tuvan throat singing, as well as a Bach solo violin partita played on the banjo. Recording companies are responding to increased consumer demand for world and traditional musics, producing all kinds of specialty collections as well as samplers for those who want a varied multicultural listening experience.

Does a recording of modern world or traditional music capture the essence of a culture's tradition? There are a number of historical field recordings by anthropologists and ethnomusicologists that carefully preserve traditional musics and ceremonies as they existed at the time of the recording. (We will study one such recording from the Republic of Uganda in a later chapter.) You can probably find some of these collections in your college or university library (the Nonesuch Explorer series and Folkways recordings are fairly standard). But music is a living art. Thus, despite efforts to preserve "authentic" musics of certain cultures, what we hear today is often a fusion of styles—traditional, art, and pop—from around the world. Some musicians reflect the strong impact of Western rock—the Algerian singer Khaled, for example—while others, such as the South African group Ladysmith Black Mambazo and the Cajun ensemble BeauSoleil, cultivate more indigenous sounds, setting them in a contemporary idiom for today's avid listeners.

SUGGESTED LISTENING:

South African music (Ladysmith Black Mambazo)
Irish music (The Chieftains)
Tibetan music (Gyütö monks)
Algerian music (Khaled) or Senegalese music (Youssou N' Dour)
Cape Verde music (Cesaria Evora) ♪
North Indian music (Ravi Shankar) ♪
Appalachian music (Yo-Yo Ma) or *Crouching Tiger, Hidden Dragon* soundtrack (Tan Dun with Yo-Yo Ma)
Cajun music (BeauSoleil)
Béla Fleck, *Live at the Quick*

Fiddle player Michael Doucet in a performance with the Cajun band BeauSoleil.

descent) and Cajuns (French colonists who settled in the Canadian maritime province of Nova Scotia, until they were exiled by the British; the word "Cajun" derives from Acadia, the former name of the Canadian region). These peoples shared French as a common language, and their musics evolved side by side. The earliest Cajun music was vocal—usually drinking songs and ballads about exile and separation from families and loved ones. Cajuns absorbed the music of southern whites and blacks into their sound and the fiddle, which often accompanied itself with a drone, became a central feature in their music. The guitar, a Spanish influence, and the accordion, introduced by German Jewish exiles, also contributed to the unique sound. While commercial Cajun bands dropped the accordion in favor of a more country-western sound, the instrument became the core of the Creole *zydeco* band. (The word *zydeco* is a phonetic spelling of *les haricots*, French for green beans.) This style arose in midcentury as a blend of African-American, Caribbean, and Cajun styles; the typical zydeco ensemble uses voice, fiddle, accordion, electric guitar, and washboard. Although some purists have tried to keep the two styles—Cajun and Creole—distinct, new generations of musicians have bridged the gap.

Both Cajun and zydeco music enjoyed widespread popularity during the late twentieth century. The Cajun group BeauSoleil and its leader Michael Doucet have been a strong force in the revival of this traditional music. In 1984, Beau-Soleil recorded the landmark album *Parlez nous à boire (Let's Talk about Drinking)*, which launched them to international fame. Since then, the group has played at New York's Carnegie Hall, been highlighted on Garrison Keillor's popular radio show *Prairie Home Companion*, been nominated for several Grammy awards, and was featured in the soundtrack for the film *The Big Easy* (1987).

Think of Me (Jongle à moi), is a traditional dance song first recorded in the 1930s by the Cajun fiddler Jean-Baptiste Fuselier. BeauSoleil's performance features violin, accordion, and vocals, accompanied by guitar, drums, bass, and

> *I won't play a song until I know every note and every word. Yes sir! Like that you can defend yourself, you don't stumble. You don't sing off time, either. . . . Like reading, you can hit each word right on the drummer's timing. Each time he'll hit, your word will fall right in line. That's music!*
>
> —ROY FUSILIER

🎧 **Listening Guide 46** 💿 CD: CHR/STD 8/70–73, SH 4/59–62

Think of Me (Jongle à moi), by BeauSoleil (3:14)

FORM:	Tune built on 8-bar phrases (verse and bridge); alternation of vocal and instrumental verse
METER:	4/4
TEXTURE:	Heterophonic
BASIS:	Traditional Cajun fiddle tune, recorded in 1930s, by J. B. Fuselier
INSTRUMENTS:	Fiddle, guitar, accordion, washboard, drums, bass, vocals

WHAT TO LISTEN FOR: Rousing dance tune, with syncopated rhythms and wide-ranging
instrumental lines.
Typical Cajun fiddle (violin) techniques (drones, double-stops, slides, and trills).
Unique timbre of accordion, blending with fiddle and guitar.
Instrumental and vocal embellishments of tune.
Text sung in Cajun French, with interjections (*yé yaillé*).
Regular structure, with 8-meausre phrases, repeated and varied;
a bridge (or *turn*) alternates with main tune.

59   0:00   Fiddle, with lively tune (8 bars), then varied (8 bars),
accompanied by ensemble (accordion, guitar, and rhythm);
opening 4 bars shown, with repeated notes and syncopations:

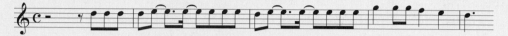

0:20   Accordion with syncopated tune (8 bars, varied from violin),
then repeated (8 bars), accompanied by fiddle and ensemble; opening 4 bars:

60   0:39   Verse 1 (8+8 bars), with rhythm accompaniment; opening verse:

O mais,   o   o   o   yé   yail · le,   Quoi   faire   t'es   comme   ça?____

TEXT

O mais, o, yé yaille,
Quoi faire t'es comme ca?
Jongle á moi, catin, bébé,
O, une fois par jour.
Yé, yé, yé, bébé,
Tu connais que moi je t'appelais
Tous les samedis soir, catin,
Jongle á moi pendant la journée.

TRANSLATION

Oh, but oh, yé yaille,
Why are you like that?
Think of me, darling baby,
At least once a day.
Yé, yé, yé, bébé,
You know that I called for you
Every Saturday night, darling,
Think of me during the day.

0:59   Fiddle, with double-stops in rhythmic idea; guitar playing running
bass line (8+8 bars).

61   1:17   Break in music, then bridge (turn) played twice (8+8 bars);
begins in high range in fiddle, then descends and becomes disjunct;
second time accompanied by cymbals; opening of bridge:

1:37   Fiddle, with tune and variation (8+8 bars).

1:56   Break in music; fiddle, with bridge; repeated with slides between notes in fiddle.

62   2:15   Verse 2, slightly varied from verse 1;
with rhythmic accompaniment; opening of verse 2:

O___ O O, yé yail - le,_____ Quoi faire t'es comme ça?_____

TEXT	TRANSLATION
O mais, o, yé yaille,	Oh, but oh yé yaille,
Quoi faire t'es comme ca?	Why are you like that?
Jongle á moi, catin, bébé,	Think of me, darling baby,
O, une fois par jour.	At least once a day.
Yé, yé, yé, bébé,	Yé, yé, yé, baby,
Tu connais que moi je t'aimais	You know that I love you
Jongle á moi, catin, bébé,	Think of me, darling baby,
Jongle á moi pendant la journées.	Every night and every day.

2:34   Fiddle, with bridge in double-stops, sliding between notes
repeated in high range, with scoops into notes (8+8 bars).

2:53   Break filled-in by guitar, leading to fiddle, with bridge;
played twice, with slides, scoops, and trills.

washboard. The tune spins out in eight-bar phrases followed by a turn, or bridge, of another eight bars. The fiddle and accordion vie throughout for the tune. You can hear some typical Cajun fiddle techniques, including _drones_ (playing a sustained tone on one string and the tune on another), _double-stops_ (playing two strings at once to produce a chord), _slides_ (moving from one pitch to another by sliding the finger on the string while bowing), and _trills_ (creating an ornament by quickly alternating between the main note and one directly above or below it). This is a toe-tapping dance music, quick-paced and rhythmic, with a highly syncopated melody that immediately draws in the listener. The texture is at times heterophonic, with various instruments elaborating on the bouncy tune. The text, in Cajun French (based on the northern French dialect spoken by the original Canadian settlers), has interjections that cannot be translated into English (for example, _yé yaille_; see Listening Guide 46).

Fiddle techniques

Ladysmith Black Mambazo and Music of South Africa

A famous and successful collaboration of differing musical cultures resulted in Paul Simon's album _Graceland_ (1986), which featured various styles of South African music. Simon was especially attracted to a style known as "township jive," the street music of Soweto, and to the musicality of South Africa's popular _a cappella_ vocal group Ladysmith Black Mambazo. The album was politically controversial in the United States, since it violated commercial sanctions against South Africa's apartheid policy; in the end, however, it did much to fur-

Graceland

Joseph Shabalala, founder and leader of the popular South African vocal group Ladysmith Black Mambazo.

in his own words

We sing as free South Africans all over the world now, and this helps develop our pride. . . . We are trying to establish a school to teach children the traditions of their indigenous culture. . . . We must not let our children forget our heritage.
—JOSEPH SHABALALA

ther the cause of the black population there. Simon called on musicians from around the world, including the popular Senegalese singer Youssou N'Dour. The album also introduced the American public to Ladysmith Black Mambazo, which won the Grammy Award for the best traditional folk recording of 1988.

The South African choral singing heard on *Graceland* exemplifies a traditional style developed by Zulu migrant workers first introduced to the Western world in the early 1950s by the folk group the Weavers in *Wimoweh* (better-known in 1961 as *The Lion Sleeps Tonight* by the Tokens), and now familiar to many through the recordings of Ladysmith Black Mambazo. Originally sung in labor camps to alleviate loneliness, this singing style became linked to protest against apartheid. The music features the call-and-response pattern typical of many African cultures, with the *a cappella* choral responses set in rich, close-knit harmonies sung in medium to slow tempos. Irregular phrasing and syncopated rhythms enliven the musical movement, and special effects such as trilled vocal glides and blues-style interjections are typical.

Ladysmith Black Mambazo has long been a voice for peace and freedom in South Africa. Their antiracist song *Kangivumanga (I Disagreed)* examplifies the group's polished style of singing as well as the urbanization of traditional choral music.

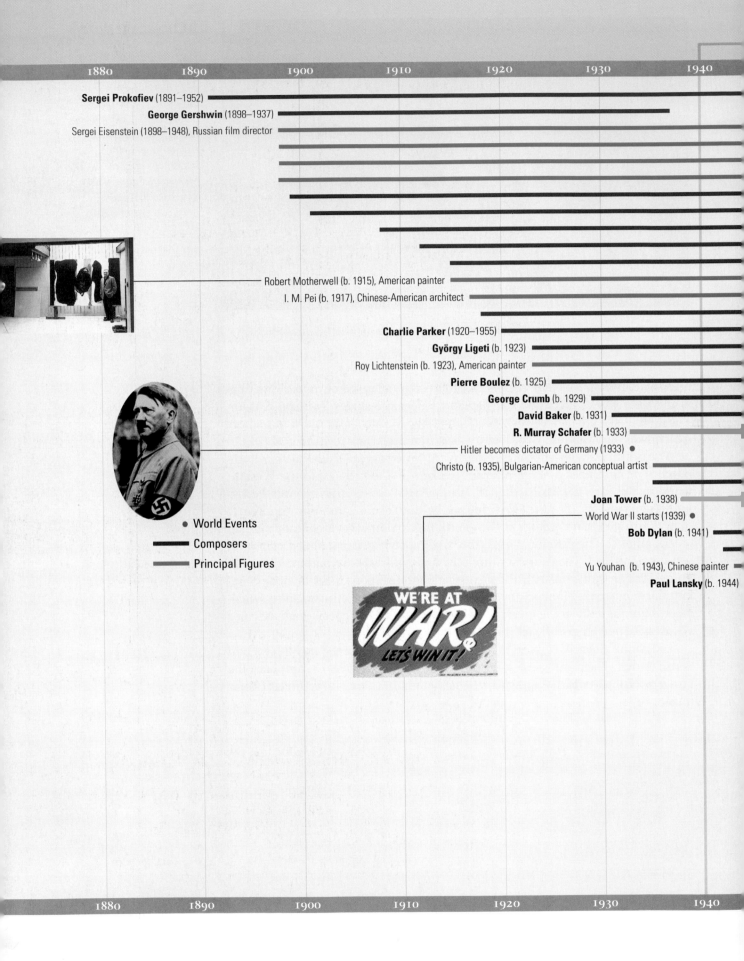

Sergei Prokofiev (1891–1952)

George Gershwin (1898–1937)

Sergei Eisenstein (1898–1948), Russian film director

Robert Motherwell (b. 1915), American painter

I. M. Pei (b. 1917), Chinese-American architect

Charlie Parker (1920–1955)

György Ligeti (b. 1923)

Roy Lichtenstein (b. 1923), American painter

Pierre Boulez (b. 1925)

George Crumb (b. 1929)

David Baker (b. 1931)

R. Murray Schafer (b. 1933)

Hitler becomes dictator of Germany (1933) ●

Christo (b. 1935), Bulgarian-American conceptual artist

Joan Tower (b. 1938)

World War II starts (1939) ●

Bob Dylan (b. 1941)

Yu Youhan (b. 1943), Chinese painter

Paul Lansky (b. 1944)

● World Events

━━ Composers

━━ Principal Figures

WE'RE AT WAR! LET'S WIN IT!

Late Twentieth Century (1940–)

1950	1960	1970	1980	1990	2000	2010

Ernest Hemingway (1898–1961), American novelist

Alexander Calder (1898–1976), American artist

Henry Moore (1898–1986), English sculptor

E. K. ("Duke") Ellington (1899–1974)

Louis Armstrong (1901–1971)

Olivier Messiaen (1908–1991)

John Cage (1912–1992)

Billie Holiday (1915–1959)

Leonard Bernstein (1918–1990)

Elvis Presley (1935–1977)

Jimi Hendrix (1942–1970)

Laurie Anderson (b. 1947), American performance artist

John Adams (b. 1947)

Bruce Springsteen (b. 1949)

Tan Dun (b. 1957)

Michael Jackson (b. 1958)

Madonna (b. 1958)

The Beatles (1960–70)

● Richard Nixon elected U.S. president (1968)

● Woodstock Festival (1969)

● First home computers (1974)

Lauryn Hill (b. 1975)

● First AIDS case reported (1981)

Nirvana (1987–94)

● Soviet Union dissolved (1991)

First free elections in South Africa (1994) ●

Princess Diana (d. 1997) ●

Terrorist attack on World Trade Center, New York (9/11/2001) ●

e Learning

unit **XXV**

The New Music

71

New Directions

"From Schoenberg I learned that tradition is a home we must love and forgo."

—LUKAS FOSS

KEY POINTS:

■ Musical trends in the second half of the twentieth century mirrored movements in the arts, including *Abstract Expressionism, Pop Art*, and *Post-Modernism*.

■ Feminist as well as ethnic art and literature flourished in the later twentieth century.

■ Modern theater and music have merged in *performance art*, a multimedia genre explored by John Cage and Laurie Anderson, among others.

■ National schools of filmmaking have developed in recent years (especially in Germany, China, and Poland).

■ Some composers moved in the direction of *total serialism*, imposing a more structured organizational system on their works, while others moved toward freer constructions (*aleatoric music, open form*).

■ European and American composers alike responded to societal changes that occurred after World War II to produce experimental, or avant-garde, music in widely varied styles and genres.

■ Canadian musicians have been leaders on the contemporary music scene, their works widely promoted by the national Canadian Music Centre (CP 22).

■ Contemporary music often calls for new and highly virtuosic instrumental or vocal effects; certain singers and instrumentalists have specialized in performing avant-garde music.

The term "new music" has been used throughout history. Nearly every generation of creative musicians produced sounds and styles that had never been heard before. All the same, the innovations of the last half of the twentieth century have outstripped the most far-reaching changes of earlier times, truly justifying the label "new music." In effect, we have witnessed nothing less than the birth of a new world of sound.

The Arts since the Mid-Twentieth Century

The increasing social turmoil since the Second World War has inevitably been reflected in the arts, which passed through a period of violent experimentation with new media, new materials, and new techniques. Artists have freed themselves from every vestige of the past in order to explore new areas of thought and feeling.

Sculptor Henry Moore's *Large Reclining Connected Forms* is an abstraction of the mother and child concept, with the fluid and supple outer form representing the female body and the contrasting interior structure an incomplete, or still emerging, form.

A trend away from objective painting led to Abstract Expressionism in the United States during the 1950s and 1960s. In the canvases of painters such as Robert Motherwell and Jackson Pollock, space, mass, and color were freed from the need to imitate objects in the real world. The urge toward abstraction was felt equally in sculpture, as is evident in the work of artists such as Henry Moore and Isamu Noguchi.

At the same time, a new kind of realism appeared in the art of Jasper Johns, Robert Rauschenberg, and their colleagues. This trend culminated in Pop Art, which drew its themes and techniques from modern urban life: machines, advertisements, comic strips, movies, commercial photography, and familiar objects connected with everyday living. A similar aim motivated artists such as Andy Warhol, Jim Dine, and Roy Lichtenstein (see p. 462).

Pop Art

Today, the term "Post-Modernism"—suggesting a movement away from formalism—is applied to a variety of styles, including conceptual art,

In Abstract Expressionism, space and mass become independent values, liberated from the need to express reality. *Elegy to the Spanish Republic No. 18*, by Robert Motherwell (1915–1991). (Museum of Modern Art, New York; © Dedalus Foundation/licensed by VAGA, New York)

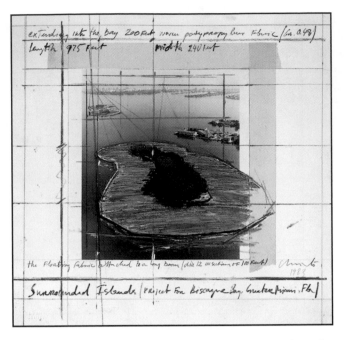

Surrounded Islands, Project for Biscayne Bay, Greater Miani, Florida, by conceptual artist Christo, was realized for two weeks in 1983.

Feminist artist Judy Chicago's *Holocaust Project Logo* (stained glass, 1992). In this exhibit, the Holocaust provides a point from which to explore issues relating to the human condition.

minimalism, and environmental art. A familiar Neoclassical structure of the Post-Modern era is I. M. Pei's *Grand Louvre Pyramid*, in Paris (see p. 464). Environmental art, sometimes called earthworks, is one manifestation of the minimalist movement, which advocates a bareness and simplicity (we will read about minimalism in music in Chapter 75). Bulgarian-born artist Christo has chosen to wrap up nature, thus drawing attention to form through concealment. One of his largest projects was *Surrrounded Islands* (1983), in Biscayne Bay, Florida, where he used six-and-a-half million feet of pink fabric floating on the water to wrap the islands (see illustration to the left).

The feminist movement has affected mainstream developments in the art world since the late 1960s by focusing attention on a lesser-known body of works and artists and on issues of gender. The collaborative projects led by Judy Chicago have contributed much to this movement: an example is the celebrated artwork *The Dinner Party* (1979), a triangular table with thirty-nine place settings, which pays homage to important women throughout history. Recently, serious attention has also been paid to global crosscurrents in the arts as well as to the artistic achievements of America's diverse ethnic communities, especially the African-American, Latino, and Native American. The African-American artist Faith Ringgold has addressed political and social issues of racial and gender bias in her rich quilts, which combine storytelling and quilt making with the "higher" art of painting (see illustration opposite). According to Ringgold, several of her quilt series examine "the complicated interrelations of black and white people struggling with injustice, inequality, oppression, and fear." The AIDS epidemic of recent decades has inspired a monumental example of public art—the AIDS Memorial Quilt, an ongoing community project intended to commemorate the many thousands who have died and to raise public awareness of this crisis. (The 79,000 names on the quilt's 45,000 panels represent only a small fraction of the victims worldwide.) The Canadian AIDS Quilt is currently developing an online memorial. This is an electronic respository of graphics, images, and words that preserves in some seventy panels the memories of loved ones lost to HIV and AIDS.

A national art of *perestroika* (openness) has arisen in countries of the former Soviet Union. This new avant-garde style is essentially a deconstruction of the "official" Soviet art. A nationalist style has developed in China as well; the canvases of Yu Youhan, for example, combine elements of pop art and the ancient Chinese art of block printing. In *Mao and Blonde Girl Analyzed* (1992; p. 462), the blonde girl, symbolic of involuntary Westernization, is juxtaposed with a portrait of the Chinese leader.

In the field of literature, poetry has lent itself to the most widespread experimentation. Many poets face the contemporary world with a profound sense of alienation. Modern American verse ranges from complex intellectualism to the Whitmanesque exuberance of the "beat generation," with a great variety of forms. In recent years, the poetry and literature of various cultural groups has received widespread attention. Among these, African-American poet Maya Angelou, American Yiddish writer Isaac Bashevis Singer, West Indian Derek Walcott, Chinese dissident playwright Gao Xingjian, and Trinidad-born British writer V. S. Naipaul have been awarded Nobel Prizes in literature.

In *Tar Beach 2*, from the colorful quilt series *Women on a Bridge*, African-American artist Faith Ringgold depicts a child's magical fantasy of flying over the George Washington Bridge.

Since drama and the novel are by their very nature based on an imitation of life, they have not remained indifferent to the new trends. The theater moved away from the social and psychological concerns that permeated the plays of Arthur Miller (such as *The Crucible*, 1953) and Tennessee Williams (*Cat on a Hot Tin Roof*, 1955) in the 1950s, turning instead to the "theater of the absurd," whose leading European proponents—Samuel Beckett (*Waiting for Godot*, 1956) and Eugene Ionesco (*Rhinoceros*, 1960)—viewed the world with a vast disillusionment. The spirit of the absurd also penetrated the novel; witness such works as *Catch 22* (1961), by Joseph Heller, and *Slaughterhouse Five* (1969), by Kurt Vonnegut, to name only two that caught the pulse of the 1960s.

Recent writers

More recent writers who have captured the attention of the literary world include British dramatist Tom Stoppard (*Rosencrantz and Guildenstern Are Dead*, 1967, based on two minor characters from Shakespeare's *Hamlet*), American playwright/screenwriter/actor Sam Shepard (*Buried Child*, 1978; *A Fool for Love*, 1983), and New York playwright Wendy Wasserstein (*The Heidi Chronicles*, 1989; *The Sisters Rosensweig*, 1993). Among the distinguished novelists of our time are Nobel laureates Saul Bellow (*Humboldt's Gift*, 1976) and Toni Morrison (*Beloved*, 1987) as well as Pulitzer Prize winners John Updike (*The Centaur*, 1963; the *Rabbit* tetralogy, 1960–91), Jane Smiley (*A Thousand Acres*, 1992), E. Annie Proulx (*The Shipping News*, 1994, of which a movie version was recently released), and Richard Russo (*Empire Falls*, 2002) to name only a few. Latin-American writers who have risen to prominence include Gabriel García Márquez, who has produced some of the great novels of our age (*One Hundred Years of Solitude*, 1967; *Love in the Time of Cholera*, 1985). Some modern writers have received attention for their uncensored portrayals of society. Tom Wolfe, a leading figure in the 1960s in literary experiments that came to be known as New Journalism, has kept his finger on the pulse of America with *The Bonfire of the Vanities* (1984–85), and Salman Rushdie's novel *The Satanic Verses* (1988), condemned by the Muslim world, has been widely recognized for its blunt attack on religious bigotry. Recently, the delightful *Harry Potter* children's series, by J. K. Rowling, has caused controversy among conservative religious groups, who claim the fantasies endorse witchcraft and wizardry.

Performance art

Linked to developments in modern theater is performance art, which combines visual stimuli with theater and music. The term "happening" was coined

Roy Lichtenstein (1923–1997) fully embraced popular mass culture in his enlarged comic strips such as *Whaam!* (1963). Acrylic on canvas. (Tate Gallery, London)

in the 1960s to describe this semi-improvised multimedia event, which was often highly dependent on audience participation. The experimental composer John Cage was intrigued by this art form (see p. 472), as is Laurie Anderson, who uses a combination of popular music, storytelling, comic routines, and high-tech equipment to address social issues.

Several trends have changed the way we look at literature. For example, deconstruction, developed in the early 1970s, is based on the concept that any text can be understood to say something quite different from what it first appears to mean; a deconstructive interpretation focuses only on the text itself, without concern for external influences, such as its context. Feminine criticism, popular since the late 1960s, questions long-standing male interpretations of texts and attempts to describe experience as depicted in literature from the female point of view. (On feminism and music, see CP 13.)

Finally, film—of all the arts the one most securely chained to popular story-telling—has also responded to the twin impulses of experimentation and ab-

In *Mao and Blonde Girl Analyzed* (1992), **Yu Youhan** (b. 1943) combines elements of Chinese peasant paintings and pop art with Socialist Realism. Acrylic on canvas.

A hyperkinetic scene of urban life, from Godfrey Reggio's spellbinding film *Koyaanisqatsi* (1983), for which Philip Glass wrote the minimalist musical score.

straction. "New wave" directors include Jean-Luc Godard (*Breathless*, 1959), Federico Fellini (*La Strada*, 1959; *8½*, 1963), Michelangelo Antonioni (*Blowup*, 1966; *The Passenger*, 1975), and Louis Malle (*My Dinner with André*, 1981; *Au revoir, les enfants*, 1987). In films like Alain Resnais's *Last Year at Marienbad* (1962) and Ingmar Bergman's *Persona* (1966), the Abstract Expressionist urge was realized on the screen.

A number of national cinemas have come into their own in the past several decades. In the 1970s, German filmmakers, among them Rainer Werner Fassbinder (*The Marriage of Maria Braun*, 1978), were world leaders in the genre. Japanese and Chinese films have also received critical attention, especially those of China's Zhang Yimou (*Raise the Red Lantern*, 1991; *The Story of Qiu Ju*, 1992), which depict tragedies suffered under the Communists. Polish filmmaker Krzysztof Kieślowski has also presented poignant views of his native country throwing off Communist rule (*Three Colors* trilogy: *Blue*, 1993; *White*, 1994; *Red*, 1994). The genre of nonnarrative film is best exemplified by American Godfrey Reggio (*Koyaanisqatsi*, 1983; *Powaqqatsi*, 1988), whose visual collages soar against the minimalist music of Philip Glass (see illustration above). Such "art films" have given us profound insights into the lives of people all over the world. We will explore the long-term marriage of film and music in popular and art cultures in Chapter 73.

The artworks mentioned above are only a few landmarks in the second half of the twentieth century, but they are enough to indicate that all the arts have become increasingly intellectual, experimental, and abstract.

Toward Greater Organization in Music

When Schoenberg based his twelve-tone method on the use of tone rows, he was obviously moving toward a much stricter organization of sound material. It

One of the things a cartoon does is to express violent emotion and passion in a completely mechanical and removed style. To express this thing in a painterly style would dilute it; the techniques I use are not commercial, they only appear to be commercial— and the ways of seeing and composing and unifying are different and have different ends.

—ROY LICHTENSTEIN

The *Grand Louvre Pyramid*, at the entrance to the expansion of the Louvre, provides a Neoclassical skylight for viewing Paris's historic museum. It was designed by the Chinese-American architect **I. M. Pei** (b. 1917).

remained for later generations to extend the tone-row principle to the elements of music other than pitch—such as durations (time values), dynamic values (degrees of loudness), or timbres. Registers and densities, types of attack, and sizes of intervals might also be organized serially. By thus extending the serial principle in all possible directions, a composer could achieve a totally organized fabric. This move toward *total serialism* resulted in an extremely complex, ultra-rational music. The composers who embraced the idea, such as Pierre Boulez and Karlheinz Stockhausen, pushed the experience of listening to music to unprecedented limits.

Total serialism

Toward Greater Freedom in Music

"My music liberates because I give people the chance to change their minds in the way I've changed mine."

—JOHN CAGE

The urge toward a totally controlled music had its counterpart in the desire for greater, even total, freedom from all predetermined forms and procedures. Music of this type emphasizes the antirational element in artistic experience: intuition, chance, the spur of the moment. Composers who wish to avoid the rational ordering of musical sound may rely on the element of chance and allow, for example, a throw of dice to determine rhythm and melody, or perhaps build their pieces around a series of random numbers generated by a computer. They may let the performer choose the order in which the sections are to be played, or indicate the general range of pitches, durations, and registers but leave it up to the performer to fill in the details. The performance thus becomes a musical "happening" in the course of which the piece is re-created afresh each time it is played.

Such indeterminate music is known as *aleatoric* (from *alea*, the Latin word for "dice"). In aleatoric music, the overall form may be clearly indicated, but the

As these two forms—human and machine—begin to merge a little bit, we're talking about technology really as a kind of new nature, something to measure against, to make rules from, to investigate.

—LAURIE ANDERSON

464

details are left to choice or chance. On the other hand, some composers, among them John Cage, will indicate the details of a composition clearly enough but leave its overall shape to choice or chance; this type of flexible structure is known as *open form*. Related to these tendencies is the increased reliance on improvisation—a technique common in music of the Baroque and earlier eras and, of course, in jazz. Traditionally, improvisation consists of spontaneous invention within a known framework and a style, so that player and listener have fairly well defined ideas of what is "good" and what is "bad." In the more extreme types of aleatory music, no such criteria are set; anything that happens is acceptable to the composer.

Contemporary attitudes have liberated not only forms but all the elements of music from the restrictions of the past. The idea that music must be based on the twelve pitches of the chromatic scale has been left far behind. Electronic instruments make possible the use of sounds that lie "in the cracks of the piano keys"—the *microtonal* intervals, such as quarter tones, that are smaller than semitones—and very skilled instrumentalists and vocalists have now mastered these novel scales, borrowed from various world musics.

Red Petals (1942), a mobile by Alexander Calder, can be compared to open form through the various leaf shapes that move freely in the air.

The Postwar Internationalism

The Second World War and the events leading up to it disrupted musical life in Europe much more than in North America, with the result that the United States forged ahead in certain areas. The first composer to apply serial organization to dimensions other than pitch was the American Milton Babbitt, and the experiments of John Cage anticipated and influenced similar attempts abroad. Earle Brown (1926–2002) was the first to use open form; Morton Feldman (1926–1987) was the first to write works that gave performers a choice. Once the war was over, the Europeans made up for lost time. Intense experimentation went on in Italy, Germany, France, England, the Netherlands, and Scandinavia. Serial and electronic music also took root in Japan, while the music of the East has in turn influenced Western composers.

A number of Europeans have achieved international reputations. The French composer Olivier Messiaen (1908–1992), a mystic and a visionary, steadfastly maintained that art is the ideal expression of religious faith. One powerful work inspired by religious mysticism is his *Quartet for the End of Time* (1941), written while he was held in a German prisoner-of-war camp and first performed in front of five thousand other prisoners at Stalag VIIA. Messiaen was drawn to nature and bird songs, in which he found an inexhaustible source of melody, and also to the free-flowing lines of Gregorian chant and the delicate bell sounds of the Javanese gamelan. These strands are woven into the colorful tapestry of his *Turangalîla-Symphony* (1948), a monumental orchestral work in ten movements.

Luciano Berio (b. 1925) is a leading figure among the radicals of the post-Webern generation in Italy. He was one of the founders of the electronic studio in Milan, which became a center of avant-garde activity, and for several years taught composition

Performance artist Laurie Anderson on tour, singing and playing electric violin for her album *Life on a String* (2001).

Canada's Vision for a Global Culture

A huge, multi-ethnic country, Canada has established a national arts identity despite its linguistic and cultural divisions and its relative youth as a nation (it achieved independence in 1867). Thus while the traditional musics of Canada are widely varied—representing the French, British, Native American, and Inuit (Eskimo) cultures—its modern art music has presented a more unified and mainstream front.

Canadian composers are notable for their interest in avant-garde techniques. With the advent of electronic music in the 1950s, Canada was quick to respond with studios around the country—in Ottawa, Toronto, Montreal, and Vancouver. Composer John Weinzweig (b. 1913) first championed twelve-tone technique in Canada; he, along with Jean Papineau-Couture of the French-Canadian community, actively sought support for new music through an organization they headed, the Canadian League of Composers. The country also boasts one of the best music information centers in the world, devoted exclusively to the promotion and dissemination of music by Canadians (see the Canadian Music Centre site on the Internet). Another important music institution is the National Youth Orchestra of Canada, whose commitment to discovering and training young musicians has contributed significantly to the high quality of Canada's performance groups.

Most contemporary Canadian composers have felt the influence of one of the country's important thinkers, Marshall McLuhan (1911–1980), who early on saw the far-reaching consequences of electronic communication. McLuhan prophesied the coming of what he called a "global village," achieved through the mass media of radio, TV, films, and com-

A Native American legend is the theme of R. Murray Schafer's *Princess of the Stars,* performed at dawn at Two Jack Lake in the Canadian Rockies as part of the 1981 Banff Arts Festival. Photo courtesy of The Banff Centre.

at the Juilliard School in New York. Berio's music exemplifies three major trends in the contemporary scene—serialism, electronic technology, and indeterminacy. A characteristic work is his well-known homage to Martin Luther King, Jr., *Sinfonia* (1969), for orchestra, organ, harps, piano, chorus, and reciters.

The German composer Karlheinz Stockhausen (b. 1928) assumed leadership in the 1950s of an international group of composers who worked at an

Lake and Mountains, by Canadian landscape painter Lawren S. Harris, which inspired *Blue Mountain*, a movement from Harry Freedman's composition *Images* (1958). (Art Gallery of Ontario)

puters—in short, a new way of experiencing the world. He firmly believed, however, that the means of communication—the medium—had more influence than the actual message. (The commonly heard phrase "the medium is the message" is the title of a book by McLuhan.) His writings had a significant impact on composer John Cage, who included selected phrases in a verbal collage (published under the title *I-VI*, 1988–89).

One Canadian composer who has responded to the ideas of both McLuhan and Cage is R. Murray Schafer (b. 1933). His early interest in new techniques of sound, notation, and mixed media, especially theater, has led him to a world-wide study of acoustic ecology. This project, known as World Soundscapes, explores the relationship between people and the sounds of the environment. Echoing McLuhan's concern for the impact of technology,

Schafer has been actively recording and preserving the sounds of the world. He also draws on the natural resources and native culture of his homeland, as in *The Princess of the Stars* (1981), a drama based on a Native American legend that is performed outdoors, at dawn, on the shore of a lake. His works expand our established notions of performance ritual—that is, the place, time, and conventions of a concert.

Schafer has also influenced the arts in Canada as an educator. He has taught at universities on both coasts, in Newfoundland and British Columbia, and has worked extensively with children in order to develop their general awareness and receptiveness to sounds. In his book *The Soundscape: Our Sonic Environment and the Tuning of the World* (1993), Shafer has broadened our definition of what music can be and has taken a pro-active stance to protect the Earth from noise pollution. He hopes this global view of sound will change the relationship between humanity and the acoustic environment.

SUGGESTED LISTENING:

Colin McPhee: *Nocturnes*, for chamber orchestra (1958)

Malcolm Forsyth: *Atayoskewin*, for orchestra (1984)

Jean Papineau-Couture: *Prouesse*, for solo viola (1986)

R. Murray Schafer: *Dream Rainbow Dream Thunder*, for orchestra (1986)

John Weinzweig: Divertimento No. 11, for English horn and orchestra (1989)

Harry Freedman: *Images: Suite on Three Canadian Paintings* (1958); *Touchpoints*, for flute, viola and harp (1994)

Alexina Louie: *Music for Heaven and Earth*, for orchestra (1990)

Henry Brant, *Ice Field* (2002)

avant-garde radio station studio in Cologne, Germany. His works pursue the possibilities of serialism, aleatoric technique, improvisation, and electronic manipulation of prerecorded tape. Pierre Boulez, the most important composer of the French avant-garde, is widely known for his activities as a conductor and as head of IRCAM (the French government's institute for composition and acoustics). The emotional content of Boulez's music extends from gentle

Pierre Boulez

lyricism to a furious Expressionism. From Messiaen, he took over a fondness of bell and percussion sounds that evoke the gamelan. His best-known work is *The Hammer Without a Master* (*Le marteau sans maître*, 1953–54; revised 1957), a suite of nine movements based on three short surrealist poems by René Char for alto voice and chamber ensemble. The music is suggestive of several non-Western cultures. The Russian composer Sofia Gubaidulina (b. 1931) stands out as a leader among women on the international scene. She brings to modern techniques a strong spiritual element. In some vocal works, she gives the voice nontextual and highly emotional utterances. Her reputation was established by her Violin Concerto entitled *Offertorium* (1980), which parodies J. S. Bach's *Musical Offering* in a Webernesque setting.

American Voices in the Postwar Era

Among the American composers who have made significant contributions to the development of new music is Elliott Carter (b. 1908), whose profound and well-crafted works have been widely praised, and who has been a strong presence on the contemporary music scene for nearly half a century. Carter's music blends European modernism with American ultra-modernism. Some of his works employ a novel technique that he calls "metric modulation," in which fluctuating tempos help create the form of a piece.

George Perle   Several composers have tried to reconcile serial procedures with tonality. None has played a more important role in this area than George Perle (b. 1915), who has retained the concept of tonal centers while using a language based on the twelve-tone scale. In 1986, Perle won the Pulitzer Prize for his Wind Quintet IV as well as a "genius" grant from the MacArthur Foundation. He is also known for his books, including *Serial Composition and Atonality* (1962), *Twelve-Tone Tonality* (1978), and *The Listening Composer* (1990).

Henry Brant   Canadian-born composer Henry Brant (b. 1913) has been a leader in spatial music. His early works were influenced by Charles Ives's ideas of spatial separation; since 1950, Brant's works have explored different spatial deployments of musicians throughout a hall. He has even moved beyond traditional concert venues, conceiving works for rooms with movable walls. Brant won the 2002 Pulitzer Prize for *Ice Field*, a work commissioned by the San Francisco Symphony for over one hundred musicians, who were placed throughout the auditorium. Brant is also interested in combining unusual timbres and styles in a kind of multicultural potpourri. He does not use electronic media in his works, and does not allow amplification.

Louise Talma   Among American women composers, Louise Talma (1906–1996), who studied with the French teacher Nadia Boulanger, is an important exponent of serialism. Much influenced by Stravinsky, Talma retains tonal qualities in her music while using advanced serial techniques as added unifying procedures. She is known for her choral works, including *La Corona* (1955) and an opera, *The Alcestiad* (1955–58), a collaboration with writer Thornton Wilder. Barbara **Barbara Kolb**   Kolb (b. 1939), the first American woman to win the prestigious Prix de Rome, has developed a personal style of serialism. Her piano work *Appello* (1976), based on Pierre Boulez's *Structures* (1952), is written in a much more expressive style of serialism than the sparse pointillism of her model.

It is impossible to name all the composers who have contributed to the myriad of contemporary styles and procedures. In the following chapters, we will explore a number of representative individuals who have helped shape and give expression to modern musical ideas, and we will consider some of the most current trends in composition, including how technology has facilitated the artistic process.

The New Virtuosity

Musical styles that differ so greatly from what is familiar call for a new breed of instrumentalists and vocalists to cope with their technical demands. We have only to attend a concert of avant-garde music to realize how far the art of piano playing or singing has moved from the world of Chopin or Schubert. The piano keyboard may be slammed with fingers, palm, or fist; or the player may reach inside to hit, scratch, or pluck the strings directly. A violinist may tap, stroke, or even slap the instrument. Vocal music runs the gamut from whispering to shouting, including all manner of groaning, moaning, or hissing along the way. Wind players have learned to produce a variety of double-stops, subtle changes of color, and microtonal progressions; and the percussion section has been enriched by an astonishing variety of noisemakers creating special effects.

We will consider here three gifted virtuoso singers, and then consider several creative minds whose music has demanded heightened levels of expression and virtuosity from such performers. One of these is the American George Crumb, who has sounded an original voice in the diverse world of avant-garde music.

Virtuoso Women Singers of the Twentieth Century

Among the extraordinary virtuosos of the new music are three American women singers who have made a significant mark on the development of contemporary styles. Bethany Beardslee (b. 1927), a soprano who is widely admired for the silvery quality and wide range of her voice, presented the

Bethany Beardslee

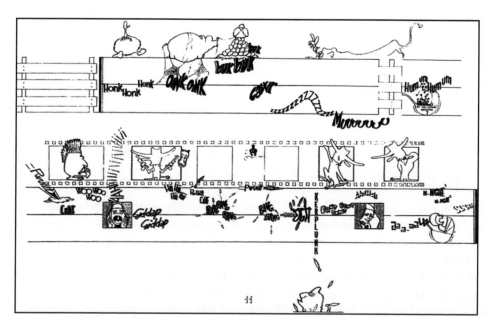

In this musical score by singer Cathy Berberian, drawings of snippets from comic strips challenge the performer to shape pictures, words, and sounds into a unified structure. *Stripsody*, for solo voice (1966).

469

American premieres of works by Schoenberg, Stravinsky, and Berg. In 1964, she was awarded a grant from the Ford Foundation to commission a work from Milton Babbitt. The resulting composition, *Philomel*, for soprano and pre-recorded tape, is based on the Roman poet Ovid's tale of a princess who is raped by the king, has her tongue cut out, and is transformed into a nightingale so she can sing of her suffering. This violent story, really an antirape statement, is told through Beardslee's virtuosic distortions and fragmentation of her voice.

Cathy Berberian
Equally noted for her vocal virtuosity was Cathy Berberian (1928–1983), a singer (and composer; see illustration on p. 469) who gained fame with her 1958 performance of *Aria*, by John Cage. In presenting the work, she had to create her own melody from the composer's purposely vague indications, singing a text in five languages and changing between numerous vocal styles, techniques, ranges, and imitations, including jazz, contralto, Sprechstimme, Marlene Dietrich (a pop singer known for her sensuous, husky voice), coloratura soprano, folk, Asian, baby, and nasal.

Jan DeGaetani
The clear and versatile voice of mezzo-soprano Jan DeGaetani (1933–1989) can be heard on recordings of early music, Schubert Lieder, Stephen Foster songs, and many contemporary pieces. She premiered, among other works, the challenging song cycle *Ancient Voices of Children*, written in 1970 by George Crumb, which we will consider. In 1973, DeGaetani was appointed to the faculty of the Eastman School of Music in Rochester, New York. She has greatly influenced the next generation of performers in her dual role as singer and teacher.

All of these women gained fame through their remarkable ability to sing avant-garde music, a talent that women musicians, especially sopranos, have developed far more than men. Contemporary music has thus created a great demand for certain female singers, and allowed them a venue for showing off their flexible voices and adventuresome spirits.

72

Contemporary Composers Look to World Music

"I believe composers must forge forms out of the many influences that play upon them and never close their ears to any part of the world of sound."

—HENRY COWELL

KEY POINTS

- Composer John Cage invented the *prepared piano* to simulate the sound of the Javanese *gamelan* orchestra. Like Cage, many experimental composers of the twentieth century found their inspiration in musics of non-Western cultures.
- The American composer George Crumb has set many texts by the Spanish poet Federico García Lorca, including five poems for his song cycle *Ancient Voices of Children*; this work uses the voice as a highly virtuosic instrument.

- Inspired by the complexity of African drumming and of gamelan music, the Hungarian composer György Ligeti experimented with the manipulation of rhythm (*additive meters* and *polyrhythm*) in his piano études.
- The royal court music of Uganda featured tuned drums that played pentatonic melodies within a dense polyrhythmic framework.
- *The Moon Reflected on the Second Springs* is a traditional Chinese piece that is now viewed as "classical" repertory, especially for the two-string fiddle (*erhu*); the performance style is highly ornamented.

Throughout the course of history, the West has felt the influence of other cultures. Twentieth-century composers, as we have seen, found inspiration in the strong rhythmic features of songs and dances from the borderlands of Western culture—southeastern Europe, Asiatic Russia, the Near East, and parts of Latin America (see world map at back of book). We have also noted how American musicians combined the powerful rhythmic impulse of African styles with the major-minor tonality of Western art music to produce the rich literature of spirituals, work songs, and shouts—and ultimately, ragtime, blues, jazz, swing, and rock.

A number of contemporary composers have responded in particular to the philosophy of the Far East, notably Zen Buddhism and Indian thought. Among them are three Californians whose work has attracted much notice: Henry Cowell, Harry Partch, and especially John Cage, whose name was associated with the avant-garde scene for over fifty years.

Important Experimenters

Henry Cowell (1897–1965) was drawn toward a variety of non-Western musics. His studies of the music of Japan, India, and Iran as well as rural Ireland and America led him to combine Asian instruments with traditional Western ensembles, as he did in his two koto concertos (1962 and 1965). (The koto, illustrated on p. 43, is a Japanese zither with thirteen strings stretched over bridges and tuned to one of a variety of pentatonic scales.) Cowell also experimented with foreign scales, which he harmonized with Western chords. The piano provided a medium for several of his innovations; two such innovations were *tone clusters*, groups of adjacent notes that are sounded with the fist, palm, or forearm, and plucking of the piano strings directly with the fingers.

The piano also lent itself to experiments with new tuning systems. One of the first to attempt microtonal music for the piano was Charles Ives, who wrote for pianos tuned a quarter tone apart. But perhaps the most serious proponent of this technique was Harry Partch (1901–1974), who single-mindedly pursued the goal of a microtonal music. In the 1920s, he evolved a scale of forty-three microtones to the octave and adapted Indian and African instruments to fit this tuning. Among his original idiophones are cloud-chamber bowls (made of glass), cone gongs (made of metal), diamond marimba (made of wood), and tree gourds. Such instruments make melody and timbre, rather than harmony, the focus of his music. Partch's performance group,

Composer Harry Partch plays one of his experimental instruments—a kind of marimba—assisted by conductor Jack Login.

called the Gate 5 Ensemble, played his works from memory; one example is *The Delusion of Fury* (1969), a large-scale ceremonial piece that employs elements of Japanese Noh drama in its first part, "On a Japanese Theme" (see illustration on p. 67), and demands that its instrumentalists make choral-voice sounds in the second part, which is titled "On an African Theme."

The Music of John Cage

"I thought I could never compose socially important music. Only if I could invent something new, then would I be useful to society."

A collage of screws, nuts, and other materials on piano strings, suggesting John Cage's prepared piano.

John Cage (1912–1992) represents the type of eternally questing artist who no sooner solves one problem than he presses forward to another. Cage exhibited an early interest in non-Western scales, which he learned from his mentor, Henry Cowell, and his abiding interest in rhythm led him to explore the possibilities of percussion instruments. He soon realized that the traditional division between consonance and dissonance had given way to a new opposition between music and noise, as a result of which the boundaries of the one were extended to include more of the other. The composer prophesied in 1937 that "the use of noise to make music will continue and increase until we reach a music produced through the aid of electrical instruments, which will make available for musical purposes any and all sounds that can be heard."

In 1938, Cage invented what he called the "prepared piano," consisting of nails, bolts, nuts, screws, and bits of rubber, wood, or leather inserted at crucial points in the strings of an ordinary grand piano. From this instrument came a myriad of sounds whose overall effect resembled that of a Javanese *gamelan* (an ensemble made up of various kinds of gongs, xylophones, drums, bowed and plucked strings, cymbals, and sometimes singers). Cage wrote a number of works for the prepared piano, notably the set of *Sonatas and Interludes* (1946–48). The music reflects the composer's preoccupation with East Asian philosophy.

Indeterminacy Cage's interest in indeterminacy, or chance, led him to compose works in which performers make choices by throwing dice. He also relied on the *I Ching* (Book of Changes), an ancient Chinese method of throwing coins or marked sticks for chance numbers, from which he derived a system of charts and graphs governing the series of events that could happen within a piece. These experiments established Cage as a decisive influence in the artistic life of the mid-twentieth century.

4′33″ Cage maintained an intense interest in exploring the role of silence. This led to his composition entitled *4′33″*, without any musical content at all, consisting of four minutes and thirty-three seconds of "silence." Audience members are expected to become aware of the sounds in the hall or outside it, the beating of their hearts, or the sounds floating around in their imagination. The piece was first performed by the pianist David Tudor in 1952. He came out onstage, placed a score on the piano rack, sat quietly for the duration of the piece, then closed the piano lid and walked off the stage. Some critics considered the piece a hoax or a not-so-clever trick. Yet Cage viewed it as one of the most radical statements he had made (and he made many) against the traditions of Western music, one that raised profound questions. What is music, and what is noise? And what does silence contribute to music? In any case, *4′33″* which can be performed by anyone on any instrument, always makes us more aware of our surroundings.

Multicultural Influences in Contemporary Society

The impulse toward a world music sound has continued beyond John Cage with such composers as Philip Glass, Terry Riley, and Steve Reich (see p. 508). Also in this category are several composers who drew on their Asian heritage as well as the traditions of the West; these include Toru Takemitsu (1930–1996) and Tan Dun, whom we will study in the chapter on film music. The result of all this activity has been to open up to the West a new world of styles, techniques, and instruments.

We have in past chapters traced how artistic impulses from disparate cultures have steadily grown closer together. Having received powerful impetus during the Second World War, this trend has been further strengthened through air travel and the media of radio, television, the press, and the Internet, all of which have made the earth a smaller place. The result is that today, artists in general and musicians in particular are more exposed to multicultural influences than anyone in earlier times could have imagined.

We will study two modern representatives of this awakening—the American composer George Crumb, whose settings of the Spanish poet Federico García Lorca are enhanced by flamenco and East Asian music, and the Hungarian composer György Ligeti, whose piano études assume the rhythmic complexity of certain African and Indonesian musics. To demonstrate these rhythmic influences, we will juxtapose one of Ligeti's études against a style he studied—traditional drumming from Uganda, in Eastern Africa. We will then explore a Chinese work played on traditional instruments that have a distinctive timbre and use a multifaceted embellishment technique; the influence of this world-music style can be heard clearly in the film score of the Chinese-American composer Tan Dun, which we will consider in the following chapter.

George Crumb and Avant-Garde Virtuosity

"Music [is] a system of proportions in the service of a spiritual impulse."

In recent years, George Crumb (b. 1929) has achieved a preeminence that is due partly to the emotional character of his music, which results from the composer's highly developed sense of the dramatic. His kind of romanticism is rare among composers of his generation. Crumb uses contemporary techniques for expressive ends that make an enormous impact in the concert hall. He has won numerous honors and awards and has been teaching composition at the University of Pennsylvania since 1965.

George Crumb

Principal Works

Orchestral music, including *Echoes of Time and the River* (1967) and *A Haunted Landscape* (1984)

Vocal music based on Lorca poetry, including *Night Music I* (1963); four books of madrigals (1965–69); *Songs, Drones, and Refrains of Death* (1968); *Night of the Four Moons* (1969); and *Ancient Voices of Children* (1970)

Chamber music, including *Black Angels* (1970), for electrified string quartet; *Lux aeterna* (*Eternal Light*, 1971), for voice and chamber ensemble (including sitar); *Vox balaenae* (*The Voice of the Whales*, 1971), for amplified instruments; *Quest* (1994), for guitar and chamber ensemble; and *Mundus Canis* (*The Dog's Mouth*, 1997) for guitar and percussion

Music for amplified piano, including 2 volumes of *Makrokosmos* (1972, 1973), *Music for a Summer Evening* (1974), and *Zeitgeist* (1988); piano music (*Processional*, 1984)

Crumb has shown a special affinity for the poetry of Federico García Lorca, the great poet who was killed by the Fascists during the Spanish Civil War and to whom the Mexican composer Silvestre Revueltas dedicated his work *Homenaje a Federico García Lorca* (see p. 405). His Lorca cycles include *Ancient Voices of Children*; *Night Music I*; four books of madrigals; *Songs, Drones, and Refrains of Death*; and *Night of the Four Moons*.

Ancient Voices of Children

Ancient Voices of Children

Ancient Voices of Children is a cycle of songs for soprano, boy soprano, oboe, mandolin, harp, electric piano, and percussion (see Listening Guide 47). Like many contemporary composers, Crumb uses the voice here like an instrument, in a vocal style he describes as ranging "from the virtuosic to the intimately lyrical."

The score abounds in unusual effects, many inspired by musics of distant cultures. The soprano opens with a fanciful *vocalise* (a wordless melody, in this case based on purely phonetic sounds) that is reminiscent of a rhapsodic East Asian melody. She sings into an electrically amplified piano, arousing a shimmering cloud of sympathetic vibrations. The pitch is "bent" to produce microtones, which typify some styles of Asian music. Included in the score are a toy piano, a harmonica, and a musical saw as well as a rich array of percussion instruments—many borrowed from other cultures—such as Tibetan prayer stones, Japanese temple bells, tuned tom-toms (high-pitched drums of African origin), Latin-American claves (wooden clappers), and maracas (a kind of rattle). Also heard are marimba, vibraphone, sleigh bells, glockenspiel plates, tubular bells, and gong (tam-tam). The composer explained why he picked this unusual combination: "I was conscious of an urge to fuse . . . unrelated stylistic elements . . . a suggestion of Flamenco with a Baroque quotation . . . , or a reminiscence of Mahler with . . . the Orient."

The first song from this cycle, *The Little Boy Is Looking for His Voice* (*El niño busca su voz*; Listening Guide 47), displays a free and fantastic character. The

in his own words

In Ancient Voices of Children *. . . I have sought musical images that enhance and reinforce the powerful yet strangely haunting imagery of Lorca's poetry. I feel that the essential meaning of this poetry is concerned with the most primary things: Life, death, love, the smell of the earth, the sounds of the wind and the sea.*

soprano part offers a virtuoso exhibition of what the voice can do in the way of cries, sighs, whispers, buzzings, trills, and percussive clicks. There are even passages marked "fluttertongue"—an effect generally associated with instruments. Throughout, Crumb captures the improvisational spirit of flamenco song. The passion is here, the sense of mystery and wonder—but in a thoroughly twentieth-century setting.

In *Ancient Voices*, Crumb found the right music for the dark intimations of Lorca's poetry. The work has justly established itself as a prime example of contemporary imagination and feeling.

Listening Guide 47

CD: CHR/STD 8/36–38, SH 4/63–65

Crumb: *Ancient Voices of Children*, First Movement   (4:09)

DATE OF WORK:	1970
GENRE:	Song cycle (5 songs and 2 instrumental interludes)
TEXT:	Poems by Federico García Lorca

WHAT TO LISTEN FOR: Opening *vocalise*, or wordless melody, with many virtuosic effects (flutter tonguing, hissing, clicking, trills); voice used instrumentally.
Rhapsodic, improvisatory-like vocal line.
Voice singing into amplified piano, producing sympathetic vibrations.
Pure timbre of boy soprano (on second verse), singing offstage.

1. *The Little Boy Is Looking for His Voice (El niño busca su voz)*
Medium: Soprano, boy soprano, electric piano, harp, tam-tam (gong), other percussion

		TEXT	TRANSLATION	DESCRIPTION
63	0:00			Opens with an elaborate vocalise for soprano, including cries, trills, other vocal gymnastics; she sings into piano with pedal down for resonance.
64	2:32	El niño busca su voz. (La tenía el rey de los grillos.) En una gota de agua buscaba su voz el niño.	The little boy is looking for his voice. (The king of the crickets had it.) In a drop of water the little boy looked for his voice.	Strophe 1—sung by soprano alone with turns, trills, hisses; she continues with low-pitched recitation.
65	3:17	No la quiero para hablar; me haré con ella un anillo que llevará mi silencio en su dedo pequeñito.	I don't want it to speak with; I will make a ring of it so that he may wear my silence on his little finger.	Strophe 2—overlaps strophe 1; boy soprano sings offstage, through cardboard tube; folk-like character to melody.

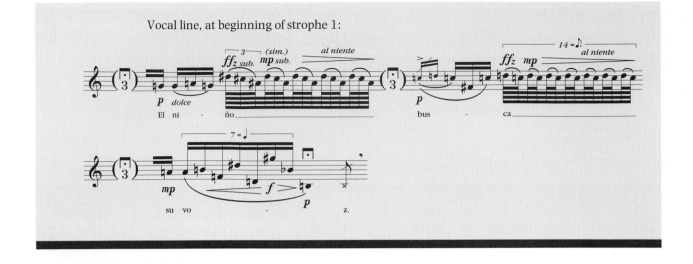

Vocal line, at beginning of strophe 1:

György Ligeti

György Ligeti's *Etudes for Piano*

György Ligeti (b. 1923), left his native Hungary in 1956 to settle first in Vienna and later in Hamburg, Germany. He was also active at the electronic music studio in Cologne and taught summer courses at Darmstadt. In Darmstadt, he worked closely with other leaders of the European avant-garde such as Stockhausen and Boulez (to whom the piece we will study is dedicated). Ligeti has been especially interested in achieving with traditional instruments the finer gradations of sound made familiar by electronic music. Through tone clusters and amalgams of sound that create a flow of shifting densities and colors, Ligeti has gone beyond focusing on fixed, recognizable pitches to working with large clusters of tones.

Ligeti developed a process of interweaving many separate strands into a complex polyphonic fabric, deriving the shape and momentum of the music from barely perceptible changes in timbre, dynamics, density, and texture. The result is a shimmering current of sound, to which he applied the term

🎺 Principal Works

Orchestral works, including *Apparitions* (1958–59), *Atmosphères* (1961), *Lontano* (1967), Piano Concerto (1985–88), and Violin Concerto (1990)

Chamber works, including Chamber Concerto (1970) and Trio for Violin, Horn, and Piano (1982)

Theater works, including *Aventures* (1962), *Nouvelles aventures* (1962–65), and *Le grand macabre* (1976)

Choral works, including *Lux aeterna* (*Eternal Light*, 1966) and *Magyar Etüdök* (*Hungarian Studies*, 1983)

Keyboard music, including *Etudes for Piano* (Book I, 1985; Book II, 1989–90)

Ligeti: *Disorder (Désordre)*, from *Etudes for Piano*, Book I

(2:18)

DATE OF WORK: 1985

MEDIUM: Solo piano

FORM: Cycles of order and disorder, achieved through a mathematical system of accents

TEMPO: Molto vivace, vigoroso, molto ritmico (very fast, vigorous, and rhythmical)

WHAT TO LISTEN FOR: Steady eighth-note rhythm, with shifting accents.

Sense of disorder and order created from mathematical planning of accents (additive meter).

Very fast pace, with points of rhythmic convergence and divergence in right and left hands.

Exploration of wide-ranging registers of piano.

66 0:00 Hands begin synchronized, with movement in eighth notes in groups of 8 (accents in patterns of 3 + 5 or 5 + 3), played legato, accents played *forte*; right hand gradually gets ahead of left by dropping one eighth note every 4 measures; dissonance increases.

Opening 7 measures, showing accents and divergence of parts:

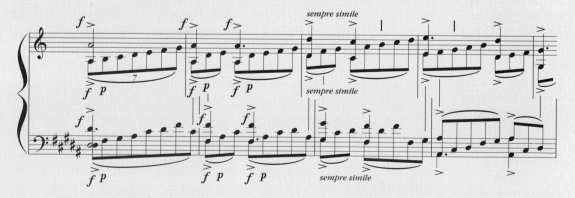

0:30   Hands finally come together again with same accents; after 4 measures, same process begins with eighth notes in right hand.

0:37   Shift in rhythmic patterns: both hands begin shortening patterns at different rates; hands and accents synchronize in pattern of 4 eighths per measure (accented 1 + 3 or 3 + 1), then diverge again as groupings change.

67   0:49   Both hands converge, then begin patterns of 3, but these are not coordinated or accented the same; piece builds to *crescendo*; bass part (left hand) drops one octave lower.

           Hands continue to diverge, *fortissimo*; briefly synchronize, then diverge again.

1:18   Hands converge at *fff* marking with all notes heavily accented; piece reaches climax.

68   1:22   Intensity and volume let down; both hands in treble range synchronized for a long time, then diverge to more rhythmic complexity and increasingly dense texture.

           Piece ends with hands ascending to upper end of keyboard.

in his own words

In Africa, cycles or periods of constantly equal length are supported by a regular beat (which is usually danced, not played). The individual beat can be divided into two, three, sometimes even four or five "elementary units" or fast pulses. I employ . . . the elementary pulse as an underlying gridwork . . . in Désordre *for accent shifting, which allows illusory pattern deformations to emerge: the pianist plays a steady rhythm, but the irregular distribution of accents leads to seemingly chaotic configurations.*

"micropolyphony." This style reached its fullest expression in his works of the early 1960s. He subsequently moved toward a style with more transparent textures and more clear-cut melodic, harmonic, and rhythmic contours. *Atmosphères*, "for large orchestra without percussion," established Ligeti's position as a leader of the European avant-garde. Together with his choral work *Lux aeterna*, it was included in the soundtrack of the classic Stanley Kubrick film *2001: A Space Odyssey* (1968), making the composer's name familiar to an international public.

Ligeti's *Etudes for Piano* illustrate another of his interests—the manipulation of rhythm. In these pieces, Ligeti experimented with illusionary rhythm, where, for example, the listener perceives a work to be much slower than it is actually played because of the recurrence of certain accented notes. Inspiration for this rhythmic treatment came from a variety of sources, including a long-held fondness for paradoxes and mathematical puzzles and the musics he had studied of certain sub-Saharan African and Indonesian cultures. Around 1980, he became aware of the player-piano works written by Conlon Nancarrow (1912–1997), an American expatriate living in Mexico, who was able to attain levels of virtuosity in rhythm and polyphony that were impossible in live performance. By punching holes in piano rolls in a certain precise way, Nancarrow could superimpose elaborate rhythmic ratios that were then automatically played on the mechanical instrument. Ligeti sought to achieve a similar effect on a normal piano with a live person performing.

The first étude from Book I, *Disorder (Désordre)*, is the most rhythmically contorted of the set. Here, Ligeti combines two distinct musical processes: an additive metric pattern (5 + 3 or 3 + 5) and a simultaneous sounding of triple patterns in one of the pianist's hands and duple patterns in the other. (See Listening Guide 48 for analysis.) These techniques make for "disorder" in the piece—the hands do not always coincide in their accents, with one hand falling behind the other, then catching up again, then lagging once more. All this proceeds at a vigorous tempo, with strongly accented notes. Thus the music whizzes by at a speed at which the ear cannot possibly disentangle the complexities involved. What you will hear is a rhythmic drive and texture of extraordinary force and energy that builds to a furious climax in the upper register of the instrument, then vanishes. Ligeti's careful mathematical planning throughout the work, and his borrowing of African concepts of additive meter and polyrhythms, are obscured by the overall perception of chaos. At the same time, the work presses the pianist's virtuosic ability to new heights.

Music from Eastern Africa

We have noted that certain musical systems of Africa were highly influential to the contemporary composer György Ligeti, in his *Etudes for Piano*. Let us investigate some of these musical elements in an example from Uganda, one of the regions that particularly interested Ligeti.

Uganda is a land-locked country in eastern Africa, bordering Kenya and Lake Victoria (for location, see world map at back of book). The peoples of Uganda—representing many different cultures—have felt significant outside influences throughout their history; they have long had contact with the Arab world and with Indonesia; they were colonized by the British, from whom they gained independence in 1962. The modern Republic of Uganda was formerly subdivided into a number of powerful kingdoms, each with its own court and ruler. We will consider a piece that was originally court music, played by a royal drum ensemble.

Among the types of musical instruments associated with this region of Africa are chordophones—musical bows, zithers, harps, lyres, and fiddles; aerophones—flutes and both end-blown and side-blown trumpets; idiophones—log xylophones and plucked metal instruments called *lamellaphones*; and membranophones—pitched and unpitched drums. The court musicians of the former King (or *Kabaka*) of Buganda (a region of Uganda on Lake Victoria) included a private harpist, a flute ensemble (accompanied by drums), a xylophone group, a band of trumpeters, and an ensemble called the *entenga*. This last group, one of the most prestigious at court, consisted of six musicians playing fifteen drums: four played twelve melody drums that were graduated in size and were tuned to notes of a pentatonic scale, while the other two accompanied them on three unpitched bass drums (see Listening Guide 49 for this arrangement). These tuned conical drums, often called *drum chimes*, have cowhide skins laced tight over both open ends; they are played with long, curved beaters (see illustration).

Like much of eastern Africa, this region developed pentatonic music. The tunes played by the drum ensembles come mostly from the vocal folk song literature. Our example, *Ensiriba ya munange Katego*, tells the story of a subchief named Kangawo, who wears a leopard-skin headband for good luck. One night, his precious headband disappears, and he feels so unprotected without his charm that he becomes ill and dies.

In the performance of *Ensiriba ya munange Katego*, the players of the melody drums enter one after the other, striking at the sides of their drums. The first melody player begins a pattern—let's call it A—which is then doubled an octave lower by the second player. The third drummer enters with two different patterns, B and C, one played in each hand. The fourth musician then joins in doubling pattern B. When the patterns are all established and the

Instrument types

Members of the entenga drum chime ensemble of Uganda.

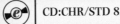
Eastern African Music: *Ensiriba ya munange Katego* (2:37)

REGION:	Kampala (former kingdom of Buganda), Uganda (Ganda tribe)
FUNCTION:	Ceremonial court music
CHARACTERISTICS:	Pentatonic melodies with gapped scale (not equidistant intervals), polyrhythm
MELODIC PATTERNS:	3 basic patterns (A, B, C), played in 2½-octave range
	5 notes in lowest octave, with lines under numbers
	5 notes in middle octave, no lines
	2 notes (½ octave) in highest octave, with lines above notes
MEDIUM:	12 tuned (melody) drums (4 players) and 3 bass drums (2 players)

WHAT TO LISTEN FOR: Entrance of tuned-drum players, one by one.
Change from playing side of drum to drum head.
3 pentatonic patterns, each played in different range.
Dense polyrhythmic structure that results from combination of
3 melodic/rhythmic patterns and bass drum.

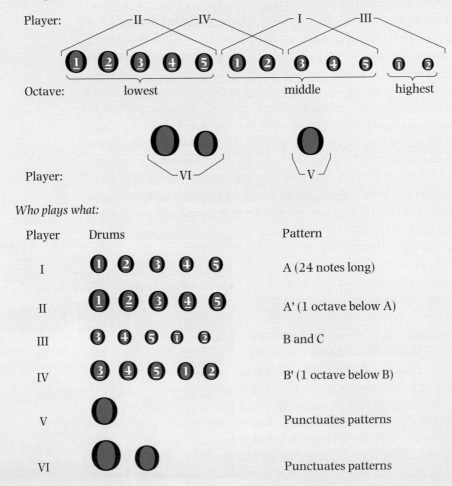

Arrangement of drums and players:

Who plays what:

Player	Drums	Pattern
I	① ② ③ ④ ⑤	A (24 notes long)
II	① ② ③ ④ ⑤	A' (1 octave below A)
III	③ ④ ⑤ ① ②	B and C
IV	③ ④ ⑤ ① ②	B' (1 octave below B)
V		Punctuates patterns
VI		Punctuates patterns

69	0:00	Players begin to establish patterns rhythmically while striking sides of their drums (producing a "clicking" sound); larger bass drums occasionally punctuate the ensemble; complexity and intensity increases as all patterns are interlocked.
70	0:19	Player I moves to drum head so that melodic pattern A is heard.
71	0:37	Next player moves to drum head, followed by the others, so that melodic pitches can be heard in a dense texture; moves at a frenetic pace; lower-pitched drum moves to drum heads, creating more depth of sound.
72	2:10	Lower-pitched drums drop out and texture thins, as one melodic pattern is heard above other parts; one drummer moves to side of drum ("clicking"); tempo slows to the end.

Resulting interlocking melodic and rhythmic patterns after all melody drums enter on drum heads (note that pitches do not align in the parts, illustrating the polyrhythmic nature of the work):

A and A': 3 4 3 4 3 1 3 3 1 4 1 1 2 3 4 5 4 2 3 4 2 5 2 2 3 4 3 4 3 1 3

B and B': $\bar{1}$ $\bar{1}$ 4 5 4 $\bar{2}$ $\bar{1}$ $\bar{2}$ 4 4 $\bar{2}$ $\bar{1}$ $\bar{2}$ $\bar{2}$ 5 4 $\bar{2}$ $\bar{1}$ 5 $\bar{2}$ 3 5 4

C: $\bar{1}$ $\bar{1}$ $\bar{1}$ 2 $\bar{2}$ $\bar{2}$ $\bar{2}$ $\bar{1}$

large bass drums have begun to punctuate the dense polyrhythmic fabric that results, the players move their strokes to the middle of the drum heads, at which point the volume level grows and the pitches of the individual lines can be heard more easily. As in the Ligeti piano étude we studied, a carefully planned musical process produces what sounds somewhat chaotic to our ears. The selection ends with a release in intensity as the drummers drop out one by one.

This is music transmitted through an oral tradition, in which an apprentice learns the repertory and technique by sitting beside an accomplished drummer. Such tuned-drum ensembles are not unique to Uganda nor to this once-famous court. Similar instruments are found in south and southeast Asia as well, offering support to the theory that the musical cultures of eastern Africa and Asia are linked. Today, this drum ensemble is seldom played, except as a vestige of Uganda's rich cultural past.

An Introduction to Chinese Traditional Music

Having seen how György Ligeti's piano étude *Disorder* draws on musical elements from African drumming—notably polyrhythms and additive meters—let us reverse the listening process to hear how a well-known Chinese piece, played on traditional instruments, inspires a modern film score (*Crouching Tiger, Hidden Dragon*) by the Chinese-American composer Tan Dun (see p. 492). We will listen first to *The Moon Reflected on the Second Springs*.

The musician who composed and first performed this work is known as Abing (1883–1950). According to the official biography written by a Chinese music historian, Abing's original name was Hua Yanjun, and he was born in Wuxi, in the eastern Chinese province of Jiangsu (see world map). Both his parents died when Abing was young; he was adopted by a Daoist monk, who taught him music. (*Daoism* is one of China's major philosophies and religions, based on the teachings of sixth-century-B.C.E. philosopher Lao-tse.) As an apprentice Daoist, Abing played in the wind and percussion ensemble of the

Abing

Man playing the erhu.

local temple. He was eventually expelled from the Daoist group for playing their music in secular settings, and became a wandering street musician. In his mid-thirties, he went blind—some say as a result of contracting syphilis.

Abing was able to make a (meager) living by singing and playing the two-stringed fiddle (*erhu*) and the lute (*pipa*). In his music, much of it improvised on the spot, he sometimes narrated the day's news as he heard it at the opium houses. Shortly before his death in 1950, Abing taped six memorable solo works; *The Moon Reflected on the Second Springs* is the most famous.

Abing's pieces are viewed as traditional music because they were created through improvisation and thus took their shape gradually, and because they have been orally disseminated in differing versions, like folk music (in this case, they have also been written down for posterity). Today, Abing's music is highly revered; it forms part of the standard repertory at music conservatories for erhu and pipa players, further blurring the lines between art and traditional music.

This humble Chinese musician would have been surprised to read some of his biographies, written under the Communist regime (which came to power in 1949), that have romanticized his life and turned him into a revolutionary hero of the people. Questions have even arisen over the descriptive title of the work we will hear, which was probably given to the composition after a long period of performance and development. Although some have searched for political meaning behind the name, most scholars believe it refers to a scenic site outside the city of Wuxi, near the Second Springs pavilion.

The Moon Reflected on the Second Springs was originally conceived for solo *erhu*, a bowed, two-string fiddle played resting upright on the upper leg, with a snakeskin-covered sound box and with its bow hairs fixed between the two strings. Our modern recorded version adds the *yangqin*, a hammered dulcimer with a trapezoidal sound box strung with metal strings that are struck (or hammered) with strips of bamboo (see illustration at right). The work is based on a pentatonic scale (D-E-G-A-B) that uses only the intervals of major seconds and minor thirds (as shown in Listening Guide 50).

The melody is made up of four musical phrases, which are repeated and ornamented with many types of embellishments (trills, slides, glissandos, grace notes, bent notes, and tremolos, among others) in a process beautifully described as "adding flowers" (*jia hua*). The haunting melody begins slowly, in a low range and rhythmically free, and then ascends very gradually and expressively. The yangqin adds depth to the linear movement, offering new melodic decoration and rhythmic pulses with its gently hammered tremolos.

Master yangqin player in performance.

The complete melodic outline of the work is heard four times, with newly invented ornamentation at each appearance. In this performance, a poignant climax is reached in the third statement of the melody, with the erhu "singing" out beautifully in the instrument's highest range. A final statement releases some of the tension and ends the work quietly. The version we hear today of *The Moon Reflected on the Second Springs* has, like most traditional pieces, been shaped over several generations since its modest beginnings, when it was performed by a blind, gifted Chinese musician.

Listening Guide 50

CD: CHR/STD 8/66–69, SH 4/73–76

Abing: *The Moon Reflected on the Second Springs* (*Er quan ying yue*)

(5:36)

DATE:	First recorded in 1950 by Abing
MEDIUM:	Erhu (2-string fiddle), with yangqin (hammered dulcimer)
GENRE:	Chinese traditional music, from Jiangsu region
SCALE:	Pentatonic (5-note), with pitches D-E-G-A-B
FORM:	4 musical phrases, repeated and elaborated
TEMPO:	Slow, with very gradual acceleration

WHAT TO LISTEN FOR: Lyrical melody made up of 4 melodic phrases, derived from pentatonic (5-note) scale.
Entire melody played 4 times, each a variation with new embellishments.
Unique timbre of bowed erhu supported by hammered yangqin.
Exploration of varied articulations and registers of solo erhu; reaches a climax in highest range.

73 0:00 Short, rhythmically free introduction by erhu is followed by lyrical melodic phrase 1, played in low range; accompanied by yangqin; ends on low G:

0:35 Melodic phrase 2—begins up an octave, in middle range and louder, with brief countermelody on yangqin; ends on sustained D:

0:48 Melodic phrase 3—higher range, begins with soft staccato note, ends on sustained pitch of G:

1:06 Melodic phrase 4—returns to middle range; serves as a short closing idea ending on D:

483

74	1:15	Returns to phrase 1 in low range, soft, with first note plucked; continuation of melodic phrases, yangqin more audible; phrase 3 extended in tremolo (fast repeated note), with rising yangqin line:

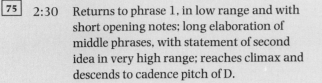

75	2:30	Returns to phrase 1, in low range and with short opening notes; long elaboration of middle phrases, with statement of second idea in very high range; reaches climax and descends to cadence pitch of D.

76	4:08	Last statement of opening phrase, now with rising interval of sixth; more trills on erhu as melody climbs through phrases; ending is extended and tempo slows down; cadence pitch is on D.

73

Music for Films

"A film is a composition and the musical composition is an integral part of the design."

—H. G. WELLS

KEY POINTS:

- Music sets the mood, helps establish the characters, and creates a sense of place and time in a film.
- There are two principal types of music in a film—*underscoring* and *source music*.
- Silent films were generally accompanied by solo piano or organ.
- Film music may be newly composed or may borrow from Classical or popular repertory; rock, country/western, and jazz gained favor in film music after the late 1940s.
- The late 1930s is considered the Golden Age of films and film music.
- The Russian composer Sergei Prokofiev wrote scores for two epic films—*Alexander Nevsky* (1938) and *Ivan the Terrible* (1944–45)—both about Russian historical figures and both directed by Sergei Eisenstein.
- Post–World War II films used music sparingly, and composers explored more modern special effects.
- The film music of John Williams marks a return to full orchestral resources and the use of *leitmotifs* (recurring themes) associated with characters or situations.

- In the 1980s, the synthesizer had a significant influence on the film music industry.
- Tan Dun's score for *Crouching Tiger, Hidden Dragon* blends Western and Far Eastern instruments and musical styles.

Music has helped to create some of the most memorable moments in film history. The opening of *2001: A Space Odyssey*, the Paris montage from *Casablanca*, and the shower scene in *Psycho* are all accompanied by music that has become an integral part of American culture. Yet most film music functions in a less spectacular manner. With the viewer's attention focused on dialogue, visual images, and general sound effects, music often goes unnoticed. Indeed, many film composers take great pride in the unobtrusive qualities of their artistic contributions. Listening to music in film can be challenging, but the effort is rewarded with a better understanding of film as an art form.

The Role of Music in Film

The most important function of music in film is to set a mood. Choices of musical style, instrumentation, and emotional quality are critical in creating the director's vision. Even the absence of music in a scene or an entire movie (Hitchcock's *Lifeboat*, 1944) can contribute to the overall tone of a film.

Mood

Most Hollywood films use music to reflect the emotions of a given scene. In *Gone With the Wind* (1939), Max Steiner's score deftly supports Scarlett O'Hara's shift from love to anger when she is rejected by Ashley at Twin Oaks. Likewise, John Williams guides the viewer's emotions at the end of *E. T.: The Extraterrestrial* (1982) from sadness at the apparent death of E. T. through joy at his recovery, excitement at the chase scene, to sadness at his final farewell. Howard Shore's score to *The Lord of the Rings: The Fellowship of the Ring* (2001) plays a major role in creating the dark, brooding mood surrounding Frodo's quest, but it also brings out the contrasting moments of humor and tenderness. Many scenes in Hollywood movies would be unthinkable, if not laughable, without musical support.

But music does not necessarily need to mirror every emotion or action on the screen. In some films, the composer will establish a single dominant theme for the entire narrative, which is sustained no matter what happens on screen. This detached approach towards music, which is more prevalent in European films, is effectively used by John Williams in his score to *Schindler's List* (1993). The music for this horrific tale of the Holocaust creates a pervading mood of sadness throughout, always reminding the viewer of the inevitability of these historic events.

Composers can sometimes create irony by supplying music that contradicts what is being shown on the screen. This technique is called *running counter to the action*. In James Horner's music to the final scene of *Glory* (1989), the triumphant music reflects the moral victory of black soldiers finally being allowed to fight in the Civil War and runs counter to the observed massacre of the black regiment. Perhaps the best-known musical/visual contradiction is the chilling climactic scene of *The Godfather* (1972). While the audience hears Bach organ music during a baptism, it sees the brutal and systematic murders of Michael

Running counter to the action

Corleone's enemies. In one bold scene, we hear Michael become Godfather to an infant in Church and see Michael become Godfather to the mob family on the streets.

Character
In addition to setting moods, music can play an important role in establishing character. The appearance of a dashing romantic hero might be accompanied by a passionate melody; the image of a soldier could be supported with a strong march; and a worldly woman might be shown with a sultry saxophone melody heard in the background. In *Titanic* (1997), music helps delineate the social levels of the principal characters. A string quartet plays elegant chamber music to the upper-deck aristocrats while Irish dance music energizes the lower levels occupied by the common people.

Place and time
Music can also help create a sense of place and time. The bagpipes in *Braveheart* (1995), the banjo in *Deliverance* (1972), and the sitar in *Gandhi* (1982) all help transport the viewer to different locales. Similarly, the addition of a harpsichord may suggest an eighteenth-century tale; the singing of Gregorian chant conjures up images of the Middle Ages; and resounding trumpet fanfares typically accompany scenes of the mighty Ancient Romans. Popular tunes can also help set a more precise date for events. Jazz music might accompany stories set in the 1920s or 1930s, while rock music from the 1960s or early 1970s might appear in a film about the Vietnam War. The soundtrack for *Forrest Gump* (1994) takes the listener on a brief history of rock and roll, as we watch Forrest grow from boyhood to manhood.

Underscoring

Source music
There are two principal types of music in a film. *Underscoring*, which is what most people think of as film music, occurs when music comes from an unseen source, often an invisible orchestra. But music can also function as part of the drama itself; this is referred to as *source music*. For example, someone may turn on a radio, a couple may enter a concert hall or a dance room, or a character may be inspired to sing. In each instance, the music stems from a logical source within the film and functions as part of the story itself. Source music can be a fascinating part of the drama. In *Rear Window* (1954), Hitchcock employs only source music, which emanates from the various apartments on the block. Source music can also tell us a great deal about a character. In *Boyz 'N the Hood* (1991), source music of classical jazz, Motown, and rap helps define the principal figures of the story.

Leitmotifs
In an attempt to create musical unity within the context of an ongoing dramatic flow, many film composers turned to models created by Liszt and Wagner and incorporated the techniques of leitmotifs (see p. 337) and thematic transformation. In *Jaws* (1975), John Williams creates a two-note oscillating leitmotif that warns the audience of the shark's presence. Perhaps inspired by Wagner's *Ring Cycle*, Williams also introduces a multitude of leitmotifs for the *Star Wars* trilogy. Each motif—the opening fanfare (which becomes the theme for Luke Skywalker), Yoda's gentle melody, and Darth Vader's intense march—supports the general nature of the character. Yet these musical motives can also be transformed to reflect totally different events. The theme for Luke Skywalker can sound sad or distorted when he is in trouble, triumphant when he is victorious. One of the finest musical moments of the trilogy occurs in *The Return of the Jedi* (1983). At the death of Darth Vader, his once terrifying theme is transformed into a gentle tune played by the woodwinds and harp (symbolizing the character's death).

Music in the Silent Film Era

On December 28, 1895, Louis and Auguste Lumière showed a series of short films to a Parisian audience. This event is generally considered the birth of cinema. During this presentation, a pianist reportedly accompanied the films by improvising on popular tunes. From the beginning, then, film music was used to establish a mood, and throughout the so-called *silent film era*, it continued to function in this manner. As films moved from vaudeville houses to nickelodeons (small shops converted to movie theaters with the usual admission price of a nickel) to the movie palaces of the 1920s, musicians enhanced the visual experience of silent films.

In the literally thousands of movie theaters that sprang up in the United States, the solo piano was the most common type of musical accompaniment for silent films. In many houses, a percussionist was added in order to create a variety of different sounds, which was particularly important for special effects. The organ was also suitable for film accompaniment, and soon special organs were built that were capable of producing a wide range of musical colors and effects, such as gunshots, animal noises, and traffic sounds.

Larger theaters featured ensembles with more musicians. A chamber orchestra of thirteen or fourteen performers, which included a piano, string quintet, and solo winds, was typical of a quality theater. The major movie palaces in cities like New York, Chicago, and Los Angeles would likely have had a full symphony orchestra numbering about fifty musicians. Special feature films were sometimes presented with over one hundred performers, including both instrumentalists and singers.

Three types of music were played during the showings of films: borrowings from Classical music, arrangements of well-known tunes (popular, patriotic, or religious), and newly composed music. Music directors of the theater generally created the music. Ideally, they would preview the film, taking notes on the

> *Nonsense. The idea originated with Richard Wagner. Listen to the incidental scoring behind the recitatives in his operas. If Wagner had lived in this century, he would have been the Number One film composer.*
>
> —MAX STEINER
> (RESPONDING TO THE IDEA THAT HE HAD INVENTED FILM MUSIC)

D. W. Griffith elevated cinema to an art form with his classic Civil War spectacle *Birth of a Nation* (1915), for which Joseph Carl Breil wrote the landmark score.

moods of various scenes. After gathering enough suitable music, often with considerable borrowings from the Classics, they would rehearse the musicians and be ready for the show.

The quality of these performances varied greatly from theater to theater. Hence filmmakers increasingly turned to composers to create original scores for their films. The French composer Camille Saint-Saëns is generally credited with writing the first original film score—for *L'Assassinat du Duc de Guise* (1908).

Joseph Carl Breil

The most important American composer of film music during the silent era is Joseph Carl Breil, who wrote the score for D. W. Griffith's landmark and controversial film *The Birth of a Nation* (1915; see illustration on p. 487). Breil's score contains all three types of music mentioned above. Substantial quotes from Classical works (for example, Wagner's *Ride of the Valkyries* used for the ride of the Klansmen), numerous quotes of patriotic tunes for the Civil War scenes, and new music featuring a number of leitmotifs establish this work as the first great American film score.

The Sound Era

In 1926, the Warner Bros. Studio unveiled the Vitaphone system, which synchronized music played on a phonograph with action shown on a reel of film. The first feature film using this technology, *Don Juan* (1926), was recorded with music performed by the New York Philharmonic. In the following year, Warner Bros. released *The Jazz Singer*, which employed synchronized background music, several songs recorded live by Al Jolson, and two brief passages of spoken words. The spoken words created an enormous public sensation, and talking pictures quickly displaced silent films.

In the transition to sound, difficulties in coordinating music and dialogue led to the temporary abandonment of music. Films from this era, such as *All Quiet on the Western Front* (1929) and *Dracula* (1930), seem eerily quiet. But advancements in technology were rapid, and *King Kong* (1933), with a full symphonic score by Max Steiner, reestablished the prominent role of music in films.

During the 1930s, quality films were produced at an unprecedented rate, and Hollywood entered a Golden Age that fostered music as a central feature of film. In shaping the physiognomy of the classical film score, Hollywood called upon the service of two composers from Vienna: Max Steiner and Eric Korngold.

Max Steiner

Max Steiner, a child prodigy, came to Hollywood in 1929. After scoring *King Kong*, he composed a number of important works before starting his masterpiece, *Gone With the Wind* (1939). For this epic film of love and war, Steiner wrote an unprecedented three hours and forty-five minutes of music. The leitmotif for Scarlett's plantation (Tara's theme) became the first blockbuster film theme and remains one of the most popular and recognizable of all movie melodies. Steiner worked on over three hundred films, and his credits include memorable works such as *Casablanca* (1942), *The Big Sleep* (1946), and *The Treasure of the Sierra Madre* (1948).

Erich Korngold

The son of a major music critic in Vienna, Erich Korngold, like Steiner, was a child prodigy. Richard Strauss, Gustav Mahler, and Giacomo Puccini were among the many admirers of the young Korngold. A master of orchestral color and thematic development, Korngold provided a model for future film composers with only a handful of film scores, his most famous being *The Adventures of Robin Hood* (1938).

After World War I, filmmakers in Europe were unable to match the commercial accomplishments of the Hollywood industry. Instead, they tended to focus more on the artistic qualities of film. Germany had a brief flourishing of filmmaking prior to Hitler's rise to power. The expressionistic film *The Cabinet of Dr. Caligari* (1919) made a sensation both in Europe and in the United States. Because of the film's distorted visions—horizontal and vertical lines are avoided and the sets are deliberately artificial—this tale of insanity became one of the earliest works to incorporate modern music.

In France, film was embraced by a significant number of art music composers. Unlike their American counterparts, who seemingly held film music in disdain, Erik Satie, Jacques Ibert, Germaine Tailleferre, Darius Milhaud, and Arthur Honegger eagerly adopted the new art form. Honegger provided music for perhaps the most remarkable French film of the 1920s, Abel Gance's *Napoleon* (1927).

Under the leadership of Lenin (1917–24), the Soviet Union also became a major force in filmmaking. As in France, the major composers of this country contributed greatly to the artistic success of their film industry. Dmitri Shostakovich composed his first film score in 1929, and completed fifteen more during the 1930s, including *The Great Citizen* (1939), which was largely created by Stalin himself. Sergei Prokofiev (1891–1953) worked on eight Soviet films. The first of these projects was a satirical film, *Lieutenant Kije* (1934), which he composed during his transition back to the Soviet Union from living abroad. The film was never realized, but a suite derived from the music has become a popular orchestral concert piece. Prokofiev's two greatest film scores were created for the Soviet Union's leading film director, Sergei Eisenstein: *Alexander Nevsky* (1938), later reshaped into a seven-movement cantata by the composer, and *Ivan the Terrible* (1944–45).

Dmitri Shostakovich and Sergei Prokofiev

The Postwar Years

Following World War II, film music underwent a number of significant changes. Due to financial constraints, the lush symphonic score of the Golden Age gradually declined, and many films used music sparingly. Composers also explored new musical styles, including the use of popular genres as well as twentieth-century art music.

Bernard Herrmann and Miklós Rózsa are two early pioneers from this period. In his first film score, for Orson Welles' classic *Citizen Kane* (1941), Herrmann creates a dark atmosphere by using low instrumental colors and tone clusters. He later continued to incorporate disturbing modernistic material in his scores for Hitchcock's *Vertigo* (1958) and *Psycho* (1960) and for Martin Scorsese's *Taxi Driver* (1976). Miklós Rózsa, who is best remembered for his scores to religious epics such as *Ben-Hur* (1959), was the first composer to use an electronic instrument in film music. In Hitchcock's *Spellbound* (1945), Rózsa added the Theremin (see p. 496) to create an eerie effect during the passages suggesting dementia.

Bernard Herrmann

Miklós Rózsa

As the film industry allowed for more daring musical sounds in films, several prominent American composers of art music turned their attention to the genre, most notably Aaron Copland and Leonard Bernstein. Copland (see p. 398) wrote music for five Hollywood feature films and received four Oscar nominations. He won the Award for Best Music, Original Score, in 1949 for *The*

Aaron Copland

Leonard Bernstein

Heiress. Bernstein (see p. 431) composed an original film score for only one movie, Elia Kazan's masterpiece *On the Waterfront* (1954). His score supports this tale of corruption and redemption with a mixture of modern and jazz elements. The powerful ending is one of the finest moments in film music. In 1961, Bernstein's Broadway hit *West Side Story* was converted to film and won a near record-breaking ten Oscars.

Dmitri Tiomkin

From the late 1940s through the 1960s, popular music gradually moved from its restricted role as source music to underscoring. Dmitri Tiomkin created a landmark score in 1952 for *High Noon* when he incorporated a country/western ballad sung by Tex Ritter, both in the opening credits and during scenes showing the isolation of Sheriff Will Kane. The tune created a public sensation, and soon popular movie themes were in demand for every Hollywood film. Perhaps the greatest composer of movie themes emerged in the 1960s. Henry Mancini created a series of major hits in films such as *Breakfast at Tiffany's* ("Moon River," 1961), *The Days of Wine and Roses* (1962), and *The Pink Panther* (1964).

Rock music came of age with Hollywood movies. In 1955, the release of *The Blackboard Jungle*, featuring *Rock Around the Clock* by Bill Haley and the Comets, propelled the song to the top of the Billboard chart, marking the beginning of the Rock era. Hollywood quickly made a movie star of Elvis Presley, who made pictures at a rate of three a year for nearly a decade. Landmark films with rock music include *The Graduate* (1967) and *Easy Rider* (1969), which created rock albums rather than just singles; *Shaft* (1971), with an Oscar-winning, full-rock score by Isaac Hayes; and *Saturday Night Fever* (1977), whose soundtrack by the Bee Gees sold over thirty million copies, smashing all previous records and creating a model for the future use of rock music in films.

> I think that the composer, because of the success of the Williams scores, is in a somewhat better position now than he has been in for some time. The attitudes appear to be a little bit looser, less doctrinaire on the part of the producers. There was one time a feeling . . . that they wanted either a rock score or a commercial score.
>
> —ELMER BERNSTEIN

Elmer Bernstein

Jerry Goldsmith

In the new environment of film music, composers needed to be versatile and be able to write in all musical styles, including modern and popular. Two of the finest craftsmen from this time are Elmer Bernstein and Jerry Goldsmith. Bernstein helped introduce jazz as underscoring in the disturbing portrayal of a drummer addicted to drugs (played by Frank Sinatra) in *The Man with the Golden Arm* (1955). He later composed such divergent scores as the energetic *The Magnificent Seven* (1960) and the thoughtful *To Kill a Mockingbird* (1962). He has maintained a prolific output that includes *Ghostbusters* (1984) and *Wild Wild West* (1999). Goldsmith likewise has had a lengthy and versatile career. His scores range from the expressionistic *Planet of the Apes* (1968) to the dark *Chinatown* (1974), the Rambo action movies, the sports tale *Hoosiers* (1986), and the terrifying *The Mummy* (1999).

Beyond *Star Wars*

Star Wars (1977) revolutionized the movie industry by inundating the audience with spectacular visual and aural effects. Critical to the phenomenal success of this film is the brilliant score by John Williams, which features a return to the colorful virtuoso symphony, the unabashed emotional underscoring, and the system of leitmotifs that were hallmarks of the film scores from the Golden Age.

John Williams

John Williams began composing for television in the 1950s, working on shows such as *Gilligan's Island*. Shifting to the big screen in the 1960s, he wrote a series of scores for disaster films, which culminated in his exhilarating score for *Jaws* (1975). By the end of the 1970s, he had established himself as Hollywood's foremost composer and had three blockbusters: *Star Wars* (1977), *Close Encounters of the Third Kind* (1977), and *Superman* (1978). During the 1980s, Williams scored six of the top ten box-office hits in the decade: the two *Star Wars* sequels, the *Indiana Jones* trilogy, and *E. T.: The Extraterrestrial*. Williams has maintained a steady output of quality film scores up to the present time. Among his best-known works in recent years are *Schindler's* List (1993), *Jurassic Park* (1995), *The Phantom Menace* (1999), and *Harry Potter and the Sorcerer's Stone* (2001).

Another important figure in the revival of the symphonic score is James Horner. A product of the music schools of both University of Southern California (USC) and University of California at Los Angeles (UCLA), he received critical attention for his music to *Star Trek II: The Wrath of Khan* (1982) and *Star Trek III: The Search for Spock* (1984). Horner created an international sensation with his song and underscoring for *Titanic* (1997). Among his other well-known scores are *Field of Dreams* (1989), *Apollo 13* (1995), and *Braveheart* (1995).

The synthesizer had a major impact on films during the 1980s (see p. 496) and has been an enormous aid to the composer, in part because of its ease in creating scores and parts. It also serves as a useful tool for the film director, who can now hear the general sound of the music before hiring a studio orchestra. The synthesizer's ability to reproduce the sounds of acoustic instruments has also led to its inclusion in the modern studio orchestra where it not only imitates the sound of individual instruments, such as a harp, piano, or drums, but also gives support to the general sound of the strings. In some films, a synthesizer has substituted for an entire orchestra, as in the Oscar-winning score to *Chariots of Fire* (1981).

Because use of the synthesizer as a performing instrument was largely the domain of popular musicians, the newest generation of film composers features a significant number who lack traditional university training. Two prominent examples of the new breed are Danny Elfman and Hans Zimmer. Elfman, the founder of the rock group Oingo Boingo, began composing film scores with

Writing the melody is the easy part. . . . But then, it's what you do with it. That's the skill, that's the art, that's what makes a great film score.
—DANNY ELFMAN

James Horner

Synthesizer

Danny Elfman

In this scene from *Star Wars*—featuring Han Solo (Harrison Ford), Obi-Wan Kenobi (Alec Guinness), Luke Skywalker (Mark Hamill), and Chewbacca (Peter Mayhew)—John Williams's score heightens the drama as the starship *Millennium Falcon* is drawn into the tractor beam of the Death Star.

Toby Maguire as the title character in *Spider-Man* (2002), with a film score by Danny Elfman.

Pee-Wee's Big Adventure (1985). Continuing to work with director Tim Burton, Elfman expanded his technique in *Beetlejuice* (1988), *Batman* (1989), *Edward Scissorhands* (1990), *The Nightmare Before Christmas* (1993), *Men in Black* (1997), and *Planet of the Apes* (2001). Elfman's most recent hit was *Spider-Man* (2002). Hans Zimmer, like Elfman, comes from a popular-music and synthesizer background. Among his early films are two Academy Award winners for Best Picture, *Rain Man* (1988) and *Driving Miss Daisy* (1989). His other well-known scores include *The Lion King* (1994), *Gladiator* (2000), and *Pearl Harbor* (2001).

In recent years, women composers have started to gain prominence in film composition. Rachel Portman became the first woman to win an Academy Award for Best Music, Original Score, for *Emma* (1996) which was based on the Jane Austen novel of the same name. Born in England and trained at Oxford, Portman also composed music for the thoughtful *Joy Luck Club* (1993) and received an Oscar nomination for her score to *The Cider House Rules* (1999). Songwriter Diane Warren has also been prominent in Academy Award presentations, receiving four nominations since 1996. Most recently, she has contributed the song *There You'll Be* for *Pearl Harbor* (2001).

During the 1990s, American composers of art music have again turned to the medium of film. Philip Glass (see p. 508), whose minimalistic style has had much popular appeal, composed music for a number of commercial films in the 1990s, including *Candyman* (1992) and *The Truman Show* (1998). John Corigliano (see p. 504), a leading figure in the New Romanticism, received an Oscar for his haunting music to *The Red Violin* (1999), played by solo violinist Joshua Bell. The score is an overarching theme and variations that incorporates Baroque, Romantic, Chinese, and modern musical styles.

Tan Dun: His Life and Music

Chinese-American composer Tan Dun and world-famous cellist Yo-Yo Ma discuss a musical score.

Like John Corigliano, Tan Dun is both a critically recognized composer of art music and a winner of an Academy Award for Best Music, Original Score, for *Crouching Tiger, Hidden Dragon* (2000). The music of Tan Dun is a fascinating post-modern blend of Asian musical traditions and Western styles, including both avant-garde and popular.

Born in Hunan Province in China, Tan Dun (b. 1957) grew up during the Cultural Revolution. When governmental restrictions were loosened, he became a leading figure in the "new wave" of Chinese composers who began to explore aspects of modern Western music. In 1983, the Chinese government, referring to his music as "spiritual pollution," banned public performances of Tan Dun's works. He came to the United States in 1986 and continued his musical studies at Columbia University in New York.

In recent years, Tan Dun has created a number of celebrated works. The opera *Marco Polo* (1995), which mixes Western avant-garde sounds with the vocal style of the Beijing Opera, won the prestigious

Chow Yun-Fat and Zhang Ziyi battle on the branches of bamboo trees in Ang Lee's *Crouching Tiger, Hidden Dragon* (2000).

Grawemeyer Award. Tan Dun composed the *Symphony 1997: (Heaven, Earth, Mankind)* for the ceremony marking the return of the city of Hong Kong to China. His *2000 Today: A World Symphony for the Millennium*—a work commissioned by the BBC, PBS Television, and Sony Classical—was broadcast to the world on January 1, 2000, on over fifty-five international television networks.

Crouching Tiger, Hidden Dragon

The film *Crouching Tiger, Hidden Dragon* is a well-made martial arts fantasy with stunning visual effects. The story involves two sets of doomed lovers. The music is composed for both Western and Chinese musical instruments. A solo cello played by the Chinese-American musician Yo-Yo Ma is featured throughout and often heard in combination with Chinese instruments. The cello's melodic material, featuring slides and quick ornaments, is directly influenced by the vocal style of the Beijing Opera. You will remember that we heard similar string effects in the Chinese traditional piece *The Moon Reflected on the Second Springs*, played on the erhu (or Chinese violin).

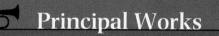
Principal Works

Orchestra music, including *On Taoism* (1985), *Orchestra Theater I* (1990), *Orchestra Theater II* (1992), *Symphony 1997 (Heaven, Earth, Mankind)* (1997), and *2000 Today: A World Symphony for the Millennium* (1999)

Chamber music, including *Ghost Opera* (1994)

3 operas: *Nine Songs* (1989), *Marco Polo* (1995), and *Orchestra Theater III* (1996)

2 films: *Fallen* (1998) and *Crouching Tiger, Hidden Dragon* (2000)

in his own words

My music is to dream without boundaries. . . . Crouching Tiger bridged East and West, romance and action, high and low cultures.

Listening Guide 51

CD: CHR/STD 8/62–65, SH 4/77–80

Tan Dun: *Farewell*, from *Crouching Tiger, Hidden Dragon* (2:25)

DATE OF WORK: 2000

BASIS: Book by Wang Du Lu; screenplay by Wang Hui Ling, James Schamus, Tsai Kuo Jung

GENRE: Film score

FORM: Theme and variations procedure

PRINCIPAL INSTRUMENTS: Cello (played by Yo-Yo Ma) and erhu (bowed Chinese fiddle), accompanied by Chinese hand drum and Western orchestra

WHAT TO LISTEN FOR:
Singing cello line with lyrical erhu countermelody and lush string accompaniment.
Silvery timbre of ehru; characteristic sliding effects between notes.
Repetitive melody (in 2 phrases) that varies in pitch, range, and dynamics with each statement (heard three times, then phrase 2 heard again).
Expressive rising 5th interval that begins main theme; heard frequently throughout.
Elaborate hand drum accompaniment.
Programmatic nature of theme; linked to film story.

77 0:00 Love theme played by cello, with interval of rising 5th at opening (pitches D-A); theme heard in 2 phrases; accompanied by sustained strings and hand drum. Ehru improvises expressive countermelody against cello line; also begins with rising line (pitches A-C-D).

78 0:34 Variation 1—duet continues between cello and ehru, with differing pitches; drum accompaniment slightly faster.

79 1:05 Variation 2—duet closer to original statement; more expressive, louder, with quicker drum accompaniment.

80 1:38 Two varied statements of 2nd phrase, with quickening drum part.

2:07 Wavering between 2 pitches at closing.

Tan Dun draws upon Western harmony, Western popular-music rhythms, avant-garde timbres, and ethnic Chinese sounds. His free mixture of musical styles is clearly evident during the closing credits. Here, he transforms the love theme, originally heard as a traditional Chinese melody played by the cello (see Listening Guide 51), into a Western popular song, *A Love Before Time*, which was nominated for an Oscar for Best Song in 2000.

The music heard in *Farewell* combines two melodies that are associated with the lovers Jen Lu and the bandit king Lo. These melodies are accompanied by both a Western string orchestra and Chinese percussion instruments. The principal love theme, played by the cello, has two equal phrases. In this excerpt, the melody is presented three times, with two additional repetitions of the second phrase at the end. At the final cadence, the cello closes with a two-note oscillation. During the film, this motive is associated with the vibrating movement of the powerful sword known as "The Green Destiny."

The erhu plays an ostinato lament in counterpoint with the cello. Entering at the cadence of the cello's first phrase, the erhu melody also has two equal phrases that continue to overlap with the cello melody throughout the passage. Each of the erhu phrases begins with the notes A-C-D. These pitches are linked with much of the thematic material that is heard throughout the film score.

Farewell

74

Technology and Music

"I have been waiting a long time for electronics to free music from the tempered scale and the limitations of musical instruments. Electronic instruments are the portentous first step toward the liberation of music."

—EDGARD VARÈSE

KEY POINTS

- The French school of *musique concrète*, which began in the late 1940s, used natural sounds recorded on magnetic tape as a new medium for composition.
- In the early 1950s, the German school of *electronische Musik* created compositions using electronically generated sounds.
- By the late 1960s, smaller, cheaper synthesizers were available to many musicians and composers.
- Digital technology, beginning with the invention of FM synthesis in the 1970s, revolutionized the world of electronic music.
- Computers have played an important role in electronic music. They can generate sounds, create compositions, and interact with synthesizers via the Musical Instrument Digital Interface (MIDI).
- The contemporary composer Paul Lansky is a prominent figure in the field of computer-assisted composition; his work *Notjustmoreidlechatter* uses linear predictive coding (LPC) to produce "unintelligible" humanlike sounds.
- Modern composers are moving toward interactive performances involving a live audience, either directly or via the Internet.
- Composers are now exploring artificial intelligence (AI) techniques in the creation of computer-generated music (CP 23).

The Technological Revolution

The most demonstrably important development in art music during the last fifty years was the emergence of electronic music. New instruments such as the Theremin, the Ondes Martenot, and the Hammond organ—all of which produce sounds electronically—predicted a future that was quickly realized by the booming revolution of technology.

Musique concrète

Two trends emerged simultaneously in the late 1940s and early 1950s: *musique concrète* in France and *electronische Musik* in Germany. The first trend (*musique concrète*) was based in Paris and headed by Pierre Schaeffer. It relied on sounds (made by any natural source, including musical instruments) that were recorded onto magnetic tape and then manipulated by various means—for example, by changing the speed of the playback, reversing the direction of the tape, or processing the sounds through external devices such as filters.

The possibility of using not only natural but also artificially generated sounds soon presented itself, and a wide variety of sound equipment came into use. Significant in this regard were the experiments begun around 1951 at Columbia University. Within a few years, studios for the production of tape **Tape music** music (an extension of *musique concrète*) sprang up in many of the chief musical centers of Europe and America. With the raw sound (either naturally or electronically produced) as a starting point, the composer could isolate its components, alter its pitch, volume, or other dimensions, play it backward, add reverberation (echo), filter out some of the overtones, or add other components by splicing and overdubbing. Even though all these operations were laborious and time-consuming—it might take many hours to process only a minute or two of finished music—composers hastened to try out and use the new medium.

Electronische Musik

The second trend occurred during the early 1950s, in Cologne, Germany, where a new studio was built exclusively for the creation of *electronische Musik*. By 1953, German composer Karlheinz Stockhausen had begun working in the new studio, where he produced his electronic masterpiece *Song of the Youths* (*Gesang der Jünglinge*, 1956), a composition integrating the human voice with electronically generated sounds. The heart of this German system was the oscillator, which could generate one of several waveforms, each capable of a different timbre. This electronically generated waveform could be subjected to filters, reverberation (by means of an echo chamber), amplifiers, and other devices that altered the sound. Eventually, these many components would be packaged together in a single console with a keyboard interface to become our modern-day *synthesizer*.

Synthesizers

The first system to present a completely integrated package of electronic components for sound generation was the RCA music synthesizer, completed in 1955. A second version of the RCA synthesizer was delivered to Columbia-Princeton's Electronic Music Center in 1959, where composers such as Milton Babbitt produced compositions using this new machine. Unfortunately, the size and cost of this device prohibited other institutions from purchasing synthesizers of their own, and very few composers had the luxury of being able to work at the Electronic Music Center. Composing on the RCA synthesizer also proved to be tedious and time con-suming, and hours were spent programming the machine to produce just a few minutes of music.

By the 1960s, however, both Robert Moog and Donald Buchla had created more compact and affordable synthesizers suited for mass production. These newer synthesizers capitalized on the transistor technology developed in the late 1950s (the RCA synthesizer used bulky vacuum tubes, whereas transistors used only a fraction of that space) and the more efficient voltage-controlled oscillator as developed by Moog. A recording called *Switched-On Bach*, made in 1968 by Walter Carlos (who later became Wendy Carlos), catapulted the synthesizer and the genre of electronic music to instant fame. The Moog synthesizer that Carlos used for the recording was quickly adopted by many musicians in the world of popular music. Carlos's synthesizer music can also be heard on the soundtracks of films such as Stanley Kubrick's *A Clockwork Orange* (1971) and *The Shining* (1980).

This initial wave of commercially available synthesizers marked the era of *analog* synthesis. But by the late 1960s, a new wave of technology known as *digital frequency modulation synthesis* had already been developed at Stanford University. Synthesis by means of frequency modulation (FM) depends on a series of sine-wave generators acting upon each other to produce new, more complex, waveforms. (These digital waveforms are represented by a string of discrete numbers as opposed to analog signals, which are continuous in nature, such as electrical current.) The rights to this new technique were sold to a company named Yamaha. It took nearly ten years before Yamaha turned FM synthesis into a commercially feasible product. In 1983, the Yamaha DX7, one of the best-selling synthesizers of all time, was unveiled and retailed for slightly under $2,000. During that same year, a standardized communications protocol known as the *Musical Instrument Digital Interface* (MIDI) was officially adopted and incorporated into all new music synthesizers. MIDI allows synthesizers not only to communicate with one another, but with other devices such as computers, signal processors, drum machines, and even mixing boards. Specially designed software allows composers to record MIDI data (such as pitch, duration, volume, etc.) on the computer for playback on one or more synthesizers. By the mid-1980s, digital sampling synthesizers, capable of digitizing short audio samples, became affordable to the average musician. Digital samplers allow performers and composers to recreate a realistic sounding grand piano, trumpet, violin, bird call, car crash, or any other sound that can be sampled. With the affordability of digital synthesizers and personal computers, and their ability to communicate with one another, the digital revolution has managed to take the world of electronic music by storm.

Computer music, however, did not wait for the invention of MIDI to become integrated with the world of electronic music. Research in this field had already begun with the pioneering work of Max Mathews at Bell Laboratories in the 1950s. While Mathews explored the idea of using a computer to synthesize sounds via his series of MUSIC software programs (eleven versions in all), other composers employed the computer to generate music compositions. Most early work in automated composition was achieved by Lejaren Hiller, who developed a software program in 1956 that subsequently "composed" the *Illiac Suite for String Quartet*. Another collaborative effort, this time with composer John Cage (see p. 472), produced the computer-generated composition *HPSCHD* (1969), featuring elements of

FM Synthesis

MIDI

Digital sampling

Robert Moog, creator of the pioneering Moog synthesizer.

Edgar Varèse's *Poème électronique* was composed as part of a multimedia show for the Philips Pavilion, designed by Le Corbusier, at the 1958 Brussels World's Fair.

indeterminacy and randomness. More recently, composers such as David Cope have employed artificial intelligence techniques to create compositions in the style of the great masters such as Bach and Mozart. (For more on computers and music, see CP 23).

Important Figures in Electronic Music

One of the pioneers of electronic music was the French composer Edgard Varèse (1883–1965), whose composition *Poème electronique* (1956–58), commissioned for a sound-and- light show at Philips Pavilion at the 1958 Brussels World's Fair, consisted of both electronic and *concrète* sounds recorded onto multichannel tape. Varèse combined natural sounds (for example, the human voice) with electronically generated sounds and subjected them to tape music techniques such as altering the tape speed, using filters, and adding reverberation. The result was recognizable sounds—voices, bells, a flying airplane—along with pulse-generated percussion sounds and synthetic tones. The pavilion design by Le Corbusier called for music to accompany both the projected images and the lighting effects in order to provide a complete audio-visual experience. The music was recorded onto multiple tape channels along with control information for the more than four hundred speakers as well as film projectors, spotlights, and an array of multicolored lamps and bulbs distributed throughout the pavilion.

Electronic music has two novel aspects. The most immediately obvious one, the possibility to create new sounds, has impelled many musicians to use the medium. Equally important, the composer of electronic music can work directly with the sounds and produce a finished work without the help of an intermediary performer.

However, combining electronic sounds with live music has also proved fertile. Works for soloist and recorded tape have become common, even "concertos" for tape recorder (or live-performance synthesizer or computer) and orchestra. **Mario Davidovsky** One important composer working in this mixed medium is Mario Davidovsky (b. 1934): among his works for tape and live performer is a series known as *Synchronisms* (1963–88), dialogues for solo instrument and prerecorded tape. No. 1, for flute and tape, is particularly effective because of the flute's purity of tone, wide range of dynamics, and agility in pitch and articulation.

Milton Babbitt Another important voice in the field of electronic music is that of Milton Babbitt (b. 1916), who was one of the first to recognize its possibilities. Babbitt's early electronic works, composed at the Columbia-Princeton Electronic Music Center, reflect his interest in assuming total control of the final musical result. But it was never his intention that the synthesizer should replace the live musician. "I know of no serious electronic composer who ever asserts that we are supplanting any other form of music. . . . We're interested in increasing the resources of music." Like Davidovsky, he saw as the next step combining electronic music with live performers, an area in which he has contributed such pathbreaking works as *Philomel* (1964) and *Phonemena* (1974), both for soprano and tape. Babbitt has been a highly influential teacher at Princeton University to several generations of talented young composers.

Pauline Oliveros (b. 1932), one of the more experimental contemporary composers, has explored mixed media and the possibilities of multichannel tape interacting with live performers and theatrical forms. Oliveros is also known for her experiments with live electronic music, in which sounds are generated and manipulated during the performance. Her developing interest in the 1970s in Asian culture and philosophy resulted in *Sonic Meditations* (1971–74), twenty-five pieces with verbal descriptions that suggest ways to make, hear, and think about sounds. Her later works look back to earlier techniques: *The Roots of the Moment* (1988), for example, combines an interactive electronic environment with a favorite instrument of hers, the accordion.

Pauline Oliveros

Electronic music has permeated the commercial world of music making in a big way. Much of the music we hear today as movie and TV soundtracks is electronically generated, although some effects resemble the sounds of conventional instruments so closely that we are not always aware of the new technology. Popular music groups have been "electrified" for some years, but now most of them regularly feature synthesizers and samplers that both simulate conventional rock band instruments and produce altogether new sounds.

Lansky: *Notjustmoreidlechatter*

"I like to project the idea that my electronic sounds don't have a supernatural origin, that they have a human origin."

Paul Lansky (b. 1944), a pioneer in digital sound synthesis, is one of the most prominent figures in the world of computer music. A faculty member at Princeton University since 1969, Lansky has received many awards, fellowships, and commissions, and has made notable contributions to music theory and music criticism.

Like most contemporary composers, Lansky has explored a number of compositional methods. Some of his early works for chamber ensembles and solo instruments reflect his interest in a twelve-tone system. For the past twenty years,

Paul Lansky

🎺 Principal Works

Chamber/instrumental works, including 2 string quartets (1967, 1971/rev. 1977), *Crossworks* (1978, for piano, flute, clarinet, violin, cello), *As If* (1981–82, for string trio with computer-generated tape), *Hop* (1993, for marimba and violin)

Electronic/computer works, including *mild und leise* (1973), *Six Fantasies on a Poem by Thomas Campion* (1979), *As it grew dark* (1983), *Guy's Harp* (1984), *Idle Chatter* (1985), *just_more_idle_chatter* (1987), *Notjustmoreidlechatter* (1988), *Smalltalk* (1988), *Not So Heavy Metal* (1989), *QuakerBridge* (1990), *The Sound of Two Hands* (1990), *Table's Clear* (1992), *Still Time* (1994), *Things She Carried* (1997, computer opera), and *Dancetracks* (1997, with Steven Mackey).

Artificial Intelligence: The Composer's New Tool

A few years ago, most people had never heard the term "artificial intelligence." It was only the recent Stanley Kubrick/Steven Spielberg movie *A. I. Artificial Intelligence* (2001) that set the term in the public's consciousness—but the movie did nothing to explain the actual technology. Artificial intelligence is certainly not new; in fact, it is roughly a half century old. This area of computer science is now working its way into all aspects of our lives, and music is no exception.

The concept of using computers for music composition dates back to the early nineteenth century with Ada Augusta (1815–1852), Countess of Lovelace. She was the daughter of the English poet

Ada Augusta, Countess of Lovelace, was able to foresee the possibilities of composing music with computers.

Lord Byron, and has often been called the world's first computer programmer. In her remarks on inventor Charles Babbage's analytical engine (1834), she conjectured that the device (considered to be the world's first computer) could do more than compute mathematical equations—it could also compose music. She was more than a century ahead of her time, but she was right.

The first applications of AI and music appeared in the 1960s and focused on the creation of expert systems (computer programs dependent on expert-level knowledge) that used rules to compose music in a given style. By the 1980s, David Cope, a longtime contributor to the field of AI and music, had developed a notable AI computer program called Experiments in Musical Intelligence (EMI). This program has successfully generated new compositions in the style of Palestrina, Bach, Mozart, and Chopin, among others. In fact, a musical "Turing test" was conducted on an unsuspecting audience who were asked to identify which piece was composed by the computer and which was by Bach. (The Turing test, invented by Alan Turing in 1950, was meant to determine whether or not a computer was truly intelligent.) Most people chose the computer composition as the "authentic" Bach work. Classical music enthusiasts and technology buffs alike can hear these compositions by David Cope's EMI on recordings such as *Bach by Design* (1993) and *Virtual Mozart* (1997).

In more recent years, AI has focused on new methods for computer composition and analysis using artificial neural networks and genetic algorithms. The unique advantage of neural networks is their ability to learn. Artificial neural networks

however, he has preferred the medium of computer-synthesized music. Lansky fully embraced computer-assisted composition in *Idle Chatter* (1985) and its two sequels, *just_more_idle_chatter* (1987) and *Notjustmoreidlechatter* (1988). In these works, the computer participates in defining and creating the compositional procedures and the complex textures. *Notjustmoreidlechatter*, which we will consider, is unified by a simple recurring tonal bass progression, over which the listener hears thousands of unintelligible synthesized word fragments.

attempt to mimic the biological processes of the human brain by digitally simulating a network of neurons, their interconnections, and the strengths of these connections. Using this approach, the computer is given multiple samples of a composer's work in the form of training data until the computer has "learned" the composer's style. Not only can the computer create new pieces of music, it can provide valuable information about a composer's works. Neural networks can provide composers, music theorists, and musicologists with new tools for understanding the great masterpieces of music.

At the forefront of many new AI applications is a new methodology known as genetic algorithms (sometimes called evolutionary algorithms). With genetic algorithms, programmers do not program the solution directly; rather, they allow a solution to evolve. This process of evolution mimics the natural, biological process by simulating reproduction, crossover, and mutation within a computer program.

Composers (and musically inclined computer scientists) have applied the techniques of evolutionary computing to the composition of music. To generate a melody, for example, the programmer would create a "population of individuals," each "individual" representing a randomly generated melodic fragment. Each melodic fragment would be able to reproduce and cross over (combine bits of their melody with bits of another melody), forming a new generation of melodic solutions. The programmer must also decide what constitutes a "good" melody (in the form of a fitness function) and then evaluate the resulting melodies accordingly. Those not meeting the criteria are eliminated (the survival of the fittest analogy), and the process continues. Mutation (randomly altering a single note, for example) can be

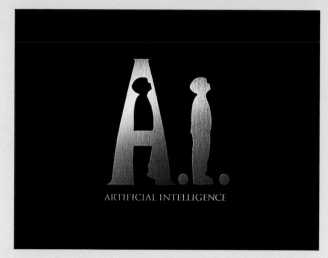

The very recognizable logo from the film *A. I. Artificial Intelligence* (2001).

introduced at any time to bring about possible new solutions. The evolutionary process may be repeated hundreds of times until a satisfactory result—in this case, a good melody—has been achieved. The programmer may choose to run the program again until all aspects of the composition have emerged: harmony, rhythm, texture, tempo, and dynamics.

As exciting as these artificial intelligence techniques are, they have yet to be fully explored. While programmers are busy writing code, scientists and engineers are working to increase the computing power of our hardware. Composers, performers, teachers, theorists, and musicologists will surely harness the power of these new supercomputers to run increasingly more sophisticated AI programs. After nearly a half century in obscurity, artificial intelligence promises to come into its own, and to realize fully Ada Augusta's prediction of computer-generated music.

The fragments first appear random, then the "chatter" becomes almost understandable and "human"; but this perception is soon lost, and the listener abandons any hope of making sense out of the "text." Lansky uses a technique called linear predictive coding (LPC) to produce a series of "frames," each of which contains information on the sound frequencies and timbral qualities that combine to make up speech at various moments. He then synthesizes a voice using these frames to control the filtering of an artificial sound produced by a buzz

in his own words

I have adopted computer music technology as a kind of aural microscope on the sounds of the world. My pieces concern themselves with the way people speak, formally and informally . . . the way they play musical instruments . . . the sounds of urban scenes and anything else whose odd shape and contour has the potential to make interesting music.

generator. White noise is mixed in to produce certain consonants, and the buzz generator controls the pitch and rhythm of the "words," giving a "humanness" to the computer-generated sounds. The resulting lively and engaging work draws the listener in to its varied speech sounds.

Lansky's broad-ranging interests extend to blues and folk music, as revealed in *Guy's Harp* (1984), for computer-processed harmonica. He has also collaborated on several works with his Princeton colleague, the electric guitarist Steven Mackey, to produce *Not So Heavy Metal* (1980) and *Dancetracks* (1994).

In recent years, contemporary composers have leaned more toward increased interactivity—not only between the composer or performer and technology, but with the audience and even the at-home listener. Interactivity at home means that a lay person—without sophisticated musical training—can participate in the musical process.

Composer Tod Machover has successfully broken down the boundary between the listener and the creator. His *Brain Opera*, which premiered in 1996 at New York's Lincoln Center, was wired into the Internet. The event was in two parts: the first an informal one, where the audiences explored and played with his electronically enhanced hyperinstruments, and a second, more formal

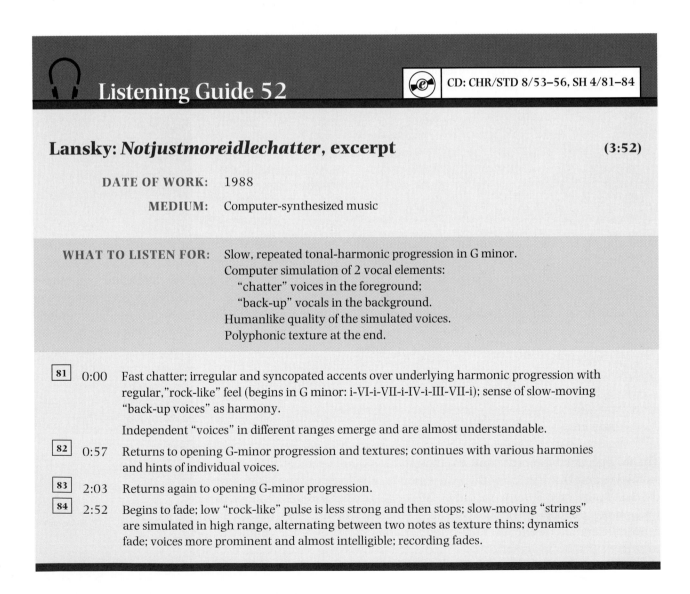

Listening Guide 52

CD: CHR/STD 8/53–56, SH 4/81–84

Lansky: *Notjustmoreidlechatter*, excerpt (3:52)

DATE OF WORK:	1988
MEDIUM:	Computer-synthesized music

WHAT TO LISTEN FOR: Slow, repeated tonal-harmonic progression in G minor.
Computer simulation of 2 vocal elements:
    "chatter" voices in the foreground;
    "back-up" vocals in the background.
Humanlike quality of the simulated voices.
Polyphonic texture at the end.

81	0:00	Fast chatter; irregular and syncopated accents over underlying harmonic progression with regular, "rock-like" feel (begins in G minor: i-VI-i-VII-i-IV-i-III-VII-i); sense of slow-moving "back-up voices" as harmony.
		Independent "voices" in different ranges emerge and are almost understandable.
82	0:57	Returns to opening G-minor progression and textures; continues with various harmonies and hints of individual voices.
83	2:03	Returns again to opening G-minor progression.
84	2:52	Begins to fade; low "rock-like" pulse is less strong and then stops; slow-moving "strings" are simulated in high range, alternating between two notes as texture thins; dynamics fade; voices more prominent and almost intelligible; recording fades.

performance that incorporated recordings from the incoming audience and from participants on the Web. After its premiere, the *Brain Opera* toured North America, Europe, and Asia, and was then updated for its installation at the House of Music in Vienna. The composer believes firmly that

> one of the great things about technology is that it can break down barriers, such as the difficulty of mastering a musical instrument or the mystery of learning musical technique. Technology lets people tap skills that they already had; it lets people use their intuition to make creative decisions without having the detailed knowledge. It will change the way we think about concerts.

We can only imagine to what new regions composers will lead their art. What is increasingly clear is that they have no intention of leaving the audience behind. Such attempts to bridge the gap between the audience and the composer through interactivity are meant to draw in a new generation of technologically savvy listeners.

I envison a time in which new works will be convincingly composed in the styles of composers long dead. . . . Musicians and non-musicians alike will interplay with programs which allow them to endlessly tinker with the styles of the composing program. . . . Machines, after all, only add and subtract. Programs that benefit from those operations are only as good as their creators.

—DAVID COPE

75

Some Current Trends

"The current state of music presents a variety of solutions in search of a problem, the problem being to find somebody left to listen."

—NED ROREM

KEY POINTS

- The current compositional styles of both *New Romanticism* and *minimalism* seek to appeal to audiences who have been alienated by the highly intellectual and structural aspects of twentieth-century music.
- *New Romanticism* favors a harmonic language from the late Romantic era, sometimes coupled with a highly virtuosic style and new instrumental combinations.
- The American composer Joan Tower's *Fanfares for the Uncommon Woman* and her orchestral work *For the Uncommon Woman* exemplify her New Romantic style, and make a feminist statement as well.
- *Minimalist music* is based on repetitive melodic, rhythmic, or harmonic patterns with few or slowly changing variations. The music can sound hypnotic (as in *new-age music*) or motor-driven and frenzied. Important exponents of this style are Steve Reich and Philip Glass.
- *Spiritual minimalism* is a recent trend characterized by a simple, nonpulsed music that stems from deep religious convictions; the Estonian composer Arvo Pärt's choral music (including *Cantate Domino canticum novum*) is a good introduction to this style.
- American composer John Adams has successfully combined elements of New Romanticism and minimalism into a *post-minimalist style*, using a lush harmonic language in his high-energy compositions (as in the Chamber Symphony).

The New Romanticism

Serial, or twelve-tone, music, with its emphasis on intellectual and constructivist aspects (the highly structural use of all musical elements), has lost some favor in recent decades to a more eclectic synthesis of familiar styles known as the New Romanticism. A number of composers felt that the time had come to close the gap between themselves and the public by restoring music to its former position as "the language of the emotions," complete with appealing melodies, regular rhythms, lush harmonies, and rich orchestral colors.

The New Romanticism has taken a variety of forms. Some composers have combined the general harmonic language of the Romantic era with other current trends, such as the New Virtuosity (see p. 469). Others have used the Romantic style or the works of a particular composer more literally. As usual, there are no clear dividing lines. Many works that are labeled as examples of the New Romanticism share techniques with serial and aleatoric music and employ the new instrumental possibilities that have opened up since the middle of the century.

Samuel Barber

The New Romanticism had an important precursor in Samuel Barber (1910–1981), whose music, suffused with feeling, leans toward the grand gestures of nineteenth-century tradition. Several of his works achieved enormous popularity, among them the light-hearted Overture to *The School for Scandal* (1932) and the elegiac *Adagio for Strings* (1936).

Ned Rorem

Ned Rorem (b. 1923), one of the most distinguished composers of his generation, has written widely in all genres, from chamber and orchestral music to opera. His songs are in the line of descent from the great French art song of the post-Romantic period.

Thea Musgrave

One of the leading exponents of the New Romanticism is the Scottish-born composer Thea Musgrave (b. 1928). She is best-known for her stage works—operas and ballets. *Mary, Queen of Scots* (1977) is a highly accessible tonal opera that draws on the history of the composer's native land. A figure from American history serves as the heroine in her opera *Harriet, the Woman Called Moses* (1985)—Harriet Tubman, who escaped from slavery and helped establish the Underground Railroad. Musgrave's *Simón Bolívar* (1995) brings to the stage the bloody story of South America's fight for independence from Spain.

David Del Tredici

Of a more recent generation of composers interested in the New Romanticism, David Del Tredici (b. 1937) stands out for the broad lyric appeal of his music. He spent some years writing large works for soprano and orchestra inspired by Lewis Carroll's *Alice's Adventures in Wonderland* and *Through the Looking Glass*. Two compositions based on these novels—*Final Alice* (1976) and *In Memory of a Summer Day* (1980)—have found special favor with the public. His recent works are more personal and introspective, including *Gay Life* (1996–2000), set to texts by Alan Ginsberg, Federico García Lorca, and Paul Monette, among others.

John Corigliano

John Corigliano's (b. 1938) music displays an imaginative use of contemporary techniques. Two of his recent works are dedicated to AIDS victims: the Symphony No. 1 (1995; subtitled the *AIDS* Symphony) and the cantata *Of Rage and Remembrance* (1996), based on the third movement of the *AIDS* Symphony, with a text that combines an emotionally intense poem by William Hoffman with a litany of victims' names. As noted earlier, Corigliano also wrote the Oscar-winning soundtrack for the 1999 art film *The Red Violin*.

Amid the late-twentieth-century composers whose experiments have produced such a wide variety of styles, Ellen Taaffe Zwilich (b. 1939) has continued the great tradition of the symphony. In 1975, Zwilich became the first woman to earn a doctorate in composition from the Juilliard School in New York. She was also the first woman to win a Pulitzer Prize in composition, granted in 1983 for her Symphony No. 1 (1982). Zwilich's loyalty to traditional forms and her reaffirmation of tonality have endeared her to concert audiences and musicians alike.

Like other New Romantics, Libby Larsen (b. 1950) has sought ways to make her music more accessible to the general audience. Some of her works express her interest in illuminating strong-minded women—among these are *Songs from Letters* (1989), a song cycle set to letters that sharpshooter Calamity Jane wrote to her daughter, and *Eleanor Roosevelt* (2000), a dramatic cantata based on the life and words of the former First Lady. Born in Minnesota, the "land of ten-thousand lakes," Larsen found inspiration in her environment for *Symphony: Water Music* (1985), which presents four sonic portraits of "the motions and rhythms of nature." The first movement, *Fresh Breeze*, pays homage to Handel's *Water Music* through a parody of the Alla hornpipe dance we heard earlier (see p. 169). This parodying technique is often referred to as *quotation music*.

In this scene from *The Red Violin* (1999), the seventeenth-century craftsman Nicolo Bussotti (Carlo Cecchi) creates a magnificent instrument. John Corigliano's film score features the virtuoso violin playing of Joshua Bell.

Quotation music

Joan Tower: *For the Uncommon Woman*

"I try to choreograph a landscape of sound that reaches people in an emotional, visceral, and formal kind of way—the formal being the sense of coherence of this landscape."

Joan Tower (b. 1938) was born in New Rochelle, New York, and grew up in South America, where her father worked as a geologist and mining engineer. She returned to the United States to attend Bennington College and Columbia University, where she received a doctorate in composition. In 1969, she founded the Da Capo Players, a performance group dedicated to new music. Tower was appointed composer-in-residence of the St. Louis Symphony in 1985 and during the next year wrote *Silver Ladders*, which earned her the prestigeous Grawemeyer Award (she was the first American to receive this honor). She has taught at Bard College in Annandale-on-Hudson, New York, since 1972.

In her early works, Tower explored the possibilities of serialism, but abandoned that technique with *Breakfast Rhythms I and II* (1974–75), for clarinet and five instruments, which turns to a more organic approach. Her chamber work *Black Topaz* (1976), for piano and six instruments, is one of a set of three "mineral" pieces that pay tribute to her father and that exemplify the composer's interest in geology. Her first orchestral work, *Sequoia* (1981), explores the disparity between the majestic size of the sequoia tree and its miniscule needles. Tower's music has been strongly influenced by that of earlier masters, including Beethoven, Stravinsky, and Copland. In her Piano Concerto (1985),

Joan Tower

Principal Works

Orchestra music, including *Sequoia* (1981), *Silver Ladders* (1986), and *For the Uncommon Woman* (1992); concertos for flute, clarinet, cello, violin, and piano (*Homage to Beethoven*, 1985; *Rapids*, 1996); *Concerto for Orchestra* (1991)

Chamber music, including *Breakfast Rhythms I and II* (1974–75), *Black Topaz* (1976), *Petroushskates* (1980), *Wings* (1981), *Fanfare for the Uncommon Woman* (Nos. 1, 2, 3, 5, 1986–93)

Stage works, including *Stepping Stones* (1993)

Works for wind ensemble, including *Fascinating Ribbons* (2001)

she pays homage to Beethoven, making prominent use of three of his piano sonatas. Her delightful chamber work *Petroushskates* (1980) combines a parody of Stravinsky's ballet *Petrushka* with a figure-skating theme.

Concertos   Tower's relationship with some of today's leading instrumental artists has led her to embrace the concerto: among her notable contributions to this genre are a Clarinet Concerto (1988), a Flute Concerto (1989), a Violin Concerto (1992) and *Rapids* (Piano Concerto No. 2, 1996), composed for Ursula Oppens, a pianist noted for her interpretation of contemporary music.

The series *Fanfares for the Uncommon Woman* makes a strong feminist statement—a rarity for Tower, who is reticent to speak about the role of gender in her music. The first of these was written in 1986 as a tribute to Aaron **Tribute to Copland**   Copland's brilliant *Fanfare for the Common Man* (1942); here, she uses the same instrumentation (brass and percussion) as Copland did, and quotes his work in the opening bars—but, she comments, her work is for "women who takes risks and are adventurous." Her third *Fanfare* (1991), commissioned by Carnegie Hall for its One Hundredth Anniversary Concert—an important and glitzy event in the classical music world—has already been played by over two hundred different ensembles, giving her widespread visibility. We will consider the fourth work in this series; however, Tower has aptly revised the title to *For the Uncommon Woman* (1992). As one reviewer noted, this is "no 'mere' fanfare; it might be better called an overture . . . it's a brilliant orchestral showpiece compacted within a four-minute span." *For the Uncommon Woman* (see Listening Guide 53), scored for full orchestra, was commissioned by the Kansas City Symphony and is dedicated to conductor JoAnn Falletta, well known for her recordings of works by women composers. A reviewer at the premiere observed that "great slabs of dissonant brass chords crunch up against each other and chattering figurations run their way through the whole orchestra." Throughout, Tower uses the large arsenal of percussion instruments to punctuate the two contrasting ideas. The work builds to a forceful, dissonant closing, letting up the tension only on the final, unison pitch. This dynamic work presents an absorbing soundscape that falls into the realm of the New Romantics while also representing Tower's unique and personal musical voice.

Listening Guide 53

CD:CHR/STD 8/47-52, SH 4/85-90

Tower: *For the Uncommon Woman*

(4:27)

DATE OF WORK: 1992

MEDIUM: Orchestra (commissioned by Kansas City Symphony)

FORM: Free (alternates two musical ideas)

WHAT TO LISTEN FOR: Alternation of 2 musical ideas: dissonant sound masses and wavering figure.
Focus on brass and percussion timbres.
High dissonance levels, punctuated by percussive accents.
Organic growth of ideas throughout work.
Release of tension in final unison note.

85 0:00 Dissonant sustained chords, at slow tempo; accented (*fp*), with swells; percussion and brass featured.

86 0:32 Quicker tempo with wavering motive in strings (in 16th notes), answered by woodwinds (in triplets). Short motivic idea grows in length, volume, and tempo.

0:59 Wavering melody played softly by 2 muted trumpets. Momentum builds, and sweeping scales lead to return of opening idea.

87 1:18 Return to dissonant sound masses, punctuated by percussion.

88 1:42 Wavering motive in woodwinds over sustained strings, then in horns.

89 2:07 Rising figure in clarinets, then dissonance builds in brass in antiphonal statements (high vs. low), trills in strings as energy level grows.

90 3:00 Return of wavering motive in full orchestra, heard in different instruments and in changing meters; idea builds, then reduced to 2-note rhythmic figure.

3:57 Coda—sustained chords, played sforzando (*sfz*); dissonant brass with percussion; tension released on final unison note, D, played *fff*.

Minimalism and Post-Minimalism

"Now that things are so simple, there's so much to do."
—MORTON FELDMAN

Independent of the New Romantics, another group of composers found their own way to simplify the musical language. They stripped their compositions down to the barest essentials in order to concentrate the listener's attention on a few basic details. This urge toward a minimal art, which first found expression in painting and sculpture, became a significant force in contemporary music during the 1970s, and has remained a strong voice.

The salient feature of *minimalist music*, as it has come to be known, is the repetition of melodic, rhythmic, and harmonic patterns with very little variation. The music changes so slowly that it can have a hypnotic effect, and indeed the term "trance music" has attached itself to some works of the minimalists. But it is a label they reject because, as they point out, their material is selected most carefully and worked out in highly disciplined procedures. One can say, however, that in minimalist music, time moves at a different pace from what most of us are accustomed to.

In simplifying melody, rhythm, and harmony within an unwavering tonality, the minimalists have turned away from the complex, highly intellectual style of the serialists. Instead, they open themselves to modes of thought emanating from Third World countries—especially the contemplative art of India

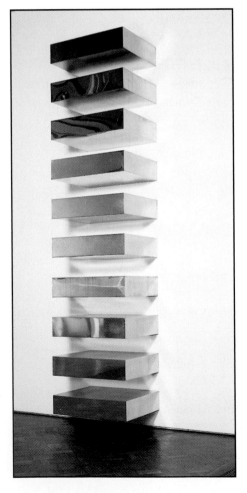

Sculptor Donald Judd uses space as a building material, along with polished copper, in this repetitive minimalist work. *Untitled* (1969).

and the quasi-obsessive rhythms of some African cultures—and to jazz, pop, and rock. Although influenced by the early ideas of John Cage, minimalists for the most part reject his interest in indeterminacy and chance. They prefer to control their sounds.

There are several kinds of minimalist music. In some works, the pulse is repeated with numbing regularity. Others are very busy on the surface, though the harmonies and timbres change very slowly. Terry Riley (b. 1935) introduced the element of pulse and the concept of tiny motivic cells that repeat in his ninety-minute masterwork *In C* (1964).

The most widely known minimalists are Steve Reich (b. 1936), whose music achieves a trancelike quality that derives from his study on non-Western—especially African—music, and Philip Glass (b. 1937). Glass studied at the University of Chicago and the Juilliard School, and in Paris on a Fulbright Scholarship. His contact with the Indian sitar player Ravi Shankar (see illustration on p. 56), influenced the composer's fascination with non-Western music. "And, of course," Glass wrote, "I was also hearing the music of Miles Davis, of John Coltrane, and the Beatles." When he returned to New York, he became convinced that "modern music had become truly decadent, stagnant, uncommunicative. Composers were writing for each other and the public didn't seem to care." It was out of this conviction that Glass evolved his own style, drawing on the musical traditions of India and Africa as well as the techniques of rock and progressive jazz. His most important works include *Glassworks* (1983) and his operas *Einstein on the Beach* (1976), *Satyagraha* (1980), and *Akhnaten* (1984).

One branch of minimalism that has developed, mostly at the hands of European composers, is a nonpulsed music inspired by religious beliefs and expressed in deceptively simple—and seemingly endless—chains of lush modal or tonal progressions. The major representatives of this deeply meditative music, often referred to as *spiritual minimalism*, are Arvo Pärt, an Estonian composer who combines the mysticism of Russian Orthodox rituals with elements of Eastern European folk music; and John Taverner (b. 1944), an English composer whose style combines elements of New Romanticism with a devout spiritualism. Taverner's powerful choral work *Song for Athene* was heard by millions at the close of the funeral service for Princess Diana on September 6, 1997; its text, "Alleluia. May flights of angels sing thee to thy rest," is drawn from Shakespeare's *Hamlet* and from the Orthodox Vigil Service.

Arvo Pärt

Arvo Pärt and Spiritual Minimalism

"Arvo Pärt's music accepts silence and death, and thus reaffirms the basic truth of life, its frailty compassionately realised, its sacred beauty observed and celebrated."

—PAUL HILLIER

Arvo Pärt (b. 1935) was born and raised in Estonia, a former republic of the Soviet Union (USSR). As a youth, Pärt studied piano, but the instrument on which he practiced needed repairs to its middle register so badly that he explored the sounds of the extreme upper and lower regions of the piano. His first acquaintance with orchestral music was as a teenager, when he congregated with his friends in the town square and listened to music piped over loudspeakers. He met his two-year military service requirement as a snare drummer in an army band, after which he studied music at the Tallinn Conservatory. While a student, he worked as a recording engineer for the Estonian State Radio, and supported himself writing music for films and stage productions.

Early years

In his early compositions, Pärt explored both Neoclassical and serial techniques. These early works are set in a Baroque imitative style. One such composition is *Collage sur B-A-C-H* (1964), in which Pärt transcribes a Bach dance

Principal Works

Orchestra works, including *Cantus in memoriam Benjamin Britten* (string orchestra and bells, 1977); concertos *Pro et contra* (for cello, 1966), and *Tabula Rasa* (for 2 violins, 1977)

Instrumental chamber works, including *Collage sur B-A-C-H* (1964) and *Fratres* (1977)

Sacred choral works, including *Credo* (for piano, chorus, and orchestra, 1968), *Cantate Domino canticum novum* (1977, rev. 1996), *St. John Passion* (1982), Seven Magnificat Antiphons (1988), *Magnificat* (1989), and *Kanon Pokajanen* (on Russian Orthodox texts, 1997)

Listening Guide 54

CD: CHR/STD 8/43–46, SH 4/91–94

Pärt: *Cantate Domino canticum novum*

(2:50)

DATE OF WORK:	1977 (rev. 1996)
MEDIUM:	SATB chorus and organ
TEXT:	Psalm 95 (Catholic Bible); Psalm 96 (Protestant Bible)

WHAT TO LISTEN FOR:
Chantlike melodies in repetitive patterns.
Free-flowing rhythms, following text, with pauses at text punctuation.
Contrasting, or mirror, motion between the voices.
Voices often paired SA and TB.
Changing textures: 1 voice, 2 voices, and 4 voices.
Tintinnabular, or bell-like, style.
Occasional harsh dissonances (intervals of 2nds).

	TEXT	TRANSLATION	VOICES (WITH ORGAN)
91 0:00	Cantate Domino canticum novum:	O sing to the Lord a new song:	Sopranos
	Cantate Domino omnis terra.	Sing to the Lord, all the earth.	
	Cantate Domino, et benedicite nomini ejus:	Sing to the Lord, bless his name;	Sopranos and Altos
	Annuntiate de die in diem salutare ejus.	Tell of his salvation from day today.	
	Annuntiate inter gentes gloriam ejus,	Declare his glory among the nations.	SATB
	In omnibus populis mirabilia ejus.	His marvelous works among all the peoples.	
92 0:35	Quoniam magnus Dominus, et laudabilis nimis:	For great is the Lord, and greatly to be praised.	Tenors
	Terribilis est super omnes deos.	He is to be feared above all gods.	
	Quoniam omnes dii gentium daemonia:	For all the gods of the people are idols;	Tenors and Basses
	Dominus autem coelos fecit.	But the Lord made the heavens.	
	Confessio et pulchritudo in conspectu ejus:	Honor and majesty are before him;	
	Sanctimonia et magnifcentia in sanctificatione ejus.	Strength and beauty are his salvation.	
93 1:09	Afferte Domino patriae gentium,	Ascribe to the Lord, o families of the peoples.	Sopranos
	Afferte Domino gloriam et honorem:	Ascribe to the Lord glory and strength;	
	Afferte Domino gloriam nomini ejus.	Ascribe to the Lord the glory due his name.	

Tollite hostias, et introite in atria ejus:	Bring an offering, and come into his courts.	Sopranos and Altos
Adorate Dominum in atria sancto ejus.	Worship the Lord in holy array.	
Commoveatur a facie ejus universa terra:	Tremble before him, all the earth;	SATB
Dicite in gentibus quia Dominus regnavit.	Say among the nations, "The Lord reigns.	

94 1:52

Etenim corexit orbem terrae qui non commovebitur:	Yea, the world is established, it shall never be moved.	Tenors
Judicabit populus in aequitate.	He will judge the peoples with equity."	
Laetentur caeli, et exsultet terra:	Let the heavens be glad, and let the earth rejoice;	Tenors and Basses
Commoveatur mare, et plenitudo eius:	Let the sea roar, and all that fills it;	
Gaudebunt campi, et omnia quae in eis sunt.	Let the field exult, and every thing in it.	
Tunc exsultabunt omnia ligna silvarium	Then shall all the trees of the wood sing for joy	SATB
A facie Domini, quia venit:	Before the Lord, for he comes;	
Quoniam venit iudicare terram.	For he comes to judge the earth.	
Judicabit orbem terrae in aequitate,	He will judge the world with righteousness,	
Et populos in veritate sua.	And the peoples with his truth.	

Duet between sopranos and altos, moving in contrary motion, showing free rhythmic notation (arrows mark stressed dissonances of interval of 2nd):

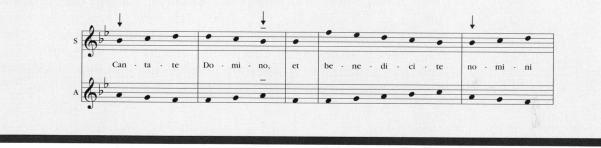

and then distorts it nearly beyond recognition. Likewise, his *Credo* (1968), for piano, chorus and orchestra, begins with a quote from the C-major Prelude of Bach's *Well-Tempered Clavier* (Book 1) that is soon fragmented and distorted. Estonian authorities were opposed to his religious texts like the Credo, but Pärt explains: "I didn't have political aims, yet I was asked exactly this question about my political aims in this Credo."

There have been several notable periods of compositional silence from Pärt; in the early 1970s, he studied medieval and Renaissance music, including chant, Notre Dame organum, and the masses of Josquin Des Prez, while at the same time working with an Estonian early music ensemble. When he returned to composition in 1976, there was a new-found spiritualism at the root of his music. He eschewed serialism in favor of a style all his own—*tintinnabulation* (after the Latin word for ringing of bells). "I created my tintinnabular style, and was declared mad. . . ." Three works from 1977

Medieval and Renaissance Music

in his own words

catapulted Pärt, and his tintinnabular sound, to international fame: *Fratres*, a chamber work that explores the interval of open fifths; *Cantus in memoriam Benjamin Britten*, for string orchestra and bells; and *Tabula Rasa*, a kind of Baroque concerto for two violins.

Pärt's religious convictions made life in the Soviet Union difficult (the state position was atheism), and in 1980 he and his family left, eventually settling in what was then West Berlin. Since 1980, Pärt has focused his creative efforts on Latin and Orthodox choral music. Pärt's choral work on Psalm 95, *Cantate Domino canticum novum* (O sing to the Lord a new song), is an alluring example of his tintinnabular style. Here, the composer returns to the simplicity of medieval chant for his inspiration: lyrical, conjunct lines move freely, always following the Latin text. At the same time, the work seems to dance along lightly, interrupted by brief moments of silence. Pärt does not use traditional notation; instead, he provides only black note-heads to indicate pitch, adding dashes to lengthen a note at the end of a phrase (one dash approximately doubles the value; two dashes triple it—the same as doubling an eighth note to equal a quarter, or tripling it to equal a dotted quarter note). This notation is very similar to notating Gregorian chant today; you can see an example in Listening Guide 2, on page 83.

Each section of Pärt's work begins with a fluid, monophonic line to which is joined a second line, or countermelody, that moves with the first, but in contrary motion, or inversion. At key points in the psalm text, the texture expands to the four-part choir (the added voices doubling in octaves, thus retaining a two-line texture), still in strict homorhythmic movement. There are clear examples of word painting, as when the full choir (SATB) proclaims "his glory among all the nations," and, near the end, announces that "all the trees of the wood sing for joy." The bell-like, or tintinnabular, style is achieved by weaving together two melodic lines that hover around a central pitch (B-flat) and by triadic pitches in the organ that seem to ring throughout. Pärt's serenely religious music rejects the sounds of modernity, returning to a purity and simplicity that reopens communication with the listener.

John Adams and Post-Minimalism

John Adams

Although both minimalism and the New Romanticism sought above all else to escape the overly intellectual world of serialism, they did so through very different paths. A composer who would respond to the emotional impulses of the New Romantics by seeking to expand the expressive gamut of minimalist music was bound to appear. John Adams (b. 1947), the best-known of the minimalist composers, answered this call. Adams was educated at Harvard University, and was thus steeped in serialism (he claimed "it was like a mausoleum where we would sit and count tone-rows in Webern"). In his dorm room, he preferred to listen to rock: "I was much inspired by certain albums that appeared to me to have a fabulous unity to them, like *Disraeli Gears*, *Abbey Road*, *Dark Side of the Moon*, and Marvin Gaye's *What's Going On?*" In 1971, he drove his Volkswagen Beetle cross-country to San Francisco, where he continues to live, and began teaching at the San Francisco Conservatory of Music in 1972. Adams quickly became an advocate for contemporary music in the Bay Area, serving as an adviser to the San Francisco Symphony and establishing its New and Unusual Music Series.

Strongly influenced by Steve Reich, Adams's music is marked by warm sonorities, a high energy level, and a more personal approach. He first gained notice with two hypnotic, minimalist works—*Phrygian Gates* (for piano, 1977) and *Shaker Loops* (for string septet, 1978)—and earned a national reputation with *Harmonium* (1980–81) and *Harmonielehre* (1984–85). With *Harmonielehre*, Adams expanded his harmonic palette to include the lush language of the late Romantic composers which he expressed with his own explosive force.

Adams attracted much attention with his opera *Nixon in China* (1987), which was a collaboration with the imaginative director Peter Sellars and the poet/librettist Alice Goodman. The opera takes place in Beijing, China, during the historic visit of former President Nixon in November 1972. Adams's score is playful and full of irony; the opera was enthusiastically received and played to sold-out houses.

The historic handshake between President Richard Nixon and Chinese Communist Party Chairman Mao Tse -tung in February 1972. The event was the inspiration for John Adam's 1987 opera *Nixon in China*.

His next opera, *The Death of Klinghoffer* (1991), touched a sensitive international nerve. Based on the 1985 hijacking of the cruise liner *Achille Lauro* by Palestinian terrorists and their murder of the Jewish-American passenger Leon Klinghoffer, this opera has been misunderstood and ill-received. Although Adams attempts to balance his portrayal of the Jews and Palestinians, the perennial clash between these two peoples and the horror of this particular event are far too upsetting for many to appreciate as art. Adam's next stage work was *I Was Looking at the Ceiling and Then I Saw the Stars* (1995), a comic, satiric work (he called it an "earthquake/romance") about the lives and loves of seven young Americans of different ethnicities, all residing in Los Angeles at the

🎺 Principal Works

Stage works, including *Nixon in China* (1987), *The Death of Klinghoffer* (1990–91), *I Was Looking at the Ceiling and Then I Saw the Sky* (1995), and *El Niño* (2000)

Orchestral works, including *The Chairman Dances* (orchestral fantasy on themes from *Nixon in China*, 1985), *Short Ride in a Fast Machine* (1986), Violin Concerto (1993), and *Lollapalooza* (1995)

Chamber music, including *Phrygian Gates* (1977), *Shaker Loops* (1978), *Grand Pianola Music* (with 3 female voices and chamber ensemble, 1982), and *Chamber Symphony* (1992)

Tape and electronic works, including *Heavy Metal* (1970) and *Hoodoo Zephyr* (1992–93)

Various arrangements, including orchestrations of some tangos by Astor Piazzola

Listening Guide 55

CD: CHR/STD 8/57–61, SH 4/95–99

Adams: *Roadrunner*, from Chamber Symphony, Third Movement

(5:52)

DATE OF WORK:	1992
MEDIUM:	Chamber orchestra (13 instruments including synthesizer); commissioned by the San Francisco Contemporary Chamber Players
OVERALL STRUCTURE:	I. *Mongrel Airs*
	II. *Aria with Walking Bass*
	III. *Roadrunner*

WHAT TO LISTEN FOR: Complex rhythmic treatment, with offbeats, syncopations, and polyrhythms.
Disjunct, short motivic ideas that are passed around the orchestra.
Furious motor-driven pace that rarely lets up.
Rhapsodic violin solo intercedes with double-stops.

95 0:00 Complex polyrhythms, with offbeats and continuous fast patterns; snare drum played on rim; occasional accented string chords punctuate the rhythms; synthesizer has disjunct, short motivic idea:

96 0:23 Solo violin in double-stops, playing short motivic idea, syncopated over bar lines; becomes very disjunct and dissonant.

0:48 Woodwinds, with accented notes and running scale lines, against dissonant accompaniment and offbeats in low strings.

97 1:15 Solo violin in double-stops, playing syncopated melodic line against running woodwind lines:

1:38 Violin continues over faster 16th-note movement, with brief trumpet interjections and accented percussion (tambourine and bass drum, cowbell, bongo drums).

2:23 Complexity level grows; rising trumpet motive moves up sequentially:
synthesizer takes up 2-note violin motive:

2:48   Reduced orchestration—Eb-clarinet dominates, against fast rhythmic accompaniment in woodwinds.

2:57   Synthesizer, moving 16th-note line; low-pitched, 2-note motive with complex accompaniment.

98   3:35   Fast-paced violin in cadenza-like solo, with drum and tambourine:

Accelerando, then slowing, with wide-ranging melody, then rocking 2-note idea.

99   4:26   Loud bass and synthesizer, with low-note interjections that are both disjunct and accented; violin continues underneath.

4:56   Woodblock enters, then trumpets—2-note idea pervades; sweeping woodwind and string lines build to *fortissimo* closing.

time of the Northridge Earthquake (1994). Most recently, he premiered *El Niño* (2000), a Nativity oratorio modeled after Handel's *Messiah*, with texts drawn from English, Spanish, and Latin sources from the pre-Christian era to mid-twentieth-century Hispanic women writers. Both these recent stage works were collaborations with Peter Sellars.

We will consider Adams's Chamber Symphony, written in 1992 for the San Francisco Contemporary Chamber Players. Adams acknowledges his debt to Arnold Schoenberg's Chamber Symphony, Op. 9, explaining that he originally set out to write a children's piece, but one day while sitting in his studio studying the score of Schoenberg's work, he became aware of his young son Sam watching old cartoons (from the 1950s) in the next room. "The hyperactive, insistently aggressive and acrobatic scores for the cartoons mixed in my head with the Schoenberg music, itself hyperactive, acrobatic and not a little aggressive, and I realized suddenly how much these two traditions had in common."

Adams's Chamber Symphony is scored for a fifteen-piece ensemble of woodwinds (including bass clarinet and contrabassoon), brass, and strings, as well as drum set and synthesizer. The work is in three movements: the first, *Mongrel Airs*, is so named because a British critic once said Adams's music "lacked breeding"; the second, *Aria with Walking Bass*, slowly unfolds over an incessant bass line; and the third, *Roadrunner*, is obviously drawn from the classic cartoon show of the same name. Highly polyphonic and virtuosic (and thus very difficult to play), *Roadrunner* races at a frenzied pace, all the while giving us the unsettling feeling that the music is being played backwards. A rhapsodic violin solo, played in double-stops, interrupts the pace in several places, as does a long, written-out violin cadenza with percussive accompaniment. The synthesizer's insistent voice is heard throughout with terse motives. Adams presses tonality here to its limit, exploring the harmonic ambiguity created by an augmented chord (G-B-D♯). In the *Chamber Symphony*, Adams successfully wed a work of symphonic proportions and weight to the transparency of chamber music.

Homage to Schoenberg

in his own words

[I am] a very emotional composer, one who experiences music on a very physical level. My music is erotic and Dionysian, and I never try to obscure those feelings when I compose.

515

Coda

"Just listen with the vastness of the world in mind. You can't fail to get the message."

—PIERRE BOULEZ

These pages have included a variety of facts—historical, biographical, and analytical—that have entered into the making of music and that we must consider if we seek to listen intelligently to music. Like all books, this one belongs to the domain of words, and words have no power over the domain of sound. They are helpful only insofar as they lead us to enjoy the music.

The enjoyment of music depends on perceptive listening, which (like perceptive anything) is achieved gradually, with practice and effort. By studying the circumstances out of which a musical work issued, we prepare ourselves for its multiple meanings; we open ourselves to that exercise of mind and heart, sensibility and imagination, that makes listening to music a unique experience. But in building up our musical perceptions—that is, our listening enjoyment—let us always remember that the ultimate wisdom rests neither in dates nor in facts. It is to be found in one place only: the sounds themselves.

Musical Notation

The Notation of Pitch

Musical notation presents a kind of graph of each sound's duration and pitch. These are indicated by symbols called *notes*, which are written on the *staff*, a series of five parallel lines separated by four spaces:

Staff

The positions of the notes on the staff indicate the pitches, each line and space representing a different degree of pitch.

A symbol known as a *clef* is placed at the left end of the staff to determine the relative pitch names. The *treble clef* (𝄞) is used for pitches within the range of the female singing voices, and the *bass clef* (𝄢) for a lower group of pitches, within the range of the male singing voices.

Clefs

Pitches are named after the first seven letters of the alphabet, from A to G. (From one note named A to the next is the interval of an *octave*.) The pitches on the treble staff are named as follows:

Pitch names

E   F   G   A   B   C   D   E   F

And those on the bass staff:

G   A   B   C   D   E   F   G   A

For pitches above and below these staffs, short extra lines called *ledger lines* can be added:

A   B   C   D   G   A   B   C   C   D   E   F   B   C   D   E

Middle C—the C that, on the piano, is situated approximately in the center of the keyboard—comes between the treble and bass staffs. It is represented by either the first ledger line above the bass staff or the first ledger line below the treble staff, as the following example makes clear. This combination of the two staffs is called the *great staff* or *grand staff*:

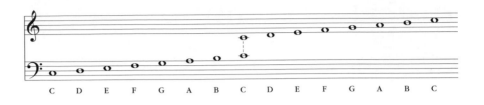

C   D   E   F   G   A   B   C   D   E   F   G   A   B   C

Accidentals

Signs known as *accidentals* are used to alter the pitch of a written note. A *sharp* (♯) before the note indicates the pitch a half step above; a *flat* (♭) indicates the pitch a half step below. A *natural* (♮) cancels a sharp or flat. Also used are the *double sharp* (×) and *double flat* (♭♭), which respectively raise and lower the pitch by two halftones—that is, a whole tone.

Key signature

In many pieces of music, where certain sharped or flatted notes are used consistently throughout, these sharps or flats are written at the beginning of each line of music, in the *key signature,* as seen in the following example of piano music. Notice that piano music is written on the great staff, with the right hand usually playing the notes written on the upper staff and the left hand usually playing the notes written on the lower:

The Notation of Rhythm

Note values

The duration of each musical tone is indicated by the type of note placed on the staff. In the following table, each note represents a duration, or *value,* half as long as the preceding one:

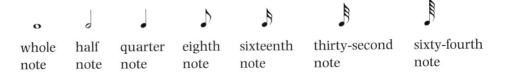

| whole note | half note | quarter note | eighth note | sixteenth note | thirty-second note | sixty-fourth note |

In any particular piece of music, these note values are related to the beat of the music. If the quarter note represents one beat, then a half note lasts for two beats, a whole note for four; two eighth notes last one beat, as do four sixteenths. The following chart makes this clear:

Notes		Beats
		(in quadruple time)

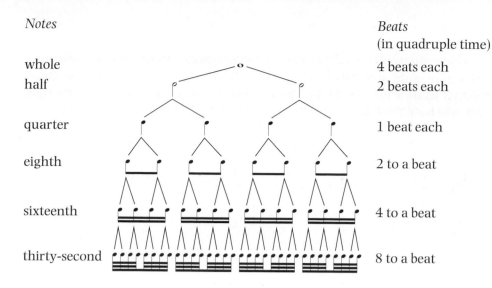

whole	4 beats each
half	2 beats each
quarter	1 beat each
eighth	2 to a beat
sixteenth	4 to a beat
thirty-second	8 to a beat

When a group of three notes is to be played in the time normally taken up by only two of the same kind, we have a *triplet*:

Triplet

If we combine successive notes of the same pitch, using a curved line known as a *tie*, the second note is not played, and the note values are combined:

Tie

beats: $4 + 4 = 8$ $2 + 4 = 6$ $1 + \frac{1}{2} = 1\frac{1}{2}$

A *dot* after a note enlarges its value by half:

Dot

beats: $2 + 1 = 3$ $1 + \frac{1}{2} = 1\frac{1}{2}$ $\frac{1}{2} + \frac{1}{4} = \frac{3}{4}$

Time never stops in music, even when there is no sound. Silence is indicated by symbols known as *rests*, which correspond in time value to the notes:

Rests

| whole rest | half rest | quarter rest | eighth rest | sixteenth rest | thirty-second rest | sixty-fourth rest |

The metrical organization of a piece of music is indicated by the *time signature*, which specifies the meter: this appears as two numbers written as in a fraction. The upper numeral indicates the number of beats within the measure; the lower one shows which note value equals one beat. Thus, the time signature 3/4 means that there are three beats to a measure, with the quarter note equal to one beat. In 6/8 time, there are six beats in the measure, each eighth note receiving one beat. Following are the most frequently encountered time signatures:

Time signature

duple meter	2/2	2/4	
triple meter	3/2	3/4	3/8
quadruple meter		4/4	
sextuple meter		6/4	6/8

Measures and bar lines

The examples below show how the system works. Notice that the *measures* are separated by a vertical line known as a *bar line*; a measure is sometimes referred to as a *bar*. As a rule, the bar line is followed by the most strongly accented beat, the ONE.

Sur le pont d'Avignon, French children's song

Clef: Treble
Key signature: None = key of C major
Meter: Duple (2/4)
Other features: Begins with pick-up note (upbeat)

Home on the Range, American song of the West

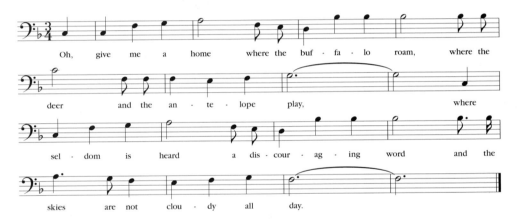

Clef: Bass
Key signature: 1 flat (B♭) = key of F major
Meter: Triple (3/4)
Other features: Pick-up note, dotted rhythms, and ties

Auld Lang Syne, Scottish traditional song

Clef: Treble
Key signature: 1 sharp (♯) = key of G major
Meter: Quadruple (4/4)
Other features: Pick-up note, dotted rhythms

Greensleeves, English traditional song

Clef: Treble
Key signature: 1 sharp (♯) = key of E minor
Meter: Sextuple (6/8)
Other features: Pick-up note, dotted rhythms, and accidentals (D♯ and C♯)

Glossary

absolute music Music that has no literary, dramatic, or pictorial program. Also *pure music*.

a cappella Choral music performed without instrumental accompaniment.

accelerando Getting faster.

accent The emphasis on a beat resulting in its being louder or longer than another in a measure.

accompagnato Accompanied; also a *recitative* that is accompanied by orchestra.

accordion A musical instrument with a small keyboard and free-vibrating metal reeds that sound when air is generated by pleated bellows.

acid rock Genre of American rock that emerged in the late 1960s, often associated with psychedelic drugs. Its style featured heavy amplification, instrumental improvisation, new sound technologies, and light shows.

adagio Quite slow.

additive meter Patterns of beats that subdivide into smaller, irregular groups (e.g., 2 + 3 + 2 + 3 = 10); common in certain Eastern European musics.

ad libitum Indication that gives the performer the liberty to omit a section or to improvise.

aerophone Instruments such as a flute, whistle, or horn that produce sound by using air as the primary vibrating means.

agitato Agitated or restless.

Agnus Dei A section of the Mass; the last musical movement of the *Ordinary*.

aleatory Indeterminate music in which certain elements of performance (such as pitch, rhythm, or form) are left to choice or chance.

alla breve See *cut time*.

allegro Fast, cheerful.

Alleluia An item from the *Proper* of the Mass sung just before the reading of the Gospel; *neumatic* in style with a long *melisma* on the last syllable of the word "Alleluia."

allemande German dance in moderate duple time, popular during the Renaissance and Baroque periods; often the first movement of a Baroque *suite*.

alto Lowest of the female voices. Also *contralto*.

andante Moderately slow or walking pace.

answer Second entry of the subject in a *fugue*, usually pitched a fourth below or a fifth above the *subject*.

anthem A religious choral composition in English; performed liturgically, the Protestant equivalent of the *motet*.

antiphonal Performance style in which an ensemble is divided into two or more groups, performing in alternation and then together.

antique cymbals Small disks of brass, held by the player one in each hand, that are struck together gently and allowed to vibrate.

arabesque Decorative musical material or a composition based on florid *embellishment*.

aria Lyric song for solo voice with orchestral accompaniment, generally expressing intense emotion; found in *opera, cantata,* and *oratorio*.

arioso Short, aria-like passage.

arpeggio Broken chord in which the individual tones are sounded one after another instead of simultaneously.

Ars Antiqua French sacred polyphonic musical style from the period c. 1160–1320.

Ars Nova Fourteenth-century French polyphonic musical style whose themes moved increasingly from religious to secular.

art rock Genre of rock that uses larger forms and more complex harmonies than other popular styles; occasionally quotes examples from classical music. Also *progressive rock*.

a tempo Return to the previous tempo.

atonality Total abandonment of *tonality* (centering in a key). Atonal music moves from one level of dissonance to another, without areas of relaxation.

attaca "Attack," proceed without a pause between movements.

augmentation Statement of a melody in longer note values, often twice as slow as the original.

aulos Double-reed pipe; played for public and religious functions in ancient Greece.

avant-garde jazz A free-style jazz that developed in the 1960s; John Coltrane was a major proponent.

bagpipe Wind instrument popular in Eastern and Western Europe that has several tubes, one of which plays the melody while the others sound the *drones,* or sustained notes; a windbag is filled by either a mouth pipe or a set of bellows *(uilleann pipes)*.

balalaika Guitar-like instrument of Russia with a triangular body, fretted neck, and three strings; often used in traditional music and dance.

ballade French poetic form and *chanson* type of the Middle Ages and Renaissance with courtly love texts. Also a Romantic genre, especially a lyric piano piece.

ballad opera English comic opera, usually featuring spoken dialogue alternating with songs set to popular tunes; also called dialogue opera.

ballet A dance form featuring a staged presentation of group or solo dancing with music, costumes, and scenery.

balungan The melodic-structural framework in Javanese music.

banjo Plucked-string instrument with round body in the form of a single-headed drum and a long, fretted neck; brought to the Americas by African slaves.

baritone Male voice of moderately low range.

baritone horn See *euphonium*.

bas Medieval category of soft instruments, used principally for indoor occasions, as distinct from *haut,* or loud, instruments.

bass Male voice of low range.

bass clarinet Woodwind instrument of the clarinet family with the lowest range.

bass drum Percussion instrument played with a large, soft-headed stick; the largest orchestral drum.

basse danse Graceful court dance of the early Renaissance; an older version of the *pavane*.

basso continuo Italian for "continuous bass." See *figured bass*. Also refers to performance group with a bass, chordal instrument (harpsichord, organ), and one bass melody instrument (cello, bassoon).

bassoon Double-reed woodwind instrument with a low range.

bass viol See *double bass*.

beat Regular pulsation; a basic unit of length in musical time.

bebop Complex jazz style developed in the 1940s. Also *bop*.

bel canto "Beautiful singing"; elegant Italian vocal style characterized by florid melodic lines delivered by voices of great agility, smoothness, and purity of tone.

bell tree Long stick with bells suspended from it, adopted from *Janissary music*.

bellows An apparatus for producing air currents in certain wind instruments (accordion, bagpipe).

bent pitch See *blue note*.

big band Large jazz ensemble popular in 1930s and 1940s, featuring sections of trumpets, trombones, saxophones (and other woodwinds), and rhythm instruments (piano, double bass, drums, and guitar).

binary form Two-part (**A-B**) form with each section normally repeated. Also *two-part form*.

biwa A Japanese lute, similar to the Chinese *pipa*.

bluegrass *Country-western* music style characterized by quick tempos, improvised instrumental solos, and high-range vocal harmonies.

blue note A slight drop of pitch on the third, fifth, or seventh tone of the scale, common in blues and jazz. Also *bent pitch*.

blues African-American form of secular folk music, related to jazz, that is based on a simple, repetitive poetic-musical structure.

bodhran Hand-held frame drum with a single goatskin head; used in Irish traditional music.

bongo A pair of small drums of differing pitches; held between the legs and struck with both hands; of Afro-Cuban origin.

bop See *bebop*.

bossa nova Brazilian dance related to the *samba*, popular in the 1950s and 1960s.

bourrée Lively French Baroque dance type in duple meter.

branle Quick French group dance of the Renaissance, related to the *ronde*.

brass instrument Wind instrument with a cup-shaped mouthpiece, a tube that flares into a bell, and slides or valves to vary the pitch. Most often made of brass or silver.

brass quintet Standard chamber ensemble made up of two trumpets, French horn, trombone, and tuba.

break Jazz term for a short improvised solo without accompaniment that "breaks" an ensemble passage or introduces an extended solo.

bridge Transitional passage connecting two sections of a composition; also *transition*. Also the part of a string instrument that holds the strings in place.

bugle Brass instrument that evolved from the earlier military, or field, trumpet.

cadence Resting place in a musical phrase; music punctuation.

cadenza Virtuosic solo passage in the manner of an improvisation, performed near the end of an aria or a movement of a concerto.

Cajun music Eclectic Louisiana traditional style that draws from French folk music as well as from music of Southern whites and blacks; fiddle is used as a solo instrument, sometimes accompanying itself with a *drone*.

cakewalk Syncopated, strutting dance of nineteenth-century origin; developed among Southern slaves in a parody of white plantation owners.

call and response Performance style with a singing leader who is imitated by a chorus of followers. Also *responsorial singing*.

canon Type of polyphonic composition in which one musical line strictly imitates another at a fixed distance throughout.

cantabile Songful, in a singing style.

cantata Vocal genre for solo singers, chorus, and instrumentalists based on a lyric or dramatic poetic narrative. It generally consists of several movements including recitatives, arias, and ensemble numbers.

cantor Solo singer or singing leader in Jewish and Christian liturgical music.

cantus firmus "Fixed melody," usually of very long notes, often based on a fragment of Gregorian chant that served as the structural basis for a polyphonic composition, particularly in the Renaissance.

capriccio Short lyric piece of a free nature, often for piano.

carol English medieval strophic song with a *refrain* repeated after each stanza; now associated with Christmas.

cassation Classical instrumental genre related to the *serenade* or *divertimento* and often performed outdoors.

castanets Percussion instruments consisting of small wooden clappers that are struck together. They are widely used to accompany Spanish dancing.

castrato Male singer who was castrated during boyhood to preserve the soprano or alto vocal register, prominent in seventeenth-and early eighteenth-century opera.

celesta Percussion instrument resembling a miniature upright piano, with tuned metal plates struck by hammers that are operated by a keyboard.

cello See *violoncello*.

celtic harp See *Irish harp*.

chaconne Baroque form similar to the *passacaglia*, in which the variations are based on a repeated chord progression.

chamber choir Small group of up to about twenty-four singers, who usually perform *a cappella* or with piano accompaniment.

chamber music Ensemble music for up to about ten players, with one player to a part.

chamber sonata See *sonata da camera*.

chanson French polyphonic song, especially of the Middle Ages and Renaissance, set to either courtly or popular poetry.

chart Colloquial or jazz term for a score or arrangement.

chimes Percussion instrument of definite pitch that consists of a set of tuned metal tubes of various lengths suspended from a frame and struck with a hammer. Also *tubular bells*.

Chinese block Percussion instrument made from a hollowed rectangular block of wood that is struck with a beater.

choir A group of singers who perform together, usually in parts, with several on each part; often associated with a church.

chorale Baroque congregational hymn of the German Lutheran church.

chorale prelude Short Baroque organ piece in which a traditional chorale melody is embellished.

chorale variations Baroque organ piece in which a chorale is the basis for a set of variations.

chord Simultaneous combination of three or more tones that constitute a single block of harmony.

chordal Texture comprised of chords in which the pitches sound simultaneously; also *homorhythmic*.

chordophone Instrument that produces sound from a vibrating string stretched between two points; the string may be set in motion by bowing, striking, or plucking.

chorus Fairly large group of singers who perform together, usually with several on each part. Also a choral movement of a large-scale work. In jazz, a single statement of the melodic-harmonic pattern.

chromatic Melody or harmony built from many if not all twelve semitones of the octave. A *chromatic scale* consists of an ascending or descending sequence of semitones.

church sonata See *sonata da chiesa*.

clarinet Single-reed woodwind instrument with a wide range of sizes.

clavecin French word for "harpsichord." See *harpsichord*.

claves A Cuban clapper consisting of two solid hardwood sticks; widely used in Latin-American music.

clavichord Stringed keyboard instrument popular in the Renaissance and Baroque that is capable of unique expressive devices not possible on the harpsichord.

clavier Generic word for keyboard instruments, including harpsichord, clavichord, piano, and organ.

closed ending Second of two endings in a secular medieval work, usually cadencing on the final.

coda   The last part of a piece, usually added to a standard form to bring it to a close.

codetta   In sonata form, the concluding section of the *exposition*. Also a brief coda concluding an inner section of a work.

collage   A technique drawn from the visual arts whereby musical fragments from other compositions are juxtaposed or overlapped within a new work.

collegium musicum   An association of amateur musicians, popular in the Baroque era. Also a modern university ensemble dedicated to the performance of early music.

colotomic structure   Cyclic, interlocking rhythmic structure in Javanese gamelan music.

comic opera   See *opéra comique*.

commedia dell'arte   Type of improvised drama popular in sixteenth- and seventeenth-century Italy; makes use of stereotyped characters.

common time   See *quadruple meter*.

compound meter   Meter in which each beat is subdivided into three rather than two.

computer music   A type of electro-acoustic music in which computers assist in creating works through sound synthesis and manipulation.

con amore   With love, tenderly.

concertante   Style based on the principle of opposition between two dissimilar masses of sound; concerto-like.

concert band   Instrumental ensemble ranging from forty to eighty members or more, consisting of wind and percussion instruments. Also *wind ensemble*.

concertina   Small, free-reed, bellows-operated instrument similar to an accordion; hexagonal in shape, with button keys.

concertino   Solo group of instruments in the Baroque *concerto grosso*.

concerto   Instrumental genre in several movements for solo instrument (or instrumental group) and orchestra.

concerto form   Structure commonly used in first movements of concertos that combines elements of Baroque *ritornello* procedure with *sonata-allegro form*. Also *first-movement concerto form*.

concerto grosso   Baroque concerto type based on the opposition between a small group of solo instruments (the *concertino*) and orchestra (the *ripieno*).

concert overture   Single-movement concert piece for orchestra, typically from the Romantic period and often based on a literary program.

conductor   Person who, by means of gestures, leads performances of musical ensembles, especially orchestra, bands, or choruses.

con fuoco   With fire.

conga   Afro-Cuban dance performed at Latin-American Carnival celebrations. Also a single-headed drum of Afro-Cuban origin, played with bare hands.

conjunct   Smooth, connected melody that moves principally by small intervals.

con passione   With passion.

consonance   Concordant or harmonious combination of tones that provides a sense of relaxation and stability in music.

continuous bass   See *basso continuo*.

continuous imitation   Renaissance polyphonic style in which the motives move from line to line within the texture, often overlapping one another.

contrabass   See *double bass*.

contrabassoon   Double-reed woodwind instrument with the lowest range in the woodwind family. Also *double bassoon*.

contralto   See *alto*.

contrapuntal   Texture employing counterpoint, or two or more melodic lines.

cool jazz   A substyle of *bebop*, characterized by a restrained, unemotional performance with lush harmonies, moderate volume levels and tempos, and a new lyricism; often associated with Miles Davis.

cornet   Valved brass instrument similar to the trumpet but more mellow in sound.

cornetto   Early instrument of the brass family with woodwind-like finger holes. It developed from the cow horn, but was made of wood.

Council of Trent   A council of the Roman Catholic Church that convened in Trent, Italy, from 1543 to 1565 and dealt with Counter-Reformation issues, including the reform of liturgical music.

counterpoint   The art of combining in a single texture two or more melodic lines.

countermelody   An accompanying melody sounded against the principal melody.

countersubject   In a figure, a secondary theme heard against the *subject;* a countertheme.

country-western   Genre of American popular music derived from traditional music of Appalachia and the rural South, usually vocal with an accompaniment of banjos, fiddles, and guitar.

courante   French Baroque dance, a standard movement of the *suite,* in triple meter at a moderate tempo.

cover   Recording that remakes an earlier, often successful, recording with a goal of reaching a wider audience.

cowbell   Rectangular metal bell that is struck with a drumstick; used widely in Latin-American music.

Credo   A section of the Mass; the third musical movement of the *Ordinary.*

crescendo   Growing louder.

crossover   Recording or artist that appeals primarily to one audience but becomes popular with another as well (e.g., a rock performer who makes jazz recordings).

crotales   A pair of small pitched cymbals mounted on a frame; also made in chromatic sets.

crumhorn   Early woodwind instrument, whose sound is produced by blowing into a capped double reed and whose lower body is curved.

cut time   A type of duple meter interpreted as 2/2 and indicated as ¢; also called *alla breve.*

cyclical form   Structure in which musical material, such as a theme, presented in one movement returns in a later movement.

cymbals   Percussion instruments consisting of two large circular brass plates of equal size that are struck sidewise against each other.

da capo   An indication to return to the beginning of a piece.

da capo aria   Lyric song in ternary, or **A-B-A,** form, commonly found in *operas, cantatas,* and *oratorios.*

decrescendo   Growing softer.

development   Structural reshaping of thematic material. Second section of *sonata-allegro form*; it moves through a series of foreign keys while themes from the exposition are manipulated.

dialogue opera   See *ballad opera.*

diatonic   Melody or harmony built from the seven tones of a major or minor scale. A *diatonic scale* encompasses patterns of seven whole tones and semitones.

Dies irae   Chant from the *Requiem Mass* whose text concerns Judgment Day.

diminuendo   Growing softer.

diminution   Statement of a melody in shorter note values, often twice as fast as the original.

disco   Commercial dance music popular in the 1970s, characterized by strong percussion in a quadruple meter.

disjunct   Disjointed or disconnected melody with many leaps.

dissonance   Combination of tones that sounds discordant and unstable, in need of resolution.

divertimento   Classical instrumental genre for chamber ensemble or soloist, often performed as light entertainment. Related to *serenade* and *cassation.*

Divine Offices   Cycle of daily services of the Roman Catholic Church, distinct from the *Mass.*

doctrine of the affections   Baroque doctrine of the union of text and music.

dodecaphonic   Greek for "twelve-tone"; see *twelve-tone music.*

dolce Sweetly.

dolente Sad, weeping.

dominant The fifth scale step, *sol*.

dominant chord Chord built on the fifth scale step, the V chord.

double bass Largest and lowest-pitched member of the bowed string family. Also called *contrabass* or *bass viol*.

double bassoon See *contrabassoon*.

double exposition In the *concerto*, twofold statement of the themes, once by the orchestra and once by the soloist.

double-stop Playing two notes simultaneously on a string instrument.

doubles Variations of a dance in a French keyboard suite.

down beat First beat of the measure, the strongest in any meter.

drone Sustained sounding of one or several tones for harmonic support, a common feature of some folk musics.

dulcimer Early folk instrument that resembles the *psaltery*; its strings are struck with hammers instead of being plucked.

duple meter Basic metrical pattern of two beats to a measure.

duplum Second voice of a polyphonic work, especially the medieval *motet*.

duration Length of time something lasts; e.g., the vibration of a musical sound.

dynamics Element of musical expression relating to the degree of loudness or softness, or volume, of a sound.

electronische Musik Electronic music developed in Germany in the 1950s that uses an oscillator to generate and alter waveforms.

embellishment Melodic decoration, either improvised or indicated through *ornamentation* signs in the music.

embouchure The placement of the lips, lower facial muscles, and jaws in playing a wind instrument.

Empfindsamkeit German "sensitive" style of the mid-eighteenth century, characterized by melodic directness and homophonic texture.

encore "Again"; an audience request that the performer(s) repeat a piece or perform another.

English horn Double-reed woodwind instrument, larger and lower in range than the oboe.

entenga Tuned drum from Uganda; the royal drum ensemble of the former ruler of Buganda.

episode Interlude or intermediate section in the Baroque *fugue*, which serves as an area of relaxation between statements of the subject.

equal temperament Tuning system based on the division of the *octave* into twelve equal *half steps*; the system used today.

erhu Bowed, two-string fiddle from China, with its bow hairs fixed between the strings; rests on the leg while playing.

espressivo Expressively.

ethnomusicology Comparative study of musics of the world, with a focus on the cultural context of music.

étude Study piece that focuses on a particular technical problem.

euphonium Tenor-range brass instrument resembling the tuba. Also *baritone horn*.

exoticism Musical style in which rhythms, melodies, or instruments evoke the color and atmosphere of far-off lands.

exposition Opening section. In the *fugue*, the first section in which the voices enter in turn with the subject. In *sonata-allegro form*, the first section in which the major thematic material is stated. Also *statement*.

falsetto Vocal technique whereby men can sing above their normal range, producing a lighter sound.

fantasia Free instrumental piece of fairly large dimensions, in an improvisational style; in the Baroque, it often served as an introductory piece to a *fugue*.

fiddle   Colloquial term for *violin*; often used in traditional music.

figured bass   Baroque practice consisting of an independent bass line that often includes numerals indicating the harmony to be supplied by the performer. Also *thorough-bass*.

film music   Music that serves either as background or foreground for a film.

first-movement concerto form   See *concerto form*.

first-movement form   See *sonata-allegro form*.

fixed forms   Group of forms, especially in medieval France, in which the poetic structure determines musical repetitions. See also *ballade, rondeau, virelai*.

flat sign   Musical symbol (b) that indicates lowering a pitch by a semitone.

fluegelhorn   Valved brass instrument resembling a bugle with a wide bell, used in jazz and commercial music.

flute   Soprano-range woodwind instrument, usually made of metal and held horizontally.

flutter tonguing   Wind instrument technique in which the tongue is fluttered or trilled against the roof of the mouth.

folk music.   See *traditional music*.

folk rock   Popular music style that combines folk music with amplified instruments of rock.

form   Structure and design in music, based on repetition, contrast, and variation; the organizing principle of music.

formalism   Tendency to elevate formal above expressive value in music, as in Neoclassical music.

forte *(f)*   Loud.

fortissimo *(ff)*   Very loud.

four-hand piano music   Chamber music genre for two performers playing at one or occasionally two pianos, allowing home or salon performances of orchestral arrangements.

free jazz   Modern jazz style developed in the 1960s by Ornette Coleman.

French horn   Medium-range valved brass instrument that can be played "stopped" with the hand as well as open. Also *horn*.

French overture   Baroque instrumental introduction to an *opera, ballet,* or *suite,* in two sections: a slow opening followed by an Allegro, often with a brief reprise of the opening.

frequency   Rate of vibration of a string or column of air, which determines pitch.

fugato   A fugal passage in a nonfugal piece, such as in the development section of a *sonata-allegro form*.

fuging tune   Polyphonic, imitative setting of a *hymn* or *psalm,* popular in Great Britain and the United States from the eighteenth century.

fugue   Polyphonic form popular in the Baroque era in which one or more themes are developed by imitative *counterpoint*.

fusion   Style that combines jazz improvisation with amplified instruments of rock.

gagaku   Traditional court music of Japan.

galliard   Lively, triple-meter French court dance.

gamelan   Musical ensemble of Java or Bali, made up of gongs, chimes, metallophones, and drums, among other instruments.

gavotte   Duple-meter Baroque dance type of a pastoral character.

genre   General term describing the standard category and overall character of a work.

Gesamtkunstwerk   German for "total artwork"; a term coined by Richard Wagner to describe the synthesis of all the arts (music, poetry, drama, visual spectacle) in his late operas.

gigue   Popular English Baroque dance type, a standard movement of the Baroque *suite,* in a lively compound meter.

gioioso   Joyous.

glee club   Specialized vocal ensemble that performs popular music, college songs, and more serious works.

glissando   Rapid slide through pitches of a scale.

glitter rock   Theatrical, flamboyant rock style popular in the 1970s.

global pop   Collective term for popular third-world musics, ethnic and traditional musics, and eclectic combinations of Western and non-Western musics. Also world beat.

glockenspiel   Percussion instrument with horizontal, tuned steel bars of various sizes that are struck with mallets and produce a bright metallic sound.

Gloria   A section of the Mass; the second musical movement of the *Ordinary*.

Goliard song   Medieval Latin-texted secular song, often with corrupt or lewd lyrics; associated with wandering scholars.

gong   Percussion instrument consisting of a broad circular disk of metal, suspended in a frame and struck with a heavy drumstick. Also *tam-tam*.

gospel music   Twentieth-century sacred music style associated with Protestant African Americans.

grace note   Ornamental note, often printed in small type and not performed rhythmically.

Gradual   Fourth item of the *Proper* of the Mass, sung in a *melismatic* style, and performed in a *responsorial* manner in which soloists alternate with a choir.

grand opera   Style of Romantic opera developed in Paris, focusing on serious, historical plots with huge choruses, crowd scenes, elaborate dance episodes, ornate costumes, and spectacular scenery.

grave   Solemn; very, very slow.

Gregorian chant   Monophonic melody with a freely flowing, unmeasured vocal line; liturgical chant of the Roman Catholic Church. Also *plainchant* or *plainsong*.

ground bass   A repeating melody, usually in the bass, throughout a vocal or instrumental composition.

grunge rock   Contemporary Seattle-based rock style characterized by harsh guitar chords; hybrid of *punk rock* and *heavy metal*.

guitar   Plucked-string instrument originally made of wood with a hollow resonating body and a fretted fingerboard; types include acoustic and electric.

habanera   Moderate duple-meter dance of Cuban origin, popular in the nineteenth century; based on characteristic rhythmic figure.

half step   Smallest interval used in the Western system; the *octave* divides into twelve such intervals; on the piano, the distance between any two adjacent keys, whether black or white. Also *semitone*.

harmonica   Mouth organ; a small metal box on which free reeds are mounted, played by moving back and forth across the mouth while breathing into it.

harmonics   Individual pure sounds that are part of any musical tone; in string instruments, crystalline tones in the very high register, produced by lightly touching a vibrating string at a certain point.

harmonium   Organ-like instrument with free metal reeds set in vibration by a bellows; popular in late-nineteenth-century America.

harmony   The simultaneous combination of notes and the ensuing relationships of *intervals* and *chords*.

harp   Plucked-string instrument, triangular in shape with strings perpendicular to the soundboard.

harpsichord   Early Baroque keyboard instrument in which the strings are plucked by quills instead of being struck with hammers like the piano. Also *clavecin*.

haut   Medieval category of loud instruments, used mainly for outdoor occasions, as distinct from *bas*, or soft, instruments.

heavy metal   Rock style that gained popularity in the 1970s, characterized by simple, repetitive ideas and loud, distorted instrumental solos.

heptatonic scale   Seven-note scale; in non-Western musics, often fashioned from a different combination of intervals than major and minor scales.

heterophonic Texture in which two or more voices (or parts) elaborate the same melody simultaneously, often the result of *improvisation*.

hip hop See *rap*.

homophonic Texture with principal melody and accompanying harmony, as distinct from *polyphony*.

homorhythmic Texture in which all voices, or lines, move together in the same rhythm.

horn See *French horn*.

hornpipe Country dance of British Isles, often in a lively triple meter; optional dance movement of solo and orchestral Baroque suite; a type of duple-meter hornpipe remains popular in Irish traditional dance music.

hymn Song in praise of God; often involves congregational participation.

idée fixe "Fixed idea"; term coined by Berlioz for a recurring musical idea that links different movements of a work.

idiophone Instrument that produces sound from the substance of the instrument itself by being struck, blown, shaken, scraped, or rubbed. Examples include bells, rattles, xylophones, and cymbals.

imitation Melodic idea presented in one voice and then restated in another, each part continuing as others enter.

improvisation Creation of a musical composition while it is being performed, seen in Baroque ornamentation, cadenzas of concertos, jazz, and some non-Western musics. See also *embellishment*.

incidental music Music written to accompany dramatic works.

inflection Small alteration of the pitch by a microtonal interval. See also *blue note*.

instrument Mechanism that generates musical vibrations and transmits them into the air.

interlude Music played between sections of a musical or dramatic work.

intermezzo Short, lyric piece or movement, often for piano. Also a comic interlude performed between acts of an eighteenth-century *opera seria*.

Internet radio Radio stations that convert their signal into digital format and transmit it over the worldwide web.

interval Distance and relationship between two pitches.

inversion Mirror or upside-down image of a melody or pattern, found in fugues and twelve-tone compositions.

Irish harp Plucked-string instrument with about thirty strings; used to accompany Irish songs and dance music (also *celtic harp*).

isorhythmic motet Medieval and early Renaissance motet based on a repeating rhythmic pattern throughout one or more voices.

Italian overture Baroque overture consisting of three sections: fast-slow-fast.

Janissary music Music of the military corps of the Turkish sultan, characterized by percussion instruments such as triangle, cymbals, bell tree, and bass drum as well as trumpets and double-reed instruments.

jarabe Traditional Mexican dance form with multiple sections in contrasting meters and tempos, often performed by *mariachi* ensembles.

jazz A musical style created mainly by African Americans in the early twentieth century that blended elements drawn from African musics with the popular and art traditions of the West.

jazz band Instrumental ensemble made up of reed (saxophones and clarinets), brass (trumpets and trombones), and rhythm sections (percussion, piano, double bass, and sometimes guitar).

jia hua Literally, "adding flowers"; an embellishment style in Chinese music using various ornamental figures.

jig A vigorous dance developed in the British Isles, usually in compound meter; became fashionable on the Continent as the *gigue*; still popular as an Irish traditional dance genre.

jongleurs Medieval wandering entertainers who played instruments, sang and danced, juggled, and performed plays.

jongleuresses Female *jongleurs*, or wandering entertainer/minstrels.

jota A type of Spanish dance song characterized by a quick triple meter and guitar and castanet accompaniment.

karaoke "Empty orchestra"; popular nightclub style from Japan where customers sing the melody to accompanying pre-recorded tracks.

kettledrums See *timpani*.

key Defines the relationship of tones with a common center or *tonic*. Also a lever on a keyboard or woodwind instrument.

keyboard instrument Instrument sounded by means of a keyboard (a series of keys played with the fingers).

keynote See *tonic*.

key signature Sharps or flats placed at the beginning of a piece to show the key of a work.

Klangfarbenmelodie Twentieth-century technique in which the notes of a melody are distributed among different instruments, giving a pointillistic texture.

koto Japanese plucked-string instrument with a long rectangular body, thirteen strings, and movable bridges or frets.

kouta A short Japanese song traditionally sung by a geisha for private or theatrical entertainment.

lamellophone Plucked idiophone with thin metal strips; common throughout sub-Saharan Africa.

lamentoso Like a lament.

largo Broad; very slow.

Latin jazz A jazz style influenced by Latin American music, which includes various dance rhythms and traditional percussion instruments.

Latin rock Subgenre of rock featuring Latin and African percussion instruments *(maracas, conga drums, timbales)*.

legato Smooth and connected; opposite of *staccato*.

Leitmotif "Leading motive," or basic recurring theme, representing a person, object, or idea, commonly used in Wagner's operas.

libretto Text, or script, of an opera, prepared by a librettist.

Lied German for "song"; most commonly associated with the solo art song of the nineteenth century, usually accompanied by piano.

Lieder Plural of *Lied*.

lining out A *call-and-response* singing practice prevalent in early America and England; characterized by the alternation between a singer leader and a chorus singing heterophonically.

liturgy The set order of religious services and the structure of each service, within a particular denomination (e.g., Roman Catholic).

lute Plucked-string instrument of Middle Eastern origin, popular in western Europe from the late Middle Ages to the eighteenth century.

lyre Ancient plucked-string instrument of the harp family, used to accompany singing and poetry.

lyric opera Hybrid form combining elements of *grand opera* and *opéra comique* and featuring appealing melodies and romantic drama.

madrigal Renaissance secular work originating in Italy for voices, with or without instruments, set to a short, lyric love poem; also popular in England.

madrigal choir Small vocal ensemble that specializes in *a cappella* secular works.

maestoso Majestic.

Magnificat Biblical text on the words of the Virgin Mary, sung polyphonically in church from the Renaissance on.

major scale Scale consisting of seven different tones that comprise a specific pattern of whole and half steps. It differs from a minor scale primarily in that its third degree is raised half a step.

mambo Dance of Afro-Cuban origin with a characteristic quadruple-meter rhythmic pattern.

mandolin Plucked-string instrument with a rounded body and fingerboard; used in some folk musics and in *country-western* music.

maracas Latin-American rattles (*idiophones*) made from gourds or other materials.

march A style incorporating characteristics of military music, including strongly accented duple meter in simple, repetitive rhythmic patterns.

marching band Instrumental ensemble for entertainment at sports events and parades, consisting of wind and percussion instruments, drum majors/majorettes, and baton twirlers.

mariachi Traditional Mexican ensemble popular throughout the country, consisting of trumpets, violins, guitar, and bass guitar.

marimba Percussion instrument that is a mellower version of the *xylophone*; of African origin.

masque English genre of aristocratic entertainment that combined vocal and instrumental music with poetry and dance, developed during the sixteenth and seventeenth centuries.

Mass Central service of the Roman Catholic Church.

mazurka Type of Polish folk dance in triple meter.

mbube "Lion"; *a cappella* choral singing style of South African Zulus, featuring *call-and-response* patterns, close-knit harmonies, and syncopation.

measure Rhythmic group or metrical unit that contains a fixed number of beats, divided on the musical staff by bar lines.

medium Performing forces employed in a certain musical work.

melismatic Melodic style characterized by many notes sung to a single text syllable.

melody Succession of single tones or pitches perceived by the mind as a unity.

membranophone Any instrument that produces sound from tightly stretched membranes that can be struck, plucked, rubbed, or sung into (setting the skin in vibration).

meno Less.

mesto Sad.

metallophone Percussion instrument consisting of tuned metal bars, usually struck with a mallet.

meter Organization of rhythm in time; the grouping of beats into larger, regular patterns, notated as *measures*.

metronome Device used to indicate the tempo by sounding regular beats at adjustable speeds.

mezzo forte (*mf*) Moderately loud.

mezzo piano (*mp*) Moderately soft.

mezzo-soprano Female voice of middle range.

micropolyphony Twentieth-century technique encompassing the complex interweaving of all musical elements.

microtone Musical interval smaller than a semitone, prevalent in some non-Western musics and in some twentieth-century art music.

MIDI Acronym for musical instrument digital interface; technology standard that allows networking of computers with electronic musical instruments.

minimalist music Contemporary musical style featuring the repetition of short melodic, rhythmic, and harmonic patterns with little variation. See also *post-minimalism* and *spiritual minimalism*.

Minnesingers Late medieval German poet-musicians.

minor scale Scale consisting of seven different tones that comprise a specific pattern of whole and half steps. It differs from the major scale primarily in that its third degree is lowered half a step.

minuet and trio An **A-B-A** form (**A** = minuet; **B** = trio) in a moderate triple meter; often the third movement of the Classical *multimovement cycle*.

misterioso Mysteriously.

modal Characterizes music that is based on modes other than major and minor, especially the early church *modes*.

mode Scale or sequence of notes used as the basis for a composition; major and minor are modes.

moderato Moderate.

modified strophic form Song structure that combines elements of strophic and through-composed forms; a variation of strophic form in which a section might have a new key, rhythm, or varied melodic pattern.

modulation The process of changing from one key to another.

molto Very.

monody Vocal style established in the Baroque, with a solo singer and instrumental accompaniment.

monophonic Single-line texture, or melody without accompaniment.

monothematic Work or movement based on a single theme.

morality play Medieval drama, often with music, intended to teach proper values.

motet Polyphonic vocal genre, secular in the Middle Ages but sacred or devotional thereafter.

motive Short melodic or rhythmic idea; the smallest fragment of a theme that forms a melodic-harmonic-rhythmic unit.

movement Complete, self-contained part within a larger musical work.

MP3 A file-compression format applied to audio files; term is short for Moving Pictures Expert Group 1 Layer 3.

MTV Acronym for music television, a cable channel that presents non-stop *music videos*.

multimovement cycle A three- or four-movement structure used in Classical-era instrumental music—especially the symphony, sonata, concerto—and in chamber music; each movement is in a prescribed tempo and form; sometimes called *sonata cycle*.

muses Nine daughters of Zeus in ancient mythology; each presided over one of the arts.

musical Genre of twentieth-century musical theater, especially popular in the United States and Great Britain; characterized by spoken dialogue, dramatic plot interspersed with songs, ensemble numbers, and dancing.

musical saw A handsaw that is bowed on its smooth edge; pitch is varied by bending the saw.

music drama Wagner's term for his operas.

music video Video tape or film that accompanies a recording, usually of a popular or rock song.

musique concrète Music made up of natural sounds and sound effects that are recorded and then manipulated electronically.

mute Mechanical device used to muffle the sound of an instrument.

nakers Medieval percussion instruments resembling small kettledrums, played in pairs; of Middle Eastern origin.

Neoclassical jazz A modern jazz style characterized by expanded tonalities, modal improvisations, and new forms; Wynton Marsalis is a proponent of this style.

neumatic Melodic style with two to four notes set to each syllable.

neumes Early musical notation signs; square notes on a four-line staff.

new age Style of popular music of the 1980s and 1990s, characterized by soothing timbres and repetitive forms that are subjected to shifting variation techniques.

new-age jazz A mellow, reflective jazz style exemplified by Paul Winter and his ensemble.

New Orleans jazz Early jazz style characterized by multiple improvisations in an ensemble of cornet (or trumpet), clarinet (or saxophone), trombone, piano, string bass (or tuba), banjo (or guitar), and drums; repertory included *blues*, *ragtime*, and popular songs.

new wave Subgenre of rock popular since the late 1970s, highly influenced by simple 1950s-style *rock and roll*; developed as a rejection of the complexities of *art rock* and *beauty metal*.

ninth chord Five-tone chord spanning a ninth between its lowest and highest tones.

nocturne "Night piece"; introspective work common in the nineteenth century, often for piano.

Noh drama A major form of Japanese theater since the late fourteenth century; based on philosophical concepts from Zen Buddhism.

nonmetric Music lacking a strong sense of beat or meter, common in certain non-Western cultures.

non troppo Not too much.

note A musical symbol denoting *pitch* and *duration*.

oboe Soprano-range, double-reed woodwind instrument.

octave Interval between two tones seven diatonic pitches apart; the lower note vibrates half as fast as the upper and sounds an octave lower.

ode Secular composition written for a royal occasion, especially popular in England.

offbeat A weak beat or any pulse between the beats in a measured rhythmic pattern.

Office See *Divine Offices*.

ondes Martenot Electronic instrument that produces sounds by means of an oscillator; invented by Maurice Martenot in 1928.

open ending The first ending in a medieval secular piece, usually cadencing on a pitch other than the final.

open form Indeterminate contemporary music in which some details of a composition are clearly indicated, but the overall structure is left to choice or chance.

opera Music drama that is generally sung throughout, combining the resources of vocal and instrumental music with poetry and drama, acting and pantomime, scenery and costumes.

opera buffa Italian comic opera, sung throughout.

opéra comique French comic opera, with some spoken dialogue.

opera seria Tragic Italian opera.

ophicleide A nineteenth-century brass instrument (now obsolete) with woodwind fingering holes; used by Berlioz, among others; the parts are generally played today on tuba.

oral tradition Music that is transmitted by example or imitation and performed from memory.

oral transmission Preservation of music without the aid of written notation.

oratorio Large-scale dramatic genre originating in the Baroque, based on a text of religious or serious character, performed by solo voices, chorus, and orchestra; similar to opera but without scenery, costumes, or action.

orchestra Performing group of diverse instruments in various cultures; in Western art music, an ensemble of multiple strings with various woodwind, brass, and percussion instruments.

orchestral bells See *chimes*.

orchestration The technique of setting instruments in various combinations.

Ordinary Sections of the Roman Catholic Mass that remain the same from day to day throughout the church year, as distinct from the *Proper*, which changes daily according to the liturgical occasion.

organ Wind instrument in which air is fed to the pipes by mechanical means; the pipes are controlled by two or more keyboards and a set of pedals.

organal style *Organum* in which the Tenor sings the melody (original chant) in very long notes while the upper voices move freely and rapidly above it.

organum Earliest kind of polyphonic music, which developed from the custom of adding voices above a plainchant; they first ran parallel to it at the interval of a fifth or fourth and later moved more freely.

ornamentation See *embellishment*.

ostinato A short melodic, rhythmic, or harmonic pattern that is repeated throughout a work or a section of one.

overture An introductory movement, as in an *opera* or *oratorio*, often presenting melodies from arias to come. Also an orchestral work for concert performance.

panpipe Wind instrument consisting of a series of small vertical tubes or pipes of differing length; sound is produced by blowing across the top.

pantomime Theatrical genre in which an actor silently plays all the parts in a show while accompanied by singing; originated in ancient Rome.

part song Secular vocal composition, unaccompanied, in three, four, or more parts.

partita See *suite*.

pas de deux A dance for two that is an established feature of classical ballet.

passacaglia Baroque form (similar to the *chaconne*) in moderately slow triple meter, based on a short, repeated base-line melody that serves as the basis for continuous variation in the other voices.

passepied French Baroque court dance type; a faster version of the *minuet*.

passion Musical setting of the Crucifixion story as told by one of the four Evangelists in the Gospels.

pastorale Pastoral, country-like.

patalon An overture from a Javanese shadow-puppet play; performed by *gamelan*.

pavane Stately Renaissance court dance in duple meter.

pedal point Sustained tone over which the harmonies change.

pélog Heptatonic (7-note) tuning used in Javanese *gamelan* music.

penny whistle See *tin whistle*.

pentatonic scale Five-note pattern used in some African, Far Eastern, and Native American musics; can also be found in Western music as an example of exoticism.

percussion instrument Instrument made of metal, wood, stretched skin, or other material that is made to sound by striking, shaking, scraping, or plucking.

perfect pitch The innate ability to reproduce any pitch without hearing it first.

performance art Multimedia art form involving visual as well as dramatic and musical elements.

period-instrument ensemble Group that performs on historical instruments or modern replicas built after historical models.

perpetuum mobile Type of piece characterized by continuous repetitions of a rhythmic pattern at a quick tempo; perpetual motion.

phasing A technique in which a musical pattern is repeated and manipulated so that it separates and overlaps itself, and then rejoins the original pattern; getting "out of phase" and back "in sync."

phrase Musical unit; often a component of a melody.

phrygian One of the church *modes* often associated with a somber mood; built on the pitch E using only white keys.

pianissimo *(pp)* Very soft.

piano *(p)* Soft.

piano Keyboard instrument whose strings are struck with hammers controlled by a keyboard mechanism; pedals control dampers in the strings that stop the sound when the finger releases the key.

pianoforte Original name for the *piano*.

piano quartet Standard chamber ensemble of piano with violin, viola, and cello.

piano quintet Standard chamber ensemble of piano with *string quartet* (two violins, viola, and cello).

piano trio Standard chamber ensemble of piano with violin and cello.

piccolo Smallest woodwind instrument, similar to the flute but sounding an octave higher.

pipa A Chinese *lute* with four silk strings; played as solo and ensemble instrument.

pitch Highness or lowness of a tone, depending on the frequency (rate of vibration).

pizzicato Performance direction to pluck a string of a bowed instrument with the finger.

plainchant See *Gregorian chant.*

plainsong See *Gregorian chant.*

plectrum An implement made of wood, ivory or another material used to pluck a *chordophone.*

poco A little.

polka Lively Bohemian dance; also a short, lyric piano piece.

polonaise Stately Polish processional dance in triple meter.

polychoral Performance style developed in the late sixteenth century involving the use of two or more choirs that alternate with each other or sing together.

polyharmony Two or more streams of harmony played against each other, common in twentieth-century music.

polyphonic Two or more melodic lines combined into a multivoiced texture, as distinct from *monophonic.*

polyrhythm The simultaneous use of several rhythmic patterns or meters, common in twentieth-century music and in certain African musics.

polytextual Two or more texts set simultaneously in a composition, common in the Medieval *motet.*

polytonality The simultaneous use of two or more keys, common in twentieth-century music.

portative organ Medieval organ small enough to be carried or set on a table, usually with only one set of pipes.

positive organ Small single-manual organ, popular in the Renaissance and Baroque eras.

post-minimalism A contemporary style that combines the lush harmonies of New Romanticism with the high-energy rhythms of minimalism; John Adams is a major exponent.

prelude Instrumental work intended to precede a larger work.

prepared piano Piano whose sound is altered by the insertion of various materials (metal, rubber, leather, and paper) between the strings; invented by John Cage.

presto Very fast.

program music Instrumental music endowed with literary or pictorial associations, especially popular in the nineteenth century.

program symphony Multimovement programmatic orchestral work, typically from the nineteenth century.

progressive rock See *art rock.*

Proper Sections of the Roman Catholic Mass that vary from day to day throughout the church year according to the particular liturgical occasion, as distinct from the *Ordinary,* in which they remain the same.

Psalms Book from the Old Testament of the Bible; the 150 psalm texts, used in Jewish and Christian worship, are often set to music.

psaltery Medieval plucked-string instrument similar to the modern zither, consisting of a sound box over which strings were stretched.

punk rock Subgenre of rock, popular since the mid-1970s; characterized by loud volume levels, driving rhythms, and simple forms typical of earlier rock and roll; often contains shocking lyrics and offensive behavior.

pure music See *absolute music.*

quadrivium Subdivision of the seven liberal arts; includes the mathematical subjects of music, arithmetic, geometry, and astronomy.

quadruple meter Basic metrical pattern of four beats to a measure. Also *common time.*

quadruple stop Playing four notes simultaneously on a string instrument.

quadruplum Fourth voice of a polyphonic work.

quartal harmony Harmony based on the interval of the fourth as opposed to a third; used in twentieth-century music.

quarter tone An interval halfway between a *half step.*

quotation music Music that parodies another work or works, presenting them in a new style or guise.

raga Melodic pattern used in music of India; prescribes pitches, patterns, ornamentation, and extramusical associations such as time of performance and emotional character.

ragtime Late-nineteenth-century piano style created by African Americans, characterized by highly syncopated melodies; also played in ensemble arrangements. Contributed to early jazz styles.

range Distance between the lowest and highest tones of a melody, an instrument, or a voice.

rap Subgenre of rock in which rhymed lyrics are spoken over rhythm tracks; developed by African Americans in the 1970s and widely disseminated in the 1980s and 1990s; the style and culture is often referred to as hip hop.

rebec Medieval bowed-string instrument, often with a pear-shaped body.

recapitulation Third section of *sonata-allegro form,* in which the thematic material of the *exposition* is restated, generally in the tonic. Also *restatement.*

recitative Solo vocal declamation that follows the inflections of the text, often resulting in a disjunct vocal style; found in opera, cantata, and oratorio.

recorder End-blown woodwind instrument with a whistle mouthpiece, generally associated with early music.

reed Flexible strip of cane or metal set into a mouthpiece or the body of an instrument; set in vibration by a stream of air.

reel Moderately quick dance in duple meter danced throughout the British Isles; the most popular Irish traditional dance type.

refrain Text or music that is repeated within a larger form.

regal Small medieval reed organ.

reggae Jamaican popular music style characterized by offbeat rhythms and chanted vocals over a strong bass part; often associated with the Christian religious movement Rastafarianism.

register Specific area in the range of an instrument or voice.

registration Selection or combination of stops in a work for organ or harpsichord.

relative key The major and minor key that share the same key signature; for example, D minor is the relative minor of F major, both having one flat.

repeat sign Musical symbol (‖: :‖) that indicates repetition of a passage in a composition.

Requiem Mass Roman Catholic Mass for the Dead.

resolution Conclusion of a musical idea, as in the progression from an active chord to a rest chord.

response Short choral answer to a solo *verse*; an element of liturgical dialogue.

responsorial singing Singing, especially in *Gregorian chant,* in which a soloist or a group of soloists alternates with the choir. See also *call and response.*

restatement See *recapitulation.*

retrograde Backward statement of melody.

retrograde inversion Mirror image and backward statement of a melody.

rhythm The controlled movement of music in time.

rhythm and blues Popular African-American music style of the 1940s through 1960s featuring a solo singer accompanied by a small instrumental ensemble (piano, guitar, acoustic bass, drums, tenor saxophone), driving rhythms, and blues and pop song forms.

ring shout Religious dance performed by African-American slaves, performed with hand clapping and a shuffle step to spirituals.

ripieno The larger of the two ensembles in the Baroque *concerto grosso*. Also *tutti.*

ritardando Holding back, getting slower.

ritornello Short, recurring instrumental passage found in both the aria and the Baroque concerto.

rock and roll   American popular music style first heard in the 1950s; derived from the union of African-American *rhythm and blues, country-western,* and pop music.

rock band   Popular music ensemble that depends on amplified strings, percussion, and electronically generated sounds.

rocket theme   Quickly ascending rhythmic melody used in Classical-era instrumental music; the technique is credited to composers in Mannheim, Germany.

romance   Originally a ballad; in the Romantic era, a lyric instrumental work.

ronde   Lively Renaissance "round dance," associated with the outdoors, in which the participants danced in a circle or a line.

rondeau   Medieval and Renaissance fixed poetic form and chanson type with courtly love texts.

rondo   Muscial form in which the first section recurs, usually in the tonic. In the Classical *multimovement cycle,* it appears as the last movement in various forms, including **A-B-A-B-A, A-B-A-C-A,** and **A-B-A-C-A-B-A.**

rosin   Substance made from hardened tree sap, rubbed on the hair of a bow to help it grip the strings.

round   Perpetual canon at the unison in which each voice enters in succession with the same melody (for example, *Row, Row, Row Your Boat*).

rounded binary   Compositional form with two sections, in which the second ends with a return to material from the first; each section is usually repeated.

rubato   "Borrowed time," common in Romantic music, in which the performer hesitates here or hurries forward there, imparting flexibility to the written note values. Also *tempo rubato.*

rumba   Latin-American dance of Afro-Cuban origin, in duple meter with syncopated rhythms.

rural blues   American popular singing style with raspy-voiced male singer accompanied by acoustic steel-string guitar; features melodic *blue notes* over repeated bass patterns.

sackbut   Early brass instrument, ancestor of the trombone.

sacred music   Religious or spiritual music, for church or devotional use.

salsa   "Spicy"; collective term for Latin-American dance music, especially forms of Afro-Cuban origin.

saltarello   Italian "jumping dance," often characterized by triplets in a rapid 4/4 time.

samba   Afro-Brazilian dance, characterized by duple meter, responsorial singing, and polyrhythmic accompaniments.

sampler   Electronic device that digitizes, stores, and plays back sounds.

Sanctus   A section of the Mass; the fourth musical movement of the *Ordinary.*

sarabande   Stately Spanish Baroque dance type in triple meter, a standard movement of the Baroque *suite.*

sarangi   Bowed chordophone from north India with three main strings and a large number of metal strings that vibrate sympathetically.

saxophone   Family of single-reed woodwind instruments commonly used in the concert and jazz band.

scale   Series of tones in ascending or descending order; may present the notes of a key.

scat singing   A jazz style that sets syllables without meaning *(vocables)* to an improvised vocal line.

scherzo   Composition in **A-B-A** form, usually in triple meter; replaced the *minuet and trio* in the nineteenth century.

secco   *Recitative* singing style that features a sparse accompaniment and moves with great freedom.

Second Viennese School   Name given to composer Arnold Schoenberg and his pupils Alban Berg and Anton Webern; represents the first efforts in *twelve-tone* composition.

secular music   Nonreligious music; when texted, usually in the vernacular.

semitone   Also known as a *half step,* the smallest interval commonly used in the Western musical system.

sequence Restatement of an idea or motive at a different pitch level.

serenade Classical instrumental genre that combines elements of chamber music and symphony, often performed in the evening or at social functions. Related to *divertimento* and *cassation*.

serialism Method of composition in which various musical elements (pitch, rhythm, dynamics, tone color) may be ordered in a fixed series. See also *total serialism*.

seventh chord Four-note combination consisting of a triad with another third added on top; spans a seventh between its lowest and highest tones.

sextuple meter Compound metrical pattern of six beats to a measure.

sforzando *(sf)* Sudden stress or accent on a single note or chord.

shake A jazz technique in which brass players shake their lips to produce a wide vibrato.

shakuhachi A Japanese end-blown flute.

shamisen Long-necked Japanese *chordophone* with three strings.

shape note Music notation system originating in nineteenth-century American church music in which the shape of the note heads determines the pitch; created to aid music reading.

sharp sign Musical symbol (♯) that indicates raising a pitch by a semitone.

shawm Medieval wind instrument, the ancestor of the oboe.

sheng A reed mouth organ from China.

side drum See *snare drum*.

simple meter Grouping of rhythms in which the beat is subdivided into two, as in duple, triple, and quadruple meters.

sinfonia Short instrumental work, found in Baroque opera, to facilitate scene changes.

Singspiel Comic German drama with spoken dialogue; the immediate predecessor of Romantic German opera.

sitar Long-necked plucked *chordophone* of northern India, with movable frets and a rounded gourd body; used as solo instrument and with *tabla*.

ska Jamaican urban dance form popular in the 1960s, influential in *reggae*.

sléndro *Pentatonic* tuning used in Javanese *gamelan* music; a gapped scale using tones 1, 2, 3, 5, 6.

slide trumpet Medieval brass instrument of the trumpet family.

snare drum Small cylindrical drum with two heads stretched over a metal shell, the lower head having strings across it; played with two drumsticks. Also *side drum*.

soft rock Lyrical, gentle rock style that evolved around 1960 in response to hard-driving *rock and roll*.

son A genre of traditional Mexican dances that combine compound duple with triple meters.

sonata Instrumental genre in several movements for soloist or small ensemble.

sonata-allegro form The opening movement of the *multimovement cycle*, consisting of themes that are stated in the first section *(exposition)*, developed in the second section *(development)*, and restated in the third section *(recapitulation)*. Also *sonata form* or *first-movement form*.

sonata cycle See *multimovement cycle*.

sonata da camera Baroque chamber sonata, usually a suite of stylized dances. Also *chamber sonata*.

sonata da chiesa Baroque instrumental work intended for performance in church; in four movements, frequently arranged slow-fast-slow-fast. Also *church sonata*.

sonata form See *sonata-allegro form*.

song cycle Group of songs, usually *Lieder*, that are unified musically or through their texts.

soprano Highest-ranged voice, normally possessed by women or boys.

source music A film technique in which music comes from a logical source within the film and functions as part of the story.

sound Vibrations perceived by the human ear; a musical sound is described by its *pitch* and its *duration*.

sousaphone Brass instrument adapted from the tuba with a forward bell that is coiled to rest over the player's shoulder for ease of carrying while marching.

spiritual Folklike devotional genre of the United States, sung by African Americans and whites.

spiritual minimalism Contemporary musical style related to *minimalism*, characterized by a weak pulse and long chains of lush progressions—either tonal or modal.

Sprechstimme A vocal style in which the melody is spoken at approximate pitches rather than sung on exact pitches; developed by Arnold Schoenberg.

staccato Short, detached notes, marked with a dot above them.

statement See *exposition*.

steamroller effect A drawn-out crescendo heard in Classical-era instrumental music; a technique credited to composers in Mannheim, Germany.

stile concitato Baroque style developed by Monteverdi, which introduced novel effects such as rapid repeated notes as symbols of passion.

stile rappresentativo A dramatic *recitative* style of the Baroque period in which melodies moved freely over a foundation of simple chords.

stopping On a string instrument, altering the string length by pressing it on the fingerboard. On a horn, playing with the bell closed by the hand or a mute.

strain A series of contrasting sections found in rags and marches; in duple meter with sixteen-measure themes or sections.

streaming audio Music that is played directly from the Web, in real time, and does not require downloading.

string instruments Bowed and plucked instruments whose sound is produced by the vibration of one or more strings. Also *chordophone*.

string quartet Chamber music ensemble consisting of two violins, viola, and cello. Also a multimovement composition for this ensemble.

string quintet Standard chamber ensemble made up of either two violins, two violas, and cello or two violins, viola, and two cellos.

string trio Standard chamber ensemble of two violins and cello or violin, viola, and cello.

strophic form Song structure in which the same music is repeated with every stanza (strophe) of the poem.

Sturm und Drang "Storm and stress"; late-eighteenth-century movement in Germany toward more emotional expression in the arts.

style Characteristic manner of presentation of musical elements (melody, rhythm, harmony, dynamics, form, etc.).

subdominant Fourth scale step, *fa*.

subdominant chord Chord built on the fourth scale step, the IV chord.

subject Main idea or theme of a work, as in a *fugue*.

suite Multimovement work made up of a series of contrasting dance movements, generally all in the same key. Also *partita* and *ordre*.

swing Jazz term coined to described Louis Armstrong's style; more commonly refers to big-band jazz.

syllabic Melodic style with one note to each syllable of text.

symphonic poem One-movement orchestral form that develops a poetic idea, suggests a scene, or creates a mood, generally associated with the Romantic era. Also *tone poem*.

symphony Large work for orchestra, generally in three or four movements.

syncopation Deliberate upsetting of the meter or pulse through a temporary shifting of the accent to a weak beat or an offbeat.

synthesizer Electronic instrument that produces a wide variety of sounds by combining sound generators and sound modifiers in one package with a unified control system.

tabla Pair of single-headed, tuned drums used in north Indian classical music.

tabor Cylindrical medieval drum.

tag Jazz term for a coda, or a short concluding section.

tala Fixed time cycle or meter in Indian music, built from uneven groupings of beats.

tambourine Percussion instrument consisting of a small round drum with metal plates inserted in its rim; played by striking or shaking.

tam-tam See *gong.*

tango A Latin American dance involving couples in tight embrace; characterized by abrupt movements and syncopated rhythms.

Te Deum Song of praise to God; a text from the Roman Catholic rite, often set polyphonically.

tempo Rate of speed or pace of music.

tempo rubato See *rubato.*

tenor Male voice of high range. Also a part, often structural, in polyphony.

tenor drum Percussion instrument, larger than the snare drum, with a wooden shell.

ternary form Three-part (**A-B-A**) form based on a statement (**A**), contrast or departure (**B**), and repetition (**A**). Also *three-part form.*

tertian harmony Harmony based on the interval of the third, particularly predominant from the Baroque through the nineteenth century.

texture The interweaving of melodic (horizontal) and harmonic (vertical) elements in the musical fabric.

thematic development Musical expansion of a theme by varying its melodic outline, harmony, or rhythm. Also *thematic transformation.*

thematic transformation See *thematic development.*

theme Melodic idea used as a basic building block in the construction of a composition. Also *subject.*

theme and variations Compositional procedure in which a theme is stated and then altered in successive statements; occurs as an independent piece or as a movement of a *multimovement cycle.*

theme group Several themes in the same key that function as a unit within a section of a form, particularly in *sonata-allegro form.*

Theremin An early electronic instrument from the 1920s, named after its inventor Leon Theremin.

third Interval between two notes that are two diatonic scale steps apart.

third stream Jazz style that synthesizes characteristics and techniques of classical music and jazz; term coined by Gunther Schuller.

thorough-bass See *figured bass.*

three-part form See *ternary form.*

through-composed Song structure that is composed from beginning to end, without repetitions of large sections.

timbales Shallow, single-headed drums of Cuban origin, played in pairs; used in much Latin-American popular music.

timbre The quality of a sound that distinguishes one voice or instrument from another. Also *tone color.*

timbrel Ancient percussion instrument related to the tambourine.

timpani Percussion instrument consisting of a hemispheric copper shell with a head of plastic or calfskin, held in place by a metal ring and played with soft or hard padded sticks. A pedal mechanism changes the tension of the head, and with it the pitch. Also *kettle-drums.*

tintinnabulation A bell-like style developed by Estonian composer Arvo Pärt, achieved by weaving conjunct lines that hover around a central pitch; from the Latin word for bell.

tin whistle Small metal end-blown flute commonly used in Irish traditional music.

toccata Virtuoso composition, generally for organ or harpsichord, in a free and rhapsodic style; in the Baroque, it often served as the introduction to a *fugue.*

tom-tom Cylindrical drum without snares.

tone A sound of definite pitch.

tonal Based on principles of major-minor tonality, as distinct from *modal.*

tonality Principle of organization around a tonic, or home, pitch, based on a major or minor scale.

tone cluster Highly dissonant combination of pitches sounded simultaneously.

tone color See *timbre*.

tone poem See *symphonic poem*.

tone row An arrangement of the twelve chromatic tones that serves as the basis of a *twelve-tone* composition.

tonic The first note of the scale or key, *do*. Also *keynote*.

tonic chord Triad built on the first scale tone, the I chord.

total serialism Extremely complex, totally controlled music in which the twelve-tone principle is extended to elements of music other than pitch.

traditional music Music that is learned by *oral transmission* and is easily sung or played by most people; may exist in variant forms. Also *folk music*.

tragédie lyrique French serious opera of the seventeenth and eighteenth centuries, with spectacular dance scenes and brilliant choruses on tales of courtly love or heroic adventures; associated with J.-B. Lully.

transition See *bridge*.

transposition Shifting a piece of music to a different pitch level.

tremolo Rapid repetition of a tone; can be achieved instrumentally or vocally.

triad Common chord type, consisting of three pitches built on alternate tones of the scale (e.g., steps 1–3-5, or *do-mi-sol*).

triangle Percussion instrument consisting of a slender rod of steel bent in the shape of a triangle, struck with a steel beater.

trill Ornament consisting of the rapid alternation between one tone and the next or sometimes the tone below.

trio sonata Baroque chamber sonata type written in three parts: two melody lines and the *basso continuo*; requires a total of four players to perform.

triple meter Basic metrical pattern of three beats to a measure.

triple-stop Playing three notes simultaneously on a string instrument.

triplet Group of three equal-valued notes played in the time of two; indicated by a bracket and the number 3.

triplum Third voice in early polyphony.

tritonic Three-note scale pattern, used in the music of some sub-Saharan African cultures.

trobairitz Female *troubadours*, composer-poets of southern France.

trombone Tenor-range brass instrument that changes pitch by means of a movable double slide; there is also a bass version.

troubadours Medieval poet-musicians in southern France.

trouvères Medieval poet-musicians in northern France.

trumpet Highest-pitched brass instrument that changes pitch through valves.

tuba Bass-range brass instrument that changes pitch by means of valves.

tubular bells See *chimes*.

turn A bridge, or alternate phrase, in Cajun dance music.

tutti "All"; the opposite of solo. See also *ripieno*.

twelve-bar blues Musical structure based on a repeated harmonic-rhythmic pattern that is twelve measures in length (I-I-I-I-IV-IV-I-I-V-V-I-I).

twelve-tone music Compositional procedure of the twentieth century based on the use of all twelve chromatic tones (in a *tone row*) without a central tone, or *tonic*, according to prescribed rules.

two-part form See *binary form*.

uilleann pipes Type of bellows-blown bagpipe used in Irish traditional music; bellows are elbow-manipulated.

underscoring A technique used in films in which the music comes from an unseen source.

union pipes See *uilleann pipes*.

unison Interval between two notes of the same pitch; the simultaneous playing of the same note.

upbeat Last beat of a measure, a weak beat, which anticipates the downbeat.

vamp Short passage with simple rhythm and harmony that introduces a soloist in a jazz performance.

verismo Operatic "realism," a style popular in Italy in the 1890s, which tried to bring naturalism into the lyric theater.

verse In poetry, a group of lines constituting a unit. In liturgical music for the Catholic Church, a phrase from the Scriptures that alternates with the *response*.

Vespers One of the *Divine Offices* of the Roman Catholic Church, held at twilight.

vibraphone A percussion instrument with metal bars and electrically driven rotating propellers under each bar that produces a *vibrato* sound, much used in jazz.

vibrato Small fluctuation of pitch used as an expressive device to intensify a sound.

vielle Medieval bowed-string instrument; the ancestor of the violin.

Viennese School Title given to the three prominent composers of the Classical era: Haydn, Mozart, and Beethoven.

viola Bowed-string instrument of middle range; the second-highest member of the violin family.

viola da gamba Family of Renaissance bowed-string instruments that had six or more strings, was fretted like a guitar, and was held between the legs like a modern cello.

violin Soprano, or highest-ranged, member of the bowed-string instrument family.

violoncello Bowed-string instrument with a middle-to-low range and dark, rich sonority; lower than a viola. Also *cello*.

virelai Medieval and Renaissance fixed poetic form and *chanson* type with French courtly texts.

virtuoso Performer of extraordinary technical ability.

vivace Lively.

vocable Nonlexical syllables, lacking literal meaning.

vocalise A textless vocal melody, as in an exercise or concert piece.

volume Degree of loudness or softness of a sound. See also *dynamics*.

waltz Ballroom dance type in triple meter; in the Romantic era, a short, stylized piano piece.

washboard A rhythm instrument used in certain styles of traditional music; an *idiophone* built from a laundry implement that is scraped with a metal rod or with the fingers.

West Coast jazz Jazz style developed in the 1950s, featuring small groups of mixed timbres playing contrapuntal improvisations; similar to *cool jazz*.

whole step Interval consisting of two half steps, or *semitones*.

whole-tone scale Scale pattern built entirely of whole-step intervals, common in the music of the French Impressionists.

wind ensemble See *concert band*.

woodwind Instrumental family made of wood or metal whose tone is produced by a column of air vibrating within a pipe that has holes along its length.

woodwind quintet Standard chamber ensemble consisting of one each of the following: flute, oboe, clarinet, bassoon, and French horn (not a woodwind instrument).

word painting Musical pictorialization of words from the text as an expressive device; a prominent feature of the Renaissance madrigal.

work song Communal song that synchronized group tasks.

xylophone Percussion instrument consisting of tuned blocks of wood suspended on a frame, laid out in the shape of a keyboard and struck with hard mallets.

yangqin A Chinese hammered dulcimer with a trapezoidal sound box and metal strings that are struck with bamboo sticks.

zither Family of string instruments with sound box over which strings are stretched; they may be plucked or bowed. Zithers appear in many shapes and are common in traditional music throughout Europe, Asia, and Africa.

Credits

Index

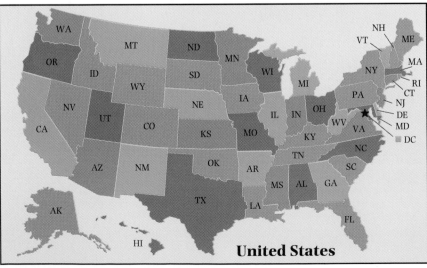

Canada

United States